WORKSHOPS IN COMPUTING
Series edited by C. J. van Rijsberg

Also in this series

ALPUK91, Proceedings of the 3rd UK Annual Conference on Logic Programming, Edinburgh, 10–12 April 1991
Geraint A. Wiggins, Chris Mellish and Tim Duncan (Eds.)

Specifications of Database Systems,
1st International Workshop on Specifications of Database Systems, Glasgow, 3–5 July 1991
David J. Harper and Moira C. Norrie (Eds.)

7th UK Computer and Telecommunications Performance Engineering Workshop,
Edinburgh, 22–23 July 1991
J. Hillston, P.J.B. King and R.J. Pooley (Eds.)

Logic Program Synthesis and Transformation,
Proceedings of LOPSTR 91, International Workshop on Logic Program Synthesis and Transformation, University of Manchester, 4–5 July 1991
T.P. Clement and K.-K. Lau (Eds.)

Declarative Programming, Sasbachwalden 1991
PHOENIX Seminar and Workshop on Declarative Programming, Sasbachwalden, Black Forest, Germany, 18–22 November 1991
John Darlington and Roland Dietrich (Eds.)

Building Interactive Systems: Architectures and Tools
Philip Gray and Roger Took (Eds.)

Functional Programming, Glasgow 1991,
Proceedings of the 1991 Glasgow Workshop on Functional Programming, Portree, Isle of Skye, 12–14 August 1991
Rogardt Heldal, Carsten Kehler Holst and Philip Wadler (Eds.)

Object Orientation in Z
Susan Stepney, Rosalind Barden and David Cooper (Eds.)

Code Generation – Concepts, Tools, Techniques
Proceedings of the International Workshop on Code Generation, Dagstuhl, Germany, 20–24 May 1991
Robert Giegerich and Susan L. Graham (Eds.)

Z User Workshop, York 1991, Proceedings of the Sixth Annual Z User Meeting, York, 16–17 December 1991
J.E. Nicholls (Ed.)

Formal Aspects of Measurement
Proceedings of the BCS-FACS Workshop on Formal Aspects of Measurement, South Bank University, London, 5 May 1991
Tim Denvir, Ros Herman and R.W. Whitty (Eds.)

AI and Cognitive Science '91
University College, Cork, 19–20 September 1991
Humphrey Sorensen (Ed.)

Algebraic Methodology and Software Technology (AMAST'91)
Proceedings of the Second International Conference on Algebraic Methodology and Software Technology, Iowa City, USA, 22–25 May 1991
M. Nivat, C. Rattray, T. Rus and G. Scollo (Eds.)

continued on back page…

Cliff B. Jones, Roger C. Shaw and Tim Denvir (Eds.)

5th Refinement Workshop

Proceedings of the 5th Refinement Workshop, organised by BCS-FACS, London, 8–10 January 1992

Published in collaboration with the British Computer Society

BCS
FACS

Springer-Verlag
London Berlin Heidelberg New York
Paris Tokyo Hong Kong
Barcelona Budapest

Cliff B. Jones, DPhil
Department of Computer Science
The University, Manchester, M13 9PL, UK

Roger C. Shaw, GIMA, MBCS
Lloyd's Register of Shipping, Lloyd's Register House
29 Wellesley Road, Croydon, Surrey, CR0 2AJ, UK

Tim Denvir, MA, CEng, MIEE, MBCS
Translimina Ltd, 37 Orpington Road
Winchmore Hill, London, N21 3PD, UK

ISBN 3-540-19752-4 Springer-Verlag Berlin Heidelberg New York
ISBN 0-387-19752-4 Springer-Verlag New York Berlin Heidelberg

British Library Cataloguing in Publication Data
5th Refinement Workshop: Proceedings of the 5th Refinement Workshop,
Organised by BCS–FACS, London, 8–10 January 1992. –
(Workshops in Computing Series)
I. Jones, Cliff B. II. Series
005.1
ISBN 3-540-19752-4

Library of Congress Cataloging-in-Publication Data
Refinement Workshop (5th : 1992 : London, England)
5th Refinement Workshop: proceedings of the 5th Refinement Workshop, London,
8–10 January / [edited by] Roger C. Shaw, Cliff B. Jones, and Tim Denvir.
p. cm. – (Workshops in computing)
ISBN 0-387-19752-4
1. Computer software–Development–Congresses. I. Shaw, Roger C.F.
II. Jones, C.B. (Cliff B.), *1944–* . III. Denvir, Tim, *1939–*. IV. Title.
V. Title: Fifth Refinement Workshop. VI. Series.
QA76.76.D47R44 1992 92–7438
005. 1–dc20 CIP

Printed in Germany

Typesetting: Camera ready by authors

34/3830-543210 Printed on acid-free paper

Preface

This volume contains the proceedings of the Fifth Refinement Workshop which was organised by the British Computer Society specialist group in Formal Aspects of Computer Science and held at Lloyd's Register of Shipping in London on 8–10 January 1992.

As its name implies, this was the fifth in a series of workshops on the theme of formal refinement. Previous events have been held in the University of York, the Open University, IBM UK Laboratories and Logica Cambridge. These workshops have become the major regular formal methods events in the UK.

The workshop hcard both refereed and invited papers. The invited speakers were Jim Grundy (Cambridge University), Roger Jones (ICL), Robin Milner (Edinburgh University), José Oliveira (Minho University), Jeannette Wing (Carnegie Mellon University), and Jim Woodcock (Oxford University). There was also a well-populated set of tool demonstrations featuring the Genesis Z Tool from Imperial Software Technology, μral from Manchester University, Specbox from Adelard, RED (Refinement Editor) from Oxford University, the RAISE Toolset from CRI, Cadiz from York Software Engineering, the SPADE Theorem Prover from Program Validation Ltd. and a refinement tool from the Victoria University of Wellington, New Zealand.

"Refinement" or "reification" in the context of rigorous software development is taken to be the process of creating more concrete representations of abstractions in a specification or design, and producing a new document which defines the same behaviour as its ancestor and which may contain extra properties or embody more design decisions and detail. There is a notion of correctness of refinements, namely that the result of the refinement is correct if it exhibits the key properties of its ancestor. The precise meaning can vary depending on the development approach and specification or design language used. Designs and specifications can be refined to executable programs. Correctness of refinement is crucial to correct development of software, and this has provided the principal motive for this series of events. Refinement has been the theme of all the refinement workshops, and each has had a particular emphasis. The fifth workshop has attempted to emphasise certain practical aspects of refinement: for the first time there has been a tools demonstration; more papers from industry have been encouraged, although obtaining them is always a problem; papers which demonstrated refinement that preserves safety and security properties were encouraged.

That progress has been made in terms of moving formal approaches of software development into industrial practice is clearly indicated by the introductory talk from Mr Patrick O'Ferrall, the Deputy Chairman of Lloyd's Register of Shipping. This is reproduced with his permission as the first paper in these proceedings.

At present the application of formal methods is perceived to be most worthwhile where there is a paramount need for correctness, particularly in safety critical applications. Applications in which lack of correctness would cause great material cost, such as high volume embedded software, electronic funds transfer or data security applications, have been slower to use formal methods but movements to do so can now be observed. At the same time the total context of software engineering, the place and role of formal methods within that context, and the relationship to other issues in the software development process such as requirements capture, design of user interfaces, cognitive modelling and many other issues are being very seriously, if uncertainly, studied. Software engineering is embarking upon a multidisciplinary path and the role of formal methods, the model of the development process and the place of refinement within it can all be expected to find themselves in new, changing and possibly unfamiliar contexts. The continual change and maturation of our science and engineering discipline leads to an exciting and vital arena of theory and practice. We can look forward to the future with expectant optimism.

The organising committee consisted of Bernard Carré (Chair), Cliff Jones (Technical Programme), Roger Shaw (Local Arrangements), Paul Smith (Publicity), John Cooke, Tim Denvir and Jeremy Jacob. We had material support from three sources: Lloyd's Register of Shipping provided lunches, refreshments and the venue with its imposing board room; Program Validation Ltd hosted a social evening at the London Transport Museum; and the Department of Trade and Industry funded some of the incidental printing and overhead costs without which a conference cannot operate. Finally we would like to thank the large number of referees who kindly devoted time and energy to reviewing the papers on a very short timescale.

May 1992

Cliff B. Jones
Roger C. Shaw
Tim Denvir

Contents

Opening Address

Mr Patrick O'Ferrall
Deputy Chairman
Lloyd's Register
71 Fenchurch Street, London, EC3M 4BS

Lloyd's Register's (LR) central purpose is to play a leading role in the setting, maintenance and application of proper standards of safety and quality for engineering systems. Traditionally we have been most active in the world's shipping industries where we have provided an independent "third party" service based on our own rules and standards for 230 years. During this century, however, this "third party" role has been increasingly extended into a wide spectrum of both land based and offshore industries.

Over the last few decades software has become an essential tool of the design process for most engineering systems. More recently, however, the trend has been for software to become an integral part of the engineering system itself with obvious implications for the safety and reliability of its operation. In consequence, therefore, all issues associated with safe and high quality software are becoming a major concern for the Society (LR).

Even today we face the problem of addressing safety critical systems in our everyday business with the advent of ships that have been designed to operate with crewing levels as low as six. Navigation, engine management systems, cargo handling can all be supervised by computer based control systems. LR is therefore focusing its attention on how such systems should be constructed if adequate levels of safety are not only to be achieved but also to be demonstrated. At the moment, LR rules effectively prohibit "sail by wire" by requiring that software systems be proved to be as reliable as hardware systems. This cannot be satisfactorily achieved at the current state of the art. However, this situation will not continue for long. When it becomes possible to demonstrate software reliability in an acceptable engineering manner, then it will be necessary for LR to approve the use of such systems within engineering products. By then we need to know how best to develop and assess such systems from the safety perspective.

It is recognised that safety critical systems, such as fly by wire control systems, are often required to achieve reliability levels of 10^{-9} failures on demand per hour yet there is no practical way that software can be empirically tested to levels beyond 10^{-4} failures on demand per hour. This factor alone has caused major debate within the industry about the desirability of developing engineering products which will fail catastrophically if the software fails. One approach proposed for addressing this problem is of course to use formal methods for specifying and formally developing correct programs. Not everyone agrees that this fully addresses the problem as it fails to focus on the adequacy of the statement of requirements nor does it address the criticism that formal methods are other than "good practice".

Nevertheless LR has identified formal methods as a key element in the package of techniques that would contribute significantly to providing an engineering discipline in the development and assessment of software.

For this reason we are participating in research projects which are contributing to the industrialisation of formal methods and we would support activities that address the major concerns of the industry. We are particularly concerned with the proper influence of formal methods in safety critical standards, the training requirements for these methods and more than anything else their application to practical problems in which they can demonstrate the level of increased confidence that can be placed on systems developed by formal methods.

I hope that this workshop will reflect on the issues and will contribute to further progress in this important area of work. I hope you will find this workshop useful and stimulating.

Concurrent Processes as Objects

Robin Milner
Laboratory for the Foundations of Computer Science
University of Edinburgh

Abstract

The π-calculus is a relatively new algebraic calculus for communicating processes, in the tradition of process algebras [1, 3, 4, 5]. It goes a step further than these in one respect: it models processes whose configuration is dynamically varying. This enrichment gives the calculus status as a general computational model. Its main character is what may be called the *object* paradigm, since it most directly represents the action and reaction among independently existing agents. It also embraces the *function* paradigm, since both functions (the λ-calculus) and data can be accurately encoded as processes.

A basic knowledge of process algebra can be got from some of the books referred to above. The π-calculus is most clearly derived from CCS [5]; it evolved through work by Nielsen and Engberg [2], and the best introduction is the two-part paper by Milner, Parrow and Walker [7]. The encoding of λ-calculus is done in detail in [6].

References

[1] Baeten, J.C.M. and Weijland, W.P., **Process Algebra**, Cambridge University Press 1990.

[2] Engberg, U. and Nielsen, M., *A Calculus of Communicating Systems with Label Passing*, Report DAIMI PB–208, Computer Science Department, University of Århus, 1986.

[3] Hoare, C.A.R., **Communicating Sequential Processes**, Prentice Hall, 1985.

[4] Hennessy, M., **Algebraic Theory of Processes**, MIT Press, 1988.

[5] Milner, R., **Communication and Concurrency**, Prentice Hall, 1989

[6] Milner, R., *Functions as Processes*, Proc. ICALP '90, Lecture Notes in Computer Science, Vol. 443, pp167–180, Springer-Verlag, 1990.

[7] Milner, R., Parrow, J. and Walker, D., *A Calculus of Mobile Processes*, Reports ECS-LFCS–89–85 and –86, Laboratory for Foundations of Computer Science, Computer Science Department, Edinburgh University, 1989. (To appear in Journal of Information and Computation.)

Formalising Dijkstra's Development Strategy within Stark's Formalism

Antonio Cau[*]
Institut für Informatik und Praktische Mathematik II
Preußerstr. 1-9
Christian-Albrechts-Universität zu Kiel
D-2300 Kiel 1, Germany

Ruurd Kuiper[†]
Department of Mathematics and Computing Science
Eindhoven University of Technology
5600 MB Eindhoven, The Netherlands

Willem-Paul de Roever[‡]
Institut für Informatik und Praktische Mathematik II
Preußerstr. 1-9
Christian-Albrechts-Universität zu Kiel
D-2300 Kiel 1, Germany

Abstract

Dijkstra introduced an enticing development strategy in a paper addressing the readers/ writers problem. This strategy is as follows: one starts with some "stupid" (in the sense that it allows undesirable computations) first try and then tries in subsequent steps to "refine" this stupid try into a better one by eliminating (some) undesirable computations. In a number of steps one strives to get a good (in the sense that it no longer contains undesirable computations) implementation for the problem. Unfortunately this strategy is not very formal. In this paper we try to make it more formal by using Stark's temporal logic based rely/guarantee formalism. We use this formalism in a special way in order to describe Dijkstra's development strategy: the part intended to describe the liveness condition is used for the more general purpose of disallowing the undesirable sequences.

1 Introduction

Current formal methods are far from solving the problems in software development. The simplest view of the formal paradigm is that one starts with a formal specification and subsequently develops a correct implementation which

[*]E-mail: ac@informatik.uni-kiel.dbp.de

[†]E-mail: wsinruur@win.tue.nl

[‡]E-mail: wpr@informatik.uni-kiel.dbp.de

is then proved to be correct. This view is too idealistic in a number of respects. First of all, most specifications of software are wrong and certainly most informal ones (unless they have been formally analyzed) contain inconsistencies [11]. Secondly, even a formal specification is produced (if at all) only after a number of iteration steps because writing a correct specification is a process whose difficulty is comparable with that of writing a correct program. This activity should therefore be structured, resulting in a number of increasingly less abstract layers with specifications which tend to increase in detail (and therefore become less readable [8]). Thirdly, even an incorrect program may describe a strategy whose specification by any other means is not as clear and has therefore at least *some* merits. This is especially the case with intricate algorithms such as those concerning specific strategies for solving the mutual exclusion problem. An interesting illustration of this third view is provided by E.W. Dijkstra's "Tutorial on the split binary semaphore" [2] in which he solves the readers/writers problem by subsequently improving an incorrect program till it is correct. If this master of style prefers to approximate and finally arrive at his correct solution using formally incorrect intermediate stages, one certainly expects that a formally correct development process for that paradigm is difficult to find! The strategy described in [2] is necessarily informal, reflecting the state of the art in 1979.

In the present paper we present a formal development strategy and its application to Dijkstra's example [2]. This formal strategy preserves the flavour of the informal strategy in that it formalises Dijkstra's argumentation in terms of incorrect approximations to a correct program and provides a formal criterion for recognising when a formally correct end product, the correct program, has finally been reached. We use Stark's formalism in order to achieve this. In this formalism a specification is separated in a safety (machine) part and a liveness (validity) part. It is this separation that enables us to handle incorrect approximations: the specific use of abstraction functions in Stark's formalism enables us to prove the correctness between machine parts, even in cases where incorrect sequences might prevent this in more rigid frameworks.

The structure of the paper is as follows. In Section 2 we introduce Stark's formalism and give some simplifications/improvements based on [3]. Furthermore we give an intuitive explanation of Stark's rely/guarantee rule for liveness properties. Stark's work was based on the rely/guarantee idea presented by Cliff Jones in [4]. We present in Section 3 the formal treatment of [2]. Section 4 contains a conclusion and mentions future work.

2 Stark's Formalism

2.1 Introduction

In this section we present Stark's formalism because papers [12, 13] are not easily accessible. We simplify his temporal logic; this simplification is based on that of [3]. Furthermore we give a more intuitive construction of the *events* of Stark's notion of composite machine and a more intuitive explanation of his rely/guarantee rule.

In Section 2.2 the notion of module is defined. In particular a distinction is made between abstract, composed and component modules. The idea is that an abstract module is implemented by a composed module which has component modules as components. Abstraction functions are defined and the notion of correct development step is defined, i.e., it is defined when a composed module implements an abstract one.

In order to relate these abstract black box notions to actual computations in Section 2.3 machines are introduced, a kind of automata. Stark's machine notion is a handy normal form to express safety properties. Lamport's notion of machine closure [1] can easily be applied to these machines. Liveness properties can be defined as global restrictions on the machine's behaviour. Stark makes a distinction between local properties and global ones, for instance, but not necessarily so, safety and liveness.

To obtain a more abstract temporal logic, doing away with the stuttering problem, Stark defines a dense linear time temporal logic. We adopt in Section 2.4 a slightly simplified/improved version of the logic as defined in [3]. The following picture illustrates the underlying model.

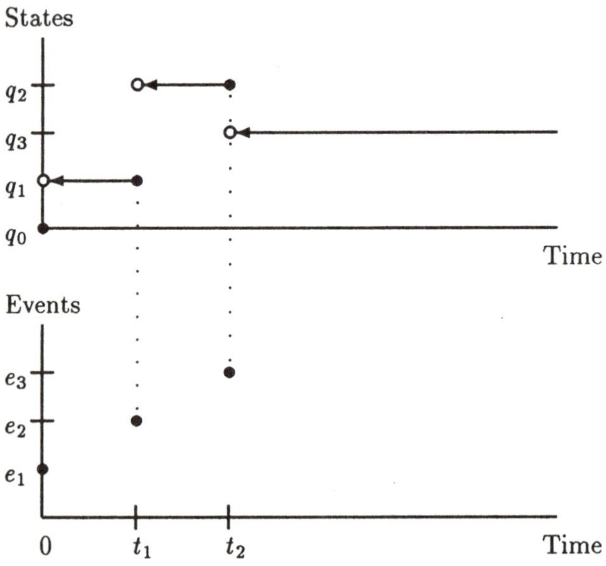

Figure 1: This picture illustrates the following: the initial state is q_0, on the occurrence of event e_1 the state changes in q_1. Between time 0 and time t_1 there are no interesting event occurrences, but only occurrences of the uninteresting stuttering event λ. So the state does not change until the next interesting event e_2 occurs.

A salient feature of the temporal logic is the "immediately after" state operator $'$, in a version which Lamport approves of according to [5].

In Section 2.5 machines and their allowed computations are related to correct development steps. The relation is expressed by verification conditions. In Section 2.6 we illustrate some of the notions of the previous sections with Lamport's soda machine example [7]. In Section 2.7 Stark's rely/guarantee notion for his proof rule is introduced. We also give an intuitive explanation of his proof rule and how he handles the problem of circular reasoning. In Section 2.8 we relate Stark's model to that of Lamport. In Section 2.9 we explain our special use of Stark's formalism in order to disallow undesirable sequences.

2.2 Modules and correct development steps

In [12] a method for specifying reactive systems is introduced. Such systems are assumed to be composed of one or more modules. A module is characterised by the specification pair $\langle E, B\rangle$ where E denotes its *interface* of possible events and B its *allowed behaviour*, as explained below.

An *event* is an observable instantaneous occurrence during the operation of a module, that can be generated by that module or its environment and that is of interest at the given level of abstraction. Also a λ_E-event which represents all uninteresting events (in Milners set up the τ event [10]) is distinguished.

The B-part of specification $\langle E, B\rangle$ characterises the allowed behaviour of the module. An *observation* x over interface E is a function from $[0, \infty)$ to E, such that $x(t) \neq \lambda$ for at most finitely many $t \in [0, \infty)$ in each bounded interval, which means that in a bounded interval only a finite number of interesting events can occur (this is the so called finite variability condition). Let $Obs(E)$ denote the set of all observations over E. Then the allowed behaviour B is a subset of $Obs(E)$. $Beh(E)$ denotes the set of all behaviours of interface E.

In Stark's view there are three kinds of modules. The first one is an *abstract* module. Such a module serves as a high level specification of a system. The second one is a *component* module which serves as a lower level specification of a system component. The third and last one is a *composite* module. This last module provides the link between the two levels.

To specify a system one needs one abstract module, one composite module and one or more component modules. An *interconnection* relates these modules with each other, i.e., it relates the interface of the composite module with the interface of the abstract module, and the interface of the composite module with each of the interfaces of the component modules.
An interconnection $\mathcal{I}$ is a pair $\langle \alpha, \langle \delta_i\rangle_{i\in I}\rangle$ where:

- α denotes a function from the interface E of the composite module to the interface A of the abstract module such that $\alpha(\lambda_E) = \lambda_A$ holds; α is called *abstraction* function.

- δ_i denotes a function from interface E of the composite module to interface F_i of the component module such that $\delta_i(\lambda_E) = \lambda_{F_i}$ holds; δ_i is called *decomposition* function.

The abstraction function α hides events from the composite machine that do not belong to the high level interface. The decomposition function δ_i hide events from the composite machine that do not belong to the component i. So intuitively the requirement about both α and the δ_i's is that uninteresting events of the composite module are not turned into interesting ones of the abstract or component modules.

The definition of interconnection can easily be extended to behaviour of the mentioned modules. When $\mathcal{I}$ is an interconnection between the interfaces of the modules, $\mathcal{I}^*$ denotes the corresponding interconnection between the behaviours of the modules.
If $\mathcal{I}$ is a pair $\langle \alpha, \langle \delta_i\rangle_{i\in I}\rangle$ then $\mathcal{I}^*$ is the pair $\langle \alpha^*, \langle \delta_i^*\rangle_{i\in I}\rangle$ where :

- α^* denotes a function from the set $Beh(E)$ of all possible behaviours of the composite module to the set $Beh(A)$ of all possible behaviours of the abstract module. If $B_E \in Beh(E)$ then $\alpha^*(B_E) \stackrel{\text{def}}{=} \{\alpha \circ x \mid x \in B_E\}$ is obtained by elementwise composition of α.

- δ_i^* denotes a function from the set $Beh(E)$ of all possible behaviours of the composite module to the set $Beh(F_i)$ of all possible behaviours of the component module. If $B_E \in Beh(E)$ then $\delta_i^*(B_E) \stackrel{\text{def}}{=} \{\delta_i \circ x \mid x \in B_E\}$.

It is the composite module that actually defines the composition of the component modules. In the examples we define this composite module in such a way that it reflects the parallel composition of the component modules. A *development step* is defined as a triple $\langle \mathcal{I}^*, S_A, \langle S_i \rangle_{i \in I} \rangle$ where

- $\mathcal{I}^*$ is the interconnection (between behaviours),

- S_A is the specification of the abstract module : $\langle A, B_A \rangle$ ($B_A \in Beh(A)$ denotes the set of allowed behaviours of the abstract module), and

- S_i is the specification of component module i : $\langle F_i, B_i \rangle$ ($B_i \in Beh(F_i)$ denotes the set of allowed behaviours of component module i).

The inverse image operator induced by the decomposition functions of an interconnection expresses the operation of composing a collection of component modules to produce the corresponding behaviour of the composite module. Hence, the composition operator associated with $\langle \delta_i^* \rangle_{i \in I}$ is the composition function $\langle \delta_i^* \rangle_{i \in I}^{-1}$, mapping the vector $\langle B_i \rangle_{i \in I}$ of allowed behaviours of the component modules to a composite module's behaviour $\langle \delta_i^* \rangle_{i \in I}^{-1}(\langle B_i \rangle_{i \in I}) \in Beh(E)$ under the definition:

$$\langle \delta_i^* \rangle_{i \in I}^{-1}(\langle B_i \rangle_{i \in I}) = \{x_E \in Obs(E) \mid \delta_i \circ x_E \in B_i \text{ for all } i \in I\} = \textstyle\bigcap_{i \in I} \delta_i^{*-1}(B_i)$$

A development step is correct if the behaviour obtained by abstracting away the internal behaviour (of the composed component modules) is also a behaviour of the abstract module; i.e., if the following holds:

$$\alpha^* \circ (\langle \delta_i^* \rangle_{i \in I}^{-1})(\langle B_i \rangle_{i \in I}) \subseteq B_A$$

2.3 Machines

Until now we have specified the allowed behaviour of a module by a set of observations. We now introduce a state-transition formalism to generate this set. In this state-transition formalism, we imagine that – at any instant of time – a module can be thought of as being in a *state*. Associated with each state is a collection of events that can occur in that state, and a description of the state change that results from the occurrence of each of those events. Thus a state-transition specification describes the desired functioning of a module in terms of a machine that generates an observation as it executes.

One can divide the properties that can be specified by the state-transition technique in two classes. The first class consists of the so called *local (safety) properties*, which describe how an event causes a state to transform to the next state. The second class consists of the so called *global properties*, which describe the relationship of events and states that cannot be directly described in terms of state-transition relations.

The local properties are specified by the above mentioned machine and the global properties are specified by defining a set of *validity conditions* on computations of that machine. The set of computations that satisfy the validity conditions is called the *set of valid computations*. The intersection of this set with the set of computations that are generated by the machine, describe the allowed behaviour of the corresponding module.

The machine M that specifies the local properties of a module is defined as follows:
$M = (E_M, Q_M, IQ_M, TR_M)$ where:

- E_M : is the interface of M; events labeled with a$\downarrow$ are input events, events labeled with a$\uparrow$ are output events and events without an arrow are internal events,
- Q_M : is the set of states of M; a state is a function from the set of observable variables Var to the set of values Val i.e. $Q_M : Var \rightarrow Val$,
- IQ_M : a non-empty subset of Q_M, the set of initial states,
- TR_M : the state-transition relation, $TR_M \subseteq Q_M \times E_M \times Q_M$, such that for all $q \in Q_M$ the stuttering step $\langle q, \lambda_{E_M}, q\rangle \in TR_M$. Furthermore M is input-cooperative (if an input comes "at the wrong moment" it should be mapped to *error*, i.e., TR_M is total for input events).

The next example illustrates how such a specification of a machine M may look like.

Example

$M = (E_M, Q_M, IQ_M, TR_M)$ where:

1. **Events:**
   $E_M : \{d_0, d_1, \lambda_d\}$
2. **States:**
   $Q_M : \{u\} \rightarrow \{0, 1, 2\}$
3. **Initial States:**
   IQ_M: $\{q \in Q_M : q(u) = 0\}$
4. **Transitions:**
   TR_M:
   $\{\langle q, e, r\rangle \in Q_M \times E_M \times Q_M :$
   (a) $(q(u) = 0 \wedge e = d_0 \wedge r(u) = 1)\vee$
   (b) $(q(u) = 1 \wedge e = d_1 \wedge r(u) = 2)\vee$
   (c) $(e = \lambda_d \wedge r(u) = q(u))\}$

end example

A *state function* over a set of states Q is a function $f : [0, \infty) \rightarrow Q$ such that for all $t \in [0, \infty)$, there exists $\varepsilon_t > 0$ such that f is constant on intervals $(t - \varepsilon_t, t] \cap [0, \infty)$ and $(t, t + \varepsilon_t]$. We write $f(t^{\leftarrow\bullet})$ for the value of the state just before and at time t (the first interval) and write $f(t^{\circ\rightarrow})$ for the value of f just after time t (the second interval). This is illustrated in the next picture where the state just before and at time t_1 equals q_1 and the state just after time t_1 equals q_2.

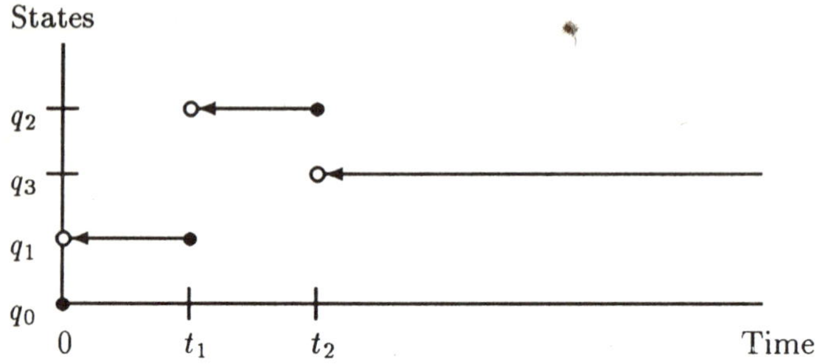

A *history* over an interface E and state set Q is a pair $X = \langle Obs_X, State_X \rangle$, where Obs_X is an observation over E (a function from $[0, \infty)$ to E). An example of such an observation is illustrated in the next picture. For example at time t_1 event e_2 occurs.

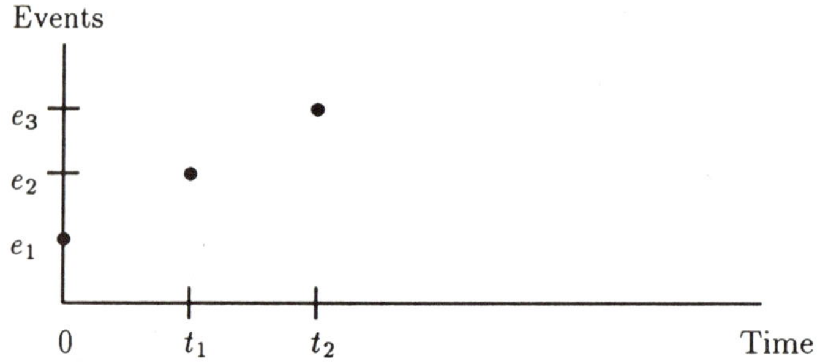

And where $State_X$ is a state function over Q as illustrated in the first picture. These two notions will be related by the notion of computation of a machine M. But first we need the notion of step at t in X.
Let $Hist(E, Q)$ denote the set of all histories over interface E and state set Q. If $X \in Hist(E, Q)$ and $t \in [0, \infty)$, then define the *step* occurring at time t in X by:
$Step_X(t) = \langle State_X(t^{\leftarrow\bullet}), Obs_X(t), State_X(t^{\circ\rightarrow}) \rangle$. An example of such a step is illustrated in the next picture whichs combines the previous two pictures. The step at time t_1 is then $\langle q_1, e_2, q_2 \rangle$.

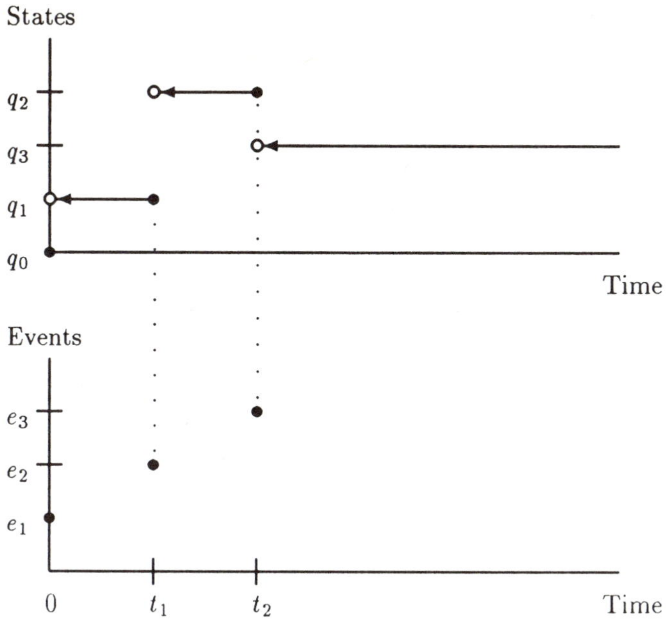

A *computation of a machine* M is a history $X \in Hist(E_M, Q_M)$ such that:

- $State_X(0) \in IQ_M$.
- $Step_X(t) \in TR_M$ for all $t \in [0, \infty)$.

Let $Comp(M)$ denote the set of all computations of M.
Let $Reachable_M$ denote the set of reachable states of M, i.e. all the states that can occur in a computation.

If V is a set of computations of M, then define $Obs(V)$ –the set of all observations generated by V – by $Obs(V) = \{Obs_X : X \in V\}$.

2.4 Stark's dense linear time logic DTL

As we have seen above the global properties are described by a set of validity conditions. Stark uses temporal logic to describe these validity conditions. Our modified temporal logic DTL looks like the one of Stark and is defined as follows:
Let F denote the set of freeze variables then a *history model* is a tuple $\langle\theta, h\rangle$, where $\theta \in F \rightarrow Val$ is an assignment to freeze variables and h a history (pair $\langle Obs_h, State_h\rangle$). Let $h^{(\tau)}$ denote the history $\lambda t.h(t + \tau)$.

Syntax

variables elements of Var
values of variables elements of Val
mapping operator $\mapsto$
state mapping from Var to Val, i.e. when for instance $Var = \{x\}$ and $Val = \{0, 1, 2\}$ then $[x \mapsto 0]$ denotes a state

freeze variables elements of F; $F \cap Var = \emptyset$
events elements of E_M
special symbols **e** and **st**
event term **e** $= f$ where f denotes an element of E_M
state terms **st** $= x$ and **st**$' = x$ where x denotes a state and $'$ is a **temporal** operator
terms can be event terms, state terms, freeze variables or function symbols
quantification over freeze variables $\forall, \exists$
formulae built from terms, relation symbols, boolean connectives, quantification and **temporal** operators $\Box$ and $\Diamond$

Semantics

Before we give the semantics of DTL we give the definition of a variant of a state q: $(q \mid x : v)$ which is defined as follows:
$(q \mid x : v)(y) = v$ for $y = x$ and $(q \mid x : v)(y) = q(y)$ for $y \neq x$.
For all freeze variables v, $v(\langle \theta, h \rangle) = \theta(v)$.
For all variables $v \in Var$, $v(\langle \theta, h \rangle) = State_h(0)(v)$.
For $[v \mapsto n]$, where $v \in Var$ and $n \in Val$, $[v \mapsto n](\langle \theta, h \rangle) = State_h(0) \mid v : n$
For e , e$(\langle \theta, h \rangle) = Obs_h(0)$.
For **st**, **st**$(\langle \theta, h \rangle) = State_h(0)$.
For **st**$'$, **st**$'(\langle \theta, h \rangle) = State_h(0^{\multimap})$.
As usual.
For function f with interpretation $\overline{f}$,
$f(t_1, ..., t_n)(\langle \theta, h \rangle) = \overline{f}(t_1(\langle \theta, h \rangle), ..., t_n(\langle \theta, h \rangle))$.
$\langle \theta, h \rangle \models R(t_1, ..., t_n)$ if $\overline{R}$ is the interpretation of R and
$\overline{R}(t_1(\langle \theta, h \rangle), ..., t_n(\langle \theta, h \rangle))$ holds;
$\langle \theta, h \rangle \models \neg\varphi$ if $\langle \theta, h \rangle \not\models \varphi$;
$\langle \theta, h \rangle \models \varphi \rightarrow \psi$ if $\langle \theta, h \rangle \models \neg\varphi$ or $\langle \theta, h \rangle \models \psi$;
$\langle \theta, h \rangle \models \exists x.\varphi$ if there exists an assignment θ' differing from θ only in the value assigned to freeze variable x such that $\langle \theta', h \rangle \models \varphi$;
$\langle \theta, h \rangle \models \Diamond\varphi$; if there exists an $t \in [0, \infty)$ such that $\langle \theta, h^{(t)} \rangle \models \varphi$;
$\langle \theta, h \rangle \models \Box\varphi$; if for all $t \in [0, \infty)$ $\langle \theta, h^{(t)} \rangle \models \varphi$;

The initial states and the transition relation can also be expressed as a DTL formula, as illustrated in the next example. Note that although we use the same names IQ_M and TR_M as in the previous example, this is in fact not correct because in the next example these are actual DTL formulae. When we refer to these names we mean from now on the DTL formulae.

Example

Same machine M as above:

1. **Events:**
   $E_M : \{d_0, d_1, \lambda_d\}$

2. **States:**
   $Q_M : \{u\} \rightarrow \{0, 1, 2\}$

3. **Initial States:**
   $IQ_M \equiv \textbf{st} = [u \mapsto 0]$

4. **Transitions:**
$TR_M \equiv (\mathbf{st} = [u \mapsto 0] \wedge \mathbf{e} = d_0 \wedge \mathbf{st}' = [u \mapsto 1]) \vee$
$(\mathbf{st} = [u \mapsto 1] \wedge \mathbf{e} = d_1 \wedge \mathbf{st}' = [u \mapsto 2]) \vee$
$(\mathbf{e} = \lambda_d \wedge \mathbf{st}' = \mathbf{st})$

end example

In the above example we used expressions like $\mathbf{st} = [u \mapsto 0]$; to increase readability we use the abbreviation $\mathbf{st}(u) = 0$ instead of the previous one.

The *enabling condition* of an event in machine M denoted by $Enabled_M(e)$ is that condition that enables the generation of that event in M. For example, $Enabled_M(d_0)$ of the previous example is condition $\mathbf{st}(u) = 0$.

In order to describe situations where an old state is updated we use the variant construct: $\mathbf{st} \mid x : v$ defined above. Furthermore we do not mention the λ-transition anymore because this transition is the same for all machines.

The local properties of a module Z can now be expressed as formula $IQ_Z \wedge \Box TR_Z$. Thus $\text{Comp}(M_Z)=\{X \in Hist(E_Z, Q_Z) \mid X \models IQ_Z \wedge \Box TR_Z\}$. The liveness properties can now be added, expressed by some extra DTL formula V_Z, the *validity condition*. The complete behaviour of module Z is the following set of histories:

$$\{X \in \text{Comp}(M_Z) \mid X \models V_Z\},$$

and is described by formula $IQ_Z \wedge \Box TR_Z \wedge V_Z$.

2.5 Machines, allowed computations, and correct development steps

As we have seen above, there are several kinds of machines -abstract, component and composite ones- and they all have a set of allowed computations. If we have an abstract machine M_A, described by temporal formula $IQ_A \wedge TR_A$, and component machines M_i, described by temporal formula $IQ_i \wedge TR_i$, and if we have furthermore an interconnection $\mathcal{I} = \langle \alpha, \langle \delta_i \rangle_{i \in I} \rangle$ that links both kinds of machine then we can construct the composite machine M_c as follows:

- The interface E_c is the same as the interface of the interconnection.
- The set of states $Q_c = Q_A \times \prod_{i \in I} Q_i$, i.e, the product of the set of states of the abstract machine with the product of the sets of states of all the component machines.
- The set of initial states of M_c we also want to describe by a temporal formula. A first try would be the following temporal formula $IQ_A \wedge \bigwedge_{i \in I} IQ_i$ but this formula consists of a part that describe the initial states of M_A and a part that describe the initial states of the M_i's. The formula must however describe the initial states of M_c. But fortunately the set of states of M_c is defined as a Cartesian product of the set of states of M_A and M_i. So if we replace every state term $\mathbf{st} = x$ in IQ_A by $\pi^A(\mathbf{st}) = x$ where π^A is just the ordinary projection function from Q_c to Q_A, then this last formula expresses the same thing as IQ_A but now in terms of the states of M_c. This replacement is denoted by $[IQ_A]_{\mathbf{Atoc}}$.

The same thing can be done for the temporal formulas IQ_i: state term $\mathbf{st} = x$ is replaced by $\pi^i(\mathbf{st}) = x$ where π^i is just the ordinary projection function from Q_c to Q_A. This replacement is denoted by $[IQ_i]_{\mathbf{itoc}}$.
So the set of initial states of M_c can be expressed by following temporal formula $IQ_c \stackrel{\text{def}}{=} [IQ_A]_{\mathbf{Atoc}} \wedge \bigwedge [IQ_i]_{\mathbf{itoc}}$.

- For describing the state-transition relation we have the same problem but now for the states and events. But fortunately we have the definition of α and δ_i's which we can use to transform event terms in TR_A and TR_i into event terms of TR_c. Event term $\mathbf{e} = d$ in TR_A is transformed into $\alpha(\mathbf{e}) = d$ and event term $\mathbf{e} = f$ in TR_i is transformed into $\delta(\mathbf{e}) = f$. Let $[f]_{\mathbf{Atoc}}$ denote the transformation of both event and state terms of a formula f in the temporal framework of the abstract machine into the temporal framework of the composite machine and let $[g]_{\mathbf{itoc}}$ denote the transformation of both event and state terms of a formula g in the temporal framework of a component machine i. Then the state-transition relation of the composite machine can now be expressed as following temporal formula $TR_c \stackrel{\text{def}}{=} \Box([TR_A]_{\mathbf{Atoc}} \wedge \bigwedge_{i\in I}[TR_i]_{\mathbf{itoc}})$.

We use the correctness definition given before in the following form:

$\langle \delta_i^* \rangle_{i\in I}^{-1}(\langle B_i \rangle_{i\in I}) \subseteq \alpha^{-1}(B_A)$.

In the present formalism, this translates to

$\langle \delta_i^* \rangle_{i\in I}^{-1}(\langle \{X \in Comp(M_i) : X \models V_i\} \rangle_{i\in I}) \subseteq \alpha^{-1}(\{X \in Comp(M_A) : X \models V_A\})$.

And this can be expressed as the following temporal formula:

$\bigwedge_{i\in I}[IQ_i \wedge \Box TR_i \wedge V_i]_{\mathbf{itoc}} \rightarrow [IQ_A \wedge \Box TR_A \wedge V_A]_{\mathbf{Atoc}}$

Due to the separation of the allowed behaviour into a machine and a validity part we can split this verification condition into two verification conditions. One applying to machines and one applying to validity conditions[1]:

- *maximality* : any event that can be generated by the system of component machines can also be performed by the abstract machine.
- *validity* : any allowed computation of each component machine corresponds with an allowed computation of the abstract machine.

More formally:

- *maximality* :
  $Comp(M_c) \models \forall e \in E_c.(Reachable_c \wedge \bigwedge_{i\in I}[Enabled_i(e)]_{\mathbf{itoc}})$
  $\rightarrow [Enabled_A(e)]_{\mathbf{Atoc}}$
  where $Reachable_c$ is a condition that checks if a state of the composite machine is reachable, $Enabled_i(e)$ is the enabling condition of the event

[1] Observe that this split can only be done when V_i and V_A concern pure liveness properties cfr. [1]. In case $V = \Box S_0 \wedge V'$ for a validity condition V, where $\Box S_0$ is the safety part and V' the pure liveness part (see [1] for this terminology) the transition relation TR of the machine in question must be described by $TR' \stackrel{\text{def}}{=} TR \wedge S_0$ and the validity part by V'.

of machine i corresponding to event e, and $Enabled_A(e)$ the enabling condition of the event of the abstract machine corresponding event to event e.

- *validity* :
  $Comp(M_c) \models (\bigwedge_{i \in I}[V_i]_{i \mathrm{to} c}) \rightarrow [V_A]_{A \mathrm{to} c}$
  where V_i is the validity condition of module i, and V_A is the validity condition of the abstract module.

Given the construction of the composite machine, maximality implies, intuitively, that all interleavings, even unfair ones, of the component machines should, after abstraction, be allowed by the abstract machine. Validity means, intuitively, that only those sequences should be allowed as complete behaviours that also satisfy some progress properties.

To prove these two conditions it is necessary to find an implementation invariant that, firstly, describes the reachable states of the composite machine in order to prove the maximality condition and, secondly, is such that it is of help in the proof of the validity condition.

The proof of the maximality condition is intuitively done as follows: one checks if for all events of the composite machine the maximality condition holds. For the proof of the validity condition Stark uses his rely/guarantee rule because the V-formulae can be written in rely/guarantee form. This rule solves the circular reasoning problem in another way than [4, 15, 9], see Section 2.7 for details.

2.6 Specification of Lamport's soda machine

In the next example, the soda machine example [7], we illustrate some of the above notions – particularly that of composite machine. The soda machine is a system in which the user deposits either a half dollar or two quarters and the machine in return dispenses a can of soda.

Example

Given two specifications of a soda-machine, show that one specification implements (i.e. refines) the other one.

The high level specification of the soda-machine :

Initially the user either deposits a quarter or a half dollar. If he deposits a quarter then the next coin can only be a quarter. If he next deposits a half dollar the machine enters the error state; if he deposits a quarter the machine dispenses a can of soda. A can of soda is also returned when he deposits a half dollar initially. If the user deposits another coin before the machine has dispensed a can of soda then the machine will also enter the error state. This informal specification is illustrated in figure 2 and written down formally in Stark's formalism as S_H:

1. **Events:**
   $E_H = \{\mathrm{de.qu}\downarrow, \mathrm{de.hd}\downarrow, \mathrm{di.so}\uparrow, \lambda_H\}$

   - de.qu$\downarrow$: the depositing of a quarter by the environment.
   - de.hd$\downarrow$: the depositing of a half dollar by the environment.

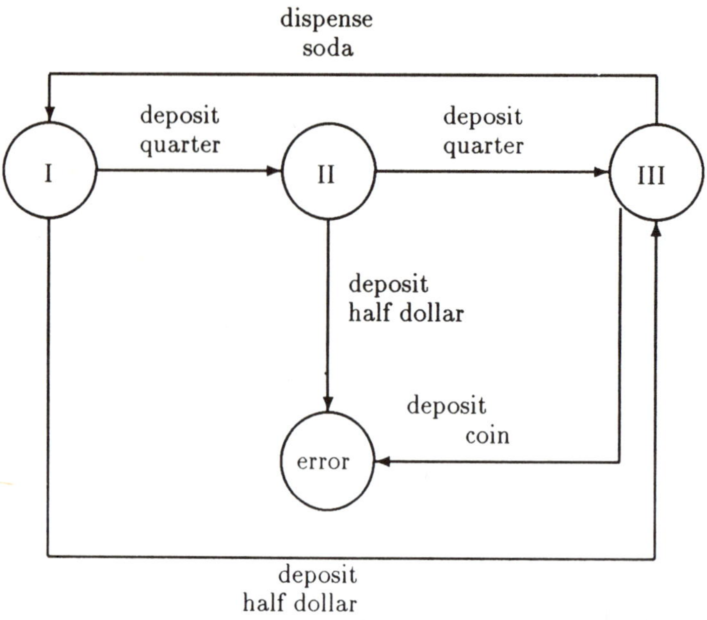

Figure 2:

- di.so↑ : the dispensing of a can of soda by M_H.

2. **States**
   $Q_H : ms \rightarrow \{I, II, III, error\}$
   $ms = I$: M_H is in state I.

3. Initial States:
   $IQ_H \equiv \mathbf{st}(ms) = I$

4. **Transitions:**
   $TR_H \equiv$

- $\mathrm{e} = \mathrm{de.qu}\!\downarrow \wedge((\mathbf{st}(ms) = I \wedge \mathbf{st}' = \mathbf{st} \mid ms : II) \vee$
  $(\mathbf{st}(ms) = II \wedge \mathbf{st}' = \mathbf{st} \mid ms : III) \vee$
  $((\mathbf{st}(ms) \neq I \vee \mathbf{st}(ms) \neq II) \wedge \mathbf{st}' = \mathbf{st} \mid ms : error))$
  If the environment deposits a quarter and M_H is in state I then it enters state II. If the environment deposits a quarter and M_H is in state II then M_H enters state III. If the environment deposits a quarter and M_H is in state III or the *error* state then M_H enters the *error* state. This latter possibility we must explicitly allow, because an machine M must be input-cooperative.

- $\mathrm{e} = \mathrm{de.hd}\!\downarrow \wedge((\mathbf{st}(ms) = I \wedge \mathbf{st}' = \mathbf{st} \mid ms : III) \vee$
  $(\mathbf{st}(ms) \neq I \wedge \mathbf{st}' = \mathbf{st} \mid ms : error))$
  If the environment deposits a half dollar and M_H is in state I then M_H enters state III. In all other states M_H enters the *error* state.

- $\mathbf{e} = \text{di.so}\uparrow \wedge \mathbf{st}(ms) = III \wedge \mathbf{st}' = \mathbf{st} \mid ms : I$
  M_H dispenses a can of soda when it is in state III and then enters state I..

5. **Validity Condition:**
   To make the example not too complicated we leave the validity condition out of the specification, but it should specify intuitively that if the user deposits a half dollar or 2 quarters then eventually the machine dispenses a can of soda.

The lower level specification :
The lower level specification is written in some programming language:

var x: { 0, 25, 50 };
    $y : \{25, 50\}$;
beginloop
    $\alpha : \langle x := 0 \rangle$;
    β : **while** $\langle x < 50 \rangle$
        do $\gamma : \langle y :=$ *deposit_coin* **only if** $x + y_{new} \leq 50 \rangle$ **else raise error**
            $\delta : \langle x := x + y \rangle$
        od;
    $\epsilon : \langle$*dispense_soda*$\rangle$
end loop
error : $\langle$*errorhandling*$\rangle$

The only construct that should need explanation is:
$\langle y :=$ *deposit_coin* **only if** $x + y_{new} \leq 50 \rangle$ **else raise error**.
The meaning is as follows: y is assigned the value of a coin only if this value plus the current value of x is less or equal 50, otherwise it will raise an error, i.e. enter the error state.
The above program is in Stark's formalism described as specification S_L:

1. **Events:**
   $E_L = \{e1, e2, e3(v)\downarrow, e4, e5\uparrow, \lambda_L : v = \{25, 50\}\}$

2. **States:**
   $Q_L : (pc \rightarrow \{\alpha, \beta, \delta, \gamma, \epsilon, error\}) \times (x \rightarrow \{0, 25, 50\}) \times (y \rightarrow \{25, 50\})$

3. **Initial States**
   $IQ_L \equiv \mathbf{st}(pc) = \alpha$

4. **Transitions:**
   $TR_L \equiv$

   - $\mathbf{e} = e1 \wedge \mathbf{st}(pc) = \alpha \wedge \mathbf{st}' = \mathbf{st} \mid pc, x : \beta, 0$
     M_L performs an internal event to make x equal 0.
   - $\mathbf{e} = e2 \wedge \mathbf{st}(pc) = \beta \wedge ((\mathbf{st}(x) < 50 \wedge \mathbf{st}' = \mathbf{st} \mid pc : \gamma) \vee$
     $(\mathbf{st}(x) \geq 50 \wedge \mathbf{st}' = \mathbf{st} \mid pc : \epsilon))$
     M_L performs an internal checking event.

- $\mathrm{e} = e3(v)\downarrow \wedge((\mathbf{st}(pc) = \gamma \wedge v + \mathbf{st}(x) \leq 50 \wedge \mathbf{st}' = \mathbf{st} \mid pc, y : \delta, v) \vee$
  $((\mathbf{st}(pc) \neq \gamma \vee v + \mathbf{st}(x) > 50) \wedge \mathbf{st}' = \mathbf{st} \mid pc : error))$
  The environment deposits a quarter or a half dollar: this may only happen if pc and x have certain values. If pc and x do not have these values M_L enters the *error* state. What coin is deposited is "remembered" by y.
- $\mathrm{e} = e4 \wedge \mathbf{st}(pc) = \delta \wedge \mathbf{st}' = \mathbf{st} \mid pc, x : \beta, \mathbf{st}(x) + \mathbf{st}(y)$
  M_L performs an internal adding event.
- $\mathrm{e} = e5\uparrow \wedge \mathbf{st}(pc) = \epsilon \wedge \mathbf{st}' = \mathbf{st} \mid pc : \alpha$
  The machine dispenses a can of soda.

5. **Validity Condition:**
   To make the example not too complicated we leave the validity condition out of the specification.

We must find a composite machine M_C and translations α and δ such that "$\alpha(M_C)$ gives M_H and $\delta(M_C)$ gives M_L". First find translations α and δ. From the definition of the abstraction and decomposition operator we know that α is a function from E_C (interface of composite machine) to E_H and δ is a function from E_C to E_L. We can construct E_C by means of a Cartesian product out of E_H and E_L using some intuition. (This construction is not from [12, 13] but in our opinion more clearly follows the intuition.)

If M_L generates $e1$ (an internal event) then M_H must generate a λ_H event thus $\langle \lambda_H; e1 \rangle$ is an event of M_C. We can do this for all the events of M_H and M_L. E_C is then as follows:
$E_C = \{\langle \lambda_H, e1 \rangle, \langle \lambda_H, e2 \rangle, \langle \mathrm{de.qu}\downarrow, e3(25)\downarrow \rangle, \langle \mathrm{de.hd}\downarrow, e3(50)\downarrow \rangle,$
$\langle \lambda_H, e4 \rangle, \langle \mathrm{di.so}\uparrow, e5\uparrow \rangle, \langle \lambda_H, \lambda_L \rangle\}$
From E_C we now can get α and δ:
Let $\langle p, q \rangle \in E_C$ then $\alpha(\langle p, q \rangle) = p$ and $\delta(\langle p, q \rangle) = q$. The construction of M_C is now easy, see Section 2.5.

In order to check that M_L implements M_H we must check:

$$\forall e \in E_C . [Enabled_L(e)]_{L\mathbf{to}c} \rightarrow [Enabled_H(e)]_{H\mathbf{to}c}$$

This formula holds, for instance in case of $e = \langle \lambda_H, e1 \rangle$:
$[Enabled_L(e)]_{L\mathbf{to}c} \equiv \pi^L(\mathrm{st})(pc) = \alpha$ and $[Enabled_H(e)]_{L\mathbf{to}c} \equiv true$ so the formula holds for case $e = \langle \lambda_H, e1 \rangle$.

end example

2.7 Stark's rely/guarantee proof rule

It is Stark's intention to prove the validity part with a proof rule. To use this proof rule it is necessary that the set of allowed computations is in a special form. This form, which is called the *rely/guarantee* form is based on Cliff Jones' original idea of including, in the rely-condition, assumptions about the other components [4]. In Stark's formalism this form is as follows: $\{X \in \mathrm{Comp}(M) : X \models R \rightarrow G\}$, i.e. the DTL logic formula V is written as $R \rightarrow G$. The R(ely)-part of this formula expresses how the module being specified relies on what its environment provides. The G(uarantee)-part of this formula expresses what the module then guarantees to provide. We now give an intuitive explanation of this proof rule.

As seen above we must show that any allowed computation of each component machine corresponds with an allowed computation of the abstract machine. The sets of allowed computations of component machine M_i and abstract machine M_A are respectively expressed as $\{X \in \text{Comp}(M_i) : X \models R_i \rightarrow G_i\}$ and $\{X \in \text{Comp}(M_A) : X \models R_A \rightarrow G_A\}$. In order to compare these sets with each other we must transform these sets into sets that specify the allowed computations of the composite machine. This means that the first set is transformed into $\{X \in \text{Comp}(M_c) : X \models [R_i]_{\mathbf{itoc}} \rightarrow [G_i]_{\mathbf{itoc}}\}$ and the second one into $\{X \in \text{Comp}(M_c) : X \models [R_A]_{\mathbf{Atoc}} \rightarrow [G_A]_{\mathbf{Atoc}}\}$. In order to facilitate the explanation of the proof rule we write $\mathcal{P} \models R_A \rightarrow G_A$ instead of $\{X \in \text{Comp}(M_c) : X \models [R_A]_{\mathbf{Atoc}} \rightarrow [G_A]_{\mathbf{Atoc}}\}$ and $\mathcal{P} \models R_i \rightarrow G_i$ instead of $\{X \in \text{Comp}(M_c) : X \models [R_i]_{\mathbf{itoc}} \rightarrow [G_i]_{\mathbf{itoc}}\}$.

There must exist some relationship between the R_A, G_A, R_i and G_i mentioned above. This relationship is as follows.

- Relationship between G_i and G_A:
  If the conjunction of the G_i's holds then G_A holds.
  Formally: $\mathcal{P} \models \bigwedge_i G_i \rightarrow G_A$.

- Relationship between R_i and R_A:
  If R_A holds then it is impossible to infer that the conjunction of the R_i's holds because the R_A only says something about the external relationship and the R_i says something about the internal relationship too. Thus R_A is not enough. We also need a condition to infer that the internal relationship holds. This condition is the conjunction of the G_i because this guarantees the internal relationship.
  Formally: $\mathcal{P} \models [R_A \wedge \bigwedge_{j \neq i} G_j] \rightarrow R_i$

This leads to the following rule to infer $\mathcal{P} \models R_A \rightarrow G_A$ from the $\mathcal{P} \models R_i \rightarrow G_i$'s: (Note: this rule is nearly the same as in [13].)

$$\frac{\mathcal{P} \models R_i \rightarrow G_i, \mathcal{P} \models [R_A \wedge \bigwedge_{j \neq i} G_j] \rightarrow R_i, \mathcal{P} \models \bigwedge_i G_i \rightarrow G_A}{\mathcal{P} \models R_A \rightarrow G_A}$$

Regrettably, this simple rule is not sound in our set-up (a similar rule is, however, sound in the setting of [4, 15, 9] because there they do not define a R/G condition to hold for a component by straightforward implication, as above, but by a more involved definition reflecting induction on the communication trace).

The reason is that one can get a cycle of proof obligations, as can be seen from the following example.

<u>Example</u>

Suppose there are two component machines. Suppose we have proven the following proof obligations:

1. $\mathcal{P} \models R_1 \rightarrow G_1$
2. $\mathcal{P} \models R_2 \rightarrow G_2$
3. $\mathcal{P} \models [R_A \wedge G_2] \rightarrow R_1$

4. $\mathcal{P} \models [R_A \wedge G_1] \rightarrow R_2$

5. $\mathcal{P} \models [G_1 \wedge G_2] \rightarrow G_A$

We want to infer $\mathcal{P} \models R_A \rightarrow G_A$ from 1–5.
Assume R_A holds.
Then we must prove that G_A holds.
Working our way backwards, we conclude: $G_1 \wedge G_2$ should hold.
Similarly, from 1 and 2 we conclude: $R_1 \wedge R_2$ should hold.
From 3 and 4 we conclude: $[R_A \wedge G_2] \wedge [R_A \wedge G_1]$ should hold.
Thus, $G_1 \wedge G_2$ should hold.
So we get the cycle $G_1 \wedge G_2 \rightarrow R_1 \wedge R_2 \rightarrow G_1 \wedge G_2$.

end example

The idea is now, that the proof obligations in the cycle can be trivially fulfilled by choosing false for all assertions involved. It is than also possible to choose R_A to be true and G_A to be false. $\mathcal{P} \models R_A \rightarrow G_A$ is than derivable, and equivalent to true implies false! Hence the rule is unsound. Stark eventually solves this problem by imposing a condition that rules out cycles. To avoid making the rule seriously incomplete by imposing such a condition, first an adaptation to reflect the dependencies between components more precisely needs to be made.

In the rule as given above we can not see the split between the internal and external relationship of a component. Therefore Stark introduces $G_{i,j}$, $G_{i,A}$, $G_{A,i}$, $R_{i,j}$, $R_{A,i}$ and $R_{i,A}$ to make this split explicit. (In the following, "environment" means the environment as seen by the abstract machine.)

- $G_{i,A}$ describes the guarantee condition from component i towards the environment.
  Note: this is the same as what the environment should rely on for component i to provide, which we denote by $R_{i,A}$.

- $R_{A,i}$ describes the rely condition of component i w.r.t. the environment.
  Note: this is the same as what the environment should guarantee towards component i, which we denote by $G_{A,i}$.

- $G_{i,j}$ describes the internal relation, i.e. what component i guarantees to component j.
  Note: this is the same as what component j should rely on component i to provide, which we denote by $R_{i,j}$.

If we use this split, the proof obligations of the rule change to:

- $\mathcal{P} \models \bigwedge_i G_{i,A} \rightarrow G_A, \mathcal{P} \models G_i \rightarrow [G_{i,A} \wedge \bigwedge_{j \neq i} G_{i,j}]$
  (this was $\mathcal{P} \models \bigwedge_i G_i \rightarrow G_A$)

- $\mathcal{P} \models R_A \rightarrow \bigwedge_i R_{A,i}, \mathcal{P} \models [R_{A,i} \wedge \bigwedge_{j \neq i} R_{j,i}] \rightarrow R_i$
  (this was $\mathcal{P} \models [R \wedge \bigwedge_{j \neq i} G_j] \rightarrow R_i$)

The resulting rule has still the same trouble as the previous one, though in a less trivial form. This is illustrated in the next example.

Example

Suppose there are two component machines. Suppose we have proven the following proof obligations:

1. $\mathcal{P} \models R_1 \rightarrow G_1$
2. $\mathcal{P} \models R_2 \rightarrow G_2$
3. $\mathcal{P} \models R_A \rightarrow [R_{A,1} \wedge R_{A,2}]$
4. $\mathcal{P} \models G_1 \rightarrow [G_{1,A} \wedge G_{1,2}]$
5. $\mathcal{P} \models G_2 \rightarrow [G_{2,A} \wedge G_{2,1}]$
6. $\mathcal{P} \models [G_{1,A} \wedge G_{2,A}] \rightarrow G_A$
7. $\mathcal{P} \models [R_{A,1} \wedge R_{2,1}] \rightarrow R_1$
8. $\mathcal{P} \models [R_{A,2} \wedge R_{1,2}] \rightarrow R_2$

We want to infer $\mathcal{P} \models R_A \rightarrow G_A$ from 1-8.
Assume R_A holds then we must prove that G_A holds.
From 6 we can conclude: $G_{1,A} \wedge G_{2,A}$ must hold.
From 4 and 5 we conclude: $G_1 \wedge G_2$ must hold.
From 1 and 2 we conclude: $R_1 \wedge R_2$ must hold.
From 7 and 8 we conclude: $[R_{A,1} \wedge R_{2,1}] \wedge [R_{A,2} \wedge R_{1,2}]$ must hold.
From 3 we conclude: $R_A \wedge R_{2,1} \wedge R_{1,2}$ must hold.
From assumption we conclude: $R_{2,1} \wedge R_{1,2}$ must hold.
Because of $R_{2,1} \equiv G_{2,1}$ and $R_{1,2} \equiv G_{1,2}$: $G_{2,1} \wedge G_{1,2}$ must hold.
From 4 and 5 we conclude: $G_1 \wedge G_2$ must hold.
So we get cycle $G_1 \wedge G_2 \rightarrow R_1 \wedge R_2 \rightarrow R_{2,1} \wedge R_{1,2} \rightarrow G_1 \wedge G_2$.

end example

Now unsoundness can be shown similarly as before. The proof obligations in the cycle can again be trivially fulfilled by choosing false for all assertions involved. It is than also possible to choose R_A and all $R_{A,i}$ to be true and G_A to be false. $\mathcal{P} \models R_A \rightarrow G_A$ is than again derivable, and the rule therefore unsound.

Stark's solution to the cycle problem is given for this version of the rule. The idea is to require that the set of $G_{i,j}$ is acyclic, i.e. to require that there can be no unbroken cyclic dependency between components.
Formally: $\{G_{i,j} : i, j \in I\}$ is acyclic if
$\mathcal{P} \models \bigvee_{k=0}^{n-1} G_{i_k, i_{k+1}}$ for all simple cycles $\{(i_0, i_1), \ldots, (i_{n-1}, i_n)\}$ in I with $i_n = i_0$. This additional information breaks the circular reasoning. This means for the above example that we have the extra proof obligation $\mathcal{P} \models G_{1,2} \vee G_{2,1}$. The last example used above illustrates how this extra proof obligation works.

Example

Suppose there are two component machines and that we have proven the proof obligations as before, together with:

9. $\mathcal{P} \models G_{1,2} \vee G_{2,1}$

Suppose R_A holds.
From 3 we infer: $R_{A,1} \wedge R_{A,2}$ holds.
From 7 and 8 and logical reasoning we infer: $(R_{2,1} \rightarrow R_1) \wedge (R_{1,2} \rightarrow R_2)$.
From 1 and 2 we infer: $(R_{2,1} \rightarrow G_1) \wedge (R_{1,2} \rightarrow G_2)$.
From 4 and 5 we infer: $(R_{2,1} \rightarrow [G_{1,A} \wedge G_{1,2}]) \wedge (R_{1,2} \rightarrow [G_{2,A} \wedge G_{2,1}])$.
With logical reasoning we infer:
$(R_{2,1} \rightarrow G_{1,2}) \wedge (R_{1,2} \rightarrow G_{2,1}) \wedge (R_{2,1} \rightarrow G_{1,A}) \wedge (R_{1,2} \rightarrow G_{2,A})$. (*)
The first two form the cycle we are discussing because
$G_{1,2} \equiv R_{1,2}$ and $G_{2,1} \equiv R_{2,1}$: $R_{2,1} \rightarrow G_{1,2} \equiv R_{1,2} \rightarrow G_{2,1} \equiv R_{2,1}$.
This cycle is broken by condition 9.
From 9 and $R_{2,1} \rightarrow G_{1,2}$ we infer with logical reasoning: $R_{1,2}$.
From 9 and $R_{1,2} \rightarrow G_{2,1}$ we infer with logical reasoning: $R_{2,1}$.
So (*) becomes: $R_{2,1} \wedge R_{1,2} \wedge (R_{2,1} \rightarrow G_{1,A}) \wedge (R_{1,2} \rightarrow G_{2,A})$.
With logical reasoning we infer: $G_{1,A} \wedge G_{2,A}$.
From 6 we infer: G_A.
So from 1-9 we can infer: $R_A \rightarrow G_A$.

end example

In [12, 13] Stark gives a soundness proof of this last rule.

2.8 Relationship with Lamport's model

The relationship between Lamport's model and the one of Stark is mainly the way how the stutter-problem is solved. This problem is as follows. Given two observations of a system, the first observation contains only consecutive snap-shots of the system that differ from each other whereas the second observation contains the same snap-shots but also some consecutive ones that are identical. This is called stuttering. Clearly these observations must be considered to be equal. The problem is: how must we do that? Both methods provide a solution. In [3] these solutions are discussed in detail, here we only give an informal description of them.

Lamport's methods [7, 6, 1] use infinite discrete state sequences as model of observations. Because of this discrete time domain, a temporal operator referring to the next state can be (and in many temporal logics is) defined. Specifications should not distinguish between sequences that are equal modulo stuttering. Therefore the use of this operator in specifications is simply forbidden.

Stark's method [12, 13, 14] uses dense time models, in which an execution is modeled by a state-valued function of the set of non-negative reals. Using dense time is based on the intuition that state changes happen only now and then, so that in between two consecutive changes there are uncountable moments at which *nothing* happens. Consequently, it is impossible to count, or express, stutter-steps, i.e., there is no next state operator.

In both frameworks there is a completeness problem if refinement mappings or relations are used to prove correctness. Intuitively, this is connected with the amount of information present in states. Abadi and Lamport, in [1], present a solution for the discrete framework, using history as well as prophesy variables, that can be also used in the dense setting.

2.9 Our use of Stark's formalism

In Stark's formalism a separation is made between the machine part (local) and the validity condition part (global), see Section 2.5. We use the validity condition part not for liveness but for deleting undesirable sequences. In the readers/writers example we will see that a deadlocked sequence is an example of such an undesirable sequence. These deadlocked sequences are removed by defining the proper validity condition. In the next section we see what such a validity condition looks like.

3 R/W-Problem in Stark's Formalism

We are now ready to apply Stark's formalism to Dijkstra's development. The readers/writers problem, described intuitively, is as follows: given N readers and M writers, a reader performs, cyclically, non-critical action `NCS` and critical action `READ`, and a writer performs, again cyclically, non-critical action `NCS` and critical action `WRITE`. We must synchronise these readers and writers in such a way that if a writer performs the `WRITE` action it is the only process that performs a critical action, i.e. mutual exclusion is required (ME). Furthermore, it is necessary that any request to execute the critical action is eventually granted, i.e. eventual access should hold (EA). It is this synchroniser that has to be developed. But before we give the development we formulate an abstract specification for the problem.

The development process has four steps: in the first step Dijkstra gives an implementation by a program that produces undesirable deadlocked sequences. In the second step Dijkstra uses the split binary semaphore technique to delete the deadlocked sequences from the first implementation; he obtains by this technique a second implementation that introduces as undesirable sequences new deadlocked ones. These deadlocked sequences are deleted in the third step resulting in a third implementation that contains as undesirable sequences unnecessarily blocking ones. These sequences are not deadlocking sequences but only sequences that are inefficient because they suspend a reader or writer unnecessarily. In the fourth step, these sequences are deleted and also the resulting implementation is cleaned up.

3.1 The abstract specification

We follow [2] and show how the informal approach used there can be formalised. Dijkstra rewrites the informal specification as follows: as a first step, he describes readers and writers by programs (whose semantics he assumes are intuitively clear):

```
reader0:  do true → NCS;READ  od
writer0:  do true → NCS;WRITE od
```

He then combines these programs into one parallel program `S0`. `S0` forms the abstract specification and is defined as follows:

$$\mathtt{S0} : \ \|_{i=1}^{N} \ \mathtt{reader0} \ \| \ \|_{j=1}^{M} \ \mathtt{writer0} \ ,$$

Where $||_{i=1}^{N}$ `reader0` is a notation for the N-fold parallel composition of `reader0`.

Finally he formulates an informal requirement to exclude from `S0` the unwanted sequences. This requirement is the same as in the introduction: ME and EA. The complete abstract specification is thus `S0` plus this requirement.

We transform `S0` into a machine M_A and the informal requirements ME and EA into V_A to get a specification a la Stark. Note: `S0` has some liveness or fairness property that is assumed a priori by Dijkstra. Which property Dijkstra assumes is not entirely clear from [2]. We assume, following Stark, that all machines have the property that if a machine is infinitely often enabled it will infinitely often make a move. This corresponds to strong fairness.

We want to specify the behaviour of the synchroniser module in an environment of readers and writers. As it is really the scheduler we wish to specify, it seems advantageous to us to single this part out as a separate component. The specification $S_A = \langle M_A, V_A\rangle$ we shall use is then as follows.

1. **Events:**
   $E_A = \{rtryi\downarrow, rruni\uparrow, rresti\downarrow, wtryj\downarrow, wrunj\uparrow, wrestj\downarrow :$
   $i \in [1,\ldots,N], j \in [1,\ldots,M]\}$
   When a *rtryi* event occurs M_A knows that *readeri* wants to execute `READ`. M_A subsequently generates a *rruni* event to signal *readeri* that it may execute `READ`. When a *rresti* event occurs M_A knows that *readeri* has finished executing `READ`. Similarly for *writerj*.

2. **States:**
   $Q_A : (\{r1,\ldots,rN\} \cup \{w1,\ldots,wM\}) \rightarrow \{tryg, rung, resg, err\}$
   $\mathbf{st}(ri) = tryg$: *readeri* wants to execute `READ`.
   $\mathbf{st}(ri) = err$: *readeri* is not functioning correctly. Note, that this is the state of the scheduler, reflecting the activities of the readers and writers.

3. **Initial States:**
   $IQ_A \equiv \bigwedge_{i=1}^{N} \mathbf{st}(ri) = resg \wedge \bigwedge_{j=1}^{M} \mathbf{st}(wj) = resg$

4. **Transitions:**
   $TR_A \equiv$

   - $e = rtryi\downarrow \wedge((\mathbf{st}(ri) = resg \wedge \mathbf{st}' = \mathbf{st} \mid ri : tryg)\vee$
     $(\mathbf{st}(ri) \neq resg \wedge \mathbf{st}' = \mathbf{st} \mid ri : err))$
     If *readeri* is functioning correctly (i.e. the synchroniser is not in the *err* state for this reader) then it goes from state *resg* to state *tryg* on the occurrence of the *rtryi* event. This event signals the synchroniser that *readeri* wants to to execute its `READ`.
   - $e = rruni\uparrow \wedge \mathbf{st}(ri) = tryg \wedge \mathbf{st}' = \mathbf{st} \mid ri : rung$
     When a reader has signaled the synchroniser that it wants to execute `READ`, the synchroniser signals with a *rruni* event that it may execute its `READ`. Note: because we follow Dijkstra the synchroniser does not check if there are writers that are currently execute their `WRITE`. We have could have done it here but then ME can be dropped from the validity conditions because it is then already specified here.
   - $e = rresti\downarrow \wedge((\mathbf{st}(ri) = rung \wedge \mathbf{st}' = \mathbf{st} \mid ri : resg)\vee$
     $(\mathbf{st}(ri) \neq rung \wedge \mathbf{st}' = \mathbf{st} \mid ri : err))$

When *readeri* has finished executing **READ**, it signals this to the synchroniser with a *rresti* event.

The writer events can be dealt with in the same way.

5. **Validity Conditions:**
V_A extracts from $Comp(M_A)$ those sequences that satisfy the mutual exclusion requirement ME: when a writer executes its **WRITE** then no other writers are executing **WRITE** and no readers executing **READ**. And V_A also extracts those sequences that satisfy the "liveness" requirement EA: when a reader or writer wants to execute its critical section it is eventually allowed to do so. Formally:
$V_A \equiv P_0 \wedge R_A \rightarrow G_A$
$P_0 \equiv \Box((\bigwedge_{j=1}^{M} \mathtt{st}(wj) \neq rung) \vee$
$\quad ((\sum_{j=1}^{M} \mathtt{st}(wj) = rung) = 1 \wedge \bigwedge_{i=1}^{N} \mathtt{st}(ri) \neq rung))$
This is the ME requirement.
$R_A \equiv \Box(\bigwedge_{i=1}^{N}(\mathtt{st}(ri) = rung \rightarrow \Diamond(\mathtt{st}(ri) = resg)) \wedge$
$\quad \bigwedge_{j=1}^{M}(\mathtt{st}(wj) = rung \rightarrow \Diamond(\mathtt{st}(wj) = resg)))$
$G_A \equiv \Box(\bigwedge_{i=1}^{N}(\mathtt{st}(ri) = tryg \rightarrow \Diamond(\mathtt{st}(ri) = rung)) \wedge$
$\quad \bigwedge_{j=1}^{M}(\mathtt{st}(wj) = tryg \rightarrow \Diamond(\mathtt{st}(wj) = rung)))$
And this the EA requirement.

3.2 The first development step

Dijkstra's next step is to translate the informally stated requirement into formal program form, i.e. to transform `reader0` and `writer0` in such a way that they satisfy the synchronisation requirement ME. We discuss this translation informally.

He introduces shared variables **aw** and **ar** and binary semaphore **mx**. Shared variable **ar** represents the number of readers which may execute their **READ**, and **aw** represents the number of writers which may execute their **WRITE**. A reader increases **ar** by 1 if it is allowed to execute its **READ** and decreases **ar** by 1 if it is finished with executing its **READ**. Since **ar** will be changed and accessed by several readers, Dijkstra protects the operation of increasing and decreasing **ar** by semaphore operations P and V on binary semaphore *mx* to ensure that only one reader changes **ar** at a time, i.e. mutual exclusion. The synchronisation requirement is brought into `reader0` by guarding the increasing operation of **ar** with condition `aw=0`, i.e., the number of writers that may execute their **WRITE** equals zero. The same can be done for `writer0`. The initial values of the shared variables are 0 and the initial value of semaphore **mx** is 1. This results in the following programs:

```
reader1:
     do true → NCS;
               P(mx);(*) if aw=0 →ar:=ar+1 fi;V(mx);
               READ;
               P(mx);ar:=ar-1;V(mx)
     od
```

```
writer1:
     do true → NCS;
               P(mx);(+) if aw=0 ∧ ar=0→aw:=aw+1 fi;V(mx);
               WRITE;
               P(mx);aw:=aw-1;V(mx)
     od
```

`S1` : $||_{i=1}^{N}$ `reader1` $||$ $||_{j=1}^{M}$ `writer1`

Dijkstra now formulates a requirement for this collection of programs. This is necessary because this collection can generate new unwanted sequences, namely sequences which can deadlock. One such sequence is for instance:

> A writer starts in the initial state and then executes `NCS;P(mx);(+)`, as result of this the value of `aw` changes in 1. A reader then executes `NCS;P(mx);(*)` and blocks in the `if-fi` clause of `(*)` because `aw=1` and the semantics of this `if-fi` is such that when no guard is fulfilled it blocks. Then no reader or writer can then execute `(*)` or `(+)` because `mx=0` and `mx` holds this value forever. The requirement is thus that these deadlocked sequences are not generated.

(Note: `S0` generates no deadlocked sequences, so `S1` generates some sequences that `S0` did not generate. The deadlocked sequences that are generated by the machine corresponding to `S1` are removed by the validity condition corresponding to `S1`, so that the set of allowed sequences of `S1` is not bigger than that of `S0`.)

We again specify `S1` plus the requirement that no deadlocked sequences are allowed in Stark's formalism. This specification must implement S_A. In Stark's formalism an implementation consists of the interconnection, the abstract specification and the component specifications. The abstract specification is S_A. We have seen that `S1` uses variables `ar,aw` and semaphore `mx`. These variables correspond to components ar, aw and mx in Stark's formalism. The PV-segments of `reader1` and `writer1` correspond to components $rn1$ and $wn1$. These are the components that take care of the synchronisation. In the next subsections we show how these component specifications are formulated in Stark's formalism.

3.2.1 Specification of a shared variable

We give a specification of a general shared variable with initial value K. Informally the specification is that the environment retrieves the current value of the shared variable with a $g(v)$ event and updates it with a $p(w)$ event. The formal specification $Ssv_K = \langle Msv_K, Vsv_K \rangle$ is as follows:

1. **Events:**
   $Esv_K = \{g(v)\downarrow, p(w)\downarrow : v, w \in Z\}$

2. **States:**
   $Qsv_K : svs \rightarrow Z$
   $\mathrm{st}(svs) = z$: the current value of the shared variable is z.

3. **Initial States:**
   $IQsv_K \equiv \mathbf{st}(svs) = K$

4. **Transitions:**
   $TRsv_K \equiv$

   - $\mathbf{e} = g(v)\downarrow \wedge v = \mathbf{st}(svs) \wedge \mathbf{st}' = \mathbf{st}$
     The environment retrieves the current value of the shared variable.
   - $\mathbf{e} = p(w)\downarrow \wedge \mathbf{st}' = \mathbf{st} \mid svs : w$
     The environment updates the current value of the shared variable.

5. **Validity Conditions:**
   All the sequences Msv_K generates are allowed, so: $Vsv_K \equiv true$.
   (In R/G form this is true→ true, i.e. no liveness requirements are imposed.)

3.2.2 The specification of a binary semaphore

We give an abstract specification of a general binary semaphore with initial value K. Informally this specification is as follows. A component that uses this semaphore signals with a tPi event that it wants to execute its P-operation. The semaphore signals with an ePi event that this component may execute its P-operation. The component signals with a Vi event that it has executed the V-operation. Note, that the validity conditions formalise the as-yet-unformalised concept of fairness used in the programs in [2]. (As will become clear later, a strong semaphore is used.)
The formal specification $SsemA_K = \langle MsemA_K, VsemA_K \rangle$ is as follows:

1. **Events:**
   $EsemA_K = \{tPi\downarrow, ePi\uparrow, Vi\downarrow : i \in \{1, \ldots, H\}\}$
   (H is the number of components using the binary semaphore.)

2. **States:**
   $QsemA_K : sems : \{sem0, sem1, err\} \times wset : \{1, \ldots, H\}$
   $\mathbf{st}(sems) = sem0$:
   A P-operation corresponds with a decrease of 1 and a V-operation corresponds with an increase of 1, so $semi$ corresponds with value i. The variable $wset$ denotes the set of indices of the components that are waiting to execute P.

3. **Initial States:**
   $IQsemA_K \equiv \mathbf{st}(sems) = semK \wedge \mathbf{st}(wset) = \emptyset$

4. **Transitions:**
   $TRsemA_K \equiv$

   - $\mathbf{e} = tPi\downarrow \wedge((i \notin \mathbf{st}(wset) \wedge \mathbf{st}' = \mathbf{st} \mid wset : \mathbf{st}(wset) \bigcup \{i\}) \vee$
     $(i \in \mathbf{st}(wset) \wedge \mathbf{st}' = \mathbf{st} \mid sems : err))$
     Component i wants to execute a P-operation on the semaphore. If component i is not in the waiting set it will be inserted.

- $e = ePi\uparrow \wedge \mathbf{st}(sems) = sem1 \wedge i \in \mathbf{st}(wset) \wedge$
  $\mathbf{st}' = \mathbf{st} \mid sems, wset : sem0, \mathbf{st}(wset)/\{i\}$
  The semaphore only generates an ePi event if the value of the semaphore equals one and component i has generated a tPi event before.
- $e = Vi\downarrow \wedge((\mathbf{st}(sems) = sem0 \wedge \mathbf{st}' = \mathbf{st} \mid sems : sem1) \vee$
  $(\mathbf{st}(sems) \neq sem0 \wedge \mathbf{st}' = \mathbf{st} \mid sems : err))$
  Component i generates a V-operation on the semaphore.

5. **Validity Conditions:**
   With $VsemA_K$ we can express the liveness properties of a semaphore. $VsemA_K$ must specify which sequences, that $MsemA_K$ generates, are allowed. This is needed because $MsemA_K$ can generate sequences in which a component i never finishes its P-operation. We express with $VsemA_K$ that $MsemA_K$ is a strong semaphore because Dijkstra apparently also uses a strong semaphore in his implementation.
   $VsemA_K \equiv RsemA_K \rightarrow GsemA_K$
   $RsemA_K \equiv \Box(\bigwedge_{i=1}^{H}(e = ePi \rightarrow \Diamond(e = Vi)))$
   $GsemA_K \equiv \Box(\bigwedge_{i=1}^{H}(e = tPi \rightarrow \Diamond(e = ePi)))$
   $MsemA_K$ relies on the environment to generate a Vi event if it has generated an ePi event itself. $MsemA_K$ guarantees then if the environment generates a tPi event that it eventually generates an ePi event.

3.2.3 Specification of component rn1

We now give the specification of component $rn1$ (the specification of $wn1$ is analogous). Component $rn1$ corresponds to the PV-segments of `reader1`. The specification $Srn1 = \langle Mrn1, Vrn1 \rangle$ is as follows:

1. **Events:**
   $Ern1 = EV \bigcup \{Vmx\uparrow, ePmx\downarrow, tPmx\uparrow\}$
   where $EV = \{try\downarrow, run\uparrow, rest\downarrow, gaw(w)\uparrow, gar(v)\uparrow, par(u)\uparrow : u, v, w \in N\}$
2. **States:**
   $Qrn1 : rs : RS1 \times rr : N \times rw : N$
   where $RS1 = \{resg, tryg, tPV1, iPV1, gaw1, gar1, par1, aPV1, rung,$
   $bPV2, tPV2, iPV2, gar2, par2, err, err1\}$
3. **Initial States:**
   $IQrn1 \equiv \mathbf{st}(rs) = resg$
4. **Transitions:**
   $TRrn1 \equiv$

   1 $e = try\downarrow \wedge((\mathbf{st}(rs) = resg \wedge \mathbf{st}' = \mathbf{st} \mid rs : tryg) \vee$
   $(\mathbf{st}(rs) \neq resg \wedge \mathbf{st}' = \mathbf{st} \mid rs : err))$
   The reader signals with a $rtry$ event to $rn1$ that it wants to execute `READ`.

   2 $e = tPmx\uparrow \wedge((\mathbf{st}(rs) = tryg \wedge \mathbf{st}' = \mathbf{st} \mid rs : tPV1) \vee$
   $(\mathbf{st}(rs) = bPV2 \wedge \mathbf{st}' = \mathbf{st} \mid rs : tPV2))$
   $rn1$ requests with a $tPmx$ event that it wants to enter a PV-section, that is, it wants access to the components ar and aw.

3 $\mathbf{e} = ePmx\uparrow \wedge$
$((\mathbf{st}(rs) = tPV1 \wedge \mathbf{st}' = \mathbf{st} \mid rs : iPV1) \vee$
$(\mathbf{st}(rs) = tPV2 \wedge \mathbf{st}' = \mathbf{st} \mid rs : iPV2) \vee$
$((\mathbf{st}(rs) \neq tPV1 \vee \mathbf{st}(rs) \neq tPV2) \wedge \mathbf{st}' = \mathbf{st} \mid rs : err1))$
The mx component signals with a $ePmx$ event that $rn1$ may enter its PV-section and thus has access to components ar and aw.

4 $\mathbf{e} = gaw(w)\uparrow \wedge \mathbf{st}(rs) = iPV1 \wedge \mathbf{st}' = \mathbf{st} \mid rs, rw : gaw1, w$
The synchroniser retrieves the current value of aw.

5 $\mathbf{e} = gar(v)\uparrow \wedge((\mathbf{st}(rs) = gaw1 \wedge \mathbf{st}' = \mathbf{st} \mid rs, rr : gar1, v) \vee$
$(\mathbf{st}(rs) = iPV2 \wedge \mathbf{st}' = \mathbf{st} \mid rs, rr : gar2, v))$
The synchroniser retrieves the current value of ar.

6 $\mathbf{e} = par(u)\uparrow \wedge$
$((u = \mathbf{st}(rr) + 1 \wedge \mathbf{st}(rs) = gar1 \wedge \mathbf{st}(rw) = 0 \wedge$
$\mathbf{st}' = \mathbf{st} \mid rs, rr : par1, u) \vee$
$(u = \mathbf{st}(rr) - 1 \wedge \mathbf{st}(rs) = gar2 \wedge \mathbf{st}' = \mathbf{st} \mid rs, rr : par2, u))$
If $rn1$ is in the first PV-section then it increases component ar with one if the current value of the aw component is zero. That means that there are no writers executing their `WRITE`. If the current value of aw is not zero, component $rn1$ will be deadlocked in its PV-section.
If $rn1$ is in the second PV-section then it decreases ar with one.

7 $\mathbf{e} = Vmx\uparrow \wedge((\mathbf{st}(rs) = par1 \wedge \mathbf{st}' = \mathbf{st} \mid rs : aPV1) \vee$
$(\mathbf{st}(rs) = par2 \wedge \mathbf{st}' = \mathbf{st} \mid rs : resg))$
After updating the ar component $rn1$ signals with a Vmx event that it leaves its PV-section.

8 $\mathbf{e} = run\uparrow \wedge \mathbf{st}(rs) = aPV1 \wedge \mathbf{st}' = \mathbf{st} \mid rs : rung$
When $rn1$ has passed first PV-section it signals with an $rrun$ event to its corresponding reader that it may execute `READ`.

9 $\mathbf{e} = rest\downarrow \wedge((\mathbf{st}(rs) = rung \wedge \mathbf{st}' = \mathbf{st} \mid rs : bPV2) \vee$
$(\mathbf{st}(rs) \neq rung \wedge \mathbf{st}' = \mathbf{st} \mid rs : err))$
The reader signals with a $rest$ event $rn1$ that it has finished `READ`.

5. **Validity Conditions:**
The set $Vrn1$ of allowed sequences of $Mrn1$ is as follows:
$Vrn1 \equiv Rrn1 \rightarrow Grn1$
$Rrn1 \equiv$

- $\Box(\mathbf{st}(rs) = rung \rightarrow \Diamond(\mathbf{st}(rs) = bPV2))$
$rn1$ relies on its reader that the execution of `READ` takes only a finite amount of time.

- $\wedge\Box(\mathbf{e} = tPmx \rightarrow \Diamond(\mathbf{e} = ePmx))$
$rn1$ furthermore relies on mx that it eventually gives the access-right if $rn1$ has asked for it.

$Grn1 \equiv$

- $\Box(\mathbf{st}(rs) = tryg \rightarrow \Diamond(\mathbf{st}(rs) = rung))$
$rn1$ then guarantees to its reader that it eventually may execute `READ` if the reader has asked for it.

- $\wedge\Box(\mathrm{e} = ePmx \rightarrow \Diamond(\mathrm{e} = Vmx))$
  $rn1$ furthermore guarantees to mx that it has the access-right only a finite amount of time.

These last two conditions remove the unwanted deadlocked sequences because it is required that when the $rn1$ component gets in its PV-segment it must eventually leave this PV-segment, i.e., not get deadlocked in it.

3.2.4 Correctness of the implementation

The implementation is correct if the maximality and the validity conditions hold. This means that we have to prove the following:
(1) Any event that can be generated by the system of component machines can also be performed by the abstract machine.
maximality:

$$Comp(M_c) \models \forall e \in E_c : (Reachable_c \wedge \bigwedge_{i=1}^{N}[Enabled_{rn1}(e)]_{ri\mathbf{to}_c} \wedge \bigwedge_{j=1}^{M}[Enabled_{wn1}(e)]_{wj\mathbf{to}_c} \wedge [Enabled_{sv0}(e)]_{ar\mathbf{to}_c} \wedge [Enabled_{sv0}(e)]_{aw\mathbf{to}_c} \wedge [Enabled_{semA1}(e)]_{mx\mathbf{to}_c}) \rightarrow [Enabled_A(e)]_{A\mathbf{to}_c},$$

where E_c denotes the interface of the composite machine. The proof that this formula holds is not difficult but rather long so we present do not present it.
(2) Any allowed computation of each component machine corresponds with an allowed computation of the abstract machine.
validity:

$$Comp(M_c) \models (\bigwedge_{i=1}^{N}[Vrn1]_{rn1\mathbf{to}_c} \wedge \bigwedge_{j=1}^{M}[Vwn1]_{wn1\mathbf{to}_c} \wedge [VsemA_1]_{mx\mathbf{to}_c} \wedge [Vsv0]_{aw\mathbf{to}_c} \wedge [Vsv0]_{ar\mathbf{to}_c}) \rightarrow [V_A]_{A\mathbf{to}_c},$$

where M_c denotes the composite machine. The proof of this can be done with the rely/guarantee rule and is not difficult but it is again too long to present it here.

3.3 The second development step

The components of the first implementation still generate sequences, i.e. deadlocked ones, which are not allowed by the validity conditions of these components. In this step we change components $rn1$ and $wn1$ because these components are responsible for the generation of these deadlocked sequences. This is the same as is done by Dijkstra: he massages `reader1` and `writer1` into `reader2` and `writer2` so that no deadlocked sequences inside a PV-segment are generated any more.

One such deadlocked sequence generated by the first implementation is as follows: suppose $rn1$ has gained the access-right for the shared variables (first PV-segment) and has executed $gar(v)$ and $gaw(w)$, suppose also $w = 1$ (a writer is executing `WRITE`). Then $rn1$ can never execute the $par(\mathbf{st}(rar) + 1)$ event , i.e., $rn1$ has deadlocked. This sequence is not allowed by $Vrn1$ because $rn1$ must guarantee that if it gets the access-right it must eventually give it back.

Dijkstra uses the split binary semaphore technique to prevent programs from becoming deadlocked inside a PV-segment. The idea is that we must prevent programs from getting the access-right (get into a PV-segment) for the shared variables if we know that they can not give it back (get deadlocked inside a PV-segment). For `reader1` this means: never let it enter the first PV-segment if `aw` does not equal zero. For `writer1` this means: never let it enter the first PV-segment if `aw` or `ar` does not equal zero. `reader1` and `writer1` never block in their second PV-segment.
How does one prevent that `reader1` gets deadlocked inside a PV-segment? This is done as follows: `reader1` chooses, when it gives the access-right back, who can have it thereafter. `Reader1` executes therefore the following piece of program as replacement for `V(mx)`:

```
CHOOSE: if true → V(m) [] aw=0 → V(r) [] aw=0 ∧ ar=0 → V(w) fi
```

We have to split `mx` in three pieces. If `aw` equals zero then a reader is allowed to enter its first PV-segment, i.e., this PV-segment is not guarded by `P(mx)` but by `P(r)`. We do this substitution for all PV-segments of `reader1` and `writer1`. So we have replaced `mx` by three other binary semaphores.
What is the initial value of these semaphores? If they all have initial value 1 then more than one program can have access-right to the shared variables, i.e., only one has initial value 1. Semaphore `r` can not have initial value 1 because if no reader wants to execute `READ` then no writer can execute `WRITE`. The same holds for semaphore `w`. Thus `m` has initial value 1. But then no reader or writer can enter the first PV-segment. The solution to this problem is that we insert a PV-segment (`P(m);CHOOSE`) in front of the first one. This is in short what Dijkstra does to prevent that `reader1` and `writer1` get deadlocked inside a PV-segment. The result of this transformation is:

```
reader2:
            do true → NCS;
                      P(m);CHOOSE;
                      P(r);ar:=ar+1;CHOOSE;
                      READ;
                      P(m);ar:=ar-1;CHOOSE
            od
writer2:
            do true → NCS;
                      P(m);CHOOSE;
                      P(w);aw:=aw+1;CHOOSE;
                      WRITE;
                      P(m);aw:=aw-1;CHOOSE
            od
```

S2 : $\|_{i=1}^{N}$ reader2 $\|$ $\|_{j=1}^{M}$ writer2

`S2` generates no sequences that can deadlock inside a PV-segment. But `S2` can generate sequences that can deadlock outside these segments, e.g. initially `reader2` can choose for a `V(w)` operation, and get blocked by a `P(r)` operation. Then no other reader or writer can enter the first PV-segment because `m` equals zero. The informal requirement is thus that no such sequences are allowed.

3.3.1 Specification of component rn2

The result of the split binary semaphore technique is that $rn1$ (and $wn1$) have to be changed because they are accessing now three semaphores instead of one. So semaphore mx has to replaced by semaphores m, r and w. We give the changes of component $rn1$, i.e., $Srn1$ changes to $Srn2 = \langle Mrn2, Vrn2\rangle$. (Note: we have numbered the transitions in the first implementation. These numbers correspond with the numbers in the following implementation, for instance, transition 2 of the first implementation is replaced by transitions 2.1 and 2.2 in the second implementation.)

1. **Events:**
   $Ern2 = EV \bigcup \{Vm\uparrow, ePm\downarrow, tPm\uparrow, Vr\uparrow, ePr\downarrow, tPr\uparrow, Vw\uparrow\}$

2. **States:**
   $Qrn2 : rs : RS2 \times rr : N \times rw : N$
   where $RS2 = RS1 \bigcup \{tPV0, iPV0, gaw0, gar0, aPV0, gaw2\}$

3. **Initial States:**
   $IQrn2 \equiv \mathbf{st}(rs) = resg$

4. **Transitions:**
   $TRrn2 \equiv$

   1 same as $TRrn1$

   2.1 $\mathrm{e} = tPm\uparrow \wedge((\mathbf{st}(rs) = tryg \wedge \mathbf{st}' = \mathbf{st} \mid rs : tPV0)\vee$
   $(\mathbf{st}(rs) = bPV2 \wedge \mathbf{st}' = \mathbf{st} \mid rs : tPV2))$
   The synchroniser signals with a tPm event that it wants to enter the first or third PV-segment.

   2.2 $\mathrm{e} = tPr\uparrow \wedge \mathbf{st}(rs) = aPV0 \wedge \mathbf{st}' = \mathbf{st} \mid rs : tPV1$
   The synchroniser signals with a tPr event that it wants to enter the second PV-segment.

   3.1 $\mathrm{e} = ePm\downarrow \wedge$
   $((\mathbf{st}(rs) = tPV0 \wedge \mathbf{st}' = \mathbf{st} \mid rs : iPV0)\vee$
   $(\mathbf{st}(rs) = tPV2 \wedge \mathbf{st}' = \mathbf{st} \mid rs : iPV2)\vee$
   $((\mathbf{st}(rs) \neq tPV0 \vee \mathbf{st}(rs) \neq tPV2) \wedge \mathbf{st}' = \mathbf{st} \mid rs : err1))$
   The synchroniser may enter the first or third PV-segment.

   3.2 $\mathrm{e} = ePr\downarrow \wedge((\mathbf{st}(rs) = tPV1 \wedge \mathbf{st}' = \mathbf{st} \mid rs : iPV1)\vee$
   $(\mathbf{st}(rs) \neq tPV1 \wedge \mathbf{st}' = \mathbf{st} \mid rs : err1))$
   The synchroniser may enter the second PV-segment.

   4 $\mathrm{e} = gaw(w)\uparrow \wedge((\mathbf{st}(rs) = iPV0 \wedge \mathbf{st}' = \mathbf{st} \mid rs, rw : gaw0, w)\vee$
   $(\mathbf{st}(rs) = iPV1 \wedge \mathbf{st}' = \mathbf{st} \mid rs, rw : gaw1, w)\vee$
   $(\mathbf{st}(rs) = iPV2 \wedge \mathbf{st}' = \mathbf{st} \mid rs, rw : gaw2, w))$
   The synchroniser retrieves the current value of aw.

   5 $\mathrm{e} = gar(v)\uparrow \wedge((\mathbf{st}(rs) = gaw0 \wedge \mathbf{st}' = \mathbf{st} \mid rs, rr : gar0, v)\vee$
   $(\mathbf{st}(rs) = gaw1 \wedge \mathbf{st}' = \mathbf{st} \mid rs, rr : gar1, v)\vee$
   $(\mathbf{st}(rs) = gaw2 \wedge \mathbf{st}' = \mathbf{st} \mid rs, rr : gar2, v))$
   The synchroniser retrieves the current value of ar.

6 $\mathbf{e} = par(u)\uparrow \wedge$
$((u = \mathbf{st}(rar) + 1 \wedge \mathbf{st}(rs) = gar1 \wedge \mathbf{st}' = \mathbf{st} \mid rs, rr : par1, u) \vee$
$(u = \mathbf{st}(rar) - 1 \wedge \mathbf{st}(rs) = gar2 \wedge \mathbf{st}' = \mathbf{st} \mid rs, rr : par2, u))$
The synchroniser increases or decreases ar.

7.1 $\mathbf{e} = Vm\uparrow \wedge((\mathbf{st}(rs) = gar0 \wedge \mathbf{st}' = \mathbf{st} \mid rs : aPV0) \vee$
$(\mathbf{st}(rs) = par1 \wedge \mathbf{st}' = \mathbf{st} \mid rs : aPV1)) \vee$
$(\mathbf{st}(rs) = par2 \wedge \mathbf{st}' = \mathbf{st} \mid rs : resg))$
The synchroniser chooses the Vm branch.

7.2 $\mathbf{e} = Vr\uparrow \wedge((\mathbf{st}(rs) = gar0 \wedge \mathbf{st}(rw) = 0 \wedge \mathbf{st}' = \mathbf{st} \mid rs : aPV0) \vee$
$(\mathbf{st}(rs) = par1 \wedge \mathbf{st}(rw) = 0 \wedge \mathbf{st}' = \mathbf{st} \mid rs : aPV1)) \vee$
$(\mathbf{st}(rs) = par2 \wedge \mathbf{st}(rw) = 0 \wedge \mathbf{st}' = \mathbf{st} \mid rs : resg))$
The synchroniser chooses the Vr branch.

7.3 $\mathbf{e} = Vw\uparrow \wedge$
$((\mathbf{st}(rs) = gar0 \wedge \mathbf{st}(rw) = 0 \wedge \mathbf{st}(rr) = 0 \wedge \mathbf{st}' = \mathbf{st} \mid rs : aPV0) \vee$
$(\mathbf{st}(rs) = par1 \wedge \mathbf{st}(rw) = 0 \wedge \mathbf{st}(rr) = 0 \wedge \mathbf{st}' = \mathbf{st} \mid rs : aPV1) \vee$
$(\mathbf{st}(rs) = par2 \wedge \mathbf{st}(rw) = 0 \wedge \mathbf{st}(rr) = 0 \wedge \mathbf{st}' = \mathbf{st} \mid rs : resg))$
The synchroniser chooses the Vw branch.

8-9 same as $TRrn1$.

5. **Validity Conditions:**
The synchroniser does not generate anymore sequences that deadlock inside a PV-segment. But it can generate sequences that deadlock outside a PV-segment. One such sequence is for instance the following one:
The synchroniser is in the initial state. Suppose a component $rn2$ enters its first PV-segment. If this component leaves the first PV-segment it can choose non-deterministically between Vr, Vw or Vm events as last event of this segment. It can for instance always choose Vm. Suppose this is the case. It then eventually is added to the waiting set of semaphore r (see the specification of the binary semaphore) because it wants to enter its second PV-segment. Another component $rn2$ (or $wn2$) can now enter its first PV-segment because the first one chose the Vm event. Suppose this happens and this component chooses also Vm as its last event of the first PV-segment. This can continue until all $rn2$ components are in the waiting set of semaphore r and all the $wn2$ components are in the waiting set of semaphore w. There is no component that can get these components out of the waiting sets, i.e., the system has deadlocked.
Hence, we must restrict $rn2$ and $wn2$ in such a way that they choose the right V-branch when they leave a PV-segment. In case of the example, the right V-branch for the last component is not Vm because there are no components that can generate tPm events as first $tP\ldots$ event on a semaphore. The last component must choose a Vr or Vw event. $Vrn2$ must express what the allowed sequences of $rn2$ are, i.e., not a deadlocked one as mentioned above.
$Vrn2 \equiv Rrn2 \rightarrow Grn2$
$Rrn2 \equiv$

- $\Box(\mathbf{st}(rs) = rung \rightarrow \Diamond(\mathbf{st}(rs) = bPV2))$
$rn2$ relies on its reader to guarantee that its execution of `READ` only takes a finite amount of time.

- $\wedge\Box(\mathrm{e} = tPm \rightarrow \Diamond(\mathrm{e} = ePm))$
  $rn2$ furthermore relies on m that it gives eventually the access-right to the shared variables of the first or last PV-segment.
- $\wedge\Box(\mathrm{e} = tPr \rightarrow \Diamond(\mathrm{e} = ePr))$
  $rn2$ furthermore relies on r that it gives eventually the access-right to the shared variables of the second PV-segment.

$Grn2 \equiv$

- $\Box(\mathbf{st}(rs) = \boldsymbol{tryg} \rightarrow \Diamond(\mathbf{st}(rs) = \boldsymbol{rung}))$
  $rn2$ guarantees to its reader that it eventually may execute `READ` if he has requested it.
- $\wedge\Box(\mathrm{e} = ePm \rightarrow \Diamond(\mathrm{e} = Vm \wedge X1))$
  $rn2$ guarantees that it has the access-right in the first or third PV-segment only a finite amount of time and chooses the Vm-branch if the number of processes that have as first coming P-operation a P-operation on `m`, is greater than zero.
- $\wedge\Box(\mathrm{e} = ePr \rightarrow \Diamond(\mathrm{e} = Vm \wedge X1))$
  $rn2$ guarantees that it has the access-right in the second PV-segment only a finite amount of time and chooses the Vm-branch if the number of processes that have as first coming P-operation a P-operation on `m`, is greater than zero.
- $\wedge\Box(\mathrm{e} = ePm \rightarrow \Diamond(\mathrm{e} = Vr \wedge X2))$
  $rn2$ guarantees that it has the access-right in the first or third PV-segment only a finite amount of time and chooses the Vr-branch if the number of processes that have as first coming P-operation a P-operation on `r`, is greater than zero.
- $\wedge\Box(\mathrm{e} = ePr \rightarrow \Diamond(\mathrm{e} = Vr \wedge X2))$
  $rn2$ guarantees that it has the access-right in the second PV-segment only a finite amount of time and chooses the Vr-branch if the number of processes that have as first coming P-operation a P-operation on `r`, is greater than zero.
- $\wedge\Box(\mathrm{e} = ePm \rightarrow \Diamond(\mathrm{e} = Vw \wedge X3))$
  $rn2$ guarantees that it has the access-right in the first or third PV-segment only a finite amount of time and chooses the Vw-branch if the number of processes that have as first coming P-operation a P-operation on `w`, is greater than zero.
- $\wedge\Box(\mathrm{e} = ePr \rightarrow \Diamond(\mathrm{e} = Vw \wedge X3))$
  $rn2$ guarantees that it has the access-right in the second PV-segment only a finite amount of time and chooses the Vw-branch if the number of processes that have as first coming P-operation a P-operation on `w`, is greater than zero.

$X1 \equiv \sum$ "components that from now on can generate a tPm event as first $tP\ldots$ event on a semaphore". > 0
$X2 \equiv \sum$ "components that from now on can generate a tPr event as first $tP\ldots$ event on a semaphore". > 0
$X3 \equiv \sum$ "components that from now on can generate a tPw event as first $tP\ldots$ event on a semaphore". > 0

3.4 The third development step

Dijkstra's solution to the problem of the newly introduced deadlocked sequences is as follows: record in a shared variable bX the number of components that can generate a P-operation on a semaphore X as their first coming P-operation. A component that executed a P-operation on X decreases bX by one. The component "knows" what its next P-operation is, so it increases the corresponding shared variable by one. The guards in the `CHOOSE` segment are changed so that the correct V-branch is chosen. The initial value of bm is $N + M$ because initially all processes have `P(m)` as their first coming P-operation. The initial value of br and bw is then of course 0. Like in the second step the initial value of m is 1 and that of ar, aw, r and w 0. The result of this transformation is as follows:

```
reader3:
          do true → NCS;
                    P(m);bm:=bm-1;br:=br+1;CHOOSE;
                    P(r);br:=br-1;ar:=ar+1;bm:=bm+1;CHOOSE;
                    READ;
                    P(m);bm:=bm-1;ar:=ar-1;bm:=bm+1;CHOOSE
          od

writer3:
          do true → NCS;
                    P(m);bm:=bm-1;bw:=bw+1;CHOOSE;
                    P(w);bw:=bw-1;aw:=aw+1;bm:=bm+1;CHOOSE;
                    WRITE;
                    P(m);bm:=bm-1;aw:=aw-1;bm:=bm+1;CHOOSE
          od

with CHOOSE: if bm>0 →V(m)
             [] aw=0 ∧ br>0 →V(r)
             [] aw=0 ∧ ar=0 ∧ bw>0 →V(w)
             fi
```

S3 : $\|_{i=1}^{N}$ reader3 $\|$ $\|_{j=1}^{M}$ writer3

S3 still generates sequences that Dijkstra does not allow. These sequences are generated because `CHOOSE` is still non-deterministic. Suppose a `reader3` can choose between a `V(m)` and a `V(r)` operation. Choosing `V(m)` causes that another `reader3` (`writer3`) can signal that it has finished executing `READ` (`WRITE`) or wants to execute `READ` (`WRITE`). A `V(r)` causes that a `reader3` can execute `READ`. Choosing `V(m)` thus unnecessarily blocks a `reader3`. So it is not a deadlocked sequence but only an inefficient sequence. The informal requirement of S3 is that no unnecessary blocking sequences are allowed. Again, not a pure liveness requirement is added.

3.4.1 Specification of components rn3

For the synchroniser this means that $rn2$ and $wn2$ have to be changed and components bm, rm and wm have to be added. The changes to $rn2$ result in $rn3$:(Note: again the numbers of the transitions of the second implementation correspond with those of the following third implementation.)

1. **Events:**
   $Ern3 = Ern2 \bigcup \{gbm(x)\uparrow, gbw(z)\uparrow, gbr(y)\uparrow, pbm(x)\uparrow, pbr(y)\uparrow : x, y, z \in N\}$

2. **States:**
   $Qrn3 : rs : RS3 \times rr : N \times rw : N \times bm : N \times br : N \times bw : N$
   where
   $RS3 = RS2 \bigcup \{gbm0, gbr0, gbw0, pbm0, pbr0, gbm1, gbr1, gbw1, pbr1, pbm1, gbm2, gbr2, gbw2, pbm2, pbm3\}$

3. **Initial States**
   $IQrn3 \equiv \mathbf{st}(rs) = resg$

4. **Transitions:**
   $TRrn3 \equiv$

   1-5 same as $TRrn2$.

   6.1 $\mathrm{e} = gbm(x)\uparrow \wedge((\mathbf{st}(rs) = gar0 \wedge \mathbf{st}' = \mathbf{st} \mid rs, bm : gbm0, x)\vee$
   $(\mathbf{st}(rs) = gar1 \wedge \mathbf{st}' = \mathbf{st} \mid rs, bm : gbm1, x)\vee$
   $(\mathbf{st}(rs) = gar2 \wedge \mathbf{st}' = \mathbf{st} \mid rs, bm : gbm2, x))$
   The synchroniser retrieves the current value of bm.

   6.2 $\mathrm{e} = gbr(y)\uparrow \wedge((\mathbf{st}(rs) = gbm0 \wedge \mathbf{st}' = \mathbf{st} \mid rs, br : gbr0, y)\vee$
   $(\mathbf{st}(rs) = gbm1 \wedge \mathbf{st}' = \mathbf{st} \mid rs, br : gbr1, y)\vee$
   $(\mathbf{st}(rs) = gbm2 \wedge \mathbf{st}' = \mathbf{st} \mid rs, br : gbr2, y))$
   The synchroniser retrieves the current value of br.

   6.3 $\mathrm{e} = gbw(z)\uparrow \wedge((\mathbf{st}(rs) = gbr0 \wedge \mathbf{st}' = \mathbf{st} \mid rs, bwgbw0, z)\vee$
   $(\mathbf{st}(rs) = gbr1 \wedge \mathbf{st}' = \mathbf{st} \mid rs, bw : gbw1, z)\vee$
   $(\mathbf{st}(rs) = gbr2 \wedge \mathbf{st}' = \mathbf{st} \mid rs, bwgbw2, z))$
   The synchroniser retrieves the current value of bw.

   6.4 $\mathrm{e} = pbm(x)\uparrow \wedge$
   $((x = \mathbf{st}(bm) - 1 \wedge \mathbf{st}(rs) = gbw0 \wedge \mathbf{st}' = \mathbf{st} \mid rs, bm : pbm0, x)\vee$
   $(x = \mathbf{st}(bm) + 1 \wedge \mathbf{st}(rs) = par1 \wedge \mathbf{st}' = \mathbf{st} \mid rs, bm : pbm1, x)\vee$
   $(x = \mathbf{st}(bm) - 1 \wedge \mathbf{st}(ns) = gbw2 \wedge \mathbf{st}' = \mathbf{st} \mid rs, bm : pbm2, x)\vee$
   $(x = \mathbf{st}(bm) + 1 \wedge \mathbf{st}(rs) = par2 \wedge \mathbf{st}' = \mathbf{st} \mid rs, bm : pbm3, x))$
   The synchroniser increases or decreases bm.

   6.5 $\mathrm{e} = pbr(y)\uparrow \wedge$
   $((y = \mathbf{st}(br) + 1 \wedge \mathbf{st}(rs) = pbm0 \wedge \mathbf{st}' = \mathbf{st} \mid rs, br : pbr0, y)\vee$
   $(y = \mathbf{st}(br) - 1 \wedge \mathbf{st}(rs) = gbw1 \wedge \mathbf{st}' = \mathbf{st} \mid rs, br : pbr1, y))$
   The synchroniser increases or decreases br.

   6.6 $\mathrm{e} = par(u)\uparrow \wedge$
   $((u = \mathbf{st}(rr) + 1 \wedge \mathbf{st}(rs) = pbr1 \wedge \mathbf{st}' = \mathbf{st} \mid rs, rr : par1, u)\vee$
   $(u = \mathbf{st}(rr) - 1 \wedge \mathbf{st}(rs) = pbm2 \wedge \mathbf{st}' = \mathbf{st} \mid rs, rr : par2, u))$
   The synchroniser increases or decreases ar.

7.1 $\mathbf{e} = Vm\uparrow \wedge((\mathbf{st}(rs) = pbr0 \wedge \mathbf{st}(bm) > 0 \wedge \mathbf{st}' = \mathbf{st} \mid rs : aPV0)\vee$
$(\mathbf{st}(rs) = pbm1 \wedge \mathbf{st}(bm) > 0 \wedge \mathbf{st}' = \mathbf{st} \mid rs : aPV1)\vee$
$(\mathbf{st}(rs) = pbm3 \wedge \mathbf{st}(bm) > 0 \wedge \mathbf{st}' = \mathbf{st} \mid rs : resg))$
The synchroniser chooses the Vm branch.

7.2 $\mathbf{e} = Vr\uparrow \wedge$
$((\mathbf{st}(rs) = pbr0 \wedge \mathbf{st}(rw) = 0 \wedge \mathbf{st}(br) > 0 \wedge \mathbf{st}' = \mathbf{st} \mid rs : aPV0)\vee$
$(\mathbf{st}(rs) = pbm1 \wedge \mathbf{st}(rw) = 0 \wedge \mathbf{st}(br) > 0 \wedge \mathbf{st}' = \mathbf{st} \mid rs : aPV1)\vee$
$(\mathbf{st}(rs) = pbm3 \wedge \mathbf{st}(rw) = 0 \wedge \mathbf{st}(br) > 0 \wedge \mathbf{st}' = \mathbf{st} \mid rs : resg))$
The synchroniser chooses the Vr branch.

7.3 $\mathbf{e} = Vw\uparrow \wedge$
$((\mathbf{st}(rs) = pbr0 \wedge \mathbf{st}(rw) = 0 \wedge \mathbf{st}(rr) = 0\wedge$
$\mathbf{st}(bw) > 0 \wedge \mathbf{st}' = \mathbf{st} \mid rs : aPV0)\vee$
$(\mathbf{st}(rs) = pbm1 \wedge \mathbf{st}(rw) = 0 \wedge \mathbf{st}(rr) = 0\wedge$
$\mathbf{st}(bw) > 0 \wedge \mathbf{st}' = \mathbf{st} \mid rs : aPV1)\vee$
$(\mathbf{st}(rs) = pbm3 \wedge \mathbf{st}(rw) = 0 \wedge \mathbf{st}(rr) = 0\wedge$
$\mathbf{st}(bw) > 0 \wedge \mathbf{st}' = \mathbf{st} \mid rs : resg))$
The synchroniser chooses the Vw branch.

8-9 same as $TRrn2$.

5. **Validity Conditions:**
Dijkstra gives priority to a Vr (Vw) event if it is possible to choose between Vr (Vw) and Vm. This informal requirement we formalise by $Vrn3$.
$Vrn3 \equiv Rrn3 \rightarrow Grn3$
$Rrn3 \equiv$

- $\Box(\mathbf{st}(rs) = rung \rightarrow \Diamond(\mathbf{st}(rs) = bPV2))$
$rn3$ relies on its reader to guarantee that its execution of `READ` only takes a finite amount of time.
- $\wedge\Box(\mathbf{e} = tPm \rightarrow \Diamond(\mathbf{e} = ePm))$
$rn3$ furthermore relies on m that it gives eventually the access-right to the shared variables of the first or last PV-segment.
- $\wedge\Box(\mathbf{e} = tPr \rightarrow \Diamond(\mathbf{e} = rePr))$
$rn3$ furthermore relies on r that it gives eventually the access-right to the shared variables of the second PV-segment.

$Grn3 \equiv$

- $\Box(\mathbf{st}(rs) = tryg \rightarrow \Diamond(\mathbf{st}(rs) = rung))$
$rn3$ guarantees to its reader that it eventually may execute `READ` if he has requested it.
- $\wedge\Box(\mathbf{e} = ePm \rightarrow \Diamond(\mathbf{e} = Vm \wedge X1))$
$rn3$ guarantees that it only takes the Vm-branch if the Vr- and Vw-branch can not be taken.
- $\wedge\Box(\mathbf{e} = ePr \rightarrow \Diamond(\mathbf{e} = Vm \wedge X1))$
$rn3$ guarantees that it only takes the Vm-branch if the Vr- and Vw-branch can not be taken.

- $\wedge\Box(\mathrm{e} = ePm \rightarrow \Diamond(\mathrm{e} = Vw \wedge X2))$
  $rn3$ guarantees that it only takes the Vw-branch if the Vm-branch can not be taken.
- $\wedge\Box(\mathrm{e} = ePr \rightarrow \Diamond(\mathrm{e} = Vw \wedge X2))$
  $rn3$ guarantees that it only takes the Vw-branch if the Vm-branch can not be taken.
- $\wedge\Box(\mathrm{e} = ePm \rightarrow \Diamond(\mathrm{e} = Vr \wedge X3))$
  $rn3$ guarantees that it only takes the Vr-branch if the Vm-branch can not be taken.
- $\wedge\Box(\mathrm{e} = ePr \rightarrow \Diamond(\mathrm{e} = Vr \wedge X3))$,
  $rn3$ guarantees that it only takes the Vr-branch if the Vm-branch can not be taken.

where

- $X1 \equiv (\mathbf{st}(bm) > 0 \wedge \neg X2 \wedge \neg X3))$
  is the condition for the Vm-branch and
- $X2 \equiv (\mathbf{st}(rw) = 0 \wedge \mathbf{st}(br) > 0)$
  is the condition for the Vr-branch and
- $X3 \equiv (\mathbf{st}(rw) = 0 \wedge \mathbf{st}(rr) = 0 \wedge \mathbf{st}(bw) > 0)$
  the condition for the Vw-branch.

3.5 The fourth development step

We have already seen how we can prevent $rn3$ to choose wrongly between Vr and Vw. Dijkstra also updates the PV-segments in such a way that only statements that are actually executed are listed. It turns out that we do not anymore need bm. Also the guards of CHOOSE get simpler. The result of this transformation is:

```
reader4:
  do true → NCS;
            P(m);br:=br+1;if aw>0 → V(m) [] aw=0 →V(r) fi;
            P(r);br,ar:=br-1,ar+1;if br=0 → V(m) [] br>0 →V(r)fi;
            READ;
            P(m);ar:=ar-1;
            if ar>0 ∨ bw=0 →V(m) [] ar=0 ∧ bw>0 → V(w) fi
  od

writer4:
  do true → NCS;
            P(m);bw:=bw+1;
            if aw>0 ∨ ar>0 → V(m) [] aw=0 ∧ ar=0 → V(w) fi;
            P(w);bw,aw:=bw-1,aw+1;V(m);
            WRITE;
            P(m);aw:=aw-1;
            if br=0 ∧ bw=0 → V(m) [] br>0 → V(r) [] bw>0 → V(w)fi
  od
```

S4 : $||_{i=1}^{N}$ reader4 $||$ $||_{j=1}^{M}$ writer4

In S4 only the last `CHOOSE` operation of `writer4` is non-deterministic, i.e. there is a choice between a `V(r)` and a `V(w)` operation. Dijkstra suggests to give priority to `V(r)`.

3.5.1 *Specification of components $Mrn4$*

In Stark's formalism these modifications leads to specification $Srn4 = \langle Mrn4, Vrn4 \rangle$ $(Swn4)$, as specified below:

1. **Events:**
   $Ern4 = Ern3 \setminus \{gbm(x)\uparrow, pbm(x)\uparrow : x \in N\}$

2. **States:**
   $Qrn4 : rs : RS4 \times rr : N \times rw : N \times br : N \times bw : N$
   where
   $RS4 = RS3 \setminus \{gaw1, gar0, gaw2, gbm0, gbw0, pbm0, gbm1, pbm1, gbm2, gbr2, pbm2, pbm3\}$

3. **Initial States:**
   $IQrn4 \equiv \mathbf{st}(rs) = resg$

4. **Transitions:**
   $TRrn4 \equiv$

   1-3 same as $TRrn3$.

   4 $\mathbf{e} = gaw(w)\uparrow \wedge \mathbf{st}(rs) = iPV0 \wedge \mathbf{st}' = \mathbf{st} \mid rs, rw : gaw0, w$
   We need the value of aw only in the first PV-segment.

   5 $\mathbf{e} = gar(v)\uparrow \wedge ((\mathbf{st}(rs) = iPV1 \wedge \mathbf{st}' = \mathbf{st} \mid rs, rr : gar1, v) \vee (\mathbf{st}(rs) = iPV2 \wedge \mathbf{st}' = \mathbf{st} \mid rs, rr : gar2, v))$
   We need the value of ar only in the second and third PV-segment.

   6.1 $\mathbf{e} = gbr(y)\uparrow \wedge ((\mathbf{st}(rs) = gaw0 \wedge \mathbf{st}' = \mathbf{st} \mid rs, br : gbr0, y) \vee (\mathbf{st}(rs) = gar1 \wedge \mathbf{st}' = \mathbf{st} \mid rs, br : gbr1, y))$
   We need the value of br only in the first and second PV-segment.

   6.2 $\mathbf{e} = gbw(z)\uparrow \wedge \mathbf{st}(rs) = gar2 \wedge \mathbf{st}' = \mathbf{st} \mid rs, bw : gbw2, z$
   We need the value of bw only in the third PV-segment.

   6.3 $\mathbf{e} = pbr(y)\uparrow \wedge$
   $((y = \mathbf{st}(br) + 1 \wedge \mathbf{st}(rs) = gbr0 \wedge \mathbf{st}' = \mathbf{st} \mid rs, br : pbr0, y) \vee$
   $(y = \mathbf{st}(br) - 1 \wedge \mathbf{st}(rs) = gbr1 \wedge \mathbf{st}' = \mathbf{st} \mid rs, br : pbr1, y))$
   The value of br is updated only in the first and second PV-segment.

   6.4 $\mathbf{e} = par(u)\uparrow \wedge$
   $((u = \mathbf{st}(rr) + 1 \wedge \mathbf{st}(rs) = pbr1 \wedge \mathbf{st}' = \mathbf{st} \mid rs, rr : par1, u) \vee$
   $(u = \mathbf{st}(rr) - 1 \wedge \mathbf{st}(rs) = gbw2 \wedge \mathbf{st}' = \mathbf{st} \mid rs, rr : par2, u))$
   The value of ar is updated only in the second and third PV-segment.

   7.1 $\mathbf{e} = Vm\uparrow \wedge$
   $((\mathbf{st}(rs) = pbr0 \wedge \mathbf{st}(rw) > 0 \wedge \mathbf{st}' = \mathbf{st} \mid rs : aPV0) \vee$
   $(\mathbf{st}(rs) = par1 \wedge \mathbf{st}(br) = 0 \wedge \mathbf{st}' = \mathbf{st} \mid rs : aPV1) \vee$
   $(\mathbf{st}(rs) = par2 \wedge (\mathbf{st}(rr) > 0 \vee \mathbf{st}(bw) = 0) \wedge \mathbf{st}' = \mathbf{st} \mid rs : resg))$
   The guards of Vm simplify to this.

7.2 $\mathbf{e} = Vr\uparrow \wedge((\mathbf{st}(rs) = pbr0 \wedge \mathbf{st}(rw) = 0 \wedge \mathbf{st}' = \mathbf{st} \mid rs : aPV0)\vee$
$(\mathbf{st}(rs) = par1 \wedge \mathbf{st}(br) > 0 \wedge \mathbf{st}' = \mathbf{st} \mid rs : aPV1))$
The guards of Vr simplify to this.

7.3 $\mathbf{e} = Vw\uparrow \wedge \mathbf{st}(rs) = par2 \wedge \mathbf{st}(bw) = 0\wedge$
$\mathbf{st}(rr) = 0 \wedge \mathbf{st}' = \mathbf{st} \mid rs : resg$
The guards of Vw simplify to this.

8-9 same as $TRrn3$

5. **Validity Conditions:**
$Vrn4 \equiv Rrn4 \rightarrow Grn4$
$Rrn4 \equiv \Box(\mathbf{st}(rs) = rung \rightarrow \Diamond(\mathbf{st}(rs) = bPV2))\wedge$
$\Box(\mathbf{e} = tPm \rightarrow \Diamond(\mathbf{e} = ePm))\wedge$
$\Box(\mathbf{e} = tPr \rightarrow \Diamond(\mathbf{e} = ePr))$
$Grn4 \equiv \Box(\mathbf{st}(rs) = tryg \rightarrow \Diamond(\mathbf{st}(rs) = rung))\wedge$
$\Box(\mathbf{e} = ePm \rightarrow \Diamond(\mathbf{e} = Vm))\wedge$
$\Box(\mathbf{e} = ePr \rightarrow \Diamond(\mathbf{e} = Vm))\wedge$
$\Box(\mathbf{e} = ePm \rightarrow \Diamond(\mathbf{e} = Vr))\wedge$
$\Box(\mathbf{e} = ePr \rightarrow \Diamond(\mathbf{e} = Vr))\wedge$
$\Box(\mathbf{e} = ePm \rightarrow \Diamond(\mathbf{e} = Vw))\wedge$
$\Box(\mathbf{e} = ePr \rightarrow \Diamond(\mathbf{e} = Vw))$

The requirement of giving priority to a `V(r)` operation is easily formulated, so we do not give it. Note that, formally speaking, we have not finished the implementation since we did not implement the abstract semaphore. Since doing so is not difficult, we leave it at that (take an implementation for a strong semaphore and transform it into this formalism).

4 Conclusion

We have shown by the formal development of Dijkstra's readers/writers program that it is indeed possible to formalise Dijkstra's development strategy of deleting undesirable sequences generated by intermediate programs. We have formalised this development within Stark's formalism which expresses separately the safety and liveness properties of a program under development. We offer the following conclusions:

- The formalisation of liveness causes no problems; we can translate the liveness conditions required for shared variables and semaphores into Stark's formalism.
- The translation of high level liveness properties into low level safety and liveness properties also causes no problems.
- The main problem is that this translation sometimes generates new, not allowed, sequences that on a higher level were previously not possible. This problem is solved by disallowing such sequences with the help of validity conditions which remove disallowed sequences from a machine. These validity conditions were originally intended in Stark's formalism to describe the liveness conditions. We have used them for *another purpose*: to extract the allowed sequences of a machine.

The last observation implies that a notion of satisfaction that uses set inclusion between sets of sequences generated by the safety parts only is not the correct one. We would nevertheless like to preserve Dijkstra's treatment of the readers/writers problem in this formalisation. From the example in the paper it can be seen how we achieve this. The proof obligation on the machine parts abstracts away differences that are caused by potential deadlock or blocking. Namely by the combined use of stutter steps as well as abstraction functions. That this does not cause inconsistencies is because of the limited corrective role of the validity condition: any liveness properties that a high level machine enables should also belong to the potential of the low level one. Only potential deadlock or blocking can be corrected. This turns out to be exactly the kind of incorrect sequences that Dijkstra allows in his approximative development. This means that the direction of the development is not only from validity conditions to machines but also from machines to validity conditions.

In future work we want to also apply Stark's formalism to the development of fault tolerant systems. Also the formalism should be changed so that machine specifications get shorter.

4.1 Acknowledgements

I would like to thank W.H.J. Feijen for drawing our attention to [2] as an example of developing a parallel program.

References

[1] M. Abadi and L. Lamport. The existence of refinement mappings. In *Third annual symposium on Logic in Computer Science*, pages 165–175, July 1988.

[2] E.W. Dijkstra. A tutorial on the split binary semaphore, 1979. EWD 703.

[3] E. Diepstraten and R. Kuiper. Abadi & Lamport and Stark: towards a proof theory for stuttering, dense domains and refinements mappings. In *LNCS 430:Proc. of the REX Workshop on Stepwise Refinement of Distributed Systems, Models, Formalisms, Correctness*, pages 208–238. Springer-Verlag, 1990.

[4] C.B. Jones. *Development methods for computer programs including a notion of interference*. PhD thesis, Oxford University Computing Laboratory, 1981.

[5] L. Lamport. What good is temporal logic. In R.E.A. Manson, editor, *Information Processing 83: Proc. of the IFIP 9th World Congress*, pages 657–668. Elsevier Science Publishers, North Holland, 1983.

[6] L. Lamport. An axiomatic semantics of concurrent programming languages. In K.R. Apt, editor, *NATO ASI SERIES, vol. F13: Logics and Models of Concurrent Systems*, pages 77–122. Springer-Verlag, January 1985.

[7] L. Lamport. A simple approach to specifying concurrent systems. *Communications of the ACM*, 32(1):32–45, January 1989.

[8] S. Lee, S. Gerhart, and W.-P. de Roever. The evolution of list-copying algorithms and the need for structured program verification. In *Proc. of 6th POPL*, 1979.

[9] J. Misra, and M. Chandy. Proofs of Networks of Processes. IEEE SE 7 (4), pp. 417-426, 1981.

[10] R. Milner. A calculus of Communicating Systems. LNCS 92, Springer-Verlag 1980.

[11] P.R.H. Place, W.G. Wood, and M. Tudball. Survey of formal specification techniques for reactive systems. Technical Report, 1990.

[12] E.W. Stark. *Foundations of a Theory of Specification for Distributed Systems.* PhD thesis, Massachusetts Inst. of Technology, 1984. Available as Report No. MIT/LCS/TR-342.

[13] E.W. Stark. A Proof Technique for Rely/Guarantee Properties. In *LNCS 206: Fifth Conference on Foundations of Software Technology and Theoretical Computer Science*, pages 369–391. Springer-Verlag, 1985.

[14] E.W. Stark. Proving entailment between conceptual state specifications. *Theoretical Computer Science*, 56:135–154, 1988.

[15] J. Zwiers, A. de Bruin, and W.-P. de Roever. A proof system for partial correctness of Dynamic Networks of Processes. In proc. of the conference on logics of programs 1983, LNCS 164, Springer Verlag 1984.

A Recursion Removal Theorem

Martin Ward
Computer Science Dept
Science Labs
South Rd
Durham DH1 3LE

March 30, 1992

Abstract

In this paper we briefly introduce a Wide Spectrum Language and its transformation theory and describe a recent success of the theory: a general recursion removal theorem. Recursion removal often forms an important step in the systematic development of an algorithm from a formal specification. We use semantic-preserving transformations to carry out such developments and the theorem proves the correctness of many different classes of recursion removal. This theorem includes as special cases the two techniques discussed by Knuth [13] and Bird [7]. We describe some applications of the theorem to cascade recursion, binary cascade recursion, Gray codes, and an inverse engineering problem.

1 Introduction

In this paper we briefly introduce some of the ideas behind the transformation theory we have developed over the last eight years at Oxford and Durham Universities and describe a recent result: a general recursion removal theorem.

We use a Wide Spectrum Language (called WSL), developed in [20,22, 22] which includes low-level programming constructs and high-level abstract specifications within a single language. Working within a single language means that the proof that a program correctly implements a specification, or that a specification correctly captures the behaviour of a program, can be achieved by means of formal transformations in the language. We don't have to develop transformations between the "programming" and "specification" languages. An added advantage is that different parts of the program can be expressed at different levels of abstraction, if required.

Refinement is defined in terms of the denotational semantics of the language: the semantics of a program $\mathbf{S}$ is a function which maps from an initial state to a final set of states. The set of final states represents all the possible output states of the program for the given input state. Using a set of states enables us to model nondeterministic programs and partially defined (or incomplete) specifications. For programs $\mathbf{S}_1$ and $\mathbf{S}_2$ we say $\mathbf{S}_1$ is refined by $\mathbf{S}_2$ (or $\mathbf{S}_2$ is a refinement of $\mathbf{S}_1$) and write $\mathbf{S}_1 \leq \mathbf{S}_2$ if $\mathbf{S}_2$ is more defined and more deterministic than $\mathbf{S}_1$. If $\mathbf{S}_1 \leq \mathbf{S}_2$ and $\mathbf{S}_2 \leq \mathbf{S}_1$ then we say $\mathbf{S}_1$ is equivalent to $\mathbf{S}_2$ and write

$\mathbf{S}_1 \approx \mathbf{S}_2$. A transformation is an operation which maps any program satisfying the applicability conditions of the transformation to an equivalent program. Thus a transformation is a special case of refinement. See [20] and [22] for a description of the semantics of WSL and the methods used for proving the correctness of transformations.

Many of the transformations of WSL programs are "refinements" in the wider sense of transforming an abstract specification or algorithm into a concrete implementation; in [23] we discuss ways of defining the relative "degree of abstractness" of semantically equivalent WSL programs.

In developing a model based theory of semantic equivalence, we use the popular approach of defining a core "kernel" language with denotational semantics, and permitting definitional extensions in terms of the basic constructs. In contrast to other work, we do not use a purely applicative kernel; instead, the concept of state is included, with primitive statements to add and remove variables to/from the state space. Together with guards and assertions, this allows specifications expressed in first order logic to be part of the language, thus providing a genuine "wide spectrum language". Unlike the CIP project [5] and others (eg [6,8]) our kernel language will have state introduced right from the start so that it can cope easily with imperative programs. Our experience is that an imperative kernel language with functional extensions is more tractable than a functional kernel language with imperative extensions. Unlike Bird [8] we did not want to be restricted to a purely functional language since this is incompatible with the aims of a true wide spectrum language.

This approach has proved highly successful, not only to the goal of refining specifications into algorithms by formal transformation (see [21,25,26]), but also working in the reverse direction: starting with an unstructured program we can transform it into a high-level specification [27].

2 The Wide Spectrum Language

Our kernel language has four primitive statements:

1. Assertion: $\{\mathbf{P}\}$
2. Guard: $[\mathbf{P}]$
3. Add variables (with arbitrary values): $add(\mathbf{x})$
4. Remove variables: $remove(\mathbf{x})$

where $\mathbf{x}$ is a sequence of variables and $\mathbf{P}$ a formula of first order logic.

An assertion is a partial **skip** statement, it aborts if the condition is false but does nothing if the condition is true. The **abort** statement {**false**} therefore always aborts. The guard statement $[\mathbf{P}]$ always terminates, it enforces $\mathbf{P}$ to be true at this point in the program.If this cannot be ensured then the set of possible final states is empty, and therefore all possible final states will satisfy any desired condition. Hence the "null guard", [**false**], is a "correct refinement" of *any* specification whatsoever. Clearly guard statements cannot be directly implemented but they are nonetheless a useful theoretical tool.

The *add*($\mathbf{x}$) statement is unrestricted in its nondeterminacy, by following it with a suitable guard we can restrict the nondeterminacy and achieve the effect of a general assignment. For example, Back's atomic description [4], written $\mathbf{x}/\mathbf{y}.\mathbf{Q}$, where $\mathbf{Q}$ is a formula of first order logic (with equality) and $\mathbf{x}$, $\mathbf{y}$ are sets of variables, is equivalent to the sequence $\{\exists \mathbf{x}.\, \mathbf{Q}\}$; *add*($\mathbf{x}$); $[\mathbf{Q}]$; *remove*($\mathbf{y}$). Its effect is to add the variables in $\mathbf{x}$ to the state space, assign new values to them such that $\mathbf{Q}$ is satisfied, remove the variables in $\mathbf{y}$ from the state and terminate. If there is no assignment to the variables in $\mathbf{x}$ which satisfies $\mathbf{Q}$ then the atomic specification does not terminate.

Morgan and others [14,15,16,17] use a different specification statement, written $\mathbf{x}$: [*Pre*, *Post*]. This statement is guaranteed to terminate for all initial states which satisfy *Pre* and will terminate in a state which satisfies *Post* while only assigning to variables in the list $\mathbf{x}$. It is thus a combination of an assignment and a guard statement. In our notation an equivalent statement is $\{Pre\}$; *add*($\mathbf{x}$); $[Post]$.

The kernel language is constructed from these four primitive statements, a set of *statement variables* (these are symbols which will be used to represent the recursive calls of recursive statements) and the following four compounds:

1. **Sequential Composition**: $(\mathbf{S}_1;\ \mathbf{S}_2)$
   First $\mathbf{S}_1$ is executed and then $\mathbf{S}_2$.

2. **Choice:** $(\mathbf{S}_1 \sqcap \mathbf{S}_2)$
   One of the statements $\mathbf{S}_1$ or $\mathbf{S}_2$ is chosen for execution. It is the strongest program refined by both $\mathbf{S}_1$ and $\mathbf{S}_2$.

3. **Join:** $(\mathbf{S}_1 \sqcup \mathbf{S}_2)$
   The join of two programs is the weakest program which refines them both.

4. **Recursive Procedure:** $(\mu X.\mathbf{S}_1)$
   Within the body $\mathbf{S}_1$, occurrences of the statement variable X represent recursive calls to the procedure.

There is a rather pleasing duality between the assertion and the guard and also between the choice and join constructs. In fact, the set of programs forms a *lattice* [11] with [**false**] as the top element, {**false**} as the bottom element, $\sqcap$ as the lattice meet and $\sqcup$ as the lattice join operators.

The kernel language is particularly elegant and tractable but is too primitive to form a useful wide spectrum language for the transformational development of programs. For this purpose we need to extend the language by defining new constructs in terms of the existing ones using "definitional transformations". A series of new "language levels" is built up, with the language at each level being defined in terms of the previous level: the kernel language is the "level zero" language which forms the foundation for all the others. Each new language level automatically inherits the transformations proved at the previous level, these form the basis of a new transformation catalogue. Transformations of the new language construct are proved by appealing to the definitional transformation of the construct and carrying out the actual manipulation in the previous level language. This technique has proved extremely powerful in the development of a practical transformation system which currently implements over four hundred transformations, accessible through a simple user interface [10].

2.1 Syntax of Expressions

Expressions include variable names, numbers, strings of the form "`text...`", the constants $\mathbb{N}$, $\mathbb{R}$, $\mathbb{Q}$, $\mathbb{Z}$, and the following operators and functions: (in the following e_1, e_2 etc. represent any valid expressions):

Numeric operators: $e_1 + e_2$, $e_1 - e_2$, $e_1 * e_2$, e_1/e_2, $e_1^{e_2}$, $e_1 \bmod e_2$, $e_1 \operatorname{div} e_2$, $\mathit{frac}(e_1)$, $\mathit{abs}(e_1)$, $\mathit{sgn}(e_1)$, $\mathit{max}(e_1, e_2, \ldots)$, $\mathit{min}(e_1, e_2, \ldots)$, with the usual meanings.

Sequences: $s = \langle a_1, a_2, \ldots, a_n \rangle$ is a sequence, the ith element a_i is denoted $s[i]$, $s[i\,..\,j]$ is the subsequence $\langle s[i], s[i+1], \ldots, s[j] \rangle$, where $s[i\,..\,j] = \langle\rangle$ (the empty sequence) if $i > j$. The length of sequence s is denoted $\ell(s)$, so $s[\ell(s)]$ is the last element of s. We use $s[i\,..]$ as an abbreviation for $s[i\,..\,\ell(s)]$. $\mathit{reverse}(s) = \langle a_n, a_{n-1}, \ldots, a_2, a_1 \rangle$, $\mathit{head}(s)$ is the same as $s[1]$ and $\mathit{tail}(s)$ is $s[2\,..]$.

Sequence concatenation: If s_1 and s_2 are sequences then $s_1 +\!\!+\, s_2 = \langle s_1[1], \ldots, s_1[\ell(s_1)], s_2[1], \ldots, s_2[\ell(s_2)] \rangle$ The *append* function, $\mathit{append}(s_1, s_2, \ldots, s_n)$, is the same as $s_1 +\!\!+\, s_2 +\!\!+ \cdots +\!\!+\, s_n$.

Subsequences: The assignment $s[i\,..\,j] := t[k\,..\,l]$ where $j - i = l - k$ assigns s the value $\langle s[1], \ldots, s[i-1], t[k], \ldots, t[l], s[j+1], \ldots, s[\ell(s)] \rangle$.

Sets: We have the usual set operations $\cup$ (union), $\cap$ (intersection) and $-$ (set difference), $\subseteq$ (subset), $\in$ (element), $\wp$ (powerset). $\{\, x \in A \mid P(x) \,\}$ is the set of all elements in A which satisfy predicate P. For the sequence s, $\mathit{set}(s)$ is the set of elements of the sequence, i.e. $\mathit{set}(s) = \{\, s[i] \mid 1 \leq i \leq \ell(s) \,\}$.

Relations and Functions: A relation is a (finite or infinite) set of pairs, a subset of $A \times B$ where A is the domain and B the range. A relation f is a function iff $\forall x, y_1, y_2.\, (((x, y_1) \in f \wedge (x, y_2) \in f) \Rightarrow y_1 = y_2)$. In this case we write $f(x) = y$ when $(x, y) \in f$.

Substitution: The expression $e[e_2/e_1]$ in which e, e_1 and $e_2$are expressions means the result of replacing all occurrences of e_1 in e by e_2. (This notation is also used for substitution in statements).

2.2 Syntax of Formulae

true and **false** are true and false conditions, **true** is defined as $\forall v.\, (v = v)$ and **false** as $\neg \forall v.\, (v = v)$. In the following $\mathbf{Q}$, $\mathbf{Q}_1$, $\mathbf{Q}_2$ etc. represent arbitrary formulae and e_1, e_2, etc. arbitrary expressions:

Relations: $e_1 = e_2$, $e_1 \neq e_2$, $e_1 < e_2$, $e_1 \leq e_2$, $e_1 > e_2$, $e_1 \geq e_2$, $even?(e_1)$, $odd?(e_1)$;

Logical operators: $\neg\mathbf{Q}$, $\mathbf{Q}_1 \vee \mathbf{Q}_2$, $\mathbf{Q}_1 \wedge \mathbf{Q}_2$;

Quantifiers: $\forall\mathbf{v}.\,\mathbf{Q}$ and $\exists\mathbf{v}.\,\mathbf{Q}$ are allowed in formulae.

2.3 Language Extensions

The first set of language extensions, which go to make up the "first level" language, are as follows. Subsequent extensions will be defined in terms of the first level language. For the purposes of this paper we will describe only a subset of the language extensions. See [22] and [20] for a more complete definition.

- Sequential composition: The sequencing operator is associative so we can eliminate the brackets:

  $\mathbf{S}_1;\ \mathbf{S}_2;\ \mathbf{S}_3;\ \ldots;\ \mathbf{S}_n \quad =_{\mathrm{DF}} \quad (\ldots((\mathbf{S}_1;\ \mathbf{S}_2);\ \mathbf{S}_3);\ \ldots;\ \mathbf{S}_n)$

- Deterministic Choice: We can use guards to turn a nondeterministic choice into a deterministic choice:

  $\underline{\text{if}}\ \mathbf{B}\ \underline{\text{then}}\ \mathbf{S}_1\ \underline{\text{else}}\ \mathbf{S}_2\ \underline{\text{fi}} \quad =_{\mathrm{DF}} \quad (([\mathbf{B}];\ \mathbf{S}_1) \sqcap ([\neg\mathbf{B}];\ \mathbf{S}_2))$

- Assignment: We can express a general assignment using *add*, *remove*, and guards:

  $\mathbf{x} := \mathbf{x}'.\mathbf{Q} \quad =_{\mathrm{DF}} \quad \{\exists\mathbf{x}.\,\mathbf{Q}\};\ add(\mathbf{x}');\ [\mathbf{Q}];$
  $add(\mathbf{x});\ [\mathbf{x} = \mathbf{x}'];\ remove(\mathbf{x}')$
  Here, $\mathbf{x}$ is a sequence of variables and $\mathbf{x}'$ is a sequence of new variables. The formula $\mathbf{Q}$ expresses the relation between the initial values of $\mathbf{x}$ and the final values. For example: $\langle x\rangle := \langle x'\rangle.(x' = x + 1)$ increments the value of the variable x. We will sometimes omit the sequence brackets around singleton sequences of variables and expressions where this causes no confusion.

- Simple Assignment: If $\mathbf{e}$ is a list of expressions and $\mathbf{x}$ a list of variables and $\mathbf{x}'$ a list of new variables, then:

  $\mathbf{x} := \mathbf{e} \quad =_{\mathrm{DF}} \quad \mathbf{x} := \mathbf{x}'.(\mathbf{x}' = \mathbf{e})$
  With this notation, the statement to increment x can be written: $x := x + 1$ (omitting the sequence brackets as discussed above).

- Stack Operations:

  $x \leftarrow e \quad =_{\mathrm{DF}} \quad x := \langle e\rangle +\!\!+\, x$

  $x \xleftarrow{\text{push}} e \quad =_{\mathrm{DF}} \quad x := \langle e\rangle +\!\!+\, x$

$$x \xleftarrow{\text{pop}} e \quad =_{\text{DF}} \quad e := x[1];\ x := x[2\,.\,.]$$

- Nondeterministic Choice: The "guarded command" of Dijkstra [12]:

$$\underline{\textbf{if}}\ \mathbf{B}_1 \rightarrow \mathbf{S}_1 \ \Box\ \mathbf{B}_2 \rightarrow \mathbf{S}_2 \ldots \Box\ \mathbf{B}_n \rightarrow \mathbf{S}_n\ \underline{\textbf{fi}}$$

$$=_{\text{DF}}$$

$$\begin{array}{l}(((\ldots(([\mathbf{B}_1];\ \mathbf{S}_1) \sqcap \\ \quad\quad ([\mathbf{B}_2];\ \mathbf{S}_2)) \sqcap \\ \quad \ldots) \sqcap \\ \ ([\mathbf{B}_n];\ \mathbf{S}_n)) \sqcap \\ ([\neg(\mathbf{B}_1 \vee \mathbf{B}_2 \vee \cdots \vee \mathbf{B}_n)];\ \mathbf{abort}))\end{array}$$

- Deterministic Iteration: We define a **while** loop using a new recursive procedure X which does not occur free in **S**:

$$\underline{\textbf{while}}\ \mathbf{B}\ \underline{\textbf{do}}\ \mathbf{S}\ \underline{\textbf{od}} \quad =_{\text{DF}} \quad (\mu X.(([\mathbf{B}];\ \mathbf{S};\ X) \sqcap [\neg\mathbf{B}]))$$

- Nondeterministic Iteration:

$$\underline{\textbf{do}}\ \mathbf{B}_1 \rightarrow \mathbf{S}_1 \ \Box\ \mathbf{B}_2 \rightarrow \mathbf{S}_2 \ldots \Box\ \mathbf{B}_n \rightarrow \mathbf{S}_n\ \underline{\textbf{od}}$$

$$=_{\text{DF}}$$

$$\begin{array}{l}\underline{\textbf{while}}\ (\mathbf{B}_1 \vee \mathbf{B}_2 \vee \cdots \vee \mathbf{B}_n)\ \underline{\textbf{do}} \\ \quad\quad \underline{\textbf{if}}\ \mathbf{B}_1 \rightarrow \mathbf{S}_1 \ \Box\ \mathbf{B}_2 \rightarrow \mathbf{S}_2 \ldots \Box\ \mathbf{B}_n \rightarrow \mathbf{S}_n\ \underline{\textbf{fi}}\ \underline{\textbf{od}}\end{array}$$

- Initialised local Variables:

$$\underline{\textbf{var}}\ \mathbf{x} := \mathbf{t} : \mathbf{S}\ \underline{\textbf{end}} \quad =_{\text{DF}} \quad add(\mathbf{x});\ [\mathbf{x} = \mathbf{t}];\ \mathbf{S};\ remove(\mathbf{x})$$

- Counted Iteration:

$$\underline{\textbf{od}} \quad =_{\text{DF}} \quad \underline{\textbf{var}}\ i := b : \underline{\textbf{while}}\ i \leq f\ \underline{\textbf{do}}\ \mathbf{S};\ i := i + s\ \underline{\textbf{od}}\ \underline{\textbf{end}}$$

- Procedure call:

$$\underline{\textbf{proc}}\ X \equiv \mathbf{S}. \quad =_{\text{DF}} \quad (\mu X.\mathbf{S})$$

- Block with local procedure:

$$\underline{\textbf{begin}}\ \mathbf{S}_1\ \underline{\textbf{where}}\ \underline{\textbf{proc}}\ X \equiv \mathbf{S}_2.\ \underline{\textbf{end}} \quad =_{\text{DF}} \quad \mathbf{S}_1[\underline{\textbf{proc}}\ X \equiv \mathbf{S}_2./X]$$

details.

2.4 Exit Statements

Our programming language will include statements of the form **exit**(n), where n is an integer, (*not* a variable) which occur within loops of the form **do** **S** **od** where **S** is a statement. These were described in [13] and more recently in [19]. They are "infinite" or "unbounded" loops which can only be terminated by the execution of a statement of the form **exit**(n) which causes the program to exit n of the enclosing loops. To simplify the language we disallow **exit**s which leave a block or a loop other than an unbounded loop.

Previously, the only formal treatments of **exit** statements have treated them in the same way as unstructured **goto** statements by adding "continuations" to the denotational semantics of all the other statements. This adds greatly to the complexity of the semantics and also means that all the results obtained prior to this modification will have to be re-proved with respect to the new semantics. The approach taken in our work, which does not seem to have been tried before, is to express every program which uses **exit** statements and unbounded loop in terms of the first level language *without* changing the language semantics. This means that the new statements will not change the denotational semantics of the kernel so all the transformations developed without reference to **exit** statements will still apply in the more general case. In fact we make much use of the transformations derived without reference to **exit**s in the derivation of transformations of statements which use the **exit** statement.

The interpretation of these statements in terms of the first level language is as follows:

We have an integer variable *depth* which records the current depth of nesting of loops. At the beginning of the program we have $depth := 0$ and each **exit** statement **exit**(k) is translated: $depth := depth - k$ since it changes the depth of "current execution" by moving out of k enclosing loops. To prevent any more statements at the current depth being executed after an **exit** statement has been executed we surround all statements by "guards" which are **if** statements which will test *depth* and only allow the statement to be executed if *depth* has the correct value. Each unbounded loop **do** **S** **od** is translated:

$$depth := n;\ \underline{\textbf{while}}\ depth = n\ \underline{\textbf{do}}\ guard_n(\mathbf{S})\ \underline{\textbf{od}}$$

where n is an integer constant representing the depth of the loop (1 for an outermost loop, 2 for double nested loops etc.) and $guard_n(\mathbf{S})$ is the statement **S** with each component statement guarded so that if the depth is changed by an **exit** statement, then no more statements in the loop will be executed and the loop will terminate. The important property of a guarded statement is that it will only be executed if *depth* has the correct value. Thus if $depth \neq n$ initially then $guard_n(\mathbf{S}) \approx \mathbf{skip}$. So for example, the program:

```
do do last := item[i];
      i := i + 1;
      if i = n + 1 then write(count); exit(2) fi;
      if item[i] ≠ last then write(count); exit(1)
                         else count := count + number[i] fi od;
   count := number[i] od
```

translates to the following:

```
depth := 1;
while depth = 1 do
        depth := 2;
        while depth = 2 do
                last := item[i];
                i := i + 1;
                if i = n + 1 then write(count); depth := depth − 2 fi;
                if depth = 2
                   then if item[i] ≠ last
                              then write(count); depth := depth − 1
                               else count := count + number[i] fi fi od;
        if depth = 1 then count := number[i] fi od
```

2.5 Action Systems

This section will introduce the concept of an *Action System* as a set of parameterless mutually recursive procedures. A program written using labels and jumps translates directly into an action system. Note however that if the end of the body of an action is reached, then control is passed to the action which called it (or to the statement following the action system) rather than "falling through" to the next label. The exception to this is a special action called the terminating action, usually denoted **Z**, which when called results in the immediate termination of the whole action system.

Our recursive statement does not directly allow the definition of mutually recursive procedures (since all calls to a procedure must occur within the procedure body). However we can define a set of mutually recursive procedures by putting them all within a single procedure. For example suppose we have two statements, $\mathbf{S}_1$ and $\mathbf{S}_2$ both containing statement variables X_1 and X_2 (where we intend $\mathbf{S}_1$ to be the body of X_1 and $\mathbf{S}_2$ to be the body of X_2). We can represent these by a single recursive program:

$$
\begin{aligned}
&x := 1;\\
&\underline{\text{proc}}\ A \equiv \underline{\text{if}}\ x = 1 \rightarrow \mathbf{S}_1[x := 1;\ A/X_1][x := 2;\ A/X_2]\\
&\qquad\qquad\ \square\ x = 2 \rightarrow \mathbf{S}_2[x := 1;\ A/X_1][x := 2;\ A/X_2]\ \underline{\text{fi}}.
\end{aligned}
$$

where an additional variable x records which procedure is required when the composite procedure A is called.

Arsac [2,3] uses a restricted definition of actions together with deterministic assignments, the binary if statement and do loops with exits: so there is no place for nondeterminism in his results. The main differences between our action systems and Arsac's are: (i) that we use a much more powerful language (including general specifications) , (ii) we give a formal definition (ultimately in terms of denotational semantics), and (iii) our action systems are simple statements which can form components of other constructs. This last point is vitally important in this application since it gives us a way to restructure the body of a recursive procedure as an action system. It is this restructuring which gives the recursion removal theorem much of its power and generality.

Definition 2.1 An *action* is a parameterless procedure acting on global variables (cf [2,3]). It is written in the form $A \equiv \mathbf{S}$ where A is a statement variable (the name of the action) and $\mathbf{S}$ is a statement (the action body). A set of (mutually recursive) actions is called an *action system*. There may sometimes be a special action (usually denoted Z), execution of which causes termination of the whole action system even if there are unfinished recursive calls. An occurrence of a statement <u>call</u> X within the action body refers to a call of another action.

The action system:

<u>**actions**</u> A_1 :
$A_1 \equiv \mathbf{S}_1$.
$A_2 \equiv \mathbf{S}_2$.
...
$A_n \equiv \mathbf{S}_n$. <u>**endactions**</u>

(where statements $\mathbf{S}_1, \ldots, \mathbf{S}_n$ must have no <u>**exit**</u>(n) statements within less than n nested loops) is defined as follows:

<u>**var**</u> *action* := "A_1";
    <u>**proc**</u> $A \equiv$
        <u>**if**</u> *action* = "A_1" $\rightarrow$ *action* := "O";
                $guard_Z(\mathbf{S}_1)$[*action* := "A_i"; A/<u>**call**</u> A_i]
        $\Box$ *action* = "A_2" $\rightarrow$ *action* := "O";
                $guard_Z(\mathbf{S}_2)$[*action* := "A_i"; A/<u>**call**</u> A_i]
        ...
        $\Box$ *action* = "A_n" $\rightarrow$ *action* := "O";
                $guard_Z(\mathbf{S}_n)$[*action* := "A_i"; A/<u>**call**</u> A_i]. <u>**end**</u>

Here *action* is a new variable which contains the name of the next action to be invoked and $guard_Z(\mathbf{S})$ is defined in a similar way to $guard_n(\mathbf{S})$ so that:

$guard_Z$(<u>**call**</u> Z) $=_{\text{DF}}$ *action* := "Z"
$guard_Z(v := e)$ $=_{\text{DF}}$ <u>**if**</u> *action* = "O" <u>**then**</u> $v := e$ <u>**fi**</u> etc.

and as soon as *action* is set to "Z" no further statements will be executed. This ensures the correct operation of the "halting" action. Here "A_1", ..., "A_n", "O" and "Z" represent a suitable set of $n + 2$ distinct constant values.

The procedure A is never called with *action* equal to "Z" (or in fact anything other than "A_1", ..., "A_n"). The assignment *action* := "O" is not really needed because the variable *action* will be assigned again before its value is tested; it is added so that we can distinguish the following three cases depending on the value of *action*:

1. Currently executing an action: *action* = "O";

2. About to call another (or the same) action (other than the terminating action): *action* = one of "A_1", ..., "A_n";

3. Have called the terminating action, all outstanding recursive calls are terminated without any statements being executed: *action* = "Z".

Definition 2.2 An action is *regular* if every execution of the action leads to an action call. (This is similar to a regular rule in a Post production system [18]).

Definition 2.3 An action system is regular if every action in the system is regular. Any algorithm defined by a flowchart, or a program which contains labels and gotos but no procedure calls in non-terminal positions, can be expressed as a regular action system.

2.6 Procedures and Functions with Parameters

For simplicity we will only consider procedures with parameters which are called by value or by value-result. Here the value of the actual parameter is copied into a local variable which replaces the formal parameter in the body of the procedure. For result parameters, the final value of this local variable is copied back into the actual parameter. In this case the actual parameter must be a variable or some other object (eg an array element) which can be assigned a value. Such objects are often denoted as "L-values" because they can occur on the left of assignment statements.

Our "definitional transformation" for a procedure with formal parameters and local variables will replace them both by global stacks. Consider the following piece of code, which contains a call to the recursive procedure F. This procedure uses a local variable a which must be preserved over recursive calls to F:

```
begin ...; F(t, v); ...
where
  proc F(x, var: y) ≡
        var a := d :
           S end.
end
```

where t is an expression, v a variable, x is a value parameter, v a value-result parameter and a a local variable which is assigned the initial value d. This is defined as:

begin
  $x := \langle\rangle$; $y := \langle\rangle$; $a := \langle\rangle$;
  ...;
  $x \xleftarrow{\text{push}} t$; $y \xleftarrow{\text{push}} v$;

$F;$
$v \stackrel{\text{pop}}{\longleftarrow} y;\ x := x[2\,..];$
...
where
proc $F \equiv$
$a \stackrel{\text{push}}{\longleftarrow} d;$
$\mathbf{S}[x[1]/x][y[1]/y][a[1]/a]$
$[x \stackrel{\text{push}}{\longleftarrow} t';\ y \stackrel{\text{push}}{\longleftarrow} v';\ F;\ v' \stackrel{\text{pop}}{\longleftarrow} y;\ x := x[2\,..]/F(t',v')];$
$a := a[2\,..].$
end

Here the substitution of $x[1]$ for x etc. ensures that the body of the procedure only accesses and updates the tops of the stacks which replace the parameters and local variables. This means that any call of F will only affect the values at the tops of the stacks x, y and a so an inner recursive call of F, which takes the form: $x \stackrel{\text{push}}{\longleftarrow} t';\ y \stackrel{\text{push}}{\longleftarrow} v';\ F;\ v' \stackrel{\text{pop}}{\longleftarrow} y;\ x := x[2\,..]$, will only affect the value of v (and global variables in **S**) and will not affect the stacks. The proof is by the theorems on invariant maintenance for recursive statements [20].

To allow side effects in expressions and conditions we introduce the new notation of "expression brackets", $\lceil$ and $\rfloor$. These allow us to include statements as part of an expression, for example the following are valid expressions:

$\lceil x := x + 1;\ x\rfloor$
$\lceil x := x + 1;\ x - 1\rfloor$

We also have conditional expressions where **if** and **fi** are used as expression brackets, for example:

if $x > 0$ **then** x **else** $-x$ **fi**

The first and second are equivalent to C's `++x` and `x++` respectively, the third is a conditional expression which returns the absolute value of x.

Note that expression brackets may be nested, for example the assignment:

$a := \lceil \mathbf{S}_1;\ b :=$ **if** $\lceil \mathbf{S}_2;\ \mathbf{Q}\rfloor$ **then** $\lceil \mathbf{S}_3;\ \mathbf{t}_1\rfloor$ **else** $\mathbf{t}_2$ **fi**; $b * b\rfloor$

is represented as:

$\mathbf{S}_1;\ \mathbf{S}_2;$ **if** $\mathbf{Q}$ **then** $\mathbf{S}_3;\ b := \mathbf{t}_1$ **else** $b := t_2$ **fi**; $a := b * b$

Definition 2.4 *Function calls:* The definitional transformation of a function call will replace the function call by a call to a procedure which assigns the value returned by the function to a variable. This variable then replaces the function call in the expression. Several calls in one expression are replaced by the same number of procedure calls and new variables. Boolean functions are treated as functions which return one of the values "*tt*" or "*ff*" (representing true and false). So a boolean function call is replaced by a formula ($b =$ "*tt*") where b is a new local variable. The statement in which the function call appeared is preceded by a procedure call which sets b to "*tt*" or "*ff*", depending on the result of the corresponding boolean function.

For example, the statement with function calls:

begin $a := F(x) + F(y)$
where
  funct $F(x) \equiv$ **if B then** $\mathbf{t}_1$ **else** $\mathbf{t}_2$ **fi**. **end**

is interpreted:

begin var r_1, r_2 :
        $F(x);\ r_1 := r;\ F(y);\ r_2 := r;$
        $a := r_1 + r_2$ **end**
where
  proc $F(x) \equiv$ **if B then** $r := t_1$ **else** $r := t_2$ **fi**. **end**

The statement:

begin
  $a := \lceil$**while** $B(x)$ **do** $x := F(x)$ **od**; $x + c\rfloor$
where
  funct $B(x) \equiv \lceil$S; $x > y\rfloor$.
  funct $F(x) \equiv$ **if B then** $\mathbf{t}_1$ **else** $\mathbf{t}_2$ **fi**.

is interpreted:

begin
  do $B(x)$; **if** $r =$ "*ff*" **then exit fi**;
    $F(x);\ x := r$ **od**;
  $a := x + c$ **where**
  proc $B(x) \equiv$ S; **if** $x > y$ **then** $r :=$ "*tt*" **else** $r :=$ "*ff*" **fi**,
    proc $F(x) \equiv$ **if B then** $r := \mathbf{t}_1$ **else** $r := \mathbf{t}_2$ **fi**. **end**

See [20] for the formal definition of generalised expressions and generalised conditions and their interpretation functions.

3 Example Transformations

In this section we describe a few of the transformations we will use later:

3.1 Expand IF statement

The if statement:

> **if** B **then** S_1 **else** S_2 **fi**; S

can be expanded over the following statement to give:

> **if** B **then** S_1; S **else** S_2; S **fi**

3.2 Loop Inversion

If the statement S_1 contains no **exits** which can cause termination of an enclosing loop (i.e. in the notation of [20] it is a *proper sequence*) then the loop:

> **do** S_1; S_2 **od**

can be inverted to:

> S_1; **do** S_2; S_1 **od**

This transformation may be used in the forwards direction to move the termination test of a loop to the beginning, prior to transforming it into a **while** loop, or it may be used in the reverse direction to merge two copies of the statement S_1.

3.3 Loop Unrolling

The next three transformations concern various forms of loop unrolling. They play an important role in the proofs of other transformations as well as being generally useful.

Lemma 3.1 *Loop Unrolling:*

> **while** B **do** S **od** $\approx$ **if** B **then** S; **while** B **do** S **od** **fi**

Lemma 3.2 *Selective unrolling of* **while** *loops:* For any condition Q we have:

> **while** B **do** S **od** $\approx$ **while** B **do** S; **if** B $\wedge$ Q **then** S **fi** **od**

Lemma 3.3 *Entire Loop Unfolding:* if $B' \Rightarrow B$ then:

> **while** B **do** S **od** $\approx$ **while** B **do** S; **if** Q **then** **while** B' **do** S **od** **fi** **od**

Each of these transformation has a generalisation in which instead of inserting the "unrolled" part after S it is copied after an arbitrary selection of the terminal statements in S.

3.4 Absorption

Definition 3.4 A *primitive statement* is any statement other than a conditional, a <u>do</u> ... <u>od</u> loop or a sequence of statements. The *depth* of a component of a statement is the number of enclosing <u>do</u> ... <u>od</u> loops around the component. A *terminal statement* is a primitive statement which is either

(i) in a terminal position, or

(ii) is an <u>exit</u>(n) at depth less than n, or

(iii) is an <u>exit</u>(n) at depth n where the outermost <u>do</u> ... <u>od</u> loop is in a terminal position.

The *terminal value* of a terminal statement <u>exit</u>(n) is n minus the depth. *Incrementing* a statement by k means adding <u>exit</u>(k) after each non-<u>exit</u> terminal statement with terminal value zero, and replacing each terminal statement <u>exit</u>(n) with terminal value zero by <u>exit</u>($n + k$).

A sequence **S**; **S**$'$ of two statements can be merged together by the *absorption* The statement **S**$'$ following **S** is "absorbed" into it by replacing all of the terminal statements of **S** which would lead to **S**$'$ by a copy of **S**$'$ incremented by the depth of the terminal statement. For example:

<u>do</u> <u>do</u> <u>if</u> $y > x$ <u>then</u> <u>exit</u> <u>fi</u>;
        $x := x - 1$;
        <u>if</u> $x = 0$ <u>then</u> <u>exit</u>(2) <u>fi</u> <u>od</u>;
    <u>if</u> $z > x$ <u>then</u> <u>exit</u> <u>fi</u> <u>od</u>;
<u>if</u> $z = x$ <u>then</u> <u>exit</u> <u>fi</u>

after absorption becomes:

<u>do</u> <u>do</u> <u>if</u> $y > x$ <u>then</u> <u>exit</u> <u>fi</u>;
        $x := x - 1$;
        <u>if</u> $x = 0$ <u>then</u> <u>if</u> $z = x$ <u>then</u> <u>exit</u>(3) <u>else</u> <u>exit</u>(2) <u>fi</u> <u>fi</u> <u>od</u>;
    <u>if</u> $z > x$ <u>then</u> <u>if</u> $z = x$ <u>then</u> <u>exit</u>(2) <u>else</u> <u>exit</u> <u>fi</u> <u>od</u>

4 The Theorem

Theorem 4.1 Suppose we have a recursive procedure whose body is an action system in the following form, in which the body of the procedure is an action system. (A <u>call</u> Z in the action system will therefore terminate only the current invocation of the procedure):

<u>proc</u> $F(x) \equiv$
    <u>actions</u> A_1 :
    $A_1 \equiv$ **S**$_1$.

$\ldots A_i \ \equiv \mathbf{S}_i.$
$\ldots B_j \ \equiv \mathbf{S}_{j0};\ F(g_{j1}(x));\ \mathbf{S}_{j1};\ F(g_{j2}(x));\ \ldots;\ F(g_{jn_j}(x));\ \mathbf{S}_{jn_j}.$
$\ldots$ **endactions**.

where $\mathbf{S}_{j1}, \ldots, \mathbf{S}_{jn_j}$ preserve the value of x and no $\mathbf{S}$ contains a call to F (i.e. all the calls to F are listed explicitly in the B_j actions) and the statements $\mathbf{S}_{j0}, \mathbf{S}_{j1} \ldots, \mathbf{S}_{jn_j-1}$ contain no action calls. There are $M+N$ actions in total: $A_1, \ldots, A_M, B_1, \ldots, B_N$.

We claim that this is equivalent to the following iterative procedure which uses a new local stack L and a new local variable m and where we have added a new action $\hat{F}$ to the action system:

```
proc F'(x) ≡
    var L := ⟨⟩, m := 0:
        actions A_1:
        A_1  ≡ S_1[call F̂/call Z].
        ...A_i ≡ S_i[call F̂/call Z].
        ...B_j ≡ S_j0; L := ⟨⟨0, g_j1(x)⟩, ⟨⟨j, 1⟩, x⟩, ⟨0, g_j2(x)⟩, ...,
                       ⟨0, g_jn_j(x)⟩, ⟨⟨j, n_j⟩, x⟩⟩ ++ L;
                 call F̂.
        ...F̂  ≡ if L = ⟨⟩ then call Z
                          else ⟨m, x⟩ ← L;
                               if m = 0 → call A_1
                               □ ... □ m = ⟨j, k⟩ → S_jk[call F̂/call Z]
                               ... fi fi. endactions
    end.
```

Proof: See [24] for the proof.

Note that any procedure $F(x)$ can be restructured into the required form; in fact (as we shall see later) there may be several different ways of structuring $F(x)$ which meet these criteria.

We will assume that the action system is *regular*, i.e. every execution of an action body leads to the call of another action. This means that the action body (and hence the current invocation of F) can only be terminated by a call to action Z. Transformations are presented in [20] to convert any action system into a regular one, perhaps with the aid of a stack. We will also assume for simplicity that all the action calls appear in terminal positions in an action body, regularity then implies that the statement at every terminal position is an action call. Any regular action system can be put into this form by repeated application of the absorption transformation of [20].

Corollary 4.2 By unfolding some calls to $\hat{F}$ and pruning, we get the following, slightly more efficient, version:

```
proc F'(x) ≡
```

$$
\begin{array}{l}
\underline{\text{var}}\ L := \langle\rangle, m := 0: \\
\quad \underline{\text{actions}}\ A_1: \\
\quad A_1 \equiv \mathbf{S}_1[\underline{\text{call}}\ \hat{F}/\underline{\text{call}}\ Z]. \\
\quad \ldots A_i \equiv \mathbf{S}_i[\underline{\text{call}}\ \hat{F}/\underline{\text{call}}\ Z]. \\
\quad \ldots B_j \equiv \mathbf{S}_{j0};\ L := \langle\langle\langle j, 1\rangle, x\rangle, \langle 0, g_{j2}(x)\rangle, \\
\qquad\qquad \ldots, \langle 0, g_{jn_j}(x)\rangle, \langle\langle j, n_j\rangle, x\rangle\rangle \mathbin{+\!\!+} L; \\
\qquad\qquad x := g_{j1}(x);\ \underline{\text{call}}\ A_1. \\
\quad \ldots \hat{F} \equiv \underline{\text{if}}\ L = \langle\rangle\ \underline{\text{then}}\ \underline{\text{call}}\ Z \\
\qquad\qquad\qquad \underline{\text{else}}\ \langle m, x\rangle \leftarrow L; \\
\qquad\qquad\qquad\quad \underline{\text{if}}\ m = 0 \rightarrow \underline{\text{call}}\ A_1 \\
\qquad\qquad\qquad\quad \square \ldots \square\ m = \langle j, k\rangle \rightarrow \mathbf{S}_{jk}[\underline{\text{call}}\ \hat{F}/\underline{\text{call}}\ Z] \\
\qquad\qquad\qquad\quad \ldots \underline{\text{fi}}\ \underline{\text{fi}}.\ \underline{\text{endactions}} \\
\underline{\text{end}}.
\end{array}
$$

In the case where $n_j = 1$ for all j, this version will never push a $\langle 0, x\rangle$ pair onto the stack. This can be significant for parameterless procedures where the number of j values is small as it can reduce the amount of storage required by the stack. In the extreme case where there is only one j value, the stack reduces to a sequence of identical elements and can therefore be represented by an integer, which simply records the length of the stack.

5 Cascade Recursion

This theorem can provide several different iterative equivalents for a given recursive procedure, depending on how the initial restructuring of the procedure body into an action system is carried out. Two extreme cases are:

1. Each action contains no more than one procedure call. This imposes no restrictions on the other statements in the body and is therefore frequently used (for example, many compilers use essentially this approach to deal with recursion). Bird [7] calls this the *direct method.*

2. Each action contains as long a sequence of procedure calls as possible. The resulting iterative program is a simple **while** loop with the stack managing all the control flow. Bird [7] describes this as the *postponed obligations* method: all the sub- invocations arising from a given invocation of the procedure are postponed on the stack before any is fulfilled.

These two special cases of the general transformation will be applied to the following simple cascade recursion schema:

$$
\begin{array}{l}
\underline{\text{proc}}\ F(x) \equiv \\
\quad \underline{\text{if}}\ \mathbf{B}\ \underline{\text{then}}\ \mathbf{T} \\
\qquad \underline{\text{else}}\ \mathbf{S}_1;\ F(g_1(x));\ M(x);\ F(g_2(x));\ \mathbf{S}_2\ \underline{\text{fi}}.
\end{array}
$$

For the direct method we restructure the body of the procedure into the following action system:

```
proc F(x) ≡
    actions A1 :
    A1 ≡ if B then T
                 else call B1 fi.
    B1 ≡ S1; F(g1(x)); call B2.
    B2 ≡ M(x); F(g2(x)); call A2.
    A2 ≡ S2; call Z. endactions.
```

Applying the general recursion removal transformation we get:

```
proc F(x) ≡
    var L := ⟨⟩, m := 0:
        actions A1 :
        A1 ≡ if B then T
                     else call B1 fi.
        B1 ≡ S1; L := ⟨⟨0, g1(x)⟩, ⟨1, x⟩⟩ ++ L; call F̂.
        B2 ≡ M(x); L := ⟨⟨0, g2(x)⟩, ⟨2, x⟩⟩ ++ L; call F̂.
        A2 ≡ S2; call F̂.
        F̂  ≡ if L = ⟨⟩ then call Z
                        else ⟨m, x⟩ ← L;
                             if m = 0 → call A1
                             □ m = 1 → call B1
                             □ m = 2 → call B2 fi fi. endactions end.
```

The action system is (naturally) regular, so we can apply the transformations in [20] to restructure the action system:

```
proc F(x) ≡
    var L := ⟨⟩, m := 0:
        do while ¬B do S1; L := ⟨⟨1, x⟩⟩ ++ L; x := g1(x) od;
           T;
           do if L = ⟨⟩ then exit(2) fi;
              ⟨m, x⟩ ← L;
              if m = 1 → M(x); L := ⟨⟨2, x⟩⟩ ++ L; x := g2(x); exit
              □ m = 2 → S2 fi od od end.
```

Note that whenever $\langle 0, g_i(x)\rangle$ was pushed onto the stack, it was immediately popped off. So we have avoided pushing $\langle 0, g_i(x)\rangle$ altogether in this version.

For the postponed obligations case we need to structure the initial action system slightly differently:

```
proc F(x) ≡
    actions A :
    A ≡ if B then T
                else call B fi.
    B ≡ S1; F(g1(x)); M(x); F(g2(x)); S2; call Z. endactions.
```

Applying the general recursion removal transformation we get:

```
proc F(x) ≡
    var L := ⟨⟩, m := 0:
        actions A :
        A  ≡ if B then T
                   else call B fi.
        B  ≡ S₁; L := ⟨⟨0, g₁(x)⟩, ⟨1, x⟩, ⟨0, g₂(x)⟩, ⟨2, x⟩⟩ ++ L; call F̂.
        F̂  ≡ if L = ⟨⟩ then call Z
                   else ⟨m, x⟩ ← L;
                        if m = 0 → call A
                        □ m = 1 → M(x); call F̂
                        □ m = 2 → S₂; call F̂ fi fi. endactions end.
```

This can be expressed as a simple **while** loop thus:

```
proc F(x) ≡
    var L := ⟨⟨0, x⟩⟩, m := 0:
        while L ≠ ⟨⟩ do
            ⟨m, x⟩ ← L;
            if m = 0 →
                    if B then T
                         else S₁;
                              L := ⟨⟨0, g₁(x)⟩, ⟨1, x⟩, ⟨0, g₂(x)⟩, ⟨2, x⟩⟩
                                                                   ++ L fi
            □ m = 1 → M(x)
            □ m = 2 → S₂ fi od end.
```

Alternatively, we can restructure so as to avoid some unnecessary pushes and pops:

```
proc F(x) ≡
    var L := ⟨⟩, m := 0:
        do while ¬B do
                S₁; L := ⟨⟨1, x⟩, ⟨0, g₂(x)⟩, ⟨2, x⟩⟩ ++ L;
                x := g₁(x) od;
          T;
          do if L = ⟨⟩ then exit(2) fi;
             ⟨m, x⟩ ← L;
             if m = 0 → exit
             □ m = 1 → M(x)
             □ m = 2 → S₂ fi od od end.
```

6 Binary Cascade Recursion

In this section we consider a special case of the cascade recursion above where the functions $g_1(x)$ and $g_2(x)$ return $x - 1$ and the test for a nonrecursive case is simply $n = 0$. Here each invocation of the function leads to either zero or two further invocations, so we use the term *binary* cascade for this schema:

$\underline{\textbf{proc}}\ G(n) \equiv$
$\quad \underline{\textbf{if}}\ n = 0\ \underline{\textbf{then}}\ \mathbf{T}$
$\qquad\qquad \underline{\textbf{else}}\ \mathbf{S}_1;\ G(n-1);\ M(n);\ G(n-1);\ \mathbf{S}_2\ \underline{\textbf{fi}}.$

where **T**, $\mathbf{S}_1$ and $\mathbf{S}_2$ are statements which do not change the value of n and M is an external procedure.

With this schema, the sequence of statements and calls to M depends only on the initial value of n. We want to determine this sequence explicitly, i.e. we want to determine how many calls of M are executed, what their arguments are and what statements are executed between the calls.

Since the functions g_i are invertable, there is no need to have n as a parameter: we can replace it by a global variable thus:

$\underline{\textbf{proc}}\ G \equiv$
$\quad \underline{\textbf{if}}\ n = 0\ \underline{\textbf{then}}\ \mathbf{T}$
$\qquad\qquad \underline{\textbf{else}}\ \mathbf{S}_1;\ n := n-1;\ G;\ M(n+1);\ G;\ n := n+1;\ \mathbf{S}_2\ \underline{\textbf{fi}}.$

It is clear that G preserves the value of n and hence G is equivalent to $G(n)$. We apply the direct method of recursion removal (discussed in the previous Section) to get:

$\underline{\textbf{var}}\ L := \langle\rangle, d := 0:$
$\quad \underline{\textbf{do}}\ \underline{\textbf{while}}\ n \neq 0\ \underline{\textbf{do}}\ \mathbf{S}_1;\ n := n-1;\ L := \langle 1\rangle +\!\!\!+\ L\ \underline{\textbf{od}};$
$\qquad \mathbf{T};$
$\qquad \underline{\textbf{do}}\ \underline{\textbf{if}}\ L = \langle\rangle\ \underline{\textbf{then}}\ \underline{\textbf{exit}}(2)\ \underline{\textbf{fi}};$
$\qquad\quad d \leftarrow L;$
$\qquad\quad \underline{\textbf{if}}\ d = 1 \rightarrow M(n+1);\ L := \langle 2\rangle +\!\!\!+\ L;\ \underline{\textbf{exit}}$
$\qquad\quad \square\ d = 2 \rightarrow \mathbf{S}_2;\ n := n+1\ \underline{\textbf{fi}}\ \underline{\textbf{od}}\ \underline{\textbf{od}}\ \underline{\textbf{end}}$

Note that since there are no parameters the stack only records control information.

The elements of the stack are either 1 or 2, so we can represent this stack by an integer c whose digits in a binary representation represent the elements of the stack. We need to distinguish an empty stack from a stack of zeros so we use the value 1 to represent the empty stack. The statement $L := \langle 1\rangle +\!\!\!+\ L$ becomes $c := 2.c+1$, $L := \langle 2\rangle +\!\!\!+\ L$ becomes $c := 2.c$ and $d \leftarrow L$ becomes $\langle d, c\rangle := \langle c \div 2\rangle$. With this representation, the translation of $\underline{\textbf{while}}\ n \neq 0\ \underline{\textbf{do}}\ S_1;\ n := n-1;\ L := \langle 1\rangle +\!\!\!+\ L\ \underline{\textbf{od}}$ which pushes n 1's onto L has the effect of multiplying c by 2^n and adding $2^n - 1$ to the result. We get:

$\underline{\textbf{var}}\ c := 1, d := 0:$
$\quad \underline{\textbf{do}}\ \underline{\textbf{for}}\ i := n\ \underline{\textbf{step}}\ -1\ \underline{\textbf{to}}\ 1\ \underline{\textbf{do}}\ \mathbf{S}_1[i/n]\ \underline{\textbf{od}};$
$\qquad c := 2^n.c + 2^n - 1;\ n := 0;$
$\qquad \mathbf{T};$
$\qquad \underline{\textbf{do}}\ \underline{\textbf{if}}\ c = 1\ \underline{\textbf{then}}\ \underline{\textbf{exit}}(2)\ \underline{\textbf{fi}};$
$\qquad\quad \langle d, c\rangle := \langle c \div 2\rangle;$
$\qquad\quad \underline{\textbf{if}}\ d = 1 \rightarrow M(n+1);\ c := 2.c;\ \underline{\textbf{exit}}$
$\qquad\quad \square\ d = 0 \rightarrow \mathbf{S}_2;\ n := n+1\ \underline{\textbf{fi}}\ \underline{\textbf{od}}\ \underline{\textbf{od}}\ \underline{\textbf{end}}$

Using the transformations in [20] we can transform this into the following:

$\underline{\textbf{var}}\ n_0 := n:$
  $\underline{\textbf{for}}\ i := n\ \underline{\textbf{step}}\ -1\ \underline{\textbf{to}}\ 1\ \underline{\textbf{do}}\ \mathbf{S}_1[i/n]\ \underline{\textbf{od}};$
  $\mathbf{T};$
  $\underline{\textbf{for}}\ c := 1\ \underline{\textbf{step}}\ 1\ \underline{\textbf{to}}\ 2^{n_0} - 1\ \underline{\textbf{do}}$
    $n := \mathrm{ntz}(c);$
    $\underline{\textbf{for}}\ i := 0\ \underline{\textbf{step}}\ 1\ \underline{\textbf{to}}\ n - 1\ \underline{\textbf{do}}\ \mathbf{S}_2[i/n]\ \underline{\textbf{od}};$
    $M(n+1);$
    $\underline{\textbf{for}}\ i := n\ \underline{\textbf{step}}\ -1\ \underline{\textbf{to}}\ 1\ \underline{\textbf{do}}\ \mathbf{S}_1[i/n]\ \underline{\textbf{od}};$
    $\mathbf{T}\ \underline{\textbf{od}};$
  $\underline{\textbf{for}}\ i := 0\ \underline{\textbf{step}}\ 1\ \underline{\textbf{to}}\ n_0 - 1\ \underline{\textbf{do}}\ \mathbf{S}_2[i/n]\ \underline{\textbf{od}}\ \underline{\textbf{end}}$

where ntz(c) is the number of trailing zeros in the binary representation of c.

For the case where $\mathbf{S}_1$ and $\mathbf{S}_2$ are both **skip** this simplifies to:

$\mathbf{T};$
$\underline{\textbf{for}}\ c := 1\ \underline{\textbf{step}}\ 1\ \underline{\textbf{to}}\ 2^n - 1\ \underline{\textbf{do}}$
  $M(\mathrm{ntz}(c) + 1);$
  $\mathbf{T}\ \underline{\textbf{od}};$

7 Example: The Gray Code

An n-bit gray code is a sequence of 2^n n-bit binary numbers (sequences of 0's and 1's of length n) starting from $00\ldots0$ such that each element of the sequence differs from the next in a single bit position (and the 2^nth element has a single bit set). We want to define a function $g(n)$ which returns an n-bit gray code. For $n = 0$ the gray code is the one element sequence $\langle\langle\rangle\rangle$. Note that there are several different n-bit gray codes for $n > 1$: the problem of finding all gray codes of a given length is equivalent to finding all the Hamiltonian cycles of a n-dimensional unit hypercube.

So suppose we have $g(n-1)$ and want to construct $g(n)$. The elements of $g(n-1)$ will be $n-1$ bit codes; hence $(\langle 0\rangle \mathbin{+\!\!+}) * g(n-1)$ and $(\langle 1\rangle \mathbin{+\!\!+}) * g(n-1)$ are disjoint gray code sequences of length 2^{n-1}. Their corresponding elements differ in only the first bit position, in particular the last element of $(\langle 0\rangle \mathbin{+\!\!+}) * g(n-1)$ differs from the last element of $(\langle 1\rangle \mathbin{+\!\!+}) * g(n-1)$ in one bit position. Thus if we reverse the sequence $(\langle 1\rangle \mathbin{+\!\!+}) * g(n-1)$ and append it to $(\langle 0\rangle \mathbin{+\!\!+}) * g(n-1)$ we will form an n-bit gray code. Thus the definition of $g(n)$ is:

$\underline{\textbf{funct}}\ g(n) \equiv$
  $\underline{\textbf{if}}\ n = 0\ \underline{\textbf{then}}\ \langle\langle\rangle\rangle$
    $\underline{\textbf{else}}\ (\langle 0\rangle \mathbin{+\!\!+}) * g(n-1) \mathbin{+\!\!+} \mathit{reverse}((\langle 0\rangle \mathbin{+\!\!+}) * g(n-1))\ \underline{\textbf{fi}}.$

This function defines $g(n)$ in terms of $g(n-1)$ and $reverse(g(n-1))$: this suggests we define $g(n)$ in terms of a function $g'(n,s)$ such that $g'(n,0) = g(n)$ and $g'(n,1) = reverse(g(n))$. Note that $reverse(g(n)) = (\langle 1 \rangle \mathbin{+\!\!+}) * g(n-1) \mathbin{+\!\!+} (\langle 0 \rangle \mathbin{+\!\!+}) * reverse(g(n-1))$. So we can define $g'(n,s)$ as follows:

```
funct g'(n, s) ≡
      if n = 0 then ⟨⟨⟩⟩
               else (⟨s⟩ ++) * g'(n − 1, 0) ++ (⟨1 − s⟩ ++) * g'(n − 1, 1) fi.
```

Finally, instead of computing $g'(n-1,s)$ and appending either $\langle 0 \rangle$ or $\langle 1 \rangle$ to each element, we can pass a third argument which is to be appended to each element of the result; i.e. define $g''(L,n,s) = (L \mathbin{+\!\!+}) * g'(n,s)$. We get the following definition of g'':

```
funct g''(L, n, s) ≡
      if n = 0 then ⟨L⟩
               else g''(⟨s⟩ ++ L, n − 1, 0) ++ g''(⟨1 − s⟩ ++ L, n − 1, 1) fi.
```

The recursive case of this version simply appends the results of the two recursive calls. This suggests we use a procedural equivalent which appends the result to a global variable r. Thus our gray code function $g(n)$ is equivalent to:

```
funct g(N) ≡
      ⌈r := ⟨⟩:
       begin
         G(⟨⟩, N, 0)
       where
         proc G(L, n, s) ≡
              if n = 0 then r := r ++ ⟨L⟩
                       else G(⟨s⟩ ++ L, n − 1, 0);
                            G(⟨1 − s⟩ ++ L, n − 1, 1) fi. end;
      r⌋.
```

Represent the stack L of bits as an integer c as in Section 6:

```
begin
  G(1, N, 0)
where
  proc G(c, n, s) ≡
       if n = 0 then r := r ++ ⟨bits(c)⟩
                else G(2.c + s, n − 1, 0); G(2.c + 1 − s, n − 1, 1) fi. end
```

where $bits(c)$ returns the sequence of bits represented by the integer c. We can combine c and s into one argument c' where $c' = 2.c + s$:

```
begin
  G(2, N)
where
```

$$
\begin{array}{l}
\underline{\mathbf{proc}}\ G(c', n)\ \equiv \\
\quad \underline{\mathbf{if}}\ n = 0\ \underline{\mathbf{then}}\ r := r +\!\!+ \langle bits(\lfloor c'/2 \rfloor)\rangle \\
\qquad\qquad \underline{\mathbf{else}}\ G(2.c', n-1);\ G(2.(c' \oplus 1) \oplus 1, n-1)\ \underline{\mathbf{fi}}.\ \underline{\mathbf{end}}
\end{array}
$$

where $a \oplus b$ is a "bitwise exclusive or" operator. Note that we always double c' whenever we decrement n; this suggests representing c' by c where $c = c'.2^n$:

$$
\begin{array}{l}
\underline{\mathbf{begin}} \\
\quad G(2^{N+1}, N) \\
\underline{\mathbf{where}} \\
\quad \underline{\mathbf{proc}}\ G(c, n)\ \equiv \\
\qquad \underline{\mathbf{if}}\ n = 0\ \underline{\mathbf{then}}\ r := r +\!\!+ \langle bits(\lfloor c/2 \rfloor)\rangle \\
\qquad\qquad \underline{\mathbf{else}}\ G(c, n-1);\ G((c \oplus 2^n) \oplus 2^{n-1}, n-1)\ \underline{\mathbf{fi}}.\ \underline{\mathbf{end}}
\end{array}
$$

We want to replace c by a global variable c'. To do this we add c' as a new ghost variable; we assign values to c' which track the current value of c:

$$
\begin{array}{l}
\underline{\mathbf{begin}}\ \underline{\mathbf{var}}\ c' := 2^{N+1}: \\
\qquad G(2^{N+1}, N) \\
\quad \underline{\mathbf{where}} \\
\qquad \underline{\mathbf{proc}}\ G(c, n)\ \equiv \\
\qquad\quad \underline{\mathbf{if}}\ n = 0\ \underline{\mathbf{then}}\ r := r +\!\!+ \langle bits(\lfloor c/2 \rfloor)\rangle;\ c' := c' \oplus 1 \\
\qquad\qquad \underline{\mathbf{else}}\ G(c, n-1);\ c' := c' \oplus 2^n; \\
\qquad\qquad\quad G((c \oplus 2^n) \oplus 2^{n-1}, n-1)\ \underline{\mathbf{fi}}.\ \underline{\mathbf{end}}\ \underline{\mathbf{end}}
\end{array}
$$

By induction on n we prove: $\{c' = c\};\ G(c, n-1) \leq \{c' = c\};\ G(c, n-1);\ \{c' = c \oplus 2^n\}$. Then at every call of G we have $c' = c$ so we can replace the parameter c by the global variable c':

$$
\begin{array}{l}
\underline{\mathbf{begin}}\ \underline{\mathbf{var}}\ c' := 2^{N+1}: \\
\qquad G(N) \\
\quad \underline{\mathbf{where}} \\
\qquad \underline{\mathbf{proc}}\ G(n)\ \equiv \\
\qquad\quad \underline{\mathbf{if}}\ n = 0\ \underline{\mathbf{then}}\ r := r +\!\!+ \langle bits(\lfloor c'/2 \rfloor)\rangle;\ c' := c' \oplus 1 \\
\qquad\qquad \underline{\mathbf{else}}\ G(n-1);\ c' := c' \oplus 2^n;\ G(n-1)\ \underline{\mathbf{fi}}.\ \underline{\mathbf{end}}\ \underline{\mathbf{end}}
\end{array}
$$

Now we have a standard binary cascade recursion for which the transformation of Section 6 gives:

$$
\begin{array}{l}
\underline{\mathbf{begin}}\ \underline{\mathbf{var}}\ c' := 2^{N+1}: \\
\qquad r := r +\!\!+ \langle bits(\lfloor c'/2 \rfloor)\rangle; \\
\qquad \underline{\mathbf{for}}\ i := 1\ \underline{\mathbf{step}}\ 1\ \underline{\mathbf{to}}\ 2^N - 1\ \underline{\mathbf{do}} \\
\qquad\quad c' := c' \oplus 2^{\mathrm{ntz}(i)+1}; \\
\qquad\quad r := r +\!\!+ \langle bits(\lfloor c'/2 \rfloor)\rangle\ \underline{\mathbf{od}}\ \underline{\mathbf{end}}\ \underline{\mathbf{end}}
\end{array}
$$

Finally, the least significant bit of c' is always ignored and the most significant bit of c' is always the 2^{N+1} bit so we can represent c' by $c = \lfloor (c' - 2^{N+1})/2 \rfloor$:

```
begin var c := 0:
          r := r ++ ⟨Nbits(c)⟩;
          for i := 1 step 1 to 2^N − 1 do
              c := c ⊕ 2^ntz(i);
              r := r ++ ⟨Nbits(c)⟩ od end end
```

where $Nbits(c) = bits(c + 2^{N+1})$.

Thus, the bit which changes between the ith and $(i+1)$th codes is the bit in position $\text{ntz}(i)$. From this result we can prove the following:

Theorem 7.1 *The ith gray code is* $i \oplus \lfloor i/2 \rfloor$.

Proof: The proof is by induction on i. Suppose $c = i \oplus \lfloor i/2 \rfloor$ is the ith gray code. Then from the program above, the $(i+1)$th gray code is $c \oplus 2^{\text{ntz}(i+1)}$. The number of trailing zeros in the binary representation of $i+1$ is simply the number of trailing ones in the binary representation of i. If i is even then the 2^0 bit is changed, while if i is odd and has k trailing ones with $k > 0$, it is easy to see that only the 2^k bit is changed.

From this we derive the following gray code generator:

```
funct g(n) ≡
    ⌈r := ⟨Nbits(0)⟩:
     for i := 1 step 1 to 2^n − 1 do
         r := r ++ ⟨Nbits(i ⊕ ⌊i/2⌋)⟩ od;
     r⌋.
```

While the previous gray code generator only told us which bit changes from one code to the next, this one calculates the ith gray code directly from i without using any previous codes.

8 Program Analysis

Since the recursion removal theorem can be applied in either direction, and because it places so few restrictions on the form of the program, it can be applied in the reverse direction as a program analysis or reverse engineering tool to make explicit the control structure of programs which use a stack in a particular way. For example, consider the following function:

```
funct A(m, n) ≡
    ⌈begin d := 0, stack := ⟨⟩:
       do do if m = 0 then n := n + 1; exit
             elsif n = 0 then stack := ⟨1⟩ ++ stack; m := m − 1; n := 1
                         else stack := ⟨0⟩ ++ stack; n := n − 1 fi od;
          do if stack = ⟨⟩ then exit(2) fi;
             d ← stack;
             if d = 0 then stack := ⟨1⟩ ++ stack; m := m − 1; exit fi;
```

```
            m := m + 1 od od end;
    n⌋.
```

This program was analysed by the REDO group at the Programming Research Group in Oxford to test their proposed methods for formal reverse engineering of source code. Their paper [9] required eight pages of careful reasoning plus some "inspiration" to uncover the specification this short program. With the aid of our theorem the analysis breaks down into three steps:

1. Restructure into the right form for application of the theorem (this stage could easily be automated);
2. Apply the theorem;
3. Restructure the resulting recursive procedure in a functional form (this stage could also be automated).

If we examine the operations carried out on the stack we see that only constant elements are pushed onto the stack, the program terminated when the stack becomes empty, and the value popped off the stack is used to determine the control flow. This suggests that we may be able to remove the stack and re-express the control flow explicitly using our theorem. The first step is to restructure the loops into an action system and collect together the "stack push" operations into separate actions:

```
var d := 0, stack := ⟨⟩ :
   actions A1 :
   A1 ≡ if m = 0 then n := n + 1; call /A
        elsif n = 0 then call B1
                    else call B2 fi.
   B1 ≡ m := m − 1; n := 1; stack := ⟨1⟩ ++ stack; call A1.
   B2 ≡ n := n − 1; stack := ⟨0⟩ ++ stack; call A1.
   /A ≡ if stack = ⟨⟩ then call Z
                      else d ← stack;
                           if d = 0 then call B3
                                    else m := m + 1; call /A fi fi.
   B3 ≡ m := m − 1; stack := ⟨1⟩ ++ stack; call A1.
   endactions end
```

Apply the transformation in Corollary (4.2) to get the recursive version:

```
proc F ≡
    actions A1 :
    A1 ≡ if m = 0 then n := n + 1; call Z
         elsif n = 0 then call B1
                     else call B2 fi.
    B1 ≡ m := m − 1; n := 1; F; m := m + 1; call Z.
    B2 ≡ n := n − 1; F; call B3.
    B3 ≡ m := m − 1; F; m := m + 1; call Z.
    endactions
```

Unfold all the actions into A_1 to get:

```
proc F ≡
    if m = 0 then n := n + 1
    elsif n = 0 then m := m − 1; n := 1; F; m := m + 1
                else n := n − 1; F; m := m − 1; F; m := m + 1 fi.
```

This procedure can be written in a functional form:

```
begin
  r := F(n, m)
where
  funct F(m, n) ≡
      if m = 0 then n + 1
      elsif n = 0 then F(m − 1, 1)
                  else F(m − 1, F(m, n − 1)) fi.
end
```

This is the famous Ackermann function [1].

9 Conclusion

In our work on the derivation of algorithms from specifications by formal refinement we find that the problem can often be broken down into the following stages:

1. Nonexecutable specification
2. Recursively defined specification
3. Recursive procedure
4. Iterative algorithm

In [22] we prove some important transformations which enable the transition from (2) to (3) to be carried out easily. In this paper we provide a general-purpose recursion removal transformation which can achieve the transition from (3) to (4). There is often more than one way to apply the theorem, with each method generating a different iterative algorithm. The aim here is not simply to improve efficiency but to discover new algorithms and prove properties of existing algorithms. An added benefit of the theorem, which illustrates its wide applicability, is that it can be applied to a given iterative algorithm which uses a stack or array in a particular way. This produces a recursive procedure which is often much easier to analyse and understand. This aspect of the work is being investigated in the "Maintainer's Assistant" project [10,28] at Durham University and the Centre for Software Maintenance Ltd. which aims to produce a prototype tool to assist a maintenance programmer to understand and modify an initially unfamiliar program, given only the source code. The project uses program transformations as a means of code analysis as well as program development.

10 References

[1] W. Ackermann, "Zum Hilbertschen Aufbau der reellen Zahlen," *Math. Ann.* 99 (1928), 118–133.

[2] J. Arsac, "Transformation of Recursive Procedures," in *Tools and Notations for Program Construction*, D. Neel, ed., Cambridge University Press, Cambridge, 1982, 211–265.

[3] J. Arsac, "Syntactic Source to Source Program Transformations and Program Manipulation," *Comm. ACM* 22 (Jan., 1982), 43–54.

[4] R. J. R. Back, *Correctness Preserving Program Refinements*, Mathematical Centre Tracts #131, Mathematisch Centrum, 1980.

[5] F. L. Bauer, B. Moller, H. Partsch & P. Pepper, "Formal Construction by Transformation—Computer Aided Intuition Guided Programming," *IEEE Trans. Software Eng.* 15 (Feb., 1989).

[6] F. L. Bauer & H. Wossner, *Algorithmic Language and Program Development*, Springer-Verlag, New York–Heidelberg–Berlin, 1982.

[7] R. Bird, "Notes on Recursion Removal," *Comm. ACM* 20 (June, 1977), 434–439.

[8] R. Bird, "Lectures on Constructive Functional Programming," Oxford University, Technical Monograph PRG-69, Sept., 1988.

[9] P. T. Breuer, K. Lano & J. Bowen, "Understanding Programs through Formal Methods," Oxford University, Programming Research Group, 9 Apr., 1991.

[10] T. Bull, "An Introduction to the WSL Program Transformer," *Conference on Software Maintenance 1990, San Diago* (Nov. 26th–29th, 1990).

[11] B. A. Davey & H. A. Priestley, *Introduction to Lattices and Order*, Cambridge University Press, Cambridge, 1990.

[12] E. W. Dijkstra, *A Discipline of Programming*, Prentice-Hall, Englewood Cliffs, NJ, 1976.

[13] D. E. Knuth, "Structured Programming with the GOTO Statement," *Comput. Surveys* 6 (1974), 261–301.

[14] C. Morgan, *Programming from Specifications*, Prentice-Hall, Englewood Cliffs, NJ, 1990.

[15] C. Morgan & K. Robinson, "Specification Statements and Refinements," *IBM J. Res. Develop.* 31 (1987).

[16] C. C. Morgan, "The Specification Statement," *ACM TOPLAS* 10 (1988), 403–419.

[17] C. C. Morgan, K. Robinson & Paul Gardiner, "On the Refinement Calculus," Oxford University, Technical Monograph PRG-70, Oct., 1988.

[18] E. L. Post, "Formal Reduction of the General Combinatorial Decision Problem," *Amer. J. Math.* (1943).

[19] D. Taylor, "An Alternative to Current Looping Syntax," *SIGPLAN Notices* 19 (Dec., 1984), 48–53.

[20] M. Ward, "Proving Program Refinements and Transformations," Oxford University, DPhil Thesis, 1989.

[21] M. Ward, "Derivation of a Sorting Algorithm," Durham University, Technical Report, 1990.

[22] M. Ward, "Specifications and Programs in a Wide Spectrum Language," Durham University, Technical Report, 1990.

[23] M. Ward, "A Definition of Abstraction," University of Durham Technical Report, 1990.

[24] M. Ward, "A Recursion Removal Theorem - Proof and Applications," University of Durham, Technical Report, 1991.

[25] M. Ward, "The Largest True Square Problem—An Exercise in the Derivation of an Algorithm," Durham University, Technical Report, Apr., 1990.

[26] M. Ward, "The Schorr-Waite Graph Marking Algorithm An Exercise in the Derivation of an Algorithm," Durham University, Technical Report , Apr., 1990.

[27] M. Ward, "Abstracting a Specification from Code," Submitted to Journal of Software Maintenance and Management, Aug., 1991.

[28] M. Ward, F. W. Calliss & M. Munro, "The Maintainer's Assistant," *Conference on Software Maintenance 1989, Miami Florida* (Oct. 16th–19th, 1989).

Demonstrating the Compliance of Ada Programs with Z Specifications

C T Sennett

Defence Research Agency
Malvern, Worcestershire, UK

Abstract

This paper describes a notation for presenting a claim that a program written in Ada satisfies a specification written in Z. The notation has both formal and informal elements: the formal elements follow the style of the refinement calculus, while the informal elements follow Knuth's literate programming style. The combination of formal and informal elements allows for selective verification, an important requirement for practical use of formal refinement.

1 Introduction

The purpose of this paper is to present a notation to support compliance claims, of which refinement forms a part. Demonstrating compliance between a program and a specification involves relating the parts of the program to the requirements in the specification with an argument for satisfaction. Refinement provides a way of giving this argument in a formal manner. This has the advantage of precision and of allowing the argument to be checked by mechanical means. Unfortunately, formal specifications are costly to develop and formal proofs even more costly to carry out. As a result, the formal process is carried out only for the critical aspects of the software. A practical system for demonstrating compliance must therefore have both formal and informal aspects and the purpose of this paper is to present a notation supporting both aspects. The specification and target languages are chosen as Z and Ada, but the principle could be extended to other languages. At the outset it should also be stated that where formal refinement is involved, the target will be a subset of Ada and our work is directed at the SPARK subset of Ada [Carre *et al* 1990]. The notation is at a preliminary state of development: the purpose of describing it now is to benefit from user reaction.

A driving force in the design of the notation has been that the intended reader is not the designer or the implementor of the software, but a third party: a customer or an evaluator or someone maintaining the software subsequently. This means the notation is primarily oriented to human use, rather than machine processing: the aim should be to support understanding of the software through an understanding of the compliancy arguments. It is just as important that the significance of a proof should be understood as that it should be correct. Consequently the aims of the notation are to give software designers and programmers a means for explaining the structure of their programs together with clear explanations of how the critical parts meet given specifications.

The understandability aim is supported by demonstrating compliance in stages. This is similar to Dijkstra's idea of step-wise program composition [Dahl *et al* 1972] or the more general idea of explaining a complicated whole in terms of its parts. To support this with a formal notation requires some principle of compositionality, which allows the parts to be independently described in such a manner that the composition of them meets the requirements placed on the whole. In other words it should be possible to specify fragments of program such that the satisfaction of these fragment specifications guarantees the satisfaction of the overall requirement. In the notation this concept appears as a *specification statement*. That is, the programming language is extended with specification statements giving a formal specification of the program fragment which is required at this position. This allows program structure to be introduced in a step-by-step fashion with the overall specification being refined by stages. The concept of the specification statement has been defined by Morgan, Back and others [see for example Morgan 1988, Back 1988], but in this paper the notation of Morgan [1990] will be followed with only minor variations.

In the notation, a refinement step takes the form

$$\textit{this} \sqsubseteq \textit{that}$$

where *this* is a label denoting a specification statement and *that* is a program fragment which may contain embedded within it further specification statements. The refinement symbol ($\sqsubseteq$, read as "is refined by") is an assertion that the right hand side bears the refinement relation to the left hand side, a formal statement requiring proof. The LHS of the relation refers to a specification statement which is characterized by the variables being altered by the statement (called the *frame*) and the pre- and postconditions of the operation which the statement specifies. The RHS of the relation is a program fragment and the refinement assertion is that for *any* given condition to hold after the operation, the weakest precondition of the RHS is always weaker than the weakest precondition of the left. This generality is what is required to guarantee composability of program fragments.

The weakest precondition approach to specifying the meaning of programs is based on the work of Dijkstra [1976]. The refinement calculus proposed by Morgan enables the refinement relation to be justified by rules depending on the program structure used and the specific operation pre- and postconditions. These rules are cast into an intuitive form: for example, the implemented operation may alter fewer variables than the frame specifies, it may have a weaker precondition and so on. If the given refinement step conforms to the rules, the refinement relation holds. Although based on Morgan's theory, and using the notational aspects of the refinement calculus, the emphasis of the notation described here is not quite the same. In particular, in the refinement calculus the aim is to *derive* the program from the specification, using the refinement calculus laws. In a sense the program is being calculated from the specification. Because this notation is aimed at compliance, the emphasis is more on calculating the verification conditions from the program and the specification. This is the more traditional approach to verification. In systems such as Gypsy [Good 1986; an introduction is in Smith and Bleech 1989], ANNA [Luckham 1990], or the SPARK examiner itself [Carre 1989], the program text is annotated with assertions which specify what must hold at various points in the program. The tools used in these systems process the annotated text to yield the verification conditions (VCs) which must be proved for the assertion to hold. For this compliance notation, the refinement steps are treated in a similar way to annotations, so the intention is that tool processing should yield VCs. The VCs may be presented using Z: they may then be verified using a Z theorem prover. Note that in the examples given in this paper, the notation for Z theorems used is that of King *et al* [1988].

Compared with the traditional VC generation process, the notation presented here has the advantage of more directly relating the annotations to the original specification. Compared with the refinement calculus approach, VC generation is more automatic: however, because they are generated automatically, the VCs may not be quite so intuitive as the refinement calculus laws.

VC generation should be derived from the semantics of the programming language, essentially as the laws of the refinement calculus are. The formal semantics of SPARK have not yet been defined, so the example VCs generated are based on intuition and modelled on the refinement laws given in Morgan [1990], supplemented when necessary for the constructions peculiar to SPARK and Ada.

Regardless of the presence or not of a formal proof, there should be a human readable justification of the statement and this is provided in narrative which separates refinement steps. This technique for presenting a formal refinement is reminiscent of a Z specification in which the formal text is interspersed with informal narrative. This seems to be a rather better way of documenting programs than relying on comments in the program text itself. The narrative text can be separated out using the file structure, and then handled as text to provide features such as paragraphs and cross-referencing. This supports a more explanatory form of documentation than is provided by the typically terse comments scattered over a program text.

The new specification statements which have been introduced within the refinement step will themselves be refined further on in the document. In order to refer to them they need to be labelled: the convention used here is that they are labelled rather like equations in a mathematical paper. This concept of labelling and step-wise development recalls Knuth's literate programming [1984]. In this technique, the program fragments are described in steps, each fragment being labelled with tags. A literate programming step consists in defining a program fragment in terms of program structure and further program fragments. This allows the program to be described in the order which suits the documentation, rather than the compiler: the compiler order can be retrieved by a simple program which analyses the text on the basis of the tags. In the paper, Knuth is fairly evangelical about the technique, an enthusiasm I share. This is a simple and low cost technique which can considerably improve the standard of documentation and reliability of software. The notation chosen therefore is a combination of Morgan and Knuth. The formal steps are given in the refinement calculus, the informal ones as a literate programming step. Each formal or informal step is separated by narrative.

The notation is a combination of three different syntaxes: that for Z predicates, used within pre and post conditions in the specification statement and in subsidiary formal development; that for SPARK, used in the program fragments; and the refinement and literate programming notation itself. In making the combination of Morgan and Knuth some minor variations have been introduced. As far as the refinement calculus is concerned, the notation requires a one-way transformation to SPARK: that is, the left hand side of a refinement statement is always a specification statement, rather than allowing one SPARK fragment to be refined into another. This restriction is to simplify the extraction of the program for compilation. A minor syntactic difference is that the specification statement is written in the form Δ *w* [*pre, post*], rather than *w:* [*pre, post*] as in Morgan. Here *w* is the set of variables changed by the statement and *pre* and *post* are Z predicates representing the pre and post conditions respectively. The change is entirely for syntactic reasons as it simplifies the parsing of the statement when going to a language such as Algol 60 or Algol 68 where declarations start in a similar manner.

Knuth's literate programming package (called Web) includes facilities for graphical mark up. These have been removed from the notation as they can be added independently. To give uniformity with the refinement calculus, the program fragments are labelled in a similar way. To allow for the processing envisaged, each program fragment must correspond to a statement or declaration in SPARK, rather than any program text. Tool processing is also supported by requiring declaration before use: this can be argued for, even from the point of view of documentation.

Two forms of processing are envisaged for this notation, namely compilation and verification condition generation. Compilation is intended to cover syntax and type checking of the specification statements and their type compatibility with the programming language statements, as well as the generation of code. This supports traceability of the specification to the code and so compilation on its own makes a useful contribution to assurance in the development process.

VC generation is required at every occurence of the $\sqsubseteq$ symbol. The details will not be described here, but the overall strategy is as follows. The LHS of a refinement step is always a label representing a specification statement, the elements of which are a frame and the pre- and postconditions. Using standard VC generation techniques, the RHS can also be expressed in this form so the refinement step can be thought of as expressing the condition:

$$\Delta\, w\ [pre, post] \sqsubseteq \Delta\, w'\ [pre', post']$$

The frame check is that $w' \subseteq w$ unless the extra variables have been introduced by a local declaration. The verification conditions are:

$pre \vdash pre'$ and $pre'_0 \wedge post' \vdash post$

The first corresponds to the weaken precondition refinement rule. In the second, pre'_0 signifies the precondition pre' with the variables in w' subscripted by 0 to indicate initial values. (A similar transformation is applied to the initial values in $post'$.)

Rather than describing the notation it will be illustrated using the example in Knuth's paper, namely a program to print the first 1,000 prime numbers. This will be formally specified and then described using the notation in a series of formal and informal steps. The description has been broken down into a number of sections as each new concept in the notation or new (SPARK) refinement rule is introduced; in addition, it is necessary to explain the example. In actual use, only the latter text would be needed in the narrative.

2 Formal specification of the example

This is very straightforward. Start first of all with the specification of prime numbers:

$$prime == \{n : \mathbb{N} \mid \neg(\exists\, i, j : \mathbb{N} \setminus \{0, 1\} \bullet i{*}j = n)\}$$

while the composite numbers are simply given by

$$not\_prime == \mathbb{N} \setminus prime$$

The prime numbers are required in order, so define the relation between successive prime numbers as follows:

$$
\begin{aligned}
\_\ next\_prime\ \_ == \{ & i, j : \mathbb{N} \\
& \mid prime\ i \wedge prime\ j \wedge j > i \wedge (i{+}1) \mathrel{..} (j{-}1) \subseteq not\_prime \\
& \bullet\ i \mapsto j \\
\} &
\end{aligned}
$$

Sequences of consecutive prime numbers starting at 2 are given by

$$
\begin{aligned}
primed == \{ & p : seq_1\, \mathbb{N} \\
& \mid p\ 1 = 2 \wedge (\forall\, i : dom\, p \setminus \{1\} \bullet (p\ (i{-}1))\ next\_prime\ (p\ i)) \\
\} &
\end{aligned}
$$

This completes the specification which is typical in that many aspects are left unspecified. For example, the fact that a 1,000 primes are wanted and how they are to be displayed have not been specified. It is not that these facts are unimportant, but they may be specified by the customer informally and without loss of precision. Formal specifications should be abstract and contain only critical detail.

3 Overall features of the notation

This section onwards can be regarded as a document written in the notation in reponse to the specification in section 2. This specification has been given in terms of a property of sets of numbers. The designer agrees with the customer that 1,000 primes are required and that they are to be printed out. The designer further implements this by putting them in an array called *p*, and then printing the array. The formal refinement will apply to the calculation of *p*, while the printing of the array will be described informally. The specification of the calculation of *p* is as follows:

```
┌─ p_primed ──
│ p : seq ℕ
├──────────
│ primed p
└──────────
```

A document in the notation consists of formal parts interspersed with informal text. Each formal part is either a compilation unit, a refinement step, a literate step or any Z phrase. There is only one compilation unit which is expanded into packages and procedures using literate steps. The inclusion of Z phrases in the syntax allows for the statement of useful theorems and for formal manipulation outside the refinement steps. In this case the Z schema definition is being used to obtain the specification in an operational form, so that it can be used in a specification statement.

The overall structure of the program is given by the next notation section, which is the compilation unit, a procedure declaration:

```
procedure print_primes is
    subtype Indexrange is Integer range 1..1000;
    type Arraytype is array (Indexrange) of Integer;
    p : Arraytype;
    <other variables of the procedure>                    (1)
begin
    Δ p [p_primed];                                        (2)
    <print table p>                                        (3)
end;
```

The angle brackets <> enclose the name of a program fragment which can stand for a sequence of statements or declarations. The name of the fragment has no significance within the notation, but following Knuth, it could be sensible to put an indication of where in the text this fragment of program is expanded. As far as the notation is concerned the text to be substituted at this position is indicated by the label, for example *(3)* in the last program fragment above. The expansion will be found in some section of notation beginning

(3) ≡

which will continue the informal development of the printing section of the program. (As there are no further differences from the Knuth notation, this informal development will not be given here.)

The item labelled *(2)* is a specification statement, using the particular form in which the precondition is true. The postcondition is a Z predicate, the schema reference *p_primed* just defined. This is a valid predicate provided the identifier *p* exists in the environment with the correct Z type. The environment is actually provided by the SPARK declarations and so rules are needed for relating Z identifiers to SPARK identifiers and Z types to SPARK types. The first of these is relatively trivial: the only problem is in deciding how to treat Z decorations. The ′ decoration, referring to values of state variables after an operation, must be dropped in a postcondition and should not be present in a precondition. Treatment of the other decorations is a matter of taste: *!* and *?* could for example be related to parameters of procedures and subscripts could simply be appended to the word part of the Z identifier. In any case, simple rules can be given for checking whether a Z identifier is present in a SPARK environment.

For the relation between Z and SPARK types, only the integer ranges and array types need be considered for this example. Within the Z text of a specification statement, it is possible to refer to an identifier declared in SPARK. An example which occurs later on is a reference to *Indexrange*. The definition of this SPARK subtype may be treated as an implicit definition of a Z term:

$$Indexrange == 1..1000$$

and this can then be used for type checking in Z. It is not possible to refer to a variable declared in Z within the SPARK text unless it has been declared in the SPARK text. In this case the problem becomes one of compatibility between an object declared simultaneously in Z and SPARK, such as p in *p_primed* in statement 2. This has Z type sets of pairs of integers ($\mathbb{P}(\mathbb{Z} \times \mathbb{Z})$) and SPARK type `array (Indexrange) of Integer`. These two declarations are treated as compatible because arrays are treated as functions on the array index and the functions are a subset of the Z pairs. The SPARK types are more restrictive than the Z types and it is necessary to take account of this extra information. The restriction arises partly in the type `Integer` which is treated as equivalent to the Z integers ($\mathbb{Z}$). This is incorrect because of the finite length of integer arithmetic, but the view taken for the notation is that word length problems should be treated by analysis of compiler output rather than being dealt with at the specification stage, so these two types are treated as equivalent.

On the other hand a user supplied range constraint should be taken into account. In this case it appears as an invariant

$$p \in Indexrange \rightarrow \mathbb{Z}$$

derived from the SPARK declaration. Invariants are part of the context at each formal step; they may be assumed in the preconditions and should be achieved in postconditions. In this case the invariant cannot be altered by the program and so it is trivially maintained. The Z operation *p_primed* has been "parachuted" into the program and this indicates how the scope differences between Z and SPARK are dealt with. Rather than introduce local declarations, packages and so on using the laws of the refinement calculus, *any* Z expression is allowed in the specification statement provided the free identifiers in the expression are present in the SPARK environment with a compatible type. This is rather akin to schema inclusion in Z. Because of the invariants the meaning of these expressions depends on the context into which they have been parachuted. For example, the statement *(2)* actually stands for the specification statement

$$\Delta\, p\, [p \in Indexrange \rightarrow \mathbb{Z},\, p\_primed \wedge p \in Indexrange \rightarrow \mathbb{Z}]$$

It is unlikely that the invariant would cause the specification to be invalid (that is, incorrectly represent the customer's requirement) but it could be inconsistent so it might be advisable to check that

$$\vdash \exists\, p : seq\, \mathbb{N} \bullet p\_primed \wedge p \in Indexrange \rightarrow \mathbb{Z}$$

The notation text given so far gives a bird's eye view of the program and indicates which part of it is formally specified. The informal part of the program, namely printing the table, can be developed as in Knuth. The formal part, concerned with the calculation of the primes, will now be developed into code.

4 Some simple refinement statements

Inevitably, the calculation proceeds with a loop, in which one prime number is increased until it is again prime, at which point it is assigned to the next position in the array *p*. The algorithm for testing prime numbers makes use of the fact that the prime numbers after 3 are odd, so it is not necessary to test the even numbers.

$odd == \{n : \mathbb{N} \mid \forall i : \mathbb{N} \bullet n \neq i + i\}$

The loop invariant is given by:

Inv1
$p : seq\ \mathbb{N}$
$j, k : \mathbb{N}$
$primed((1..(k\text{-}1)) \lhd p)$
$j = p(k\text{-}1)$
$odd\ j$

The variable *k* is the current position in the array and previous elements of the array have been filled with the prime numbers in order: *j* is the current prime number. For those unfamiliar with the Z mathematical toolkit, the symbol $\lhd$ represents the operator which delivers the function in its right hand argument restricted to the domain specified by the set in the left hand argument. The variables *j* and *k* must be declared before *Inv1* can be used and they are introduced with some Knuth notation:

(1) ≡ `j, k : Integer;`

The left hand side of the ≡ symbol is the label of a program fragment, the right hand side is SPARK text, in this case required to be a declaration list. With this, the following refinement step becomes valid:

$(2) \sqsubseteq \Delta\, j, k, p[Inv1 \wedge k = last\ Indexrange + 1]$

The frame has been widened to include *j* and *k* which is only allowed immediately after their introduction. Note that SPARK does not have blocks as compound statements so all the local declarations must appear in the procedure heading. Various Z functions need to be defined to correspond to Ada qualifiers: in this case *last* is equivalent to the Z library function *max*.

The VC output for this step is

$Inv1 \wedge k = last\ Indexrange + 1 \wedge p \in Indexrange \rightarrow \mathbb{Z}$
$\vdash$
p_primed

the proof of which is immediate.

The first value of *k* for which the loop invariant holds is 3, so the loop needs to be preceded by an intialization:

$\sqsubseteq \Delta\, j, k, p\ [Inv1 \wedge k = 3];$ *(4)*
$\Delta\, j, k, p\ [Inv1 \wedge k = 3, Inv1 \wedge k = last\ Indexrange + 1]$ *(5)*

To economise on labels, the left hand side of a refinement relation may be omitted, as in this case and it then refers to the *last unlabelled specification statement*. This differs from Morgan's notation in which it refers to the current statement as a whole. In this particular instance the two are the same, but this will not be so for future steps. Because this breaks with the usual conventions for equations, this may be an undesirable decision, but the expectation is that users of the notation will quickly become accustomed to the convention.

The VCs to be output in this case are trivially true: for a sequence of statements the precondition is that for the first statement and the postcondition that for the last. In this case they are identical with the specification statement being refined.

5 Postponing the order of refinement

Statement *(4)* corresponds to the initialization necessary before entering the main loop. There is a problem here because the algorithm used to test for a prime number uses working variables which also need initialization. The initialization must be done at this point in the program, but the logical place to introduce the code in the notation is nearer to the test itself. This after all is the whole point of literate programming. This is not a problem for the Knuth notation as the initialization code can simply be introduced as an extension to this section using the symbol +≡ at the appropriate place. For the formal development on the other hand, it is necessary to record the state achieved so that the initialization can be shown to be correct. This is achieved using an assumption which is labelled and refined into further initialization code later on. In effect the use of assumptions in this way is a convention which fits in with the overall aims of the notation. As in Morgan, assumptions are written $\{pre\}$ and are abbreviations for the specification statement $[pre, true]$. Given that a state *post* has been achieved, an assumption $\{post'\}$ generates the VC:

$$post \vdash post'$$

In other words, after having achieved a postcondition, you are entitled to assume it. The assumption states that the precondition holds and that anything may be done, provided no variables are changed. The notation allows the frame to be widened to include introduced variables which can then be initialized appropriately.

Statement *(4)* is refined as follows:

```
(4) ⊑ p(1) := 2;   p(2) := 3;   j := 3;   k := 3;
      {Invl ∧ k = 3}                                          (6)
```

The assumption *(6)* is developed into initialization code in section 8 below.

A series of assignment statements as in this step can be represented in terms of a substitution of expressions for the identifiers appearing in the left hand sides of the assignments. If the postcondition of the operation being refined is *post*, the sequence of statements is represented by the specification statement $\Delta\, w\ [post', post]$, where $post'$ is the result of carrying out the substitutions on *post* and *w* the set of variables being assigned to. Consequently, if the precondition of the statement being refined is *pre*, the VC output should be $pre \vdash post'$.

6 Introduction of loops

A refinement step of the form

```
Δ w [pre, post] ⊑ while G
                  loop Δ w' [pre', post']
                  end loop;
```

is allowable if $w' \subseteq w$ and if the following VCs hold:

$pre \vdash \neg G' \vee G' \wedge pre'$

$post' \wedge G' \vdash pre'$

$post' \wedge \neg G' \vdash post$

G' is the Z equivalent of the SPARK expression G. For these VCs to be valid, G must not change state: fortunately this holds for SPARK expressions as side effects are forbidden to functions. In the case of the loop statement, *(5)*,

```
(5)⊑ while k /= Indexrange'last + 1
     loop  Δ j, k, p [Invl, Invl]
     end loop;
```

The VCs generated in this case are trivially proved. For proof of termination it is also necessary to exhibit a variant which bounds the number of iterations through the loop. This has not yet been provided for in the notation. For the case of the current step, the variant is the variable *k*, which increases from 3 to 1,000 with each step through the loop.

To refine the body of the loop, define an intermediate state in which *j* has been increased to the next prime:

```
— Interl ————————————
| p : seq ℕ
| j, k : ℕ
|————————————————
| primed((1..(k-1)) ◁ p)
| p(k-1) next_prime j
| odd j
—————————————————————
```

Using this, the body of the loop is refined as follows:

$\sqsubseteq \Delta j\ [Invl, Interl];$ (7)
$\Delta p\ [Interl, Invl_{[k+1/k]}];$ (8)
$\Delta k\ [Invl_{[k+1/k]}, Invl];$ (9)

Recall first of all that a blank on the left hand side of a refinement statement refers to the last unlabelled specification statement, so the body of the loop, rather than the loop itself, is being refined. In statement *(8)*, the subscript in the postcondition is intended to denote a substitution of *k+1* for *k*. The meaning of these statements is simply, increase *j* until it is the next prime number, assign it at the appropriate place in *p* and then step on *k*. The last two statements are easily refined:

```
(8)⊑ p(k) := j;

(9)⊑ k := k + 1;
```

The specification statement *(9)* is in the standard form for assignment. Statement *(8)* involves array assignment which is rather more complicated.

To implement statement *(7)*, it is useful to have an identifier for the value of *j* when it was last prime, which is introduced as follows:

$(7) \sqsubseteq \textbf{con}\ lastj : \mathbb{N} \bullet \Delta j\ [lastj = j \wedge Invl,\ lastj\ next\_prime\ j]$

The logical constant *lastj* may not appear in the SPARK code, but is available to simplify the predicates in the specification statement. The postcondition has been simplified to show that the only significant thing which has to be achieved is to make *j* the next prime after the last one. This step generates the following VCs:

$$Inv1 \vdash \exists\ lastj : \mathbb{N} \bullet lastj = j \land Inv1$$

and

$$Inv1_{[j0/j]};\ j, lastj : \mathbb{N}$$
$$lastj = j_0 \land lastj\ next\_prime\ j$$
$$\vdash$$
$$Inter1$$

The first VC justifies the introduction of *lastj* and expresses the precondition constraint while the second is the postcondition constraint. Again, these are simply proved by rewriting.

7 The *exit* statement

The current specification statement is achieved by increasing *j* until it is again prime and the natural construction for programming this uses the Ada exit statement. The exit statement itself may be introduced at some depth within a conditional statement and so it is difficult to generate VCs directly. The solution adopted is to use an ***until*** annotation as follows:

$\Delta\ w\ [pre, post] \sqsubseteq$ **while** G_1
    until G_2
    loop $\Delta\ w'\ [pre', post']$
    end loop;

This generates the following VCs:

$$pre \vdash \neg G_1' \lor G_1' \land pre'$$
$$post' \land G_1' \vdash pre'$$
$$(post' \land \neg G_1') \lor G_2 \vdash post$$

where G_1' is the Z equivalent of G_1. The ***until*** annotation is not executeable code and is ignored by the compiler. If $\neg G_1$ is achieved, the loop is terminated with the post condition satisfied. However, an ***until*** annotation allows the introduction of an exit statement when G_2 has been achieved. In a context in which a condition *post* has been achieved, the statement

```
exit when G;
```

will generate the VC:

$$post \land G' \vdash G_2$$

and will achieve the postcondition

$$post \land \neg G'$$

where G' is the Z equivalent of G. As usual, all the guards must be free from side effects: G and G_1 are SPARK expressions, while G_2 is a Z predicate.

To apply this to the current statement it is necessary to define another loop invariant. This expresses states in which j is increased through the composite numbers:

Inv2

$p : seq\ \mathbb{N}$
$j, k, lastj : \mathbb{N}$

$prime\ lastj \wedge odd\ j$
$j \geq lastj \wedge (lastj+1) .. (j-1) \subseteq not\_prime$
$primed((1..(k-1)) \lhd p)$

With this, the loop is introduced in the form in which G_1 is true, that is, without the ***while*** part:

$\sqsubseteq$ ***until*** $Inv2 \wedge j > lastj \wedge prime\ j$
  loop $\Delta j\ [Inv2, Inv2]$ *(10)*
  end loop;

The VCs generated (after simplifications involving true and false) are:

$Inv1;\ lastj : \mathbb{N};\ lastj = j$
$\vdash$
$Inv2$

and

$Inv2;\ j > lastj \wedge prime\ j$
$\vdash$
$lastj\ next\_prime\ j$

The variant for this loop is j which increases from *lastj* to the next prime. Euclid's theorem can be used to show that such a number exists and so sets an upper bound on the number of iterations in the loop. This upper bound is of course rather large for a practical demonstration of termination.

8 Introduction of variables with invariants

The body of the loop should increase j and exit if it is prime. To test this, it is of course only necessary to test whether j is divisible by the prime numbers, which are handily stored in p. Furthermore it is not necessary to test all of the primes in p as any factor of j will be less than the square root of j. Consequently it is useful to maintain two working variables which contain the index of the least prime whose square is greater than j, and also the square itself. These are related by an invariant:

ord_inv

$p : seq\ \mathbb{N}$
$j, k : \mathbb{N}$
$ord, square : \mathbb{N}$

$square = (p\ ord) * (p\ ord)$
$j < square$
$ord < k$

The predicate *ord* < *k* is necessary because *p ord* must have been calculated. This invariant has the useful property

$$ord\_inv;\ primed((1..(k\text{-}1)) \lhd p) \wedge odd\ j$$
$$\vdash$$
$$not\_prime\ j \Leftrightarrow (\exists\ x, n : \mathbb{N} \mid n \in 2..(ord\text{-}1) \bullet j = x * (p\ n))$$

The restriction on *n* in the existential quantification to *2..(ord-1)* arises because *p 1* is 2 and *j* is odd.

This concept of an invariant is supported by special features in the notation so it is worth discussing the need for them and the consequences of having them. Invariants have already been introduced during the discussion on types and the intention is that they are predicates which may be introduced into the context of a refinement step. An invariant may be assumed in a precondition and should be achieved in a postcondition: the formal refinement step should be understood in these terms. This implicit context to the refinement statements allows the visible notation to be simpler, thus concentrating the attention on the significant features of the step. Thus the motivation for this is similar to the introduction of a frame in a specification statement, which implicitly asserts that all the variables not in the frame are unchanged.

For this to be a sensible usage, the invariant must be relatively trivially achieved and obviously there will be differences of opinion as to what is trivial and what is not. For type invariants, the maintenance of a range constraint is often trivial, but occasionally extremely significant. In the case of this example, the invariant idea seems to be well suited to the explanation. The only purpose of the variables *ord* and *square* is to capture their relation to the sequence of primes and the current value of *j* and it is useful to introduce them in a way which makes this clear. Variables linked by an invariant are declared in the usual way. In this case the Knuth +≡ symbol is used to extend the first program fragment:

```
(1) +≡ ord, square : Integer;
```

Unlike a type invariant which is automatically established at declaration, an invariant of this nature needs to be explicitly established. Furthermore, an invariant controlling two variables cannot be established with one statement, so there must be occasions within the formal development when the invariant does not hold and therefore may not appear within the context. What is required are clear rules which usefully serve the purposes of the notation and allow the correct verification conditions to be generated.

The scheme proposed is to assert the invariant once it has been established, using an annotation:

invariant *inv;*

If the state *post* has been achieved, this will generate the VC:

$$post \vdash inv$$

Thereafter, the invariant is added to pre- and postconditions as with type invariants. To maintain the invariant, another annotation is used:

maintain *inv;*

In this case, the invariant is added to the first precondition only. When re-established, the ***invariant*** annotation is used again. The use of a ***maintain*** annotation allows the frame to be widened to include the dependent variables. In order to identify which these are, the invariant must be a named schema. For our example, the invariant is established as follows:

(6) ⊑ Δ *ord, square* $[Invl \wedge k = 3,$ *(11)*
$Invl \wedge k = 3 \wedge ord\_inv];$
invariant *ord_inv;*
$\{Invl \wedge k = 3 \wedge ord\_inv\}$ *(12)*

(11) ⊑ `ord := 2;   square := 9;`

The assumption *(12)* allows for the initialisation of yet more working variables.

The rules for the treatment of introduced variables and invariants can be illustrated in the following tree which displays the development of the program so far.

```
p, Indexrange
procedure
 1 begin  2 ;                         3 end
 j, k     ↓
 |        ↓
 |        4 ;          5
 |        ↓            |
 |        ◊ ; 6        |
 |            |        ↓
 |            |        loop
 |            |        ↓
 |            |        7  ;   8 ; 9
 |            |        |      ↓   ↓
 |            |        |      ◊   ◊
 |            |        ↓
 |            |        ↓
 |            |        loop
 |            |        ↓
 ↓            ↓        10
 ord,         ↓ ; 12   |
 square       ◊   |    |
 |                |    |
 |                |    |
```

The textual order of description if from top to bottom, the program order from left to right. The refinement steps are indicated by arrows descending from the specification statements which gave rise to them and the nodes of the tree have an indication of the program structure used in the development while the ◊ symbols indicate code.

For introduced variables *not* linked by an invariant, the frame may be widened once for each arm of the tree which is still (in the textual order) being developed. For these variables, no assumption about the values of the introduced variables can be propagated between the arms of the tree, so each of these places where the frame is widened can be treated as a separate local declaration. With an invariant, information is being propagated through the context. All of the development of *(5)* for example, is required to maintain *ord_inv*. This means the verification conditions cannot be calculated until the text has been entirely processed.

With a sensible invariant, the refinement steps prior to the introduction of the invariant should remain valid. In the case of this example, the development of *(7)* is still in terms of specification statements, so the invariant is implicitly present in the pre- and postconditions. Statements *(8)* and *(9)* have already been refined into code, but fortunately these maintain the invariant.

9 Introduction of Boolean values

The next complication concerns the introduction of Boolean variables. Z does not have a Boolean type, as the set membership and equality predicates are used to express truth or falsity. However, for the refinement calculus it is necessary to have a model for the SPARK Boolean values and the operators on them. This has been implicitly used in translating between Z predicates involving the logical connectives and the SPARK *and* and *or* operators. The next step in the example program development introduces a Boolean variable so it is necessary, in the Z part of the notation, to specify what happens to it. Consequently an explicit Z model of Booleans is required, defined as follows:

Boolean ::= true | false

[X]

$(\_\ mem\ \_) : (X \times \mathbb{P}\,X) \rightarrow Boolean$
$(\_\ neq\ \_) : (X \times X) \rightarrow Boolean$
$(\_\ and\ \_) : (Boolean \times Boolean) \rightarrow Boolean$
$not : Boolean \rightarrow Boolean$

$\forall\, x : X;\ S : \mathbb{P}\,X;\ b : Boolean$
$\bullet\ b = x\ mem\ S \Leftrightarrow b = true \wedge x \in S \vee b = false \wedge x \notin S$
$\forall\, x, y : X;\ b : Boolean$
$\bullet\ b = x\ neq\ y \Leftrightarrow x \neq y \wedge b = true \vee x = y \wedge b = false$
$\forall\, a, b, c : Boolean$
$\bullet\ a\ and\ b = c \Leftrightarrow$
$a = true \wedge b = true \wedge c = true$
$\vee$
$c = false \wedge (a = false \vee b = false)$
$\forall\, a, b : Boolean$
$\bullet\ a = not\ b \Leftrightarrow a = true \wedge b = false \vee a = false \wedge b = true$

This defines in turn the Boolean analogues of the membership and inequality predicates and the connectives which are needed for this example, namely the analogues of $\wedge$ and $\neg$. Returning to the program once more, it is required to refine the body of the loop, statement *(10)*, which must increase *j* and exit if it is prime. The "primeness" of *j* will be held in the boolean variable *jprime*, introduced as follows:

(1) +≡ `jprime : Boolean;`

The loop body is now refined by:

(10) ⊑ $\Delta\, j\ [Inv2, Inv2 \wedge j = j_0 + 2]$; *(13)*
$\Delta\, jprime\ [Inv2, Inv2 \wedge jprime = j\ mem\ primes]$; *(14)*
exit when `jprime;`

In other words, increase *j* by 2 (because *j + 1* will be even), give to *jprime* the meaning *j* is a prime number, and exit if it is true. The notation j_0 refers to the initial value of *j*, as in Morgan. Statement *(13)* alters *j* and so it is necessary to re-establish *ord_inv*:

(13) ⊑ ***maintain*** *ord_inv;*
`j := j + 2;`
$\Delta\, ord, square\ [odd\ j \wedge j - 2 < square \wedge Inv2, ord\_inv]$;
invariant *ord_inv;*

```
⊑ if j = square
  then Δ ord, square [j = square ∧ Inv2, ord_inv];
  end if;

⊑ ord := ord + 1;
  square := p(ord) * p(ord);
  {ord_inv};                                        (15)
```

The introduction of the conditional statement follows the standard refinement rules. The refinement holds because if the new value of $j < square$ the invariant is automatically maintained. As Knuth discusses in his paper, the proof that after incrementing *ord*, it remains less than *k* (as required by *ord_inv*), depends on some advanced number theory. The assumption *(15)* is left to provide for the maintenance of another invariant to be defined later.

10 Refinement rules for looping within a range

The next step in the example uses a *for* loop in which the controlled variable takes on values which are successive members of a range. This has the advantage that the variant is provided explicitly. The general refinement step will be of the form:

```
Δ w [pre, post] ⊑ for id in range
                  loop Δ w' [pre', post']
                  end loop;
```

This generates VCs as follows:

$$pre \vdash \exists\ id : range \mid id = first\ range \bullet pre'$$

$$post'_{[id+1/id]} \vdash pre'$$

$$\exists\ id : range \mid id = last\ range \bullet post' \vdash post$$

The existential quantifier is necessary as the loop variable is local to the loop. The substitution of *id+1* for *id* in the postcondition is necessary as the loop variable is incremented in the loop itself. This rule can be justified as an iterated sequential composition: the precondition is satisfied for the first element of the range; the loop body steps it on to be the precondition for the next operation when the loop variable has been incremented and the final operation satisfies the specified post condition.

The statement to be refined *(13)* is a test for the primeness of *j*, which is true if none of the primes computed so far is a factor. The test for one integer being a factor of another is given by the following relation:

$$\_factor\_of\_ == \{i, n : \mathbb{N} \mid \exists\ j : 2 \mathrel{..} (n-1) \bullet i*j = n \bullet i \mapsto n\}$$

The loop consists of testing successive members of the array *p* and exiting once one is found to be a factor of *j* in which case it is not prime and *jprime* is set to false. The loop invariant is given by the following schema, where *n* is the loop variable.

```
Inv3
p : seq ℕ
j, n, ord : ℕ
jprime : Boolean
-----------------------------------
∀ m : 2 .. (n-1) • ¬((p m) factor_of j)
jprime = true
```

Using this, the test for j being prime is:

```
(14) ⊑ jprime := true;
       for n in Integer range 2 .. ord-1
       until (p n) factor_of j ∧ jprime = false
       loop  Δ jprime [Inv3, Inv3 ∧ ¬((p n) factor_of j)]
       end loop;
```

This generates the following VCs:

$jprime = true \wedge Inv2 \vdash \exists\, n : \mathbb{N} \mid n = 2 \bullet Inv3$

$(\exists\, n : \mathbb{N} \mid n = ord - 1 \bullet Inv3 \wedge \neg((p\ n)\ factor\_of\ j))$
$\vee$
$(\exists\, n : 2 \,..\, (ord\text{-}1) \bullet (p\ n)\ factor\_of\ j \wedge jprime = false)$
$\vdash$
$Inv2 \wedge jprime = j\ mem\ primes$

The initialisation of *jprime* to true is necessary when the loop is not executed (when *ord* is equal to 2). The body of the loop is refined as follows:

```
⊑ Δ jprime [Inv3, (p n) factor_of j ⇔ jprime = false];      (16)
  exit when not jprime;
```

The last operation, *(16)*, is to test whether a given prime is a factor of j. For this an array *mult*, of the odd multiples of the primes is kept. They are incremented until greater than or equal to j. If equal then that particular prime is a factor, but not otherwise. This gives another invariant as follows:

```
mult_inv
p, mult : seq ℕ
ord, j : ℕ
-----------------------------------
∀ n : 2 .. (ord-1)
•    odd mn ∧ pn factor_of mn
     mn < j ∨ mn - (2*pn) < j ≤ mn
  where
     mn == mult n
     pn == p n
```

The upper bound of the array *mult* is determined by the number of primes it is necessary to consult and consequently is the maximum value attained by *ord*. This in turn is determined by the largest prime, but as this is what is being calculated, the constraint is expressed in terms of the available variables:

```
┌─ ord_max_inv ────────
│ ord, ord_max : ℕ
├──────────────────
│ ord ≤ ord_max
└──────────────────
```

With this, the SPARK declaration of *mult* is given by

```
(1) +≡ ord_max : constant Integer := 30;
       subtype mult_index_type is Integer range 2..ord_max;
       type mult_type is array (mult_index_type) of Integer;
       mult : mult_type;
```

The invariant on *mult* is established automatically by the initialisation of *ord*:

```
(12) ⊑ invariant mult_inv;
```

and further maintained as *ord* increases:

```
(15) ⊑ maintain mult_inv;
       mult(ord - 1) := j;
       invariant mult_inv;
```

The test now becomes

```
(16) ⊑ maintain mult_inv;
       Δ mult [mult_inv, mult_inv ∧ mult n ≥ j];                          (17)
       invariant mult_inv;
       Δ jprime [mult n ≥ j, jprime = (mult n) neq j];                    (18)
```

```
(17) ⊑ while mult(n) < j
       loop mult(n) := mult(n) + p(n) + p(n);
       end loop;
```

```
(18) ⊑ jprime := mult(n) /= j;
```

All formal statements have now been refined to code and the development is complete.

11 Conclusions

The aim of this paper has been to present an idea on how to combine the formal method of refinement with the informal method of natural language justification. The resulting notation is not intended to support the creative part of the design process, but rather that of recording the design once it is complete. It seems unlikely that anyone would *design* this program using this rather cumbersome formal notation: rather, they would use the programming language on its own, as acceptability for the designer has been a major consideration in its definition. After the design is complete the notation provides a splendid way of explaining why it is correct, but that is a different matter from arriving at the design in the first place. Even from the point of view of explanation, the standard presentation of the program in compilation order conveys an overall picture which supplements the detailed description provided by the notation.

The notation therefore should be judged on its success at increasing the assurance that a program at the algorithmic level is correct. The example has shown that the amount of detail introduced for the formalization may be kept within bounds and is certainly not excessive. The gain has been a complete formalization of every aspect of the algorithm which is necessary for correctness, apart from the range checks on arithmetic and loop termination. The ability to generate the formal verification condition in a form suitable for human inspection in itself adds to assurance and further assurance can then gained by carrying out the proofs mechanically.

The notation, at its current state of development, is tentative. There seem to be no major obstacles to the extension of the refinement aspects to all the elements of SPARK from the syntactic point of view, but from the semantic point of view a large amount of work needs to be done to give the verification aspects proper foundations.

References

Back, R J R (1988). A calculus of refinements for program derivations. Acta Informatica, 25, 593 - 624.

Dahl, O-J, Dijkstra, E W and Hoare, C A R (1972). Structured programming, Academic Press, London and New York.

Dijkstra, E W (1976). A discipline of programming, Prentice Hall, Englewood Cliffs.

Carre, B A (1989). Reliable programming in standard languages. In *High Integrity Software*, Sennett, C T (ed), Pitman, London.

Carre, B A, Jennings, T J, Maclennan, F J, Farrow, P F and Garnsworthy, J R (1990). SPARK - The SPADE Ada Kernel. Program Validation Ltd, 26 Queens Terrace, Southampton SO1 1BQ.

Good, D I (1986). Report of Gypsy 2.05, Institute for Computer Science, University of Texas at Austin.

King S, Sorensen I H, Woodcock J, (1988). Z: grammar and concrete and abstract syntaxes, Programming Research Group Technical Monograph PRG-68, University of Oxford.

Knuth, D E, (1984). Literate programming, Computer Journal, 27, 2, pp 97 - 111.

Luckham, D C (1990). Programming with specifications. Springer Verlag Texts and Monographs in Computer Science.

Morgan C C (1988). The specification statement, TOPLAS 10, 3.

Morgan C C (1990). Programming from specifications. Prentice Hall International Series in Computer Science.

Smith, P and Bleech, N (1989). Practical experience with a formal verification system, in *High Integrity Software* Sennett, C T (ed), Pitman London.

Methods and Tools for the Verification of Critical Properties

Roger Bishop Jones
International Computers Limited,
Eskdale Road, Winnersh, Berks, England, RG11 5TT.
Phone: +44 734 693131, E-mail: R.B.Jones@win0109.uucp

Abstract

This paper discusses methods for the formal treatment of critical systems. The discussion is based on experience at ICL in the application of formal methods to the development of highly assured secure systems.

Problems arising in the use of the standard paradigm for specification and refinement in Z are identified and discussed. Alternative methods which overcome some of these difficulties are presented.

A fully worked example is provided showing how the prototype ICL Z proof support tool may be used to specify and verify the critical properties of a secure system.

The paper argues that effective use of formal methods in establishing, with high levels of assurance, that critical systems meet their critical requirements demands methods distinct from those typically advocated for general applications.

1 Introduction

This paper is neither a report on research undertaken in formal methods nor a description of an industrial application of such methods.

It is a discussion of methods, based upon experience at ICL in applications of formal methods to the development of highly assured secure systems, and illustrated by an example small enough to permit relevant proofs to be included in the paper. A subsidiary theme is the work we have undertaken at ICL to establish tools supporting proof in the specification language Z. The proof scripts in the paper illustrate the use of the prototype ICL Z proof tool.

section 2 - methodological discussions

The primary methodological issues illustrated by the examples in the paper are introduced.

section 3 - ICL proof support for Z

This paper illustrates the use of the ICL Z support tools, which have been used to produce the paper, to syntax and type check the specifications contained in it and in the development and checking of the formal proofs. A brief description of these tools is given together with information on how the various formal sections of the document are to be interpreted.

These formal sections include not only Z specifications but also proof scripts for input to the proof tool and output from the proof tool as it processes these scripts.

section 4 - a formal model of a secure system

The paper begins with a presentation of a specification of a secure system in a fairly traditional way as a collection of Z schemas describing the operations of the system. This serves to illustrate some of the difficulties which motivate the alternative methods which form the main subject of the paper.

The primary difficulty identified at this stage is that specification of *a* secure system does not settle the question of what it is for a system to be secure, and to be able to verify that a system is secure one needs in the first instance a formal definition of *security*, not merely an example of a secure system.

section 5 - a specification of critical requirements

Having identified a need for a specification of critical requirement, an example of such a specification is furnished.

section 6 - a formal model of a system architecture

The first stage in the design and implementation of a system meeting the formalised critical requirements is to establish a system architecture which can be shown to guarantee satisfaction of the requirements. Such an architecture is exhibited, followed by a proof that it does indeed ensure conformance to the critical requirements.

section 7 - a model of a secure kernel

The correctness proposition for the architectural design asserts that a system correctly constructed from subsystems having certain critical properties will meet the critical requirements for the system. We now proceed to exhibit a (mathematical model of a) subsystem having the required critical property. The proof that the kernel does guarantee that the system is secure is shown in full.

section 8 - system correctness proposition

For completeness the overall system is defined and its correctness proposition stated.

2 Methodological Discussions

For over 5 years ICL has been developing and delivering to external customers formal machine checked proofs about secure systems. This paper attempts to identify and illustrate some of the special concerns that arise in the use of formal methods for the development of very high assurance systems. No deep insights are reflected in the methods we have adopted, which flow naturally from a preoccupation with properties of systems. Nevertheless, we are aware of few examples of published material on this topic. Rob Arthan presents similar methods applied to the specification of the critical properties of a proof tool in the proceeding of VDM 91 [1]. Jeremy Jacob discusses some of the problems in refining specifications of secure systems in [5].

The main methodological issues raised in this paper are:

- The need to verify critical systems against a specification of critical requirements.
- The form of specifications, and the distinction between a specification of critical requirements and a full functional specification.
- The traditional notion of refinement and its relationship with the meaning of specifications.
- The limitations of the traditional notion of specification for expressing critical requirements.
- The need for an explicit formalisation of the claim to be verified.

I propose to focus primarily upon two recommendations.

2.1 Formalisation of Critical Requirements

The first recommendation is that formal treatments of critical systems should begin with formalisation of *critical properties* and that the primary objective of the formal treatment should be to establish that the system as implemented will have these properties.

This contrasts with the more common perception that the formal treatment begins with an abstract formal specification of the system and that the primary objective of the formal treatment is to establish that the system as implemented is "correct" with respect to this initial specification. Often the desirability of proving critical properties of specifications is mentioned as a way of checking the correctness of a system specification, without any prior mention of the need to formalise these properties, as if these properties are in general straightforward and obvious enough to deserve no attention until we feel it necessary to prove them.

We advocate that in the case of *critical* systems (whether security or safety critical) the specification of critical properties should be regarded as the most important aspect of the formal treatment, since these represent the most crucial aspects of the requirements on the system being developed. There is no reason to suppose that either a specification or a design can be undertaken successfully if these critical requirements have not first been established.

The connection implicit in this discussion between critical *requirements* and critical *properties* is important. Critical requirements cannot in general be adequately expressed other than by stating a *property* of systems, which is not the same thing as a *model* of *a system*. Safety and security are properties not models.

2.2 Caution about Refinement

My second recommendation is that care should be taken to ensure that the models of the system which are used in this process are clearly understood, and are adequate for the purposes in hand.

Particularly the reader is warned to beware of the use of models which are intended to permit "operation refinement" (as defined, for example, in *The Z Notation* [8] section 5.5). The reason why he should beware of such models is that properties possessed by such models need not be enjoyed by "correct" refinements of them under the normal rules of refinement. It is therefore not adequate to write a specification in Z of a system, prove that this specification has the required critical properties, and then refine to an implementation using the normal rules of operation refinement. Similar considerations also apply to data refinement.

This does not mean that such models may not be used. It means that proof of critical properties cannot in general be mediated by a proof that an incomplete specification of the system has the required properties.

The reason why these problems arise is that a model of this kind is by convention regarded as not specifying the possible inputs to the system. So called "pre-conditions" are interpreted not as constraining the possible inputs to the system, but as constraining the scope of applicability of the constraints imposed by the post-conditions and state-invariants. The system specifier wishing to ensure that, whatever the behaviour of the operator, a system will not behave dangerously, will find that a legitimate refinement of his system may introduce further possible inputs, and that the behaviour of the system when receiving these inputs is in no way constrained by any invariants or post-conditions which the original specifications contained.

The presumption that systems can be shown to be secure by showing that a model of the system is secure, and then proving that the system is correctly refined from the model has never featured in the methods used by ICL for high assurance secure systems. This kind of problem in the development of secure systems has been discussed in the literature by Jeremy Jacob [5].

The kind of properties of models which are preserved under refinement have been called "safety properties". This unfortunate terminology might suggest to the reader that the problems discused here arise only in the development of secure systems, and not in the development of safety critical systems. There is however no reason to suppose that the critical properties required of safety critical systems are "safety properties" in this technical sense. Using the term "reckless refinement" to describe refinements which permit liberalisation of the pre-condition without preservation of state invariants or post-conditions, then "safety properties" are those which are indifferent to reckless refinement. It is doubtful that any safety critical systems have critical properties which are indifferent to reckless refinement.

Reckless refinement is like permitting an extra cockpit control to be introduced which overrides all the safety features in the flight control software.

3 ICL Proof Support for Z

3.1 Background

The ICL Secure Systems High Assurance Team has grown from the need to use formal methods in the development of highly assured secure systems.

The dominant formal specification notation in the UK for such applications is Z[7], and the evaluation guidelines for secure systems call not only for formal specifications, but also for proofs.

At the time when ICL was establishing its capability in this area the Z notation was less stable and well defined than it now is, and lacked good tool support. We nevertheless wanted to obtain early experience of undertaking formal proof and therefore spent some time looking at proof support tools for languages other than Z. Some experience was obtained in the use of the NQTHM theorem prover (often called the Boyer-Moore prover after its authors [2]), and also of the HOL system developed at the University of Cambridge by Mike Gordon and others [3].

The HOL system was felt to be more suitable for our applications for two main reasons.

The first reason was that the language supported by the system, a polymorphic version of Church's simple theory of types (using Milner-style type polymorphism [6]), was closer in its logical expressiveness to Z than the quantifier-free first order logic supported by NQTHM.

The second factor was that the HOL system was one of the LCF family [4]. This meant that the role of the user of the tool in the proof development process was more fully recognised, and a powerful meta-language (ML) was available for the user to use in programming proofs. The flexibility of the system for adaptation to tasks not anticipated by the developers of the system was felt to be greater than that of NQTHM.

We found that HOL as a language was close enough to Z that the kind of specifications we were then writing could be manually translated into HOL without great difficulty. This provided the beginnings of our practical experience in constructing formal machine checked proofs. The flexibility and extendibility afforded by the LCF paradigm enabled us to progressively customise the HOL system towards support for reasoning about specifications translated from Z, and we were able to acquire gradually a deeper understanding of these languages and of the relationship between them.

By mid 1988 we were sufficiently convinced of the merits of the HOL system that when an opportunity arose to undertake a technology research and development project our proposal was based around an industrial re-implementation of the HOL system. One of our objectives was to achieve best possible proof support for Z, but at the time of submitting the proposal we were uncertain about how close that would be, and our proposal was therefore non-committal. The language had by this time been given a formal semantics (although incomplete) by Spivey [7], but there was no sign of progress on proof rules. Compared with the stark simplicity of HOL, Z seemed a very complex language, and contained some features which seemed logically controversial. One of particular concern was the fact that variables in the signatures of schemas effectively occur in expressions in which they do not syntactically occur. The rules for free and bound occurrences of variables would either have to be very unusual, or else these concepts would not be adequate to express the necessary side conditions on the logical rules. Other oddities include the lack of distinction between variables and constants (which makes side conditions non-local).

We proposed to continue to support proof for Z via HOL. We felt that a re-implementation of the HOL system following industrial quality control processes was desirable and that this would give us valuable further experience with the technology to enable us to provide best achievable support for Z. Early into the project further investigations led us to conclude that full support for the Z language as then defined was feasible by this route, and since then this has been one of the primary objectives of our work on proof support.

3.2 The ICL Z Proof Tool

A prototype Z proof tool has been under development for some time. This prototype is built on the prototype ICL HOL system. The prototype ICL HOL system has now been superseded by a product quality implementation, and Z proof support is now being re-implemented on the new version of ICL HOL.

The prototype Z tool is sufficiently powerful to permit illustration of the methods described in this paper, and also to give some indication of the proof style which will be supported by the product standard Z tool.

We have not felt that our objectives in relation to proof support could be achieved if substantial improvements in support for the preparation of Z scripts were attempted at the same time, and therefore the preparation of scripts is undertaken using standard text editors, though benefiting from the use of extended fonts. The development method is document based, where the documents are LaTeXsource scripts interspersed with formal text in a "close to wysiwyg" format. This paper is such a script.

During the preparation of a script the developer may have running concurrently with the text editor an interactive session of the ICL Z tool, which will undertake the syntax and type checking of specifications in an incremental manner, and will support interactive development of proof scripts.

In the case of specification checking this may be achieved interactively by the use of cut-and-paste from the editor into the proof tool. As the specification is entered and checked, theories are built up containing the formal specifications. Proofs of conjectures relating to the specifications may be undertaken at any time, and the resulting theorems, once proven, may be stored in theories with the specifications.

The entire process may be rerun in batch mode to ensure that the resulting document is complete and correct.

The proof system is based on the LCF paradigm, under which proof scripts are essentially programs in standard ML which compute the required theorems via abstract data types which ensure that all computations of theorems correspond to admissible inferences in the supported logic. Proof scripts of this kind are not usually intelligible without seeing the intermediate goals displayed by the proof tool during the development of the proof. If proof scripts are intended to be read without resort to the tool they are therefore best annotated with output from the proof tool showing these intermediate goals.

This document is a "literate script" containing, in addition to informal narrative, formal specifications and annotated proof scripts. Specifications are all in the language "Z". They are preceded by a small Z on the left of the page, and where not enclosed by a box according to the Z conventions, a vertical bar on the left makes clear the extent of the formal material.

The proof script proper is in the language ML (in fact "standard" ML), and is marked by vertical bars on the left starting with the characters "ML". Output from the proof tool has been included in the document, again distinguished by a vertical bar on the left, in this case headed by 'HOL output'. Descriptions of some of the proof facilities available are included in the narrative. The output displayed is not quite verbatim. To improve the readability of the paper I have added newlines to overcome shortcomings of the pretty printer in the prototype. Some of the duplication of output which is beneficial in an interactive session using a scrolling teletype interface has been eliminated, "..." marking the place where non-current subgoals, or irrelevant assumptions have been listed.

The detailed formal scripts presented demonstrate how our prototype tool provides assistance in finding proofs as well as in checking them. It illustrates some of the additional complexity arising in Z proofs relative to proofs in HOL, and some of the mechanisms so far developed for dealing with these complications.

4 A Formal Model of a Secure System

The use of formal techniques in systems developments may be beneficial even if no proofs are undertaken.

Our concern in this paper however, is not with the use of formal techniques in this (rather informal) manner. We are concerned with formal techniques which are appropriate where proofs are to be undertaken to give higher levels of assurance that the system under development will have certain critical properties, such as "security" or "safety".

In such cases, it is our belief that a prerequisite of obtaining value from undertaking proof is to obtain some *formal* statement of what is to be proven.

In order to make effective use of formal techniques to obtain high assurance it is necessary to establish formally the proposition of which we seek assurance.

This may seem to be an obvious requirement, but it is a requirement which is not supported by standard methods. In the case of 'model oriented' specifications in Z there is in general no single formal entity which represents the system as a whole. In 'model oriented' specification methods the conventional paradigm is to have (or to hope for) a tool which will generate proof obligations. What is proven is a set of propositions (perhaps generated by this tool), which are expected to amount to a correctness result, even though the proposition which these proof obligations establish is not itself expressed or proven by the proof system.

4.1 Informal Description of Security

"Security" is meant , for the purposes of this paper in the narrow sense of preserving the confidentiality of classified information. A secure system is one which stores data classified according to its 'sensitivity'. 'sensitivity' is a measure of how serious unauthorised disclosure of the information is considered to be.

Sensitivity classifications are normally (partially) ordered, and in the following examples they will be modelled by natural numbers. Every user of the system has a clearance, which is also a natural number. The system is required to permit a user to access only data whose classification is not greater than the user's clearance.

Transfer of information from an entity of a certain classification to an entity having a lower classification is known as a downgrade. The system is required not to connive in the downgrade of information. This means that the system itself will not undertake a transfer of information which might reduce the classification of the information.

The user himself may be entitled both to read highly classified data, and to write to more lowly classified data. If so he may take notes himself from highly classified data and use the information obtained while modifying lowly classified data. In doing so he will be committing a breach of security. The system will not be able to prevent such breaches, but it will prevent all breaches which it is able to detect. In particular the user will not be permitted to copy a highly classified object into a lowly classified object by instructions to the system.

4.2 The Model

The following example is presented as an example of a specification in the Z model-oriented style of a system purporting to meet the requirements informally described in the previous section. It is not offered as a realistic specification of a secure system. Its primary purposes are:

- to clarify by formal example the informal notion of secure system
- to illustrate some of the points subsequently raised about the role of this kind of specification in the development of critical systems

The proof tool keeps specifications in theories and we therefore introduce a new theory for the specification to follow:

ML

```
load_theory "Z_Lib_rel";
new_theory "example1";
```

We have no interest in the form of data to be stored by our computer system, and therefore introduce a "given set" for this data.

Z

$$[DATA]$$

We do however require that the system stores data together with a *classification*. For simplicity we assume that all data at a given class is stored together indexed by its classification, and we use non-negative numeric values as classification marks.

Z

STATE

$$classified\_data : \mathbb{N} \leftrightarrow DATA$$

A transition of the system will be, at bottom, a state transformation.

Z

ΔSTATE

$$STATE; STATE'$$

Since all the operations permitted must be initiated by some user, and the user's clearance is needed to determine whether the operation is permitted, we model the system as having an unconditional input providing this clearance. Authentication of users is in practice an important problem, but for present purposes we will assume that by means unspecified the input value *clear* is known to be the clearance of the user who initiates the operation and receives the output from the operation.

z

OPERATION

$\Delta STATE$;
clear? $:\mathbb{N}$

The informal critical requirement is that no operation permits "downflow" of information. This means that information does not flow from any *DATA* in the state to *DATA* with a numerically lower classification.

With this in mind we specify two operations which plausibly meet the informally stated requirement. First the *READ* operation, which enables the user to retrieve information from the classified information store.

z

READ

OPERATION;
class? $:\mathbb{N}$;
data! $: DATA$

$class? \in dom\ classified\_data$
$\wedge\ class? \leq clear?$
$\wedge\ data! = classified\_data\ class?$
$\wedge\ classified\_data' = classified\_data$

The first two clauses of the predicate belong to the pre-condition of the operation. It is the second of these which ensures that the operation is 'secure' by preventing a user from reading data whose classification is higher than the user's clearance.

The *COMPUTE* operation permits the user to undertake computations and to store the results of the computations in the classified data store.

z

COMPUTE

OPERATION;
class? $:\mathbb{N}$;
computation? $:(\mathbb{N} \nrightarrow DATA) \rightarrow DATA$

$class? \in dom\ classified\_data$
$\wedge\ class? \geq clear?$
$\wedge\ classified\_data'$
$= \quad classified\_data \oplus$
$\{class? \mapsto computation?\ (0\ ..\ clear? \lhd classified\_data)\}$

In this case the clause in the pre-condition of the operation which is necessary to ensure that the operation is secure is $class? \geq clear?$. The difference between the two operations in this area is because *class?* in this operation is a destination for information not a source. This clause does not suffice, but is supplemented by the fact that the state is filtered of highly classified data before being used in the computation. This ensures that the user is not permitted access to information for which he is not cleared.

These two operations are supplied as representatives of secure operations. Examples of insecure operations may be obtained by omitting the constraint on *class?* in either of the above operations.

4.3 Discussion of Specification

4.3.1 specification of systems or of properties of systems

In the previous section we have supplied a specification of a simple system. The state of the system contains a classified data store. Two operations have been specified which we believe to be "secure" in a sense characterised informally in the narrative.

It is clear that even in this simple specification minor errors might have resulted in the specified system not meeting our informal notion of security. In fact an earlier version of this very simple example survived a week before I realised that it was not secure. In a realistic system specification, which would be considerably more complex, the risk of the system described being insecure *because of errors in the specification* becomes significant. No amount of care or proof in designing and implementing a system from such a specification would result in the system being secure.

We would like to be able to use formal techniques to establish whether a system specified in this (or some other way) is secure. For this purpose a specification of a secure system is not sufficient. What is needed is a specification of the property of being secure, only then are we in a position to judge whether any specified system is secure.

The reader might object that the problem facing us is one of infinite regress. No matter where we start our formal work there is a risk that errors will be made, and these errors will not be formally checkable against some previous specification. Nevertheless, it is our experience that a specification of what it is to be secure (of our *critical property*) is much simpler than the complete specification of some particular secure system. The activity of formalising the critical requirement is one in which the specifier focuses exclusively on the aspects of the system of highest concern. The informal assessment of the critical requirements is likely to be more effective because of this focus, and because of the *smaller* specifications which result.

4.3.2 further problems

Even as a specification of a system, what we have offered cannot be accepted, though superficially plausible, as a specification of a secure system.

This is because the standard rules of refinement, which fill an important gap between the formal meaning of the specification and its *true* meaning, will permit this specification to be refined by liberalisation of the pre-condition into specifications which are no longer even superficially those of secure systems.

To ensure that this cannot formally be refined into an insecure system it is necessary to specify what happens when the preconditions are not met. This is exacerbated in Z by the fact that the formal precondition is not what it might appear to be. Thus the formal precondition includes the state invariant on the initial state (you may not assume that the system states satisfy the invariant), and also includes the predicate implicit in the declaration of the input variables. The specification can legitimately be refined to one in which *clear?* is a negative integer, and the behaviour of the system in such circumstances is not constrained unless a schema is supplied in which this is not explicitly or implicitly in the precondition.

These considerations are important in the treatment of critical systems, and may be the origin of the belief among some that formal methods (in general) can specify what a system must do, but cannot specify what it must not do.

My list is not exhausted. A further difficulty in some applications (including security) is that this form of specification confuses looseness and non-determinism. A non-deterministic system is one which does not always exhibit the same behaviour when supplied with the same inputs and initial state. Non-deterministic systems are particularly problematic when confidentiality is at issue. There are special problems in deciding when information flows are occurring in non-deterministic systems, so that there is as yet no consensus on what it means to say that a system is secure (in the narrow sense of enforcing confidentiality) if it is non-deterministic. The formalisation of security given below is essentially a property of deterministic systems, and so cannot be applied to a system model which may be interpreted as or refined to a non-deterministic system.

If we were to attempt to formalise the notion of information flow security for non-deterministic systems, then it is unlikely that the kind of model of a non-deterministic system provided by a Z schema would be satisfactory. In order to make statements about information flow through non-deterministic systems it is necessary to know not only the possible outcomes of an operation, but also the probability distribution. Even a very small amount of noise on a channel may render all transitions possible without significantly impairing the ability of the channel to transmit information.

So a Z schema, interpreted as a specification of an operation, not only fails to provide the means of specifying deterministic systems, but provides models of non-deterministic systems which may not be adequate for some purposes. This is not to be construed as a criticism of the language Z, which is a rich notation for classical set theory well able to cope with any mathematical modelling task. It is a criticism of the narrow view that systems should or can be modelled by Z schemas, and the normal interpretation of such models.

5 A Specification of Critical Requirements

ML

```
new_theory "example2";
```

The specification of critical requirements avoids detail about the specific operations supported by the system, and we therefore use 'given sets' to represent the inputs and outputs.

z

$$[IN,OUT]$$

The state of our system is similar to that in the previous example. Classifications of data and clearances of users are modelled by natural numbers, more sensitive data having numerically higher classifications.

Since there is only one component in the state it is simpler not to use a schema.

z

$$\mathbf{STATE2} == \mathbb{N} \nrightarrow DATA$$

A system is modelled as a transition function. This is to be regarded as a single function modelling all the permissible transitions of the system. We require that the system is a total function.

z

$$\mathbf{SYSTEM} == (\mathbb{N} \times IN \times STATE2) \rightarrow (STATE2 \times OUT)$$

We now attempt to capture (in fact *define*) what it means to say that such a system is *secure*. The intended meaning here concerns the nature of the information flows permitted by the system. The requirement will be expressed by two properties concerning the information flowing to the output of the system, and the information flowing between different classes of data within the state.

The constraint on information flowing to the output is that none of this information comes from data classified more highly than the clearance associated with the input (which is to be understood as the clearance of some user supplying the input and receiving the output).

This is expressed by saying that the output will be the same if the state before the transition differed only in data classified more highly than the input.

z

$$\mathbf{out\_secure} : \mathbb{P}\, SYSTEM$$

$$\forall sys{:}SYSTEM \bullet sys \in out\_secure \Leftrightarrow$$

$$\begin{array}{l} (\forall\, clear{:}\mathbb{N};\ inp{:}IN;\ s,s'{:}STATE2 \\ \mid (0\,..\,clear \lhd s) = (0\,..\,clear \lhd s') \\ \bullet \qquad\qquad second\,(sys\,(clear, inp, s)) \\ \qquad = \qquad second\,(sys\,(clear, inp, s'))) \end{array}$$

The constraint on flows within the state are that the information flowing to any data in the state should be derived exclusively from information in the state which is classified no higher than the destination data.

z

$$\mathbf{state\_secure} : \mathbb{P}\, SYSTEM$$

$$\forall sys{:}SYSTEM \bullet sys \in state\_secure \Leftrightarrow$$
$$(\forall class, clear{:}\mathbb{N};\ inp{:}IN;\ s,s'{:}STATE2$$
$$\mid (0 \mathinner{..} class \lhd s) = (0 \mathinner{..} class \lhd s')$$
$$\bullet \quad 0 \mathinner{..} class \lhd (first\,(sys\,(clear, inp, s)))$$
$$= \quad 0 \mathinner{..} class \lhd (first\,(sys\,(clear, inp, s'))))$$

A further property involving the flows of information from the input value would also be appropriate, but is omitted for the sake of simplicity. The security property is then simply the conjunction of these two properties.

z

$$\mathbf{secure} : \mathbb{P}\, SYSTEM$$

$$\forall sys{:}SYSTEM \bullet sys \in secure \Leftrightarrow sys \in state\_secure \wedge sys \in out\_secure$$

6 A Formal Model of a Secure System Architecture

The system may be implemented minimising the critical function, by implementing a secure *KERNEL*, which is required to enforce security, and an untrusted *APPLICATION*.

The kernel is a subsystem which will control the running of the application, giving access to the data store at a level which is appropriate to the clearance of the current user of the system. When a command is initiated the system is supplied with the clearance of the user. This information is used by the kernel to control access by the application to the data store.

6.1 Component Types

The application is modelled as if it were a system itself, except that it need not concern itself with security, and is therefore not supplied with the clearance parameter associated with each operation.

z

$$\mathbf{APPLICATION} == (IN \times STATE2) \rightarrow (STATE2 \times OUT)$$

In general a security kernel will be capable of controlling an application because the processor on which it runs has hardware protection facilities which make this possible. More detailed and realistic models of this kind of system would therefore be expected to show how such features of the hardware supported the enforcement of security.

However, secure systems can be built using processors which do not have such protection features, at the cost either of disallowing assembly level implementations of applications and regarding the compiler as a critical subsystem, or of arranging for the application to be interpreted by the kernel rather than executed by the hardware.

The following model of a kernel is most plausible in these contexts. The application could be a functional program, provided to the kernel for invocation as appropriate, or any other sort of program to be interpreted by the kernel.

The kernel is modelled as a function which when supplied with an *APPLICATION* will yield a *SYSTEM*.

z

$$\mathbf{KERNEL} == APPLICATION \rightarrow SYSTEM$$

6.2 Construction

Given the way the kernel has been modelled, the construction of a system from a kernel and an application is trivial.

z

$$\mathbf{construction} : APPLICATION \times KERNEL \rightarrow SYSTEM$$

$$\forall appl{:}APPLICATION;\ kernel{:}KERNEL \bullet construction\,(appl, kernel) = kernel\ appl$$

6.3 Critical Requirements on Components

The architecural thinking here goes little further than that there will be a kernel and it will be responsible for enforcing the security of the system. The critical requirements on the kernel can therefore say simply that the kernel must be capable of discharging this responsibility, i.e. that whatever application is supplied to the kernel, the resulting system will be secure.

z

$$\mathbf{secure\_kernel} : \mathbb{P}\ KERNEL$$

$$\forall kernel{:}KERNEL \bullet kernel \in secure\_kernel \Leftrightarrow (\forall appl{:}APPLICATION \bullet (construction\,(appl, kernel)) \in secure)$$

6.4 Architecture Correctness Proof

We are now in a position to formulate a conjecture expressing the claim that the architectural design modelled above suffices for the construction of secure systems.

The conjecture states that whenever a system is built using *construction* from a kernel which is a *secure_kernel* together with any application, then the resulting system will be *secure*. The fact that no conditions on the nature of the application are expressed indicates that the application need not be trusted to behave in any particular way. Whatever the behaviour of the application the system will be secure.

This claim is trivial and so is its proof, since it follows directly from the *definition* of a *secure_kernel*.

Nevertheless the machine proof will be exhibited, as our first introduction to the mechanics of proof.

Though proof checking in LCF-like systems (including ICL HOL) is undertaken on forward inferences from axioms to theorems, the normal interactive proof style is a backward style supported by a "goal package". The goal package is responsible for translating the results of the goal oriented backward proof search into a fully checked forward proof.

The proof is initiated by first giving the conjecture to the goal package as follows:

ML
```
zset_goal([],⟦∀kernel:KERNEL;appl:APPLICATION •
        kernel ∈ secure_kernel ⇒ secure (construction (appl,kernel))⟧);
```

The system echoes back the goal and awaits instructions on how to approach the proof of the goal.

HOL output
```
(∀kernel: KERNEL; appl: APPLICATION | true • ((kernel ∈ secure_kernel)
⇒ ((construction (appl, kernel)) ∈ secure)))
```

Since the proof of the conjecture hinges entirely upon the definition of *secure_kernel* we need to use the definition to expand the goal.

The procedure *z_specification* may be used to retrieve from the theory a theorem consisting of the conjunction of the predicate implicit in the declaration part of the specification and the explicit predicate. The combination is sufficient to justify rewriting the goal, but its form is not suitable for use by the rewriting facilities. This is because the explicit predicate is quantified, and its use depends upon establishing that the expression to be rewritten falls in the range of quantification. A similar HOL definition would suffice for rewriting, because quantification is permitted only over *types* and type checking alone establishes applicability of the definition. In Z, quantification is over sets (which may or may not be co-extensive with types), and type checking alone will not establish applicability of a quantified equation or equivalence; some proof is required.

In the case of axiomatic definitions of sets (i.e. properties) in this form it is possible to derive from the combination of the declaration and predicate parts of the specification an unconditional free variable form of the definition, which is more convenient for rewriting. A derived rule `iff_simp` is provided to undertake this derivation and its result is as follows.

ML
```
val secure_kernel_sim =
        iff_simp (z_specification "-" "secure_kernel");
```

HOL output
```
val secure_kernel_sim = ⊢ ((kernel ∈ secure_kernel) ⇔ ((kernel ∈ KERNEL) ∧
(∀appl: APPLICATION | true • ((construction (appl, kernel)) ∈ secure)))):thm
```

Since this equivalence is unconditional it may be used to expand out the goal using a general purpose rewriting tactic a follows:

ML
```
ze (Zrewrite_tac[secure_kernel_sim]);
```

HOL output
```
(∀kernel: KERNEL; appl: APPLICATION | true •
  (((kernel ∈ KERNEL) ∧
  (∀appl: APPLICATION | true • ((construction (appl, kernel)) ∈ secure)))
  ⇒ ((construction (appl, kernel)) ∈ secure)))
```

The goal has now become logically complex, and the proof may be progressed by repeating *Zstrip_tac*, a tactic suitable for use on goals whose top level connective is a propositional connective or a universal quantifier.

ML
```
ze (REPEAT Zstrip_tac);
```

The resulting goal is in the form of a *conclusion* to be proven, together with a number of *assumptions* which are available for use in the proof. The assumptions are listed first, each enclosed in square brackets, followed by the conclusion to be established.

HOL output
```
1 subgoal
  [(kernel ∈ KERNEL)]
  [(appl ∈ APPLICATION)]
  [(∀appl: APPLICATION | true • ((construction (appl, kernel)) ∈ secure))]

((construction (appl, kernel)) ∈ secure)
```

Further progress now depends on choice of a suitable value for instantiation of the generalisation in the assumptions. This case is sufficiently simple that the instantiation will be found by *Zres_tac*.

ML
```
ze Zres_tac;
```

HOL output
```
subgoal proved
```

The theorem arising from proof of the conjecture may now be stored in the theory.

ML
```
zsave_top_thm "architecture_secure";
```

HOL output

$val\ it = \vdash (\forall kernel: KERNEL;\ appl: APPLICATION \mid true \bullet$
$((kernel \in secure\_kernel) \Rightarrow ((construction\ (appl, kernel)) \in secure))) : thm$

This very simple example has exhibited some of the basic machinery used for conducting proofs using the ICL Z proof tool.

It has also shown that conjectures about which subsystems of critical systems are themselves critical may be susceptible of formal proof. The fact that critical requirements were specified only on the kernel and not on the application indicates that in this architecture the application is not a critical component.

7 A Model of a Secure Kernel

7.1 The Model

We may now proceed to the definition of a function which we believe to be a *secure_kernel*. We call this an implementation for present purposes. In another context we might regard this as a functional specification or a design.

The specification is sufficiently explicit that it could be manually translated to a similar program in a functional programming language, though it is more plausible as a rather abstract model of a kernel which would be elaborated somewhat before implementation.

The kernel adopts two measures to ensure that the application does not violate the security policy (the critical requirement). Firstly it ensures that the application does not have access to information which the user is not cleared to see. This is modelled by the kernel supplying the application with a filtered copy of the classified data store from which highly classified data has been removed. Secondly it ensures that the application does not transfer information from highly classified data into data classified lower. This is modelled by the kernel filtering the classified data store returned from the application, discarding lowly classified data before using this to update the state of the system.

Z

kernel_implementation : $KERNEL$

$\forall\ clear{:}\mathbb{N};\ inp{:}IN;\ state{:}STATE2;\ appl{:}APPLICATION \bullet$

$kernel\_implementation\ appl\ (clear, inp, state) =$

$((state \oplus ((0\ ..\ (clear-1)) \lhd\!\!\!- (first\ (appl\ (inp, (0\ ..\ clear) \lhd state)))),$
$second\ (appl\ (inp, (0\ ..\ clear) \lhd state))))$

7.2 The Correctness Proof

The fact that the *kernel_implementation* is a *secure_kernel* is not a trivial consequence of the definitions.

It is however a sufficiently straightforward consequence that full details of an interactive proof session establishing this result can be given. The level of complexity of the example was engineered with this in mind.

7.2.1 mathematical lemmas

A number of lemmas of a purely mathematical nature are required in this proof.

Some of these are results about set theory which are straightforwardly provable in the course of the main proof. A tactic is prepared here to deal with these proofs automatically.

The primary proof facilities available are of the following three kinds:

- stripping

  The tactic **Zstrip_tac** embodies the basic techniques for dealing with propositional connectives, including skolemisation of quantifiers where appropriate.

  Repeating *Zstrip_tac* progresses the proof through to the point at which further progress depends upon instantiation of generalisations in assumptions or on the provision of witnesses for existential conclusions of subgoals.

  In the case that the goal or subgoal is a propositional tautology this is automatically discharged by repeating *Zstrip_tac*.

- resolution

  Identifying candidate values for instantiation of universal assumptions or witnesses for existential conclusions is typically undertaken in resolution based systems using unification. Some limited but basic facilities described as forms of resolution in the HOL system have been adapted for use in Z proofs. These provide only for instantiation of universal assumptions (and stripping of the results) using pattern matching rather than unification. Despite these limitations they are effective in proving a useful class of predicate calculus results with minimal user intervention.

- rewriting

  General rewriting facilities are available in HOL, and these have been adapted for use with Z (the adaptations concern the "built-in" rewriting equations and the support of the more elaborate quantifiers in Z).

Useful classes of results in elementary set theory can be proven with a single proof strategy using these facilities.

Where a conjecture consists of an equation or other relation (most frequently $\subseteq$), or a logical combination of such predicates, where the operands are expressions involving various operators over sets, the following strategy will often suffice for its proof.

First the goal should be rewritten using theorems which characterise the relations or operators in terms of the members of operands and results. In the case of equality the relevant theorem is "the axiom of extensionality" (though it isn't an *axiom* in our system). This asserts that two sets are equal if and only if they have the same members. Rewriting with the axiom of extensionality converts an equation over sets into a generalised equivalence of two assertions about set membership. The analogous theorem for $\subseteq$ results in a generalised implication. Theorems characterising operators over sets serve to "push in" membership assertions over complex terms, giving membership assertions involving subterms. Such a theorem for set union would assert that an element is a member of the union of two sets if and only if it is a member of one set or of the other. Using a list of theorems which covers each of the predicates and operators in the goal will translate an assertion in set theory to (an instance of) an assertion in the predicate calculus. For simple set equations this will usually be a generalised propositional tautology and stripping will suffice to prove it. For more complex goals stripping followed by resolution and finally rewriting with assumptions will frequently solve the problem.

By inspection of our specification we can identify the predicates and operators over sets which are likely to occur in set theoretic lemmas required in the proof. This enables us to put together a tactic which will be capable of solving these problems. During the course of the proof this tactic can be enhanced as necessary if it is found to be insufficient.

The operators used in the specification are $\lhd$, $⩤$ and $\oplus$. It turns out that both equality and $\subseteq$ appear in the required lemmas.

The following list of theorems suffices for all the proofs required:

ML

```
[Zset_eq_thm, ⊆_thm, ◁_thm1, ⩤_thm4, ⊕_thm, first_thm];
```

HOL output

$$
\begin{aligned}
&val\ it = \\
&\quad [\vdash ((x = y) = (\forall z\colon U \mid true \bullet ((z \in x) \Leftrightarrow (z \in y)))), \\
&\quad \vdash ((P \subseteq Q) \Leftrightarrow (\forall z\colon U \mid true \bullet ((z \in P) \Rightarrow (z \in Q)))), \\
&\quad \vdash ((x \in (S \lhd R)) \Leftrightarrow ((x \in R) \wedge ((first\ x) \in S))), \\
&\quad \vdash ((x \in (S ⩤ R)) \Leftrightarrow ((x \in R) \wedge \neg((first\ x) \in S))), \\
&\quad \vdash ((x \in (A \oplus B)) \Leftrightarrow \\
&\qquad\qquad ((x \in B) \vee ((x \in A) \wedge \neg(\exists y\colon U \mid true \bullet (((first\ x), y) \in B))))), \\
&\quad \vdash ((first\ (x, y)) = x)] : thm\ list
\end{aligned}
$$

The theorem about *first* is included because *first* is introduced by several of the theorems, and ordered pairs are introduced by $\oplus$*_thm*. Between them they yield expressions of the form $first(x, y)$, and the proofs depend on simplification of these expressions.

A tactic may be defined using the proof strategy described above as follows:

ML

```
val SET_TAC = EVERY
 [Zrewrite_tac[Zset_eq_thm, ⊆_thm, ◁_thm1, ⩤_thm4, ⊕_thm, first_thm],
 REPEAT Zstrip_tac, Zres_tac, Zres_tac, Zasm_rewrite_tac[]];
```

HOL output

val SET_TAC = fn : tactic

Informally this says:

1. rewrite with the relevant theorems

2. strip the resulting goal

3. do two steps of "resolution" (forward inference on the assumptions)

4. rewrite the remaining subgoals using the available assumptions

The tactic may be used where the current goal is (an instance of) a theorem of the target group.

The proof may be faster if this tactic operates on the bare set theoretic fact rather than some complex instantiation of it, and therefore use of the following derived rule may be preferred. This takes a term which expresses a conjecture, and returns the corresponding theorem if it can be proven using *SET_TAC*, otherwise it fails.

ML
```
fun SET_RULE t = TAC_PROOF(([],t),SET_TAC);
```

HOL output
```
val SET_RULE = fn : TERM -> thm
```

Use of *SET_RULE* has the advantage of improving the intelligibility of the proof script by explicitly citing the theorem to be used in the script.

Two other lemmas are required which depend upon a better developed theory of arithmetic than is currently available for Z in the prototype. It is most convenient for present purposes to introduce these as new axioms, though they might instead have been cited as assumptions on the theorem to be proven.

ML
```
val le..lemma1 = new_axiom "le..lemma1" ⟦x ≤ y ⇒ (0 .. x) ⊆ (0 .. y)⟧;
val le..lemma2 = new_axiom "le..lemma2" ⟦¬ x ≤ y ⇒ (0 .. y) ⊆ (0 .. (x − 1))⟧;
```

7.2.2 application lemmas

It is convenient to convert the predicates defined in the specification into free variable equations as follows:

ML
```
val secure_sim = iff_simp (z_specification "–" "secure");
val state_secure_sim = iff_simp (z_specification "–" "state_secure");
val out_secure_sim = iff_simp (z_specification "–" "out_secure");
```

HOL output

$$
\begin{array}{l}
val\ secure\_sim = \vdash \\
\quad ((sys \in secure) \Leftrightarrow ((sys \in SYSTEM) \land \\
\qquad ((sys \in state\_secure) \land (sys \in out\_secure)))) : thm
\end{array}
$$

$$
\begin{array}{l}
val\ state\_secure\_sim = \vdash \\
\quad ((sys \in state\_secure) \Leftrightarrow ((sys \in SYSTEM) \land \\
\qquad (\forall class: \mathbb{N}; clear: \mathbb{N}; inp: IN; s: STATE2; s': STATE2 \\
\qquad \mid (((0 .. class) \lhd s) = ((0 .. class) \lhd s')) \bullet \\
\qquad (((0 .. class) \lhd (first\ (sys\ (clear, inp, s)))) \\
\qquad = ((0 .. class) \lhd (first\ (sys\ (clear, inp, s')))))))) : thm
\end{array}
$$

$$
\begin{array}{l}
val\ out\_secure\_sim = \vdash \\
\qquad ((sys \in out\_secure) \Leftrightarrow ((sys \in SYSTEM) \land \\
\qquad (\forall clear: \mathbb{N}; inp: IN; s: STATE2; s': STATE2 \\
\qquad \mid (((0 .. clear) \lhd s) = ((0 .. clear) \lhd s')) \bullet \\
\qquad ((second\ (sys\ (clear, inp, s))) = (second\ (sys\ (clear, inp, s'))))))) : thm
\end{array}
$$

Axiomatic descriptions of functions cannot be converted into theorems supporting unconditional rewriting (unless their domain happens to be a type). It is useful to have separate names for the two parts of the predicate associated with such a definition (the predicate implicit in the declaration part, and the explicit predicate).

ML

```
val [kidec, kipred] =
        CONJUNCTS (z_specification "–" "kernel_implementation");
val [condec, conpred] =
        CONJUNCTS (z_specification "–" "construction");
```

HOL output

```
val kidec = ⊢ (kernel_implementation ∈ KERNEL) : thm

val kipred =
  ⊢
  (∀clear: ℕ; inp: IN; state: STATE2; appl: APPLICATION | true •
        (((kernel_implementation appl) (clear, inp, state)) =
        ((state ⊕ ((0 .. (clear − 1)) ⩤
                (first (appl (inp, ((0 .. clear) ◁ state)))))),
                (second (appl (inp, ((0 .. clear) ◁ state))))))
: thm

val condec =
  ⊢ (construction ∈ ((APPLICATION × KERNEL) → SYSTEM)) : thm

val conpred =
  ⊢
  (∀appl: APPLICATION; kernel: KERNEL | true •
  ((construction (appl, kernel)) = (kernel appl)))
: thm
```

7.2.3 the main goal

Our objective is to prove that *kernel_implementation* is a *secure_kernel*.

ML

```
zset_goal([],⟦kernel_implementation ∈ secure_kernel⟧);
```

HOL output

```
(kernel_implementation ∈ secure_kernel)
```

First we expand the goal using definitions of *secure_kernel*, *secure*, *state_secure* and *out_secure*, and "strip" the resulting goal.

ML

```
ze (    Zrewrite_tac[kidec, secure_kernel_sim, secure_sim,
                state_secure_sim, out_secure_sim]
        THEN REPEAT Zstrip_tac);
```

HOL output

Note: *tactic produced 2 duplicated subgoals*
3 subgoals

$[(appl \in APPLICATION)]$
$[(clear \in \mathbb{N})]$
$[(inp \in IN)]$
$[(s \in STATE2)]$
$[(s' \in STATE2)]$
$[(((0 \,..\, clear) \lhd s) = ((0 \,..\, clear) \lhd s'))]$

$((second\ ((construction\ (appl, kernel\_implementation))\ (clear, inp, s)))$
$=$
$(second\ ((construction\ (appl, kernel\_implementation))\ (clear, inp, s'))))$

$[(appl \in APPLICATION)]$
$[(class \in \mathbb{N})]$
$[(clear \in \mathbb{N})]$
$[(inp \in IN)]$
$[(s \in STATE2)]$
$[(s' \in STATE2)]$
$[(((0 \,..\, class) \lhd s) = ((0 \,..\, class) \lhd s'))]$

$(((0 \,..\, class) \lhd$
$(first\ ((construction\ (appl, kernel\_implementation))\ (clear, inp, s))))$
$=$
$((0 \,..\, class) \lhd$
$(first\ ((construction\ (appl, kernel\_implementation))\ (clear, inp, s')))))$

$[(appl \in APPLICATION)]$

$((construction\ (appl, kernel\_implementation)) \in SYSTEM)$

The two subgoals listed first derive from the two properties (*out_secure* and *state_secure*) which a system must have in order to be secure.

The subgoal listed last (which is the *current* subgoal), is typical of the proof obligations arising in Z from the use of sets as if they were types. The decidable type-checking undertaken when the specification is entered leaves proof obligations of this kind which we would hope in due course to provide better automation for.

The proof makes use of the predicates implicit in the declarations of "construction" and "kernel_implementation" together with the following theorems about the cartesian product and function space constructors:

ML

```
[Z_pair_×_sym, fun_app_thm];
```

HOL output

$val\ it = [\vdash (((x \in X) \land (y \in Y)) \Leftrightarrow ((x, y) \in (X \times Y))),$
$\vdash (\forall f : (X \to Y); x : X \mid true \bullet ((f\ x) \in Y))\ ] : thm\ list$

We use forward inference on the assumptions by "resolution" to prove the subgoal, first adding the required declarations into the assumptions and then resolving with the rules.

ML
```
ze (EVERY[      ASSUME_TAC condec,
                ASSUME_TAC kidec,
                Zimp_res_tac Z_pair_×_sym,
                Zimp_res_tac fun_app_thm]);
```

This discharges the current subgoal.

HOL output
```
subgoal proved
2 subgoals
...
```

7.2.4 the state_secure subgoal

The next subgoal corresponds to demonstrating that a system built using the kernel has the *state_secure* property.

HOL output

$$[(appl \in APPLICATION)]$$
$$[(class \in \mathbb{N})]$$
$$[(clear \in \mathbb{N})]$$
$$[(inp \in IN)]$$
$$[(s \in STATE2)]$$
$$[(s' \in STATE2)]$$
$$[(((0 \,..\, class) \lhd s) = ((0 \,..\, class) \lhd s'))]$$

$$(((0 \,..\, class) \lhd (first\ ((construction\ (appl, kernel\_implementation))\ (clear, inp, s))))$$
$$=$$
$$((0 \,..\, class) \lhd (first\ ((construction\ (appl, kernel\_implementation))\ (clear, inp, s')))))$$

The subgoal is now progressed by expanding *construction* and *kernel_implementation*.

ML
```
ze (EVERY[      ASSUME_TAC kidec,
                Zimp_res_rewrite_tac conpred,
                Zimp_res_rewrite_tac kipred,
                Zrewrite_tac [first_thm]]);
```

HOL output

1 subgoal

$[(appl \in APPLICATION)]$
...
$[(((0 \mathinner{..} class) \lhd s) = ((0 \mathinner{..} class) \lhd s'))]$
$[(kernel\_implementation \in KERNEL)]$

$$(((0 \mathinner{..} class) \lhd (s \oplus ((0 \mathinner{..} (clear - 1)) \ntriangleleft (first\,(appl\,(inp, ((0 \mathinner{..} clear) \lhd s)))))))$$
$$=$$
$$((0 \mathinner{..} class) \lhd (s' \oplus ((0 \mathinner{..} (clear - 1)) \ntriangleleft (first\,(appl\,(inp, ((0 \mathinner{..} clear) \lhd s'))))))))$$

Now we have to think for a few moments to find a proof strategy. If $clear \leq class$ then $(0..clear) \subseteq (0..class)$ and, given:

$$(((0..class) \lhd s) = ((0..class) \lhd s'))$$

we can conclude that:

$$(0..clear) \lhd s) = (0..clear) \lhd s'$$

This fact may be used to rewrite the goal, changing the second occurence of s to s'. The resulting goal will be provable using:

$$(((0..class) \lhd s) = ((0..class) \lhd s'))$$

once more, with the theorem:

$$x \lhd z = x \lhd z' \Rightarrow x \lhd (z \oplus y) = x \lhd (z' \oplus y)$$

If $\neg clear \leq class$ then $0..class \subseteq 0..(clear - 1)$, and the theorem:

$$(A \subseteq B) \Rightarrow (A \lhd z) = (A \lhd z') \Rightarrow (A \lhd (z \oplus (B \ntriangleleft s))) = (A \lhd (z' \oplus (B \ntriangleleft s')))$$

suffices to prove the subgoal.

A case split on the proposition $clear \leq class$ is therefore chosen.

This is the only point at which the proof is not routine. The proof tool does not help you to discover the proof plan, this can only be done by scrutinising the subgoal and coming to an understanding of why it is true. This does not mean that I had to go away and do a pencil and paper proof before attempting the machine proof. Describing the proof plan was more difficult than formulating it, the description was written after the proof had been completed, and completing the formal proof on the machine was not much more difficult than describing the informal proof on paper.

The structure of the proof is not unconnected with the the intuition behind the design of the kernel. This involves the use of two filtering operations on classified data stores. The case split used reflects the fact that for data at some classification just one of these filters is sufficient to ensure that this data item does not receive downgraded information. Which filter is needed depends upon whether the class is less than the clearance of the user. If it is, a filter prevents the data being updated, if it is not, the other filter ensures that no more highly classified data is used in the computation of the new value.

The following command initiates the case split:

ML
```
ze (ASM_CASES_TAC⟦clear ≤ class⟧);
```

This gives two subgoals differing only in their last assumptions:

HOL output

2 subgoals

$[(appl \in APPLICATION)]$

...

$[(((0 \mathinner{..} class) \lhd s) = ((0 \mathinner{..} class) \lhd s'))]$

$[(kernel\_implementation \in KERNEL)]$

$[\neg(clear \leq class)]$

$$(((0 \mathinner{..} class) \lhd (s \oplus ((0 \mathinner{..} (clear - 1)) \unlhd (first\,(appl\,(inp, ((0 \mathinner{..} clear) \lhd s)))))))$$
$$=$$
$$((0 \mathinner{..} class) \lhd (s' \oplus ((0 \mathinner{..} (clear - 1)) \unlhd (first\,(appl\,(inp, ((0 \mathinner{..} clear) \lhd s'))))))))$$

$[(appl \in APPLICATION)]$

...

$[(((0 \mathinner{..} class) \lhd s) = ((0 \mathinner{..} class) \lhd s'))]$

$[(kernel\_implementation \in KERNEL)]$

$[(clear \leq class)]$

$$(((0 \mathinner{..} class) \lhd (s \oplus ((0 \mathinner{..} (clear - 1)) \unlhd (first\,(appl\,(inp, ((0 \mathinner{..} clear) \lhd s)))))))$$
$$=$$
$$((0 \mathinner{..} class) \lhd (s' \oplus ((0 \mathinner{..} (clear - 1)) \unlhd (first\,(appl\,(inp, ((0 \mathinner{..} clear) \lhd s'))))))))$$

The first of the previously cited arithmetic lemmas, $(\vdash x \leq y \Rightarrow 0..x \subseteq 0..y)$ is now used:

ML
```
ze (Zimp_res_tac le..lemma1);
```

reducing the conjecture to a result which can be seen to follow from purely set-theoretic principles:

HOL output

1 subgoal

$[(appl \in APPLICATION)]$

...

$[(((0 \mathinner{..} class) \lhd s) = ((0 \mathinner{..} class) \lhd s'))]$

$[(kernel\_implementation \in KERNEL)]$

$[(clear \leq class)]$

$[((0 \mathinner{..} clear) \subseteq (0 \mathinner{..} class))]$

$$(((0 \mathinner{..} class) \lhd (s \oplus ((0 \mathinner{..} (clear - 1)) \unlhd (first\,(appl\,(inp, ((0 \mathinner{..} clear) \lhd s)))))))$$
$$=$$
$$((0 \mathinner{..} class) \lhd (s' \oplus ((0 \mathinner{..} (clear - 1)) \unlhd (first\,(appl\,(inp, ((0 \mathinner{..} clear) \lhd s'))))))))$$

The truth of this goal is too subtle for *SET_TAC*, and it is easiest shown by first deriving and rewriting with $(0..clear) \lhd s = (0..clear) \lhd s'$.

ML

```
ze (Zimp_res_rewrite_tac (SET_RULE
        ⟦(A ⊆ B) ⇒ (B ◁ z) = (B ◁ z') ⇒ (A ◁ z) = (A ◁ z')⟧));
```

HOL output

1 subgoal

$[(appl \in APPLICATION)]$
...
$[(((0 .. class) \lhd s) = ((0 .. class) \lhd s'))]$
$[(kernel\_implementation \in KERNEL)]$
$[(clear \leq class)]$
$[((0 .. clear) \subseteq (0 .. class))]$
$[((((0 .. class) \lhd z) = ((0 .. class) \lhd z'))$
$\Rightarrow (((0 .. clear) \lhd z) = ((0 .. clear) \lhd z')))]$
$[(((0 .. clear) \lhd s) = ((0 .. clear) \lhd s'))]$

$(((0 .. class) \lhd$
$(s \oplus ((0 .. (clear - 1)) \lhd (first\ (appl\ (inp, ((0 .. clear) \lhd s')))))))$
$=$
$((0 .. class) \lhd$
$(s' \oplus ((0 .. (clear - 1)) \lhd (first\ (appl\ (inp, ((0 .. clear) \lhd s'))))))))$

This goal can now be discharged with the assistance of *SET_RULE*.

ML

```
ze (Zimp_res_rewrite_tac(
        SET_RULE ⟦x ◁ z = x ◁ z' ⇒ x ◁ (z ⊕ y) = x ◁ (z' ⊕ y)⟧));
```

HOL output

subgoal proved

We now return to the second case in the proof of the *state_secure* property.

HOL output

1 subgoal
$[(appl \in APPLICATION)]$
...
$[(((0 .. class) \lhd s) = ((0 .. class) \lhd s'))]$
$[(kernel\_implementation \in KERNEL)]$
$[\neg(clear \leq class)]$

$(((0 .. class) \lhd$
$(s \oplus ((0 .. (clear - 1)) \lhd (first\ (appl\ (inp, ((0 .. clear) \lhd s)))))))$
$=$
$((0 .. class) \lhd$
$(s' \oplus ((0 .. (clear - 1)) \lhd (first\ (appl\ (inp, ((0 .. clear) \lhd s'))))))))$

The proof of this depends on the the second of the arithmetic lemmas:

$$(\vdash \neg(x \leq y) \Rightarrow 0..y \subseteq 0..(x - 1))$$

together with the non-trivial but automatically provable result from set theory shown below:

ML
```
ze (EVERY[
 Zimp_res_then MP_TAC le..lemma2,
 UNDISCH_TAC ⟦(((0 .. class) ◁ (s⊕STATE2)) = ((0 .. class) ◁ s'))⟧,
 Zrewrite_tac[SET_RULE
         ⟦(A ◁ z) = (A ◁ z') ⇒ (A ⊆ B) ⇒
                    (A ◁ (z ⊕ (B ⩤ s))) = (A ◁ (z' ⊕ (B ⩤ s')))⟧]]);
```

This completes the subgoal relating to the *state_secure* property.

HOL output
```
subgoal proved
```

7.2.5 the out_secure subgoal

The final subgoal corresponds to demonstrating that a system built using the kernl has the *out_secure* property.

HOL output
```
1 subgoal
 [(appl ∈ APPLICATION)]
...
 [(((0 .. clear) ◁ s) = ((0 .. clear) ◁ s'))]

((second ((construction (appl, kernel_implementation)) (clear, inp, s)))
=
(second ((construction (appl, kernel_implementation)) (clear, inp, s'))))
```

We are now left with the subgoal corresponding to the property *out_secure*. Once again we begin by rewriting with the specifications of *construction* and *kernel_implementation*.

ML
```
ze (EVERY[      ASSUME_TAC kidec,
                Zimp_res_rewrite_tac conpred,
                Zimp_res_rewrite_tac kipred,
                Zasm_rewrite_tac [second_thm]]);
```

In this case this is sufficient to prove the subgoal and also completes the proof of the main goal.

HOL output
```
subgoal proved
main goal proved
val it = () : unit
```

ML
```
zsave_top_thm "kernel_secure";
```

HOL output

$val\ it = \vdash (kernel\_implementation \in secure\_kernel) : thm$

8 System Correctness Proposition

Even though we have said nothing about the behaviour of the application, we have done enough formal modelling to establish that a system built from *kernel_implementation* and an application using *construction* will be secure.

If the application is loosely specified as:

Z

$$\textbf{application} : APPLICATION$$

$$true$$

and the system as:

Z

$$\textbf{system} : SYSTEM$$

$$system = construction(application, kernel\_implementation)$$

The claim that this system is secure may then be expressed:

Z

$$\vdash ? \quad system \in secure$$

The proof of this conjecture is trivial given the two previous results.

9 Concluding Remarks

9.1 Methods

We have given tiny illustrations of formal methods similar to those which we have used in our applications over the past few years, together with some explanation of why these methods have been thought desirable (which inevitably appear as criticisms of more widely accepted methods).

I hope that this will help to broaden the debate about what formal methods are good for, and to encourage the view that formal notations such as Z are a flexible resource which can and should be used to support a variety of different methods, varying according to the application domain and the particular concerns which the formal modelling is intended to address.

9.2 Tools

This paper has illustrated the use of the prototype Z proof tool developed by ICL to a point at which it is possible to reason about small systems with reasonable facility. We have learned a great deal from this activity, and some of these lessons have been fed back into the design of the product quality ICL HOL system which is now being used for a re-implementation of the Z proof tool. The resulting tool is expected to be significantly improved on the tool used in preparing this paper, and we hope that it will be suitable for the much larger proofs required in the development of critical systems.

The challenge for non-critical systems is to bring automated reasoning about formal specifications to the point at which this can yield tangible *productivity* benefits. This demands not only developments in tools, but open minds and further innovation in methods and notations.

9.3 Acknowledgements

Both the methods and the tools are the result of teamwork, in a context in which publication of results and distribution of credit are subsidiary considerations. All the present and past members of the High Assurance Team at ICL Secure Systems have contributed to the work reported in this paper, as well as the many academics whose work we have exploited, particularly the groups at the Universities of Cambridge and Oxford who have been responsible for the development of HOL and Z.

The members of the High Assurance Team are: Rob Arthan, Kevin Blackburn, Adrian Hammon, Barry Homer, David King, Gill Prout, Geoff Scullard, Roger Stokes and myself.

References

[1] R.D. Arthan. Formal Specification of a Proof Tool. In S.Prehn and W.J.Toetenel, editors, *VDM '91, Formal Software Development Methods, LNCS 551*, volume 551, pages 356–370. Springer-Verlag, 1991.

[2] R.S. Boyer and J.S. Moore. *A Computational Logic Handbook.* Academic Press, 1988.

[3] Michael J.C. Gordon. HOL:A Proof Generating System for Higher-Order Logic. In G. Birtwistle and P. A. Subrahmanyam, editors, *VLSI Specification, Verification and Synthesis.* Kluwer, 1987.

[4] Michael J.C. Gordon, Arthur J. Milner, and Christopher P. Wadsworth. *Edinburgh LCF. Lecture Notes in Computer Science. Vol. 78.* Springer-Verlag, 1979.

[5] Jeremy Jacob. On The Derivation of Secure Components. *proc 1989 IEEE Symposium on Security and Privacy*, pages 242–247, 1989.

[6] R.Milner. A Theory of Type Polymorphism in Programming. *Journal of Computer and System Sciences*, 17:348–375, 1978.

[7] J.M. Spivey. *Understanding Z.* Cambridge University Press, 1988.

[8] J.M. Spivey. *The Z Notation: A Reference Manual.* Prentice-Hall, 1989.

Index of Formal Names

Refinement and Confidentiality

Colin O'Halloran
DRA
Malvern, Worcs. U.K.

Abstract

As computer systems become more powerful and cheaper they permeate more of our everyday life. With this greater reliance on the automated processing and movement of our personal information comes a duty to demonstrate that computer systems are secure. Unfortuneately refinement which preserves "functional" properties does not necessarily preserve properties concerning the confidentiality of information. In this paper a way of describing confidentiality properties independently from "functional" properties is described. The paper goes on to show when "functionality" and confidentiality can be preserved by refinement.

1 Introduction

At the moment refinement is a costly process in time and expertise, because of this it seems to be most suited to the production of safety-critical or secure systems where the cost can be justified. It is in the production of secure systems however where the use of functional refinement appears to fail. It is possible to specify a design of a system that exhibits some confidentiality properties and to refine that specification, using standard laws of refinement, into one that violates the confidentiality properties.

Example 1 In this paper the notation and theory of CSP is taken from [6]. If

$$P \triangleq a \rightarrow P \text{ and } Q \triangleq b \rightarrow Q$$

then for the system $P||Q$ an agent who can only see b events cannot tell what a events might have occurred. If

$$S \triangleq a \rightarrow b \rightarrow S$$

then S is a refinement of $P||Q$ in CSP, but the same agent seeing a b event knows that the event a must have occurred. The refinement has transformed the system $P||Q$ into a less "secure" one. $\triangle$

The other standard forms of refinement, for example [12], can also lead to "insecure" systems, this has been examined in [8].

One of the goals of specification is to liberate a designer of a system from considering **how** a system goes about achieving **what** is required. Unfortunately one of the most popular ways of specifying a system's confidentiality is to state **how** it functions and then assert that this means the system is secure. If refinement is used to produce the implementation then problems can arise.

If the specification is behaviourally equivalent to the implementation then one of the main goals of specification, abstraction, may have been lost.

Fortunately refinement and confidentiality can be reconciled, for example in [5] a sufficient condition for a refinement to preserve the confidentiality property of non-interference [3] is proved. In some situations non-interference is too restrictive, [16], and in others it is too weak, therefore a way of specifying general confidentiality properties and their behaviour under refinement is required.

In this paper category theory is used to place constraints on systems so that they satisfy some requirement for confidentiality. A framework for refinement relative to this constraint is then defined; and finally some initial results on valid refinements and their composition are established. The abstract categorical approach is applicable to many models of computation such as timed traces and refusals. Preliminary work on other models of computation include Petri nets and relational databases.

In section 2 an outline is given of a categorical approach to specifying confidentiality properties using information flow, this is a generalization of the work presented in [7]. The category theoretic approach allows the results to be applied more easily than if a conventional set theoretic approach had been taken. An example is given of a simple confidentiality specification and a system which satisfies it.

In section 3 some simple conditions for when a system satisfies a confidentiality specification are proved. In addition various results are proved about how a system, which satisfies a functional and confidentiality specification, can be composed with other such systems. These results indicate that the construction of a large system with confidentiality properties can be broken down into a number of simpler components which can then be assembled together.

2 A categorical construction of information flow

In this section an outline of the categorical approach to reasoning about information flow is described, for a full technical account the reader is referred to [13] or [15]. For the original formulation of this approach to reasoning about confidentiality the reader is referred to [7] or [9]. A category consists of a collection of objects and a collection of arrows between those objects. Examples of categories include preorders, where the objects are elements of the preorder and the ordering relation provides the unique arrow between two objects, and monoids, where there is a single object and monoid composition provides the arrows from the object back to itself. For an introduction to category theory see [4, 1].

To describe and reason about information flow the categorical approach is at two levels: the first is at an abstract level where no concrete interpretation is put upon the objects and arrows of the category; at the second level the objects can be instantiated with, for example, sets and the arrows with, for example, relations, this gives a concrete category. In an abstract category general definitions and results can be formulated independently of any one model of computation. In each concrete category the general results can be specialized to give powerful results in particular models of computation.

To provide an intuition for what an object in an abstract information flow category is consider what an everyday object, such as a flower or a chair, is. A flower can be observed in a number of ways and one can define the object *flower* as being the collection of all the observations associated with a flower: what it looks like; what it feels like; what it smells like and so on. A particular flower is a binding of all the possible observations of that flower, this binding can in some sense be thought of as the flower object. Similarly a computer system can also be regarded as the sum of the observations which can be made of it. At the physical level this would include the heat it radiates, its shape as well as the response it makes to input. At an abstract level the system might just be the set of all possible observable behaviours such as the events it can participate in or can refuse to participate in.

An observation of a system is some "snapshot" of that system, it may include everything the system has actually done up to that point. The observation of a system is one aspect of that system and can be represented as an object also, although it may not be as complex as the system object. The objects of an information flow category, or Iflow category, therefore include systems as well as observations of those systems. The arrows in an Iflow category provide a link between objects. If an object represents the behaviours of something then an arrow to another object is interpreted as meaning that the behaviours of the source object are consistent with the behaviours of the target object.

From an observation of a system one can also infer information about the behaviour of that system. For example from all the possible behaviours of a system one can infer from an observation that some of those behaviours could not have occurred, even if they are not directly observable, an example of this kind of inference arises from the observation of a b event in example 1. In an Iflow category the object representing inferred behaviour of a system has an arrow to both the object representing the system and the object representing the observation of that system. The object representing the strongest inference one can make from an observation of a system coincides with the categorical product of the observation and that system.

Categorical product is the fundamental construction which is used for constructing an inference of a system from an observation. The bold step is also taken of composing systems together via categorical product. Using the same categorical construction simplifies the theory needed to reason about confidentiality. Systems are also composed via the dual of product, coproduct. Product and coproduct composition of systems turn out to, more or less, coincide with parallel and choice composition of systems. To avoid exceptions to theorems developed in the abstract category all small products and coproducts are assumed to exist (the requirement for *small* products and coproducts is a category theoretic condition which means that any collection of objects which is a *set* has a product or a coproduct respecitively). To apply the theory developed in the abstract category suitable restrictions are assumed in the concrete categories. Product and coproduct also form the basis for defining conjunction and disjunction for a calculus for reasoning about inferences, or confidentiality statements, described in [13].

An initial object is assumed so that an inconsistent inference can be represented and thus avoided. This assumption is part of our desire to make the theory in the abstract category unexceptional, that is uniform. The initial object also has a rôle to play in making confidentiality statements where one doesn't care about the confidentiality properties of a system. This is analogous to allowing a specification of a system to be 'false', in which case any system would satisfy such a specification.

If an inconsistent inference arises then any further observation combined with that inference, using product, should be inconsistent; this makes categorical product strict. This strictness condition is necessary to build the calculus for reasoning about confidentiality statements. Another condition which is used to introduce implication and negation into the calculus is that when product is viewed as a functor it preserves coproducts.

The description and motivation for an information flow category can be summarised as: an information flow category, $\mathcal{IF}$, includes systems and observations of those systems as objects and satisfies these four assumptions:

- $\mathcal{IF}$ has all small products and coproducts.
- In $\mathcal{IF}$ the product of any object c with an initial object, **0**, is isomorphic to **0**.
- If b is an object of $\mathcal{IF}$ then the functors

  $$\lceil b \times \_ \rceil(x) = b \times x$$

  are assumed to preserve colimits over $\mathcal{IF}$.

In a preorder category product is greatest lower bound and coproduct is least upper bound; recall that small products and coproducts is a category theoretic condition which means that any collection of objects which is a *set* has a product or coproduct respectively, the general definition of products and coproducts means that such collections might not be sets. Any lattice satisfies the first postulate when it is viewed as a preorder category. Another example of a category which has small products and coproducts is **Set**, which has sets as objects and total functions between sets as arrows. The product of two objects in **Set** is cartesian product and coproduct is disjoint union. Note that in the category **Set** the product of all sets is not small because the collection of all sets is not a set, therefore although all small products exists in **Set** an arbitrary product does not. The condition that all small coproducts exist implies that an initial object exists, this is because the coproduct of the empty set of objects is an initial object. An initial object is a generalization of the bottom element of a preorder. In the category **Set** the initial object is the empty set. With the previous assumptions the semantic definition of a confidentiality statement can be given.

Definition 1 (Confidentiality Statements) *A confidentiality statement, $\mathcal{S}$, is a functor from $\mathcal{IF}$ to $\mathcal{IF}$ such that there exists a natural transformation to the identity functor of $\mathcal{IF}$:*

$$\mathcal{S} \stackrel{\bullet}{\rightarrow} Id_{\mathcal{IF}}$$

◇

A confidentiality statement takes an observation and gives another object representing the limit of inference which one wants. That is, given an observation, the functor specifies the most that can be inferred from that observation. The functor, by its definition, preserves any relationship between observations and the maximum inference.

If P is a system then the functor $\lceil P \times \_\rceil$ is a confidentiality statement, it gives the most that can be inferred about the system P from an observation. When a confidentiality statement, $\mathcal{S}$, has a natural transformation to $\lceil P \times \_\rceil$, then P is said to satisfy $\mathcal{S}$. The natural transformation condition for a confidentiality statement is because without it behaviours which were inconsistent with an observation could be used to limit the inference on that observation; this would be meaningless and could never be satisfied by any system P, since $\lceil P \times \_\rceil$ always has a natural transformation to the identity functor.

The work described in [13] or [15] shows how given these elementary definitions a calculus of confidentiality statements can be constructed which has a sound axiomatization and rule of inference, taken from non-intuitionistic logic. In this calculus flexible confidentiality requirements can be formalized and systems can be shown to satisfy these confidentiality specifications. Before looking at a specific information flow category some notation is introduced.

Notation

$\wedge_{\mathrm{IF}}$ and $\vee_{\mathrm{IF}}$ denote the operators for conjunction and disjunction respectively in the calculus of confidentiality statements constructed in [15].

A concrete Iflow category

Because of constraints of space only one example of a concrete Iflow category is given. Two other instances of Iflow categories involving timed traces and refusals are described in [14]. The category of refusal behaviours is not a preorder although it does have a wide subcategory (i.e. has all the objects of the refusal category in the subcategory) which is a preorder and where the ordering reflects refinement. Preliminary work on a Petri net formulation described in [11] indicates that this is a fourth instance. To illustrate the abstract definitions of an Iflow category a concrete category over one of the simplest semantic models for CSP, that is sets of traces, is defined.

Definition 2 (Safety-Iflow) *The objects of Safety-Iflow are all pairs of the form:*

$$(A, T)$$

where A is any subset of an alphabet Σ and T is any subset of A^*, $A = \{\}$ only when $T = \{\langle\rangle\}$ (and not when $T = \{\}$).

An arrow exists from (A, T) to (B, U) if and only if

$$B \subseteq A \wedge T \upharpoonright B \subseteq U \text{ and is denoted } (A, T) \preceq (B, U)$$

◇

Safety-Iflow is shown to satisfy the four postulates for an information flow category in [13] and [15]. A confidentiality statement over Safety-Iflow is a monotonic function which gives a result which is less than its argument. In Safety-Iflow confidentiality statements have a particular representation.

Definition 3 *If (A, T) is an object of Safety-Iflow then*

From $l : A^* \mid C$ **MAY_INFER** $P(tr)$ **Over** B^*

denotes the monotonic function which maps the object $(A, \{l\})$, drawn from the set $\{\, (A, \{t\}) \mid t \in A^* \wedge C \,\}$ (where C is a predicate constraining the set A^*), to an object denoted by $(B, P(tr))$ (where $P(tr)$ is a predicate with a free variable tr over B^*) such that

$$(B, \{\, tr : B^* \mid P(tr) \,\}) \preceq (A, \{l\})$$

◇

Note that because $(B, \{\, tr : B^* \mid P(tr) \,\}) \preceq (A, \{l\})$ the monotonic function

From $l : A^* \mid C$ **MAY_INFER** $P(tr)$ **Over** B^*

has a natural transformation to the identity function via the arrows of the partial order, that is the $\preceq$ relation, thus any monotonic function of this form is a confidentiality statement over Safety-Iflow. If the constraining predicate C is *true* then for the rest of the paper it shall be omitted.

Example 2 A confidentiality statement which captures a well known property in the field of information flow security is the following:

From $l : \{b\}^*$
MAY_INFER $tr \upharpoonright \{b\} = l \wedge tr \upharpoonright \{b\} = tr \backslash \{a\} \upharpoonright \{b\}$
Over $\{a, b\}^*$

This confidentiality statement is over potential observations of a system characterized by the set

$$\{\, (\{b\}, \{l\}) \mid l \in \{b\}^* \,\}$$

The pair which gives the limit of inference denotes another object of Safety-Iflow where the second component is the characteristic predicate for a set of traces. Informally the confidentiality statement says that for any observation of b events the interaction of a events must not interfere with that observation. Any system which satisfies this specification will have the property that interactions through $\{a\}$ will non-interfere with interactions through $\{b\}$. That is whatever b events are observed there is no way of inferring what a events might have occurred.

△

If an object (A, T) is such that T is prefix closed and non-empty then that object is a system with alphabet A. In example 2, a confidentiality specification over a set of potential observations was defined. In general not all of the observations over which a specification is defined will be possible observations of a particular system. In this case it is not sensible to compare a system with its confidentiality specification outside of the set of its possible observations and some restriction is needed. The particular observations of a system P can be precisely characterized in Safety-Iflow.

Definition 4 *If P is a system and W is a set of subsets of the alphabet of P, denoted αP, then*

$$P_W \triangleq \{(\alpha(w), t \restriction \alpha(w)) \mid w : W \wedge t \in \tau P\}$$

that is P_W is the set of observations through a sub-alphabet of P such that there is a corresponding trace in P. $\diamond$

Example 3 If

$$P = (\{a, b, c\}, \{\langle\rangle, \langle a\rangle, \langle a, b\rangle\})$$

and

$$W = \{\{a\}, \{c\}\}$$

then

$$P_W = \{((\{c\}, \{\langle\rangle\}), (\{a\}, \{\langle\rangle\}), (\{a\}, \{\langle a\rangle\}))\}$$

$\triangle$

The set P_W in example 3 gives all the possible observations which could be made of P by a user who had only the event a available. In more realistic examples there would be a number of users each with a different set of events available to each user, this would provide each user with a different view or window onto the system. The next definition shows how a system can be compared with a confidentiality specification with respect to its possible observations.

Definition 5 (**s-sat**^{W}) *If P is a system and $\mathcal{S}$ is a confidentiality statement then P is said to satisfy $\mathcal{S}$ through the sub-alphabets of W, denoted*

$$P \ \textbf{s-sat}^{W} \ \mathcal{S}$$

if and only if

$$(P_W \lhd \mathcal{S}) \stackrel{\bullet}{\rightarrow} (P_W \lhd \lceil P \times \_\rceil)$$

that is there is a natural transformation from $\mathcal{S}$ (restricted to P_W) to $\lceil P \times \_\rceil$ (when it is restricted to P_W). $\diamond$

The constraint that there is a natural transformation from the confidentiality statement to the product of the system with its observations, means that at each observation one can infer less than that specified by the confidentiality statement. An example of the use of confidentiality statements to specify the confidentiality requirement of a message filter is now given.

Example 4 If *Input* denotes messages on a input channel and *Conf* and *Unclass* denote messages on confidential and unclassified channels then a functional specification for a message filter is that it behaves like a buffer.

$$BUFFER\_SPEC \triangleq tr \restriction (Conf \cup Unclass) \leq tr \restriction Input$$

The messages input are output, via the channels *Conf* and *Unclass*, in the same order and without anything being added or removed. For convenience the set of messages on the confidential and unclassified channel are grouped together.

$$CU \triangleq Conf \cup Unclass \text{ and } CUI \triangleq Conf \cup Unclass \cup Input$$

An object of Safety-Iflow which corresponds to the buffer specification is

$$S \triangleq (CUI, \{tr : CUI^* \mid BUFFER\_SPEC\})$$

S establishes what the functional behaviour of a message filter is but says nothing about its confidentiality properties. If

$$CONSISTENCY \triangleq tr \upharpoonright Unclass = l$$

is the predicate which links possible inferences back to the trace of an observation l; and

$$CONFIDENTIALITY \triangleq tr \upharpoonright Conf \in Conf^*$$

is the predicate which states that the most that can be inferred is that some trace of confidential communication has taken place (the predicate is equivalent to *true*, but is written as above to indicate that it is confidential messages that we are interested in); and

$$FILT\_INFERENCE \triangleq CONSISTENCY \wedge CONFIDENTIALITY$$

then a confidentiality specification for a message filter is

$$\mathcal{S} \triangleq \left\{ \begin{array}{l} \textbf{From } l : Unclass^* \\ \textbf{MAY\_INFER } FILT\_INFERENCE \textbf{ Over } CU^* \end{array} \right.$$

This confidentiality specification says that the most that can be inferred from an observation of events visible to an unclassified user is that any number of confidential events might have occurred. Given the safety and confidentiality specifications, candidate systems can be checked against them. If

$$SECURE\_FILTER \triangleq input?x \rightarrow \left(\begin{array}{l} y \rightarrow conf!x \rightarrow SECURE\_FILTER \\ \| \\ n \rightarrow unclass!x \rightarrow SECURE\_FILTER \end{array} \right)$$

then *SECURE_FILTER* receives a message and depending on some external agent, which decides whether a message is confidential or not, and outputs the message on the confidential or unclassified channel. Note that if desired the external agent's actions can be specified separately and conjoined with the buffer specification.

Hiding the events $\{y, n\}$ which determine whether a message is confidential or not gives a system which satisfies the buffer specification.

$$SECURE\_FILTER \backslash \{y, n\} \textbf{ sat } S$$

Because the confidentiality specification is in terms of only confidential and unclassified events it is necessary to restrict *SECURE_FILTER* appropriately. It can be shown, using techniques from [14], that the restricted system satisfies the confidentiality specification. Another way of showing that this satisfaction holds will be demonstrated later in the paper.

$$SECURE\_FILTER \upharpoonright CU \ \ \mathbf{s\text{-}sat}^{\{Unclass\}} \ \mathcal{S}$$

△

Note that in the previous example the specification for the buffer can be replaced by a specification of a system which delivers messages according to some priority scheme, the confidentiality specification is independent of the "functional" specification. Confidentiality statements capture only confidentiality specifications and can be re-used for different functional requirements.

3 Refinement

In this section the composition of systems, functional and confidentiality specifications is considered with respect to refinement. A proposition is proved which gives a necessary condition for a system to satisfy functionality and confidentiality. The term functionality is used loosely, functionality can be a safety specification or include liveness, and timeliness constraints.

Assumption It is assumed for the rest of this paper that functional specifications as well as systems and observations are objects in an Information flow category.

A safety specification in Safety-Iflow is just a non-empty set of traces, in the categories for timed traces and refusals a "functional" specification is a set of timed traces and set of trace refusal pairs respectively; these functional specifications reflect timeliness and liveness constraints respectively. In the rest of the section results are given about how systems respect confidentiality and functionality under product and coproduct. The refinement discussed in this section concerns functional rather than information flow refinement. To state the proposition concerning satisfaction of functionality and confidentiality the following auxiliary definition is made.

Definition 6 *If $\mathcal{IF}$ has a preorder subcategory, denoted $\mathcal{IF}_{\sqsubseteq}$, which models functional refinement then $P \sqsubseteq Q$ denotes the unique arrow from the object Q to the object P.*

$P \not\sqsubseteq Q$ denotes the fact that there are no arrows from the object Q to the object P. ◇

If P and Q are systems and S is a functional specification then

$$P \sqsubseteq Q$$

means that Q is better than P, or Q is a refinement of P.

$$P \, \mathbf{sat} \, S$$

means that $S \sqsubseteq P$. This follows the convention in CSP where if $traces(Q) \subseteq traces(P)$ then $P \sqsubseteq Q$ or if the failures of Q are a subset of the failures of P then again $P \sqsubseteq Q$. For Petri nets the existence of an implementation morphism (as defined in [11]) from N to N' reflects a refinement. The following proposition generalises a result due to He Jifeng, [10].

Proposition 1 *If* Func *is a functional specification, S a confidentiality statement and P* **sat** Func, *that is* Func $\sqsubseteq P$ *then*

$$\exists l : \mathrm{Func}_W \cdot \mathrm{Func} \not\sqsubseteq \mathcal{S}(l)$$
$$\Longrightarrow$$
$$\nexists P \cdot l \in P_W \ \wedge \ P\ \mathbf{sat}\ \mathrm{Func} \wedge P \ \ \mathbf{s\text{-}sat}^{\mathrm{w}} \ \ \mathcal{S}$$

that is if there is an observation, l, for which there are no arrows from $\mathcal{S}(l)$ to Func *then there is no system P, with the observation l, which can satisfy both the functional and confidentiality specifications.*

Proof Suppose for a contradiction that $\mathrm{Func} \not\sqsubseteq \mathcal{S}(l)$ but

$$\exists P \cdot l \in P_W \wedge \mathrm{Func} \sqsubseteq P \wedge P \ \ \mathbf{s\text{-}sat}^{\mathrm{w}} \ \ \mathcal{S}.$$

Now

$$\mathrm{Func} \sqsubseteq P \Longrightarrow \mathrm{Func} \times l \sqsubseteq P \times l \tag{1}$$

by definition of product, but

$$\begin{aligned}
P \ \ \mathbf{s\text{-}sat}^{\mathrm{w}} \ \ \mathcal{S} \ &\Longrightarrow (P_W \ \rhd \mathcal{S}) \stackrel{\bullet}{\rightarrow} (P_W \ \rhd \lceil P \times _\rceil) \\
&\quad [\text{By definition of } \ \mathbf{s\text{-}sat}^{\mathrm{w}} \ .] \\
&\Longrightarrow \forall l : P_W \cdot P \times l \sqsubseteq \mathcal{S}(l) \\
&\quad [\text{By definition of } \stackrel{\bullet}{\rightarrow}.] \\
&\Longrightarrow \forall l : P_W \cdot \mathrm{Func} \times l \sqsubseteq \mathcal{S}(l) \\
&\quad [\text{By 1 above and transitivity of } \sqsubseteq.] \\
&\Longrightarrow \forall l : P_W \cdot \mathrm{Func} \sqsubseteq \mathcal{S}(l) \\
&\quad [\text{By definition of product.}]
\end{aligned}$$

that is there is always and arrow from $\mathcal{S}(l)$ to Func, this contradicts our hypothesis, therefore proving the proposition. □

This proposition tells the designer that if they find an observation, such that the allowable inference associated with that observation has no arrow to the object representing the desired functionality of a system, then that observation must be removed by the refinement.

Example 5 Consider the following simple confidentiality specification

$$\begin{aligned}
&\mathbf{From}\ \langle\rangle : \{x,y\}^* \ \mathbf{MAY_INFER}\ tr \in \{\langle\rangle, \langle b\rangle\}\ \mathbf{Over}\ \{x,y,b\}^* \\
&\mathbf{From}\ \langle x\rangle : \{x,y\}^* \ \mathbf{MAY_INFER}\ tr \in \{\langle x\rangle, \langle b,x\rangle\}\ \mathbf{Over}\ \{x,y,b\}^* \\
&\mathbf{From}\ \langle y\rangle : \{x,y\}^* \ \mathbf{MAY_INFER}\ tr \in \{\langle y\rangle, \langle y,b\rangle\}\ \mathbf{Over}\ \{x,y,b\}^*
\end{aligned}$$

If the system

$$P \triangleq (b \to x \to STOP \mid y \to b \to STOP)$$

is taken as the functional specification then this is represented by the object

$$P' = (\{x, y, b\}, \{\langle\rangle, \langle b\rangle, \langle b, x\rangle, \langle y\rangle, \langle y, b\rangle\}).$$

The observation $(\{x, y\}, \{\langle x\rangle\})$ is mapped, by the above confidentiality statement, to the object $(\{x, y, b\}, \{\langle x\rangle, \langle b, x\rangle\})$, but there is no arrow from this to P' since $\langle x\rangle \notin P'$. Any refinement of P cannot allow the observation $(\{x, y\}, \{\langle x\rangle\})$ if it is to satisfy the above confidentiality specification. The system

$$Q \triangleq (b \to STOP \mid y \to b \to STOP)$$

is a refinement of P which does not have the offending observation and by inspection satisfies the above confidentiality specification when it is restricted to the observations $Q_{\{\{x,y\}\}}$, that is $(\{x, y, b\}, \{\langle\rangle\})$ and $(\{x, y, b\}, \{\langle y\rangle\})$. $\triangle$

A functional refinement relation generally reflects the fact that one system is more constrained or predictable. This means that one is more certain about what a system will do, the opposite of confidentiality. The conflict between confidentiality and functional refinement has been described in [8]. Restricting our attention to preorder categories leads to some simple but very useful results.

Theorem 1 *In $\mathcal{IF}_{\sqsubseteq}$ if $S \sqsubseteq P$ and $T \sqsubseteq Q$ are refinements of S by P and T by Q respectively then the usual refinement properties hold:*

i) $S \sqsubseteq P \wedge T \sqsubseteq Q \Longrightarrow S \times T \sqsubseteq P \times Q$

ii) $S \sqsubseteq P \wedge T \sqsubseteq Q \Longrightarrow S + T \sqsubseteq P + Q$

Proof **i)** and **ii)** follow by definition of categorical product and coproduct. □

This is important because it allows the construction of large functional specifications and systems from simpler components via the categorical operators of product and coproduct. In concrete categories product and coproduct turn out to be familiar operators. The construction of large systems from simpler components applies to confidentiality as well as functionality.

Corollary 1

$$S \sqsubseteq P \;\wedge\; T \sqsubseteq Q \;\wedge\; P \textbf{ s-sat}^{\text{w}}\; \mathcal{S} \;\wedge\; Q \textbf{ s-sat}^{\text{w}}\; \mathcal{T}$$
$$\Longrightarrow$$
$$S \times T \sqsubseteq P \times Q \;\wedge\; P \times Q \textbf{ s-sat}^{\text{w}}\; \mathcal{S} \wedge_{\text{IF}} \mathcal{T}$$

Proof

By theorem 1 and a result proved in both[13] and [14]. □

As indicated the importance of product and coproduct in the results given lies in their instantiation in concrete categories.

Lemma 1 *In Safety-Iflow if P and Q are processes and S and T are trace specifications then*

$$\begin{aligned} P \times Q &= P \| Q \\ P + Q &= P [\!] Q \\ S \times T &= S(tr \upharpoonright \alpha S) \wedge T(tr \upharpoonright \alpha T) \end{aligned}$$

Proof

See [14] or [13] □

The construction of concrete categories should be done in such a way that coproduct and especially product correspond to some meaningful construction. In the category of timed traces categorical product corresponds to parallel composition, [14]; in the refusals category product is not quite parallel composition, but from the point of view of reasoning about confidentiality properties it is equivalent, [14]; to be precise there is a natural transformation between both product and parallel composition, when they are used as functors for determining the inference from an observation. In [11] the categorical product of two Petri nets corresponds to their parallel composition and coproduct to non-deterministic choice. This category is of particular theoretical interest because, by applying appropriate constraints, the semantics of a range of process algebras can, in principle, be modelled by Petri nets.

Example 6 Suppose a buffer is required which may store no more than a hundred messages. A specification for such a buffer is

$$FIN\_BUFFER\_SPEC \triangleq tr \upharpoonright (Rest \cup Unclass) \leq^{100} tr \upharpoonright In$$

where *Rest* is the set of messages on a restricted channel and *Unclass* is the set of messages on the unclassified channel of example 4. For convenience the following abbreviation is made.

$$RUI \triangleq Rest \cup Unclass \cup In$$

The object denoted by the specification *FIN_BUFFER_SPEC* is

$$T \triangleq (RUI, \{tr : RUI^* \mid FIN\_BUFFER\_SPEC\})$$

To define the confidentiality specification, in this case, it is necessary to define some auxiliary functions on traces. The first function selects the odd numbered elements from a sequence of events.

$$odd(\langle\rangle) = \langle\rangle$$
$$odd(l^\frown\langle u\rangle) = \begin{cases} odd(l)^\frown\langle u\rangle & \textit{If } \#l \textit{ is even} \\ odd(l) & \textit{else} \end{cases}$$

For example

$$odd(\langle u, v, w\rangle) = \langle u, w\rangle.$$

The counterpart of the function odd is the function *even*.

$$even(\langle\rangle) = \langle\rangle$$
$$even(l^\frown\langle u\rangle) = \begin{cases} even(l)^\frown\langle u\rangle & \textit{If } \#l \textit{ is odd} \\ even(l) & \textit{else} \end{cases}$$

For example

$$even(\langle u, v, w\rangle) = \langle v\rangle.$$

The final function on traces which is used in the confidentiality specification is $\downarrow$ which is defined and used in [6]. The function $\downarrow$ *channelname* restricts a trace to messages on the named channel. For example

$$\langle rest.x, rest.y, unclass.x\rangle \downarrow rest = \langle x, y\rangle.$$

These functions are composed together in the confidentiality specification to act on traces, for example

$$\begin{aligned} odd(\langle rest.x, rest.y, unclass.x\rangle \downarrow rest) &= \langle x\rangle \\ &= odd(\langle unclass.x\rangle \downarrow unclass) \end{aligned}$$

and

$$even(\langle rest.x, rest.y, unclass.x\rangle \downarrow rest) = \langle y\rangle$$

The confidentiality specification consists of three requirements.

$$CONSISTENT \triangleq tr \upharpoonright Unclass = l$$

The first requirement insists that any inferred behaviour must be consistent with an observation, although l is free in this predicate it will be bound in the actual specification.

$$KNOWN \triangleq odd(tr \downarrow Rest) = l \downarrow Unclass$$

The second requirement insists that the first message passed along the restricted channel, and then every odd numbered communication, must be consistent with the message passed down the unclassified channel.

$$RESTRICT \triangleq even(tr \downarrow Rest) \in Mess^*$$

The final requirement is that any message can be passed down the restricted channel and that it cannot be influenced by the communications on the unclassified channel. Putting these together gives the following confidentiality specification.

$$\mathcal{T} \triangleq \begin{cases} \textbf{From } l : Unclass^* \\ \textbf{MAY\_INFER } CONSISTENT \wedge KNOWN \wedge RESTRICT \\ \textbf{Over } RU^* \end{cases}$$

where $RU \triangleq Rest \cup Unclass$

The confidentiality specification states that when a message is output on the unclassified channel then one can infer that two messages may have been input, but one cannot infer the value of the first message received on the input channel. All that can be inferred about it is that it can be output along the restricted channel. This specification allows some inference to be made about messages output on the restricted channel but places limits on it. Note also that the restricted channel interferes with the unclassified channel. If

$$R\_FILTER \triangleq (in?x \rightarrow in?y \rightarrow rest!x \rightarrow rest!y \rightarrow unclass!x \rightarrow R\_FILTER)$$

then

$$R\_FILTER \ \mathbf{sat} \ T \wedge (R\_FILTER \upharpoonright RU) \ \ \mathbf{s\text{-}sat}^{\{\mathrm{Unclass}\}} \ \ \mathcal{T}$$

R_FILTER will be proved to satisfy $\mathcal{T}$ later in example 7. By corollary 1 and lemma 1 we can take the system, *SECURE_FILTER*, of example 4 and place it in parallel with *R_FILTER* and know that *SECURE_FILTER*||*R_FILTER* satisfies the specifications S and T and the confidentiality specifications $\mathcal{S}$ and $\mathcal{T}$. That is

$$(SECURE\_FILTER \backslash \{y, n\}) || R\_FILTER$$
$$\mathbf{sat}$$
$$S(tr \upharpoonright \alpha SECURE\_FILTER) \wedge T(tr \upharpoonright \alpha R\_FILTER)$$

and

$$(SECURE\_FILTER \upharpoonright CU) || (R\_FILTER \upharpoonright RU) \ \ \mathbf{s\text{-}sat}^{\{\mathrm{Unclass}\}} \ \ \mathcal{S} \wedge_{\mathrm{IF}} \mathcal{T}.$$

In Safety-Iflow $\mathcal{S} \wedge_{\mathrm{IF}} \mathcal{T}$ can be combined to give one confidentiality statement.

$$\mathcal{S} \wedge_{\mathrm{IF}} \mathcal{T}$$
$$=$$
$$\left\{ \begin{array}{l} \textbf{From } l : Unclass^* \\ \textbf{MAY\_INFER } FILT\_INFERENCE \wedge REST\_INFERENCE \\ \textbf{Over } (RU \cup CU)^* \end{array} \right.$$

where

$$REST\_INFERENCE \triangleq CONSISTENT \wedge KNOWN \wedge RESTRICT$$

△

In order to state the rest of the results on refinement the following definition is made.

Definition 7 $\bigwedge X$ *and* $\bigvee X$ *denote the greatest lower bound and least upper bound of a set* X. ◇

Expressing a confidentiality requirement as a function over a set of observations is a natural way of specifying confidentiality, especially if the confidentiality property is discretionary. To compare a system or functional specification with such a confidentiality specification means that the system (or functional specification) has to be used to define a function for determining actual inference. Although this can be done, and leads to tractable proof techniques, it is also possible to collapse a confidentiality specification down into a single object, which (although an unintuitive representation of confidentiality) is simpler to compare with systems and functional specifications. The following theorem shows that confidentiality can be reasoned about on the same level as systems, observations and functional specifications.

Theorem 2 *In $\mathcal{IF}_{\sqsubseteq}$ if W is a set of subsets of the alphabet of P and $\mathcal{S}$ is a confidentiality statement then*

$$P \sqsubseteq \bigvee \mathcal{S}(\!| P_W |\!) \Longrightarrow P \ \textbf{s-sat}^{W} \ \mathcal{S}$$

Proof By definition of least upper bound (or coproduct) we have

$$\forall o : O \cdot P \sqsubseteq \mathcal{S}(o).$$

By definition of product and the fact that by its definition $\mathcal{S}$ has a natural transformation to the identity it must be the case that

$$\forall o : O \cdot P \times o \sqsubseteq \mathcal{S}(o).$$

Now

$$\begin{aligned} \forall o : O \cdot P \times o \sqsubseteq \mathcal{S}(o) &\iff \mathcal{S} \stackrel{\bullet}{\rightarrow} \lceil \bigvee \mathcal{S}(\!| P_W |\!) \times \_\rceil \\ &\iff \lceil \bigvee \mathcal{S}(\!| P_W |\!) \times \_\rceil \stackrel{\bullet}{\leftarrow} \mathcal{S} \end{aligned} \qquad (2)$$

since in a preorder category the natural transformation diagram commutes because of uniqueness of arrows. Finally we have

$$P \sqsubseteq \bigvee \mathcal{S}(\!| P_W |\!) \iff \lceil P \times \_\rceil \stackrel{\bullet}{\leftarrow} \lceil \bigvee \mathcal{S}(\!| P_W |\!) \times \_\rceil$$

[By definition of product and uniqueness of arrows in a preorder.]

$$\Longrightarrow \lceil P \times \_\rceil \stackrel{\bullet}{\leftarrow} \mathcal{S}$$

[By 2 above and transitivity of $\stackrel{\bullet}{\leftarrow}$.]

$$\iff P \ \textbf{s-sat}^{W} \ \mathcal{S}$$

□

This theorem states that, in an information flow category in which there exists a wide preorder sub-category reflecting refinement, a sufficient condition for "secure" functional refinement can be expressed as being in an interval. The upper bound of the interval in the preorder is the functional specification and the lower bound is the least upper bound of the image of the confidentiality statement. The theorem allows a designer to take a confidentiality statement, calculate the least upper bound and thus generate a proof obligation for secure refinement. If this condition is not met the system may still be secure since it is only a sufficient condition.

Example 7 If $\mathcal{T}$ and *R_FILTER* are as defined in example 6 with $W = \{Unclass\}$ then

$$\bigvee \mathcal{S}(\!| R\_FILTER_W |\!)$$
$$= (RU, \bigcup_{l \in Unclass^*} \{tr : RU^* \mid CONSISTENT \wedge KNOWN \wedge RESTRICT\})$$
$$= (RU, \{tr : RU^* \mid \exists l \in Unclass^* \cdot CONSISTENT \wedge KNOWN \wedge RESTRICT\})$$
$$= \left(RU, \left\{ tr : RU^* \;\middle|\; \begin{array}{l} tr \upharpoonright Unclass \in Unclass^* \\ \wedge \\ odd(tr \downarrow Rest) = tr \upharpoonright Unclass \\ \wedge \\ even(tr \downarrow Rest) \in Mess^* \end{array} \right\} \right)$$

From this point it is simple, but tedious, to show

$$tr \in \bigvee \mathcal{S}(\!| R\_FILTER_W |\!) \Longrightarrow tr \in traces(R\_FILTER \upharpoonright RU).$$

Establishing this means that by theorem 2

$$R\_FILTER \ \textbf{s-sat}^{\{\text{Unclass}\}} \ \mathcal{T}$$

This proves the claim made in example 6. △

The next theorem shows that with an additional assumption a necessary and sufficient condition can be used for refinement.

Corollary 2 *In $\mathcal{IF}_{\sqsubseteq}$, if P is a system, $\mathcal{S}$ is a confidentiality statement over observations P_W through a set of alphabets W, and*

$$\lceil \bigvee \mathcal{S}(\!| P_W |\!) \times \_\rceil = (P_W \rhd \mathcal{S})$$

then

$$P \sqsubseteq \bigvee \mathcal{S}(\!| P_W |\!) \Longleftrightarrow P \ \textbf{s-sat}^{\text{W}} \ \mathcal{S}$$

Proof

By the same proof as theorem 2 except

$$\lceil P \times \_\rceil \stackrel{\bullet}{\leftarrow} \lceil \bigvee \mathcal{S}(\!| P_W |\!) \times \_\rceil \Longrightarrow \lceil P \times \_\rceil \stackrel{\bullet}{\leftarrow} \mathcal{S}$$

can be strengthened to

$$\lceil P \times \_\rceil \stackrel{\bullet}{\leftarrow} \lceil \bigvee \mathcal{S}(\!| P_W |\!) \times \_\rceil \Longleftrightarrow \lceil P \times \_\rceil \stackrel{\bullet}{\leftarrow} \mathcal{S}$$

since $\lceil \bigvee \mathcal{S}(\!| P_W |\!) \times \_\rceil = (P_W \rhd \mathcal{S})$. □

This very useful result can be used in the practical development of systems. An example of when this holds comes from example 4.

Example 8 If $\mathcal{S}$ and *SECURE_FILTER* are as defined in example 4 and $W = \{Unclass\}$ then

$$\bigvee \mathcal{S}(\!|\ SECURE\_FILTER_W\ |\!) = (CU, CU^*)$$

therefore for any observation $(Unclass, \{l\})$ in $SECURE\_FILTER_W$

$$\begin{aligned}
&\lceil \bigvee \mathcal{S}(\!|\ SECURE_FILTER_W\ |\!) \times _\rceil\ (Unclass, \{l\})\\
&= \lceil (CU, CU^*) \times _\rceil\ (Unclass, \{l\})\\
&= (CU, CU^*) \times (Unclass, \{l\})\\
&= (CU, \{\, tr : CU^* \mid tr \restriction Unclass = l\,\})\\
&= (CU, \{\, tr : CU^* \mid tr \restriction Unclass = l \wedge tr \restriction Conf \in Conf^*\,\}
\end{aligned}$$

therefore

$$\lceil \bigvee \mathcal{S}(\!|\ SECURE\_FILTER_W\ |\!) \times \_\rceil = (SECURE\_FILTER_W\ \rhd \mathcal{S})$$

Now $(CU, traces(SECURE\_FILTER) \restriction CU) = (CU, CU^*)$ and

$$\bigvee \mathcal{S}(\!|\ SECURE\_FILTER_W\ |\!) = (CU, CU^*)$$

therefore by corollary 2 it must be the case that

$$(SECURE\_FILTER \restriction CU)\ \textbf{s-sat}^{\{Unclass\}}\ \mathcal{S}.$$

This proves the claim made at the end of example 4. △

Some other simple but useful corollaries follow from theorems 1 and 2.

Corollary 3 *In* $\mathcal{IF}_{\sqsubseteq}$, *if* $\mathcal{S}$, $\mathcal{T}$ *are confidentiality statements over observations* P_W *and* Q_W *respectively through windows in* W, *and*

$$P \sqsubseteq \bigvee \mathcal{S}(\!|\ P_W\ |\!) \wedge Q \sqsubseteq \bigvee \mathcal{T}(\!|\ Q_W\ |\!)$$

then

i) $P \times Q\ \textbf{s-sat}^{W}\ \mathcal{S} \wedge_{\mathrm{IF}} \mathcal{T}$

and

ii) $P + Q\ \textbf{s-sat}^{W}\ \mathcal{S} \vee_{\mathrm{IF}} \mathcal{T}$

Proof

$$\begin{aligned}
P \sqsubseteq \bigvee \mathcal{S}(\!|\ P_W\ |\!) \wedge Q \sqsubseteq \bigvee \mathcal{T}(\!|\ Q_W\ |\!) &\implies P \times Q \sqsubseteq \bigvee \mathcal{S}(\!|\ P_W\ |\!) \times \bigvee \mathcal{T}(\!|\ Q_W\ |\!)\\
&\quad \text{[by theorem 1]}\\
&\implies P \times Q\ \textbf{s-sat}^{W}\ \mathcal{S} \wedge_{\mathrm{IF}} \mathcal{T}\\
&\quad \text{[by theorem 2]}
\end{aligned}$$

This proves i).

$$P \sqsubseteq \bigvee \mathcal{S}(\!| P_W |\!) \wedge Q \sqsubseteq \bigvee \mathcal{T}(\!| Q_W |\!) \implies P + Q \sqsubseteq \bigvee \mathcal{S}(\!| P_W |\!) + \bigvee \mathcal{T}(\!| Q_W |\!)$$

[by theorem 1]

$$\implies P + Q \ \textbf{s-sat}^{W} \ \mathcal{S} \vee_{\mathrm{IF}} \mathcal{T}$$

[by theorem 2]

This proves ii). □

This corollary states that if the systems P and Q have the minimal amount of behaviour required for the confidentiality statements $\mathcal{S}$ and $\mathcal{T}$, then their product and coproduct will satisfy the conjunction and disjunction respectively of $\mathcal{S}$ and $\mathcal{T}$. This allows a designer to produce components which meet separate requirements, expressed as a minimal set of behaviours, and still be able to compose them together to meet all the requirements simultaneously.

Example 9 Extending examples 7 and 8, corollary 3 gives

$$(R\_FILTER \upharpoonright RU) \| (SECURE\_FILTER \upharpoonright CU) \ \textbf{s-sat}^{\{\mathrm{Unclass}\}} \ \mathcal{T} \wedge_{\mathrm{IF}} \mathcal{S}$$

and

$$(R\_FILTER \upharpoonright RU) [\!] (SECURE\_FILTER \upharpoonright CU) \ \textbf{s-sat}^{\{\mathrm{Unclass}\}} \ \mathcal{T} \vee_{\mathrm{IF}} \mathcal{S}$$

△

The next corollary extends corollary 3 to include functionality.

Corollary 4 *In $\mathcal{IF}_{\sqsubseteq}$, if $\mathcal{S}$, $\mathcal{T}$ are confidentiality statements, S and T are functional specifications such that*

$$S \sqsubseteq P \sqsubseteq \bigvee \mathcal{S}(\!| P_W |\!) \wedge T \sqsubseteq Q \sqsubseteq \bigvee \mathcal{T}(\!| Q_W |\!)$$

then

$$\text{i) } S \times T \sqsubseteq P \times Q \sqsubseteq \bigvee \mathcal{S}(\!| P_W |\!) \times \bigvee \mathcal{T}(\!| Q_W |\!)$$

and

$$\text{ii) } S + T \sqsubseteq P + Q \sqsubseteq \bigvee \mathcal{S}(\!| P_W |\!) + \bigvee \mathcal{T}(\!| Q_W |\!)$$

Proof

By theorem 1 and corollary 3. □

This theorem guarantees that if a designer has managed to find components which meet desired functional and security requirements then they can be combined to meet the combined functional and security requirements.

4 Conclusion

Specifications for general confidentiality properties can be given for systems separately from functional specifications. In general a confidentiality specification will conflict with a functional specification, however with care the conflict can be reconciled. Informally a functional specification provides an "upper" bound for a system and a confidentiality specification provides a "lower" bound. The act of "classical" refinement moves a system away from the "upper" bound towards the "lower" bound. A system will satisfy both the functional and confidentiality specification if refinement keeps the new system within this interval.

The results given show that if systems satisfy their individual functional and confidentiality specifications then their composition via categorical product and coproduct satisfy the product and coproduct of their specifications. In concrete instances, such as Safety-Iflow, this means that CSP parallel and choice composition preserve functionality and confidentiality. In the concrete categories for timed traces, refusals and Petri nets the product and coproduct operators take on similar interpretations. In a category designed to reason about inference in a relational database product and coproduct would correspond to relational operations.

The categorical approach to treating confidentiality, systems and refinement means that the results given are quite general. Other concrete categories include a category of timed traces and a category of refusals. Other possible categories might include relations, and timed refusals. The strength of the approach can be seen in the simple proofs, without the clutter of a particular model of computation and the generality of the results. An essential part of any future work in this area would be realistic case studies on how to apply the results given.

5 Acknowledgements

I would like to thank my colleagues at RSRE and the PRG for their encouragement and advice, especially Jeremy Jacob, Joseph Goguen and John McDermid. Thanks also to my anonymous referees.

References

[1] Michael Barr and Charles Wells, **Category theory for computing science**, Prentice Hall International, 1990.

[2] Jim Davies and Steve Schneider, **An Introduction to Timed CSP**, Technical Monograph PRG-75, Oxford University Computing Laboratory, Programming Research Group, 11 Keble Road, Oxford OX1 3QD. ISBN 0-902928-57-0, 1989.

[3] J. A. Goguen and J. Meseguer, Security policies and security models, **Proceedings 1982 IEEE Symposium on Security and Privacy, Oakland.**

[4] R. Goldblatt, **Topoi, the categorial analysis of logic.** North Holland, 1984

[5] J. Graham-Cumming and J.W. Sanders, On the refinement of Non-Interference, **Proceedings 1991 IEE Computer Security Foundations Workshop, IV. Franconia**

[6] C.A.R. Hoare, **Communicating sequential processes**, Prentice Hall International, ISBN 0-13-153289-8. 1985

[7] J.L Jacob, Security specifications, **Proceedings 1988 IEEE Symposium on Security and Privacy**, Oakland.

[8] J.L Jacob, Security refinement is not Ordinary refinement, **Proceedings 1989 Workshop in Refinement**, Open University, Milton Keynes.

[9] Specifying Security Properties, in C. A. R. Hoare, editor, **Developments in Concurrency and Communication**, (the proceedings of the Year of Programming Institute in Concurrent Programming), Addison Wesley, 1990

[10] He Jifeng, Private communication 1989.

[11] J. Meseguer & U. Montanari, Petri Nets Are Monoids: A New Algebraic Foundation for Net Theory. **Proceedings of the IEEE Symposium On Logic In Computer Science** 1988.

[12] C. Morgan, Programming from Specifications, **Prentice Hall International,** 1990.

[13] C.O'Halloran, A Calculus of Information Flow, **Proceedings of the European symposium on research in computer security, Toulouse, France,** October 1990.

[14] C.O'Halloran, Category theory and information flow applied to computer security, *DPhil. thesis*, Oxford University (Submitted 1991).

[15]
C.O'Halloran, A Calculus of Information Flow (specifying confidentiality requirements), **RSRE Report** No. 92001, 1992.

[16]
C.O'Halloran, Boots, a secure CCIS **RSRE Report** No. 92002, 1992.

Software Reification using the SETS Calculus

José N. Oliveira
DI/INESC, Universidade do Minho
Braga, Portugal

Abstract

SETS is an emerging reification calculus for the derivation of implementations of *model-oriented* specifications of abstract data types.

This paper shows how *abstraction invariants* can be synthesized by calculation in SETS, and the potential of this calculus for assessing, comparing or classifying specifications.

The main results of the paper are concerned with a functorial approach to reification, particularly *wrt.* the systematic implementation of recursive data domains on non-recursive run-time environments. A final example of this class of implementations is provided.

1 Introduction

Research in software technology has shown the need for splitting software design in two complementary steps: *formal specification* first (in which a mathematical text is written prescribing "what" the intended software system should do) and then *implementation* (in which machine code is produced instructing the hardware about "how" to do it).

In general, there is more than one way in which a particular machine can accomplish "what" the specifier bore in mind. Thus, the relationship between specifications and implementations is one-to-many, that is, specifications are more *abstract* than implementations. In fact, specifications are intended to be read, understood and reasoned about by humans. They prescribe behaviour rather than describe it. Implementations are intended to be executed by machines, as efficiently as possible. The programming "tricks" introduced for the sake of efficiency (in implementations) are thus irrelevant details at specification level. In summary, the "epistemological gap" between specifications and implementations is far from being a "smooth" one and is the major concern of the so-called *reification* (or *refinement*) technology, a recent branch of software engineering using formal methods.

Of course, one wants an implementation to behave exactly in the way prescribed by its specification. Thus the notion of *formal correctness* is central to any reliable reification discipline.

In the well-known *constructive style* for software development [19, 20] design is factored into as many "mind-sized" design steps as required. Every intermediate design is first proposed and then proved to follow from its antecedent. Despite improving the primitive approach to correctness (full implementation prior to the overall correctness argument), such an "invent-and-verify" style is often impractical due to the complexity of the mathematical reasoning involved in real-life software problems.

Recent research seems to point at alternative reification styles. The idea is to develop a *calculus* allowing *programs* to be actually calculated from their specifications. In this approach, an intermediate design is drawn from a previous design according to some *law* available in the calculus, which must be *structural* in order for the components of an expression to be refined in isolation (*i.e.* pre-existing refinement results can be "re-used"). Proof discharge is achieved by performing structural calculation instead of proofs from first principles. This is the point of a calculus, as witnessed elsewhere in the past (*cf.* the differential and integral calculi, linear algebra, *etc.*). After a decade of intensive research on the foundations of *formal methods* for software design, one is tempted to forecast that the 1990s will witness the maturation phase of software technology, developing and using tools based on formal calculi.

The target of this paper is to describe the evolution of a particular reification calculus — SETS — whose foundations can be found elsewhere [34, 35, 22]. We start by overviewing related work on reification calculi. For conciseness, this overview is concerned only with calculi for *static semantics*, that is, the very important area of *event reification* is deliberately left out. (The reader is referred to *e.g.* [26, 2, 18, 44, 21] for results in this area.) We proceed to a summary of SETS taken from [35] but adding further basic results. The main results of the paper are presented in section 4 and have to do with reasoning about recursive data types. The scope of these results is illustrated in section 5. The last two sections contain some conclusions and suggestions for future work.

2 Overview of Reification Calculi for Software Design

Wirth's "formula" *Algorithms + Data Structures = Programs* [46] has become famous as the title of a mandatory textbook on structured programming since the mid 1970s. It may be regarded as being probably the first, widespread message that *programs "are" algebraic structures* — *cf. Operators + Sets = Algebras* — which has become the 'moto' of a vast amount of research undertaken in the last two decades on applying universal algebra to computer programming, namely to the formalization of *abstract data types* [14, 12], to *denotational semantics* [11, 31], to *concurrent processing* [25, 16, 15, 27], to *formal specification languages* [5, 28] *etc.*

One of the schools of thought in algebraic specification is termed *model oriented*, or *constructive* because specifications are written explicitly as *models*, *i.e.* algebras, instead of being axiomatically defined. Constructive specification languages (such as VDM [20] and Z [43]) allow nondeterministic operators and local states, and work with *relational algebras* [32], that is, the above "formula" becomes *Relations + Sets = (Relational) Algebras*.

The algebraic-model approach to programming has the benefit that, whatever is said about (or happens to) programs, can always be decomposed across two complementary axes: the *data* programs deal with (*i.e.* data-structures) and the *operations* which manipulate them (*e.g.* procedures, functions *etc.*).

Reification is no exception in this respect. The way the VDM practitioner proceeds from abstract specifications to more concrete models (closer and closer to a target machine, or available programming language) is by "model-refinement". VDM recommends that one of the above axes — *data-refinement* — be considered first, possibly encompassing several iterations. Once a satisfactory *implementation-model* is reached, refinement decisions are then taken on the orthogonal direction (*algorithmic-refinement*) so as to, eventually, reach executable code (*e.g.* in PL/1, PASCAL *etc.*).

This view is in slight contrast with [30, 29], where *data-refinement* is regarded as a special case of *algorithmic-refinement*, being the action of replacing an abstract type by a more concrete type in a program, while preserving its algorithmic structure. The corresponding refinement calculus stems from an extension of Dijkstra's calculus [9] of *predicate transformers*. Such a "calculational style" was first introduced by [17] in a relational setting.

Backus' Turing Award paper [3] has become the 'ex-libris' of a vast collection of works on calculating algorithmic refinements in a *functional* setting, *cf.* the well-known *program transformation* school (see for instance [4, 7, 28]). Reference [7] is one of the first in the literature to characterize functional data-refinement by calculation (transformation). Reference [33] shows how to apply this strategy in the relational (*pre/post*-condition) context of the VDM methodology.

However, a slight difficulty persists in both relational and functional data-refinement: one has to choose (*i.e.* guess) the *abstraction invariant* which links abstract values to concrete values. Such an invariant, which in the functional style can be factored into a *concrete invariant* and an *abstraction function* [30], can be hard to formulate in practical, realistic examples. It would be preferable to be able to *calculate* such an invariant. That is to say, one needs calculi for the stepwise refinement of the data themselves.

This is precisely the main target of the SETS calculus which is the subject of this paper. Because its emphasis is on data structuring laws independently of algorithmic control, we regard it as a "pure" data-refinement calculus when compared to the approaches described above. It is grounded on elementary properties of the cartesian closed category of *Sets* [24] which underlies formal specification in the *constructive* (model-oriented) style. It is therefore easy to understand and to use in reasoning about software models. Following the pragmatical presentation of [35], most category theoretical notions will be replaced by set-theoretical ones.

3 Overview of the SETS Calculus

In this section we present a summary of SETS which is sufficient for the understanding of the main results of this paper (see [35] for further details). Some basic algebraic terminology is required first. For space economy, we stick to "functional" algebraic notation, the appropriate generalization to *non-deterministic* or *relational* algebras being available from *e.g.* [32].

3.1 Basic Terminology

Given a set Ω of function symbols, and a set S of *sorts* ("types"), a *signature* Σ is a syntactical assignment $\Sigma : \Omega \rightarrow (S^\star \times S)$ of a functionality to each function symbol; as usual, we will write $\sigma : s_1 \ldots s_n \rightarrow s$ or $s_1 \ldots s_n \xrightarrow{\sigma} s$ as shorthands of $\Sigma(\sigma) = \langle <s_1, \ldots, s_n>, s \rangle$. Let *Sets* denote the class of all finite or denumerable sets [1] operated by set-theoretical functions. Let these be denoted by $f : X \rightarrow Y$ or $X \xrightarrow{f} Y$, where X and Y are sets.

A Σ-*algebra* $\mathcal{A}$ is a semantic assignment described by a *functor*

$$\mathcal{A} : \Sigma \rightarrow Sets$$

that is, $\mathcal{A} = \langle \mathcal{A}_\Omega, \mathcal{A}_S \rangle$ where $\mathcal{A}_S$ maps sorts to corresponding carrier-sets, $\mathcal{A}_\Omega$ maps operator-symbols to set-theoretical functions, and

$$\mathcal{A}_\Omega(\sigma) : \mathcal{A}_S(s_1) \times \ldots \times \mathcal{A}_S(s_n) \rightarrow \mathcal{A}_S(s) \tag{1}$$

holds. Subscripts Ω and S may be omitted wherever they are clear from the context, *e.g.* by writing

$$\mathcal{A}(\sigma) : \mathcal{A}(s_1) \times \ldots \times \mathcal{A}(s_n) \rightarrow \mathcal{A}(s)$$

instead of expression (1).

A particular Σ-algebra is the one whose carrier-set for each sort $s \in S$ contains all the "words" (*terms*, or *morphisms*) that describe objects of that sort:

$$W_\Sigma(s) \stackrel{def}{=} C(s) \cup \{\sigma(t_1, \ldots, t_n) | \ \sigma : s_1 \ldots s_n \rightarrow s \wedge \forall 1 \leq i \leq n : t_i \in W_\Sigma(s_i)\}$$

where

$$C(s) \stackrel{def}{=} \{\sigma \in \Omega | \ \Sigma(\sigma) = \langle <>, s \rangle\}$$

is the set of all "constants" of type s.

In model-oriented specification, a software module is specified by producing a *model*, which is just a Σ-algebra $\mathcal{A}$, for a particular signature Σ describing its syntactical structure.

3.2 Underlying Formalisms

Given a specification model $\mathcal{A} : \Sigma \rightarrow Sets$, a *reified model* (or refinement) of $\mathcal{A}$ is any other model $\mathcal{B} : \Sigma \rightarrow Sets$ such that there is an epimorphism (*abstraction map*) from $\mathcal{B}$ to $\mathcal{A}$. In general, $\mathcal{B}$ is more *redundant* a model than $\mathcal{A}$, in the sense that a given abstract value $x \in \mathcal{A}(s)$, for some sort $s \in S$, may be represented (reified, refined) in $\mathcal{B}$ by more than one value in $\mathcal{B}(s)$. Take, for instance, the usual reification of finite sets in terms of arbitrary finite lists. The empty set $\emptyset$ is implemented by a single list value, the empty list $<>$. But any other set, *e.g.* $\{a, b\}$, has many list representatives, *e.g.* $<a, b>$, $<b, a>$, $<b, a, b>$, the abstraction map being the usual *elems* function [19].

The collection of all (surjective) abstraction maps, one for each sort $s \in S$, makes up an epimorphism $h : \mathcal{B} \longrightarrow \mathcal{A}$ [2]. The algorithmic structure of $\mathcal{A}$ is

[1] Following the terminology of [1], by a *denumerable* set A we mean a set whose cardinal number $card(A)$ equals $\aleph_0 = card(\mathbb{N})$.

[2] The so-called *final* approach to reification [45] imposes h to be unique. See section 7 for a discussion about this point.

preserved by $\mathcal{B}$ in the sense that every epimorphism h is a homomorphism, and thus,

$$\mathcal{A}(\sigma)(h(b_1),\ldots,h(b_n)) = h(\mathcal{B}(\sigma)(b_1,\ldots,b_n)) \tag{2}$$

for every n-ary Σ-operator σ applied to (correctly type-checked) n-arguments in $\mathcal{B}$ [3].

In our calculational style, instead of conjecturing $\mathcal{B} : \Sigma \rightarrow Sets$ and proving that there is an epimorphism from $\mathcal{B}$ to $\mathcal{A}$, we want to effectively calculate $\mathcal{B}$ from $\mathcal{A}$, gradually synthesizing the appropriate epimorphism, as explained in the sequel. We will concentrate on data-level transformations, for the sake of brevity. See [35] for a refinement theorem which fits such transformations to the preservation of algorithmic behaviour. Section 5 will provide an illustration of model calculation in SETS, combining data-level and operation-level transformations.

3.3 On Redundancy Orderings

The SETS calculus is "naively" based on the cardinality ordering $A \preceq B$ among sets:

$$A \preceq B \stackrel{def}{=} \exists B \stackrel{f}{\rightarrow} A : f \textit{ is surjective.} \tag{3}$$

where f plays the rôle of an *abstraction map* such as discussed above (section 3.2). We will write $A \preceq_f B$ wherever we want to keep track of abstraction maps in $\preceq$-reasoning. For instance,

$$2^A \preceq_{elems} A^\star \tag{4}$$

for A a finite set. The ordering $\preceq$ is reflexive and transitive, and $\preceq$-antisymmetry induces set-theoretical isomorphism [35]. Transitivity means that one can chain $\preceq$-steps and synthesize overall abstraction maps, that is

$$A \preceq_f B \wedge B \preceq_g C \Rightarrow A \preceq_{f \circ g} C \tag{5}$$

The finitary version of (5), for n $\preceq$-reasoning steps, is

$$\underbrace{A \preceq_{f_1} A_1 \preceq_{f_2} \cdots \preceq_{f_n} A_n}_{f = f_1 \circ \cdots \circ f_n}$$

Reflexivity is naturally established by identity maps,

$$A \preceq_{1_A} A$$

while $\preceq$-antisymmetry

$$A \preceq_f B \wedge B \preceq_g A \Rightarrow A \cong B$$

enforces two isomorphisms f, g for finite A, B ($g = f^{-1}$, in particular).

Unfortunately, many reification steps cannot be described by facts of the form $A \preceq B$, because B is "too wide" a data model and contains invalid

[3] For improved readability, subscripts S, Ω, s, $s_1, \ldots, s_n$ have been omitted from (2), *cf.* [35].

representatives of A. For instance, there is an implementation of sets in terms of lists which is "finer" than (4) because one wants to leave out lists which contain repeated elements (for the sake of efficiency, maybe). The basic fact we can assert in this case is

$$2^A \preceq_{elems} \{l \in A^\star \mid inv(l)\} \tag{6}$$

where

$$\begin{array}{rcl} inv : A^\star & \longrightarrow & 2 \\ l & \rightsquigarrow & len(l) = card(elems(l)) \end{array} \tag{7}$$

where $2 \cong \{TRUE, FALSE\}$ denotes the set of Boolean values, and len, $elems$ and $card$ are well-known list and set operators [19].

Validity predicates such as inv (7) have become known in the literature as *data-type invariants.* Because of the need for data-type invariants, the ordering above is too "strong". As is explained in [35], (3) may be superseded by the ordering

$$A \trianglelefteq B \stackrel{def}{=} \exists S \subseteq B : A \preceq_f S. \tag{8}$$

Let ϕ denote the characteristic function of S in B [35]. Then

$$A \trianglelefteq_f^\phi B \tag{9}$$

may be written to mean exactly the same thing as (8). For instance, instead of (6), we will write

$$2^A \trianglelefteq_{elems}^{inv} A^\star \tag{10}$$

Subscripts f, ϕ in (9) may be omitted wherever implicit in the context. Invariant ϕ determines the *domain* of the abstraction map f, which can be regarded as a *partial* surjection from B to A [4].

This wider notion of a redundancy ordering ($\trianglelefteq$) enjoys the same properties as $\preceq$, *e.g.*

$$A \trianglelefteq_{1_A}^{\lambda a.TRUE} A$$

etc. It is relevant to see how invariants are synthesized by transitivity:

$$A \trianglelefteq_f^\phi B \wedge B \trianglelefteq_g^\gamma C \Rightarrow A \trianglelefteq_{f \circ g}^\rho C$$

for

$$\rho(c) = \gamma(c) \wedge \phi(g(c)) \tag{11}$$

---

[4] Strictly speaking, the $\preceq$ and $\trianglelefteq$ orderings are mathematically equivalent, since $A \preceq B \Rightarrow A \trianglelefteq B$ (let $S = B$) and $A \trianglelefteq B \Rightarrow A \preceq B$ (choose an arbitrary $a \in A$ and "totalize" f by setting $f(b) = a$ for every $b \notin S$). However, such a "totalized" abstraction map f would be semantically unnatural and confusing, a being represented by valid and invalid data at the same time!

It is better to retain the partial nature of f explicit by using the $\trianglelefteq$-notation, $\preceq$ being a shorthand used to denote $\trianglelefteq$-facts such that f is total.

where logical conjunction ($\wedge$) should be regarded as a non-strict connective at its second argument (*e.g.* $FALSE \wedge \bot = FALSE$). For a chain of n $\trianglelefteq$-steps,

$$\trianglelefteq_i \begin{cases} f_i \\ \phi_i \end{cases}$$

the overall abstraction map and invariant are given by:

$$\trianglelefteq \begin{cases} f \stackrel{def}{=} \bigcirc_{i=1}^{n} f_i \\ \phi \stackrel{def}{=} \lambda x.\ \bigwedge_{i=n}^{1} \phi_i((\bigcirc_{j=i+1}^{n} f_j)(x)) \end{cases} \qquad (12)$$

3.4 A Redundancy Calculus

Readers familiar with model specification such as in VDM are aware that a limited number of set-theoretical constructs is enough for modelling fairly elaborate abstract objects. In *Sets*, such "primitive" constructs are,

- *cartesian product* of two sets A and B (*cf.* records):

  $$A \times B = \{\langle a, b\rangle \mid a \in A \wedge b \in B\}$$

- *disjoint union* of two sets A and B (*cf.* variant records):

  $$A + B = (\{1\} \times A) \cup (\{2\} \times B)$$

- *exponentiation* (A raised to a finite set B, see examples below):

  $$A^B = \{f \mid f : B \to A\}$$

On top of these one can build the following *derived* constructs:

- finite subsets of a finite set A (*cf.* set of A in VDM):

  $$2^A$$

- finite binary relations from A to B (*cf.* set of $(A \times B)$ in VDM):

  $$2^{A \times B}$$

- finite partial maps from A to B (*cf.* map A to B in VDM):

  $$A \hookrightarrow B = \bigcup_{K \subseteq A} B^K$$

- finite sequences on a set A (*cf.* seq of A in VDM):

  $$A^\star = \bigcup_{n \geq 0} A^{\overline{n}}$$

  where each exponent $\overline{n}$ denotes the initial segment of $\mathbb{N}$ whose cardinality is n. For simplicity, we will write n instead of $\overline{n}$, and therefore 0 instead of the empty set $\emptyset$.

- union types (*cf.* [*A*] in VDM):

$$A + 1 \tag{13}$$

  where 1 stands for any singleton set, *cf.* [35]. Typically, $1 \cong \{NIL\}$.

A last ("meta") construct is recursive definition,

$$X \cong \mathcal{F}(X)$$

where X is the name of a data sort and $\mathcal{F}$ is a *Sets*-expression ("functor") involving the above primitive or derived constructs. For example, the following recursive VDM syntax for abstract *decision trees*,

$$\begin{array}{rcll} DecTree & :: & Q: \ What & /^{*} \textit{Question or Decision} \ ^{*}/ \\ & & R: \ Answer \xrightarrow{m} DecTree & /^{*} \textit{Subtrees} \ ^{*}/ \\ What & = & \ldots & \\ Answer & = & \ldots & \end{array}$$

(where decisions are modelled by *DecTree* nodes with no answers) is written in the *Sets* notation as follows:

$$DecTree \cong What \times (Answer \hookrightarrow DecTree) \tag{14}$$

The following theorem is central to the SETS calculus.

Theorem 1 ($\trianglelefteq$-Monotonicity of *Sets*-constructs) *The Sets-constructs $\times$ and $+$ are monotone* wrt. *the $\trianglelefteq$-ordering (8); exponentiation requires isomorphical exponents.*

That is, given Sets-objects A, B, X, Y, M, N such that $A \trianglelefteq X$, $B \trianglelefteq Y$ and $M \cong N$, then facts

$$A \times B \trianglelefteq X \times Y \tag{15}$$

$$A + B \trianglelefteq X + Y \tag{16}$$

$$A^M \trianglelefteq X^N \tag{17}$$

hold.

Outline of Proof: *Let*

$$A \trianglelefteq^{\phi}_{f} X, \quad B \trianglelefteq^{\varphi}_{g} Y, \quad M \cong_h N \tag{18}$$

Then

1. *Equation (15):*

$$A \times B \trianglelefteq^{\phi \times \varphi}_{f \times g} X \times Y$$

where the product of two functions f and g is "parallel application" [24] [5]

$$(f \times g)\langle a, b \rangle = \langle f(a), g(b) \rangle \tag{19}$$

and the product of two predicates ϕ and φ is "parallel conjunction"

$$(\phi \times \varphi)\langle a, b \rangle = \phi(a) \wedge \varphi(b)$$

[5] *For improved readability, functional application involving tupled arguments,* e.g. $f(\langle x_1, \ldots, x_n \rangle)$, *will be abbreviated to* $f\langle x_1, \ldots, x_n \rangle$ *or* $f(x_1, \ldots, x_n)$.

2. *Equation (16):*

$$A + B \trianglelefteq_{f+g}^{\phi+\varphi} X + Y$$

where the sum of two functions f and g is [24]

$$\left\{ \begin{array}{lcl} (f+g)\langle 1, a\rangle & = & \langle 1, f(a)\rangle \\ (f+g)\langle 2, b\rangle & = & \langle 2, g(b)\rangle \end{array} \right. \quad (20)$$

and the sum of two predicates ϕ and φ is

$$\left\{ \begin{array}{lcl} (\phi+\varphi)\langle 1, a\rangle & = & \phi(a) \\ (\phi+\varphi)\langle 2, b\rangle & = & \varphi(b) \end{array} \right.$$

3. *Equation (17): Since M and N have the same cardinality, say m, then*

$$\begin{array}{lcl} A^M & \cong & A^m \\ & \cong & \underbrace{A \times \ldots \times A}_{m} \end{array}$$

and

$$\begin{array}{lcl} X^N & \cong & X^m \\ & \cong & \underbrace{X \times \ldots \times X}_{m} \end{array}$$

cf. *(23) below. That is, (17) can be reduced to a finitary version of (15) in which we have*

$$A^m \trianglelefteq_{f^m}^{\phi^m} X^m$$

where

$$\begin{array}{l} f^m\langle a_1, \ldots, a_m\rangle = \langle f(a_1), \ldots, f(a_m)\rangle \\ \phi^m\langle a_1, \ldots, a_m\rangle = \forall 1 \leq i \leq m : \phi(a_i) \end{array} \quad (21)$$

Alternatively, we may define the overall abstraction map t and invariant τ in

$$A^M \trianglelefteq_t^\tau X^N$$

as follows, for $\sigma \in X^N$ and h the isomorphism between M and N (18):

$$\begin{array}{lcl} t(\sigma) & = & f \circ \sigma \circ h^{-1} \\ \tau(\sigma) & = & \forall n \in dom(\sigma) : \phi(\sigma(n)) \end{array}$$

It remains to be proved that all composite abstraction maps above are surjective, which is not hard work, cf. *[22].* □

By this theorem, the components of each data domain of a *Sets* expression can be refined in isolation, allowing for the stepwise introduction of redundancy in formal models of software.

3.4.1 The ≅-Subcalculus

The SETS calculus is fairly rich in algebraic properties. A collection of ≅-equalities is given in [35] which establishes that, up to set-theoretical isomorphism, *Sets* may be regarded as a commutative semiring under $\times$ and $+$. Therefore, it makes sense to write finitary products

$$A_1 \times \ldots \times A_n \tag{22}$$

as well as finitary disjoint unions

$$A_1 + \cdots + A_n \quad \textit{that is} \quad \sum_{i=1}^{n} A_i$$

and we have

$$\underbrace{A \times \ldots \times A}_{n} \cong A^n \tag{23}$$

$$\underbrace{A + \ldots + A}_{n} \cong n \times A \tag{24}$$

as expected.

Concerning exponentiation, we recall the following laws from [35]:

$$A^0 \cong 1 \tag{25}$$

$$A^{(B+C)} \cong A^B \times A^C \tag{26}$$

$$A^1 \cong A \tag{27}$$

$$1^A \cong 1 \tag{28}$$

$$(A \times B)^C \cong A^C \times B^C \tag{29}$$

$$C^{A \times B} \cong \left(C^B\right)^A \tag{30}$$

$$A \hookrightarrow B \cong (B+1)^A \tag{31}$$

and note that

$$A^\star \cong \sum_{n \geq 0} A^n \tag{32}$$

$$A \hookrightarrow B \cong \sum_{K \subseteq A} B^K \tag{33}$$

since

$$\begin{aligned} A \neq B &\Rightarrow X^A \cap X^B = \emptyset \\ A \cap B = \emptyset &\Rightarrow A \cup B \cong A + B \end{aligned}$$

Many other basic results are derivable within this subcalculus. The following one will be useful in the sequel:

$$\begin{aligned} 2^A &\cong (1+1)^A \\ &\cong A \hookrightarrow 1 \end{aligned} \tag{34}$$

(= finite sets can be modelled by finite maps), *cf.* $2 \cong 1+1$ (24) and (31).

A more interesting example of $\cong$-reasoning is the following: let us re-write (14) avoiding semantically biased symbols such as *DecTree*, *What*, *Answer* and using more "neutral" symbols such as T, I, A:

$$T \cong I \times (A \hookrightarrow T) \tag{35}$$

Now let $A \cong 2$. Then

$$\begin{aligned} I \times (A \hookrightarrow T) &\cong I \times (2 \hookrightarrow T) \\ &\cong I \times (T+1)^2 \\ &\cong I \times (T+1) \times (T+1) \end{aligned}$$

— *cf.* (31) and (23) — and (35) becomes

$$T \cong I \times (T+1) \times (T+1) \tag{36}$$

Let us now compare (36) against the following VDM abstract data model of *genealogical diagrams* (the "pedigree view" of family relationship):

GenDia ::	I :	*Ind*	/* *data about an individual* */	(37)
	F :	[*GenDia*]	/* *genealogy of his/her father (if known)* */	
	M :	[*GenDia*]	/* *genealogy of his/her mother (if known)* */	

Clearly, (36) and (37) are the "same" data model (recall (13)). We conclude that *genealogical diagrams* "are" particular cases of *decision trees*, that is, if a package implementing the latter is available, then it may be *re-used* to implement the former. Of course, a full comparison between both models should examine the algorithmic structure as well [6]. But the point of this example is just to show the usefulness of SETS in comparing or assessing data specification.

3.4.2 The $\trianglelefteq$-Subcalculus

Equations (4) and (10) above record basic results about implementing finite sets. Most other $\trianglelefteq$-results concern the reification of finite partial maps.

Recall laws (25) to (30) concerning exponentiations, that is, sets of total maps. It would be useful if such laws were to hold for partial maps, that is, for expressions of the form $A \hookrightarrow B$ instead of B^A. It can be easily checked that only (26) and (25) are in fact preserved, *cf.* respectively,

$$\begin{aligned} (B+C) \hookrightarrow A &\cong (A+1)^{B+C} \\ &\cong (A+1)^B \times (A+1)^C \\ &\cong (B \hookrightarrow A) \times (C \hookrightarrow A) \end{aligned} \tag{38}$$

and

$$\begin{aligned} 0 \hookrightarrow A &\cong (A+1)^0 \\ &\cong 1 \end{aligned}$$

[6] For instance, making decisions in *DecTree* corresponds exactly to ascending genealogical data in *GenDia*, for a fixed *menu* (set of available "answers") at every "decision" level: $2 \cong \{father, mother\}$.

Concerning (27) and (28) we obtain slightly different results: for (28) see (34); for (27) we have

$$\begin{aligned} 1 \hookrightarrow A &\cong (A+1)^1 \\ &\cong A+1 \end{aligned}$$

still in the $\cong$-subcalculus, *cf.* (31) and (27) itself. The remaining two laws lead to $\trianglelefteq$-results, as follows.

(29) "holds" at $\hookrightarrow$-level provided that $\trianglelefteq$ replaces $\cong$,

$$A \hookrightarrow B \times C \trianglelefteq (A \hookrightarrow B) \times (A \hookrightarrow C) \tag{39}$$

cf. [35]. The $\hookrightarrow$-version of the "currying" law of exponentiation (30) is another $\trianglelefteq$-result,

$$(A \times B) \hookrightarrow C \trianglelefteq A \hookrightarrow (B \hookrightarrow C) \tag{40}$$

and not the desirable

$$(A \times B) \hookrightarrow C \cong A \hookrightarrow (B \hookrightarrow C)$$

because the expected currying and uncurrying maps are, respectively, not surjective and partial — think of those values in $A \hookrightarrow (B \hookrightarrow C)$ containing the empty map in their range. The invariant induced by (40) is thus

$$\phi(\sigma) \stackrel{def}{=} \{\,\} \notin rng(\sigma)$$

The law "symmetrical" *wrt.* (40) is therefore not valid, although a somewhat more involved fact holds,

$$A \hookrightarrow (B \hookrightarrow C) \trianglelefteq 2^A \times ((A \times B) \hookrightarrow C) \tag{41}$$

which is a particular case of

$$A \hookrightarrow D \times (B \hookrightarrow C) \trianglelefteq (A \hookrightarrow D) \times ((A \times B) \hookrightarrow C) \tag{42}$$

(let $D = 1$ and apply basic properties of $\times$ and (34)). The invariant induced by (42) is

$$\phi(\sigma, \sigma') \stackrel{def}{=} \pi_1[dom(\sigma')] \subseteq dom(\sigma) \tag{43}$$

where $\pi_1[dom(\sigma')]$ means $\{\pi_1(p) |\ p \in dom(\sigma')\}$, for π_1, π_2 the standard product selector maps:

$$\begin{aligned} \pi_1(a,b) &= a \\ \pi_2(a,b) &= b \end{aligned}$$

This invariant recommends that all $a \in A$ found in $\sigma \in A \hookrightarrow D$ which cannot be found in $\sigma' \in A \times B \hookrightarrow C$ are exactly the entries, at abstract level, to be mapped to the empty map (in $B \hookrightarrow C$), *cf.* the corresponding abstraction map:

$$f(\sigma, \sigma') \stackrel{def}{=} \{a \mapsto \langle \sigma(a), \{b \mapsto \sigma'(a,b) |\ \langle a,b \rangle \in proj(a,\sigma')\}\rangle |\ a \in dom(\sigma)\} \tag{44}$$

where

$$proj(a, \sigma') \stackrel{def}{=} \{\langle a', b \rangle \in dom(\sigma') |\ a' = a\}$$

On the other hand, the $\trianglelefteq$-subcalculus encompasses $\hookrightarrow$ -laws which cannot be adapted from similar results concerning exponentiation. For instance,

$$(B+C)^A \not\cong B^A \times C^A$$

and yet we have the following map-decomposition law:

$$A \hookrightarrow (B+C) \trianglelefteq_f^\phi (A \hookrightarrow B) \times (A \hookrightarrow C) \tag{45}$$

for

$$\begin{aligned} \phi(\sigma,\rho) &\stackrel{def}{=} dom(\sigma) \cap dom(\rho) = \emptyset \\ f(\sigma,\rho) &\stackrel{def}{=} i_1 \circ \sigma \cup i_2 \circ \rho \ . \end{aligned}$$

where i_1, i_2 are the standard co-product injection maps:

$$\begin{aligned} i_1(a) &= \langle 1, a \rangle \\ i_2(a) &= \langle 2, a \rangle \end{aligned}$$

Laws such as (39,41,42) and (45) play an important rôle in finite map reification. They can be used to "decompose" complex/nested maps into tuples of simpler maps. Recalling from [35] how immediate it is to refine finite maps into binary relations,

$$A \hookrightarrow B \trianglelefteq_{mkf}^{fdp} 2^{A \times B} \tag{46}$$

for [7]

$$fdp(R) \stackrel{def}{=} \forall \langle a,b \rangle, \langle a',b' \rangle \in R : a = a' \Rightarrow b = b' \tag{47}$$

$$mkf(R) \stackrel{def}{=} \{a \mapsto the(\{x \in B |\ a\ R\ x\}) |\ \langle a,b \rangle \in R\} \tag{48}$$

it makes sense to say that the $\trianglelefteq$-subcalculus fragment studied above is just what we need in order to refine elaborate, finite-map based data models into relational database schemata. This will become apparent from the illustration which will be given in section 5. But we need further, more ambitious $\trianglelefteq$-results concerning recursion removal.

4 Dealing with Recursive Data Models

Equations (14) and (36) presented above are examples of recursively defined data models in *Sets*. Many others could have been presented since recursion

[7] The partial operator

$$the : 2^A \rightarrow A$$

yields the unique element of a singleton set, that is,

$$the(\{a\}) = a$$

while $the(\{a,b\})$, $the(\emptyset)$ are undefined expressions.

normally provides "elegant" solutions for a wide range of problems, namely:

$$X \cong 1 + A \times X \quad /*\textit{finite lists on } A\ */ \tag{49}$$

$$X \cong 1 + A \times X^2 \quad /*\textit{binary trees on } A\ */ \tag{50}$$

$$X \cong 1 + A \times X^\star \quad /*\textit{generic trees on } A\ */$$

$$X \cong V + A \times X^\star \quad /*\textit{formal terms on } V \textit{ and } A\ */$$

etc.

What can we do about refining a recursive data model?

Some languages support recursion directly (*e.g.* LISP) but may others do not (*e.g.* FORTRAN). Languages such as PASCAL are "half-way through" — recursion is supported in an indirect way by providing *pointers* to *dynamic storage* ("heaps"). Programming with pointers is error-prone (*cf.* pointer undefinedness, non-termination caused by cyclic referencing *etc.*) and tends to produce "tricky" code (pointers are data-structuring counterparts of "gotos" [46]). A way of overcoming this situation is to think of a generic rule for refining recursive data structures into safe non-recursive ones, thus ruling out non-systematic use of pointers [8].

By way of motivation, let us recall Fielding's VDM *representation 1* of abstract mappings [10],

$$\begin{array}{l} S1 = [Bt1] \\ Bt1 :: S1\ Key\ Data\ S1 \end{array} \tag{51}$$

which means nothing more than recursive definition (50) in *Sets* (let $A \cong Key \times Data$). *Representation 2* presented in the same work [10] "maps a binary tree onto linear storage":

$$\begin{array}{l} S2 :: ROOT : [Ptr]\ ARRAY : Ptr \xrightarrow{m} Node2 \\ Node2 :: [Ptr]\ Key\ Data\ [Ptr] \end{array} \tag{52}$$

The abstract schema of (52) in *Sets* is

$$S2 \cong (K+1) \times ARRAY$$

$$ARRAY \cong K \hookrightarrow Key \times Data \times (K+1)^2$$

for an abstract domain $K \cong \mathbb{N}$ of pointers, *cf.* Ptr in (52).

From [10] we know that (52) refines (51) under a fairly elaborate datatype invariant ensuring pointer definedness and absence of pointer loops. A similar invariant is required to justify the following well-known "linked-list" representation of finite lists (49):

$$X_1 \cong (K+1) \times (K \hookrightarrow A \times (K+1))$$

Can these two "recursion removing" reification steps be generalized?

We may conjecture that, if X_1 is a fixpoint solution of a recursive definition in *Sets* of the form

$$X \cong 1 + \mathcal{G}(X), \tag{53}$$

[8] Much in the same way that one can do "Structured Programming with Goto Statements" *cf.* [23].

then

$$X_1 \trianglelefteq_f^{\phi} (K+1) \times (K \hookrightarrow \mathcal{G}(K+1)) \qquad (54)$$

for $K \cong \mathbb{N}$. For this conjecture to hold we need to find which f, ϕ are generically induced by $\mathcal{G}$. We will show below that an elegant way of doing it is to regard $\mathcal{G}$ as a polynomial (endo)functor in *Sets* [24].

Some necessary concepts about functors in *Sets* will be given next, adapted from [24] where the same concepts can be found under the appropriate categorial generalization.

4.1 Polynomial Functors

Let A, B, C be objects in *Sets*. Let $f : A \rightarrow B$ be a morphism in *Sets* and let $1_C : C \rightarrow C$ denote the identity morphism on C. Then C may be regarded as the *constant functor*

$$C : Sets \longrightarrow Sets \qquad (55)$$

such that $C(A) = C$ and $C(f) = 1_C$.

Let $\mathcal{F}, \mathcal{G} : Sets \longrightarrow Sets$ be functors. Define their *product*

$$\mathcal{F} \times \mathcal{G} : Sets \longrightarrow Sets$$

by $(\mathcal{F}\times\mathcal{G})(A) = \mathcal{F}(A)\times\mathcal{G}(A)$ and by $(\mathcal{F}\times\mathcal{G})(f) = \mathcal{F}(f)\times\mathcal{G}(f)$, *cf.* (19). For instance, $\mathcal{F}(X) = X \times C$ defines the product functor of the identity functor $\lambda X.X$ and the constant functor C (55), and we have $\mathcal{F}(f)\langle a, c\rangle = (f \times 1_C)\langle a, c\rangle = \langle f(a), c\rangle$.

We may have n-ary products of functors, of which $\mathcal{F}(X) = X^n$ is a particular case. For f the same morphism as above, we will have $\mathcal{F}(f) = f^n : A^n \rightarrow B^n$, *cf.* (21).

The notion of a product functor has a dual — the *co-product functor* (or sum of two functors) — which resorts to (20):

$$\begin{array}{rcl} \mathcal{F}+\mathcal{G} & : & Sets \longrightarrow Sets \\ (\mathcal{F}+\mathcal{G})(A) & = & \mathcal{F}(A)+\mathcal{G}(A) \\ (\mathcal{F}+\mathcal{G})(f) & = & \mathcal{F}(f)+\mathcal{G}(f) \end{array}$$

Co-product functors may also be iterated to n-arguments.

Finally, we are ready to define what a *polynomial functor* is — every functor $\mathcal{F} : Sets \longrightarrow Sets$ which is either a constant functor or the identity functor, or the composition or (finitary) product or sum of other polynomial functors, is said to be *polynomial*.

For instance,

$$\mathcal{F}(X) = 1 + A \times X \qquad (56)$$

(*cf.* (49)) is a polynomial functor and so is $\mathcal{F}(X) = X^\star$, *cf.* (32). $\mathcal{F}(X) = C \hookrightarrow X$ is also polynomial for C a finite exponent (*cf.* $C \hookrightarrow X \cong (X+1)^C$ and [24]) and we have

$$\begin{array}{rcl} (C \hookrightarrow f)(\sigma) & = & f \circ \sigma \\ & = & \{c \mapsto f(\sigma(c)) \mid c \in dom(\sigma)\} \end{array} \qquad (57)$$

The following result is valid in *Sets* [24]: every polynomial functor

$\mathcal{F} : Sets \longrightarrow Sets$

may be put into the canonical form:

$$\begin{aligned} \mathcal{F}(X) &\cong C_0 + (C_1 \times X) + (C_2 \times X^2) + \cdots + (C_n \times X^n) \\ &= \sum_{i=0}^{n} C_i \times X^i \end{aligned} \tag{58}$$

For instance, for $\mathcal{F}(X) = X^\star$ we have every $C_i = 1$, since

$$\begin{aligned} X^\star &\cong \sum_{i \geq 0} X^i \\ &\cong \sum_{i \geq 0} 1 \times X^i \end{aligned}$$

(recall (32) and the fact that 1 is the identity of $\times$ [9]).

A suggestive result for converting polynomial functors into canonical form is *Newton's binomial formula* itself,

$$(A + B)^n \cong \sum_{p=0}^{n} {}^nC_p \times A^{n-p} \times B^p \tag{59}$$

as illustrated by the following treatment of the "pedigree" functor

$$\mathcal{F}(T) = I \times (T + 1)^2$$

of section 3.4.1. We will have,

$$\begin{aligned} \mathcal{F}(T) &= I \times (T + 1)^2 \\ &\cong I \times (T^2 + 2 \times T + 1) \\ &\cong I \times T^2 + 2 \times I \times T + I \end{aligned}$$

which literally means: *"about an individual I either both father and mother are known (T^2), or one of either father or mother are known ($2 \times T$), or both father and mother are unknown (1)".*

Combining (58,59) with the map-decomposition law (45), we obtain a general rule for decomposing a mapping of the form

$A \hookrightarrow \mathcal{F}(X)$

into a cartesian product of mappings, *i.e.*

$$\Pi_{i=0}^{n}(A \hookrightarrow C_i \times X^i) \tag{60}$$

each of which may in turn be refined into tabular form, *cf.* relational data-base design.

Finally, with the aid of polynomial functors we may extend theorem 1 as follows:

---

[9] We regard a denumerable sum of polynomial functors as being a polynomial functor.

Table 1: Summary of Functorial Calculus

$\mathcal{F}(X)$	$\mathcal{F}(f)$	$\mathcal{F}(\phi)$
X	f	ϕ
C	1_C	$\lambda c.TRUE$
2^X	$2^f = \lambda s.\{f(x) \mid x \in s\}$	$2^\phi = \lambda s.\forall b \in s : \phi(b)$
$X^\star$	$f^\star = \lambda l.< f(x) \mid x \leftarrow l >$	$\phi^\star = \lambda l.\forall 1 \leq i \leq length(l) : \phi(l(i))$
X^C	$f^C = \lambda \sigma . f \circ \sigma$	$\phi^C = \lambda \sigma . \forall c \in C : \phi(\sigma(c))$
$C \hookrightarrow X$	$C \hookrightarrow f = \lambda \sigma . f \circ \sigma$	$C \hookrightarrow \phi = \lambda \sigma . \forall x \in rng(\sigma) : \phi(x)$
$\mathcal{G}(X) \times \mathcal{H}(X)$	$\mathcal{G}(f) \times \mathcal{H}(f)$	$\lambda(x,y).\mathcal{G}(\phi)(x) \wedge \mathcal{H}(\phi)(y)$
$\mathcal{G}(X) + \mathcal{H}(X)$	$\mathcal{G}(f) + \mathcal{H}(f)$	$\lambda x . \begin{cases} x = \langle 1, a \rangle & \Rightarrow \mathcal{G}(\phi)(a) \\ x = \langle 2, b \rangle & \Rightarrow \mathcal{H}(\phi)(b) \end{cases}$
$\mathcal{G}(X) + 1$	$\lambda x . \begin{cases} x = \langle 2, NIL \rangle & \Rightarrow x \\ x = \langle 1, a \rangle & \Rightarrow \langle 1, \mathcal{G}(f)(a) \rangle \end{cases}$	$\lambda x . \begin{cases} x = \langle 2, NIL \rangle & \Rightarrow TRUE \\ x = \langle 1, a \rangle & \Rightarrow \mathcal{G}(\phi)(a) \end{cases}$

Theorem 2 *Let $\mathcal{F}$ be a polynomial (endo)functor in Sets. If*

$$A \trianglelefteq_f^\phi B \tag{61}$$

then

$$\mathcal{F}(A) \trianglelefteq_{\mathcal{F}(f)}^{\mathcal{F}(\phi)} \mathcal{F}(B) \tag{62}$$

Proof: *It is performed by induction on the structure of polynomial functor $\mathcal{F}$. Sum and product (and exponentiation) have been dealt with in theorem 1.*

The base case concerning the identity functor $\mathcal{F}(X) = X$ is trivial, since $\mathcal{F}(f) = f$ and $\mathcal{F}(\phi) = \phi$, i.e. *(62) reduces to (61). The other base case concerns the constant functor $\mathcal{F}(X) = C$. We have $\mathcal{F}(f) = 1_C$ and $\mathcal{F}(\phi) = \lambda b.TRUE$, (62) holding trivially.* □

This theorem provides an elegant, functorial strategy for computing complex abstraction invariants throughout a reification process. Although $\mathcal{F}(X) = 2^X$ is not polynomial [24], (62) still holds for this functor, for finite A and B [22]. Table 1 presents a summary of this "functorial calculus" for the most common *Sets* constructs.

4.2 A Result for Recursion Removal

We now come back to our conjecture about (54). The result which will be presented below is applicable to recursive definitions of the form

$$X \cong \mathcal{F}(X) \tag{63}$$

of which (53) is a particular case, let $\mathcal{F}(X) = 1 + \mathcal{G}(X)$.

Let $(X_0, \delta : \mathcal{F}(X_0) \rightarrow X_0)$ be a fixpoint of functor $\mathcal{F}$ (63) in *Sets*. A least fixpoint solution to (63) is guaranteed for every *co-continuous* functor $\mathcal{F}$. Moreover, every polynomial functor is co-continuous [24].

We want to discuss the following reification step:

$$X_0 \trianglelefteq_f^\phi K \times (K \hookrightarrow \mathcal{F}(K)) \tag{64}$$

for K a domain of "pointers" such that $K \cong \mathbb{N}$. (64) will hold provided that we define a surjection

$$f : K \times (K \hookrightarrow \mathcal{F}(K)) \longrightarrow X_0$$

which is total over $\{\langle k, \sigma\rangle \in K \times (K \hookrightarrow \mathcal{F}(K)) | \; \phi(k, \sigma)\}$. We start by temporarily assuming that $\sigma \in K \hookrightarrow \mathcal{F}(K)$ is a total function, and draw the following diagram

$$\begin{array}{c} K \\ \downarrow \sigma \\ \mathcal{F}(K) \end{array} \tag{65}$$

Assuming a given piece of "linear storage" σ ("database"), let f_σ denote the function which, for each "pointer" $k \in K$, retrieves the value of X_0 corresponding to a σ "scan" starting from k. We may add f_σ to (65), that is

$$\begin{array}{ccc} X_0 & \stackrel{f_\sigma}{\longleftarrow} & K \\ & & \downarrow \sigma \\ & & \mathcal{F}(K) \end{array}$$

Since (X_0, δ) is a fixpoint of $\mathcal{F}$, we may add δ to the above diagram, and obtain

$$\begin{array}{ccc} X_0 & \stackrel{f_\sigma}{\longleftarrow} & K \\ \delta \uparrow & & \downarrow \sigma \\ \mathcal{F}(X_0) & & \mathcal{F}(K) \end{array}$$

Finally, our diagram may be "closed" by $\mathcal{F}(f_\sigma)$,

$$\begin{array}{ccc} X_0 & \stackrel{f_\sigma}{\longleftarrow} & K \\ \delta \uparrow & & \downarrow \sigma \\ \mathcal{F}(X_0) & \stackrel{\mathcal{F}(f_\sigma)}{\longleftarrow} & \mathcal{F}(K) \end{array} \tag{66}$$

since $\mathcal{F}$ ia a functor.

The equation implicit in commutative diagram (66) is

$$f_\sigma(k) = \delta(\mathcal{F}(f_\sigma)(\sigma(k)))$$

We may write $f(k, \sigma)$ instead of $f_\sigma(k)$, obtaining the following abstraction map for (64)

$$\begin{array}{rcl} f & : & K \times (K \hookrightarrow \mathcal{F}(K)) \longrightarrow X_0 \\ f(k, \sigma) & \stackrel{def}{=} & \delta(\mathcal{F}(f_\sigma)(\sigma(k))) \end{array} \tag{67}$$

Let us see an example involving polynomial functor (56). $(A^\star, \delta)$ is a well-known fixpoint solution of this functor [24, 35] for

$$\begin{array}{rcl} \delta & : & 1 + A \times A^\star \longrightarrow A^\star \\ \delta(x) & \stackrel{def}{=} & \left\{ \begin{array}{lcl} <> & \Leftarrow & x = \langle 1, NIL\rangle \\ cons(a, l) & \Leftarrow & x = \langle 2, \langle a, l\rangle\rangle \end{array} \right. \end{array} \tag{68}$$

For $\mathcal{F}(f_\sigma)$ we obtain

$$\begin{array}{rcl} \mathcal{F}(f_\sigma)(x) & = & (1 + A \times f_\sigma)(x) \\ & = & (1_1 + 1_A \times f_\sigma)(x) \\ & = & \left\{ \begin{array}{lcl} x & \Leftarrow & x = \langle 1, NIL \rangle \\ \langle 2, \langle a, f_\sigma(l) \rangle \rangle & \Leftarrow & x = \langle 2, \langle a, l \rangle \rangle \end{array} \right. \end{array} \tag{69}$$

Composing (69) with (68) we obtain, following (67),

$$f(k, \sigma) \stackrel{def}{=} \left\{ \begin{array}{lcl} <> & \Leftarrow & \sigma(k) = \langle 1, NIL \rangle \\ cons(a, f_\sigma(k')) & \Leftarrow & \sigma(k) = \langle 2, \langle a, k' \rangle \rangle \end{array} \right.$$

which is written in a more "palatable" notation, as follows:

$$\begin{array}{rcl} f(k, \sigma) & \stackrel{def}{=} & if\ is\text{-}NIL(\sigma(k)) \\ & & then\ <> \\ & & else\ \ let\ \ \sigma(k) = \langle a, k' \rangle \\ & & \qquad\ \ in\ \ \ cons(a, f(k', \sigma)) \end{array}$$

Removing the assumption that σ is a total function, we have to face pointer undefinedness — $\sigma(k)$ in (67) is undefined wherever $k \notin dom(\sigma)$ and other pointers k' in the range of σ, reachable from k, may be in the same situation.

Pointer reachability can be characterized by the transitive closure $<^+_{\mathcal{F}}$ of the following ordering on K, induced by $\mathcal{F}$ and σ:

$$k_1 <_{\mathcal{F}} k \stackrel{def}{=} k \in dom(\sigma) \wedge k_1 \in_{\mathcal{F}} \sigma(k) \tag{70}$$

where logical conjunction is once again regarded as non-strict (*cf.* (11)), and $\in_{\mathcal{F}}$ is structurally defined, for polynomial $\mathcal{F}$, as follows:

$$\begin{array}{rcl} k \in_C x & \stackrel{def}{=} & FALSE \\ k \in_{\lambda X.X} x & \stackrel{def}{=} & k = x \\ k \in_{\mathcal{F} \times \mathcal{G}} \langle x, y \rangle & \stackrel{def}{=} & k \in_{\mathcal{F}} x \vee k \in_{\mathcal{G}} y \\ k \in_{\mathcal{F}+\mathcal{G}} x & \stackrel{def}{=} & \left\{ \begin{array}{lcl} k \in_{\mathcal{F}} y & \Leftarrow & x = \langle 1, y \rangle \\ k \in_{\mathcal{G}} z & \Leftarrow & x = \langle 2, z \rangle \end{array} \right. \end{array} \tag{71}$$

The following invariant for (64) prevents reachable pointers being undefined:

$$\begin{array}{rcl} \phi(k, \sigma) & \stackrel{def}{=} & let\ \ P = \{k\} \cup \{k' \in K \mid k' <^+_{\mathcal{F}} k\} \\ & & in\ \ \ P \subseteq dom(\sigma) \end{array}$$

However, this invariant is insufficient if we want to restrict our interpretation of recursion to least fixpoints [24], that is, if we want to guarantee that $f(k, \sigma)$ does not yield infinite results. It remains to enforce that P is a well-founded set *wrt.* $<_{\mathcal{F}}$:

$$\begin{array}{rcl} \phi(k, \sigma) & \stackrel{def}{=} & let\ \ P = \{k\} \cup \{k' \in K \mid k' <^+_{\mathcal{F}} k\} \\ & & in\ \ \ P \subseteq dom(\sigma) \wedge \\ & & \qquad \forall \emptyset \subset C \subseteq P : \exists m \in C : \forall k' <_{\mathcal{F}} m : k' \notin C \end{array} \tag{72}$$

For instance, let $\mathcal{F}(X) = C \hookrightarrow \mathcal{G}(X)$. It is not hard to obtain $\in_{\mathcal{F}}$ for this case,

$$k \in_{C \hookrightarrow \mathcal{G}} x \stackrel{def}{=} \exists c \in dom(x) : k \in_{\mathcal{G}} x(c) \tag{73}$$

Condition (73) will be helpful in understanding the illustration of calculated reification which will be presented in section 5.

The proofs about the surjectiveness of f (67), for $(X_0, \delta : \mathcal{F}(X_0) \longrightarrow X_0)$ a finite or denumerable fixpoint of $\mathcal{F}$, and its termination over ϕ (72), are too lengthy to be pursued here, and are available from [22]. The first of these proofs is inductively performed over the structure of polynomial functor $\mathcal{F}$, and requires $K \cong \mathbb{N}$.

It is interesting to analyze the meaning of (64) for a few simple, particular cases of $\mathcal{F}$:

- Constant functor $\mathcal{F}(X) = C$. $(C, 1_C)$ is of course a fixpoint of $\mathcal{F}$. From (67) and (55) we obtain abstraction map

$$\begin{array}{rcl} f & : & K \times (K \hookrightarrow C) \longrightarrow C \\ f(k,\sigma) & \stackrel{def}{=} & \delta(\mathcal{F}(f_\sigma)(\sigma(k))) \\ & = & 1_C(C(f_\sigma)(\sigma(k))) \\ & = & 1_C(1_C(\sigma(k))) \\ & = & \sigma(k) \end{array}$$

  From (70) and (71) we obtain an empty ordering $<^+_{\mathcal{F}}$ on pointers (K), whereby invariant (72) reduces to

$$\phi(k,\sigma) \stackrel{def}{=} k \in dom(\sigma) \tag{74}$$

  as expected. This particular case corresponds to a popular programming technique (typical of C or PASCAL): instead of handling C data directly (statically stored), the program handles *dynamic* references to them.

- Same as above, for $C = 0$. This case trivializes (63) to the definition $X \cong 0$ of an empty data domain; note that $K \times (K \hookrightarrow \mathcal{F}(K))$ becomes $K \times (K \hookrightarrow 0)$ which reduces to

$$\begin{array}{rcl} K \times (K \hookrightarrow 0) & \cong & K \times \bigcup_{X \subseteq K} 0^X \\ & \cong & K \times 0^0 \end{array}$$

  That is, $\sigma : 0 \longrightarrow 0$ is bound to be completely undefined, and $dom(\sigma) = \emptyset$; then $k \in dom(\sigma) = FALSE$ and (74) reduces to

$$\phi(k,\sigma) \stackrel{def}{=} FALSE$$

  As expected, we are led to the empty reification (every datum is invalid).

- Identity functor $\mathcal{F}(X) = X$. This case trivializes (63) to $X \cong X$, which accepts any fixpoint $(X_0, \delta : X_0 \longrightarrow X_0)$ for δ a bijection. Let us see how the least fixpoint interpretation implicit in (72) reduces this case to the previous one ($X_0 = 0$), by showing that definedness and well-foundedness cannot be met at the same time.

Assuming that P is well-founded *wrt.* $k_1 <_{\lambda X.X} k$ (which we abbreviate to $k_1 < k$ and is logically equivalent to $k \in dom(\sigma) \wedge k_1 = \sigma(k)$), we have

$$\exists m \in P : \sigma(m) \notin P \tag{75}$$

But if $m \in P$ then m is reachable from k ($m <^+ k$), $m \in dom(\sigma)$ and $\sigma(m) < m$. Then

$$\sigma(m) < m <^+ k$$

i.e. $\sigma(m) <^+ k$, which entails $\sigma(m) \in P$ and contradicts (75). Thus the conjunction of definedness and well-foundedness in (74) is impossible, and we obtain

$$\phi(k, \sigma) \stackrel{def}{=} FALSE$$

Equation (72) is a generalization of some invariant definitions found in the VDM literature, *cf. e.g.* [10, 47, 48]. It also is less constrained in the sense that only the set P of pointers in σ reachable from k is affected by non-circularity and definedness restrictions ([10, 48] constrain $dom(\sigma)$ as a whole).

Some algorithmic flavour can be added to (72) by introducing an auxiliary function

$$reach(k, \sigma) \stackrel{def}{=} \{k\} \cup \{k' \in K \mid k' <^+_{\mathcal{F}} k\}$$

(that is, $P = reach(k, \sigma)$) subject to transformations as follows:

$$\begin{array}{ll} reach(k, \sigma) \stackrel{def}{=} & \\ & \{k\} \cup \{k' \in K \mid k' <^+_{\mathcal{F}} k\} \\ = & \{k\} \cup \left\{ \begin{array}{lll} \emptyset & \Leftarrow & k \notin dom(\sigma) \\ \bigcup_{k' <_{\mathcal{F}} k} \{k'\} \cup \{k'' \in K \mid k'' <^+_{\mathcal{F}} k'\} & \Leftarrow & k \in dom(\sigma) \end{array} \right. \\ = & \{k\} \cup \left\{ \begin{array}{lll} \emptyset & \Leftarrow & k \notin dom(\sigma) \\ \bigcup_{k' <_{\mathcal{F}} k} reach(k', \sigma) & \Leftarrow & k \in dom(\sigma) \end{array} \right. \end{array}$$

The test for definedness may be encapsulated in a predicate

$$defined(k, \sigma) \stackrel{def}{=} P \subseteq dom(\sigma)$$

Since $P = reach(k, \sigma)$ we obtain, after the expected substitutions and transformations:

$$defined(k, \sigma) \stackrel{def}{=} \left\{ \begin{array}{lll} FALSE & \Leftarrow & k \notin dom(\sigma) \\ \forall k' <_{\mathcal{F}} k : defined(k', \sigma) & \Leftarrow & k \in dom(\sigma) \end{array} \right.$$

Note that both *reach* and *defined* do not compute the intended set-theoretical fixpoint implicit in the transitive closure of $<_{\mathcal{F}}$ wherever this relation is cyclic. A $<_{\mathcal{F}}$-cycle is detected wherever we revisit the same $k \in K$. Since cycle detection matches with wellfoundedness testing, one may put everything together and write

$$\phi(k,\sigma) = \phi_{aux}(k,\sigma,\emptyset) \tag{76}$$

where

$$\phi_{aux}(k,\sigma,C) \stackrel{def}{=} \begin{cases} FALSE & \Leftarrow \quad k \notin dom(\sigma) \vee k \in C \\ \forall k' <_{\mathcal{F}} k : \phi_{aux}(k',\sigma,C \cup \{k\}) & \Leftarrow \quad k \in dom(\sigma) \end{cases} \tag{77}$$

5 An Illustration of Calculated Reification

The *Sets*-model *DecTree* for decision trees presented above (14) will be explored in this section and subject to a series of calculations, illustrating the main results of this paper. Refinement steps will be indexed by natural numbers to make it easy to apply rule (12) for inferring abstraction maps and data-type invariants.

This exercise about *DecTree* is a simplified version of a similar exercise reported in [40], a project where legal knowledge about public property records, expressed in terms of decision trees, had to be incorporated in a pre-existing relational database system.

5.1 Data-level Reification

Recursion removal according to (64) is the first transformation applicable to (14). One obtains

$$DecTree \quad \trianglelefteq_1 \quad DecTree_1$$

where

$$DecTree_1 \quad = \quad K \times (K \hookrightarrow What \times (Answer \hookrightarrow K)) \tag{78}$$

Before proceeding, let us think a little about what has been achieved in $DecTree_1$ (78). Two interpretations (at least) are admissible:

1. For K a domain of *pointers*,

$$K \hookrightarrow What \times (Answer \hookrightarrow K) \tag{79}$$

   models a heap-segment of dynamic storage. In PASCAL (where the heap is "hidden" in the run-time system) we would write something like [10]

```
type  DecTree1 =  ^DecTree;
      DecTree =   record
                  Q: What;                          (80)
                  R: array [Answer] of ^DecTree
                  end;
```

[10] Strictly speaking, (80) is a further refinement of (79) because PASCAL pointers implement $K+1$ rather than K (the 1 alternative corresponds to the `nil` value). Therefore, an invariant over (80) will be required ruling the `nil` alternative out of `DecTree1`.

2. For K a domain of *object names*, (79) models the object database

   $$name \longrightarrow object$$

   implicit in an object-oriented programming environment [47]. This is better suggested by the following VDM "sugaring" of (78):

$$\begin{array}{rcrl} DecTree_1 & :: & ObjName: & K \\ & & Archive: & ObjBase \\ ObjBase & = & \multicolumn{2}{l}{K \xrightarrow{m} Attributes} \\ Attributes & :: & Q: & What \\ & & SubObjs: & Answer \xrightarrow{m} K \end{array}$$

Let us proceed via law (42):

$$\begin{array}{rcl} DecTree_1 & = & K \times (K \hookrightarrow What \times (Answer \hookrightarrow K)) \\ & \trianglelefteq_2 & K \times ((K \hookrightarrow What) \times ((K \times Answer) \hookrightarrow K)) \\ & = & DecTree_2 \end{array} \tag{81}$$

For K a state descriptor, $DecTree_2$ accepts the following interpretation:

- $(K \times Answer) \hookrightarrow K$ = *state transition diagram* of a (deterministic) *finite state automaton* ($Answer$ = input stimuli);
- the first factor $k \in K$ in (81) = current state of the automaton;
- $K \hookrightarrow What$ = semantic table assigning a meaning to each state.

Step 2 led us to a lower level where we met "good old friends": finite state automata can be implemented using *arrays* and *jumps*! Carrying on our reasoning,

$$\begin{array}{rcl} DecTree_2 & = & K \times ((K \hookrightarrow What) \times ((K \times Answer) \hookrightarrow K)) \\ & \trianglelefteq_3 & K \times (2^{K \times What} \times 2^{(K \times Answer) \times K}) \\ & = & DecTree_3 \\ & \cong_4 & K \times (2^{K \times What} \times 2^{K \times Answer \times K}) \\ & = & DecTree_4 \end{array}$$

cf. (46) and (22). Our final model,

$$DecTree_4 = K \times (2^{K \times What} \times 2^{K \times Answer \times K}) \tag{82}$$

is nothing but a relational database schema for implementing $DecTree$ in terms of two database files (tables) where K plays the rôle of a domain of *keys*.

In summary, our reasoning can be sketched by

$$DecTree \trianglelefteq_1 DecTree_1 \trianglelefteq_2 DecTree_2 \trianglelefteq_3 DecTree_3 \cong_4 DecTree_4 \tag{83}$$

5.2 Inference of the Abstraction Map and Data-type Invariant

The overall abstraction map of (83) can be inferred via (12), *i.e.*

$$f(k, \langle t, t' \rangle) = f_1(f_2(f_3(f_4(k, \langle t, t' \rangle))))$$

where f is obtained by functorial composition of abstraction maps f_1 to f_4, as follows: f_4 is given by

$$f_4 = 1_K \times (1_{2^{K \times What}} \times 2^f)$$

where

$$(A \times B) \times C \cong_f A \times B \times C$$

that is,

$$f_4(\langle k, \langle t, t' \rangle \rangle) \quad = \quad \langle k, \langle t, \{ \langle \langle k, a \rangle, k' \rangle | \ \langle k, a, k' \rangle \in t' \} \rangle \rangle$$

In a similar way, f_3 resorts to the mkf abstraction map (48) between relations and functions,

$$f_3 \quad = \quad 1_K \times (mkf \times mkf)$$

and f_2 is simply

$$f_2 = 1_K \times f$$

where f is given by (44). Finally,

$$\begin{array}{rcl} f_1(k, \sigma) & = & f_\sigma(k) \\ f_\sigma(k) & \stackrel{def}{=} & \mathit{let} \quad \sigma(k) = \langle w, \sigma' \rangle \\ & & \mathit{in} \quad \langle w, \{ a \mapsto f_\sigma(\sigma'(a)) | \ a \in dom(\sigma') \} \rangle \end{array} \qquad (84)$$

cf. (67,19) and (57). Then

$$\begin{array}{rcl} f_3(f_4(\langle k, \langle t, t' \rangle \rangle)) & = & \langle k, \langle mkf(t), mkf(\{ \langle \langle k, a \rangle, k' \rangle | \ \langle k, a, k' \rangle \in t' \}) \rangle \rangle \\ & = & \langle k, \langle \{ k \mapsto w | \ \langle k, w \rangle \in t \}, \{ \langle k, a \rangle \mapsto k' | \ \langle k, a, k' \rangle \in t' \} \rangle \rangle \end{array}$$

and

$$\begin{array}{l} f_2(f_3(f_4(\langle k, \langle t, t' \rangle \rangle))) = \\ \qquad \langle k, \{ x \mapsto \langle w, \{ a \mapsto k' | \ \langle k'', a, k' \rangle \in t' \wedge k'' = x \} \rangle | \ \langle x, w \rangle \in t \} \rangle \end{array} \qquad (85)$$

Combining (85) with (84) we obtain, after some simplifications

$$\begin{array}{rl} f(k, \langle t, t' \rangle) \stackrel{def}{=} & \mathit{let} \quad w = the(\{ \pi_2(r) | \ r \in t \wedge \pi_1(r) = k \}) \\ & \mathit{in} \quad \langle w, \{ a \mapsto f(k', \langle t, t' \rangle) | \ \langle k'', a, k' \rangle \in t' \wedge k'' = k \} \rangle \end{array} \qquad (86)$$

The overall data-type invariant can be calculated in similar way,

$$\phi(k, \langle t, t' \rangle) = \phi_3(f_4(k, \langle t, t' \rangle)) \wedge \phi_2(f_3(f_4(k, \langle t, t' \rangle))) \wedge \phi_1(f_2(f_3(f_4(k, \langle t, t' \rangle))))$$

since ϕ_4 is universally true. ϕ_3 resorts to fdp (47),

$$\phi_3 = (\lambda k.TRUE) \times fdp \times fdp$$

and ϕ_2 is given by (43). It may be checked that $\phi_2(f_3(f_4(k, \langle t, t' \rangle)))$ reduces to $\pi_1[t'] \subseteq \pi_1[t]$. Then

$$\begin{array}{lll} \phi_3(f_4(k, \langle t, t' \rangle)) & = & TRUE \wedge fdp(t) \wedge fdp(\{\langle\langle k, a\rangle, k'\rangle \mid \langle k, a, k'\rangle \in t'\}) \\ & = & fdp(t) \wedge fdp(\{\langle\langle k, a\rangle, k'\rangle \mid \langle k, a, k'\rangle \in t'\}) \end{array} \quad (87)$$

Further calculating $fdp(\{\langle\langle k, a\rangle, k'\rangle \mid \langle k, a, k'\rangle \in t'\})$ in (87) yields

$$\forall \langle k_1, a, k_1' \rangle, \langle k_2, b, k_2' \rangle \in t' : (k_1 = k_2 \wedge a = b) \Rightarrow k_1' = k_2'$$

Finally, ϕ_1 (72) is based on the ordering

$$\begin{array}{lll} k_1 < k & \stackrel{def}{=} & k \in dom(\sigma) \wedge \\ & & (FALSE \vee \exists a \in dom(\pi_2(\sigma(k))) : k_1 = \pi_2(\sigma(k))(a)) \\ & \Leftrightarrow & k \in dom(\sigma) \wedge \;\; let \quad \sigma' = \pi_2(\sigma(k)) \\ & & \qquad\qquad\quad in \quad \exists a \in dom(\sigma') : k_1 = \sigma'(a) \end{array}$$

cf. (73). Recalling (76,77) above, we may reduce $\phi_1(f_2(f_3(f_4(k, \langle t, t' \rangle))))$ to $aux(k, t, t', \emptyset)$ where

$$aux(k, t, t', C) \stackrel{def}{=}$$
$$\left\{ \begin{array}{lll} FALSE & \Leftarrow & k \notin \pi_1[t] \vee \\ & & k \in C \\ \forall r \in \{\pi_1(s) = k \mid s \in t'\} : aux(\pi_3(r), t, t', C \cup \{k\}) & \Leftarrow & k \in \pi_1[t] \end{array} \right. \quad (88)$$

Putting everything together, we finally obtain the following (non-trivial) datatype invariant over (82):

$$\begin{array}{l} \phi(k, \langle t, t' \rangle) = \\ \quad (\forall \langle k, w \rangle, \langle k', w' \rangle \in t : k = k' \Rightarrow w = w') \wedge \\ \quad (\forall \langle k_1, a, k_1' \rangle, \langle k_2, b, k_2' \rangle \in t' : (k_1 = k_2 \wedge a = b) \Rightarrow k_1' = k_2') \wedge \\ \quad \pi_1[t'] \subseteq \pi_1[t] \wedge \\ \quad aux(k, t, t', \emptyset) \end{array} \quad (89)$$

where aux is the recursive auxiliary predicate given by (88).

5.3 Operation Reification

From the operations which are expected over type *DecTree* we select the following,

$$\begin{array}{l} decide : DecTree \times Answer \rightarrow DecTree \\ decide(\sigma, a) \stackrel{def}{=} \; let \quad m = dom(\pi_2(\sigma)) \\ \qquad\qquad\qquad\quad in \quad \left\{ \begin{array}{lll} \sigma & \Leftarrow & a \notin m \\ (\pi_2(\sigma))(a) & \Leftarrow & a \in m \end{array} \right. \end{array} \quad (90)$$

which specifies the action of picking a particular answer a available at the root menu of decision tree σ and selecting the corresponding sub-tree (if a is a valid answer).

We want to calculate the reification of *decide* at reification-level 4, that is *wrt.* $DecTree_4$ (82). Following [7, 33], we start by building the corresponding (commutative) reification diagram:

$$
\begin{array}{ccc}
DecTree \times Answer & \xrightarrow{\ decide\ } & DecTree \\
\uparrow {\scriptstyle f \times 1_{Answer}} & & \uparrow {\scriptstyle f} \\
DecTree_4 \times Answer & \xrightarrow[\ decide_4\ ]{} & DecTree_4
\end{array}
$$

which leads to equation

$$f(decide_4(k, \langle t, t' \rangle, a)) = decide(f(k, \langle t, t' \rangle), a) \tag{91}$$

where $decide_4$ is regarded as the unknown and f is abstraction map (86). Substituting (90) in (91) we obtain

$$
\begin{array}{rcl}
f(decide_4(k, \langle t, t' \rangle, a)) & = & decide(f(k, \langle t, t' \rangle), a) \\
& = & let \quad m = dom(\pi_2(f(k, \langle t, t' \rangle))) \\
& & in \quad \left\{ \begin{array}{lcl} f(k, \langle t, t' \rangle) & \Leftarrow & a \notin m \\ (\pi_2(f(k, \langle t, t' \rangle)))(a) & \Leftarrow & a \in m \end{array} \right.
\end{array}
$$

Assuming the following definitions, which specify usual *projection/ selection* relational operators,

$$
\begin{array}{l}
proj : \{1, \ldots, n\} \times 2^{A_1 \times \ldots \times A_n} \longrightarrow \bigcup_{i=1}^{n} 2^{A_i} \\
proj(i, t) \stackrel{def}{=} \{\pi_i(r) | \ r \in t\} = \pi_i[t]
\end{array}
$$

and

$$
\begin{array}{l}
sel : (\sum_{i=1}^{n} A_i) \times 2^{A_1 \times \ldots \times A_n} \longrightarrow 2^{A_1 \times \ldots \times A_n} \\
sel(\langle i, a \rangle, t) \stackrel{def}{=} \{r \in t | \ a = \pi_i(r)\}
\end{array}
$$

it is easy to show that

$$dom(\pi_2(f(k, \langle t, t' \rangle))) = proj(2, sel(\langle 1, k \rangle, t'))$$

and that

$$
\begin{array}{rll}
(\pi_2(f(k, \langle t, t' \rangle)))(a) = & let & t'' = sel(\langle 1, k \rangle, t') \\
& & t''' = sel(\langle 2, a \rangle, t'') \\
& & k' = the(proj(3, t''')) \\
& in & f(k', \langle t, t' \rangle)
\end{array}
$$

Then

$$
\begin{array}{l}
f(decide_4(k, \langle t, t' \rangle, a)) = \\
\qquad let \quad m = proj(2, sel(\langle 1, k \rangle, t')) \\
\qquad in \quad f(\left\{ \begin{array}{lcl} \langle k, \langle t, t' \rangle \rangle & \Leftarrow & a \notin m \\ let \quad k' = the(proj(3, sel(\langle 2, a \rangle, sel(\langle 1, k \rangle, t')))) & \Leftarrow & a \in m \ ) \\ in \quad \langle k', \langle t, t' \rangle \rangle & & \end{array} \right.
\end{array}
\tag{92}
$$

Removing f from both sides of (92) we obtain

$$
\begin{array}{l}
decide_4(k, \langle t, t' \rangle, a) \stackrel{def}{=} \\
\quad let \quad m = proj(2, sel(\langle 1, k \rangle, t')) \\
\qquad\quad k' = \left\{ \begin{array}{ll} k & \Leftarrow \; a \notin m \\ the(proj(3, sel(\langle 2, a \rangle, sel(\langle 1, k \rangle, t')))) & \Leftarrow \; a \in m \end{array} \right. \\
\quad in \quad \langle k', \langle t, t' \rangle \rangle
\end{array}
$$

which implements the expected "pointer-handling" operation in a relational database programming style. It should be noted that $decide_4$ is not a unique solution to (91) because f (86) is non-injective. Other valid solutions might "garbage collect" t and t' by removing all entries accessed by k (which will not be revisited, *cf.* invariant (89)).

6 Conclusions

The research described in this paper extends the work on the SETS calculus reported in [34, 35]. The $\trianglelefteq$-subcalculus is studied in much more detail and includes generic results for refining recursive data models.

Many laws of SETS are trivial from a strict mathematical viewpoint. What appears to be relevant is their use in the context of model-oriented reification. The synthesis of arbitrarily complex abstraction maps and data-type invariants induced by data refinement, resorts to a "functorial" approach whose compactness pays off the initial effort in understanding its categorial foundation. However, it is apparent from the final example of the paper that "pen and pencil" inference of such maps and invariants may become fairly laborious tasks in sizeable, real-life reifications. Resorting to a functional transformation tool (*e.g.* a system such as NUPRL [6] or ERIL [8]) may be of some help in this respect.

Section 5 illustrates how dramatically the complexity of data-type invariants may increase throughout reification. This provides good evidence of how insecure informal designs may become if invariants are either ignored or misrecorded.

7 Future Work

The SETS calculus is still in its infancy and there are several lines along which it may be developed.

7.1 Foundations

The categorial foundations of SETS need further investigation, particularly with respect to its naive basis on set-theoretical *cardinality*. Apparently, one is free to choose an abstraction map (surjection) $f : B \to A$ between two domains A and B such that $A \trianglelefteq B$. But this freedom appears to be available only at very basic data domains (*e.g.* *elems* from sequences to sets) and is denied by the *functorial* strategy adopted in this paper for structural composition of data refinements. In fact, it would be "unnatural" to choose an abstraction map

$$g : \mathcal{F}(B) \to \mathcal{F}(A)$$

other than $\mathcal{F}(f)$ if f is the "natural" abstraction map between B and A, *cf.* theorem 2. Such a *functorial* naturalness of some abstraction maps (and corresponding invariants) is even more evident wherever recursion is around, *cf.* section 4.

This brings to mind Wand's *final algebra* approach to specification [45] [11]:

> [...] for any object A of K, there is only one morphism in K from A to W. (There is only one "reasonable" abstraction map for each data type representation A, *i.e.*, each "concrete" value in A may reasonably represent only one "abstract" value in W.) [...] that is: *an abstract data type is a final object in the category of its representations* [...]

In this *final* approach to refinement, epimorphism (2) will become *unique* and reifications will have to form a *comma category* [45].

Alternatively, some kind of "ordering" is required on multiple reification. In fact, there seems to be no "best" way in which a given data domain A may be reified by some other domain B. Which of the following "limits" is better from a calculation viewpoint: is it to have as much redundancy as necessary to avoid invariants on B? or is it to introduce as many invariants as necessary in order for A to be isomorphic to the corresponding subset of B? The latter alternative provides unique solutions to algorithmic refinements (recall section 5.3), but invariants grow in complexity. Moreover, this problem has model-theoretical implications with non-determinism, observational equivalence, implementation bias *etc.* [32, 38].

Other aspects which may require better foundations are "context-sensitive" transformations [35], "ad hoc" invariants [39] and recursion handling [12] [22]. The main result of the paper should be extended from polynomial to co-continuous functors, in a category theoretical setting.

7.2 Operation Refinement

SETS claims no originality on operation refinement. Section 5.3 illustrated how "program transformation"-like reasoning can be used to calculate functional refinements. But other techniques could have been used, *e.g.* the "Oxford calculus" [30, 29]. In fact, it is straightforward to combine this calculus with SETS, as is apparent from the following quotation from [30]:

> An *abstraction invariant AI* is chosen which links the abstract variables a and the concrete variables c. [...] In many cases, the abstraction invariant is *functional* [...] and can always be written as a conjunction
>
> $$(a = AF(c)) \land CI(c)$$
>
> where AF we call the *abstraction function* and CI the *concrete invariant*.

[11] In the following quotation from [45], W is an "abstract data type" and K is the category of representations of W.

[12] Note that some interesting reification steps actually *introduce* (rather than remove) recursion [7]. This kind of reification is particularly relevant *wrt.* parallel runtime environments.

in which one immediately identifies a $\trianglelefteq_{AF}^{CI}$-refinement step which may be calculated using SETS rather than being simply "chosen".

7.3 "Reverse" Calculation

Another direction of future research is (formal) *reverse specification*. Some experimentation carried out by the author suggests that SETS may become useful in reversing pre-existing code, by performing calculations in the reverse direction, that is $\trianglerighteq$-calculations instead of $\trianglelefteq$-calculations (from implementation to specification). As a side effect, such pieces of code are likely to be improved since code-level invariants may be unveiled which were never recorded in the documentation.

7.4 Horizontal Refinement and Classification

Yet another potential application of the calculus concerns *horizontal refinement* [13], that is the decomposition of large software systems in terms of re-usable *components* [41]. Many laws of *Sets* work in this direction, particularly the ones which "push the $\times$ construct outwards" — *e.g.* (38), (39), (42), (45), (60) *etc.* — because they help in factorizing complex state structures of monolithic designs into collections of simpler structures which may have been dealt with already, and may thus be re-used.

The hierarchical *classification* and retrieval of re-usable abstract models is suggested above in section 3.4.1 and has been further developed in [36] and [37], where a *repository* of such models is hierarchically organized in terms of the subterm instantiation ordering on the *Sets* expressions which denote the classes of their internal states. The same repository records $\trianglelefteq$-reification relationships among components.

Acknowledgements

The author wishes to thank Isabel Jourdan (Dept. of Mathematics, University of Coimbra) for her comments on earlier drafts of this paper. This work has been partly supported by the JNICT council under PMCT contracts nrs. 87/63 and 87/66.

References

[1] Arbib M.A., Kfoury A., Mool R.N. *A Basis for Theoretical Computer Science.* Texts and Monographs in Computer Science (D.Gries Ed.), Springer-Verlag, 1981.

[2] Aceto L., Hennessy M. *Towards Action-refinement in Process Algebras.* Computer Science Report 3/880, University of Sussex.

[3] Backus J. *Can Programming Be Liberated from the von Neumann Style? A Functional Style and Its Algebra of Programs.* CACM 21(8):613-641, Aug. 1978.

[4] Burstall R.M., Darlington J. *A Transformation System for Developing Recursive Programs.* JACM 24(1):44-67, Jan. 1977.

[5] Burstall R.M., Goguen J.A. *An Informal Introduction to Specifications Using Clear.* In *The Correctness Problem in Computer Science* (Boyer R.S., Moore J.S.—Eds.), 185–213, Academic Press, 1981.

[6] Constable R.L. *et al. Implementing Mathematics in the Nuprl Proof Development System.* Prentice-Hall International, 1986.

[7] Darlington J. *Program Transformation.* In *Funct. Prog. and Its Applications: An Advanced Course*, Univ. of Newcastle. Cambridge Univ. Press, 1982.

[8] Dick J.J. *ERIL User's Manual v. R1.6a.*, RAL-88-055, September, 1988.

[9] Dijkstra E.W. *A Discipline of Programming.* Prentice-Hall, 1976.

[10] Fielding E. *The Specification of Abstract Mappings and Their Implementation as B^+-Trees.* PRG-18, Oxford Univ., Sep. 1980.

[11] Goguen J.A., Thatcher J.W., Wagner E.W., Wright J.B. *Initial Algebra Semantics and Continuous Algebras.* JACM 24:1, 68-95, January 1977.

[12] Goguen J., Thatcher J.W., Wagner E.G. *Initial Algebra Approach to the Specification, Correctness and Implementation of Algebraic Data Types.* Current Trends in Prog. Technology, Vol.IV, Prentice-Hall, 1978.

[13] Goguen J.A. *Reusing and Interconnecting Software Components.* IEEE Computer, 19(2), 16–28, February 1986.

[14] Guttag J.V., Horning J.J. *The Algebraic Specification of Abstract Data Types.* Acta Informatica 10, 27-52, 1978.

[15] Hennessy M. *Algebraic Theory of Processes.* MIT Press Series in the Foundations of Computing, 1988.

[16] Hennessy M., Milner R. *Algebraic Laws for Nondeterminism and Concurrency.* JACM 32(1):137–161, Jan. 1985.

[17] Hoare C.A.R., He J.F., Sanders J.W. *Prespecification in Data Refinement.* Inf. Proc. Letters 25, 71-76, 1987.

[18] Jifeng H. *Process Refinement.* In *The Theory and Practice of Refinement*, McDermid (Ed.), Butterworths, 1989.

[19] Jones C.B. *Software Development — A Rigorous Approach.* Prentice-Hall, 1980.

[20] Jones C.B. *Systematic Software Development Using VDM.* Prentice-Hall, 1986.

[21] Jones C.B. *Interference Resumed.* Technical Report UMCS-91-5-1, University of Manchester, 1991.

[22] Jourdan I.S. *Reificação de Tipos Abstractos de Dados: Uma Abordagem Matemática.* M.Sc. thesis, University of Coimbra, 1991 (in Portuguese).

[23] Knuth D. *Structured Programming with Goto Statements.* ACM Comp. Surveys, 6:(4), Dec. 1974.

[24] Manes E.G., Arbib M.A. *Algebraic Approaches to Program Semantics.* Springer-Verlag, 1986.

[25] Milner R. *Flowgraphs and Flow Algebras.* JACM 26(4):794–818, Oct. 1979.

[26] Milner R. *Interpreting One Concurrent Calculus in Another.* Proc. of the Int. Conference on Fifth Generation Computer Systems, 321–326, 1988.

[27] Milner R. *Communication and Concurrency.* Prentice-Hall International, Series in Computer Science (C.A.R.Hoare Ed.), 1989.

[28] Möller B. (Ed.) *A Survey of the Project CIP: Computer-aided, Intuition-Guided Programming Wide Spectrum Language and Program Transformations.* Report TUM-I8406, T. Universität München, July 1984.

[29] Morgan C. *Programming from Specification.* Prentice-Hall International, 1990.

[30] Morgan C., Gardiner P.H.B. *Data Refinement by Calculation.* Acta Informatica 27, 481-503, 1990, Springer-Verlag.

[31] Mosses P. *Abstract Semantic Algebras!* Report DAIMI PB-145, Aarhus University, July 1982.

[32] Nipkow T. *Nondeterministic Data Types: Models and Implementations.* Acta Informatica 22, 629-661, Springer-Verlag, 1986.

[33] Oliveira J.N. *The Transformational Paradigm as a Means of Smoothing Abrupt Software Design Steps.* Technical Report CCES-JNO:R2/85, University of Minho, December 1985.

[34] Oliveira J.N. *Refinamento Transformacional de Especificações (Terminais).* Actas das XII *Jornadas Luso-Espanholas de Matemática,* Vol.II, 412-417, 4-8 Maio 1987, Braga, Portugal (in Portuguese).

[35] Oliveira J.N. *A Reification Calculus for Model-Oriented Software Specification.* Formal Aspects of Computing, Vol.2, 1-23, 1990, Springer-Verlag.

[36] Oliveira J.N. *In CASE You Use Formal Methods ... or Formal Methods Just In CASE!* Invited communication, CASE'91 Symposium, Braga, Portugal, 10–11 May 1991 (in Portuguese).

[37] Oliveira J.N. *Especificação Formal de Programas.* Lecture Notes for M.Sc. Course in Computing, University of Minho, 1991 (in Portuguese).

[38] Oliveira J.N. *A Note on $\trianglelefteq$-Calculation, Nondeterminism and Implementation Bias.* DI/INESC Technical Report (in preparation).

[39] Oliveira J.N. *Hash Tables: A Case Study in $\trianglelefteq$-Calculation.* DI/INESC Technical Report (in preparation).

[40] Pacheco O. *Concepção de um Sistema Pericial para o Registo Predial.* Relatório de Estágio, LESI, U.Minho, Braga 1990 (in Portuguese).

[41] ROSE Consortium — E.S.F. *The ROSE Subproject.* Presentation at the Workshop on Reuse of Software Development Components, Joint Organization CEC-ESF, Berlin, 25-26 October 1989.

[42] Shaw R.C., Jones C.B. *Case Studies in Systematic Software Development.* Prentice-Hall, 1990.

[43] Spivey J.M. *The Z Notation — A Reference Manual.* Prentice-Hall International, Series in Computer Science (C.A.R.Hoare Ed.), 1989.

[44] Vogler W. *Bisimulation and Action Refinement.* Technical Report INFO-05-90-120-480/1.-FMI, T. Universität München, 1990.

[45] Wand M. *Final Algebraic Semantics and Data Type Extensions.* JCSS 19, 27-44, 1979.

[46] Wirth N. *Algorithms + Data Structures = Programs.* Prentice-Hall Int., 1976.

[47] Wolczko M. *Semantics of Object-oriented Languages.* Tech. Report UMCS-88-6-1, U.Manchester, 1988.

[48] Wolczko M. *Garbage Collection.* in [42], 211-233.

Classification of Refinements in VDM*

Morten Elvang-Gøransson

Department of Computer Science, Technical University of Denmark

Lyngby, Denmark

Abstract

A classification of different kinds of VDM refinements is given. Based on this classification a more appealing explanation of an example from the VDM literature can be given.

1 Introduction

The traditional refinement concept of VDM is defined in [3]. This refinement concept is in the style of Hoare [1] and formalizes the requirement for one specification, the concrete, to be a correct refinement of another specification, the abstract. The formal requirements are expressed as the refinement proof obligations and by these most refinements can be handled. There is however reported examples of refinements that seem to be acceptable but which cannot be verified because of incompleteness in the refinement proof obligations. In this paper we show how the traditional refinement concept of VDM may be generalized to cover a wider class of refinements. The generalized refinement concept gives rise to a notion of partial correctness, which is briefly discussed. The improvement with respect to the traditional refinement proof obligations is illustrated by showing a single example of their increased expressive power.

For the reader acquainted with VDM we emphasize that our notion of refinement corresponds to what is called 'data reification' in [3]. 'Operation decomposition' is not considered. We also emphasize that the kind of refinements that can be handled is of the same nature as those described in [3]. Thus the expressive power of the VDM refinement concept is not increased significantly, but moderately.

We start by giving an introduction to VDM [3] and by resuming the traditional refinement proof obligations for *normal* refinements. We shall define a more general class through a re-definition of the proof obligations. Generalized refinement proof obligations are defined first for *partial* refinements and then for *biased* refinements. Based on this (non disjoint) classification of refinements into normal, partial and biased we revisit an example from [2] and give a more appealing explanation than the one offered there. We conclude with some technical remarks about the relevance of this work.

---

*The work on this paper has been supported by The Danish Technical Research Council (STVF).

2 VDM and normal refinements

VDM is a model oriented specification method: the behaviour of a software system is specified by defining abstract data types which model the state of the system and operations over these types. Data types and operations are expressed in *Meta-IV* – the specification language of VDM. Meta-IV has both applicative and imperative constructs, but in this paper we only use the applicative ones. The aim is to introduce the concepts which are essential for understanding VDM, rather than specific pieces of notation.

Data types can be constructed from a fixed set of basic types and a number of type constructors. The basic types include natural numbers (**N**), integers (**Z**), booleans (**B**) and a few more. Type constructors include those for forming finite sets, finite lists, tuples (cartesian products), and subtypes. If S and T are VDM data types and $inv\text{-}T\colon T \rightarrow \mathbf{B}$ is a total predicate, then the following denote constructed types of the above mentioned kinds:

$$T\text{-}\mathsf{set} \qquad T^* \qquad S \times T \qquad T \ \mathsf{where}\ inv\text{-}T(x)$$

The basic and constructed types have a number of predefined operators such as set membership, list concatenation, arithmetic operators and so on[1].

Operations are defined over basic or constructed types. Operations can either be given a direct definition, by recursion and already defined operations, or an implicit definition by pre- and postconditions. The precondition restricts the arguments to which the operation is applicable. The postcondition is a predicate which relates the arguments to the result(s) of the application in a style similar to that employed in Hoare-logic (see e.g. [1]). The word *function* is sometimes used for directly defined operations. In general operations are considered only as state transformers.

A VDM *specification* consists of a number of data type and operation definitions. A VDM *development* is a sequence of specifications, the first being regarded as the *abstract specification* and the successive ones as *design steps*. Each level of specification in the development should be more *concrete* than its predecessor.

When considering the correctness of specifications we distinguish between *consistency* and *validity*. To *validate* a specification, means to increase one's confidence that it is really a model of the the system which the specifier had in mind. In addition, specifications must be internally *consistent*, which means that all operations must be well defined. In this paper we shall not be concerned with validation and consistency proof obligations, and they are not discussed further.

A (concrete) specification is said to be a *refinement* of another (abstract) specification if a number of conditions hold. These conditions are called *refinement proof obligations*. An abstract specification A is correctly represented by a concrete specification R if there exists a retrieve function $retr\colon Rep \rightarrow Abs$, such that:

[1]The constructed types are 'parameterizable' and the operators over them are polymorphic. For example, the type of lists is parameterized by the type of elements in the list; built-in list operators such as concatenation work equally well for lists of either natural numbers or booleans.

- the state *Rep* of *R* is adequate to represent the state *Abs* of *A*:

$$\forall a: Abs \cdot \exists r: Rep \cdot retr(r) = a \tag{1}$$

This is known as the *adequacy proof obligation*, and it ensures that there are enough elements in the concrete state to represent all the elements in the abstract state.

- for each operation OP_R in R modeling an operation OP_A in A the domains are 'similar':

$$\forall r: Rep \cdot pre\text{-}OP_A(retr(r)) \Rightarrow pre\text{-}OP_R(r) \tag{2}$$

This is known as the *domain rule*, and it requires that preconditions in the concrete representation are not strengthened.

- the results of applying abstract and concrete operations are 'similar' for 'similar' states: for all $\overleftarrow{r}, r: Rep$,

$$\begin{aligned}&(pre\text{-}OP_A(retr(\overleftarrow{r})) \wedge post\text{-}OP_R(\overleftarrow{r}, r))\\ &\Rightarrow\ post\text{-}OP_A(retr(\overleftarrow{r}), retr(r))\end{aligned} \tag{3}$$

This is known as the *result rule*, and requires that the postcondition in the concrete specification is not weakened.

If the specification is given by use of direct definitions, then the domain rule is (almost) the same, but the result rule becomes:

$$\forall r: Rep \cdot (pre\text{-}f_A(retr(r)) \Rightarrow f_A(retr(r)) = retr(f_R(r))) \tag{4}$$

for each operation f_R in R modeling f_A in A. Note, that (4) is more restrictive than (3) because implicitly defined operations need not be deterministic. There is a further requirement that initial states, e.g. a_0, in the abstract specification are represented by initial states, e.g. r_0, in the concrete specification, e.g.:

$$retr(r_0) \;=\; a_0 \tag{5}$$

The initial states proof obligation is not discussed further in this paper. If R represents A and (1–4) have been discharged, then R is a full model of A. We also say that there is a full refinement from A to R. (1–4) are called the traditional refinement proof obligations, and they characterize normal refinements.

3 Partial refinements

An example of a *partial refinement* is an abstract stack, which allows for an arbitrary number of items to be pushed, implemented by a concrete stack, which only allows a limited number of items to be pushed. A partial refinement is thus a refinement where the adequacy proof obligation does not hold in its usual form, because some of the abstract states lack a concrete state to represent them. As a result, each concrete operation will either fail or produce a result similar to the abstract operation. In other words a partial representation does not have the full model property. This can be expressed by changing the adequacy proof obligation to:

$$\forall a: Abs \cdot P(a) \;\Rightarrow\; (\exists r: Rep \cdot retr(r) = a)$$

where P tells which objects of *Abs* that are represented in *Rep*. If P is always true, then this coincides with the traditional adequacy proof obligation, and if P is always false, then we have a full collapse. Full collapses can be avoided by validating that P is not always false. We call P the *characteristic predicate* associated to the partial refinement from A to R.

To formalize that each operation must either succeed - if possible - or fail, the domain rule becomes a bit more complicated. We must ensure that as much as possible is done in the partial representation: for all r: *Rep*,

$$\begin{aligned}&pre\text{-}OP_A(retr(r))\\&\quad\Rightarrow\; [(pre\text{-}OP_R(r)) \lor \forall a: A \cdot post\text{-}OP_A(retr(r), a) \;\Rightarrow\; \neg P(a)]\end{aligned}$$

The generalized result rule has a strengthened antecedent in the implication: for all $\overleftarrow{r}, r$: *Rep*,

$$\begin{aligned}&(pre\text{-}OP_A(retr(\overleftarrow{r})) \land pre\text{-}OP_R(\overleftarrow{r}) \land post\text{-}OP_R(\overleftarrow{r}, r))\\&\quad\Rightarrow\; post\text{-}OP_A(retr(\overleftarrow{r}), retr(r)).\end{aligned}$$

The rule (4) is modified similarly. For normal refinements the generalized proof obligations work as usual, so they seem to be acceptable generalizations of the traditional proof obligations. For partial refinements they tell 'to what degree' the structure of the abstract specification has been preserved by the concrete specification: the characteristic predicate P from the generalized adequacy proof obligation tells how much of A that has been preserved in R, and the generalized domain rule ensures that the concrete operations represent the abstract operations as 'far as they can'. The generalized result rule is weakened to protect against undefinedness in the partial representation, and the degree of weakening is expressed exactly by the occurrence of the characteristic predicate in the domain rule.

There are examples of partial refinements where a satisfying characteristic predicate cannot be found. Consider a case where an abstract specification defines finite sets and is implemented by lists of limited length where the same element can occur several times. For this refinement a characteristic predicate requiring the abstract sets to be of cardinality less than 2 would be the only way to discharge the generalized proof obligations. Situations like this should not be seen as a defect of the generalized proof obligations, but rather as a tool for checking how reasonable such refinements are.

Some partial refinements give rise to models that behave very nicely. The property of a *submodel* is illustrated by the following example. Consider the abstract:

$$Abs = \mathbf{N}$$

$$add(m, n) \triangleq m + n$$

and concrete specification:

$Rep = \mathbf{N}$

where

$$inv(n) \triangleq (n \bmod 2 = 0)$$

$$plus(m, n) \triangleq m + n$$

Rep is a partial model for *Abs*, with the characteristic predicate in the refinement being:

$$P_A(n) \Leftrightarrow (inv(n))$$

Neither the domain rule nor the result rule will become more complicated in this case. Thus there are examples of refinements that are partial, but where the concrete specification has nice properties. Such refinements can conveniently be described by the generalized proof obligations for partial refinements. We have chosen the word submodels for the concrete specifications in such partial refinements, because the partialness of the refinement does not result in some operations being undefined (in the sense expressed by the generalized domain rule). One example of a refinement with this property can be found in the 'Heap storage' defined by George [4]. The example[2] is rather big, so we do not repeat it here. Another example of a submodel will occur in §6.

4 Biased refinements

In [2, §3] the problems arising from *biased specifications* are discussed. A specification is biased if there exists different states that cannot be distinguished by any of the operations in the specification. A typical example of a *biased refinement* is a biased abstract specification modeling sets by the unordered lists of their elements, implemented by an unbiased concrete specification where sets are modeled by ordered lists. The problems for the traditional VDM refinements arise if the abstract specification is 'more biased' than the concrete specification in a refinement, because the adequacy proof obligation cannot be discharged, due to the lack of a retrieve function that will make it possible to discharge the adequacy proof obligation. The way Jones remedy for this problem is by replacing the retrieve function with a relation, cf. the end of this section. We shall try to resolve the problems without skipping the retrieve function.

Since in a biased refinement certain states cannot be distinguished by any operation, this induces an equivalence relation on the states. We simply define

[2]Specifically we are referring to the refinement denoted '2_3' [4, pp. 203–6].

that all states that cannot be distinguished by any operation are equal under $=_{BIAS}$.

More formally, the $=_{BIAS}$ relation is the largest congruence relation over states, S, such that:

$$(s =_{BIAS} s') \Rightarrow \begin{cases} \text{for all } f_S\colon S \to S, & f_S(s) =_{BIAS} f_S(s') \\ \text{for all } f_B\colon S \to T, & f_B(s) = f_B(s') \end{cases} \tag{6}$$

where T is some type without bias. Here we have implicitly assumed that the preconditions of the operations are trivially true. The definition can easily be adapted to situations where this is not the case.

For refinements we do not require the $=_{BIAS}$ relation itself, but will accept any congruence relation, $=_S$ over S that satisfies (6). Note, that the standard equality relation, $=$, over S will always be the least relation that satisfies (6) and $=_{BIAS}$ will be the largest. The definition (6) is easily modified to also cover implicitly defined operations:

$$(\overleftarrow{s} =_S \overleftarrow{s'}) \Rightarrow \begin{cases} \text{for all } OP_S\colon S \to S, \\ \quad post(\overleftarrow{s}, s) \Rightarrow \exists s' \cdot s =_S s' \wedge post(\overleftarrow{s'}, s') \\ \text{for all } OP_B\colon S \to T, \\ \quad post(\overleftarrow{s}, t) \Rightarrow post(\overleftarrow{s'}, t) \end{cases} \tag{7}$$

Since no operation can distinguish states equal under $=_S$ it follows that for preconditions:

$$(s =_S s') \Rightarrow (pre(s) \Leftrightarrow pre(s'))$$

We can now generalize the traditional proof obligations to cover biased refinements. There is a (normal) biased refinement from A to R, if there exists a congruence relation, $=_A$ and a retrieve function, $retr\colon Rep \to Abs$, such that:

$$\forall a\colon Abs \cdot \exists r\colon Rep \cdot retr(r) =_A a$$

$$\forall r\colon Rep \cdot pre_A(retr(r)) \Rightarrow pre_R(r)$$

If A and R are defined with implicitly defined operations, then $=_A$ must have the property (7), and:

$$\forall \overleftarrow{r}, r\colon Rep \cdot \left(\begin{array}{l} pre_A(retr(\overleftarrow{r})) \wedge post_R(\overleftarrow{r}, r) \\ \quad \Rightarrow \exists a\colon Abs \cdot retr(r) =_A a \wedge post_A(retr(\overleftarrow{r}), a) \end{array} \right)$$

If A and R are defined with directly defined operations, then $=_A$ must have the property (6), and:

$$\forall r\colon Rep \cdot pre_A(retr(r)) \Rightarrow f_A(retr(r)) =_A retr(f_R(r))$$

The formal definition of $=_A$ requires a closed set of operations over Abs. If new operations are added, the validity of $=_A$ with respect to (6) or (7) must be established for each of these, and in this sense the concept of some specification being biased with respect to $=_A$ is non-monotonic.

Jones concludes the discussion in [3, §9.3] by suggesting some generalized proof obligations. The idea, taken from [5], is to replace the retrieve function by a relation and to skip the adequacy proof obligation. For a biased refinement this relation could be defined as $\{(a, r) \mid retr(r) =_{BIAS} a\}$ and from here the further relations to our approach are immediate. The present author finds the problems concerning partial refinements much more interesting and the characterization of biased refinements arose from the attempts to give a satisfying characterization of partial refinements within the aims of a generalization of the traditional proof obligations for VDM.

5 A general concept for VDM refinements

Hitherto we have considered generalized proof obligations for either partial or biased refinements. Combining the two generalizations, the proof obligations for a biased partial refinement with implicit definitions are as follows:

$$\forall a : Abs \cdot P_A(a) \;\Rightarrow\; \exists r : Rep \cdot retr(r) =_A a$$

$$\forall r : Rep \cdot \left(\begin{array}{l} pre_A(retr(r)) \\ \quad \Rightarrow\; (pre_R(r)) \vee \forall a : A \cdot post_A(retr(r), a) \;\Rightarrow\; \neg P_A(a) \end{array} \right)$$

$$\forall \overleftarrow{r}, r : Rep \cdot \left(\begin{array}{l} (pre_A(retr(\overleftarrow{r})) \wedge pre_R(\overleftarrow{r}) \wedge post_R(\overleftarrow{r}, r)) \\ \quad \Rightarrow\; \exists a : Abs \cdot retr(r) =_A a \wedge post_A(retr(\overleftarrow{r}), a) \end{array} \right)$$

A concrete specification R is a *partial correct* representation of an abstract specification A, if there exists a retrieve function, a characteristic predicate, and a congruence relation such that the generalized proof obligations can be discharged. If the characteristic predicate is not trivially true, then all properties of the abstract specification might not be preserved by the concrete specification. This is why the word partial correctness is used. As an example of partial correctness, consider an abstract stack with the property:

$$\forall s : Stack, e : Elem \cdot pop(push(e, s)) = e$$

For a concrete specification with a limit on the number of items on the stack this property would not be preserved. Instead a partial correct representation would have the property:

$$\forall s : Stack, e : Elem \cdot pre\text{-}push(s) \;\Rightarrow\; pop(push(e, s)) = e$$

Such properties can be extracted from the abstract properties and thus gives rise to a *syntactic* notion of *property inheritance*. This notion of property inheritance seems to be a valuable tool in connection with partial refinements. For biased refinements there are no problems with correctness preservation, provided that the congruence relation defined in (6–7) also is a congruence relation for any property of the abstract specification. As a consequence property inheritance for biased refinements is unproblematic.

6 Example

We finish by solving the following example, which was given in [2] to show the incompleteness of the traditional refinement proof obligations. ARB is an operation that in a non-deterministic way returns a new natural number each time it is 'called'.

$$s_0 = \{\,\}$$

$$ARB\ (\overleftarrow{s}: \mathbf{N}\text{-}\mathbf{set})\ r: \mathbf{N},\ s: \mathbf{N}\text{-}\mathbf{set}$$
$$\mathsf{pre\ true}$$
$$\mathsf{post}\ (r \notin \overleftarrow{s}\,) \wedge (s = \overleftarrow{s} \cup \{r\})$$

Let ARB_n be the following specification:

$$n_0 = 0$$

$$ARB_n\ (\overleftarrow{n}: \mathbf{N})\ r, n: \mathbf{N}$$
$$\mathsf{pre\ true}$$
$$\mathsf{post}\ (r = \overleftarrow{n}\,) \wedge (n = \overleftarrow{n} + 1)$$

The ARB_n operation implements ARB in some sense, but this cannot be justified by the traditional proof obligations, because of the lack of a retrieve function. Trying to solve this with the adequacy rule adapted to implementation bias in the abstract specification ARB will not change anything, because the specification of ARB is simply not biased! Instead the problems can be solved by considering ARB_n as a partial representation of ARB. The characteristic predicate is:

$$SN(s) \;=\; (0 \in s \wedge \mathsf{dense}(s)) \vee (s = \{\,\}).$$

The retrieve function is defined as:

$$retr: \mathbf{N} \rightarrow \mathbf{N}\text{-}\mathbf{set}$$
$$retr(n) \;\triangleq\; \{i \mid 0 \leq i < n\}$$

Note, that for all n it is true that $SN(retr(n))$. The generalized adequacy proof obligation:

$$\forall s: \mathbf{N}\text{-}\mathbf{set} \cdot SN(s) \;\Rightarrow\; \exists n: \mathbf{N} \cdot retr(n) = s$$

holds, because the witness is simply $(\mathsf{max}(s) + 1)$ or 0 for all s such that $SN(s)$. The generalized domain rule:

$$\forall n: N \cdot \textit{pre-ARB}(retr(n)) \;\Rightarrow\; [\textit{pre-ARB}_n(n) \vee \ldots]$$

holds, because both preconditions are void, i.e. in the sense of §3 ARB_n is a submodel of ARB. Finally, since both preconditions are void, the generalized result rule:

$$\forall \overleftarrow{n}, r, n: \mathbf{N} \cdot \textit{post-ARB}_n(\overleftarrow{n}, r, n) \;\Rightarrow\; \textit{post-ARB}(retr(\overleftarrow{n}), r, retr(n))$$

is easily seen to hold.

7 Final remarks

We have defined a more general refinement concept for VDM than the traditional one. For normal un-biased refinements the generalized proof obligations are identical to the traditional proof obligations and the generalized ones cover a strictly larger class of refinements. Biased refinements are correctness preserving without any restrictions, and certain properties can be preserved for partial refinements.

The main contribution of this paper is materialized in the improved understanding offered for the example in §6. The improvement is based on the classification of refinements and the generalized proof obligations that characterize each such class. Although the concept of a partial refinement is well known, the present author is not aware of any attempts to adapt the refinement concept of VDM to also cover such. The explanation offered for biased refinements is new as well, but is in range of the one offered by Jones [3].

The generalized refinement concept is less general than those defined for algebraic specifications [5, 6], but the extra generality seems to be without value in practice, since it allows for some artificial examples where the structure of the concrete specification is too poor to represent the abstract specification in a meaningful way.

Acknowledgement

I'm thankful to Professor Ole-Johan Dahl, Professor Cliff B. Jones, Juan Bicarregui and Lindsay Groves for comments on earlier versions of this paper.

References

[1] C.A.R. Hoare. *Proof of correctness of data representations.* Acta Informatica 1, pp. 271-281. 1972.

[2] C.B. Jones. *VDM Proof Obligations and their Justification.* VDM'87, LNCS 252, pp. 260-286. 1987.

[3] C.B. Jones. *Systematic Software Development Using VDM.* 2nd ed. Prentice Hall International. 1990.

[4] C.B. Jones, R.C.F. Shaw (eds). *Case studies in systematic software development.* Prentice Hall International. 1990.

[5] T. Nipkow. *Non-Deterministic Data Types: Models and Implementations.* Acta Informatica, 22, pp. 629-661, 1986.

[6] O. Schoett. *Behavioural correctness of data representations.* Department of Computer Science. University of Edinburgh. CSR-185-85. April 1985.

Constructive Refinement of First Order Specifications

Andrew Gravell
Department of Electronics and Computer Science
University of Southampton
Southampton England

Abstract

A refinement calculus is a formal system that enables a program to be derived from its specification in such a way that the program is correct by construction. A number of workers have developed such systems which are mainly based on a predicate transformer semantics. In this paper an alternative system is proposed, which is based instead on predicates in first order logic. This is a simpler framework, and its strengths and weaknesses are explored. In addition, the paper introduces a simplified form of the loop construction rule whose only side-conditions are purely syntactic.

1 Introduction

The concept of a formal system is well known. Axioms and rules of inference are the logician's tools of choice. Formal systems can be (at least in part) mechanised, and any mechanical system for manipulating formulae is, necessarily, a formal one. It is not a surprise therefore, that work in program transformation and refinement has led to the development of formal systems for carrying out such derivations. Such a formal system I will call a program calculus. Two examples of program calculi are Morgan's refinement calculus [Morgan 90] and the CIP system of program transformation ([Bauer 85, 87]), which is also the basis of a recent textbook [Partsch 90].

The danger of inconsistency in a formal system is well-known. In the case of a formal system of logic (or, more briefly, a logic), inconsistency leads to proofs of theorems that are not true. In the case of a program calculus, inconsistency allows the derivation of programs that do not in fact meet their specifications.

New formal systems are in fact often inconsistent, and require adjustment to avoid the problem. An example of such a problem occurred in the development of many-typed equational logic, where the use of empty types could lead to incorrect conclusions. Once the problem had been noted, a minor change to the rules of inference was sufficient to rectify it [Goguen 81]. Similarly there has been discussion recently of a problem in the Unity logic [Sanders 91], though it seems that there, the inconsistency is only apparent, as it results from misapplying one of the rules of inference.

Note the similarity between these problems in the development of formal systems and the familiar problems of program development itself. If we hope to use a program calculus to improve our confidence in the programs we develop, then it must be a program calculus that we trust. That means it must be simple, stable, and well-understood.

Simple, stable and well-understood formal systems that are also computationally universal are Peano's natural numbers, and Zermelo-Fraenkel set theory. The richness of set theory is useful in specifications, as shown by the popularity of the model-oriented specification languages, Z and VDM. VDM specifications differ from Z specifications largely by use of a pre- and post-condition pair, which is also the basis for Morgan's refinement calculus. In contrast, a program calculus based on Z-F set theory would perhaps be better suited for the implementation of Z specifications, as these consist essentially of single predicates rather than predicate pairs.

Thus in this paper I propose the use of an extended Z-F set theory for use as a language for specification, and program development. The extension consists purely of syntactic sugar: all the extensions are simply abbreviations for expressions already present in the theory. There are no new rules of inference: instead there is a collection of general theorems about the extended notation that simplify the creation of derivations or proofs of programs.

1.1 Benefits of an Untyped System

Note that Z-F set theory is an untyped system; there are no types, as every value is just a set. This neatly avoids some complications of typed programs, such as the need to show that intermediate values satisfy their type constraints. Nonetheless, types are popular in computing, and it is worth considering some of the arguments in their favour, and why they are not significant in this context.

1. Using types allows compilers or type-checkers to detect automatically many simple errors. However, if the program is formally proved correct, then it is certain that there are no typing errors. Thus program proof subsumes automatic type-checking.

2. Type declarations help the reader to understand the program. Of course, they can be retained as helpful comments.

3. Use of types, for example in the Z notation, helps to avoid the familiar paradoxes of set theory such as Russell's paradox. But in Z-F set theory, these paradoxes are avoided in a different way, by restricting the power of set comprehension.

4. Associating a type with each variable allows the compiler to produce better code. This is a good point. However, it is often possible to infer types (in the programming sense) by static analysis. Where efficiency is an overriding concern, it is probable that the final untyped program will be translated (possibly by hand) into a typed language such as C.

Note also that an untyped framework can lead to simpler and more elegant specification. Consider a program that calculates the nth power set of $\{0,1\}$. Some possible observations of this program would be

N	RESULT
0	$\{0,1\}$
1	$\{\{\},\{0\},\{1\},\{0,1\}\}$
2	$\{\{\},\{\{\}\},\{\{0\}\},\{\{1\}\},\{\{0,1\}\},\{\{\},\{0\}\},\{\{\},\{1\}\},$ $\{\{\},\{0,1\}\},\{\{0\},\{1\}\},\{\{0\},\{0,1\}\},\{\{1\},\{0,1\}\},$ $\{\{\},\{0\},\{1\}\},\{\{\},\{0\},\{0,1\}\},\{\{\},\{1\},\{0,1\}\},$ $\{\{0\},\{1\},\{0,1\}\},\{\{\},\{0\},\{1\},\{0,1\}\}\}$

A natural specification of this program in an untyped notation is just

$$result' = \mathcal{P}^n\{0,1\}$$

No doubt this program can also be specified in a typed notation such as Z by some complicated trick using free types. However, the specification would surely be longer and less clear than the above.

Thus, there are certainly arguments in favour of specifying and deriving programs using an untyped notation, based on Z-F set theory.

1.2 Structure of the Paper

The rest of this paper develops the extended Z-F notation, which I call Z-F′. The notation is introduced and defined in the next section, section 2. The notation consists of three extensions to the Z-F theory; the use of primed variables, partial functions and undefined expressions, and the programming operators. In section 3, the execution mechanism is considered, leading to an operational semantics, and the restrictions which must be satisfied for a specification to be considered executable. Section 4 introduces the notion of refinement, and covers the most commonly used laws of refinement. These laws are illustrated in section 5 where four simple programs are derived from their specifications in a rigorous way. Section 6 discusses shortcomings of the notation and of this paper, while section 7 compares this approach with that of other workers. An appendix lists briefly a larger collection of useful refinement laws.

2 Towards A First Order Refinement Calculus

We will take as our starting point one of the possible axiomatisations of Z-F set theory, it does not greatly matter which. In practice of course, most derivations in computing are constructed with the help of a library of theorems about standard data types, and depend only indirectly on the exact statement of the basic axioms. In addition, it is rare for a proof in computer science to rely on one of the controversial axioms such as the axiom of choice.

The base notation is assumed to include the predicate symbols for membership and equality ($\in=$). It also includes the following set-theoretic operators $\cup\cap\setminus\mathcal{P}\times$ and the set and pair constructors $(\{.\}(.,.))$. These operators are sufficient to allow the construction of (a model of) the natural numbers, sequences and arrays, which then provide a good basis for the construction of further data types for use in programming. We assume that these extensions have been or will be added as required. We deal below with the problems caused by introducing partial functions into the theory.

In this paper I in fact use only the integers and sets of integers, and the familiar functions and relations $+ - >$ *mod* and so on.

We extend the syntax of set theory using the principle of definition (see for example [Mendelson 87] page 80): each formula (and each proof) in the extended set theory can be translated into an equivalent formula (or proof) in the base language. However, once translated, the formula will be longer and harder to understand. Thus, syntactic extension is for convenience, and does not increase the logical power of the language. Note that in fact it is possible to define a set theory with just the relation $\in$. All other relations, operators and constants can be added to this set theory by syntactic extension.

2.1 Use of Primed Variables

The first extension is to assume that the set of variables is partitioned into two sets, the unprimed variables (such as x, y, aab) and primed ones (such as x', y', aab') which are in one-one correspondence through the function of priming, which maps each unprimed variable onto a primed one, and vice versa ($prime(x) = x', prime(x') = x$). We also allow expressions and formulae to be primed - a primed expression (or formula) stands for the same expression (or formula) but with all variables replaced by their primed versions. For example $(x + y' - 1)' = x' + y - 1$.

This extended set of variables is still countable, so there are many possible schemes for mapping these names back into the original set of names.

The *operational* interpretation of an unprimed variable is that it refers to the value of a program variable *before* execution, while the corresponding primed variable refers to the value of the *same* program variable *after* executing the program. Thus the equality $x' = x + 1$ is interpreted operationally as an *assignment* that increments x, and the conjunction $x' = y \wedge y' = x$, which is called a *multiple assignment*, is interpreted as the operation that swaps x and y. This convention does not affect the *logical* interpretation that the two variables x and x' are different. Through this trick, the different worlds of imperative programming and logic are brought together. As the use of primed variables is a distinctive feature of the notation, it is known as Z-F′ (Z-F set theory with primed variables).

2.2 Partial Functions and Undefined Expressions

The next extension allows the use of sets as functions in the logic. Whereas the set-theoretic operators of the base language are total, sets cannot represent total functions in Z-F (otherwise their domain would be the universal set which is impossible). We must therefore consider cases where a partial function is applied to a value outside its domain. Various solutions to this problem have been adopted; a common one is to introduce an undefined value. Here we adopt a somewhat unusual solution. In keeping with our goal of defining a syntactic extension of Z-F set theory, we simply define how to translate formulae containing partial functions into the base language of set theory.

First we associate with each expression e the formula $defined(e)$ which is defined recursively.

$defined(x) \mathrel{\widehat{=}} true$
where x is a variable

$defined(op(e)) \mathrel{\widehat{=}} defined(e)$
where op is a unary operator such as $\mathcal{P}$

$defined(f(e)) \mathrel{\widehat{=}} defined(f) \land defined(e) \land \exists_1 y \bullet (e, y) \in f$
where f is an expression (a partial function)

and so on for operators and functions with more than one argument. Following the usual conventions, I will use infix notation such as $x + y$ for applications of partial functions as well as prefix notation such as $g(x, y)$.

Next we give rules that can be applied recursively to remove applications of partial functions from a formula.

$$x = f(e) \mathrel{\widehat{=}} defined(f(e)) \land (e, x) \in f$$
$$x \in f(e) \mathrel{\widehat{=}} \exists y \bullet y = f(e) \land x \in y$$
$$f(e) \in x \mathrel{\widehat{=}} \exists y \bullet y = f(e) \land y \in x$$

and so on.

As a consequence, a formula that contains an undefined expression is considered to be meaningful, and is either true, or false, even though the undefined expression itself is not considered meaningful. For example the formula $x = 1 \ mod \ 0$, which is a sugared form of $x = mod(1, 0)$, is in fact short for $\exists_1 y \bullet ((1,0), y) \in mod \land ((1,0), x) \in mod$, which is *false* as $\neg \exists y \bullet ((1,0), y) \in mod$. Conversely, $x \neq 1 \ mod \ 0$ is *true*, as it is short for $\neg(x = 1 \ mod \ 0)$, and we have just seen that $x = 1 \ mod \ 0$ is *false*.

(The formula *true* stands for some tautology such as $\forall x \bullet x = x$, and *false* is, of course, defined as an abbreviation for $\neg true$.)

We note that this treatment of undefined expressions violates the substitutivity of equality. For example $(1, 0) = (1, 0)$ is true, but $mod(1, 0) = mod(1, 0)$ is false, so $e1 = e2$ does not necessarily imply $f(e1) = f(e2)$. That step is only justified when $f(e1)$ is defined. However, a weaker form of substitution of equals still holds: $x = 1 \ mod \ 0$ is false, which implies anything, so $x = 1 \ mod \ 0 \Rightarrow f(x) = f(1 \ mod \ 0)$ as expected. In general

$$e1 = e2 \land defined(f(e1)) \Leftrightarrow f(e1) = f(e2)$$

Similarly, there is a modified form of the one-point rule

$$\exists x \bullet P(x) \land x = e \Leftrightarrow P(e) \land defined(e)$$

The reason for adopting this convention is that it allows us to treat failing assignments such as $x' = 1 \ mod \ 0$ as being logically equivalent to *false*, which is the unsatisfiable specification. Thus, it enables execution failures to be handled in the same classical framework that we use for specifications. This benefit, in my opinion, outweighs the disadvantages described above. Introducing, say, an undefined value into Z-F set theory would involve extra complications that are hard to justify. For example in pure Z-F set theory $x = \{\} \Leftrightarrow \forall y \bullet y \notin x$. This property would no longer hold in Z-F extended with an undefined value.

By analogy with equality, we adopt definitions of inequality which ensure only sensible formulae are true. For example $1 \ mod \ 0 > 1 \ mod \ 0$ is false as $1 \ mod \ 0$ is not defined, and $1 > x$ is false if x is not a number

Thus the law of trichotomy only holds for numbers, leading to the conditional law

$$x \in \mathcal{Z} \wedge y \in \mathcal{Z} \Rightarrow (x > y \vee x = y \vee x < y)$$

Conversely

$$x < y \Rightarrow x \in \mathcal{Z} \wedge y \in \mathcal{Z}$$

2.3 Programming Operators

The third and final extension introduces operators that are necessary for programming and reasoning about programs.

Pre-Condition

The pre-condition of a formula P is another formula which determines the initial conditions under which P can be satisfied. If the primed variable (or variables) of P is (or are) x' (so x' may stand for a list of variables) then *pre* P is defined as follows

$$pre\ P \mathrel{\hat{=}} \exists\, x' \bullet\ P$$

The operator *pre* is not a programming operator, but will be used in the definition of ; (operational composition), which is a programming operator.

Conditional: IF

The keyword *IF* introduces a conditional operation. If A is an assertion (a formula with no primed variables), and P and Q are formulae then *IF A THEN P ELSE Q* is defined as follows

$$\begin{aligned}&IF\ A\ THEN\ P\ ELSE\ Q \mathrel{\hat{=}}\\ &\quad (A \wedge P \wedge q' = q) \vee (\neg A \wedge Q \wedge p' = p)\end{aligned}$$

where the variable(s) q' are those that occur primed in Q and not in P, while the variable(s) p' are those that occur primed in P and not in Q. The extra conjuncts $q' = q$ and $p' = p$ ensure that variables that are unmentioned by one branch of the conditional are unchanged.

Furthermore *IF A THEN P* is defined as

$$IF\ A\ THEN\ P \mathrel{\hat{=}} IF\ A\ THEN\ P\ ELSE\ true$$

Sequential Composition

The operator ; denotes the combination of two operations. If P and Q are formulae, and the primed variable(s) x' of P occur primed in Q, while the primed variables y' of P do not occur primed in Q, then $P;\ Q$ is defined as

$$\begin{aligned}&P;\ Q \mathrel{\hat{=}}\\ &\quad (\exists\, s, t \bullet\ P(s/x', t/y') \wedge Q(s/x, t/y) \wedge y' = t) \wedge\\ &\quad (\forall\, x', y' \bullet\ P \Rightarrow (pre\ Q)(x'/x, y'/y))\end{aligned}$$

Here s and t are fresh variables. The formula $P(s/x', t/y')$ is P with free occurrences of x' replaced by s and y' by t, and so on.

This definition has two parts. The first part alone would describe relational (or angelic) composition. The quantifier simply asserts the existence of some intermediate state between the operations P and Q. As before, the equation(s) $y' = t$ is (or are) conjoined to ensure that variables unmentioned in Q are unchanged. The second part of the definition ensures that the combined operation P; Q can only succeed when any choice made by P would be acceptable to Q. This makes the operation composition demonic, so that it will fail if at all possible.

Iteration: WHILE

The keyword *WHILE* introduces a loop. If A is an assertion, and P is a formula with primed variable(s) x then *WHILE A DO P* is defined as

$$\begin{aligned}&\mathit{WHILE}\ A\ \mathit{DO}\ P \mathrel{\widehat{=}}\\&\quad(\exists s \bullet \mathit{TRACE} \land \exists m \bullet \neg A(s(m)/x) \land x' = s(m))\land\\&\quad(\forall s \bullet \mathit{TRACE} \Rightarrow \exists m \bullet \neg A(s(m)/x))\end{aligned}$$

where the variables s, n and m are fresh, and the auxiliary predicate *TRACE* is defined as follows:

$$\begin{aligned}&\mathit{TRACE} \mathrel{\widehat{=}} x = s(0)\land\\&\quad\forall n \bullet ((n \in \mathcal{N} \Leftrightarrow \mathit{defined}(s(n)))\land\\&\quad(\mathit{IF}\ A \land \mathit{pre}\ P\ \mathit{THEN}\ P)(s(n)/x, s(n+1)/x'))\end{aligned}$$

The variable s here represents any infinite sequence of values that can be generated by executing the formula *IF A* $\land$ *pre P THEN P* repeatedly. (Incorporating *pre P* in the test ensures that the conditional is total, and thus that there are indeed infinite traces.) The first part of the definition of *WHILE* again defines relational closure or an angelic loop. This conjunct is satisfied when iterating *IF A* $\land$ *pre P THEN P can* establish $\neg A$. The second part of the definition ensures that the loop only succeeds when *any* possible sequence of choices made by P guarantees termination.

The definition gives the expected meaning to loops in which the body P is non-deterministic. This is important as it allows us to iterate over arbitrary formulae, not just programs.

Local Block

The keyword *LOCAL* introduces a local block with extra, local, variables. If P is a formula, and x is a variable (or list of variables) then *LOCAL* $x \bullet P$ is defined as

$$\mathit{LOCAL}\ x \bullet P \mathrel{\widehat{=}} \exists x' \bullet P$$

With these definitions, a simple version of deterministic imperative programming has been defined as a syntactic extension of standard set theory.

2.4 Laws of Programming

In this extended set theory many of the familiar laws of programming such as

$$IF\ A\ THEN\ P\ ELSE\ Q = IF\ \neg A\ THEN\ Q\ ELSE\ P$$
$$P;\ (Q;\ R) = (P;\ Q);\ R$$
$$WHILE\ A\ DO\ S = IF\ A\ THEN\ (S;\ WHILE\ A\ DO\ S)$$

can then be proved to follow from the standard axioms and inference rules. In the laws above, equality is interpreted as double implication, so that the first equation is short for

$$\vdash IF\ A\ THEN\ P\ ELSE\ Q \Leftrightarrow IF\ \neg A\ THEN\ Q\ ELSE\ P$$

This abuse of notation is justified by the replacement theorem of predicate calculus (see for example [Mendelson 87] page 63).

Note that some of the familiar laws of programming do *not* hold, or hold only in a modified form. For example, usually

$$\begin{aligned} &IF\ true\ \ THEN\ x := 1\ ELSE\ y := 2 \\ &= x := 1 \end{aligned}$$

In Z-F′ the equivalent does not (quite) hold. Indeed

$$\begin{aligned} &IF\ true\ \ THEN\ x' = 1\ ELSE\ y' = 2 \\ &= (true \wedge x' = 1 \wedge y' = y) \vee (\neg true \wedge y' = 2 \wedge x' = x) \\ &= (x' = 1 \wedge y' = y) \\ &\neq (x' = 1) \end{aligned}$$

3 Execution

3.1 Operational Semantics

The operational semantics of ZF' is naturally based upon deduction. Certain of the laws of programming permit the left to right reduction of initialised programs. For instance, the law

$$x = c;\ y' = f(x) \equiv x = c \wedge y' = f(c)$$

permits the initialising assertion to be conjoined with the following assignment. Evaluation of $f(c)$, say to the constant d, then gives rise to the equivalent formula $x = c \wedge y' = d$. Similar laws can be given for *IF* and *WHILE* . It follows by induction on the length of the program P, plus the number of loop unfoldings still to come, that

$$STATE;\ P$$

can be reduced to the equivalent formula

$$STATE2$$

by repeated application of these laws, at least, so long as the following conditions are satisfied

1. $STATE$ and $STATE2$ are both conjunctions of equations such as $x = c$ and $y' = d$, for constants c and d.

2. $STATE$ includes each unprimed variable of P

3. $STATE \vdash pre\ P$

4. P is a program, that is to say a collection of assignments (equations such as $y' = f(x)$ combined using the executable operators ; *IF* *WHILE* and *LOCAL*.

Thus an execution of a program P consists of

1. an input stage during which the user supplies an initial state

2. a computation stage during which the supplied equations are used to reduce the definition of the P to give the final state, and

3. an output stage when the final (primed) values are reported to the user.

It is the user's responsibility to make sure that the supplied values satisfy the three conditions given above. If the values are not satisfactory, then the computation stage may fail to terminate, so that the output stage is never reached.

The logical theorem

$$\vdash STATE;\ P \Leftrightarrow STATE2$$

where $STATE$ and $STATE2$ satisfies the three conditions given above, models the execution exactly, and is called an observation of the program P.

In general, an arbitary formula P may allow many results, so we must weaken this definition to allow observations of non-deterministic operations. An observation of such a formula P is a pair of formulae $STATE$ and $STATE2$ satisfying the conditions above for which

$$\vdash STATE;\ P \Leftarrow STATE2$$

This allows us to define the semantics of an arbitrary formula P as the set of all such pairs. Where P is a program, this set of pairs defines a function from states to states. This semantics has the desirable property that the functional composition of the semantics of P and Q is exactly the semantics of the operational composition $P;\ Q$, for any programs P and Q.

3.2 Executability Restrictions

In the previous section we defined a program to be any formula that is constructed using executable operators out of executable sub-formulae. The basic executable formulae are assignments, such as $x' = e$, and also multiple assignments, such as $x' = e1 \wedge y' = e2$ (where x' and y' are primed variables, and $e, e1$, and $e2$ are executable expressions). The executable operators are ; *IF* *WHILE* and *LOCAL*.

Thus, by this definition, $(x' = 4 \wedge y' = 5);\ IF\ z > 3\ THEN\ x' = x + 1$ is executable, as it is a multiple assignment followed by a conditional operation.

However $(x' = 4 \vee y' = 5)$; $IF\ z > 3\ THEN\ x' = x + 1$ is not executable, since $\vee$ is not an executable operator. (However, this is a valid formula.)

In addition, there are a number of minor restrictions such as the requirement that the variables assigned in a multiple assignment statement must be disjoint. Furthermore, there must be restrictions on expressions that allow them to be evaluated. Similarly, tests (or guards) in conditionals and loops must be executable.

An important point is that these restrictions must be syntactic, so that it is mechanical to check whether a formula is executable: when performing computer assisted refinement, it is reassuring to know that the computer will be able to tell when you have finished.

It is also required that all input, output and intermediate values be representable in a computer. We will assume for simplicity unlimited storage in the computer, so that the representable values are precisely the finite ones. This places the requirement that all executable operators must preserve finiteness, but fortunately the set-theoretic operators such as $\cup$ do indeed yield finite results when given finite operands.

The most important restriction, and one that is forced through the use of two valued logic, is that the execution of tests (or guards) in conditionals and loops must terminate. This means that functions called within tests must be total, or more generally must have computable domains. For example:

$$\begin{aligned}
& IF\ x = e\ THEN\ P \\
\equiv\ & IF\ defined(e) \wedge x = e\ THEN\ P \\
\equiv\ & IF\ defined(e)\ THEN \\
& \quad defined(e) \wedge IF\ x = e\ THEN\ P \\
\equiv\ & IF\ defined(e)\ THEN \\
& \quad \exists\, y' \bullet\ y' = e \wedge IF\ x = y'\ THEN\ P \\
\equiv\ & IF\ defined(e)\ THEN \\
& \quad LOCAL\ y \bullet\ y' = e \wedge IF\ x = y'\ THEN\ P
\end{aligned}$$

which can be implemented (using a law which will be covered below) by

$$\begin{aligned}
& IF\ defined(e)\ THEN \\
& \quad LOCAL\ y \bullet\ y' = e;\ IF\ x = y\ THEN\ P
\end{aligned}$$

Thus if $defined(e)$ is executable, or has an executable equivalent, then this implementation will be executable even when the original formula was not. Thus, to be executable, a formula must

1. be constructed of assignments combined using the executable operators
2. contain only finite constant values
3. contain only operators that preserve finiteness, and
4. contain only terminating function calls inside any test.

4 Refinement

Sometimes, program development is like the first steps taken above, where one formula is replaced by a logically equivalent one that happens to be executable.

At other times, a formula has to be replaced by one which is not logically equivalent to it, but which is actually better (terminates more often, is more deterministic). This is called refinement. The definition we would like to use is that $P1$ is refined by $P2$ if $P1$ can be replaced by $P2$ in any executable context C, without the difference being observable.

This definition is higher order (as it involves proving something for every context C) and would lead to long and complex proofs, so we take instead a definition that allows us to conduct proofs in standard predicate calculus.

$$P1 \sqsubseteq P2$$

is an abbreviation for three (second order) properties

$$\begin{array}{l} \mathit{pre}\ P1 \vdash \mathit{pre}\ P2 \\ \mathit{pre}\ P1 \wedge P2 \vdash P1 \\ \mathit{alphabet}(P1) = \mathit{alphabet}(P2) \end{array}$$

where the alphabet of a formula is just the set of its free variables.

The first two are the familiar conditions of relational refinement. The third condition follows from our model of execution. Executing a formula will lead to the user being prompted for values for each free unprimed variable. Success in execution will lead to a value for each free primed variable being printed on the screen. This means that the user can observe the alphabet of a formula. To be a satisfactory replacement, $P2$ must therefore have the same alphabet as $P1$. In practice, this extra restriction is not a problem as calculating the alphabet of a formula is mechanical.

Furthermore, this third condition prevents us from making unsound refinements. For example, we would not expect to be able to refine $x' = 1$ by $x' = 1 \wedge y' = 1$ since the latter program alters y. Yet both programs have the pre-condition *true*, and moreover $x' = 1 \wedge y' = 1 \vdash x' = 1$ is certainly a theorem. However $\mathit{alphabet}(x' = 1) = \{x'\} \neq \{x', y'\} = \mathit{alphabet}(x' = 1 \wedge y' = 1)$. Thus the alphabet condition prevents us from introducing assignments to arbitrary new variables during refinement.

It is easy to see that refinement, as defined above, is a transitive relation.

From the definition it also follows that $P1 \sqsubseteq P2$ and $P2 \sqsubseteq P1$ precisely when $\vdash P1 \Leftrightarrow P2$ and $\mathit{alphabet}(P1) = \mathit{alphabet}(P2)$. We write $P1 \equiv P2$ as an abbreviation for this, just as we write $P1 = P2$ for the (second order) property $\vdash P1 \Leftrightarrow P2$.

Note that these properties are proof-theoretic, not model-theoretic. Since the logic is incomplete, there will be formulae that are semantically equivalent, but for which we cannot say $P1 \equiv P2$, since there is no (first order) proof. This is the down-side of committing to a particular logic. The positive aspect of this commitment is that it becomes possible to develop an extensive collection of theorems, proofs and proof strategies that can be re-used in later developments, for example by mechanising them.

Perhaps the most important theorems are those which show that the programming operators are monotonic with respect to refinement. This property, and the fact that refinement is a transitive relation, provides the theoretical justification for the development method of top-down, stepwise refinement, and indeed the definitions of the programming operators and of refinement were carefully chosen to ensure these properties.

Also useful is the observation that if $P \equiv Q$ then $C(P) \equiv C(Q)$ for any context C (not just one built using the executable operators). This again follows from the replacement theorem of predicate calculus. More generally if $P = Q$ and $alphabet(C(P)) = alphabet(C(Q))$ then $C(P) \equiv C(Q)$. These laws allows sub-formulae to be manipulated according to the familiar laws of predicate calculus, so long as the set of free variables in the main formula is unchanged.

4.1 A Refinement Calculus

Some of the laws of refinement can be expressed in the style of a refinement calculus (following [Back 78], [Morris 87] and [Morgan 90]).

Refining Disjunctions

If the specification is given in the form of a disjunction, then it can be implemented using a conditional operation. This law is known as *conditional introduction*.

$$P \vee Q \sqsubseteq IF\ pre\ P\ THEN\ P\ ELSE\ Q \qquad \text{(IC1)}$$

Another form of *conditional introduction*, assuming A is an assertion, is

$$(A \wedge P) \vee (\neg A \wedge Q) \sqsubseteq IF\ A\ THEN\ P\ ELSE\ Q \qquad \text{(IC2)}$$

Refining Conjunctions

More usually, the specification is a conjunction. Sometimes it is possible to just drop one of the conjuncts. If the formula Q is deterministic (at most one final value is possible for each possible input value), and every variable of P occurs in Q, then the law of *deterministic conjunct* is

$$P \wedge Q \sqsubseteq Q \qquad \text{(DC)}$$

In general, a further proof is required to show that a formula is deterministic. However, if P is a program (or executable formula), then P is guaranteed to be deterministic, and as mentioned above, we can check mechanically whether P is a program. Thus a side-condition such as *P is deterministic* is usually interpreted as meaning *P is a program.*

Sometimes the two conjuncts can be executed in sequence. For example, if the primed variables of P do not occur (primed or unprimed) in Q, then the law *introduce sequence* is

$$P \wedge Q \sqsubseteq P;\ Q \qquad \text{(IS1)}$$

Suppose instead that the primed variable(s) of P, call it x', occurs primed (but not unprimed) in Q. Then another form of *introduce sequence* is

$$P \wedge Q \sqsubseteq (P \wedge (pre\ Q(x/x'))(x'/x));\ Q(x/x') \qquad \text{(IS2)}$$

The renaming here is tedious, but quite natural in practice. More of a problem is the occurrence of $pre\ Q(x/x')$. This can be dropped immediately if P is deterministic (*deterministic conjunct*) or if $Q(x/x')$ is known to be total.

Introducing Iteration

The following law (*loop introduction*) is used to introduce loops. Here I (the loop invariant) must be an equivalence, while v is an expression.

$$\begin{aligned}&I \wedge v \geq 0 = v'\\ &\sqsubseteq IF\ v > 0\ THEN\ (I \wedge v' = 0)\\ &\equiv WHILE\ v > 0\ DO\ (I \wedge v > v' \geq 0)\end{aligned} \tag{IL}$$

The formula $v \geq 0 = v'$ is short for the conjunction $v \geq 0 \wedge 0 = v'$ and so on. Three examples of equivalence formulae are $e = e'$, $A \wedge A'$, and $e = e' \wedge A \wedge A'$, for any expression e and assertion A. Thus, three special cases of *loop introduction* are

$$\begin{aligned}&e = e' \wedge v \geq 0 = v'\\ &\sqsubseteq WHILE\ v > 0\ DO\ (e = e' \wedge v > v' \geq 0)\end{aligned} \tag{IL1}$$

and

$$\begin{aligned}&A \wedge A' \wedge v \geq 0 = v'\\ &\sqsubseteq WHILE\ v > 0\ DO\ (A \wedge A' \wedge v > v' \geq 0)\end{aligned} \tag{IL2}$$

$$\begin{aligned}&e = e' \wedge A \wedge A' \wedge v \geq v' = 0\\ &\sqsubseteq WHILE\ v > 0\ DO\ (e = e' \wedge A \wedge A' \wedge v > v' \geq 0)\end{aligned} \tag{IL3}$$

Postulating the Implementation

Finally, there may be times when it is not easy to re-arrange the specification into a form which permits one of the laws above to be applied. In that case, sometimes one must postulate a possible implementation. The law *postulate Q* permits this. Providing the variables in Q all occur in P

$$P \sqsubseteq IF\ pre\ (P \wedge Q)\ THEN\ P \wedge Q\ ELSE\ P \tag{PQ}$$

The hope is that this conditional will simplify somehow. For example, using laws of IF, we can see (*postulate and prove Q*)

$$P \sqsubseteq P \wedge Q \tag{PPQ}$$

providing $\vdash (pre\ P \wedge Q) \vee \neg pre\ P$. Moreover, if Q is deterministic and includes all variables occurring in P we also have (*postulate and prove deterministic Q*)

$$P \sqsubseteq Q \tag{PPDQ}$$

Manipulating Assertions

An important body of laws permits the manipulation of assertions, also called assumptions. These (as mentioned above) are formulae with no primed variables.

Assertions can be introduced in a number of ways. If A is an assertion then the following laws hold

$$P \equiv pre\ P \wedge P \tag{IP}$$

$$A;\ P \equiv A \wedge P \tag{IA1}$$

$$IF\ A\ THEN\ P\ ELSE\ Q \equiv IF\ A\ THEN\ A \wedge P\ ELSE\ Q \tag{IA2}$$

$$IF\ A\ THEN\ P\ ELSE\ Q \equiv IF\ A\ THEN\ P\ ELSE\ \neg A \wedge Q \tag{IA3}$$

$$WHILE\ A\ DO\ P \equiv WHILE\ A\ DO\ A \wedge P \tag{IA4}$$

$$WHILE\ A\ DO\ P \equiv (WHILE\ A\ DO\ P);\ \neg A \tag{IA5}$$

The next three laws allow assertions to be moved forwards and back through compositions

$$P;\ (A \wedge Q) \sqsubseteq (P \wedge A');\ (A \wedge Q) \tag{IA6}$$

$$P \wedge A';\ Q \equiv (P \wedge A');\ (A \wedge Q) \tag{IA7}$$

$$\begin{aligned} &A;\ IF\ B\ THEN\ P\ ELSE\ Q \\ &\equiv A;\ IF\ B\ THEN\ A \wedge P\ ELSE\ A \wedge Q \end{aligned} \tag{IA8}$$

Assertions can be used in a number of ways, for example to re-express the test in a conditional or loop,

$$\begin{aligned} &IF\ A\ THEN\ P\ ELSE\ Q \\ &\sqsubseteq IF\ A \wedge pre\ P\ THEN\ P\ ELSE\ Q \end{aligned} \tag{ET1}$$

$$\begin{aligned} &IF\ A\ THEN\ P\ ELSE\ Q \\ &\sqsubseteq IF\ A \vee \neg pre\ Q\ THEN\ P\ ELSE\ Q \end{aligned} \tag{ET2}$$

$$\begin{aligned} &A;\ IF\ B\ THEN\ P\ ELSE\ Q \\ &\equiv A;\ IF\ C\ THEN\ P\ ELSE\ Q \end{aligned} \tag{ET3}$$

$$\begin{aligned} &A;\ WHILE\ B\ DO\ (A \wedge P \wedge A') \\ &\equiv A;\ WHILE\ C\ DO\ (A \wedge P \wedge A') \end{aligned} \tag{ET4}$$

In the last two laws above, B and C must be assertions such that $\vdash A \Rightarrow (B \Leftrightarrow C)$, and $alphabet(B) = alphabet(C)$.

The final law allows assertions to be dropped when they are no longer needed. Let A be an assertion, and P any formula. Then, in any executable context $C(P)$,

$$C(A \wedge P) \sqsubseteq C(P) \tag{DA}$$

provided $alphabet(C(A \wedge P)) = alphabet(C(P))$

Two special cases of this law are

$$A;\ P \sqsubseteq P \tag{DA1}$$

$$P;\ A \sqsubseteq P \tag{DA2}$$

where, in each case, we must have $alphabet(A) \subseteq alphabet(P)$.

4.2 Applicability Conditions

Note the applicability conditions of these laws of refinement. Some laws have no applicability condition and can be used freely. Some laws have an applicability condition that is purely syntactic, so can be checked mechanically. Others (such as *postulate and prove Q*) have semantic applicability conditions, which cannot, in general, be checked mechanically. Every time such a law is used, it is necessary to make a further sub-proof in order to check that the applicability conditions are satisfied. Such sub-proofs break up the linear flow of a derivation, making it harder to carry out, and, afterwards, harder to read. The temptation is to avoid checking the applicability conditions at all, which can be dangerous. Clearly, we should prefer laws with no applicability conditions at all, or with ones which are purely syntactic. We have given examples of laws that permit the introduction of each of the programming constructs. Using these laws it is possible to derive a program without generating the need for further sub-proofs. Of course, there are other reasons for choosing to perform a sub-proof, for example if the main part of a formula is unchanged by a number of steps, it may be clearer to separate out the sub-formula which is changing and manipulate only that. Since programs are often extremely large formulae, program derivation inevitably involves sub-proofs. The aim of the refinement laws above is thus, not to avoid sub-proofs, but to allow the program designer to choose when to start them.

Using these laws, programs are developed by a method that repeats each of three steps: first *re-arrange* the specification using standard logic until one of the refinement laws applies, then *apply* the refinement law, and finally *simplify* the resulting formula. This process is complete when it results in a formula that is executable. Clearly, in re-arranging and simplifying the formulae, you are likely to perform the equivalent of a sub-proof of an applicability condition. Thus you should not expect the derivation to be made any shorter simply by using laws with no applicability conditions.

More succinctly, laws without side-conditions allow derivations that are straighter, not necessarily shorter.

5 Using the Laws to Develop Simple Programs

In this section two simple programs are derived using the laws given above.

5.1 First Example: minimum of two numbers

We start with the following specification:

$$min2 \mathrel{\widehat{=}} (z' = x \vee z' = y) \wedge z' \leq x \wedge z' \leq y$$

The problem here is to remove the apparent non-determinism in the assignment to z. If we postulate the solution $z' = x$ (and this is not difficult, since this assignment appears already in the specification) we find the following refinement

$$\sqsubseteq \text{ postulate } z' = x \text{ (PQ)}$$
$$IF\ pre\ (min2 \wedge z' = x)\ THEN\ (min2 \wedge z' = x)\ ELSE\ min2$$

A quick calculation (which could easily be automated) tells us that

$$pre\ (min2 \wedge z' = x)$$
$$\equiv \exists z' \bullet (z' = x \vee z' = y) \wedge z' \leq x \wedge z' \leq y \wedge z' = x$$

$\equiv$ using the one-point rule

$(x = x \vee x = y) \wedge x \leq x \wedge x \leq y$

$\equiv x \leq y$

From now on we will elide trivial simplifications such as this. Thus

$min2$

$\sqsubseteq$ equivalent predicate

$IF\ x \leq y\ THEN\ min2 \wedge z' = x\ ELSE\ min2$

$\sqsubseteq$ introduce assertions (IA2, IA3)

$IF\ x \leq y\ THEN\ x \leq y \wedge min2 \wedge z' = x$
$ELSE\ \neg(x \leq y) \wedge min2$

$\sqsubseteq$ deterministic conjunct (DC)

$IF\ x \leq y\ THEN\ x \leq y \wedge z' = x$
$ELSE\ \neg(x \leq y) \wedge min2$

$\equiv$ expanding definition of $min2$

$IF\ x \leq y\ THEN\ x \leq y \wedge z' = x$
$ELSE\ \neg(x \leq y) \wedge (z' = x \vee z' = y) \wedge z' \leq y \wedge z' \leq x$

$\equiv$ simplifying

$IF\ x \leq y\ THEN\ x \leq y \wedge z' = x\ ELSE\ x > y \wedge z' = y$

$\sqsubseteq$ drop assertions (DA)

$IF\ x \leq y\ THEN\ z' = x\ ELSE\ z' = y$

We note that this solution is, in fact, logically equivalent to the original specification. This, however, is not particularly interesting. What matters more is that we have a refinement which is executable.

5.2 First Example (Alternative Approach)

Note that this simple example can be solved more simply by standard reasoning. Since the final implementation will involve a conditional, we start by distributing the disjunction.

$min2$

$\equiv (z' = x \wedge z' \leq x \wedge z' \leq y) \vee (z' = y \wedge z' \leq x \wedge z' \leq y)$

$\equiv (z' = x \wedge x \leq x \wedge x \leq y) \vee (z' = y \wedge y \leq x \wedge y \leq y)$

$\equiv (z' = x \wedge x \leq y) \vee (z' = y \wedge y \leq x)$

$\sqsubseteq$ introduce conditional (IC1)

$IF\ pre(z' = x \wedge x \leq y)\ THEN\ (z' = x \wedge x \leq y)$
$ELSE\ (z' = y \wedge y \leq x)$

$\equiv$ simplifying

$IF\ x \leq y\ THEN\ (z' = x \wedge x \leq y)\ ELSE\ (z' = y \wedge y \leq x)$

$\sqsubseteq$ drop assertions (DA)

$IF\ x \leq y\ THEN\ z' = x\ ELSE\ z' = y$

Note the repeated need to simplify formulae such as $pre(z' = x \wedge x \geq y)$, which is trivial, since the equation involving z' allows a direct application of the one-point rule. Such tasks can and should be delegated to a machine. Mechanical support would allow many of the trivial simplification steps to be omitted in the derivations above. The emergence of programmable, interactive theorem proving tools such as B suggests that this level of automation may indeed be feasible [Neilson 90].

5.3 Second Example: Greatest Common Divisor

We start with the specification

$$\begin{aligned} gcd \mathrel{\widehat{=}} {} & x > 0 \wedge y > 0 \wedge \\ & z' = max\{t \mid x \ mod\ t = 0 \wedge y \ mod\ t = 0\} \end{aligned}$$

To simplify the following, we define the greatest common divisor as a partial function (that is, as a set of pairs).

$$\begin{aligned} g \mathrel{\widehat{=}} \{ & ((x, y), z) \mid \\ & x > 0 \wedge y > 0 \wedge \\ & z = max\{t \mid x \ mod\ t = 0 \wedge y \ mod\ t = 0\}\} \end{aligned}$$

As is well known, implementing gcd relies on first proving some useful properties of this function such as

$$g(x, y) = g(y, x) \qquad \text{(G1)}$$

$$x > y \Rightarrow g(x, y) = g(x - y, y) \qquad \text{(G2)}$$

$$defined(g(x, y)) \Rightarrow x \geq g(x, y) \wedge y \geq g(x, y) \qquad \text{(G3)}$$

$$defined(g(x, x)) \Rightarrow x = g(x, x) \qquad \text{(G4)}$$

In a similar way, the implementation of $min2$ relied on some familiar properties of inequality.

We progress by introducing local copies of x and y.

gcd

$\equiv z' = g(x, y)$

$\equiv \exists x', y' \bullet x' = g(x, y) \wedge y' = g(x, y) \wedge z' = x'$

$\equiv$ definition of $LOCAL$, sequence introduction (IS1)

$\quad LOCAL\ x, y \bullet\ (x' = g(x, y) \wedge y' = g(x, y));\ z' = x$

$\equiv$ using following definition

$\quad LOCAL\ x, y \bullet\ gcd2;\ z' = x$

We now must implement the multiple assignment, which is not executable, as we do not have an executable definition of g. We therefore introduce the new definition

$$gcd2 \mathrel{\widehat{=}} x' = g(x, y) \wedge y' = g(x, y)$$

We will use a loop to refine this, so we need a suitable variant and invariant. These are found by trial and error. The fourth property above (G4) tells us $gcd2 \Rightarrow g(x', y') = g(x, y)$. That suggests $g(x, y)$ as an invariant. From the third property above (G3), we can see that x and y will both decrease toward their greatest common divisor. This suggests $x + y - 2 * g(x, y)$ as a suitable variant. Some important properties of this expression are

$$defined(g(x, y)) \Rightarrow x + y - 2 * g(x, y) \geq 0 \quad \text{(G5)}$$

$$x + y - 2 * g(x, y) = 0 \Rightarrow x = y \quad \text{(G6)}$$

$$defined(g(x, y)) \Rightarrow (x + y - 2 * g(x, y) > 0 \Leftrightarrow x \neq y) \quad \text{(G7)}$$

Thus, we can re-express $gcd2$ as

$$\begin{array}{l}
gcd2 \\
\equiv x + y - 2 * g(x, y) \geq 0 \wedge \\
\quad x' + y' - 2 * g(x', y') = 0 \wedge \\
\quad g(x', y') = g(x, y) \\
\sqsubseteq \text{ introduce assertion, and loop (IP, IL1)} \\
\quad defined(g(x, y)) \wedge \\
\quad WHILE\ x + y - 2 * g(x, y) > 0\ DO \\
\qquad x + y - 2 * g(x, y) > \\
\qquad x' + y' - 2 * g(x', y') \geq 0 \wedge \\
\qquad g(x', y') = g(x, y) \\
\sqsubseteq \text{ equivalent loop test, drop assertion (G5, G6, ET4, DA)} \\
\quad WHILE\ x \neq y\ DO \\
\qquad x + y - 2 * g(x, y) > \\
\qquad x' + y' - 2 * g(x', y') \geq 0 \wedge \\
\qquad g(x', y') = g(x, y) \\
\sqsubseteq \text{ simplifying, introducing assertions (IA4, IP)} \\
\quad WHILE\ x \neq y\ DO \\
\qquad x \neq y \wedge defined(g(x, y)) \wedge \\
\qquad x + y > x' + y' \wedge \\
\qquad g(x', y') = g(x, y) \\
\sqsubseteq \text{ using following definition} \\
\quad WHILE\ x \neq y\ DO \\
\qquad body \\
body \mathrel{\widehat{=}} x \neq y \wedge defined(g(x, y)) \wedge \\
\quad x + y > x' + y' \wedge \\
\quad g(x', y') = g(x, y) \\
\sqsubseteq \text{ postulate } x' = x - y \wedge y' = y \text{ (PQ)} \\
\quad x \neq y \wedge defined(g(x, y)) \wedge \\
\quad IF\ pre\ (body \wedge x' = x - y \wedge y' = y)\ THEN \\
\qquad body \wedge x' = x - y \wedge y' = y \\
\quad ELSE\ body \\
\sqsubseteq \text{ simplify test, deterministic conjunct (G2, DC)}
\end{array}$$

$x \neq y \wedge defined(g(x, y)) \wedge$
$IF\ x - y > 0\ THEN\ x' = x - y \wedge y' = y$
$ELSE\ body$

$\sqsubseteq$ move assertions forward (IA3, IA8, DA)

$IF\ x - y > 0\ THEN\ x' = x - y \wedge y' = y$
$ELSE\ x \neq y \wedge defined(g(x, y)) \wedge \neg(x - y > 0) \wedge body$

$\equiv$ simplifying (G5, G7, DA)

$IF\ x - y > 0\ THEN\ x' = x - y \wedge y' = y$
$ELSE\ x < y \wedge body$

$\sqsubseteq$ postulate $x' = x \wedge y' = y - x$ which is deterministic (PDQ)

$IF\ x - y > 0\ THEN\ x' = x - y \wedge y' = y$
$ELSE\ x < y \wedge (IF\ x < y\ THEN\ x' = x \wedge y' = y - x\ ELSE\ body)$

$\sqsubseteq$ exploit assertion (ET3)

$IF\ x - y > 0\ THEN\ x' = x - y \wedge y' = y$
$ELSE\ x < y \wedge (IF\ true\ THEN\ x' = x \wedge y' = y - x\ ELSE\ body)$

$\sqsubseteq$ simplify *IF* and drop assertion (DA)

$IF\ x - y > 0\ THEN\ x' = x - y \wedge y' = y$
$ELSE\ x' = x \wedge y' = y - x$

5.4 Second Example: (Alternative Approach)

We can arrive at a different implementation by introducing and maintaining the extra assertion $x \geq y$. This second implementation is motivated by the following facts.

$$g(x, y) = g(max2(x, y), min2(x, y)) \qquad \text{(G8)}$$

$$x > y \Rightarrow g(x, y) = g(x\ mod\ y, y) \qquad \text{(G9)}$$

$$x > y \Rightarrow x\ mod\ y < y \qquad \text{(G10)}$$

We start with the multiple assignment derived in the previous refinement.

$gcd2 \mathrel{\widehat{=}} x' = g(x, y) \wedge y' = g(x, y)$

$\equiv x' = g(max2(x, y), min2(x, y)) \wedge y' = g(max2(x, y), min2(x, y))$

$\equiv$ one point rule

$\exists\, a', b' \bullet\ a' = max2(x, y) \wedge b' = min2(x, y)$
$\wedge x' = g(a', b') \wedge y' = g(a', b')$

$\sqsubseteq$ introduce sequence, drop redundant local variables (IS1)

$x' = max2(x, y) \wedge y' = min2(x, y);$
$x' = g(x, y) \wedge y' = g(x, y)$

$\equiv$ introduce assertion (IA7)

$x' = max2(x, y) \wedge y' = min2(x, y);$
$x \geq y \wedge x' = g(x, y) \wedge y' = g(x, y)$

$\equiv$ using following definition

$x' = max2(x, y) \wedge y' = min2(x, y);$
$gcd3$

$gcd3 \mathrel{\widehat{=}} x \geq y \wedge x' = g(x, y) \wedge y' = g(x, y)$

$\equiv$ predicate calculus (G3, G4)

$x \geq y \wedge x' \geq y' \wedge$
$g(x', y') = g(x, y) \wedge$
$x - g(x, y) > x' - g(x', y') = 0$

$\sqsubseteq$ introduce loop (IL3)

$x \geq y \wedge$
$WHILE\ x - g(x, y) > 0\ DO$
$\quad x \geq y \wedge x' \geq y' \wedge$
$\quad g(x', y') = g(x, y) \wedge$
$\quad x - g(x, y) > x' - g(x', y') \geq 0$

$\equiv$ using following definition

$x \geq y \wedge$
$WHILE\ x - g(x, y) > 0\ DO$
$\quad body2$

$\equiv$ as $x \geq y \vdash x > g(x, y) \Leftrightarrow x > y$ (ET4, DA)

$WHILE\ x > y\ DO\ body2$

$body2 \mathrel{\widehat{=}} x \geq y \wedge x' \geq y' \wedge$
$g(x', y') = g(x, y) \wedge$
$x - g(x, y) > x' - g(x', y') \geq 0$

$\equiv$ predicate calculus

$x \geq y \wedge x' \geq y' \wedge$
$g(x', y') = g(x, y) \wedge$
$x > x'$

$\sqsubseteq$ postulate $x' = y \wedge y' = x\ mod\ y$

$x \geq y \wedge$
$IF\ pre(body2 \wedge x' = y \wedge y' = x\ mod\ y)\ THEN$
$\quad body2 \wedge x' = y \wedge y' = x\ mod\ y$
$ELSE\ body2$

$\sqsubseteq$ simplify test

$x \geq y \wedge$
$IF\ x \geq y\ THEN$
$\quad body2 \wedge x' = y \wedge y' = x\ mod\ y$
$ELSE\ body2$

$\sqsubseteq$ simplify test, drop assertion (ET3, DA)

$IF\ true\ THEN$
$\quad body2 \wedge x' = y \wedge y' = x\ mod\ y$
$ELSE\ body2$

$\sqsubseteq$ simplifying

$body2 \wedge x' = y \wedge y' = x\ mod\ y$

$\sqsubseteq$ deterministic conjunct (DC)

$x' = y \wedge y' = x\ mod\ y$

6 Weaknesses of Z-F′

The notation, method and refinement calculus presented in this paper are not as yet suitable for deriving any but simple examples. In this section I consider some of the weaknesses of Z-F′.

A number of the laws (IC1, IS2, PQ, IP, ET1, ET2) require a pre-condition to be calculated. While, on the one hand this is trivial, as the pre-condition operator is just a sugared form of existential quantifier, on the other hand, simplifying this quantifier may involve significant reasoning. This is certainly a potential difficulty, and only more experience of using the refinement calculus will tell us whether pre-condition calculation will indeed be a major part of the required effort.

I have suggested that, in assess the utility of refinement laws, only semantic applicability conditions are important. However, many of the laws given apply only if certain syntactic conditions are met that constrain the alphabets of the formulae involved. While these conditions are easy to check mechanically, it is rather easy to make a mistake when performing derivations by hand. This is, of course, no worse than the problem of manipulating quantified predicates where many of the laws have freeness conditions. Nonetheless, these side-conditions, and human fallibility suggest that any program derivation carried out with mechanical support must be suspect. That includes the ones in this paper! In Morgan's refinement calculus, the set of active variables is listed explictly in the frame. In Z-F′ the alphabet of a formula is implicit, and is not necessarily obvious. For example, consider

$$x' = x + 1;\ y' = 2 \quad \text{alphabet} = \{x, x', y\}$$
$$x' = 2;\ y' = x + 1 \quad \text{alphabet} = \{x', y\}$$

In the second example, it might appear that the variable x occurs free. However, it is hidden by the existential quantifier in the definition of sequential composition. This contributes to the difficulty of checking the syntactic side-conditions.

Another example confirms the subtle, and sometimes non-intuitive nature of reasoning about alphabets.

$$x = 1;\ LOCAL\ x \bullet\ y' = x$$
$\equiv$ introduce assertion (IA1)
$$x = 1 \wedge LOCAL\ x \bullet\ y' = x$$
$\equiv$ definition of $LOCAL$
$$x = 1 \wedge \exists\, x' \bullet\ y' = x$$
$\equiv$ predicate calculus
$$x = 1 \wedge y' = x$$
$\equiv$ substitution of (defined) equals
$$x = 1 \wedge y' = 1$$
$\not\sqsubseteq$ alphabets are different
$$y' = 1$$

Thus, as in section 4, the requirement to preserve the alphabet during refinement prevents the assertion from being dropped.

I have presented here a programming language and refinement calculus suitable only for small programs. To be realistic, I would also have to consider large-scale structuring mechanisms such as modules or packages. This would also allow data refinement to be added to the calculus. In addition, we have considered only briefly the small-scale structuring mechanisms such as procedures and functions. In particular, the formalism lacks a method for providing recursive definitions of partial functions. Instead, we have concentrated on iteration, and the derivation of iterative procedures.

Once these omissions have been rectified, it would be interesting to carry out some larger formal refinements.

To save space, the refinement laws have been quoted here without proof. A simple example of a proof will give an idea of what is involved. I will show that the *LOCAL* operator is monotonic with respect to the refinement ordering.

Theorem: Suppose the two formulae P and Q are such that $P \sqsubseteq Q$. Then, for any variable x, $LOCAL\ x \bullet\ P \sqsubseteq LOCAL\ x \bullet\ Q$.

Proof: We must demonstrate that the three refinement conditions are satisfied. We are given that P is refined by Q, which is to say

$$pre\ P \Rightarrow pre\ Q \qquad \text{(H1)}$$

$$pre\ P \wedge Q \Rightarrow P \qquad \text{(H2)}$$

$$alphabet(P) = alphabet(Q) \qquad \text{(H3)}$$

and we must prove the three corresponding facts about the *LOCAL* formulae.

We start by considering the alphabet (free variables) of each formula. If x' does not belong to the alphabet of P then

$LOCAL\ x' \bullet\ P$

$\Leftrightarrow$ by definition

$\quad \exists\, x' \bullet\ P$

$\Leftrightarrow$ assuming x' is not free in P

$\quad P$

In this case also, x does not belong to the alphabet of Q either (they are the same by H3), and $LOCAL\ x' \bullet\ Q \Leftrightarrow Q$. Thus, in this case it is trivial that, since $P \sqsubseteq Q$, $LOCAL\ x \bullet\ P \sqsubseteq LOCAL\ x \bullet\ Q$. We will therefore assume from now on that x' is in the alphabet of P (and Q).

Let us call the primed free variable(s) of $(LOCAL\ x \bullet\ P)$ z'. Then the primed variable(s) of P are x', z'. Now

$pre(LOCAL\ x \bullet\ P)$

$\Leftrightarrow$ by definition of *LOCAL*

$\quad pre(\exists\, x' \bullet\ P)$

$\Leftrightarrow$ definition of *pre*

$\quad \exists\, z' \bullet (\exists\, x' \bullet\ P)$

$\Leftrightarrow$ predicate calculus

$\exists z', x' \bullet P$

$\Leftrightarrow$ since z', x' are the primed variables of P

$pre\ P$

$\Rightarrow$ by hypothesis (H1)

$pre\ Q$

$\Leftrightarrow$ by symmetry

$pre(LOCAL\ x \bullet Q)$

This demonstrates that the first refinement condition holds.

Consider now the second refinement condition.

$pre(LOCAL\ x \bullet P) \wedge LOCAL\ x \bullet Q$

$\Leftrightarrow$ by previous result

$pre\ P \wedge LOCAL\ x \bullet Q$

$\Leftrightarrow$ by definition of $LOCAL$

$pre\ P \wedge \exists x' \bullet Q$

$\Leftrightarrow$ since x' not free in $pre\ Q$

$\exists x' \bullet pre\ P \wedge Q$

$\Rightarrow$ predicate calculus and hypothesis (H2)

$\exists x' \bullet P$

$\Leftrightarrow$ by definition of $LOCAL$

$LOCAL\ x \bullet P$

This demonstrates that the second refinement condition holds.

For the third refinement condition, note that

$alphabet(LOCAL\ x \bullet P)$

$= alphabet(P) \setminus \{x'\}$

$= alphabet(Q) \setminus \{x'\}$ using hypothesis H3

$= alphabet(LOCAL\ x \bullet Q)$

End of Proof.

7 Comparison with other work

This paper presents a notation, Z-F$'$, and a framework for program derivation and proof. It is similar to Rick Hehner's predicative methodology [Hehner 84, 86], but there are also a number of technical differences. Hehner's predicates must be total (that is, for each input, there must be at least one output that satisfies the predicate). An unfortunate consequence of this is that $P \wedge Q$ may fail to be a valid specification even if both P and Q are. Conjunction is an extremely valuable operator in specification which it is important to be able to use freely. However, insisting that specifications are total does allows Hehner to use *true* (a specification that constrains no output variable) for failure, so that refinement in his framework is just reverse implication ($P \sqsubseteq Q$ means $P \Leftarrow Q$). In contrast, the definition of refinement that is adopted here is complex and inelegant. However, in the method propounded here, the definition is rarely used directly, as the laws of refinement are used instead. Furthermore, these laws do provide guidance by guiding the developer towards particular formulae that match the left hand side of one of the rules.

A technical weakness of Hehner's work is that recursion and iteration are defined by taking the limit of a countable sequence of predicates. This is not adequate in the case of unbounded non-determinism [Dijkstra 86]. Note, however, that in more recent work Hehner gives fixpoint semantics to loops [Hehner 91].

A major source of ideas that inspired this approach is Morgan's refinement calculus [Morgan 90]. Indeed, the approach adopted here can be seen as an attempt to recreate Morgan's calculus in a language of predicates, rather than predicate transformers. The different framework leads to some technical distinctions. In the approach adopted here there is no frame, and no separate pre-condition; rather both frame and pre-condition are implicit. An advantage of using one predicate (or two states) rather than two (each of one state) is that this avoids the need for logical constants. Another point (from [Gilmore 91]) is that, with certain operations, giving an explicit pre-condition may lead to inelegant duplication. Compare for example the Z-style specification

$$x' \in \mathcal{N} \wedge x' * x' = y$$

with (in Morgan's notation)

$$x : [\exists x : \mathcal{N} \bullet \; x * x = y, x * x = y]$$

Furthermore, though Morgan's refinement calculus is a natural fit with VDM-style specifications, the approach adopted here would seem to work better with Z-style specifications. Some advice is offered ([King 90]) that allows Morgan's refinement calculus to be used in conjunction with Z, but to me it seems counter-productive to switch notations in mid-development.

A key message of this paper is that it is important to have laws with no, or with purely syntactic, side-conditions. Morgan has such laws for conditional, sequence, and loops. However, introducing an assignment in his refinement calculus requires a feasibility check, which is a semantic side-condition. Since assignments are rather common, this represents a significant effort. In the approach considered here assignments can be introduced with a syntactic check only. As assignments are deterministic, a special case of the *deterministic conjunct* law is

$$P(x') \wedge x' = e \sqsubseteq x' = e$$

and similarly for multiple assignments. Thus in this approach there are (essentially) no semantic side-conditions while in Morgan's there is just one. The law in question is Morgan's law of assignment:

$$w, x : [pre, post] \sqsubseteq w := e \qquad \text{providing } \vdash pre \Rightarrow post(e/w)$$

In contrast, consider a textbook on Z [Potter 91] which offers a loop law with 5 semantic side-conditions (proof obligations). A recent text book on VDM

[Jones 90] improves over this with just 3. Of course, these loop laws offer the advantage of being complete. However, it is important to recognise the existence of special cases which require (permit) fewer proof obligations.

Morgan's calculus uses a sophisticated system of labelling conventions for sub-formulae, whereas Hehner's style is to name sub-formulae explicitly. This seems to be largely a matter of taste. However, it is certainly helpful to name sub-programs when using laws such as *postulate Q*, since these introduce repeated occurrences of the original left hand side. For this reason, I also prefer to name sub-formulae.

Ralph Back [Back 90] provides a thorough overview of the lattice of predicate transformers. Under the refinement ordering defined here, single state predicates fail to be a lattice (so that one cannot take arbitrary meets and joins), and also fail to be complete (closed under limits). Working in a complete lattice offers similar theoretical advantages to using complex numbers to solve (real-valued) polynomial equations. For example, Morgan exploits the existence of infeasible predicate transformers, or miracles, in data refinement [Morgan 88]. It is yet to be seen whether there is any equivalent device that can be employed when using an approach based on first-order logic.

Acknowledgements

I would like to record my gratitude to the two anonymous referees who reviewed the initial draft of this paper, and pointed out many errors, both large and small. They also made helpful suggestions for improving the structure of the paper. I have tried to act on their suggestions, but any remaining problems are, of course, my own fault.

A Laws of Refinement

This collection of laws simply includes those that have proved useful in deriving programs. There has been no attempt to ensure that the collection is complete.

Laws of Pre-Condition

$(pre\ P) \wedge P \equiv P$

$pre(P \vee Q) \equiv pre\ P \vee pre\ Q$

$pre\ A \equiv A$ provided A is an assertion

$pre(A \wedge P) \equiv A \wedge pre\ P$ provided A is an assertion

$pre(x' = e) \equiv defined(e)$
$pre(x' = e1 \wedge y' = e2) \equiv defined(e1) \wedge defined(e2)$
and so on

$pre(P;\ Q) \equiv pre\ P \wedge \forall x' \bullet\ P \Rightarrow Q(x'/x)$

$pre(IF\ A\ THEN\ P\ \ ELSE\ \ Q) \equiv IF\ A\ THEN\ pre\ P\ ELSE\ pre\ Q$

$pre(WHILE\ A\ DO\ P) \equiv (\forall s \bullet\ TRACE \Rightarrow \exists m \bullet\ \neg A(s(m)/x))$

Laws of Composition

$(P;\ Q);\ R \equiv P;\ (Q;\ R)$

$A;\ P \equiv A \wedge P$ provided A is an assertion

$P \wedge A';\ Q \equiv P \wedge A';\ A \wedge Q$
provided A is an assertion

$true;\ P \equiv P$
$P;\ true \equiv P$

$x' = e;\ P(x, y') \equiv x' = e \wedge P(y', f(e))$

$x' = e;\ y' = f(x) \equiv x' = e \wedge y' = f(e)$

Laws of Conditionals

$IF\ TRUE\ THEN\ B\ ELSE\ C = B$

$IF\ A\ THEN\ P\ ELSE\ P = P$

$IF\ A\ THEN\ B\ ELSE\ C \equiv IF\ \neg A\ THEN\ C\ ELSE\ B$

$IF\ A\ THEN\ P\ ELSE\ Q$
$\equiv IF\ A\ THEN\ (A \wedge P)\ ELSE\ Q$
$\equiv IF\ A\ THEN\ P\ ELSE\ (\neg A \wedge Q)$
$\equiv IF\ A\ THEN\ (A \wedge P)\ ELSE\ (\neg A \wedge Q)$

$(IF\ A\ THEN\ P\ ELSE\ Q);\ R$
$\equiv IF\ A\ THEN\ (P;\ R)\ ELSE\ (Q;\ R)$

$P;\ (IF\ A\ THEN\ R\ ELSE\ S)$
$\equiv IF\ A\ THEN\ P;\ R\ ELSE\ P;\ R$
provided the primed variables of P do not occur unprimed in A

$x' = e;\ IF\ A(x)\ THEN\ P(x)\ ELSE\ Q(x)$
$\equiv IF\ A(e)\ THEN\ (x' = e;\ P(x))\ ELSE\ (x' = e;\ Q(x))$

$A;\ IF\ B\ THEN\ P\ ELSE\ Q$
$\equiv A;\ IF\ C\ THEN\ P\ ELSE\ Q$
provided $\vdash A \Rightarrow (B \Leftrightarrow C)$

Other Laws

$LOCAL\ x \bullet\ P \equiv LOCAL\ y \bullet\ P(y'/x')$
provided y' is not free in P

$LOCAL\ x \bullet\ (P;\ y' = x) \equiv P(y'/x')$
provided y' is not free in P

$LOCAL\ x \bullet\ (x' = e;\ P) \equiv defined(e) \wedge P(e/x)$
provided x' is not free in P

$LOCAL\ x \bullet\ P(y, x');\ Q(x, y') \equiv P(y, y');\ Q(y, y')$

$WHILE\ A\ DO\ P \equiv IF\ A\ THEN\ P;\ WHILE\ A\ DO\ P$

$WHILE\ A\ DO\ P \equiv (WHILE\ A\ DO\ P);\ \neg A$

$WHILE\ A\ DO\ P \equiv WHILE\ A\ DO\ A \wedge P$

$A \wedge \mathit{WHILE}\ B\ \mathit{DO}\ A \wedge P \wedge A'$

$\equiv A \wedge \mathit{WHILE}\ C\ \mathit{DO}\ A \wedge P \wedge A'$

provided $\vdash A \Rightarrow (B \Leftrightarrow C)$

Monotonicity of Program Constructors

Suppose $P1 \sqsubseteq P2$. Then we can replace $P1$ by $P2$ in any executable context:

$P1;\ Q \sqsubseteq P2;\ Q$
$Q;\ P1 \sqsubseteq Q;\ P2$

$\mathit{IF}\ A\ \mathit{THEN}\ P1\ \mathit{ELSE}\ Q \sqsubseteq \mathit{IF}\ A\ \mathit{THEN}\ P2\ \mathit{ELSE}\ Q$
$\mathit{IF}\ A\ \mathit{THEN}\ Q\ \mathit{ELSE}\ P1 \sqsubseteq \mathit{IF}\ A\ \mathit{THEN}\ Q\ \mathit{ELSE}\ P2$

$\mathit{WHILE}\ A\ \mathit{DO}\ P1 \sqsubseteq \mathit{WHILE}\ A\ \mathit{DO}\ P2$

$\mathit{LOCAL}\ x \bullet\ P1 \sqsubseteq \mathit{LOCAL}\ x \bullet\ P2$

Where $P1 \equiv P2$ then we can replace $P1$ by $P2$ in *any* context C:

$C(P1) \equiv C(P2)$

Where $P1 = P2$ and $\mathit{alphabet}(C(P1)) = \mathit{alphabet}(C(P2))$ then

$C(P1) \equiv C(P2)$

Improving Executability

$A;\ P \sqsubseteq P$

provided A is an assertion, $\mathit{alphabet}(A) \subseteq \mathit{alphabet}(P)$

$P;\ A \sqsubseteq P$

provided A is an assertion, $\mathit{alphabet}(A) \subseteq \mathit{alphabet}(P)$

$P;\ A \wedge Q \sqsubseteq P \wedge A';\ A \wedge Q$

provided A is an assertion

$(A \wedge P) \vee (\neg A \wedge Q) \sqsubseteq \mathit{IF}\ A\ \mathit{THEN}\ P\ \mathit{ELSE}\ Q$

provided A is an assertion

$A \wedge P \sqsubseteq \mathit{IF}\ A\ \mathit{THEN}\ P\ \mathit{ELSE}\ Q$

provided $\mathit{alphabet}(Q) \subseteq \mathit{alphabet}(A \wedge P)$

$A \wedge P \sqsubseteq \mathit{IF}\ A\ \mathit{THEN}\ P$

provided the primed variables of P occur unprimed in A

$A \wedge P \sqsubseteq (A \vee B) \wedge P$

provided B is an assertion and $\mathit{alphabet}(B) \subseteq \mathit{alphabet}(A \wedge P)$

$A \wedge P \sqsubseteq P$

provided A is an assertion and $\mathit{alphabet}(A) \subseteq \mathit{alphabet}(P)$

$P \wedge Q \sqsubseteq Q$

provided Q is deterministic, $\mathit{alphabet}(P) \subseteq \mathit{alphabet}(Q)$

$P \wedge Q \sqsubseteq P;\ Q$

provided the primed variables of P do not occur in Q

$P \wedge Q \sqsubseteq P \wedge (\mathit{pre}\ Q(x/x'))(x'/x);\ Q(x/x')$

provided the primed variables of P occur only primed in Q

$P \wedge Q \sqsubseteq P;\ Q(x/x')$
provided the primed variables of P occur only primed in Q, and P is deterministic

$P \wedge Q \sqsubseteq P;\ Q(x/x')$
provided the primed variables of P occur only primed in Q, and $Q(x/x')$ is total

$P \vee Q \sqsubseteq IF\ pre\ P\ THEN\ P\ ELSE\ Q$

$IF\ A\ THEN\ P\ ELSE\ Q$
$\sqsubseteq IF\ A \wedge pre\ P\ THEN\ P\ ELSE\ Q$

$IF\ A\ THEN\ P\ ELSE\ Q$
$\sqsubseteq IF\ A \vee \neg pre\ Q\ THEN\ P\ ELSE\ Q$

$P \sqsubseteq IF\ pre(P \wedge Q)\ THEN\ P \wedge Q\ ELSE\ P$
provided $alphabet(Q) \subseteq alphabet(P)$

$P \sqsubseteq P \wedge Q$
provided $pre(P \wedge Q) \vee \neg pre\ P$

$P \sqsubseteq Q$
provided $pre(P \wedge Q) \vee \neg pre\ P$, Q is deterministic, and $alphabet(P) = alphabet(Q)$

$I \wedge v \geq 0 = v'$
$\sqsubseteq IF\ v > 0\ THEN\ I \wedge v' = 0$
$\equiv WHILE\ v > 0\ DO\ I \wedge v > v' \geq 0$
provided I is an invariant formula, v is an expression with no un-primed variables

Deterministic Formulae

A formulae $P(x, x')$ is deterministic if and only if

$$pre\ P \Rightarrow \exists_1\, x' \bullet\ P$$

Note that this is a semantic property. However, the following theorems allow certain formulae to be shown to be deterministic on a purely syntactic basis.

- If P is executable, P is deterministic.
- If P is deterministic and A is an assertion then $A \wedge P$ is deterministic.
- If P is deterministic, and the primed variables of Q all occur in P then $P \wedge Q$ is deterministic.

Invariants

A formula I is an invariant, or an equivalence formula, if it satisfies the following conditions:

1. Each primed variable(s), say x', of I must also occur unprimed in I.
2. I must be reflexive ($pre\ I \wedge x' = x \Rightarrow I$).

3. I must be symmetric ($I \Rightarrow I(x/x', x'/x)$).

4. I must be transitive ($I(y/x') \wedge I(y/x) \Rightarrow I$).

Note that this is a semantic property. However, the following theorems allow certain formulae to be shown to be invariants on a purely syntactic basis.

If A is an assertion, and e is an expression of only un-primed variables, then the following formulae are invariants.

$$A \wedge A'$$

$$e = e'$$

$$A \wedge A' \wedge e = e'$$

References

Back 78 *On the Correctness of Refinement Steps in Program Development.* R J R Back. PhD Thesis A-1978-4, Department of Computer Science, University of Helsinki, 1978.

Back 90 *Duality in Specification Languages: A Lattice-theoretical Approach.* R J R Back, J von Wright. Acta Informatica, vol 27, pages 583-625, 1990.

Bauer 85 *The Munich Project CIP (vol I).* F L Bauer et al. Springer Verlag Lecture Notes in Computer Science 183, 1985.

Bauer 87 *The Munich Project CIP (vol II).* F L Bauer et al. Springer Verlag Lecture Notes in Computer Science 292, 1987.

Dijkstra 86 *A Simple Fixpoint Argument Without the Restriction to Continuity.* E W Dijkstra, A J M van Gasteren. Acta Informatica, vol 23, pages 1-7, 1986.

Gilmore 91 *Correctness-Oriented Approaches to Software Development.* S Gilmore. PhD Thesis CST-76-91, Department of Computer Science, University of Edinburgh, April 1991.

Goguen 81 *Completeness of Many-Sorted Equational Logic.* J A Goguen and J Meseguer. SIGPLAN Notices, vol 16, no 7, pages 24-32, 1981.

Hehner 84 *Predicative Programming Parts I and II.* Communications of the ACM, vol 27, pages 134-151, 1984.

Hehner 86 *Predicative Methodology.* E C R Hehner, L E Gupta, A J Malton. Acta Informatica, vol 23, pages 487-505, 1986.

Hehner 91 *A Practical Theory of Programming (draft).* E C R Hehner. Department of Computer Science, University of Toronto, July 1991.

Jones 90 *Systematic Software Development Using VDM (second edition).* C B Jones. Prentice Hall, 1990.

King 90 *Z and the Refinement Calculus.* S King. Report PRG 79, Programming Research Group, Oxford, February 1990.

Mendelson 87 *Introduction to Mathematical Logic (third edition).* E Mendelson. Wadsworth Brooks, 1987.

Morgan 88 *Data Refinement using Miracles.* C C Morgan. Information Processing Letters, vol 26, no 5, pages 243-246, January 1988.

Morgan 90 *Programming from Specifications.* C C Morgan. Prentice Hall, 1990,

Morris 87 *A Theoretical Basic for Stepwise Refinement and the Programming Calculus.* J M Morris. Science of Computer Programming, vol 9, no 3, pages 287-306, 1987.

Nielson 90 *Machine Support for Z: the zedB tool.* D Nielson. Z User Workshop (Oxford 90), ed J E Nicholls, pages 105-128, Springer-Verlag, 1991.

Partsch 90 *Specification and Transformation of Programs.* H A Partsch. Springer Verlag, 1990.

Potter 91 *An Introduction to Formal Specification and Z.* B Potter, J Sinclair, D Till. Prentice Hall, 1991.

Sanders 91 *Eliminating the Substitution Axiom from UNITY Logic.* B A Sanders. Formal Aspects of Computing, vol 3, no 2, pages 189-205, 1991.

A Model of the Refinement Process

Maurice Naftalin
Department of Computing Science, University of Stirling
Stirling, Scotland FK9 4LA

Abstract

It is increasingly accepted that the top-down model of the design process is not realistic. Designers often work at many levels of abstraction simultaneously, applying insights gained at one level to modify both specifications and designs at other levels. A development method which will accommodate such opportunistic insights must allow the designer to view and modify the developing design at a variety of different abstraction levels. We propose a design representation suitable for program derivation, intended to support this requirement and to record some non-formal aspects of the design. The model is presented in the form of a VDM specification, together with an outline of a visual editing system for it.

1 Introduction

Refinement calculi (*e.g.* [Back78], [Morris89], [Morgan90]) are currently the focus of much interest as a promising method of formally developing programs from specifications. On a small scale, they provide an attractive method of verifiable program construction; the separation between specifications and executable programs is abolished in a single language (the "specification language"), and development from an initial specification or abstract program takes place in a series of small steps each of which replaces a specification-language construct by one nearer the concrete program. The same idea is present in VDM ([Jones90]); the main difference is that a calculus provides a set of laws whose application allows the calculation of each refinement step.

On a large scale, these approaches encounter the difficulty that the hybrid objects created in the course of a development are large and in general difficult to manage. Normally, this problem is evaded[1]; derivations concentrate on each step in isolation, with the overall structure presented as chains of refinement steps connected by branch-points represented in an ad-hoc way. It is usually understood that the overall structure is a tree of some sort, but this is not normally made explicit. This effective absence of structure makes the management of large derivations difficult; to take only two examples, the collection of code and the recording of alternative derivations must be done informally.

The problems of managing large derivations are a minor inconvenience, however, compared to the cognitive problems caused by an absence of explicit derivation structure. There is strong evidence (*e.g.* [Guindon87], [Visser87], [Visser90], [Sumiga88]) that experienced designers work in an *opportunistic* manner, in which the focus of their attention shifts unpredictably in order to solve sub-problems as these present themselves. In particular, insights gained at one level of the design are applied at other, possibly higher, levels. This is hardly feasible in the absence of some structure which can record such non-systematic insights. Design methods lacking such structure impose (whatever the intentions of their originators) an unrealistically rigid top-down strategy, unattractive to would-be users.

The alternative is to provide users with a structure in which individual refinement steps can be embedded and which will facilitate opportunistic design by providing a kind

[1] [Back91] is an exception; §7 compares this work with the present proposal

of map of the entire derivation. One such structure is presented here, together with a visualisation system for it. Such a structure is bound to be a matter for controversy, as to be useful it must embody some model for the process of design by refinement, and therefore some notion of how designers really work (or how they "should" work) in a formal development method. In §2 we describe a simple version of this design structure by means of its VDM specification, written (almost entirely) in the standard form VDM-SL ([Dawes91]); §3 gives a brief example of its use; §4 enhances the model to allow operations corresponding to a more realistic design model; §5 provides a sketch of a refinement editor based on the proposed design structure, and §6 discusses the merits of the approach.

2 Constructing Refinement Graphs

In its simplest form, the design process model proposed here consists of a repetition of development stages, each one of which consists of two activities: refinement (which, within one stage, may involve a number of individual refinement steps) and summarisation. The outcome of the refinement activity of a single stage is called a *refinement tree*. Following summarisation, a new development stage begins the development of a new refinement tree.

The new tree, initially a summarised version of the culminating refinement tree of the previous stage, is linked to it in a structure called a *refinement graph*, which is a representation of the entire design. It is a graph rather than a chain, because alternative derivations can cause divergence in the development; these divergent developments may subsequently reconverge. Top-down design requires that all changes should be to the latest tree in one of these divergent developments, since each of these represents the latest stage in one of the alternative designs; indeed, strictly speaking, top-down design allows only extensions, not modifications, even to these. This section specifies the operations necessary to extend refinement trees and graphs. In practice, designers will often wish to modify work done both in the latest and in earlier stages, the latter requiring global changes to the refinement graph. Operations to support this mode of working are described in §4.

We shall take as a running example in this paper the development of a square root program (figure 1) from [Morgan90]. In our terms, figure 1 is a linearised representation of a refinement tree at some stage in the development (we shall see that this is not necessarily the final stage). This example is chosen simply to make the exposition clearer: the proposed framework is not restricted to the language or laws of Morgan's refinement calculus, nor even to any particular refinement relation. The only restrictions on the applicability of the framework to a refinement system (refinement relation and specification language) is that the refinement relation must be a preorder (*i.e.* reflexive and transitive) and compositional operators of the specification language must be monotonic with respect to it.

2.1 The type *Reftree*

We first develop the type of refinement trees. We begin by considering the various partial trees that preceded figure 1 in the development. The simplest of these is line 1 alone[2]. This is a fragment of syntax in the specification language. Since we intend to define refinement trees without reference to a particular specification language, we distinguish only two types of syntactic constructs: those which contain no separately refinable syntactic components (we call these *Atom*), and those composed by some

[2] References to "lines" in figure 1 are actually to fragments of specification language syntax represented, in most cases, by groups of physical lines.

1··· $\textbf{var}\ r, s\colon \mathbb{N} \bullet$
$r := \lfloor\sqrt{s}\rfloor$

2··· $= \quad r\colon[\mathsf{true}\ , r^2 \leq s < (r+1)^2]$

3··· $\sqsubseteq \quad \textbf{var}\ q\colon \mathbb{N} \bullet$
$q, r\colon[\mathsf{true}\ , r^2 \leq s < q^2 \wedge r+1 = q]$

4··· $\sqsubseteq \quad I \mathrel{\widehat{=}} r^2 \leq s < q^2 \bullet$
$q, r\colon[\mathsf{true}\ , I \wedge r+1 = q]$

5··· $\sqsubseteq \quad q, r\colon[\mathsf{true}\ , I];$ (iii)
$q, r\colon[I\ , I \wedge r+1 = q]$ ◁

$\sqsubseteq \quad \textbf{do}\ r+1 \neq q \rightarrow$
6··· $q, r\colon[r+1 \neq q, I, q-r < q_0 - r_0]$ ◁
$\textbf{od}$

$\sqsubseteq \quad \textbf{var}\ p\colon \mathbb{N} \bullet$
7··· $p\colon[r+1 < q, r < p < q];$ (iv)
$q, r\colon[r < p < q, I, q-r < q_0 - r_0]$ ◁

$\sqsubseteq \quad \textbf{if}\ s < p^2 \rightarrow q\colon[s < p^2 \wedge p < q, I, q < q_0]$ (v)
8··· $[\,]\ s \geq p^2 \rightarrow r\colon[s \geq p^2 \wedge r < p, I, r_0 < r]$ (vi)
$\textbf{fi}$

9··· (iii) $\sqsubseteq \quad q, r := s+1, 0$

10··· (iv) $\sqsubseteq \quad p := (q+r) \div 2$ "Binary chop"

11··· (v) $\sqsubseteq \quad q := p$

12··· (vi) $\sqsubseteq \quad r := p$

Figure 1: Square root development history
(from [Morgan90], reproduced by kind permission of Prentice Hall)

operator from other refinable constructs. An adequate description of the latter is as pairs combining the operator with a sequence of operands[3].

This reasoning leads to the following initial attempt at a type definition for abstract syntax trees in the specification language:

$AST = Atom \mid Oprnode$

[3] It would be natural to consider syntactic composites as tuple types, each containing the appropriate number and type of operands for a particular operator. Unfortunately this approach would compromise the aim of language-independence. The present approach is not fully satisfactory either, in that it is not parameterised on the language definition. It is interesting to consider how the specification of a refinement system could be abstracted away from the specification language definition in a satisfactory way.

$$\begin{aligned} \textit{Oprnode}_1 :: \quad & \textit{opr} : \textsf{token} \\ & \textit{subtrees} : \textit{AST}^* \end{aligned}$$

In order to allow a freestanding syntax tree (like line 1 of figure 1) to be a refinement tree, we define

$$\textit{Reftree} = \textit{AST} \mid \ldots$$

To complete the definition of *Reftree*, consider the refinement tree consisting of lines 1 and 2 together. We call this structure a *refinement*; it connects a source AST (the object being refined) with a target, which (in this case) is also an AST. So the appropriate types are[4]

$$\textit{Reftree} = \textit{AST} \mid \textit{Refmt}$$

$$\begin{aligned} \textit{Refmt}_1 :: \ & \textit{source} : \textit{AST} \\ & \textit{target} : \textit{AST} \end{aligned}$$

On adding line 3 to the refinement tree, it becomes apparent that the definition of $\textit{Refmt}_1$ is not adequate. Lines 2 and 3 together conform to it, but in order to relate line 1 to this composite object requires *Refmt* to be redefined:

$$\begin{aligned} \textit{Refmt} :: \ & \textit{source} : \textit{AST} \\ & \textit{target} : \textit{Reftree} \end{aligned}$$

These types accommodate the addition of lines 4 and 5 to the refinement tree, but still do not allow further progress after line 5. This is clearly an *Oprnode* with operator ";", of which the operands (the two constructs "$q, r{:}\,[\cdots, \cdots]$") are both to be further refined (as shown by the symbols at the right-hand side of the figure) whereas the type of $\textit{Oprnode}_1$ allows only (unrefined) ASTs as components. The obvious solution is to change this type to

$$\begin{aligned} \textit{Oprnode} :: \quad & \textit{opr} : \textsf{token} \\ & \textit{subtrees} : \textit{Reftree}^* \end{aligned}$$

and with this we have the types summarised in figure 2; these are the basis for the discussion in the rest of §2.

For simplicity, we will usually implicitly adapt the definition of *Reftree* to

$$\textit{Reftree} = \textit{Refmt} \mid \textit{Oprnode} \mid \textit{Atom}$$

and we will also omit the appropriate injection and projection functions.

The following simple example is the refinement tree containing the lines 5, 6 and 9 from figure 1.

$$\begin{aligned} & \textit{mk-Oprnode}(\text{";"}, [\\ & \qquad \textit{mk-Refmt}(\text{"}q, r{:}\,[\textsf{true}\,, I]\text{"}, \text{"}q, r{:}= s+1, 0\text{"}), \\ & \qquad \textit{mk-Refmt}(\text{"}q, r{:}\,[I, I \wedge r+1 = q]\text{"}, \\ & \qquad\quad \textit{mk-Oprnode}(\text{"do od"}, [\\ & \qquad\qquad \text{"}\,r+1 \neq q\text{"}, \\ & \qquad\qquad \text{"}q, r{:}\,[r+1 \neq q, I, q-r < q_0 - r_0]\text{"}))]) \end{aligned}$$

2.2 Invariant on *Reftree*

We first define an auxiliary function *refmts*, which collects the set of refinements at all levels in a refinement tree.

[4] Records have been chosen in preference to representing a refinement as a map or relation between ASTs for two reasons: first, they provide a better notation for expressing operations which compress the tree by replacing nodes with their descendants, and second, that the use of a map to model refinement would constrain the designer to use the same refinement for a particular construct wherever it occurred in the refinement tree.

$$Reftree = AST \mid Refmt$$

$$AST = Atom \mid Oprnode$$

$$\begin{aligned} Oprnode :: \quad opr &: \mathsf{token} \\ subtrees &: Reftree^* \end{aligned}$$

$$\begin{aligned} Refmt :: source &: AST \\ target &: Reftree \end{aligned}$$

Figure 2: Type Definition for Refinement Trees

$refmts : Reftree \rightarrow Refmt\text{-set}$

$refmts(rt) \ \triangleq$
  cases rt of
  $mk\text{-}Refmt(-, t) \ \rightarrow \{rt\} \cup refmts(t)$
  $mk\text{-}Oprnode(-, s) \rightarrow \bigcup\{refmts(x) \mid x \in \text{elems } s\}$
  others $\rightarrow \{\}$
  end

This is now used to define the invariant on *Reftree*:

$inv\text{-}Reftree(rt) \ \triangleq$
  $\forall r \in refmts(rt) \cdot refmts(r.source) = \{\}$

The invariant excludes the possibility that a non-atomic AST that is the source of a refinement (a compound statement being optimised, for example) could properly contain a (syntactic) subtree which is also the source of a refinement.

2.3 Collecting Refinement Trees

A key operation on refinement trees is *collection*. This summarises the result of refinement by flattening a refinement tree. Nodes which have been refined disappear, replaced by their descendants in the tree. For example, collecting the tree represented by figure 1 gives the code of the square root program; collecting the partial derivation represented by lines 1, 2 and 3 gives the refinement tree consisting of line 3 alone; collecting the subtree of the example above (lines 5, 6 and 9 of figure 1) gives

$mk\text{-}Oprnode(\text{“;”}, [$
  $\text{“}q, r := s + 1, 0\text{”},$
  $mk\text{-}Oprnode(\text{“do od”}, [$
    $\text{“}r + 1 \neq q\text{”},$
    $\text{“}q, r: [r + 1 \neq q, I, q - r < q_0 - r_0]\text{”}])])$

In order to allow collection to be used selectively, it is defined on a subtree of a given refinement tree. The collection function *collect_subtree* therefore takes two arguments, the first being the root of a refinement tree and the second being a *path*. Informally, a path is a means of “navigating” from the root of a refinement tree to some component subtree. We are not particularly concerned here with the detail of how paths can be modelled, but for the sake of completeness an appendix gives a simple representation together with corresponding definitions of the following functions:

$paths$: $Reftree \rightarrow Path$-set

paths returns the set of all paths valid for the tree of its argument.

$find\_subtree$: $Reftree \times Path \rightarrow Reftree$

find_subtree returns the value of the subtree of its first argument found by the path of its second. It requires as a precondition that the path should be valid for that tree.

$replace\_subtree$: $Reftree \times Path \times Reftree \rightarrow Reftree$

replace_subtree replaces with the tree of its third argument the subtree of its first argument found by the path of its second. Again the path must be valid for the first argument.

Using these auxiliary functions, we are now ready to define collection of a subtree (as specified by a path) of a given tree:

$collect\_subtree\ (rt: Reftree, p: Path)\ ct: Reftree$
pre $p \in paths(rt)$
post $ct =$
    let $subtree = find\_subtree(rt, p)$ in
    $replace\_subtree(rt, p, collect(subtree))$

$collect : Reftree \rightarrow Reftree$

$collect(rt)\ \triangleq$
    cases rt of
    $mk\text{-}Refmt(-, t) \rightarrow collect(t)$
    $mk\text{-}Oprnode(o, s) \rightarrow mk\text{-}Oprnode(o, [collect(s(i)) \mid i \in \text{inds}\ s])$
    others $\rightarrow rt$
    end

2.4 Refinement Graphs

Recall (from the introduction to §2) that we propose to model an entire derivation by a directed graph of refinement trees. The simplest representation for this is a binary relation on refinement trees; in order to allow duplicate trees, however, we provide each tree with a unique identifying tag (not further specified here) and record the relation on these tags:

$$\begin{aligned} Refgraph :: \quad & ttrees : Tag \xrightarrow{m} Reftree \\ & derivns : (Tag \times Tag)\text{-set} \end{aligned}$$

In order for *Refgraph* to fulfil its intended purpose of enabling the designer to record the culmination of each stage of the development and the connection between the stages, two refinement trees *left* and *right* should be connected in a refinement graph only if *right* is a *development* of *left*. More precisely, *right* should be either an extension (by refinement) of *left* or an extension (by refinement) of the result of collecting some subtree of *left*. The most straightforward way of imposing this condition on refinement graphs is to prevent collection from being applied to an arbitrary refinement tree, instead restricting its application to copies made for the purpose (this constraint, which corresponds to strict top-down development, will be relaxed in §4).

The situation described above is formalised in the invariant on *Refgraph*:

$$inv\text{-}Refgraph : Refgraph \rightarrow \mathbf{B}$$

$$\begin{aligned}
&inv\text{-}Refgraph(rg) \;\triangleq \\
&\quad (\forall rt \in \mathsf{rng}\; rg.ttrees \cdot inv\text{-}Reftree(rt)) \wedge \\
&\quad \mathsf{dom}\; rg.derivns \cup \mathsf{rng}\; rg.derivns \subseteq \mathsf{dom}\; rg.ttrees \wedge \\
&\quad \forall mk\text{-}(left, right) \in rg.derivns \cdot \\
&\qquad \exists p \in paths(rg.ttrees(left)) \cdot \\
&\qquad\quad pruned(collect_subtree(rg.ttrees(left), p), rg.ttrees(right))
\end{aligned}$$

(The operators dom , rng and (later) $\triangleleft$ are assumed to have their usual meaning applied to binary relations: VDM-SL does not define these operators on relations).

Of the clauses in the invariant, the first ensures that every tree in the graph is well-formed, the second that every tag in the *derivns* component of the graph corresponds to a defined tree, and the third formalises the relation between refinement trees described above. The predicate *pruned* is defined as follows.

$$pruned : Reftree \times Reftree \rightarrow \mathbf{B}$$

$$\begin{aligned}
&pruned(little, big) \;\triangleq \\
&\quad \mathsf{cases}\; big \;\mathsf{of} \\
&\quad mk\text{-}Refmt(bs, bt) \rightarrow \mathsf{cases}\; little \;\mathsf{of} \\
&\qquad\qquad mk\text{-}Refmt(ls, lt) \rightarrow ls = bs \wedge pruned(lt, bt) \\
&\qquad\qquad \mathsf{others} \rightarrow little = bs \\
&\qquad\qquad \mathsf{end} \\
&\quad mk\text{-}Oprnode(bo, bs) \rightarrow \mathsf{cases}\; little \;\mathsf{of} \\
&\qquad\qquad mk\text{-}Oprnode(lo, ls) \rightarrow lo = bo \wedge prwise_pruned(ls, bs) \\
&\qquad\qquad \mathsf{others} \rightarrow \mathsf{false} \\
&\qquad\qquad \mathsf{end} \\
&\quad \mathsf{others}\; little = big \\
&\quad \mathsf{end}
\end{aligned}$$

pruned(l, b) holds if $b = l$ or if b extends l by refinement.

$$prwise\_pruned : Reftree^{*} \times Reftree^{*} \rightarrow \mathbf{B}$$

$$\begin{aligned}
&prwise_pruned(littles, bigs) \;\triangleq \\
&\quad \mathsf{len}\; littles = \mathsf{len}\; bigs \wedge \\
&\qquad \forall i \in \mathsf{inds}\; littles \cdot pruned(littles(i), bigs(i))
\end{aligned}$$

2.5 Construction Operations on Refinement Graphs

This section describes the two operations necessary for extending refinement trees and graphs.

$$\begin{aligned}
&REFINE\; (t{:}\, Tag, p{:}\, Path, tgt{:}\, AST) \\
&\mathsf{ext\ wr}\; RG \;:\; Refgraph \\
&\mathsf{pre}\; t \in \mathsf{dom}\; RG.ttrees - \mathsf{dom}\; RG.derivns \wedge \\
&\quad p \in paths(RG.ttrees(t)) \wedge \\
&\quad refmts(find_subtree(RG.ttrees(t), p)) = \{\,\}
\end{aligned}$$

post let $oldtree = \overleftarrow{RG}.ttrees(t)$ in
let $newsubtree = mk\text{-}Refmt(find\_subtree(oldtree, p), tgt)$ in
let $newtree = replace\_subtree(oldtree, p, newsubtree)$ in

$$RG = \mu(\overleftarrow{RG}, ttrees \mapsto \overleftarrow{RG}.ttrees \dagger \{t \mapsto newtree\})$$

The arguments to *REFINE* are a tag (identifying a tree) and a path which together locate the node that is to be refined, and the *AST* which is to be the object of the refinement. The precondition ensures that the tree to be refined is not the source of some development (because in that case it could not be refined – in this simple model – while preserving the invariant), that the tagged tree and the path together validly locate some *AST* in the refinement graph, and that this *AST* is not already the source of some refinement, either wholly or in part.

It will be seen that *REFINE*, as defined here, is not necessarily correctness preserving. In an instantiation of this system incorporating a specific refinement relation and specification model, a further precondition could be added to *REFINE* ensuring that the only correct refinements could be added to the design. Such a constraint would be too rigid for opportunistic methods, however; a more flexible solution would be to allow a mixture of derivation and verification in the design.

$COPY\_AND\_COLLECT\ (t: Tag, p: Path)$
ext wr $RG\ :\ Refgraph$
pre $t \in \mathrm{dom}\ RG.ttrees \wedge$
$p \in paths(RG.ttrees(t))$
post let $newtree = collect\_subtree(RG.ttrees(t), p)$ in
let $nt = newtag()$ in

$$RG.ttrees = \overleftarrow{RG}.ttrees \dagger \{nt \mapsto newtree\} \wedge$$
$$RG.derivns = \overleftarrow{RG}.derivns \cup \{mk\text{-}(t, nt)\}$$

The tree identified by the tag becomes the source of a new development which has as its target the result of collecting it at the position specified by the path. The pseudo-function *newtag* used in the postcondition of this operation generates a unique tag. This informality is to avoid, for the sake of readability, the addition of a further state component representing the last tag used.

3 Example Development

In this section we place the linearised refinement tree of figure 1 in a possible line of development of the square root program. For the sake of illustration, the development is divided into phases, although this division is necessarily somewhat contrived for such a small program. The full development in [Morgan90] contains two additional refinement steps between lines 1 and 2 (of figure 1), giving $RT1$ as the refinement tree recording the derivation from line 1 to line 2:

$$\begin{aligned} RT1 = mk\text{-}Refmt(&mk\text{-}Oprnode(\text{“var”}, [\text{“}r, s{:}\, \mathbb{N}\text{”}, \text{“}r{:=} \lfloor\sqrt{s}\rfloor\text{”}]),\\ &mk\text{-}Refmt(\text{“}r{:}\, [\mathrm{true}\ , r = \lfloor\sqrt{s}\rfloor]\text{”},\\ &\quad mk\text{-}Refmt(\text{“}r{:}\, [\mathrm{true}\ , r \le \sqrt{s} < r+1]\text{”}, \text{“}r{:}\, [\mathrm{true}\ , r^2 \le s < (r+1)^2]\text{”}))) \end{aligned}$$

Broadly speaking, $RT1$ contains a record of the transition from an abstract program “written for the client” to a specification “written for the programmer” (Morgan). Although the detail of this transition should be preserved, it will not be required during the subsequent development; we therefore prevent it from appearing later by collecting $RT1$ at its root, giving

“$r{:}\, [\mathrm{true}\ , r^2 \le s < (r+1)^2]$”

as a summary of the first phase of development; for the second phase this is extended by lines 3 and 4 to give

$$\begin{array}{ll}
RT2 = \textit{mk-Refmt}(\text{“}r\text{: [true}, r^2 \leq s < (r+1)^2]\text{”}, & \\
\quad\quad \textit{mk-Oprnode}(\text{“var”}, [& \\
\quad\quad\quad \text{“}q\text{: N”}, & \\
\quad\quad\quad \textit{mk-Refmt}(\text{“}q, r\text{: [true}, r^2 \leq s < q^2 \wedge r+1 = q]\text{”}, & \star \\
\quad\quad\quad\quad \text{“}I \mathrel{\hat{=}} r^2 \leq s < q^2 \bullet q, r\text{: [true}, I \wedge r+1 = q]\text{”})])) &
\end{array}$$

$RT2$ contains the new starting-point provided by $RT1$ after that is collected, together with the second phase of the development, from the “programmer's specification” to the introduction of the invariant.

Often the process of finding an invariant involves rearranging the conditions composing the specification. As a rule, such rearrangements are omitted from the final presentation of the derivation for the sake of showing a “clean” development, even though such omissions can make the derivation hard to understand subsequently. In the system proposed here they can be retained in the record of the development “so far”, but eliminated by collection from the summary carried forward to the next phase of development. In the present example collection of the starred subtree of $RT2$ eliminates the detail represented by the root node of that subtree.

$$\begin{array}{ll}
RT3 = \textit{mk-Refmt}(\text{“}r\text{: [true}, r^2 \leq s < (r+1)^2]\text{”}, & \\
\quad \textit{mk-Oprnode}(\text{“var”}, [& \star \\
\quad\quad \text{“}q\text{: N”}, & \\
\quad\quad \textit{mk-Refmt}(\text{“}I \mathrel{\hat{=}} r^2 \leq s < q^2 \bullet q, r\text{: [true}, I \wedge r+1 = q]\text{”}, & \\
\quad\quad\quad \textit{mk-Oprnode}(\text{“;”}, [& \\
\quad\quad\quad\quad \textit{mk-Refmt}(\text{“}q, r\text{: [true}, I]\text{”}, \text{“}q, r := s+1, 0\text{”}), & \\
\quad\quad\quad\quad \textit{mk-Refmt}(\text{“}q, r\text{: }[I, I \wedge r+1 = q]\text{”}, & \\
\quad\quad\quad\quad\quad \textit{mk-Oprnode}(\text{“do od”}, [& \\
\quad\quad\quad\quad\quad\quad \text{“ }r+1 \neq q\text{”}, & \\
\quad\quad\quad\quad\quad\quad \textit{mk-Refmt}(\text{“}q, r\text{: }[r+1 \neq q, I, q-r < q_0 - r_0]\text{”}, & \\
\quad\quad\quad\quad\quad\quad\quad \textit{mk-Oprnode}(\text{“var”}, [& \\
\quad\quad\quad\quad\quad\quad\quad\quad \text{“}p\text{: N”}, & \\
\quad\quad\quad\quad\quad\quad\quad\quad \textit{mk-Oprnode}(\text{“;”}, [& \\
\quad\quad\quad\quad\quad\quad\quad\quad\quad \textit{mk-Refmt}(\text{“}p\text{: }[r+1 < q, r < p < q]\text{”}, \text{“}p := (q+r) \div 2\text{”}), & \\
\quad\quad\quad\quad\quad\quad\quad\quad\quad \textit{mk-Refmt}(\text{“}q, r\text{: }[r < p < q, I, q-r < q_0 - r_0], & \\
\quad\quad\quad\quad\quad\quad\quad\quad\quad\quad \textit{mk-Oprnode}(\text{“if fi”}, [& \\
\quad\quad\quad\quad\quad\quad\quad\quad\quad\quad\quad \text{“}s < p^2\text{”}, & \\
\quad\quad\quad\quad\quad\quad\quad\quad\quad\quad\quad \textit{mk-Refmt}(\text{“}q\text{: }[s < p^2 \wedge p < q, I, q < q_0]\text{”}, \text{“}q := p\text{”}), & \\
\quad\quad\quad\quad\quad\quad\quad\quad\quad\quad\quad \text{“}s \geq p^2\text{”}, & \\
\quad\quad\quad\quad\quad\quad\quad\quad\quad\quad\quad \textit{mk-Refmt}(\text{“}q\text{: }[s \geq p^2 \wedge r < p, I, r_0 < r]\text{”}, \text{“}r := p\text{”}) & \\
\quad\quad]))]))]))]))])) &
\end{array}$$

$RT3$ contains a summary of earlier design stages carried forward from the collection of $RT2$, together with its extension by the development phase from the introduction of the invariant to the production of code.

Collection of the starred subtree of $RT3$ gives the specification–implementation pair $RT4$, of which the implementation part is pure code. (This is the “collected code” of [Morgan90], p.167).

$RT4 = mk\text{-}Refmt(\text{“}r\text{: [true }, r^2 \leq s < (r+1)^2]\text{”},$
$\quad mk\text{-}Oprnode(\text{“var”}, [$
$\quad\quad \text{“}q\text{: N”},$
$\quad\quad mk\text{-}Oprnode(\text{“;”}, [$
$\quad\quad\quad \text{“}q, r := s+1, 0\text{”},$
$\quad\quad\quad mk\text{-}Oprnode(\text{“do od”}, [$
$\quad\quad\quad\quad \text{“ }r+1 \neq q\text{”},$
$\quad\quad\quad\quad mk\text{-}Oprnode(\text{“var”}, [$
$\quad\quad\quad\quad\quad \text{“}p\text{: N”},$
$\quad\quad\quad\quad\quad mk\text{-}Oprnode(\text{“;”}, [$
$\quad\quad\quad\quad\quad\quad \text{“}p := (q+r) \div 2\text{”},$
$\quad\quad\quad\quad\quad\quad mk\text{-}Oprnode(\text{“if fi”}, [\text{“}s < p^2\text{”}, \text{“}q := p\text{”}, \text{“}s \geq p^2\text{”}, \text{“}r := p\text{”}]$

$\quad\quad))]))]))]))$

The refinement graph corresponding to the development of $RT1$ through $RT4$ is linear, as no alternative derivations have been considered. It is (making obvious but arbitrary choices for the tags)

$mk\text{-}Refgraph($
$\quad \{\text{“}RT1\text{”} \mapsto RT1, \text{“}RT2\text{”} \mapsto RT2, \text{“}RT3\text{”} \mapsto RT3, \text{“}RT4\text{”} \mapsto RT4\},$
$\quad \{mk\text{-}(\text{“}RT1\text{”}, \text{“}RT2\text{”}), mk\text{-}(\text{“}RT2\text{”}, \text{“}RT3\text{”}), mk\text{-}(\text{“}RT3\text{”}, \text{“}RT4\text{”})\})$

Naturally, the development need not end at this point. Further transformations such as optimisation or compilation fit equally well into the present framework.

4 Editing Refinement Graphs

We now extend the model evolved in §2 and used there to define operations for extending refinement trees and graphs. The new version will enable the definition of operations which can modify existing parts of a refinement graph, while maintaining the consistency of the whole. The purpose of allowing such modification is not only to correct mistakes, but also to deviate from the top-down model to accomodate opportunistic insights: for example, a designer concentrating on high-level design who nevertheless wished to record an insight about implementation might extend a refinement tree downwards to include this insight, intending to return at a later time to complete the detail of the intermediate stages thus generated. The editing operations described in this section are intended to support this manner of working.

4.1 The Revised Type *Refgraph*

The central change is in the relation ***derivns***, from one which links entire refinement trees to one which links individual *ASTs*. The information required to uniquely specify an *AST* in a refinement graph is its location, specified by the tag of its tree, and its path within that tree. These are combined in a new data type ***Locn***. A pair of *AST*s *mk-*(*left*, *right*) is in ***derivns*** if *right* has been generated from *left* as part of the process of copying an entire refinement tree (as a result such pairs will always be textually identical) and possibly subsequently collecting it. We will sometimes refer to one element of these pairs as the ***predecessor*** or ***successor*** of the other.

The enhanced model contains the types shown in figure 3.

4.2 Invariant on *Refgraph*

The invariant for this enhanced type is as follows:

$$
\begin{aligned}
&Reftree = AST \mid Refmt\\
&AST = Atom \mid Oprnode\\
&Oprnode :: \quad opr : \mathsf{token}\\
&\qquad\qquad subtrees : Reftree^*\\
&Refmt :: source : AST\\
&\qquad\qquad target : Reftree\\
&Locn :: t : Tag\\
&\qquad\quad p : Path\\
&Refgraph :: \quad ttrees : Tag \xrightarrow{m} Reftree\\
&\qquad\qquad derivns : (Locn \times Locn)\text{-}\mathsf{set}
\end{aligned}
$$

Figure 3: Revised Type Definitions for Refinement Graphs

$$
\begin{aligned}
&inv\text{-}Refgraph : Refgraph \to \mathbf{B}\\
&inv\text{-}Refgraph(rg) \;\triangleq\\
&\quad \mathsf{let}\ all\_locs = \{mk\text{-}(t,p) \mid t \in \mathsf{dom}\ rg.ttrees, p \in paths(rg.ttrees(t))\}\ \mathsf{in}\\
&\quad (\forall rt \in \mathsf{rng}\ rg.ttrees \cdot inv\text{-}Reftree(rt)) \hfill \wedge\\
&\quad \mathsf{dom}\ rg.derivns \cup \mathsf{rng}\ rg.derivns \subseteq all\_locs \hfill \wedge\\
&\quad (\forall mk\text{-}(left, right) \in rg.derivns \cdot\\
&\qquad \exists ps: Path^* \cdot\\
&\qquad\quad (\forall i \in \mathsf{inds}\ ps \cdot ps(i+1) \in\\
&\qquad\qquad\qquad paths(seq\_coll\_st(rg.ttrees(left.t), ps(1,\ldots,i))))) \wedge\\
&\qquad\quad pruned(seq\_coll\_st(rg.ttrees(left.t), ps), rg.ttrees(right.t))) \hfill \wedge\\
&\quad (\forall mk\text{-}(left, right) \in rg.derivns \cdot\\
&\qquad \forall r' \in prefixes(right.p) \cdot\\
&\qquad\quad \exists l' \in prefixes(left.p) \cdot\\
&\qquad\qquad mk\text{-}(mk\text{-}Locn(l', left.t), mk\text{-}Locn(r', right.t)) \in rg.derivns) \hfill \wedge\\
&\quad (\forall l \in all\_locs \cdot \forall t \in \mathsf{dom}\ rg.ttrees \cdot no\_predecessor\_in(l,t,rg) \Rightarrow\\
&\qquad \forall l' \in all\_locs \cdot\\
&\qquad\quad l'.t = l.t \wedge l.p \in prefixes(l', p) \;\Rightarrow\; no\_predecessor\_in(l', t, rg)) \hfill \wedge\\
&\quad (\forall \{t1, t2\} \in \mathsf{dom}\ rg.ttrees \cdot\\
&\qquad is\_1\text{-}1(\{mk\text{-}(l,r) \mid mk\text{-}(l,r) \in rg.derivns \cdot l.t = t1 \wedge r.t = t2\})
\end{aligned}
$$

The first three clauses in this invariant correspond to the three clauses in the invariant of the earlier version (§2.4). The first ensures that every tree in the graph is well-formed, and the second that every location in the *derivns* component corresponds to an *AST* in the graph. The third clause specifies that two refinement trees can be connected (at any level) in the graph only if the second one is an extension of a tree resulting from a sequence of collection operations on the first (this generalisation of the earlier version allows the subsequent definition of an operation of collection *in situ*). The function *seq_coll_st*, defined below, formalises this.

The last three clauses constrain the properties of the *derivns* relation. The first of them states that if two locations are linked, then all those "above" the right-hand (*i.e.* successor) one are linked to some location above the left-hand one. (It uses the function *prefixes*, which returns the set of all prefixes of a given path; a specification is given in the appendix). The second clause ensures that if some location has no predecessor in a given tree, then neither has any of those "below" it (the function *no_predecessor_in*, which this clause uses, is defined below). The third specifies that the relation *derivns*, restricted to any two trees, is a bijection (the definition of the predicate *is_1-1* is omitted).

$$\begin{array}{l} \mathit{seq\_coll\_st}\ (\mathit{rt}: \mathit{Reftree}, \mathit{ps}: \mathit{Path}^*)\ \mathit{ct}: \mathit{Reftree} \\ \textsf{pre hd}\ \mathit{ps} \in \mathit{paths}(\mathit{rt}) \\ \textsf{post}\ \mathit{ct} = \textsf{if}\ \mathit{ps} = [\,] \\ \qquad\qquad \textsf{then}\ \mathit{rt} \\ \qquad\qquad \textsf{else}\ \mathit{seq\_coll\_st}(\mathit{collect\_subtree}(\mathit{rt}, \textsf{hd}\,\mathit{ps}), \textsf{tl}\,\mathit{ps}) \end{array}$$

$$\begin{array}{l} \mathit{no\_predecessor\_in}\ (\mathit{loc}: \mathit{Locn}, \mathit{tg}: \mathit{Tag}, \mathit{rg}: \mathit{Refgraph})\ \mathit{res}: \mathbf{B} \\ \textsf{pre}\ \mathit{tg} \in \textsf{dom}\ \mathit{rg.ttrees} \\ \textsf{post}\ \mathit{res} = \neg\,\exists p \in \mathit{paths}(\mathit{rg.ttrees}(\mathit{tg})) \cdot \mathit{mk}\text{-}(\mathit{mk}\text{-}\mathit{Locn}(\mathit{tg}, p), \mathit{loc}) \in \mathit{rg.derivns} \end{array}$$

4.3 Editing Operations on Refinement Graphs

In editing a refinement graph it should be possible to insert, copy, cut and paste elements of the graph – that is, trees, subtrees and individual nodes. Care has to be taken in defining these operations, however, to choose a set which will provide good editing facilities while preserving the invariant on refinement graphs. The set proposed includes the following operations:

- *COPY*
- *COLLECT*

Combined, these two operations have the effect of the operation COPY_AND_COLLECT. Their separation is necessary to allow collection to be specified on any location of any tree.

- *REFINE*: Generalised, this operation can be applied to any refinement tree, whether or not it is the source of a development.
- *ONE_LEVEL_COLLECT*: this operation collapses a single refinement link, rather than all those in a subtree.
- *REMOVE*: this operation removes either an entire refinement tree (together with all its links in the graph) or a subtree without predecessors.
- *INSERT*: this operation replaces a subtree (one without predecessors) of a refinement tree with a refinement having as its source a supplied *AST* and as its target the old subtree.

These operations must all be specified to make corresponding changes in all successors of the node being edited. The editor will further require cut, copy, and paste variants of these operations. In addition, syntax-editing operations will be required specific to each of the operators (*oprs*) which can compose an *AST*.

Of these operations, we specify only *COPY* and *COLLECT*, as these are sufficient to convey the requirements of the new model.

$COPY\ (t: Tag)$
ext wr RG : $Refgraph$
pre $t \in \text{dom}\ RG.ttrees$
post let $nt = newtag()$ in
  let $tt = \overleftarrow{RG}.ttrees(t)$ in
  $RG.ttrees = \overleftarrow{RG}.ttrees \dagger \{nt \mapsto tt\} \wedge$
  $RG.derivns = \overleftarrow{RG}.derivns \cup$
    $\{mk\text{-}(mk\text{-}Locn(t,p), mk\text{-}Locn(nt,p)) \mid p \in paths(tt)\}$

The post-condition specifies that the new tree is to be added to the set of trees in the graph and that every location in it is to be linked to its correspondent in the original tree.

$COLLECT\ (t: Tag, p: Path)$
ext wr RG : $Refgraph$
pre $t \in \text{dom}\ RG.ttrees$
post let $coll\_locs = \text{rng}(mk\_Locn(t,p) \lhd \overleftarrow{RG}.derivns^{+})$ in
  $RG.ttrees = \overleftarrow{RG}.ttrees \dagger$
    $\{cl.t \mapsto collect\_subtree(\overleftarrow{RG}.ttrees(cl.t), cl.p) \mid cl \in coll\_locs\} \wedge$
  $RG.derivns = \{mk\text{-}(l', r') \mid mk\text{-}(l, r) \in \overleftarrow{RG}.derivns \cdot$
    $new\_locn(l, l', coll\_locs) \wedge new\_locn(r, r', coll\_locs)\}$

The let expression in the postcondition sets $coll\_locs$ to the set of all successors (direct and indirect) ($\overleftarrow{RG}.derivns^{+}$ is the transitive closure of $\overleftarrow{RG}.derivns$). Then every tree containing one of these successor nodes is collected in the same way as the original, and successor links reconstructed, where possible.

$new\_locn : Locn \times Locn \times Locn\text{-set} \to \mathbf{B}$

$new\_locn(before, after, coll\_locs) \quad \triangleq$
  let $coll\_locs' = \{t \mapsto p \mid mk\text{-}Locn(t,p) \in coll\_locs\}$ in
  let $change = before.t \in \text{dom}\ coll\_locs' \wedge$
    $coll\_locs'(before.t) \in prefixes(before.p)$ in
  $(\neg\, change \;\Rightarrow\; after = before) \wedge$
  $(change \;\Rightarrow\; refmts\_elided(before.p, after.p, coll\_locs'(before.t)))$

new_locn returns true if its second argument is the result of changing its first by collecting any of the locations in its third argument. The first let expression makes use of the fact that a node can have at most one successor in any one tree to form a function from tags to paths, the second formalises the fact that a location will only be altered by collection if the location being collected is "above" it in its tree. The predicate $refmts\_elided$ returns true if its second argument is the new path to the node specified by the first argument after collection of the location specified by the third argument. Its specification, which is dependent on the representation for $Path$, is in the appendix.

5 A Refinement Editor

The example of §3 makes clear not only that management of these complex data structures requires machine assistance, but that a more intuitive notation is vital to the useability of the system. A refinement editor designed to meet these two requirements is therefore under development; this section provides a brief description.

The editor has the role, besides doing whatever housekeeping is possible automatically, of supporting the construction and modification of refinement graphs in a way that maximises their potential to facilitate browsing of the design and application of opportunistic insights. For this reason, it provides two visualisations for these graphs: a detailed one for making changes to individual components, and one for overviews and for locating the detailed view within the design as a whole. We now briefly illustrate the overview notation; [Naftalin91] explains the detailed view.

The central idea in the overview visualisation is illustrated in figure 4, which is a graphical depiction of the example refinement tree of §2.1. This figure is intended to be seen in the following way: the *AST*s "q, r: [true , I]" and "q, r: [$I, I \wedge r+1 = q$]", together with the ";" composing them, are in the plane of the paper. Directly behind them (but staggered in the diagram, for visibility) are the *AST*s to which they are refined. Components of the same *AST*s are always visualised as being in the same xy plane. Broken lines indicate refinement relations connecting objects in different planes.

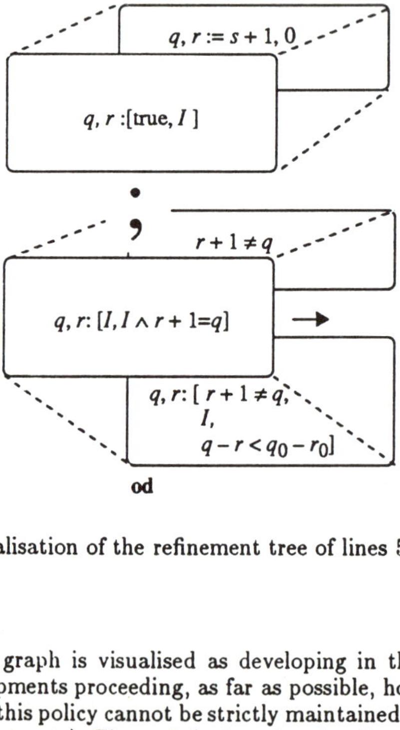

Figure 4: Visualisation of the refinement tree of lines 5, 6 and 9 from figure 1

The refinement graph is visualised as developing in the plane of the paper with sequences of developments proceeding, as far as possible, horizontally from left to right (although of course this policy cannot be strictly maintained in the presence of branching sequences of developments). Figure 5 depicts the visualisation of the refinement graph of §3. The shading convention of this figure (although not of the notation itself) is that *AST*s produced by refinement in each tree are shown shaded in that tree; *AST*s produced by refinement in an earlier tree are shown unshaded.

The editor maintains this picture of the developing design. All the operations listed above can (in principle) be performed on this image. The interface is of the "noun-verb" type, with a current location (required by all the operations) being selected either by a mouse-click or by use of commands for navigating through and between the constituent refinement trees.

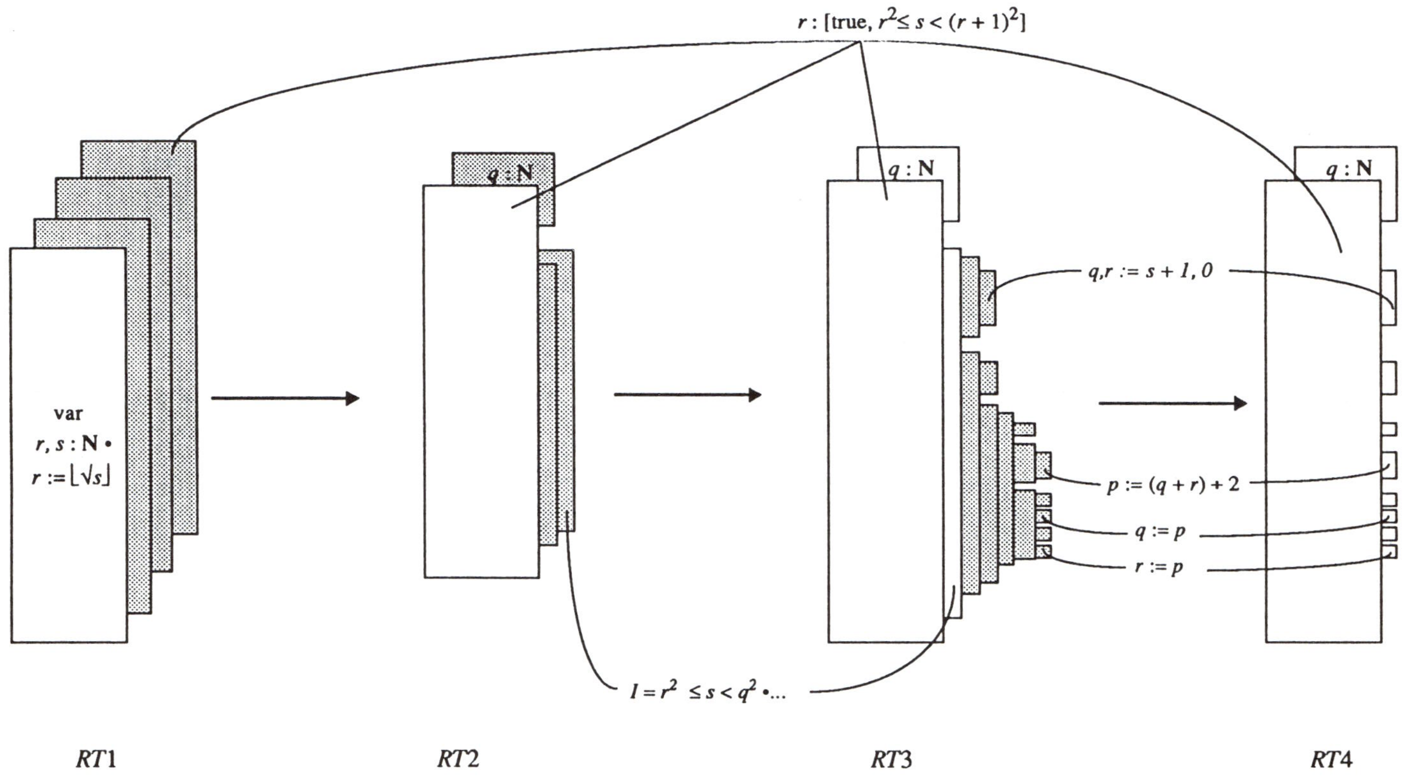

Figure 5: Refinement Graph for Square Root Development

6 Discussion

The introduction suggested that, to be more useable, formal methods of program development must be placed within a design framework which will also support opportunistic design strategies. Such a framework would have to be based on an explicit representation of the derivation, one which would allow the designer to record incomplete, as-yet-unverified, and even erroneous designs. Subsequently we have given a brief but formal outline of such a representation. The basic formalisation is quite concise, but should be extensible to deal with the many practical requirements encountered by a formal development support system.

We therefore propose refinement graphs as a contribution to solving the problem of making formal methods more useable. They fulfil the original goal of permitting opportunistic exploration of the design space (providing the designer is permitted to build them up in a non-systematic way), and lend themselves to a visualisation that supports such exploration. Further, they offer good facilities for dividing developments into phases and systematically summarising information from previous phases so as to allow a coherent summary of the development to be presented while retaining detail of its actual progress. They are suitable for support by a refinement editor, and a sketch has been given of one that can both provide machine assistance with the housekeeping tasks associated with formal refinement and support the visualisation of the unfolding design.

It is possible to imagine many improvements that could be made to the system outlined here. At the most simple level, a development support system must associate a great deal of "extra" information with each object. For example, specifications, refinements, refinement trees and developments should all be accompanied by informal annotations; refinements must (eventually) be accompanied by formal justification, and so on. At a more fundamental level, the view of the development provided by a refinement graph alone will be inadequate for a system of any complexity. Other views, recording for example data flow or invocation relationships, would need to be included to make a "full-strength" system.

Finally, although little attention has been given here to the question of correctness, facilities for supporting demonstrations of correctness are, in the long term, a key component of the editor. Such facilities should be available to assist both in generating derivation steps, and in supporting verification by generating verification conditions and assisting in the proof process, in the style of, for example *mural* [Jones91].

7 Related Work and Acknowledgements

The framework presented here is primarily designed for refinement systems which place both specifications and algorithms in the same semantic framework, so that a meaning can be given to mixed objects containing both specifications and algorithms. VDM is inherently such a system, but the idea was first explored systematically by Ralph Back ([Back78]) and has been further investigated by many authors over a long period; I have been influenced in particular by Carroll Morgan's work ([Morgan88], [Morgan90]).

The problem of organising and visualising large derivations has received little attention. An exception is [Back91], which proposes a system of *refinement diagrams* similar to the visualisation presented here. The most important difference between the two visualisations is that because in refinement diagrams refinement and development (as defined in §2.4) take place along the same axis, the facilities for separating a program development into phases and summarising the result of each are not so well developed. Confining refinement diagrams to two dimensions has the further consequence that they are very large when unfolded; thus it is necessary to define an outliner, not required in the present work because outlining facilities are inherent in the notation.

I am indebted to Simon Jones for many very helpful discussions on the ideas of this paper. Ralph Back made helpful comments on an earlier paper, stimulating the development of the ideas in the present work. An anonymous referee made constructive remarks.

References

[Back78] R. J. R. Back, *On the correctness of refinement steps in program development.* Report A-1978-4, Department of Computer Science, University of Helsinki, 1978.

[Back91] R. J. R. Back, "Refinement Diagrams". In *Proceedings of the Fourth BCS Refinement Workshop*, Springer-Verlag, 1991.

[Dawes91] J. Dawes, *The VDM-SL Reference Guide.* Pitman, 1991.

[Guindon87] R. Guindon, H. Krasner and B. Curtis, "Breakdowns and processes during the early activities of software design by professionals". *In* G. Olson, S. Sheppard and E. Soloway (eds), *Empirical Studies of Programmers: Second Workshop.* Ablex (Norwood, N.J.), 1987.

[Jones90] C. B. Jones, *Systematic Software Development Using VDM, 2nd edn.* Prentice-Hall International, 1990.

[Jones91] C. B. Jones et al., *mural: A Formal Development System.* Springer-Verlag, 1991.

[Morgan88] C. Morgan, K. Robinson and P. Gardiner, *On the Refinement Calculus.* Technical Monograph PRG-70, Oxford University Computing Laboratory, Programming Research Group.

[Morgan90] C. Morgan, *Programming from Specifications.* Prentice-Hall International, 1990.

[Morris89] J. M. Morris, "Laws of Data refinement". *Acta Informatica*, Vol.26, pp.309–332, 1989.

[Naftalin91] M. Naftalin, *A Visual Refinement System.* Technical Report TR73, University of Stirling Department of Computing Science, 1991.

[Petre90] M. Petre, "Expert programmers and programming languages". *In* T. Green *et al* (eds.), *Psychology of Programming*, Academic Press, 1990.

[Petre91] M. Petre, "Shifts in reasoning about software and hardware systems: must operational models underpin declarative ones?". Invited paper presented at The Third Workshop of the Psychology of Programming Interest Group (Huddersfield, January 1991).

[Sumiga88] J. H. Sumiga, J. I. A. Siddiqi, and B. Khazaei, "Use of a Blackboard Framework to Model Software Design". *Proceedings of the Sixth Symposium on Empirical Foundations of Information and Software Sciences*, Atlanta, Ga, 1988.

[Visser87] W. Visser, "Strategies in programming programmable controllers: a field study on a professional programmer". *In* G. Olson, S. Sheppard and E. Soloway (eds), *Empirical Studies of Programmers: Second Workshop.* Ablex (Norwood, N.J.), 1987.

[Visser90] W. Visser and J.-M. Hoc, "Expert Software Design Strategies". *In* T. Green *et al* (eds.), *Psychology of Programming*, Academic Press, 1990.

Appendix: A Representation for *Path*

The representation given here for *Path* is a sequence of natural numbers. Informally, we observe that in descending from the root of a refinement tree, choices can be made only at an *Oprnode*. A positive integer can be used to select the appropriate member of the sequence of refinement trees composing such a node. 0 is reserved to prescribe the descent of a refinement. An empty path locates the current subtree.

$Path = \mathbf{N}^*$

Informal descriptions of the purpose of the following functions are given in §2.3 and §4.2.

$paths : Reftree \to Path\text{-set}$

$paths(rt) \;\;\triangleq\;\; \{p\colon Path \mid is\_valid\_path(rt, p)\}$

$is\_valid\_path : Reftree \times Path \to \mathbf{B}$

```
is_valid_path(rt, p)  ≜
    if p = []
    then true
    else let hdp = hd p  in
        cases rt  of
        mk-Refmt(−, t)    → hdp = 0 ∧ is_valid_path(t, tl p)
        mk-Oprnode(−, s) → hdp ∈ inds s ∧ is_valid_path(s(hdp), tl p)
        others  → false
        end
```

```
find_subtree (rt: Reftree, p: Path) st: Reftree
pre p ∈ paths(rt)
post st =
    cases p  of
    []               → rt
    (0) ⌢ rest       → find_subtree(rt.target, rest)
    (n + 1) ⌢ rest → find_subtree(rt.s(n + 1), rest)
    end
```

```
replace_subtree (root: Reftree, p: Path, newsubt: Reftree) res: Reftree
pre p ∈ paths(root)
post res =
    if p = []
    then newsubt
    else cases root  of
        mk-Refmt(s, t)    → mk-Refmt(s, replace_subtree(t, tl p, newsubt))
        mk-Oprnode(o, s) → mk-Oprnode(o, s †
                                {hd p ↦ replace_subtree(s(hd p), tl p, newsubt)})
        end
```

$prefixes : Path \rightarrow Path\text{-set}$

$prefixes(p) \quad \triangleq \quad \{p(1, \ldots, n) \mid n \in \{1, \ldots, \mathsf{len}\, p\}\}$

$refmts\_elided\ (old, new, coll\_path: Path)\ res: \mathbf{B}$

$\mathsf{pre}\ coll\_path \in prefixes(old)$

$\mathsf{post}\ res = coll\_path \frown [old(i) \mid i \in \{\mathsf{len}\, coll\_path + 1, \ldots, \mathsf{len}\, old\} \cdot old(i) \neq 0]$

A Window Inference Tool for Refinement

Jim Grundy*
Computer Laboratory, University of Cambridge
Cambridge, England

Abstract

This paper proposes a refinement tool based on a style of reasoning called *window inference*. Window inference allows a user to transform one expression into another while maintaining some specified relationship between them. A program refinement tool is described which combines window inference with an approach to refinement that treats programs as predicates.

1 Introduction

The goal of the work described in this paper is the construction of a tool that supports program refinement. The approach chosen combines two previously distinct concepts: theorem proving through window inference, and reasoning about programs as if they were predicates.

Goal-oriented reasoning is a popular method of proving theorems. This is reflected in the goal-oriented interfaces associated with many proof tools. Reasoning with such systems begins by stating the goal, and progresses by simplifying the goal, or by breaking it into several subgoals whose collective truth would establish the original goal. This style of reasoning is well suited to developing correct software through *verification*. Verification is a process where a program is proposed as an implementation of a specification, and then a proof of the correctness of the program with respect to the specification is attempted. Because goal-oriented reasoning relies on users knowing what they want to prove in advance, it is not well suited to *refinement*. Refinement is a process which begins with a program specification, and progresses by applying correctness-preserving transformations to the specification. The process ends when the specification has been transformed into one that is phrased in an executable subset of the specification language. The result of the refinement process is, like verification, a program which has been proved correct with respect to the specification. However, unlike verification, it is not usual to know the precise form of the program before the refinement is commenced.

Window inference is a style of reasoning where the user is invited to transform one expression into another expression, while preserving some relationship between them. We conjecture that just as goal-oriented reasoning is a natural style of reasoning for developing provably correct software by verification, window inference is a natural style of reasoning for developing provably correct software by refinement.

*The author is supported by the Australian Defence Science & Technology Organisation.

The approach taken here is to represent programs and specifications as predicates. Window inference is used to manipulate the predicates while preserving a correctness relation between them. In doing so we hope to show that window inference is a natural style of reasoning for solving refinement problems. Our implementation of window inference is an interface to the HOL proof assistant [21]. Treating programs as predicates allows us to easily exploit the theorem proving ability of an existing system, like HOL.

2 Window inference

Window inference is a style of reasoning where the user can transform an expression or restrict attention to a subexpression and transform it. While restricting attention to a subexpression, the user can transform the subexpression without affecting the rest of the expression. While transforming a subexpression, the user can make assumptions based on the context of the subexpression. For example, suppose a user wished to transform the expression $A \wedge B$; this can be done by transforming A under the assumption B. It is legitimate to assume B while transforming A, because if B is false, the enclosing expression $A \wedge B$ is false regardless of A. For a more detailed explanation of window inference and its implementation in the HOL system, the user is referred to [9].

Window inference was first described by John Staples and Peter Robinson [20], and implemented by their theorem prover Demo2 [22]. Their work is extended here so that window inference can be applied refinement problems.

Implementing window inference within a mature theorem prover brings some advantages over the direct implementation approach used with Demo2. The user gains immediate access to the existing tools in that theorem prover for rewriting, checking tautologies, etc., as well as the ability to move between window inference and the other styles of reasoning supported by the host system. Implementing window inference in an LCF-style [19] system like HOL, where theorems are represented by a secure datatype, brings the further advantage that inconsistent results cannot be obtained through errors in the interface.

2.1 Windows and theorems

Within a window inference system, reasoning is conducted with a stack of windows. Each window has a *focus*, F, which is the expression to be transformed; a set of formulae Γ, called the *assumptions*, which can be assumed in the context of the window; and a relation R, that must relate the focus and the expression to which it is transformed. All relations used with the system must be preorders[1]. Using a notation derived from that of [20], a window is written as follows:

$$\begin{array}{l} \ !\ \Gamma \\ R \star F \end{array}$$

The focus of a window can be an expression of any type.

Each window *holds* a theorem which relates the current focus of the window to the original focus of the window. Examples of these theorems appear throughout the text beside the windows that hold them.

[1] A preorder is a relation that is both reflexive and transitive.

2.1.1 Creating a window stack

To begin reasoning with a window inference system, the user creates a window stack. Creating a window stack to transform an expression F_0 under the assumptions Γ, while preserving the relation R, results in the stack containing the single window below:

$!\ \Gamma$	theorem:
$R \star F_0$	$\Gamma \vdash F_0\ R\ F_0$

The window initially holds the theorem that F_0 is related to itself. This follows from the requirement that R is reflexive.

2.1.2 Transforming a window

Consider this window:

$!\ \Gamma$	theorem:
$R \star F_n$	$\Gamma \vdash F_n\ R\ F_0$

A transformation of the focus of a window from F_n to F_{n+1} must be justified by a theorem of the following form:

$$\Gamma \vdash F_{n+1}\ R\ F_n$$

We combine this theorem with the one held by the window, using the fact that R is transitive. The resulting theorem shows that the new focus, F_{n+1}, is related to the original focus, F_0.

$$\frac{\Gamma \vdash F_{n+1}\ R\ F_n \qquad \Gamma \vdash F_n\ R\ F_0}{\Gamma \vdash F_{n+1}\ R\ F_0}$$

This inference means that the focus can be transformed, and that doing so results in the following window:

$!\ \Gamma$	theorem:
$R \star F_{n+1}$	$\Gamma \vdash F_{n+1}\ R\ F_0$

We can use any of the existing tools in the HOL system to derive the theorem required to justify a transformation. Because the HOL system is built on top of a general purpose programming language, ML, users can write their own functions to automate the proofs of common transformations, such as rewriting.

2.1.3 Subwindows

The opening and closing of a subwindow is controlled by special inference rules called *window rules.* Opening a subwindow pushes a new window onto the stack. The components of the subwindow are extracted from the relevant window rule. Closing the subwindow pops the top window from the stack and uses the theorem it held to infer, using the window rule, how to transform the window below.

The general form of a window rule is as follows:[2]

$$\frac{\gamma, \Gamma \vdash f' \; r \; f}{\Gamma \vdash F[f'] \; R \; F[f]}$$

- $F[f]$ is the original focus of the parent window.
- f is the original focus of the subwindow.
- f' is some transformed focus of the subwindow.
- $F[f']$ is the correspondingly transformed focus of the parent window.
- R is the relation preserved by the parent window.
- r is the relation preserved by the subwindow.
- Γ is the set of assumptions which hold in the parent window.
- γ is the set of assumptions which, in addition to Γ, hold in the subwindow.

The only restriction placed on window rules is that they must, of course, be valid rules of inference.

To illustrate the use of a window rule, consider that all windows have this form:

$! \; \Gamma$	theorem:
$R \star F[f]$	$\Gamma \vdash F[f] \; R \; F_0$

We choose to open a subwindow on the expression, f. The resulting window, which is pushed onto the stack, appears below:

$! \; \Gamma$	theorem:
$! \; \gamma$	$\gamma, \Gamma \vdash f \; r \; f$
$r \star f$	

We can now transform the subwindow as shown:

$! \; \Gamma$	theorem:
$! \; \gamma$	$\gamma, \Gamma \vdash f' \; r \; f$
$r \star f'$	

Using the theorems held by the subwindow and the parent window, an appropriate instance of the window rule, and the transitivity of R; the following inference is built:

$$\frac{\dfrac{\gamma, \Gamma \vdash f' \; r \; f}{\Gamma \vdash F[f'] \; R \; F[f]} \qquad \Gamma \vdash F[f] \; R \; F_0}{\Gamma \vdash F[f'] \; R \; F_0}$$

This inference justifies closing the subwindow, which is popped from the stack. The parent window is then transformed to the following:

[2] The notation $E[e]$ denotes the substitution of e for some distinguished free occurrence of a subexpression within E.

$$\begin{array}{ll} ! \ \Gamma & \text{theorem:} \\ R \star F[f'] & \Gamma \vdash F[f'] \ R \ F_0 \end{array}$$

2.2 Example

Suppose we wish to simplify the predicate $(A \Rightarrow B) \wedge A$ by transforming it to a simpler predicate to which it is equal. We begin by creating a window stack containing only the window below.

$$\begin{array}{ll} & \text{theorem:} \\ = \star (\boxed{A \Rightarrow B}) \wedge A & \vdash ((A \Rightarrow B) \wedge A) = ((A \Rightarrow B) \wedge A) \end{array}$$

We enclose the subexpression $A \Rightarrow B$ in a box to indicate that we want to open a subwindow on it. The system chooses an appropriate window rule, in this case:

$$\frac{Y \vdash X' = X}{\vdash (X' \wedge Y) = (X \wedge Y)}$$

Using this rule, instantiated appropriately, a new window is pushed onto the stack. Only the top window of the stack is displayed.

$$\begin{array}{ll} ! \ A & \text{theorem:} \\ = \star A \Rightarrow B & A \vdash (A \Rightarrow B) = (A \Rightarrow B) \end{array}$$

The focus of this window can be simplified using its assumption:

$$\begin{array}{ll} ! \ A & \text{theorem:} \\ = \star B & A \vdash B = (A \Rightarrow B) \end{array}$$

The window is then closed. Its removal from the stack reveals the window below which is transformed as follows:

$$\begin{array}{ll} & \text{theorem:} \\ = \star B \wedge A & \vdash (B \wedge A) = ((A \Rightarrow B) \wedge A) \end{array}$$

The theorem held by the top window of the stack states that the transformed focus, $B \wedge A$, is a simplification of the original focus, $(A \Rightarrow B) \wedge A$.

2.3 Reusing rules

To build a window inference system it is *not* necessary to compile a library of window rules that cover every position at which a user may wish to open a window and preserve every relation the user may wish to work with. Techniques for substituting and composing rules can be used to implement a system that, with only three basic window rules, allows users to open a window on any subexpression and substitute equal expressions for each other. This basic system can then be incrementally extended to use contextual information and preserve more general relations by adding more window rules.

2.3.1 *Composing rules*

Suppose a user wants to open a subwindow on the subexpression B in the focus of the following window:

$$\begin{array}{l} ! \ \Gamma \\ = \star (A \wedge \boxed{B}) \wedge C \end{array}$$

It is not necessary to have a window rule for this specific case. A rule can be built by composing the rule for opening on the right-hand side of a conjunction with the rule for opening on the left-hand side of a conjunction, as follows:

$$\cfrac{\cfrac{X, Z, \Gamma \vdash Y' = Y}{Z, \Gamma \vdash (X \wedge Y') = (X \wedge Y)}}{\Gamma \vdash ((X \wedge Y') \wedge Z) = ((X \wedge Y) \wedge Z)}$$

Using a rule built in this way is equivalent to opening a window at $A \wedge B$ and then opening a window at B. In this case, opening a window at B would result in the window below:

$$\begin{array}{l} ! \ \Gamma \\ ! \ C \\ ! \ A \\ = \star B \end{array}$$

Each window rule is stored with information about the position of the focus of the subwindow within that of the parent. When asked to open a window at a position for which no specific window rule is stored, the system builds a substitute by composing window rules that descend the parse tree of the focus to the desired position.

2.3.2 *Stronger rules*

Suppose that the following is the current window:

$$\begin{array}{l} ! \ \Gamma \\ R \star F[\boxed{f}] \end{array} \qquad \begin{array}{l} \text{theorem:} \\ \Gamma \vdash F[f] \ R \ F_0 \end{array}$$

Suppose also that the user wishes to open a window on f, but the system does not contain a window rule for opening at f that preserves R directly. However, it is still possible to open a window at f if there is a rule for opening at f that preserves a relation S that is stronger[3] than R. An appropriate window rule can be built by composing the rule preserving S with the rule that S is stronger than R as follows:

$$\cfrac{\cfrac{\gamma, \Gamma \vdash f' \ s \ f}{\Gamma \vdash F[f'] \ S \ F[f]}}{\Gamma \vdash F[f'] \ R \ F[f]}$$

[3]A relation S is *stronger* than R if the following inference is valid:

$$\frac{\vdash x \ S \ y}{\vdash x \ R \ y}$$

Using this rule, the window can be opened as shown below:

$$\begin{array}{r l} ! & \Gamma \\ ! & \gamma \\ s \star & f \end{array}$$

The system stores information about the relative strength of relations together with inference rules for transforming theorems about stronger relations into theorems about weaker relations. When asked to open a window at a given position preserving a relation for which no specific window rule is stored, the system builds an appropriate substitute by composing a window rule preserving a stronger relation with an inference rule to weaken the relation.

2.3.3 Basic rules

Expressions in the HOL system can be described by the following grammar:

$$\begin{array}{r l l} E ::= & v & \text{— variable} \\ | & c & \text{— constant} \\ | & E_f\ E_a & \text{— application} \\ | & \lambda v.\ E & \text{— abstraction} \end{array}$$

It can be seen from the grammar that there are only three positions within an expression at which a subwindow can be opened. These appear below, along with the window rules that justify opening at that position.

- on the operator of an application:

$$\frac{\Gamma \vdash E'_f = E_f}{\Gamma \vdash (E'_f\ E_a) = (E_f\ E_a)}$$

- on the operand of an application:

$$\frac{\Gamma \vdash E'_a = E_a}{\Gamma \vdash (E_f\ E'_a) = (E_f\ E_a)}$$

- on the body of an abstraction:[4]

$$\frac{\Gamma \vdash E' = E[v'/v]}{\Gamma \vdash (\lambda v'.\ E') = (\lambda v.\ E)} [\ v' \text{ not free in } \Gamma \text{ or } \lambda v.\ E\ ]$$

These three window rules can be composed to reach any subexpression of a focus. Also, each of the rules preserves equality, which is as strong as any reflexive relation. Therefore, when used in conjunction with the techniques presented in sections 2.3.1 and 2.3.2, these three rules are enough to implement a basic window inference system. More rules would be added to such a system to allow the use of contextual information, and the direct preservation of weaker, more general, relations.

---

[4]The notation $E[e/v]$ denotes substitution of e for the variable v in the expression E, while renaming bound variables to avoid capture.

2.4 Lemmas

When transforming a focus, it is permissible to use any theorem where the hypotheses are a subset of the assumptions of the window. Such theorems are said to be *applicable* in the context of the window. The system has an extensible set of theorems called $\mathcal{L}$. The conclusions of the applicable theorems in $\mathcal{L}$ are displayed along with the assumptions of the window. These extra components of the window are called *lemmas*. To distinguish lemmas from assumptions, lemmas are prefixed with '¡'. However, it is not necessary to make the distinction as they can be used interchangeably. Lemmas and assumptions are referred to collectively as the *context* of a window.

2.4.1 Subwindows on assumptions

Often a user wants to make use of a fact that follows indirectly from the context of a window. We facilitate this style of reasoning by allowing the user to derive new lemmas by opening subwindows in the context. When a user opens a subwindow on a term in the context, that term becomes the focus of the new window. The context of the parent window is available in the subwindow. The user can then transform the focus to derive a new fact. Upon closing the subwindow this fact is added to the set of relevant theorems, $\mathcal{L}$. Any theorem added in this way is applicable in the context of the parent window.

For example consider the following window:

$!\ A$	theorem:
$!\ \boxed{A \Rightarrow B}$	$A \Rightarrow B, A \vdash B = F$
$= \star\, B$	
	$\mathcal{L} = \{\}$

The user could open a subwindow on the assumption $A \Rightarrow B$.

$!\ A$	theorem:
$\Leftarrow \star\, A \Rightarrow B$	$A \vdash (A \Rightarrow B) \Leftarrow (A \Rightarrow B)$
	$\mathcal{L} = \{\}$

Using the assumption A, this window can be transformed to:

$!\ A$	theorem:
$\Leftarrow \star\, B$	$A \vdash B \Leftarrow (A \Rightarrow B)$
	$\mathcal{L} = \{\}$

The user now closes the subwindow. The theorem it held is automatically simplified to the one below, and then added to $\mathcal{L}$.

$$A \Rightarrow B, A \vdash B$$

Returning to the parent window, there is a new lemma, B, that will help the user complete the proof:

$!\ A$	theorem:
$!\ A \Rightarrow B$	$A \Rightarrow B, A \vdash B = F$
$¡\ B$	
$= \star\, B$	$\mathcal{L} = \{A \Rightarrow B, A \vdash B\}$

3 Programs are predicates

This section gives a unified treatment of programs and specifications as predicates. In doing so we avoid the need for a special calculus for reasoning about programs. Our presentation is similar to those given by Tony Hoare [15] and Eric Hehner [12, 13].

Early work on the development of correct software [14] defined a language by using axiomatic semantics. Reasoning about programs was restricted to what could be accomplished using the axioms that defined the language. More recent works [1, 17, 18] define refinement calculi by giving programs and specifications a meaning in terms of weakest preconditions [5]. By taking a definitional, rather than an axiomatic, approach this work gives us the freedom to use classical logic to reason about programs. However, the reasoning is complicated because we must reason about predicates representing the meanings, expressed as weakest preconditions, of programs. By treating programs and specifications as predicates, not only are we free to use classical logic to reason about them, but we can manipulate them directly as terms in the logic.

The treatment of programs as predicates allows us to reason about them using existing theorem provers, thus avoiding many of the difficulties of providing tool support for reasoning about programs. Programmable proof tools, like HOL, can be customised into refinement tools. Many years of effort and experience have already been invested in tools for classical logic, like the HOL system. The duplication of the security and reasoning ability of these tools for a special program calculus would be a time consuming task. A better approach is to treat programs as predicates and exploit the years of effort and experience embodied in existing tools.

We should note that some tools, like HOL, are flexible enough to allow the formalisation of a refinement calculus based on weakest preconditions. This has been done by Ralph Back and Joakim von Wright [2]. However we conjecture that reasoning about programs is easier and more direct when they are simply treated as predicates.

3.1 Specifying with predicates

The behaviour of a computer can be specified by a predicate over its initial and final states. The state of a computer is a vector of program variables, for example (x, y, z), which is referred to collectively as $\vec{\sigma}$. Each individual variable in the state is referred to by its name. The initial value of a variable v is denoted by $\grave{v}$, while the final value of a variable v is denoted by $\acute{v}$.

	Components	*Abbreviation*
State	(x, y, z)	$\vec{\sigma}$
Initial State	$(\grave{x}, \grave{y}, \grave{z})$	$\grave{\vec{\sigma}}$
Final State	$(\acute{x}, \acute{y}, \acute{z})$	$\vec{\sigma}'$

The meaning of the predicate S when used as a specification is as follows:

> Given an initial state $\grave{\vec{\sigma}}$, the computer should reach a final state $\vec{\sigma}'$ such that $S[\grave{\vec{\sigma}}, \vec{\sigma}']$ holds.

For example, consider the specification below:

$$\grave{y} > 0 \Rightarrow \acute{z} = \grave{x} \div \grave{y}$$

The informal interpretation of this predicate is:

> Given an initial state where $\grave{y} > 0$ holds, the computer should reach a final state where $\acute{z} = \grave{x} \div \grave{y}$ holds. If $\grave{y} > 0$ does not hold in the initial state, any final state is acceptable.

Not all specifications can be implemented. Consider the predicate false as a specification. This specification asks for a program that, when executed in any initial state, terminates in a final state such that those two states satisfy the predicate false. However, the predicate false is unsatisfiable, so this specification is impossible to meet. Alternatively, any program terminating in a state that met this specification would be a *miracle*. A miracle is an implementation that is correct with respect to every specification. Other specifications, although seemingly less ambitious, also require miraculous behaviour if their implementations are to terminate. Consider the specification below:

$$\grave{y} > 0 \wedge \acute{z} = \grave{x} \div \grave{y}$$

When invoked with an initial state where $\grave{y} > 0$, a program must terminate with a final state where $\acute{z} = \grave{x} \div \grave{y}$ to meet this specification. However, for an initial state where $\grave{y} > 0$ does not hold, no final state can satisfy the specification.

3.2 Refining with predicates

Rather than consider the problem of program refinements that preserve total correctness, let us consider the easier problem of program refinements that preserve partial correctness. A refinement P is partially correct with respect to a specification S if:

> For all initial states $\grave{\vec{\sigma}}$, there is no final state $\acute{\vec{\sigma}}$ such that $P[\grave{\vec{\sigma}}, \acute{\vec{\sigma}}]$ holds, meaning P could terminate in that state, and $S[\grave{\vec{\sigma}}, \acute{\vec{\sigma}}]$ does not, meaning that termination in that state would be contrary to the specification.

If we recast our definition of partial correctness in formal notation, we can see that P is partially correct with respect to S precisely when P implies S.

$$\begin{array}{lll} & \forall \grave{\vec{\sigma}}.\ \neg\exists \acute{\vec{\sigma}}.\ P[\grave{\vec{\sigma}}, \acute{\vec{\sigma}}] \wedge \neg S[\grave{\vec{\sigma}}, \acute{\vec{\sigma}}] & \text{[Partial Correctness]} \\ \equiv & \forall \grave{\vec{\sigma}}, \acute{\vec{\sigma}}.\ \neg(P[\grave{\vec{\sigma}}, \acute{\vec{\sigma}}] \wedge \neg S[\grave{\vec{\sigma}}, \acute{\vec{\sigma}}]) & \text{[Quantifier Negation]} \\ \equiv & \forall \grave{\vec{\sigma}}, \acute{\vec{\sigma}}.\ \neg P[\grave{\vec{\sigma}}, \acute{\vec{\sigma}}] \vee \neg\neg S[\grave{\vec{\sigma}}, \acute{\vec{\sigma}}] & \text{[De Morgan]} \\ \equiv & \forall \grave{\vec{\sigma}}, \acute{\vec{\sigma}}.\ \neg P[\grave{\vec{\sigma}}, \acute{\vec{\sigma}}] \vee S[\grave{\vec{\sigma}}, \acute{\vec{\sigma}}] & \text{[Double Negation]} \\ \equiv & \forall \grave{\vec{\sigma}}, \acute{\vec{\sigma}}.\ P[\grave{\vec{\sigma}}, \acute{\vec{\sigma}}] \Rightarrow S[\grave{\vec{\sigma}}, \acute{\vec{\sigma}}] & \text{[Material Implication]} \end{array}$$

Since implication is a preorder, we are able to use window inference to transform specifications into implementations while preserving partial correctness.

Here are a few simple refinements that preserve partial correctness, the specification appears to the right of the implication, while its refinement appears to the left:

$$\vdash ((\acute{x} = \grave{x} + 1) \wedge (\acute{y} = \grave{y})) \Rightarrow (\acute{x} > \grave{x})$$

$$\vdash (\acute{z} = \grave{x} \times \grave{y}) \Rightarrow ((\grave{x} > 0) \Rightarrow (\acute{z} = \grave{x} \times \grave{y}))$$

There are two ways in which a program can be partially correct with respect to a given specification. The first, and most desirable, way is for the program to terminate in a state satisfying the specification. The second is for the program not to terminate. It follows, therefore, that a program that never terminates is partially correct with respect to every specification. The only predicate that implies every predicate is false, so false must be the meaning of a nonterminating program. Because we are considering partial correctness, the predicate false represents a nonterminating program, not a program which terminates in a state satisfying the predicate false (a miracle). Alternatively, we could say that a nonterminating program *is* a miracle with respect to partial correctness.

Here are a few simple refinements which cannot be further refined into programs that will terminate for all initial states:

$$\vdash \mathsf{false} \Rightarrow (\acute{z} = \grave{x} \times \grave{y})$$

$$\vdash (\grave{x} > 0 \land \acute{z} = \grave{x} \times \grave{y}) \Rightarrow (\acute{z} = \grave{x} \times \grave{y})$$

Although the question of refinements preserving total correctness is not properly addressed in this paper, section 5.1 outlines a method that could be used to establish the termination of programs derived using the techniques described here.

3.3 Programming with predicates

For the sake of simplicity we will work with a small deterministic programming language. Any expression in the logic can be part of a specification. However, only a subset of expressions are executable. We will not give a complete definition of which expressions are executable. For example, the the decision on whether an expression like *length*(l), denoting the length of the list l, is executable is left to the reader. However, one might reasonable expect that expressions like $1 + 2$ will be executable, while expressions like $\int_a^b f(x)\ dx$ will not. Note that one condition an expression must meet in order to be executable is that all the variables in the expression must be drawn from the initial state, $\grave{\vec{\sigma}}$. The statements in our language include the null statement, parallel assignment, conditional, sequential composition, and a general recursion construct. The meaning of each of these statements and the conditions under which they are executable are described below:

skip

The skip statement does nothing. The state after executing skip is the same as the state before.

$$\mathsf{skip} \stackrel{\mathrm{def}}{=} \acute{\vec{\sigma}} = \grave{\vec{\sigma}}$$

The skip statement is always executable.

$\vec{v} := \vec{x}$

The parallel assignment statement $\vec{v} := \vec{x}$ assigns the vector of expressions $\vec{x}$ to the vector of variables $\acute{\vec{v}}$ and leaves the rest of the state unchanged. For example, imagine our state is the vector of variables (w, x, y, z) then, the desired meaning for the assignment statement $(w, x) := (1, 2)$ is as follows:

$$((\acute{w}, \acute{x}) = (1, 2)) \land ((\acute{y}, \acute{z}) = (\grave{y}, \grave{z}))$$

In general, the meaning of an assignment statement is expressed as:[5]

$$(\vec{v} := \vec{x}) \overset{\text{def}}{=} \Big((\vec{v}\,' = \vec{x}) \wedge ((\vec{\sigma}\,' - \vec{v}\,') = (\grave{\vec{\sigma}} - \grave{\vec{v}}))\Big)$$

An assignment statement $\vec{v} := \vec{x}$ is executable if each of the expressions in $\vec{x}$ is executable.

if C then P else Q

The conditional statement behaves according to P if the guard C holds, otherwise it behaves according to Q. This meaning is captured by the following definition:

$$(\textsf{if } C \textsf{ then } P \textsf{ else } Q) \overset{\text{def}}{=} ((C \Rightarrow P) \wedge (\neg C \Rightarrow Q))$$

A conditional is executable if the guard is an executable expression and both the then and else clauses are executable.

$P; Q$

A computer executing the sequential composition $P; Q$ behaves according to P and then according to Q. A sequential composition $P; Q$ relates an initial and final state if there exists some intermediate state such that P relates the initial and the intermediate states, and Q relates the intermediate and final states.

$$(P; Q) \overset{\text{def}}{=} \exists \vec{\sigma}.\ P[\vec{\sigma}/\vec{\sigma}\,'] \wedge Q[\vec{\sigma}/\grave{\vec{\sigma}}]$$

A sequential composition $P; Q$ is executable if both P and Q are executable.

label l. P

The general recursion statement is used for creating loops. For example, the following program decrements a nonnegative x until it reaches 0:

$$\textsf{label } l.\ \textsf{if } \grave{x} = 0 \textsf{ then skip else } (x := \grave{x} - 1;\ l)$$

We describe the meaning of a recursive statement as the least upper bound of an ever-improving sequence of approximations to its meaning. The sequence of approximations used to describe label l. P is:

$$\textsf{false}, P[\textsf{false}/l], P\big[P[\textsf{false}/l]/l\big], \ldots$$

Our first approximation, false does not relate any initial and final states — precisely those states related by executing the body of the recursive statement zero times. Our second approximation relates those states related

[5] The notation $\vec{v} - \vec{u}$ denotes the vector containing the elements of $\vec{v}$ except those occurring in $\vec{u}$.

by executing the body of the loop precisely once. The third approximation relates those states related by executing the body of the loop once or twice, and so on. The nth term in the sequence is:[6]

$$(\lambda l.\ P)^n(\mathsf{false})$$

We define the meaning of a recursive statement as the least upper bound of this sequence. The least upper bound is the predicate that relates any pair of states related by some term in the sequence, and no others.

$$\mathsf{label}\ l.\ P \stackrel{\text{def}}{=} \exists n.\ (\lambda l.\ P)^n(\mathsf{false})$$

The operational intuition behind the definition is that two states are related by a recursive statement if they are related by executing the statement some finite number of times. The definition has the following properties:

- If f is a function on predicates that is monotonic with respect to $\Rightarrow$, and is or-continuous[7] — which all executable functions are, then $\mathsf{label}\ l.\ f(l)$ is a fixed point of f.
- The meaning of an infinite loop is false, which agrees with our expectation that a nonterminating program should be partially correct with respect to all specifications.

The recursive statement label l. P is executable if, assuming l is executable, P is executable.

Each statement in our programming language has now been given a meaning as a predicate. By treating programs as predicates we can use them to refine specifications, as below:

$$\vdash (x := \grave{x} + 1) \Rightarrow (\acute{x} > \grave{x} \wedge \acute{y} = \grave{y})$$

$$\vdash (\mathsf{if}\ C\ \mathsf{then}\ P\ \mathsf{else}\ P) \Rightarrow P$$

$$\vdash (\mathsf{label}\ l.\ P) \Rightarrow P \qquad [l \text{ is not free in } P]$$

---

[6] The notation $f^n(a)$ is defined by:

$$f^n(a) \stackrel{\text{def}}{=} \begin{cases} a & , n = 0 \\ f\big(f^{n-1}(a)\big), & n > 0 \end{cases}$$

[7] A function f is or-continuous if the following theorem holds about it:

$$\forall n.\ P_n \Rightarrow P_{n+1} \vdash f\big(\exists n.\ P_n\big) = \big(\exists n.\ f(P_n)\big)$$

3.3.1 Nonstandard predicates

The notation proposed for use with program refinement is not quite that of standard logical notation. Fortunately the difference is small and our notation can be regarded as a slight syntactic sugaring of standard notation. To understand why, it is best to look at an example. Consider the specification below:

$$\acute{x} = \grave{x} + 1;\ \acute{x} = \grave{x} + 1$$

The intended meaning of this partial program is that x should be incremented, and then x should be incremented again. Although in keeping with standard programming practice, this notation is unusual because the term contains two instances of $\acute{x}$ (and $\grave{x}$) that, despite having the same name, are different variables. Similarly, the first $\acute{x}$ and the second $\grave{x}$ in the term are the same variable, despite having different names. In standard logical notation, variables with the same name in the same scope are the same variable, while variables with different names are different variables. This means that sequential compositions, when expressed in a program like notation, are not standard logical terms. However, the meaning of a sequential composition, as defined in section 3.3, is a standard logical term. Since we wish to express our programs in a familiar notation, and reason about them using classical logic, we regard sequential compositions as syntactic sugar for their meanings. For example, assuming σ_0 and σ_1 are the initial and final states, our original specification is syntactic sugar for a term of the following form:

$$\exists \sigma_m .\ x_m = x_0 + 1 \wedge x_1 = x_m + 1$$

Our notation is more general than previously described. In addition to writing $\grave{x}$ to denote the value of x before the current statement, we also write $\grave{\grave{x}}$ to denote the value of x before that, and $\grave{\grave{\grave{x}}}$ for the value of x before that, and so on. Similarly, while $\acute{x}$ denotes the value of x after the current statement, x'' denotes the value of x after that, and so on. Consider the following specification which uses multiple priming:

$$\acute{x} = \grave{x} + 1;\ \acute{x} = \grave{\grave{x}} + 1$$

The meaning of this specification is that x should be incremented once. The form of the specification suggests that x should be incremented twice, but that the result of the first increment is ignored when calculating the second. Again, assuming that σ_0 and σ_1 are the initial and final states, this specification is syntactic sugar for standard notation of the form below:

$$\exists \sigma_m .\ x_m = x_0 + 1 \wedge x_1 = x_0 + 1$$

Note that while expressions involving multiple primes, like $\grave{\grave{x}}$ and x'', can be valuable in specifications, they are not executable.

It is also important to note that, because of the nature of the syntactic sugaring, the same term can have different syntactic sugarings in different contexts. Consider the following term:

$$x_1 = x_0 + 1$$

If σ_0 and σ_1 are our initial and final states, then this term would correspond to the following specification:

$$\acute{x} = \grave{x} + 1$$

However, if this term were a subterm in a larger specification, it might appear differently. Consider our previous example, in which this term was the second part of a sequential composition. In that context the term was represented by the following syntactic sugar:

$$\acute{x} = \grave{\grave{x}} + 1$$

The program refinement tool that is being built based on the ideas described here runs on top of the HOL system. The HOL system is designed for proving theorems in classical logic. Translation software is placed between the user and the HOL system ensuring that while the user sees the program like notation, the theorem prover works with the corresponding standard notation.

4 A refinement tool

We now describe a program refinement tool which combines a treatment of programs as predicates with a window inference system to transform the predicates while preserving partial correctness. Once combined with an interface that presents the user with a program like notation rather than standard notation, a window inference system would be customised for program refinement in the following way.

- A set of commands that automate, or partly automate, common program refinement steps is added to the system. Because the HOL system is programmable, users can add their own commands to automate refinements they frequently repeat.
- A collection of window rules to allow a user to refine a partial program by refining its components is added to the system. These window rules should also allow the user to exploit the contextual information inherent in a program.

4.1 Refinement laws

The following are examples of the kind of refinements that are so simple and common that we would expect them to be automated by commands. Such commands are analogous to the laws of a refinement calculus [1, 17, 18]. The validity of each of these refinements follows from the semantics of the programming language.

- It is possible to refine the focus of a window to skip whenever the assumption that the initial and final states are the same implies that the focus is true.

$$\frac{\acute{\vec{\sigma}} = \grave{\vec{\sigma}} \vdash P}{\vdash \mathsf{skip} \Rightarrow P}$$

- The focus of a window can be refined to an assignment statement whenever the focus is **true** under the assumption that the assignment has taken place.

$$\frac{\vec{v}'' = \vec{x}, (\vec{\sigma}' - \vec{v}'') = ({}^{\backprime}\vec{\sigma} - {}^{\backprime}\vec{v}) \vdash P}{\vdash (\vec{v}{:=}\vec{x}) \Rightarrow P}$$

- Any focus can be refined with a conditional statement.

$$\frac{}{\vdash (\textsf{if } B \textsf{ then } P \textsf{ else } P) \Rightarrow P}$$

  The choice of the guard B is arbitrary.

- The focus, P, of any window can be refined by giving it a label, l, that does not occur free in P. The **label** statement records P and an invariant I of the user's choosing, which must follow from the context of the window.

$$\frac{\vdash I}{\vdash (\textsf{label}_{(P,\,I)} l.\ P) \Rightarrow P}$$

- Any focus P can be refined by first executing some Q and then P.

$$\frac{}{\vdash (Q;P[\ldots, {}^{\backprime\backprime\backprime}\vec{\sigma}, {}^{\backprime\backprime}\vec{\sigma} / \ldots, {}^{\backprime\backprime}\vec{\sigma}, {}^{\backprime}\vec{\sigma}]) \Rightarrow P}$$

  Note that the variables in P are renamed so that they still refer to the values they held before any refinement was made. If they were not renamed, the inference rule would require a side condition stating that Q does not alter the variables. No actual renaming takes place. The apparent renaming is a consequence of the same standard term having a different syntactic sugaring when placed in a different context.

4.2 Window rules

The window inference system requires a database of window rules to allow the user to navigate around partial programs and exploit the contextual information to be found in them. The window rules should allow the user to refine partial programs by refining their components. Below are examples of the kinds of window openings that users want to perform:

- Opening a subwindow on the **then** clause of a conditional, we can assume the guard holds.

Window	*Subwindow*
$!\ \Gamma$	$!\ \Gamma$
$\Rightarrow \star$ if B then	$!\ B$
$\boxed{X}$	$\Rightarrow \star X$
else	
Y	

A similar rule allows us to open a subwindow on the **else** clause of a conditional and assume that the guard is **false**.

- Opening at the second statement in a sequential composition, we can assume the first statement has just been executed.

Window	*Subwindow*
$! \ \Gamma$	$! \ \Gamma[\ldots, \grave{\grave{\vec{\sigma}}}, \grave{\vec{\sigma}}, \vec{\sigma}', \vec{\sigma}'', \ldots / \ldots, \grave{\grave{\grave{\vec{\sigma}}}}, \grave{\grave{\vec{\sigma}}}, \grave{\vec{\sigma}}, \vec{\sigma}', \ldots]$
$\Rightarrow \star Q; \boxed{P}$	$! \ Q[\ldots, \grave{\grave{\vec{\sigma}}}, \grave{\vec{\sigma}}, \vec{\sigma}', \vec{\sigma}'', \ldots / \ldots, \grave{\grave{\grave{\vec{\sigma}}}}, \grave{\grave{\vec{\sigma}}}, \grave{\vec{\sigma}}, \vec{\sigma}', \ldots]$
	$\Rightarrow \star P$

  Note the renaming on the first and the context statement moving their variables one step into the past. No actual renaming takes place. The apparent renaming is a consequence of the same standard terms having a different syntactic sugaring when viewed from a different context.

  Similarly we can open a subwindow on the first statement of a composition and assume that the second statement is just about to be executed.

- Opening inside the body of a **label**, we can assume that the invariant holds, and that for all initial and final states, $\vec{\sigma}_1$ and $\vec{\sigma}_2$, if the invariant holds on the initial state, then the label implements the original specification.

Window	*Subwindow*
$! \ \Gamma$	$! \ \Gamma$[state variables are renamed out of the history]
$\Rightarrow \star \mathsf{label}(P, I)^{l}.$	$! \ I$
$\boxed{P'}$	$! \ \forall \vec{\sigma}_1, \vec{\sigma}_2.\ (I \Rightarrow (l \Rightarrow P))[\vec{\sigma}_1, \vec{\sigma}_2]$
	$\Rightarrow \star P'$

  The apparent renaming occurs because the variables in the assumptions can no longer be assumed to be those representing the states immediately before, or after, the current state.

5 A refinement example

To demonstrate the refinement techniques described so far, we conclude with an example. The specification we are to refine states that x is to be multiplied by y and the result put in z. Let us assume that multiplication is not an executable expression, the effect is to be achieved through repeated addition.

Because we are only preserving partial correctness, it would be possible to refine our specification to an infinite loop. However, we avoid taking that path. We begin by making our specification the focus of a window that preserves partial correctness (i.e. logical implication).

Window: 1

$$\Rightarrow \star \acute{z} = \grave{x} \times \grave{y}$$

We shall refine the specification using a variable t from outside the scope of the specification. The idea is to find a recursive solution which maintains the values of x and y, and the invariant $z = x \times t$, while advancing the value of t

towards that of y. Our first step is to rephrase the specification in terms of t, we would like to establish $\acute{t} = \grave{y}$ in a state where $\acute{z} = \grave{x} \times \acute{t}$.

$$\Rightarrow\star\ \acute{t} = \grave{y} \wedge \acute{z} = \grave{x} \times \acute{t}$$

We prefix our specification with an initialisation that will maintain x and y, and establish our invariant that $z = x \times t$. Typically we might choose the assignment $(t, z) := (0, 0)$ to implement the initialisation. However, there are many possible implementations. The refinement will progress more easily if we simply state the properties our initialisation must satisfy. Note that creating the sequential composition changes the appearance of the variables in our original specification. This is because they still refer to the values held at the beginning of the specification.

$$\begin{array}{l}\Rightarrow\star\ \acute{x} = \grave{x} \wedge \acute{y} = \grave{y} \wedge \acute{z} = \acute{x} \times \acute{t};\\ \quad \boxed{\acute{t} = \grave{\grave{y}} \wedge \acute{z} = \grave{\grave{x}} \times \acute{t}}\end{array}$$

We continue the refinement by opening a subwindow on our original specification, leaving the refinement of the initialisation until later.

Window: 1.1

$$\begin{array}{l}\quad !\ \grave{x} = \grave{\grave{x}} \wedge \grave{y} = \grave{\grave{y}} \wedge \grave{z} = \grave{x} \times \grave{t}\\ \Rightarrow\star\ \acute{t} = \grave{\grave{y}} \wedge \acute{z} = \grave{\grave{x}} \times \acute{t}\end{array}$$

Since our initialisation maintained the values of x and y, we have assumptions stating that $\grave{x} = \grave{\grave{x}}$ and $\grave{y} = \grave{\grave{y}}$. We can use these assumptions to remove the multiple priming from $\grave{\grave{x}}$ and $\grave{\grave{y}}$ in the focus.

$$\Rightarrow\star\ \acute{t} = \grave{y} \wedge \acute{z} = \grave{x} \times \acute{t}$$

We have decided to implement the current specification recursively. To allow this, we give it a label, L. The invariant we choose to associate with L is $z = x \times t$ which we know holds in our current state because $\grave{z} = \grave{x} \times \grave{t}$ appears as a conjunct of the context of this window.

$$\Rightarrow\star\ \mathsf{label}\ L.\ \boxed{\acute{t} = \grave{y} \wedge \acute{z} = \grave{x} \times \acute{t}}$$

To continue the refinement we open a subwindow inside the label construct. In our new context we can assume the invariant holds and that for all states where the invariant holds, a recursive call to L refines the original specification.

Window: 1.1.1

$$\begin{array}{l}\quad \vdots\\ \quad !\ \grave{z} = \grave{x} \times \grave{t}\\ \quad !\ \forall \vec{\sigma}_1, \vec{\sigma}_2.\ z_1 = x_1 \times t_1 \Rightarrow (L \Rightarrow (t_2 = y_1 \wedge z_2 = x_1 \times t_2))\\ \Rightarrow\star\ \acute{t} = \grave{y} \wedge \acute{z} = \grave{x} \times \acute{t}\end{array}$$

We use a conditional statement to partition the specification into two cases about the guard $\grave{t} = \grave{y}$.

$$\begin{array}{l} \Rightarrow\star\ \textsf{if}\ \grave{t} = \grave{y}\ \textsf{then} \\ \qquad \acute{t} = \grave{y} \wedge \acute{z} = \grave{x} \times \acute{t} \\ \quad \textsf{else} \\ \qquad \acute{t} = \grave{y} \wedge \acute{z} = \grave{x} \times \acute{t} \end{array}$$

The case in which $\grave{t} = \grave{y}$ holds is simple, and can be refined to skip.

$$\begin{array}{l} \Rightarrow\star\ \textsf{if}\ \grave{t} = \grave{y}\ \textsf{then} \\ \qquad \textsf{skip} \\ \quad \textsf{else} \\ \qquad \boxed{\acute{t} = \grave{y} \wedge \acute{z} = \grave{x} \times \acute{t}} \end{array}$$

The case where $\grave{t} = \grave{y}$ does not hold is the more difficult. We concentrate our attention there by opening a subwindow on the **else** clause. In this context we can assume $\grave{t} \neq \grave{y}$.

Window: 1.1.1.1

$$\begin{array}{l} \quad \vdots \\ \quad !\ \grave{z} = \grave{x} \times \grave{t} \\ \quad !\ \forall \vec{\sigma}_1, \vec{\sigma}_2.\ z_1 = x_1 \times t_1 \Rightarrow (L \Rightarrow (t_2 = y_1 \wedge z_2 = x_1 \times t_2)) \\ \quad !\ \grave{t} \neq \grave{y} \\ \Rightarrow\star \acute{t} = \grave{y} \wedge \acute{z} = \grave{x} \times \acute{t} \end{array}$$

We refine our specification by prefixing it with another that maintains x, y, and the invariant, and will later be refined to ensure progress towards making t equal to y. Again, note the change in the appearance of x and y as our specification is placed into the context of a sequential composition.

$$\begin{array}{l} \Rightarrow\star\ \acute{x} = \grave{x} \wedge \acute{y} = \grave{y} \wedge \acute{z} = \acute{x} \times \acute{t}\,; \\ \quad \boxed{\acute{t} = \grave{\grave{y}} \wedge \acute{z} = \grave{\grave{x}} \times \acute{t}} \end{array}$$

We leave the refinement of the first specification for later, and open a window on the second. In the context of the second statement we can assume that the values of x and y, and the invariant have been maintained.

Window: 1.1.1.1.1

$$\begin{array}{l} \quad \vdots \\ \quad !\ \grave{\grave{z}} = \grave{\grave{x}} \times \grave{\grave{t}} \\ \quad !\ \boxed{\forall \vec{\sigma}_1, \vec{\sigma}_2.\ z_1 = x_1 \times t_1 \Rightarrow (L \Rightarrow (t_2 = y_1 \wedge z_2 = x_1 \times t_2))} \\ \quad !\ \grave{\grave{t}} \neq \grave{\grave{y}} \\ \quad !\ \grave{x} = \grave{\grave{x}} \wedge \grave{y} = \grave{\grave{y}} \wedge \grave{z} = \grave{x} \times \grave{t} \\ \Rightarrow\star \acute{t} = \grave{\grave{y}} \wedge \acute{z} = \grave{\grave{x}} \times \acute{t} \end{array}$$

In our current context we can assume that the previous specification has just been executed. We therefore know that $\grave{x} = \grave{\grave{x}}$ and $\grave{y} = \grave{\grave{y}}$. Using these assumptions we can remove the multiple primes from $\grave{\grave{x}}$ and $\grave{\grave{y}}$ in the focus.

$$\Rightarrow\star \acute{t} = \grave{y} \wedge \acute{z} = \grave{x} \times \acute{t}$$

We have now refined our focus to an instance of our original specification. We want to refine it further with a recursive call to L. To facilitate this step, we open a subwindow on the assumption about L, and derive the fact required.

Window: 1.1.1.1.1.1

$$\vdots$$
$$!\ \grave{x} = \grave{\grave{x}} \wedge \grave{y} = \grave{\grave{y}} \wedge \grave{z} = \grave{x} \times \grave{t}$$
$$\Leftarrow\star \forall \vec{\sigma}_1, \vec{\sigma}_2.\ z_1 = x_1 \times t_1 \Rightarrow (L \Rightarrow (t_2 = y_1 \wedge z_2 = x_1 \times t_2))$$

We instantiate $\vec{\sigma}_1$ and $\vec{\sigma}_2$ with the states $\grave{\vec{\sigma}}$ and $\vec{\sigma}'$.

$$\Leftarrow\star\ \grave{z} = \grave{x} \times \grave{t} \Rightarrow (L \Rightarrow (\acute{t} = \grave{y} \wedge \acute{z} = \grave{x} \times \acute{t}))$$

The focus can be simplified because we know the invariant holds in this context.

$$\Leftarrow\star\ L \Rightarrow (\acute{t} = \grave{y} \wedge \acute{z} = \grave{x} \times \acute{t})$$

We close this window and return to its parent. In the parent window we now have a lemma that states that L refines the focus.

Window: 1.1.1.1.2

$$\vdots$$
$$¡\ L \Rightarrow (\acute{t} = \grave{y} \wedge \acute{z} = \grave{x} \times \acute{t})$$
$$\Rightarrow\star\ \acute{t} = \grave{y} \wedge \acute{z} = \grave{x} \times \acute{t}$$

Using the new lemma we refine the focus with a recursive call to L.

$$\Rightarrow\star\ L$$

Having completely implemented the focus of the window, we close it and return to its parent. In the parent window, the first part of the sequential composition is yet to be refined.

Window: 1.1.1.2

$$\vdots$$
$$!\ \grave{z} = \grave{x} \times \grave{t}$$
$$!\ \grave{t} \neq \grave{y}$$
$$\Rightarrow\star\ \acute{x} = \grave{x} \wedge \acute{y} = \grave{y} \wedge \acute{z} = \acute{x} \times \acute{t};$$
$$L$$

This specification states that we should maintain the values of x and y, and the invariant $z = x \times t$. Although we are only preserving partial correctness, we would like our implementation to be a program which terminates. To this end, we also require the implementation of this specification to advance t towards the value of y, without exceeding it. Assuming that we have initialised t to some value less than y, we achieve this with a parallel assignment that increments t and adds x to the value of z. Such an assignment maintains x and y, advances t towards the value of y, and maintains the invariant $z = x \times t$.

$$\Rightarrow\star\ (t, z) := (\grave{t} + 1, \grave{z} + \grave{x});$$
$$L$$

We can now close this window, and all those above. Returning to the top level, we see that the refinement is complete except for the initialisation.

Window: 2

$\Rightarrow \star\, \acute{x} = \grave{x} \wedge \acute{y} = \grave{y} \wedge \acute{z} = \acute{x} \times \acute{t};$
label L.
if $\grave{t} = \grave{y}$ then
skip
else
$(t, z) := (\grave{t} + 1, \grave{z} + \grave{x});$
L

Our initialisation can be trivially refined with a parallel assignment that sets both t and z to zero.

$\Rightarrow \star\, (t, z) := (0, 0);$
label L.
if $\grave{t} = \grave{y}$ then
skip
else
$(t, z) := (\grave{t} + 1, \grave{z} + \grave{x});$
L

The refinement process is now complete. The focus of the window is a program and the theorem held by the window states that the program refines the original specification.

5.1 Termination

The example just presented has proved only the partial correctness of the implementation. The question of how to make refinements which guarantee total correctness, while still using this treatment of programs as predicates, is an open one. However, the interested reader might like to consider the following possibility. With the exception of the recursive statement, all the statements in our small programming language must terminate. Proving the termination of a program is therefore achieved by proving the termination of each of the recursive statements in the program. In window 1.1.1.1.1.1 of the example above, we showed, by proving that the invariant held, that a recursive call to the label L would implement our original specification. It was this step that enabled us to introduce recursion into the implementation. If in order to prove that a recursive call would implement our specification, we not only had to show that the invariant held, but also that some variant function had decreased with respect to some well-founded ordering, then we would have been prevented from developing a nonterminating solution.

6 Related work

One of the strengths of the window inference style of reasoning is its ability to allow the user access to contextual information. The general desirability of having access to contextual information has been noted by Leonard Monk [16] and Francisco Corella [4].

Window inference was first described by Peter Robinson and John Staples [20]. Their work is extended here by removing their restriction that window inference must preserve an equivalence relation. The window inference system described here can be tailored to allow the user to preserve any preorder between expressions. The extension to allow the preservation of more general relationships is necessary for the application of window inference to refinement problems. The inspiration for building a window inference system in HOL came from using Robinson and Staples's own theorem prover, Demo2 [22]. Demo2 is similar to the system described here, except that Demo2 allows only the preservation of equivalence relations, and it automatically manipulates lemmas to make them applicable in more general contexts.

The use of predicates to describe specifications and implementations has been well known to members of the hardware verification community for some time [10, 6]. Verification is achieved, as it is here, by proving that an implementation implies its specification. Mike Gordon's work [6] has also involved the mechanisation of his ideas within the HOL system. Recent work by Andy Gordon and others investigates the building of hardware transformation systems inside the HOL proof assistant [3].

There have been other attempts to mechanise programming theory within the HOL system. Notably, Mike Gordon's work on Hoare logic [7], and Ralph Back and Joakim von Wright's work on their refinement calculus [2].

Eric Hehner has worked extensively on the treatment of programs as predicates [11, 12, 13]. Tony Hoare has also used predicates to describe specifications and programs [15]. Our convention of using $\grave{v}$ and $\acute{v}$ to denote the initial and final values of some variable v is derived from the notation used in Eric Hehner's earlier work [11]. However, the use of multiple priming to refer to variables in the past and future has not previously been explored. The treatment of programs as predicates presented in this paper is largely inspired by Eric Hehner's more recent work [12, 13], and by the work of Tony Hoare [15]. That work, like ours, has logical implication as its correctness relation. The treatment of programs as predicates presented here differs from theirs primarily by giving a different meaning to recursion.

Elsewhere in these proceedings Andy Gravell presents another approach to the treatment of programs as predicates [8]. Andy Gravell's predicates are terms in an untyped first-order logic, where ours are terms in a typed higher-order logic. That work gives a different interpretation to predicates, one like that of the Z specification language. This different interpretation of predicates requires the use of a refinement relation that is more complex than logical implication.

7 Conclusion

This paper described a method of reasoning, called window inference. We conjecture that window inference is better for refinement applications than goal-oriented styles of reasoning. Window inference has the following strengths:

- Window inference supports users who wish to solve problems by concentrating on subproblems. This means that window inference supports stepwise refinement by allowing users to decompose specifications and refine the components individually.

- Window inference allows the user to make arbitrarily fine manipulations of an expression. This is important when the form of the solution is of as much importance as the existence of a solution itself, as is the case when deriving programs from their specifications.

- Window inference allows the user to make use of the information implicit in the context of a subproblem. For example, when refining the **then** clause of a conditional it is helpful to assume that the guard of the conditional holds.

- Window inference supports the preservation of an arbitrary preorder when transforming an expression. This is important for the application of window inference to refinement where we wish to preserve correctness.

A correspondence between window inference and the sequent calculus notation has been outlined. This correspondence serves to reassure the reader that window inference is a valid and practical style of reasoning, and as a guide to the implementation of a window inference interface for programmable proof systems based on the sequent calculus, such as HOL. A window inference interface to the HOL system has already been built based on the ideas described here and earlier in [9].

A unified treatment of programs and specifications as predicates is presented in the paper together with a description of how to use window inference to manipulate these predicates. The 'Programs are Predicates' approach to refinement has the following advantages:

- As predicates, programs are terms in our logic. This means that we can reason about programs more directly than if we had to reason about them via some other semantics.

- Existing proof systems like HOL can be easily customised for reasoning about programs.

- The refinement relation is logical implication. Implication is a simple, well-understood relation, that intuitively fits the role of a refinement relation. There is already much support for proving theorems about implication in HOL and other theorem proving systems.

It should also be noted that it is not necessary to adopt the 'Programs are Predicates' approach to refinement in order to use window inference. Window inference could also form the basis of a refinement tool using one of the weakest precondition based refinement calculi.

Acknowledgements

I am grateful for the support of the Australian Defence Science & Technology Organisation. I am also grateful to Mike Gordon for his guidance and supervision.

I would like to thank the following people who have read and provided comments on drafts of this paper: Joakim von Wright of the Åbo Akademi, Institutionen för Informationsbehandling & Mathematiska Institutet; Andy Gordon, Mike Gordon, John Harrison, Mats Larsson, Tom Melham, and Monica Nesi of the Cambridge University, Computer Laboratory; Maris Ozols of the Australian Defence Science & Technology Organisation, Information Technology Division; Katherine Eastaughffe of the Oxford University, Computing Laboratory; David Carrington, Ian Hayes, and Nigel Ward of the Queensland University, Department of Computer Science; and Andy Gravell of the Southampton University, Department of Electronics & Computer Science. The comments of these people have greatly improved the quality of this paper. Any remaining flaws in the paper are, of course, my own doing.

References

[1] R.-J. R. Back. On correct refinement of programs. *Journal of Computer and System Sciences*, 23(1):49–68, Feb. 1981.

[2] R.-J. R. Back and J. von Wright. Refinement concepts formalised in higher-order logic. *Formal Aspects of Computing*, 2(3):247–272, July 1990.

[3] R. J. Boulton, A. D. Gordon, M. J. C. Gordon, J. R. Harrison, J. M. J. Herbert, and J. P. van Tassel. Experience with embedding hardware description languages in HOL. In R. Boute, T. Melham, and V. Stavridou, editors, *Proceedings of the Conference on Theorem Provers in Circuit Design: Theory, Practice and Experience*, The University of Nijmegen, The Netherlands, June 1992. IFIP, North Holland.

[4] F. Corella. What holds in a context? *Journal of Automated Reasoning*, to appear.

[5] E. W. Dijkstra. *A Discipline of Programming.* Prentice Hall Series in Automatic Computation. Prentice Hall, Englewood Cliffs, United States, 1976.

[6] M. J. C. Gordon. Why higher-order logic is a good formalism for specifying and verifying hardware. In G. J. Milne and P. A. Subrahmanyam, editors, *Formal Aspects of VLSI Design: Proceedings of the Edinburgh Workshop on VLSI*, pages 153–177, Edinburgh, Scotland, 1985. North Holland.

[7] M. J. C. Gordon. Mechanizing programming logics in higher-order logic. In G. M. Birtwistle and P. A. Subrahamanyam, editors, *Current Trends in Hardware Verification and Theorem Proving: Proceedings of the 1988 Banff Workshop on Hardware Verification*, chapter 10, pages 387–439. Springer-Verlag, Berlin, Germany, 1989.

[8] A. Gravell. Constructive refinement of first-order specifications. In C. B. Jones, B. T. Denvir, and R. C. Shaw, editors, *Proceedings of the 5th Refinement Workshop*, Lloyd's Register, London, England, Jan. 1992. BCS-FACS, Springer-Verlag.

[9] J. Grundy. Window inference in the HOL system. In P. J. Windley, M. Archer, K. N. Levitt, and J. J. Joyce, editors, *The Proceedings of the International Tutorial and Workshop on the HOL Theorem Proving System and its Applications*, University of California at Davis, Aug. 1991. ACM/IEEE, IEEE Computer Society Press.

[10] F. K. Hanna and N. Daeche. Specification and verification using higher-order logic. In C.-J. Koomen and T. Moto-oka, editors, *Proceedings of the 7th International Conference on Computer Hardware Description Languages and Their Applications*, pages 418–, Tokyo, Japan, Aug. 1985. IFIP, North Holland.

[11] E. C. R. Hehner. Predicative programming — part 1. *Communications of the ACM*, 27(2):134–143, Feb. 1984.

[12] E. C. R. Hehner. Termination is timing. In J. L. A. van da Snepscheut, editor, *Proceedings of Mathematics of Program Construction — 375th Aniversary of the Groningen University, International Conference,* volume 375 of *Lecture Notes in Computer Science*, pages 36–47. Springer-Verlag, Berlin, Germany, June 1989.

[13] E. C. R. Hehner. A practical theory of programming. *Science of Computer Programming*, 14(2-3):133–158, 1990.

[14] C. A. R. Hoare. An axiomatic basis for computer programming. *Communications of the ACM*, 12(10):576–580,583, Oct. 1969.

[15] C. A. R. Hoare. Programs are predicates. *Philosophical Transactions of the Royal Society of London — Series A: Mathematical and Physical Sciences*, 312(1522):475–490, Oct. 1984.

[16] L. G. Monk. Inference rules using local contexts. *Journal of Automated Reasoning*, 4(4):445–462, Dec. 1988.

[17] C. C. Morgan. The specification statement. *ACM Transactions on Programming Languages and Systems*, 10(3):403–419, July 1988.

[18] J. M. Morris. A theoretical basis for stepwise refinement and the programming calculus. *Science of Computer Programming*, 9(3):287–306, Dec. 1987.

[19] L. C. Paulson. *Logic and Computation: Interactive Proof with Cambridge LCF*, volume 2 of *Cambridge Tracts in Theoretical Computer Science.* Cambridge University Press, Cambridge, England, 1987.

[20] P. J. Robinson and J. Staples. Formalising the hierarchical structure of practical mathematical reasoning. *Logic and Computation*, to appear.

[21] SRI International, Cambridge Research Center, Millers Yard, Mill Lane, Cambridge CB2 1RQ, England. *The HOL System*, 2nd edition, July 1991.

[22] T. G. Tang, P. J. Robinson, and J. Staples. The demonstration proof editor Demo2. Technical Report 175, Key Centre for Software Technology, Department of Computer Science, University of Queensland, QLD 4072, Australia, Dec. 1990.

Using Metavariables in Natural Deduction Proofs

T. Clement
Department of Computer Science,
University of Manchester, Manchester, England.

Abstract

A method of proof construction is suggested based on the introduction and later instantiation of metavariables in natural deduction proofs. This is shown to be useful in program synthesis, where the unknown program can itself be represented by a parameterised metavariable, through an example which also illustrates some larger scale strategies for proof construction. Some conclusions are drawn concerning the mechanical support of this approach to proof construction, with particular reference to μral [J⁺91]

1 Introduction

Program verification and program synthesis both depend heavily on the construction of proofs connecting implementations to specifications. In order to make rigorous development feasible, then, we must have techniques for constructing large numbers of what are for the most part fairly straightforward proofs with relatively little effort.

Here we shall be concerned with constructing proofs in the natural deduction style of [Jon90]. A natural deduction logic is presented as a set of proof rule schemas: for example

$$\frac{e2}{e1 \vee e2}\,\boxed{\vee\text{-I-left}} \qquad \frac{e1}{e1 \vee e2}\,\boxed{\vee\text{-I-right}}$$

$$\frac{e1 \vee e2 \quad e1 \vdash e \quad e2 \vdash e}{e}\,\boxed{\vee\text{-E}} \qquad \frac{e1 \vee e2}{e2 \vee e1}\,\boxed{\vee\text{-comm}}$$

The parts of the rules above the line are the hypotheses: below the line we have the conclusion. The conclusion is a formula, which may contain metavariables standing for terms, formulae or types. ($e1$, $e2$ and e in the rules above are metavariables standing for formulae.) A hypothesis is either a formula or a sequent, which has hypotheses of its own to the left of the turnstile and a conclusion to the right. Rules are given names for easy reference.

We may construct proofs of some (derived) rules using the others: the primitive rules are the axioms of the theory while the others are lemmas. The following is a proof of $\vee$-*comm* using the other rules.

h1 from $e1 \vee e2$		
1.h1	from $e1$	
1.c	infer $e2 \vee e1$	$\vee$-I-left[1.h1]
2.h1	from $e2$	
2.c	infer $e2 \vee e1$	$\vee$-I-right[2.h1]
c infer $e2 \vee e1$		$\vee$-E[h1,1,2]

A proof consists of a series of labelled lines and boxes. The first lines are the hypotheses of the rule to be proved (labelled h_i), and the last line, labelled c is the conclusion. A line contains a formula, while a box contains a sub-proof, with local hypotheses and conclusions. Each line of the proof (and the boxes) except for the hypotheses has a justification, which is usually the name of a rule which has that line as an instance of its conclusion, and the labels of preceding lines and boxes containing the corresponding instances of its hypotheses. (An ordinary hypothesis will correspond to a line, a sequent hypothesis to a box with hypotheses and conclusions instances of those of the sequent.) Lines of a box may be referenced only within that box.

Our goal is to construct such proofs. There is no reason why this has to be done by adding new lines in the form they appear in the final proof, although this is how proof construction is often seen. As an alternative, consider a partially completed proof, where some of the lines remain to be justified. To continue the construction, we can take such a line, A, and find a rule $\frac{H_1 \ldots H_n}{C}\boxed{\mathrm{R}}$ and substitution θ of metavariables by metaterms of the appropriate kinds such that $C\theta = A\theta$ (so θ is a unifier of A and C). (If proof and rule have metavariables in common, we should rename them to remove the overlap before unifying.) The new proof will be the old proof extended by the lines H_i and then substituted by θ throughout. The justification of $A\theta$ is now rule R applied to the antecedent lines: these lines are obviously an instance of the rule produced by θ. The rest of the justifications remain unchanged: they are valid because they recorded instances of rules when first introduced, we have created instances of those instances by applying the same substitution to each line at each step, and an instance of an instance is itself an instance. When the proof is complete, the conclusion will therefore be a logical consequence of the hypotheses, although these may be instances of the hypotheses and conclusion we began with.

If we interpret variables in clauses as metavariables in proof rules standing for terms, the clausal resolution used in Prolog and elsewhere can be seen as just an instance of this approach. (In Prolog, this gives a more direct account of the significance of answers than the usual refutation proof interpretation.) In the natural deduction setting, we gain extra power from the possibility that metavariables stand for predicates and types, perhaps with parameters, as well as terms. The penalty for this, of course, is the increased difficulty of the unification. By analogy, we shall call this approach to proof construction rule resolution. Unlike clausal resolution it does not remove the need to select a proof rule at each step, although conversely we do not pay the penalty of a large and unintuitive reconstruction of the theory to put it into clausal form. In constructing proofs we use it in a goal-directed way.

In conventional proof, the rule to be proved is stated before we start and we do not want to instantiate any metavariables that it may contain as this will change what we are proving. Rule resolution will only differ from line by line construction, then, if metavariables are introduced during the proof and later instantiated. Metavariables are introduced when we apply a rule which has metavariables in its hypotheses which do not appear in the conclusion, as in the case of $e1$ and $e2$ in $\vee$-E. The advantage of leaving them uninstantiated when we apply the rule is the old advantage of resolution techniques over saturation techniques: if the value is left open where it is of no significance, it can be fixed later (while applying another rule) in a way that makes that later step of the proof go through. That is, we are avoiding forward planning in the proof construction, looking to see how later steps of the proof will go, which reduces the effort of applying each step. The longer delayed the instantiation, the more benefit we obtain. As a simple example, consider constructing the proof of $\vee$-*comm* above by applying rule resolution to the conclusion using $\vee$-E.

h1	from $e1 \vee e2$	
1	$e3 \vee e4$	<Justif>
2.h1	from $e3$	
2.c	infer $e2 \vee e1$	<Justif>
3.h1	from $e4$	
3.c	infer $e2 \vee e1$	<Justif>
c	infer $e2 \vee e1$	$\vee$-E[1,2,3]

We rename $e1$ and $e2$ in the rule to $e3$ and $e4$, and since they appear in the hypotheses only they are uninstantiated by rule resolution. Having chosen and applied the rule, we can now see that line 1 can be justified easily by reference to the hypothesis if we take $e3$ as $e1$ and $e4$ as $e2$, although it still remains to be seen if lines 2.c and 3.c can be justified. In trivial cases like this, we shall usually unify new hypotheses with existing proof lines as a second phase of rule resolution rather than clutter our proofs with repeated lines.

There are circumstances when it *is* useful to instantiate metavariables in the rule statement during the proof construction. These are essentially when we use metavariables to express the fact that we do not know exactly what we are trying to prove. For example, we can express a program synthesis problem by using a (parameterized) metavariable to stand for the term that will evaluate to a value satisfying a specification.

$$\frac{}{\forall x{:}\, X \cdot \text{pre-}op[x] \;\Rightarrow\; \text{post-}op[x, f[x]]}\;\boxed{f\text{-synthesis}}$$

Constructing the proof will instantiate f to a term that can be evaluated to give a result for the operation.

A similar situation arises when we want to divide up a proof under construction into a series of lemmas. We expect to instantiate metavariables within a proof as we continue the construction, so when we extract a line as the conclusion of a new lemma, it is only reasonable to allow the proof of the lemma to instantiate metavariables in that conclusion. Applying the lemma may also instantiate metavariables in the main proof. In a similar way, since goal directed reasoning introduces new hypothesis lines in need of justification, it is reasonable to allow the proof of a lemma to add to the hypotheses of the lemma statement, and thus generate extra lines in the main proof when it is used. Our standard strategy is to begin with no hypotheses on a lemma and find out exactly what is needed as we go. This idea will be amply illustrated in the example which follows.

2 An example of a synthesis

In this section, we shall illustrate the use of rule resolution in synthesis through a small example (with a fairly long proof): the synthesis of an identity substitution on terms from the starting point

$$\frac{}{\forall t\colon \mathit{Term} \cdot t \bullet s = t} \boxed{\text{Identity substitution}}$$

with s a metavariable. (Unlike the synthesis problems described in the introduction, in this case we are synthesising a constant, so s has no parameters.) This example arose as part of a larger synthesis of a unification algorithm: unification is a widely used test case for formalisation and synthesis [MW81, Pau85, Fit90, Vad90]. It will also illustrate some larger scale strategies for applying rule resolution.

One common way to establish universal properties is by induction. This is particularly common in function synthesis, since in order to prove a property of some $f[x]$ by induction, we must express it in terms of instances of f on smaller terms. This leads naturally to an interpretation as a recursive algorithm. However, there are many different induction schemes leading to different recursive algorithms, and the details of the induction to be used only become apparent when we discover which induction hypotheses help us to establish the general goal. We should like to use a general induction scheme to delay the decision until we have the information needed to take it, rather than fixing a particular scheme now, and to use metavariables to express the generality so we can exploit rule resolution to propagate the details when the decision is made. The Noetherian induction used in [MW80] requires only a well-founded ordering on the induction type, and states that if we can prove that a property holds for some arbitrary element of the type under the assumption that it holds for all smaller elements, we can deduce that it holds for all elements. We can state this formally as

$$\frac{\{t\colon T, \forall t'\colon T \cdot t' \sqsubset t \ \Rightarrow\ P[t']\} \vdash P[t]}{\forall x\colon T \cdot P[x]} \boxed{\text{Noetherian induction}}$$

where $\sqsubset$ is a predicate metavariable. (An alternative approach to induction which also exploits metavariables, but in a very different way, is described in [BSH90].)

After applying Noetherian induction, we have the following partial proof:

1.h1 from t: *Term*
1.h2 and $\forall t'$: *Term* $\cdot (t' \sqsubset t) \Rightarrow ((t' \bullet s) = t')$
1.c infer $(t \bullet s) = t$ <Justif>
c infer $\forall t$: *Term* $\cdot (t \bullet \{\,\}m) = t$ Noetherian induction[1]

We note that, had we used

$$\frac{x{:}\,X \vdash P[x]}{\forall x{:}\,X \cdot P[x]}\ \boxed{\forall\text{-I}}$$

(the other commonly used rule for establishing a universally quantified formula), the partial proof would have been the same except for hypothesis 1.h2. Noetherian induction is thus more powerful (and hence in some sense a better choice of rule) than $\forall$-*I*.

For reasons that will become apparent, it is convenient to introduce a lemma to establish $t \bullet s = t$ before continuing with the proof proper.

$$\frac{}{t \bullet s = t}\ \boxed{\text{Identity substitution lemma 1}}$$

The obvious place to start a goal-directed proof is by rewriting the application of $\bullet$. In this proof framework, we use

$$\frac{s1 = s2 \quad s2 = s3}{s1 = s3}\ \boxed{=\text{-trans}}$$

to introduce a metavariable $s2$, instantiate it by using a defining rule for the operation, and then show the rewritten form equal to t. There is a choice of two rules, $\bullet$ *Variable definition* and $\bullet$ *CompoundTerm definition*, each of which will also instantiate t since they deal with particular cases of terms. Let us use the variable rule, giving

1 v: *VarSymbol* <Justif>
2 s: *Substitution* <Justif>
3 $(mk\text{-}Variable[v] \bullet s) =$
$(if\ (v \in dom[s])\ then\ (s\ at\ v)\ else\ mk\text{-}Variable[v])$
$\bullet$ Variable definition (wff)[1,2]
4 $(if\ (v \in dom[s])\ then\ (s\ at\ v)\ else\ mk\text{-}Variable[v]) =$
$mk\text{-}Variable[v]$ <Justif>
c infer $(mk\text{-}Variable[v] \bullet \{\,\}m) = mk\text{-}Variable[v]$ =-trans[3,4]

The obvious way to justify line 4 is by showing that v is not in $dom[s]$. To justify this, we need to be able to use a rule for *dom*, which we prepare for by introducing a metavariable d equal to $dom[s]$.

1	v: *VarSymbol*	**<Justif>**
2	s: *Substitution*	**<Justif>**
3	$(mk\text{-}Variable[v] \bullet s) =$ $(if(v \in dom[s])then(s\ at\ v)else\ mk\text{-}Variable[v])$	$\bullet$ Variable definition (wff)[1,2]
4	$(mk\text{-}Variable[v]{:}\ X)$	**<Justif>**
5	$\neg(v \in d)$	**<Justif>**
6	$dom[s] = d$	**<Justif>**
7	$\neg(v \in dom[s])$	=-subs-left[5,6]
8	$(if(v \in dom[s])then(s\ at\ v)\ else\ mk\text{-}Variable[v]) =$ $mk\text{-}Variable[v]$	Condition-false[4,7]
c	infer $(mk\text{-}Variable[v] \bullet s) = mk\text{-}Variable[v]$	=-trans[3,4]

These proofs are being conducted in LPF [BCJ84], where it is sometimes necessary to show that a term is defined. This leads in this case to line 4, where we establish that the else part of the if has a type. This is easy to discharge, instantiating X to *Variable*. Elsewhere, we shall have to justify explicit assertions of the definedness of formulae, which will be written δf. We can establish line 5 with $d = \{\,\}$, then line 6 with $s = \{\,\}m$ by single rule applications. We must prove that $\{\,\}m$ is a substitution, which we shall do by appeal to an easy lemma.

This is as far as we can go. We are left with a line which we cannot justify, which, as promised, we shall make a hypothesis. The complete proof is

h1	from v: *VarSymbol*	
1	$\{\,\}m$: *Substitution*	$\{\,\}m$:Substitution
2	$(mk\text{-}Variable[v] \bullet \{\,\}m) =$ $(if(v \in dom[\{\,\}m])then(\{\,\}m\ at\ v)else\ mk\text{-}Variable[v])$	$\bullet$ Variable definition (wff)[h1,1]
3	$(mk\text{-}Variable[v]{:}\ Variable)$	Variable formation[h1]
4	$\neg(v \in \{\,\})$	$\{\,\}$ is empty[]
5	$dom[\{\,\}m] = \{\,\}$	dom $\{\,\}m$ defn[]
6	$\neg(v \in dom[\{\,\}m])$	=-subs-left[4,5]
7	$(if(v \in dom[\{\,\}m])then(\{\,\}m\ at\ v)\ else\ mk\text{-}Variable[v]) =$ $mk\text{-}Variable[v]$	Condition-false[3,6]
c	infer $(mk\text{-}Variable[v] \bullet \{\,\}m) = mk\text{-}Variable[v]$	=-trans[2,7]

The resulting rule, which we can now name in a more meaningful way, is

$$\frac{v{:}\ VarSymbol}{mk\text{-}Variable[v] \bullet \{\,\}m = mk\text{-}Variable[v]} \quad \boxed{\text{Identity substitution variable lemma}}$$

It is more specific than the lemma we originally proposed. We were expecting that s would be instantiated, but not that t would be. We cannot complete the original proof using this lemma alone, because we shall not be able to discharge the hypothesis we introduced.

At the start of the proof of the lemma, we made an arbitrary choice in using the • *Variable definition* rule rather than the • *CompoundTerm definition* rule to rewrite $t \bullet s$. If we take the other choice we might hope either to get a suitable lemma for the original proof (in which case we chose wrongly before) or something that we can combine with the previous lemma to complete the proof. The rewriting immediately makes it apparent that the former is not the case, by introducing an instance of t again, and some obvious equality reasoning yields the partial proof

1 s: *Substitution* <Justif>
2 f: *FnSymbol* <Justif>
3 $args$: (*Term**) <Justif>
4 $(mk\text{-}CompoundTerm[f, args] \bullet s) =$
$mk\text{-}CompoundTerm[f, args \bullet s]$
• Compound definition (wff)[1,2,3]
5 $mk\text{-}CompoundTerm[f, args]: CompoundTerm$
CompoundTerm-formation[2,3]
6 $mk\text{-}CompoundTerm[f, args] = mk\text{-}CompoundTerm[f, args]$
=-self-I[5]
13 $(args \bullet s) = args$ <Justif>
14 $mk\text{-}CompoundTerm[f, args \bullet s] = mk\text{-}CompoundTerm[f, args]$
=-subs-left[6,13]
c infer $(mk\text{-}CompoundTerm[f, args] \bullet s) = mk\text{-}CompoundTerm[f, args]$
=-trans[4,14]

(To save space in this and later proofs, we shall show only the new lines at each stage. To make it easier to visualise the entire proof, the line numbers will be those of the completed version.)

Once again, we shall create a lemma

$$\frac{}{args \bullet s = args}$$ identity substitution lemma 2

and attack it through rewriting the application of •. Again, there are two defining rules. The first leads (on making the only antecedent a hypothesis) to the proof

h1 from s: *Substitution*
c infer $([] \bullet s) = []$ • [] definition[h1]

In fact, for this case the lemma is equivalent to the • [ ] *definition* rule. The other leads through some obvious equational reasoning to a partial proof from which no further progress can be made (except by applying the • definition rules again)

1	$t\colon Term$	**<Justif>**
2	$ts\colon (Term^*)$	**<Justif>**
3	$s\colon Substitution$	**<Justif>**
4	$(cons[t, ts] \bullet s) = cons[t \bullet s, ts \bullet s]$	• list definition (wff)[1,2,3]
5	$cons[t, ts]\colon (Term^*)$	cons-form[1,2]
6	$cons[t, ts] = cons[t, ts]$	=-self-I[5]
7	$(t \bullet s) = t$	**<Justif>**
8	$cons[t \bullet s, ts] = cons[t, ts]$	=-subs-left[6,7]
9	$(ts \bullet s) = ts$	**<Justif>**
10	$cons[t \bullet s, ts \bullet s] = cons[t, ts]$	=-subs-left[8,9]
c	infer $(cons[t, ts] \bullet s) = cons[t, ts]$	=-trans[4,10]

We can make these into hypotheses to give the lemma

$$\frac{t\colon Term \quad ts\colon Term^* \quad s\colon Substitution \qquad t \bullet s = t \quad ts \bullet s = ts}{cons[t, ts] \bullet s = cons[t, ts]}\ \boxed{\text{identity substitution list lemma}}$$

How can we use these lemmas to make progress on the proof we suspended? Our aim is to justify in the suspended proof the hypotheses we can not justify in the lemmas. This will require the introduction of some further hypotheses for the list case. The form of the missing hypotheses (the same condition on a sublist of the list in the conclusion) strongly suggests an inductive proof. However, direct use of

$$\frac{\{a\colon A, s\colon A^*, P[s]\} \vdash P[cons[a, s]] \quad P[[\,]]}{\forall x\colon A^* \cdot P[x]}\ \boxed{\text{Sequence induction}}$$

(from which $args \bullet s = args$ could be derived by $\forall$-E) will not justify $t \bullet s = t$. Indeed, until we have proved $t \bullet s = t$ for all t, there is no reason to expect that all sequences of terms are left unchanged by s, which is what *Sequence induction* would establish. Using induction will prove that the property holds for some set of term sequences (which we want to include *args*), but that set does not seem to be the whole type. We can restrict it by introducing a predicate that the lists must satisfy, and in this context it is no surprise that this will be introduced by a metavariable. This idea of quantification over a restricted range is captured by the proof rule

$$\frac{t\colon X \quad Q[t] \quad \forall x\colon X \cdot Q[x] \Rightarrow P[x]}{P[t]}\ \boxed{\forall\text{-cond-E}}$$

Applying this backwards, using sequence induction on the $\forall$, and opening up the implication gives the new lines

7 $Q[args]$ <Justif>
8 $\delta Q[[]]$ <Justif>
9.h1 from $Q[[]]$
9.c infer $([] \bullet s) = []$ <Justif>
10 $Q[[]] \Rightarrow (([] \bullet s) = [])$ $\Rightarrow$-I[8, 9]
11.h1 from $ts: (Term^*)$
11.h2 and $t: Term$
11.h3 and $Q[ts] \Rightarrow ((ts \bullet s) = ts)$
11.1 $\delta Q[cons[t, ts]]$ <Justif>
11.2.h1 from $Q[cons[t, ts]]$
11.2.c infer $(cons[t, ts] \bullet s) = cons[t, ts]$ <Justif>
11.c infer $Q[cons[t, ts]] \Rightarrow ((cons[t, ts] \bullet) = cons[t, ts])$ $\Rightarrow$-I[11.1,11.2]
12 infer $\forall x: Term^* \cdot Q[x] \Rightarrow ((x \bullet s) = x)$ Sequence induction[10,11]
13 $(args \bullet s) = args$ $\forall$-cond-E[3,7,12]

and at this point we can apply the two lemmas to justify lines 9.c and 11.2.c. In the latter case, we create some new lines to justify, one of which follows from the induction hypothesis (as we would hope) under a further assumption.

9.h1 from $Q[[]]$
9.c infer $([] \bullet s) = []$ $\bullet$ [] definition
11.h1 from $ts: (Term^*)$
11.h2 and $t: Term$
11.h3 and $Q[ts] \Rightarrow ((ts \bullet s) = ts)$
11.1 $\delta Q[cons[t, ts]]$ <Justif>
11.2.h1 from $Q[cons[t, ts]]$
11.2.2 $(t \bullet s) = t$ <Justif>
11.2.3 $Q[ts]$ <Justif>
11.2.4 $(ts \bullet s) = ts$ $\Rightarrow$-E-left[11.h3,11.2.3]
11.2.c infer $(cons[t, ts] \bullet s) = cons[t, ts]$
identity substitution list lemma[11.h2,11.h1,1,11.2.2,11.2.4]

Now we can choose Q: the minimum properties it must have are to establish lines 11.2.1 and 11.2.2. Let us then introduce the constant q (with one expression parameter) and defining axioms

$$\frac{}{q[[\,]]}\ \boxed{\text{q []}}$$

$$\frac{t: Term \quad ts: Term^*}{q[cons[t, ts]] = (t \bullet s = t) \wedge q[ts]}\ \boxed{\text{q cons}}$$

which are precisely the axioms that would result from translating the recursive VDM definition

$$q(ts) \;\triangleq\; \textsf{cases } ts \textsf{ of}$$
$$[\,] \rightarrow \textsf{true}$$
$$\textsf{cons}(t', ts') \rightarrow t' \bullet s = t' \wedge q(ts')$$
$$\textsf{end}$$

We can show that $q[ts]$ always has a Boolean value, justifying lines 8 and 11.1. Lines 11.2.2 and 11.2.3 follow from the axiom and $\wedge$-E (left and right). The only remaining obligation is to establish $q[args]$, which must be treated as a hypothesis, giving the lemma

$$\frac{s\colon Substitution \quad f\colon FnSymbol \quad args\colon Term^* \quad q[args]}{mk\text{-}CompoundTerm[f, args] \bullet s = mk\text{-}CompoundTerm[f, args]} \quad \boxed{\text{identity substitution compound lemma}}$$

We now return to the original proof of *identity substitution synthesis*. Once again, we need a way of combining the two lemmas which we have created by rewriting $t \bullet s$ and discharging their hypotheses. We can hope that the induction hypothesis will be useful in this. Since both lemmas cover particular cases, we appear to need a case analysis, and the standard way of introducing a case split is $\vee$-*E*.

1.2	$e1 \vee e2$	<Justif>
1.3.h1	from $e1$	
1.3.c	infer $(t \bullet s) = t$	<Justif>
1.4.h1	from $e2$	
1.4.c	infer $(t \bullet s) = t$	<Justif>
1.c	infer $(t \bullet \{\,\}m) = t$	$\vee$-E[1.2,1.3,1.4]

To apply the lemmas, we must have t of the appropriate form in each case: this takes some equality reasoning to make t equal to some metavariable which can then be matched against the lemma conclusions. The variable case also instantiates s to $\{\,\}m$.

1.3.h1	from $e1$	
1.3.1	$f\colon FnSymbol$	<Justif>
1.3.2	$args\colon (Term^*)$	<Justif>
1.3.3	$q[args]$	<Justif>
1.3.4	$(mk\text{-}CompoundTerm[f, args] \bullet \{\,\}m) = mk\text{-}CompoundTerm[f, args]$	identity substitution compound lemma[1.3.1,1.3.2,1.3.3]
1.3.5	$mk\text{-}CompoundTerm[f, args] = t$	<Justif>
1.3.c	infer $(t \bullet \{\,\}m) = t$	=-subs-right[1.3.4,1.3.5]

1.4.h1	from $e2$	
1.4.1	v: *VarSymbol*	**<Justif>**
1.4.2	$(mk\text{-}Variable[v] \bullet \{\,\}m) = mk\text{-}Variable[v]$	identity substitution variable lemma[1.4.1]
1.4.3	$mk\text{-}Variable[v] = t$	**<Justif>**
1.4.c	infer $(t \bullet \{\,\}m) = t$	=-subs-right[1.4.2,1.4.3]

Lines 1.3.5 and 1.4.3 can be established by appeal to the rules for introducing *mk-* terms: this instantiates the new metavariables f, $args$ and v to $s\text{-}f[t]$, $s\text{-}args[t]$ and $s\text{-}v[t]$ respectively, and introduces a new hypothesis that t is a *CompoundTerm* or *Variable* respectively. These seem like appropriate choices for $e1$ and $e2$, and line 1.2 is now easily justified.

1.1	t: (*CompoundTerm* | *Variable*)	unfolding from 1.h1
1.2	(t: *CompoundTerm*) $\vee$ (t: *Variable*)	|-destr[1.1]
1.3.h1	from t: *CompoundTerm*	
1.3.1	$s\text{-}f[t]$: *FnSymbol*	s-f-formation[1.3.h1]
1.3.2	$s\text{-}args[t]$: $(Term^*)$	s-args-formation[1.3.h1]
1.3.3	$q[s\text{-}args[t]]$	**<Justif>**
1.3.5	$mk\text{-}CompoundTerm[s\text{-}f[t], s\text{-}args[t]] = t$	CompoundTerm-introduction[1.3.h1]
1.3.c	infer $(t \bullet \{\,\}m) = t$	=-subs-right[1.3.4,1.3.5]
1.4.h1	from t: *Variable*	
1.4.1	$s\text{-}v[t]$: *VarSymbol*	s-v-formation[1.4.h1]
1.4.2	$(mk\text{-}Variable[s\text{-}v[t]] \bullet \{\,\}m) = mk\text{-}Variable[s\text{-}v[t]]$	identity substitution variable lemma[1.4.1]
1.4.3	$mk\text{-}Variable[s\text{-}v[t]] = t$	Variable-introduction[1.4.h1]
1.4.c	infer $(t \bullet \{\,\}m) = t$	=-subs-right[1.4.2,1.4.3]

This leaves the justification of line 1.3.3, for which we might expect to use the as yet unused induction hypothesis (by choosing a well-founded ordering $\sqsubset$). This says that under some circumstances, $t' \bullet \{\,\}m = t'$. A little insight into its recursive characterization shows that $q[args]$ is equivalent to $t \bullet s = t$ holding for every element t of $args$. If we formalise (one direction of) this as a lemma

$$\frac{ts\colon Term^* \quad \forall t\colon Term \cdot t \in elems[ts] \;\Rightarrow\; t \bullet s = t}{q[ts]} \;\boxed{\text{q lemma}}$$

then we can use rule resolution followed by unification of its second hypothesis against the induction hypothesis of the proof to complete the proof. We have chosen a particular predicate: a term is smaller than another if it is one of its immediate subterms. This is not transitive, and so is not an order, but its transitive closure is a well-order, and that is enough to justify the induction. (Since syntheses will often produce the one-step relation rather than the closure, this form of Noetherian induction may be more useful than insisting that the relation itself is a well-order). We should of course have formalised the restriction on the relation in the *Noetherian induction* proof rule and now discharge the extra hypothesis in the proof. This has not been done due to some technical difficulties in formulating a definition of "well-ordered" within the logic used for these proofs. Adding $WellOrdered[\sqsubset^+]$ as a hypothesis without defining it would at least have served as a reminder in the proofs.

The completed proof of *Identity substitution* is

1.h1	from t: *Term*	
1.h2	and $\forall t'$: *Term* $\cdot$ $(t' \in elems[s\text{-}args[t]]) \Rightarrow ((t' \bullet \{\}m) = t')$	
1.1	t: (*CompoundTerm* | *Variable*)	unfolding from 1.h1
1.2	(t: *CompoundTerm*) $\vee$ (t: *Variable*)	|-destr[1.1]
1.3.h1	from t: *CompoundTerm*	
1.3.1	$s\text{-}f[t]$: *FnSymbol*	s-f-formation[1.3.h1]
1.3.2	$s\text{-}args[t]$: (*Term**)	s-args-formation[1.3.h1]
1.3.3	$q[s\text{-}args[t]]$	q lemma[1.3.2,1.h2]
1.3.4	$(mk\text{-}CompoundTerm[s\text{-}f[t], s\text{-}args[t]] \bullet \{\}m) = mk\text{-}CompoundTerm[s\text{-}f[t], s\text{-}args[t]]$	identity substitution compound lemma[1.3.1,1.3.2,1.3.3]
1.3.5	$mk\text{-}CompoundTerm[s\text{-}f[t], s\text{-}args[t]] = t$	CompoundTerm-introduction[1.3.h1]
1.3.c	infer $(t \bullet \{\}m) = t$	=-subs-right[1.3.4,1.3.5]
1.4.h1	from t: *Variable*	
1.4.1	$s\text{-}v[t]$: *VarSymbol*	s-v-formation[1.4.h1]
1.4.2	$(mk\text{-}Variable[s\text{-}v[t]] \bullet \{\}m) = mk\text{-}Variable[s\text{-}v[t]]$	identity substitution variable lemma[1.4.1]
1.4.3	$mk\text{-}Variable[s\text{-}v[t]] = t$	Variable-introduction[1.4.h1]
1.4.c	infer $(t \bullet \{\}m) = t$	=-subs-right[1.4.2,1.4.3]
1.c	infer $(t \bullet \{\}m) = t$	$\vee$-E[1.2,1.3,1.4]
c	infer $\forall t$: *Term* $\cdot$ $(t \bullet \{\}m) = t$	Noetherian induction[1]

3 Mechanical support for proof construction

The proofs of the previous section have been carried out using the μral proof assistant [J$^+$91]. This supports a theory store, containing a heirarchy of theories. Each theory contains constants defining its language, which are subdivided into expression constants and type constants; and proof rule schemas defining the properties of some of the constants, perhaps in terms of constants from ancestor theories. Other constants are defined by syntactic equivalence. A constant in μral can represent a function or predicate application by being given parameters, which may be expressions or types. For example, $\wedge$ is a constant in the Propositional Logic theory with two expression parameters (and a pretty-printing rule which says it is to be presented as $[\![e_1]\!] \wedge [\![e_2]\!]$ rather than as $\wedge[[\![e_1]\!], [\![e_2]\!]]$).

The standard assistant comes with theories for propositional and predicate typed LPF and for the standard VDM data structures: integers, tuples, union types, subtypes, and finite sets, maps and sequences. These form the VDM BASE theory. The proper theory of terms and substitutions used here, which inherits the VDM BASE theory, is listed in appendix A.

The proofs have been constructed with the μral justification tool. In its simplest use, an (optional) conclusion line and zero or more hypothesis lines or boxes are selected from the partial proof. (When doing a goal-directed construction, we always select a conclusion and no hypotheses.) A proof rule is also selected, and the justification tool presents the possible instances of the rule that match the selections. When an instance is selected, the tool displays any extra hypotheses that are not already in the proof, and a new conclusion if none was selected at the start. The proof can be searched to see if any of the "new" hypotheses are actually already present. Once the user is happy with the proof step, the new lines and boxes can be added to the proof, where the conclusion is annotated by the proof rule and hypothesis lines used in its derivation.

Because the justification tool provides only substitution of rules, the rule resolution in the proofs constructed here has been performed by hand editing of the metavariables in the proofs to the desired instance, and clearly mechanisation of this would be helpful. The presence of function and predicate metavariables in μral makes the unification problem undecideable. However, Huet's algorithm [Hue75] provides semidecideability of unifiability, with unifiers where they exist generated in a useful order. This algorithm has been implemented in μral and is provided as part of the tactic language. The principal difficulty is likely to be the large number of unifiers for any given proof rule and goal line. Even with the existing justification tool, synthesis proofs can generate too many instances to be conveniently searched, and the extra freedom of unification will make this (unboundedly) worse. Some way of restricting to "expected" instances will be needed. The search for existing lines containing the hypotheses of the rule instance also needs to be extended to a unification.

Once substitutions have been found, there is already support in μral for applying them to the local metavariables of the proof. This is sufficient for conventional proofs of pre-stated rules but, as we have seen, proof construction may also involve modification of the thing being proved by instantiating metavariables and adding hypotheses. No facilities are provided for doing either of these, since they conflict with μral's goal of maintaining a consistent theory store. (Changing the definition of a rule potentially invalidates all the proofs which use it.) This is not a problem during synthesis because we have not yet used the lemmas we are developing. In any case, proofs may be invalidated in the existing μral (after a warning) when rules they depend on are edited manually, so the means of resolving problems is in place and all that is lacking is the means to make changes from inside a proof. We may be able to restore consistency after the instantiation of a metavariable in a proof rule by instantiating a corresponding metavariable in the proof which uses it throughout, without invalidating that proof.

We intend to develop these enhancements to μral and validate them by continuing the synthesis of the unification algorithm.

4 Summary and conclusions

The central idea of this paper is that proofs can be made easier to construct if the decisions to be made at each step of the proof can be made simpler. Our major contribution to this is the use of rule resolution to avoid having to choose not only rules but also their instances. The motivation is that the correct instance may not become apparent until later in the proof. There are many cases in the example proofs here where the amount of lookahead needed to choose the appropriate instance is trivial. We may have an existing line which would immediately justify an instance of a rule hypothesis, as in the proof of $\vee$-*comm* in the introduction and many type assertions in the example; or we may have an instance in mind when we select the rule, as when we rewrite a function application to an instance of its definition. If rule resolution is made as easy to use as the regular justifications of μral, we lose nothing in these common cases, and there are occasional surprises even at this level.

There are other situations where the lifetime of the metavariable is longer and the planning of its value correspondingly more difficult (although, at least with hindsight, we would not argue that it is impossible in the example here). The proof rules *Noetherian induction* and $\forall$-*cond-E* generated particularly long lived metavariables, and represent a deliberate policy of designing proof rules to use metavariables to leave decisions (induction schemes and ranges of quantification here) open until we have the evidence to take them. We believe that more such rules remain to be proposed.

The choice of proof rule remains the critical decision at each step. Clearly, there will be many rules which can have their conclusions unified with a given proof line (including rules like $\vee$-*E* which have a metavariable as a conclusion: these are not uncommon). In practice, we have almost always chosen "obvious" rules with direct relevance to the thing to be proved. This is partly a result of the proof strategy we have adopted: case analysis rules (including structural induction) are not considered until we have developed the cases to be combined and can see what means of combination is appropriate. It also reflects the fact that this, like most syntheses, is not a difficult proof. Some choices, such as which defining rule to use when rewriting a function, turned out to be false choices since all the alternatives had to be considered to complete the proof.

We also have a choice of when to make a line a lemma. The strategy used here is to stop when there is no obvious way onward without repeating a line of reasoning (in which case, we use induction to justify the line by hypothesis instead). However, if we had made $\neg(v \in dom[s])$ a hypothesis in the proof of *identity substitution variable lemma* instead of continuing the proof and instantiating, we should eventually have constructed a proof of the more general theorem that substitutions do not affect terms whose variables are not in their domain. Without perfect planning, we shall sometimes regret decisions, and at that stage the ease of proof construction will depend on how easily pieces of proof can be recycled into new proofs. Subdividing a proof into lemmas is one way of making pieces re-usable, and the one best supported by μral, but the decision to split off a lemma is itself a piece of forward planning. The strategy we have used here is to introduce a lemma at any point where there is more than one proof rule which seems obviously applicable.

Some choice is inevitable in program synthesis, since we are constructing a particular algorithm out of many to implement the specification. Our aim is to limit the choices to, and motivate those choices as, programming decisions.

The longest lived metavariables are those introduced by the statement of the synthesis problem. The standard approach to program synthesis is to prove constructively that there exists some value for each input which satisfies the specification of the operation. (In VDM terms, synthesis is a proof of the implementability proof obligation.)

$$\frac{}{\forall x: X \cdot \exists y: Y \cdot \text{post-}op[x, y]} \boxed{op \text{ implementable}}$$

The restriction to constructive proof ensures that we must establish the existence by exhibiting a value with the property, thus giving a result for an implementation to produce. In a natural deduction setting, this corresponds to using

$$\frac{a: X \quad P[a]}{\exists x: X \cdot P[x]} \boxed{\exists\text{-I}}$$

to introduce a metavariable a to be instantiated. Introducing it explicitly into the initial synthesis problem has several advantages. The main one is that, since the proof must instantiate it (unless all expressions satisfy the condition), we need make no explicit restriction to constructivity in the logic. Nonconstructive proofs can be useful in establishing properties of synthesised values. Using parameterised metavariables also makes the dependence of the result on the input explicit, which allows the proof to synthesise the program rather than the program being extracted from the proof in a separate phase.

There are also advantages when synthesising partial functions. It is not always obvious how to express the precondition algorithmically so that it can be tested, which suggests that we need a way to synthesise it. The specification of the precondition can be taken as the syntactic equivalence $\text{pre-}op[x] \equiv \exists y: Y \cdot \text{post-}op[x, y]$. With this definition, *op-implementable* is (classically) trivial by design, but *f-synthesis* is not. The proof construction will result in a set of proof lines which can be discharged from pre-*op*. Since they also imply the existence of an (explicit) result, they must also imply the precondition and hence are equivalent to it, but they are likely to be in a more algorithmic form. This approach to the synthesis of preconditions is in the style of Z [PST91].

Finally, it is clear that μral (and most other proof support systems) has a restricted view of the inherently exploratory process of proof construction. We have sketched some improvements to μral that would be of great help in the proposed style of proof construction. We expect that other styles would suggest further improvements.

A The theory of terms and substitutions

A.1 Terms

$$Term \equiv Variable \mid CompoundTerm$$

$$\frac{f\colon FnSymbol \quad args\colon Term^*}{mk\text{-}CompoundTerm[f, args]\colon CompoundTerm}\ \boxed{\text{CompoundTerm-formation}}$$

$$\frac{t\colon CompoundTerm}{mk\text{-}CompoundTerm[s\text{-}f[t], s\text{-}args[t]] = t}\ \boxed{\text{CompoundTerm-introduction}}$$

$$\frac{mk\text{-}CompoundTerm[f, args]\colon CompoundTerm}{s\text{-}args[mk\text{-}CompoundTerm[f, args]] = args}\ \boxed{\text{s-args-defn}}$$

$$\frac{mk\text{-}CompoundTerm[f, args]\colon CompoundTerm}{s\text{-}f[mk\text{-}CompoundTerm[f, args]] = f}\ \boxed{\text{s-f-defn}}$$

$$\frac{t\colon CompoundTerm}{s\text{-}args[t]\colon Term^*}\ \boxed{\text{s-args-formation}} \qquad \frac{t\colon CompoundTerm}{s\text{-}f[t]\colon FnSymbol}\ \boxed{\text{s-f-formation}}$$

$$\frac{v\colon VarSymbol}{mk\text{-}Variable[v]\colon Variable}\ \boxed{\text{Variable-formation}}$$

$$\frac{t\colon Variable}{mk\text{-}Variable[s\text{-}v[t]] = t}\ \boxed{\text{Variable-introduction}}$$

$$\frac{mk\text{-}Variable[v]\colon Variable}{s\text{-}v[mk\text{-}Variable[v]] = v}\ \boxed{\text{s-v-defn}} \qquad \frac{t\colon Variable}{s\text{-}v[t]\colon VarSymbol}\ \boxed{\text{s-v-formation}}$$

A.2 Substitutions

$$Substitution \equiv \langle m\colon map[VarSymbol, Term].inv\text{-}Substitution[m]\rangle$$

$$\frac{s\colon map[VarSymbol, Term]}{\begin{array}{l} inv\text{-}Substitution[s] = \\ \forall v\colon VarSymbol \cdot v \in dom[s] \Rightarrow \neg(s\ at\ v = mk\text{-}Variable[v]) \end{array}}\ \boxed{\text{inv-Substitution defn (wff)}}$$

A.3 Applying substitutions

$$\frac{s\colon Substitution \quad f\colon FnSymbol \quad args\colon Term^*}{\begin{array}{c} mk\text{-}CompoundTerm[f, args] \bullet s = \\ mk\text{-}CompoundTerm[f, args \bullet s] \end{array}}\ \boxed{\text{• CompoundTerm definition (wff)}}$$

$$\frac{s\colon Substitution \quad v\colon VarSymbol}{\begin{array}{l} mk\text{-}Variable[v] \bullet s = \\ \quad if\ v \in dom[s]\ then\ s\ at\ v\ else\ mk\text{-}Variable[v] \end{array}}\ \boxed{\text{• Variable definition (wff)}}$$

$$\frac{s\colon Substitution}{[\,] \bullet s = [\,]}\ \boxed{\bullet\ \{\,\}m\ \text{definition}}$$

$$\frac{t\colon Term \quad ts\colon Term^* \quad s\colon Substitution}{cons[t, ts] \bullet s = cons[t \bullet s, ts \bullet s]}\ \boxed{\text{• list definition (wff)}}$$

References

[BCJ84] H. A. Barringer, J. H. Cheng, and C. B. Jones. A logic covering undefinedness in program proofs. *Acta Informatica*, 21:251–269, 1984.

[BSH90] A. Bundy, A. Smaill, and J. Hesketh. Turning eureka steps into calculations in automatic program synthesis. In S.L.H. Clarke, editor, *Proceedings of UK IT 90*, pages 221–6, 1990.

[Fit90] J. S. Fitzgerald. Unification: specification and development. In *Case Studies in Systematic Software Development*, pages 127–161. Prentice-Hall International, 1990.

[Hue75] G. Huet. A unification algorithm for typed lambda calculus. *Theoretical Computer Science*, 1:27–57, 1975.

[J+91] C. B. Jones et al. *mural: A Formal Development Support System.* Springer-Verlag, 1991.

[Jon90] C. B. Jones. *Systematic Software Development Using VDM.* Prentice-Hall International, 2nd edition, 1990.

[MW80] Z. Manna and R. Waldinger. A deductive approach to program synthesis. *ACM Transactions on Programming Languages and Systems*, 2:90–121, 1980.

[MW81] Z. Manna and R. Waldinger. Deductive synthesis of the unification algorithm. *Science of Computer Programming*, 1:5–48, 1981.

[Pau85] L. C. Paulson. Verifying the unification algorithm in LCF. *Science of Computer Programming*, 5:143–170, 1985.

[PST91] B. Potter, J. Sinclair, and D. Till. *An Introduction to Formal Specification and Z.* Prentice-Hall International, 1991.

[Vad90] S. Vadera. Building a theory of unification. In *Case Studies in Systematic Software Development*, pages 163–193. Prentice-Hall International, 1990.

A Tactic Driven Refinement Tool

Lindsay Groves
Victoria University of Wellington
Wellington, New Zealand

Raymond Nickson
Victoria University of Wellington
Wellington, New Zealand

Mark Utting
University of New South Wales
Sydney, Australia

Abstract

This paper describes a refinement tool we are developing, with special emphasis on the use of tactics. The operation of the tool is illustrated by stepping through the derivation of a selection sort algorithm. Several aspects of the tool and its implementation are then discussed in more detail, stressing the way in which the tool assists the user in deriving programs using the refinement calculus.

1 Introduction

The advent of the refinement calculus (e.g. [Back, 1988], [Morgan, 1990], and [Morris, 1987]) has taken us a step closer to the goal of developing programs along with proofs of their correctness (e.g. [Dijkstra, 1968], [Floyd, 1971]). Applying the refinement calculus to problems of any size, however, requires a large amount of formula manipulation which is both tedious and error prone. Revising a derivation to correct an earlier error (e.g. a loop invariant that was not strong enough), or to solve a slightly different problem, is a particularly unwelcome task. This situation suggests the need for software tools to support the use of the refinement calculus, just as proof editors have been developed to support the use of various logical calculi (e.g. [Constable *et al.*, 1986], [Paulson, 1987], [Ritchie and Taylor, 1988]).

This paper describes a tool we are developing to assist a user deriving programs using the refinement calculus. Our primary goal in designing this tool is to provide a basis for investigating the formal derivation of programs from specifications. We are interested in seeing just how much of the development process can reasonably and usefully be automated. In particular, we are interested in developing strategies for program development using the refinement calculus, and in finding ways of encoding these strategies so that they can be reused[1]. We achieve this using *tactics* comparable to those used in proof editors.

The specification and programming constructs supported by our tool are basically those described in the first 11 chapters of [Morgan, 1990], i.e. we support the usual language of guarded commands (with iteration but, as yet, no procedures), along with local blocks (**var**), types and invariants, and logical

[1] We believe that reusing software development strategies is ultimately at least as promising as reusing components.

constants (**con**), and have limited support for data refinement. The tool uses a user-assisted, theory-driven rewriter to discharge proof obligations. The tool is implemented in SICStus Prolog [Carlsson and Widén, 1988] and runs under the X Window System [Scheifler and Gettys, 1986], using the XWIP X interface for Prolog [Kim, 1989].

The aim of this paper is to discuss some of the more interesting aspects of our tool, showing how the tool assists the user in deriving programs using the refinement calculus. To illustrate a number of basic features of the tool and the general style of use, we begin by describing the derivation of a selection sort algorithm (Section 2). We then discuss some aspects of the tool in more detail, specifically how it handles formula manipulation (Section 3), the way refinements are recorded and how this information is used to navigate the recorded program derivation and rerun derivations (Section 4), and the use of tactics (Section 5). We conclude with a brief comparison with related systems, and our plans for further development of the tool.

2 Deriving selection sort

To illustrate some basic features of our refinement tool, we will describe several of the steps involved in refining a sort specification into a selection sort, emphasising the way the user interacts with the refinement tool. We also show how the tool can be used to obtain a printed record of refinement steps. All refinements at this stage are done using primitive refinement rules (essentially those described in [Morgan and Robinson, 1987], with a few additions); we discuss the use of more powerful rules and tactics in Section 5. Selection sort is one of the simplest sort algorithms to derive formally, but is large enough to illustrate various problems and alternatives that arise when using a tool to support refinement.

The refinement tool is largely mouse and menu driven. After invoking the tool, the user is presented with a window containing several buttons corresponding to pop-up menus and a program display area. Given that we already have the sort specification in a file, we use the mouse to select the *Load* command in the *Programs* menu. This pops up a dialogue box and we enter the name of the file containing the specification[2]. The tool loads the specification and displays it, as shown in Figure 1.

This specification is fairly concise because we have an underlying theory of sequences that defines permutations, ascending sequences etc. This theory also defines subsequences and orderings on subsequences, and provides rewrite rules for reasoning about ordering on sequences, which are used later in the derivation. Each stored specification declares the theories that it requires; they are then loaded automatically when the specification is loaded. Additionally, if a theory is loaded manually during a derivation, that fact is recorded in the stored derivation so it can be reloaded if the derivation is run again[3].

---

[2] We could also have entered the specification directly, using the *Load from Keyboard* command and later saved the specification thus entered in a file.

[3] We are considering promoting these "uses" declarations to be part of the specification/programming language. Then we shall require additional refinement rules to add such declarations, and to remove them when they are no longer required, in much the same way that local constants, definitions and invariants are added and eliminated.

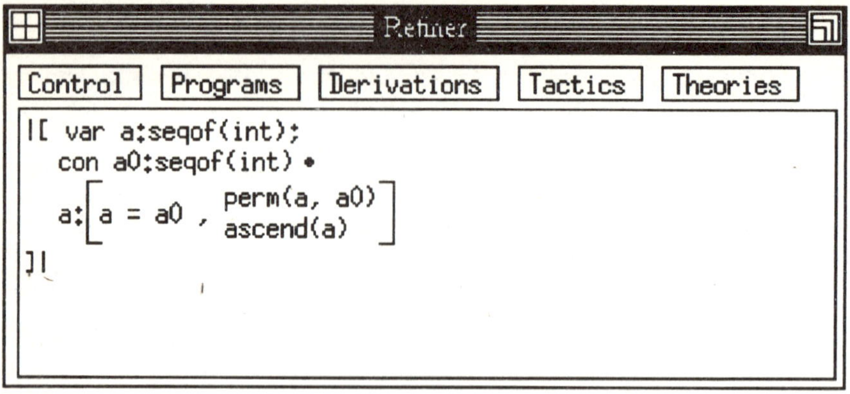

Figure 1: Screen dump showing initial specification

The program display in Figure 1 is produced by a pretty printer, which indents programs and predicates automatically, breaks long lines at their outermost operators, and stacks conjunctive predicates in assertions. The appearance of user-defined predicates and operators can be specified within the theory that defines them. The pretty printer forms an integral part of the refinement tool, and can produce both X windows displays and LaTeX output. All program and refinement step examples in this section were generated automatically using the tool.

2.1 Algorithmic refinement

The selection sort algorithm requires a loop with a local variable that partitions the array into a sorted and an unsorted part, so our first task is to introduce a local variable. Clicking the mouse on the initial specification statement brings up the left-hand menu in Figure 2. Selecting *Refine* from this menu brings up the right-hand menu in Figure 2 which contains a list of primitive rules that may be applied to the specification statement. After selecting the *Introduce New Local Variables* rule, we are prompted to enter a list of variable names, for which we enter n. The result of this refinement step is then displayed:

$$
\begin{array}{l}
[\![\ \mathbf{var}\ a : seqof(int); \\
\quad \mathbf{con}\ a0 : seqof(int) \bullet \\
\qquad [\![\ \mathbf{var}\ n \bullet \\
\qquad\quad \begin{matrix} n \\ a \end{matrix} : \left[\ a = a0 \ , \ \begin{matrix} perm(a,\ a0) \\ ascend(a) \end{matrix} \ \right] \\
\qquad]\!] \\
]\!]
\end{array}
$$

Next we need to split the specification statement into two further specification statements. The first will be refined into code to initialise the variables used

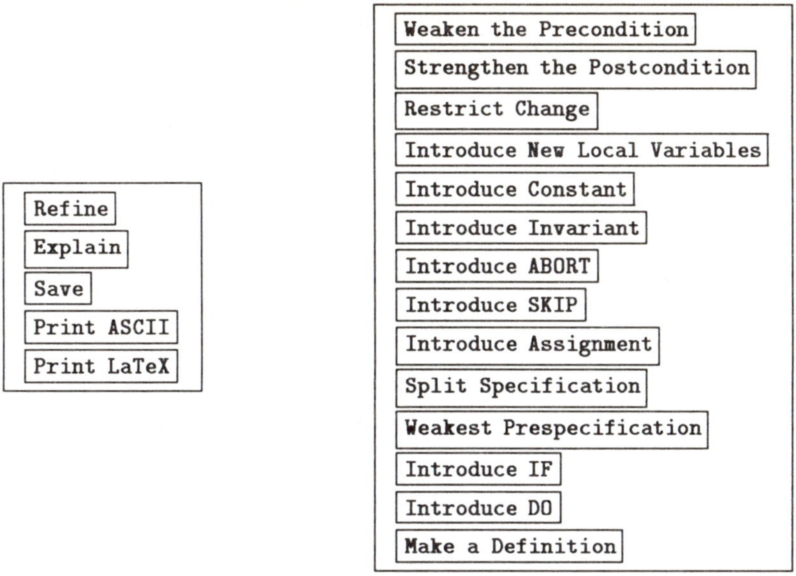

Figure 2: Specification statement menus

in the loop, the second will be refined to the loop, the intermediate assertion will be the loop invariant. The choice of loop invariant is a crucial design decision, since it largely determines the kind of algorithm we end up with. In order to obtain a selection sort, we construct the loop invariant from the postcondition by adding a suitable constraint on the range of n, $n \in 0 \,..\, \#a$ ($\#a$ is the length of a), and replacing $ascend(a)$ by $ascend(a[0:n]) \wedge a[0:n] \leq a[n:\#a]$. In our theory of sequences, the subsequence denoted by $a[i:j]$ includes the lower bound i, but excludes the upper bound j. The sequence comparison $a \leq b$ is true for sequences a and b iff all elements in a are less than or equal to all elements in b. To perform this step we select the *Split Specification* rule as above, which requires an intermediate assertion. The tool creates a structure editor window containing the postcondition of the specification being split, and we edit it to produce the assertion:

$$perm(a, a0) \wedge ascend(a[0:n]) \wedge n \in 0 \,..\, \#a \wedge a[0:n] \leq a[n:\#a]$$

Rather than showing the resulting program in full again, we will illustrate another feature of the tool. Clicking on either of the new specification statements, we get a menu which includes two new commands, *Elide* and *Undo*. Selecting *Undo* will simply undo the last refinement step, taking us back to the previous program (this can be done repeatedly until we get back to the original specification). We can then proceed to refine it again, perhaps in a different way. Selecting *Elide* will replace the two specification statements by the specification from which they were obtained. The result *looks* the same as if we had undone the last refinement step, but the refinement is still there; we can then select *Expand* to see the refined version again. This facility allows us to hide away part of the program that we are not currently interested in[4]. As well as the *Expand* command, there is an *Expand and Print* command which produces a LaTeX description of this refinement step. If we elide the sequential statement just introduced and then select *Expand and Print*, the following output is obtained:

$$\begin{array}{l} n \\ a \end{array} : \left[a = a0 \;,\; \begin{array}{l} perm(a,\, a0) \\ ascend(a) \end{array} \right]$$

$$\sqsubseteq \text{ split spec} \left(\begin{array}{l} perm(a,\, a0) \\ ascend(a[0:n]) \\ n \in 0\,..\,\#a \\ a[0:n] \le a[n:\#a] \end{array} \right)$$

$$\begin{array}{l} n \\ a \end{array} : \left[a = a0 \;,\; \begin{array}{l} perm(a,\, a0) \\ ascend(a[0:n]) \\ n \in 0\,..\,\#a \\ a[0:n] \le a[n:\#a] \end{array} \right] ;$$

$$\begin{array}{l} n \\ a \end{array} : \left[\begin{array}{l} perm(a,\, a0) \\ ascend(a[0:n]) \\ n \in 0\,..\,\#a \\ a[0:n] \le a[n:\#a] \end{array} \;,\; \begin{array}{l} perm(a,\, a0) \\ ascend(a) \end{array} \right]$$

The first of these specification statements can now be refined to code. We select the *Introduce Assignment* rule and specify $n := 0$ as the assignment statement to be used. This refinement step requires the following side condition to be proved:

$$\left(\begin{array}{l} a \in seqof(int) \\ a0 \in seqof(int) \\ a = a0 \end{array} \right) \Rightarrow \left(\begin{array}{l} perm(a,\, a0) \\ ascend(a[0:0]) \\ 0 \in 0\,..\,\#a \\ a[0:0] \le a[0:\#a] \end{array} \right)$$

The refinement tool proves this automatically by simplification, using rewriting rules from the sequence and arithmetic theories:

- $perm(a, a0)$ is implied by $a = a0$, since the sequence theory has an axiom that identical sequences are permutations;
- $ascend(a[0:0])$ rewrites to **true**, since $a[0:0]$ is an empty sequence and an empty sequence is trivially ascending;
- $0 \in 0\,..\,\#a$ is rewritten to $0 \le 0 \land 0 \le \#a$. The first conjunct reduces to **true** by a rule in the arithmetic theory, and the second because '#s is always non-negative' is an axiom in the sequence theory; and
- $a[0:0] \le a[0:\#a]$ rewrites to **true** since $\le$ for sequences is trivially true by definition if one of its arguments is the empty sequence.

---

[4] *Undo* and *Elide* can be applied to any part of the program, so a whole sequence of steps can be undone or elided. In the latter case, the steps can then be expanded again one at a time, allowing a derivation to be illustrated as if it were being done again.

Next we need to refine the second specification statement to a loop. Before doing this, however, we observe that two conjuncts of the loop invariant ($perm(a,\ a0)$ and $n \in 0\,..\,\#a$) will be preserved throughout the body of the loop, so we can move them to a *local invariant*. Local invariants [Morgan, 1989] generalize the usual type declarations in programming languages and help to reduce the size of subsequent specification statements. Unlike a loop invariant, which need only be true before and after each execution of a loop body, a local invariant must be true at *every* point within the block. Using the *Introduce Invariant* rule and printing the refinement step as described above, we obtain:

$$\begin{array}{l} n \\ a \end{array} : \left[\begin{array}{l} perm(a,\ a0) \\ ascend(a[0:n]) \\ n \in 0\,..\,\#a \\ a[0:n] \le a[n:\#a] \end{array} ,\quad \begin{array}{l} perm(a,\ a0) \\ ascend(a) \end{array} \right]$$

$$\sqsubseteq \quad \text{intro inv}\begin{pmatrix} perm(a,\ a0) \\ n \in 0\,..\,\#a \end{pmatrix}$$

$$\begin{array}{l} [\![\, \mathbf{inv}\ perm(a,\ a0) \wedge n \in 0\,..\,\#a \bullet \\ \quad n, a : \left[\begin{array}{l} ascend(a[0:n]) \\ a[0:n] \le a[n:\#a] \end{array} ,\quad ascend(a) \right] \\ ]\!] \end{array}$$

We are now ready to introduce the loop itself, using the *Introduce DO* rule. We enter the guard ($n \neq \#a$), the loop invariant ($ascend(a[0:n]) \wedge a[0:n] \le a[n:\#a]$[5]), and the variant expression ($\#a - n$). We also need a name ($var0$) for the initial value of the variant, so the postcondition can require the variant to decrease. The *Introduce DO* rule will declare this for us by adding a **con** declaration inside its body[6]. Figure 3 shows the resulting program.

Most of the remainder of the derivation proceeds without offering much further insight into the operation of the tool, so we do not describe it in the same level of detail as the above.

First we make progress in the loop by introducing the assignment $n := n+1$, which will reduce the variant. This time, we use the *Weakest Prespecification* rule, so the tool calculates the weakest precondition for $n := n + 1$, and we avoid having to manually calculate and type the intermediate assertion.

Next we introduce an inner loop (with counter i) to find the position ($small$) of the smallest element in $a[n:\#a]$. As before, we also get a **con** declaration for the logical constant ($var1$) that holds the initial value of the variant. The body contains an assignment to update i and an **if** statement that we introduce with the *Introduce IF* rule, supplying the guards.

Now we want to swap $a[small]$ with $a[n]$. To do this, we use the *update* operator defined in our theory of sequences, which takes a sequence and a list of substitutions each of the form $index := value$, and returns an updated sequence.

[5] The other conjuncts of the loop invariant ($perm(a,\ a0)$ and $n \in 0\,..\,\#a$) are already in the local invariant, so we do not need to repeat them. If we do repeat them, they will be simplified away.

[6] This is how the rule in [Morgan, 1990] works, though there the **con** is left implicit; we are somewhat unhappy with a primitive rule that introduces both constructs at once, but for now see no alternative.

$$
\begin{array}{l}
[\![\,\mathbf{var}\ a : seqof(int);\\
\quad \mathbf{con}\ a0 : seqof(int) \bullet\\
\quad\quad [\![\,\mathbf{var}\ n \bullet\\
\quad\quad\quad n := 0;\\
\quad\quad\quad [\![\,\mathbf{inv}\ perm(a,\ a0) \wedge n \in 0\,..\,\#a \bullet\\
\quad\quad\quad\quad \mathbf{do}\ n \neq \#a \rightarrow\\
\quad\quad\quad\quad\quad [\![\,\mathbf{con}\ var0 \bullet\\
\quad\quad\quad\quad\quad\quad \begin{array}{l} n \\ a \end{array} : \left[\begin{array}{ll} n \neq \#a & ascend(a[0:n]) \\ \#a - n = var0 & a[0:n] \leq a[n:\#a] \\ ascend(a[0:n]) & 0 \leq \#a - n \\ a[0:n] \leq a[n:\#a] & \#a - n < var0 \end{array} \right]\\
\quad\quad\quad\quad\quad]\!]\\
\quad\quad\quad\quad \mathbf{od}\\
\quad\quad\quad]\!]\\
\quad\quad]\!]\\
]\!]
\end{array}
$$

Figure 3: Outer loop of sort program

We use *Introduce Assignment* once again to introduce $a := update(a, [n := a[small], small := a[n]])$, and the tool discharges the necessary proof successfully.

The final step required to turn this into code is to eliminate the local invariant and the **con** declarations. To remove the invariant, we distribute it inwards through sequence, **if**, **do** and declarations, and prove that each assignment statement maintains the appropriate condition. There is a refinement rule for each of these operations. To eliminate **con** declarations, we use a rule that simply removes the declaration if the declared logical constant does not appear in the block. This applies here, since we have removed all references to $a0$, $var0$ and $var1$ with our earlier refinements. The resulting program is shown in Figure 4.

2.2 Data refinement

We make no presumptions about what data type operations are allowed in code. The derivation above uses the data type constructor *seqof*, whose properties are defined in our theory of sequences. If our target programming language does not support sequences directly, we will have to data refine the program in Figure 4, perhaps introducing concrete variables b (an array of integers) and l (an integer, giving the length of a)[7].

[7] We ignore the problem of how big the array b should be. Declaring a as a variable at the top of the specification (and all refinements thereof) is simply a convenience; if we take it literally, then the specification as a whole can be refined by **skip**. The intention is that a is a parameter to the abstract program, and b and l are parameters to the concrete

```
[[var a : seqof(int) •
    [[var n •
        n := 0;
        do n ≠ #a →
            [[var small ;
              var i •
                small, i := n, n + 1;
                do i ≠ #a →
                    if a[i] ≤ a[small] →
                        small := i
                    [] a[i] ≥ a[small] →
                        skip
                    fi;
                    i := i + 1
                od
            ]];
            a := update(a, [n := a[small], small := a[n]]);
            n := n + 1
        od
    ]]
]]
```

Figure 4: The completed program

We do this by applying the refinement rule *Data Refine Block* to the entire program. This rule is just like any other; it is applied to a program statement and changes it to another program statement that is an (algorithmic) refinement of it. The data refinement rule applies *only* to blocks that declare variables, however. Upon selecting this rule, we are asked to specify the abstract variables to be removed (a, in this case), the concrete variables that will replace them (b and l), and the coupling invariant $l = \#a \wedge (\forall j \in 0\,..\,\#a \bullet a[j] = b[j])$ that defines the relationship between abstract and concrete[8]. The tool will then calculate the result of the above refinement, using the method described in [Morgan and Gardiner, 1990].

This refinement rule breaks the spirit of the tool somewhat, since we have generally tried to keep the rules simple, and this rule requires the data refinement to percolate right through the structure of the block. We are considering how data refinement might be incorporated more comfortably into the tool. One approach is to introduce individual data refinement rules, each of which performs data refinement on a single language construct. These rules need to be parameterized by the lists of abstract and concrete variables, and by the

program. Many real programming languages allow arrays to be used as formal parameters to procedures without specifying the size of the arrays.

[8] Note that the indexing operator (_[_]) is overloaded, being used for indexing both sequences and arrays.

abstraction invariant. Unlike the current data refinement rule that operates on a block, the individual rules do not represent algorithmic refinements, so they would have to be applied in a more controlled context[9].

3 Formula manipulation

Program derivation offers many opportunities for a tool to assist with formula manipulation. Many refinement rules have side-conditions that must be checked before the rule can be applied. Some rules also require us to calculate the result of their application; often the results of such calculations can be simplified to good effect before showing them to the user.

Our refinement tool incorporates a theory-based rewrite system for formula manipulation. A theory is a collection of related predicates and operators, together with the rewrite rules that apply to them. Each rewrite rule defines a collection of equivalences, and if necessary the conditions under which the equivalences hold.

3.1 Simplifying formulas

After applying a refinement rule, the resulting specifications frequently contain predicates that are trivially true or can easily be simplified significantly. This occurs in the derivation in Section 2 with the introduction of the invariant. The refinement rule that introduces an invariant does not itself remove the invariant from the pre- and postcondition, since the invariant may not explicitly occur there. Rather, the invariant is introduced, and then the rewriter is invoked, as it always is after a refinement. When rewriting assertions the rewriter considers the *context*, which includes local definitions in scope (Section 3.2) and local invariants. In a context that includes $perm(a, a0)$ as an invariant, that will always simplify to **true**, and if it occurs as a conjunct, the rewriter eliminates it. This means that predicates that are trivially implied by the context are automatically removed from specification statements, which often makes the resulting specifications easier to comprehend.

To fulfil this rôle, The rewriter needs to be closely integrated with the refinement tool. Trivial simplifications should be carried out before the user sees the predicates. However, the rewriter must not attempt too much simplification, or simplification at an inappropriate time. Even obvious tautologies, such as $x \leq a \vee x \geq a$, should not be removed automatically, since the user may have introduced them deliberately — perhaps as a preliminary step to building an if statement. In its rôle as an automatic simplifier, the rewriter will only perform rewrites that make the specification more readable. It achieves this by restricting its rule base to a set of rules that the theory writer has identified as 'automatic' simplification rules.

A second function of the rewriter is to perform user-triggered rewrites. Sometimes it is useful to represent equivalences that are not suitable for automatic rewriting. For example, it might be useful to be able to expand an instance of $ascend(s[l : h])$ to its definition, $(\forall i \in l \,..\, h - 1 \bullet s[i] \leq s[i + 1])$,

[9] A high-level rule could then be provided (using an adaptation of the tactic mechanism of section 5) that applies the individual rules to the statements within a block in a way that guarantees algorithmic refinement of the block as a whole.

but it is certainly not desirable to always expand it in this way. Such rewrites are undertaken by 'user' simplification rules; they will only be applied when requested by the user. User rewrite rules have names. When the user selects an expression and requests a rewrite, the system will present a menu of named rules whose left-hand sides match the expression. If the user selects one of these rules, the rule is applied, just as a refinement rule is applied when refining a statement. It is the responsibility of the theory writer to ensure that any rules in a theory preserve equivalence, just as it is the responsibility of the programmer adding refinement rules to the system to ensure that they really represent refinements.

The third use to which we put the simplifier is as a theorem prover. Often all or part of the side-condition of a refinement or rewrite rule can be expressed as an assertion. For example, the *Introduce SKIP* rule applies if $pre \Rightarrow post$ can be proved. Other side-conditions are expressed outside the assertion language, for example 'v does not occur free in $post$'. When side-conditions are assertions, we simply pass the condition to the simplifier; if it can be simplified to **true** it is considered discharged, otherwise the user is asked to vouch for its validity. This rôle for the simplifier is much less closely coupled with the tool than the other two; in fact, the task could usefully be performed by a separate special-purpose theorem proving engine. Our intention, though, is for the tool itself to be that engine, as described above; as well as editing program derivations, we can edit logic proofs.

3.2 Abstraction mechanisms

An important technique for making specifications readable is to define high level predicates and other operators that relate closely to the problem being specified. Where the definitions are expected to be useful in more than one problem, it makes sense to include them in a theory, like the theory of sequences used in Section 2. Sometimes, though, it is useful to introduce a definition that will only be used in a localized piece of a derivation. A *local definition* introduces a name for a formula and may take parameters. The scope of a local definition is limited to a single block of the program, so the body of the definition may contain free references to program variables that are global to that block. For example, in the selection sort derivation, we could have introduced the local definition $sorted\_upto(N) \mathrel{\widehat{=}} ascend(a[0:N])$, which would have simplified several of the assertions used in the derivation.

When definitions are introduced by the user, additional named user rewrite rules become applicable to appropriate expressions within the scope of the definition; these allow the user to request folding and unfolding of definitions. Instances of locally defined predicates and operators in expressions will not be expanded unless explicitly requested.

4 Program derivation trees

Central to the operation of our refinement tool is a data structure, which we call a program derivation tree, that records a complete history of the derivation of the current program. It is used to generate the display of the current program, to allow the user to alter the way in which the current program is displayed, to undo refinement and rewrite steps, and to replay all or part of the derivation. Indeed, the tool is based on the view that the user is editing a program derivation, rather than manipulating a program[10]. In this section we discuss the structure of a program derivation tree and show how it supports these various features of the tool.

4.1 Recording refinements

For any program being derived, the derivation tree maintains a complete history of the derivation at any stage. The current program is not stored explicitly — it is implicit in the derivation tree.

The derivation tree uses a uniform representation for assertions, for program statements and expressions, and for refinements. This representation is designed to allow easy manipulation of all these objects with a consistent interface.

Each statement type, logical connective, functor and predicate used in programs, expressions and assertions is represented as a triple (a Prolog term), identifying:

- the sort of object represented, e.g. 'sequence statement', 'quantifier', 'associative operator', etc.,

- the *fixed* components of the object, that is, those that are not subject to individual refinement or other manipulation, e.g. the list of variable names in an assignment statement, or the name of the quantifier or operator itself in an assertion or expression, and

- the *non-fixed* components of the object, e.g. the arguments of a logical connective, the substatements of a sequential composition, or the expressions on the right-hand side of an assignment.

An object that has been edited (either a statement that has been refined or an assertion or expression that has been rewritten) has the editing operation represented explicitly. Thus, a refinement step is represented by a structure containing the original statement (initial part) and the result of refinement (final part), together with the refinement rule used and any data supplied to it, and any proof obligation arising from the refinement that the tool could not trivially discharge[11].

If we think of the representation of a program as a tree with component edges pointing downwards, refinements can be thought of as horizontal edges representing successive versions of a subtree. In this way we can store many different versions of the tree, yet share their common components. The horizontal edges in our derivation trees are similar to horizontal lines in Back's

---

[10] We could equally well choose to display something other than the current program. We are currently working on a graphical display of the refinement tree itself using diagrams like Back's Refinement Diagrams [Back, 1991], with facilities to control the portion and level of detail of the derivation that is displayed.

[11] We do not actually store proof obligations yet. When we do, we intend to use the tool itself to help discharge those obligations; each refinement step or non-trivial rewrite will have a proof obligation stored with it, and that obligation is only considered discharged if it represents a chain of rewrites terminating in the constant **true**. A derivation can only be considered valid if all its proof obligations are discharged.

refinement diagrams [Back, 1991]; however, we do not currently represent alternative refinements.

This representation only orders transformations that have been applied to a particular part of the program, rather than recording the precise sequence in which transformations were performed. This means that we can elide or undo transformations of one part of the program quite independently of unrelated transformations elsewhere, irrespective of the order in which they were actually performed.

4.2 Navigating the derivation tree

The normal display presented to the user is a single window showing the current program, obtained by collecting the leaves of the derivation. We currently do not display rules, data or proof obligations, though we are considering the best way to do this.

The user is given a simple way of navigating around the derivation tree, either to peruse the derivation itself, to hide parts of the derivation that are not of immediate interest, or to discard parts of it that are incorrect. When the user points (by depressing the mouse button) at a position in the displayed program, the tool finds the node in the derivation tree corresponding to the smallest program construct containing that position (this may be a single identifier, an expression, statement, compound statement, block, etc.) and highlights that structure. Moving the mouse whilst holding the button down will alter the portion of the program (tree) selected, which is reflected in the highlighting. After selecting a portion of the program in this way, selecting *Elide* from the resulting menu, causes the initial part of the refinement step that produced that construct to be displayed, rather than the final part. Similarly selecting *Expand* causes the final part to be displayed again. Selecting *Undo* causes the final part to be discarded, replacing the refinement step by its initial part (the final part is saved elsewhere for possible later reapplication). The user can also elide away the refinement, and then *Cut* off the subtree rooted at that position.

The mechanism we have just described also applies to rewriting steps. Each non-trivial rewrite step (i.e. each rewrite step that was not performed automatically) is also represented in the derivation tree, so they can be elided and expanded or undone in the same way. Rewrite rules are named, and the user can apply a rewrite in exactly the same manner as applying a refinement step.

4.3 Rerunning derivations

An important facility in a refinement tool is the ability to rerun a sequence of refinement steps on a modified specification. We may wish to rerun a complete derivation in order to derive a program for a problem which is similar to one we have already solved, or because we omitted part of the specification. Alternatively, we may wish to rerun only part of the derivation, for example, because we discover that a loop invariant was too weak, or because we realise we should have introduced a local variable, constant, definition or invariant. To address this need, we have a very simple mechanism that steps through a stored derivation, attempting to apply each refinement step at precisely the same place it was applied in the original. At each step, the user is consulted to determine whether the rule should be applied as before, applied with modified arguments, or whether a different refinement or rewrite should be applied.

To rerun part of a derivation, the user can use the *Elide* command to hide the erroneous refinement, save the derivation subtree rooted at the incorrect step, cut away the subtree, redo the erroneous step or add the omitted step, then rerun the saved refinements as described above.

5 Tactics

Performing program derivations using only primitive refinement rules, as we did in Section 2, is rather like programming in machine language. Having decided to introduce a loop, we then had to do several steps before doing so. We would need essentially the same steps for any counted loop, so it would be preferable to be able to do this with one command. Situations like this are very common in program refinement; being able to take advantage of them is important in making a refinement tool usable. An important goal of our research is to investigate the strategies used in performing refinements, with a view to understanding what is involved in the reuse of program derivations.

In our refinement tool, we allow a sequence of refinement steps to be packaged as a *tactic*. A tactic is like a stored derivation; but it is more general in that it can take parameters, can interact with the user, make calculations based on parts of the subject statement or other data supplied to it, and can branch. Tactics thus allow a greater degree of abstraction.

Our tactic language is essentially a programming language itself, whose primitives are refinement rules. As our tool is implemented in Prolog, the tactic language is also embedded in Prolog and we make extensive use of Prolog's capabilities in representing and applying primitive rules and tactics. Prolog is used directly in a computation rôle within tactics, where we make extensive use of user-defined predicates.

Since tactics are built up from primitive refinement rules, we begin by describing the representation and application of primitive refinement rules.

5.1 Primitive refinement rules

Each primitive refinement rule has the following components:

- a *short name*, used to identify the rule within the system and in printed refinements;
- a *long name*, used to identify the rule to the user, for example, in menus;
- a *subject pattern* which describes the kind of structure the rule can be applied to;
- a *result pattern* which describes the result of the rule;
- a list of parameters for which values must be obtained before the rule can be applied (these are represented as Prolog variables);
- a Prolog goal, known as the *getparms goal* (for want of a better name), to be used in obtaining parameter values; and

- a *body*, a Prolog goal used to check any side condition on the rule and compute any additional values required to complete the instantiation of the result pattern.

When the user selects the *Refine* command (as described in Section 2), the tool attempts to match the subject pattern of each primitive rule against the program construct selected, which we call the *subject*. Only those primitive rules whose subject pattern matches the selected subject are included in the menu of rules presented to the user. This matching is done using Prolog's unification; any variables in the rule's subject pattern will be instantiated by a successful match. Prolog variables do not normally occur in the program being transformed; where they do[12], they will not be bound by subject matching.

When the user selects a rule, the getparms goal is called to obtain values for any parameters required by the rule, typically by interacting with the user. Provided this goal succeeds, the body of the rule is called. If this succeeds, the subject subtree is replaced by a refinement node that relates the subject to the instantiated result pattern.

```
-- Split Specification
primitive_rule split_spec(Mid)
                        [edit_assertion(Pre implies Post, Mid)]:
  Vars:[Pre,Post] --> ( Vars:[Pre,Mid] ; Vars:[Mid,Post] ).
```

Figure 5: The *Split Specification* primitive refinement rule

Figure 5 shows the *Split Specification* rule that splits a specification by introducing an intermediate assertion. The long name is introduced with `--`. The second line identifies the rule as a primitive rule, and gives its short name and the parameter list (`(...)`). The third line gives the getparms goal (`[...]`). If the parameter **`Mid`** is not supplied when the rule is applied[13], the user is asked to edit an assertion containing **`Pre`** and **`Post`** to obtain it. The subject pattern (on the left of `-->`) matches any specification statement, and the result (after `-->`) is the expected sequence of two specification statements. The rule takes the single parameter **`Mid`** which is the intermediate assertion. The rule has no body, since there is no side condition and nothing further to calculate.

The *Introduce Assignment* rule shown in Figure 6 has a single parameter, `V:=E`, which is the actual assignment statement to introduce; if this is not supplied, the getparms goal will ask the user to enter the assignment. The subject of the rule is a specification statement, and the result is the assignment statement supplied as a parameter. The body of the rule (introduced with **`where`**) verifies that the supplied assignment is indeed a refinement of the specification, by checking that all the variables assigned to are in the frame, substituting **`E`** for **`V`** in the postcondition, and showing that the resulting assertion is implied by the precondition (using **`implies`**, which invokes the simplifier). We have

[12] For convenience, we implement parameterized local definitions using Prolog variables.

[13] This will always be the case when the rule is applied manually, but not when it is invoked by a tactic (see Section 5.2).

a number of Prolog predicates that we use in writing rule bodies; the use of Prolog makes it very easy to add new facilities required when coding new rules.

```
-- Introduce Assignment
primitive_rule intro_assign(V:=E)[get_assignment(V:=E)]:
   Vars:[Pre,Post] --> V:=E
   where
      (
        subset(V, Vars),
        substitute(V, Post, E, NewPre),
        implies(Pre, NewPre)
      ).
```

Figure 6: The *Introduce Assignment* primitive refinement rule

The result pattern of a primitive refinement rule is an arbitrary statement pattern, normally involving one or more of the variables bound by matching the subject, obtaining parameters or executing the body. This means that the tool does not guarantee the soundness of refinement rules, and each rule and its Prolog representation must be carefully checked before adding it to the system.

Our primitive refinement rules are intentionally very low-level, and few in number. This gives us more confidence in the soundness of the tool. Essentially, there is one rule for introducing each type of program construct, and a few rules for manipulating specifications. The set of rules is based on those given in [Morgan and Robinson, 1987], together with several low-level rules for new program constructs such as local invariants. Our intention is that more powerful rules be provided in the form of tactics.

5.2 The tactic language

A tactic is similar in form to a primitive refinement rule, but more general. The short name, long name, subject pattern, parameter list, and getparms goal are the same as for primitive rules. A tactic also has a *condition* part, introduced by `when`, which is used to check whether the tactic is applicable. The body, introduced by <<, specifies a sequence of refinement steps, possibly including further tactics, to be performed; it can also call Prolog goals to obtain data to supply to those refinement steps.

Tactics do *not* have explicit result patterns; the result of applying the tactic is found by actually applying the refinements in its body. The general form of a tactic appears in Figure 7, and examples are shown in Figures 8, 9, 10 and 11; these examples are discussed later.

Tactics are invoked by selecting a subject statement and then selecting a tactic from a menu, in the same way that primitive refinement rules are applied. The system checks all available tactics by matching their subject patterns against the subject statement and checking their conditions. Only those tactics passing these checks are included in the menu of applicable tactics. As well as binding variables by matching the subject statement against the subject pat-

```
-- long name
tactic short name(parameter list) [getparms]
   when condition:
   subject pattern <<
   body.
```

Figure 7: The general form of a tactic

tern, bindings can be obtained in the proof of the applicability condition itself. This happens naturally given that the implementation language is Prolog.

When a tactic is selected, the getparms goal is called to obtain values for any parameters not already supplied, just as for primitive refinement rules. If all parameters have been supplied by the caller, getparms is not called at all. Next, the condition is checked again since the parameter binding may have altered the validity of the condition, or constrained it further so that the condition itself can bind other variables. Provided the condition succeeds again, the body of the tactic is executed.

The language in which tactic bodies are written parallels the target programming language. The primitives of the tactic language (analogous to assignment and specification statements) are *refinement steps* and *goals*, and there are constructors to combine the primitives sequentially, conditionally and alternately, just as in the target language. Any tactic can also invoke another tactic (cf. procedure call), so repetition in tactics can be implemented by recursion. An application of recursion in tactics is the elimination of invariants; the *Eliminate_Invariant* tactic examines the construct inside the invariant and applies the appropriate primitive rule. If the result itself contains invariants, they will be eliminated by recursive calls on *Eliminate_Invariant* itself.

A refinement step invokes either a primitive refinement rule or another tactic. The general form is:

refine *subject* **using** *step* **giving** *result*

where:

- *subject* specifies the part of the current statement to which the rule is to be applied,
- *step* specifies either a primitive refinement rule or a tactic and supplies whatever parameters the calling tactic chooses to provide, and
- *result* is a pattern that matches the result of the called rule or tactic — this is optional and is used to allow components of the result to be referred to by later steps in the calling tactic.

A tactic may choose to provide values for some or all of the parameters required by the rule or tactic it calls. Any parameters for which values are not supplied will be handled using the getparms goal as described earlier. Since parameters are implemented as Prolog variables, not supplying a parameter is implemented by passing an unbound variable. If the parameter gets a value within the refinement step, the variable becomes bound and the resulting value automatically becomes available to the calling tactic for later use.

A refinement step *succeeds* if its subject matches the pattern of the rule or tactic called, the condition succeeds (in the case of a tactic), its parameters can be obtained, and the body of the called rule or tactic succeeds. Otherwise the refinement step *fails*.

A *tactic goal* is a Prolog goal, much like a condition or getparms goal. The goal is called, and it can succeed (possibly binding variables) or fail. Refinement steps are the only means by which a tactic can modify the subject statement; goals are used to obtain the data for future refinement steps (for example, by allowing the user to edit the pre- and postcondition to obtain an intermediate assertion for the *Split Specification* rule), but cannot directly alter the subject itself. This means we can never write an 'incorrect' tactic: a tactic will either fail completely or perform a valid refinement.

Refinement steps and goals can be combined using *sequential*, *conditional* and *alternate* composition. These are analogous to the ;, $\rightarrow$ and $[]$ operators in the target programming language, and are implemented directly in Prolog as *and* (`,`), *then* (`->`) and *or* (`;`) respectively. Refinement steps or goals that fail are analogous to miracles, since one interpretation for miracles is that they cause backtracking to the most recent demonic choice.

To execute a sequential composition of tactic bodies, the first component is executed; if it fails, the composition as a whole fails. If the first component succeeds, the second component is executed; failure there causes backtracking into the first component just as in Prolog. If both components succeed, the composition succeeds.

A conditional composition of tactic bodies (written $B1$ `->` $B2$) succeeds if both components succeed; it differs from a sequential composition in that success of its first component *commits* the search, so failure of the second component does not cause backtracking into the first. This follows exactly the Prolog interpretation of `->`, with which it is implemented.

An alternate composition of bodies succeeds if either component succeeds, and fails if both fail. The components are tried in the order written. The branches of an alternation will often be conditional bodies, whose conditions are Prolog goals.

5.3 Hierarchies of tactics

As we begin to develop tactics, it becomes apparent that we need an hierarchy of tactics of increasing complexity, in which tactics at each level are defined in terms of lower level tactics. The lowest level in this hierarchy contains the primitive refinement rules, as discussed above. At present we have two levels of fairly simple tactics, which we call derived rules and goal-directed rules, followed by several levels of more complex tactics, which we call strategies.

5.3.1 Derived Rules

The simplest form of tactic, just above the primitive rules, are what we call *derived rules*. These are refinements that could well be considered basic rules and are easily built by composing two or three primitive rules. Many of the rules given in [Morgan, 1990] are treated as derived rules in our tool; indeed most of the derived rules we have implemented so far have been motivated by those in [Morgan, 1990].

Figure 8 shows the tactic for the *Leading Assignment* derived rule, which splits a specification statement into an assignment statement and a specification statement addressing that part of the original not satisfied by the assignment. This version of the *Leading Assignment* rule can only be applied when the variable to be assigned does not occur in the precondition of the subject[14].

```
-- Leading Assignment
tactic leading_assignment(V:=E)[get_assignment(V:=E)]
   when free_of_var(V, Pre):
   Vars:[Pre,Post] <<
      (
        refine Vars:[Pre,Post]
           using split_spec(Pre and V=E)
           giving ( AssSpec ; Rest ),
        refine AssSpec using intro_assign(V:=E)
      ).
```

Figure 8: The *Leading Assignment* derived rule

The subject of this tactic will match any specification statement. The condition checks that the variable given in the assignment statement passed as the parameter does not occur in the precondition of the subject. The body is a sequence of two refinement steps. The first step applies the *Split Specification* rule to the subject of the tactic as a whole (**Vars:[Pre,Post]**); its result is a sequential composition (**AssSpec ; Rest**). The second step applies the *Introduce Assignment* rule to the **AssSpec** specification statement from the first step; its result is not used further, so no 'giving' clause is required.

5.3.2 Goal-Directed Rules

The next level of tactics are what we call *goal-directed rules.* They typically inspect the postcondition of the subject specification statement to work out what refinement to perform.

Figure 9 shows a tactic which generalises the *Leading Assignment* derived rule discussed above. This tactic examines the postcondition of the subject and extracts from it all conjuncts of the form $V = E$ or $E = V$, where V is a variable and E is an expression. If there is more than one such conjunct, it presents a menu of goals and allows the user to select one. The selected goal is then used to introduce an assignment of the form $V := E$. If this assignment satisfies the whole postcondition, the *Introduce Assignment* primitive rule is used, otherwise the *Leading Assignment* derived rule is used.

In the condition part of this tactic, the **setof** call[15] makes a list of all conjuncts of the postcondition (**Post**) of the form **V=E** or **E=V** where **V** is in

[14] We also have a more general tactic that does not impose this restriction.

[15] **setof(Term,Goal,Set)** is a Prolog built-in predicate that produces a set **Set** of all terms **Term** for which **Goal** is true.

```
-- Leading Assignment (auto)
tactic auto_leading_assignment()[]
   when (
          setof( V=E,
                 X^Y^ (
                        is_conjunct_of(Post, X=Y),
                        ( V=X, E=Y ; V=Y,E=X ),
                        member(V, Vars)
                      ),
                 Goals),
        ):
   Vars:[Pre, Post] <<
      (
        select_goal(Goals, V=E),
        (
          % try the assignment rule:
          refine Subj using intro_assign(V:=E)
        ;
          % otherwise:
          refine Subj using leading_assignment(V:=E)
        )
      ).
```

Figure 9: The *Leading Assignment* goal-directed rule

the frame of the subject specification (**Vars**). Since **setof** fails if it finds no satisfying terms, the tactic is not applicable if there are no such conjuncts. If it succeeds, **Goals** will be bound to the list of satisfying goals.

In the body, which will only be executed if the condition succeeds, **Goals** is passed to a Prolog predicate **select_goal**, which returns (in $V = E$) the single goal if there is only one, or presents a menu if there is more than one. Then the primitive *Introduce Assignment* rule is tried using the assignment obtained from the selected goal as data. If this succeeds, the tactic succeeds, otherwise the tactic invokes the *Leading Assignment* derived rule, which will always succeed (though it may leave an infeasible specification as the second component of its result).

5.3.3 Strategies

Above derived and goal-directed rules are further levels of tactics that embody more general strategies. We have concentrated so far on tactics for building special-purpose loops; these allow the user to introduce a variable, initialize a loop and make progress within its body, all with a single interaction. One of the simplest tactics embodies Gries' *Replace a Constant by a Variable* strategy [Gries, 1981], which prompts the user for invariant, guards and variant (see Figure 10). Built on top of this are more specialised tactics requiring less interaction, for example for iterating upwards over a sequence, which calculates the invariant itself (with the call on **replace_selective**) from the form of the postcondition of the subject (see Figure 11). The Prolog predicates used in these tactics are described in Figure 12.

```
-- Loop:  Replace a Constant by a Variable
tactic replace_constant(NewVar, Const, Invariant,
                        Variant, LogicalConst)
       [make_new_variable(NewVar),
        get_invariant_replace(Post, NewVar, Const, Invariant),
        get_variant(Variant),
        make_new_locical_const(LogicalConst)]
   when has_quantifier(Post):
   Vars:[Pre, Post] <<
     (
       refine Subj
         using intro_variables(NewVar)
         giving |[ var NewVar * S1 ]|,
       refine S1
         using strengthen_post(Invariant and NewVar=Const)
         giving S2,
       refine S2
         using split_specification(Invariant)
         giving ( S3 ; S4 ),
       refine S4
         using intro_do(NewVar/=Const, Invariant,
                        Variant, LogicalConst)
     ).
```

Figure 10: Tactic for building a loop by replacing a constant by a variable

5.4 Maintaining a tactic library

At present there is little support in the refinement tool for writing and organizing tactics. We have a simple tactic debugger, which allows us to trace the execution of tactics, reporting the stages in matching a tactic (subject unification and condition checking) and in execution (refinement steps and Prolog goals). Since tactics are interpreted within Prolog, we can also use the Prolog debugger[16].

The refinement tool assumes that tactics are organized into files. Currently, these files are simply consulted by Prolog, so they can contain **ensure_loaded** goals[17] to maintain the hierarchy. The tool also allows the user to load a file of

[16] Ideally, we would use a high-level, configurable Prolog debugger such as OPIUM [Ducassé and Emde, 1991] to make all the debugger facilities available, but at a level that is relevant to the tactic writer.

[17] **ensure_loaded** is a built-in Prolog predicate that will load a file if it has not already been loaded in the current session.

```
-- Loop:  Iterate Upwards over a Sequence
tactic up_sequence(NewVar,LogConst)
                   [make_new_variable(NewVar)]
   when has_quantifier(Post, QV, QV in Low..High):
   Vars:[Pre, Post] <<
        (
        replace_selective(High, NewVar, Post, Post1),
        Inv = (Post1 and NewVar in Low..High),
        refine Subj
           using replace_constant(NewVar, High, Inv,
                                  High-NewVar, LogConst)
           giving ( Init ;
                    do Guard -> |[ con LogConst * Body ]| od ),
           refine Init
              using following_assignment(NewVar:=Low),
           refine Body
              using following_assignment(NewVar:=NewVar+1)
              giving ( Maint ; Update ),
           refine Maint
              using restrict_change(Vars)
        ).
```

Figure 11: Tactic for building a loop iterating upwards over a sequence

has_quantifier/1,3 determines whether its (assertion) argument contains a quantifier; the three-argument version returns the quantified variable and its range.

get_invariant_replace/4 replaces some **Constant** in **Post** by **NewVar** giving **Invariant**, asking the user for direction when necessary.

get_variant/1 obtains a variant function from the user.

replace_selective/4 asks the user to selectively replace **High** by **NewVar** in **Post** giving **Post1**.

Figure 12: Prolog predicates used in above tactics

tactics while it is running. Once loaded, though, the tactics form a flat name-space. When the user requests a menu of tactics, the menu will contain all the applicable tactics that are currently loaded, in no particular order.

We envisage that the system will eventually retain the hierarchical organization of tactics once they are loaded, and by default present only the highest-level applicable tactics, with some kind of browser allowing the user to drop down to the lower tactics (and ultimately to the primitive rules) when desired. This approach could be furthered by replacing the long name of a tactic by a structured description, containing keywords and other labels that a browser could search for. The browser could then be configured to display only those tactics whose descriptions match the user's stated interests at a given point in the derivation. It seems very likely that such a sophisticated browser will be essential to manage a tactic library of any significant size, and hence to make the tool practical for a wide range of non-trivial problems.

6 Related work

Very few descriptions of tools to support software development using the refinement calculus appear to have been published. Vickers [Vickers, 1990] describes a refinement editor, also implemented in Prolog, based around the idea of the user editing a string describing the complete sequence of refinement operations performed thus far. Carrington and Robinson [Carrington and Robinson, 1990] describe a refinement tool, implemented using the Cornell Synthesizer Generator, which produces a sequence of refinement steps of the sort presented in [Morgan, 1990]. Neither of these papers provides much detail about their systems, but both systems appear to be fairly rudimentary. Both support a simpler language than we do (neither supports local definitions, invariants or constants, or data refinement), neither supports tactics, and neither appears to have a well-integrated simplifier or theorem prover. Back and von Wright [Back and von Wright, 1990] describe an implementation of the refinement calculus within HOL. This is a valuable exercise from the point of view of verifying the soundness of the refinement rules, but it seems doubtful that this approach will lead to a very usable tool.

Many features of our refinement tool can be found in a variety of other systems, including program transformation systems, proof editors, and structure editors. Detailed comparisons with these systems is, however, not possible without also comparing the kinds of software development being supported, which would itself be a major undertaking.

The notion of constructing programs by a sequence of correctness preserving transformations is found in various program transformation systems [Partsch and Steinbrüggen, 1983]. The most relevant of these appears to be the Munich CIP system [Bauer *et al.*, 1985, Bauer *et al.*, 1987]. CIP uses a wide-spectrum language, based on algebraic semantics, which allows non-algorithmic specifications to be expressed, and provides a large library of transformations and an engine for performing transformations and proving applicability conditions (proof obligations). Their system supports a wider range of specification and programming features than ours. Different rules may preserve different semantic relations, but program refinement does not appear to be among them.

Systems such as *mural* [Jones et al., 1991], RAISE [Neilson et al., 1989] and the B-tool [Abrial *et al.*, 1991] support the style of rigourous software development in which successive versions of a specification are posited and each proved to be a correct refinement of its predecessor. The steps in such a development, and consequently the proof obligations to be discharged, are generally more complex than those resulting from the application of a single rule of the refinement calculus. These systems thus have a greater emphasis on proofs, rather than on the selection and application of program-oriented rules, and successive versions of the specification are constructed by the user, rather than being calculated by the system. The theory structure used in our rewriter is similar to that in *mural*.

Many similar features, including the use of tactics, can also be found in proof editors such as Nuprl [Constable *et al.*, 1986], LCF [Paulson, 1987], and IPE [Ritchie and Taylor, 1988]. In these systems, the primary emphasis is again on proofs, with programs being extracted as a by-product.

The refinement tool we have described is an outgrowth of our earlier work developing a tool [Groves and Nickson, 1988] based on weakest preconditions [Dijkstra, 1976]. Our move to base the tool on the refinement calculus was prompted by a desire for the system to be based on a more formal theory of program development, so that we could explore issues such as the reuse and composition of program developments. Our work with that tool had, however, already taken us some way towards the refinement calculus. We had an internal representation for specifications that closely resembled specification statements, including the specification of variables that could be changed (the frame), though we did not have a formal semantics for these specifications nor for partial programs containing them. The rules for constructing programs were based primarily on the weakest precondition definitions for the programming language and the kinds of "goal directed" strategies presented in [Dijkstra, 1976] and [Gries, 1981], where considerable heuristic guidance is drawn from the structure of the postcondition. The increased formality of the refinement calculus means that a single step in our earlier system now corresponds to a series of more primitive refinement steps in which the purpose of each step is less obvious. We are attempting to address this problem by the use of derived rules and tactics. Indeed, many of our tactics are similar to the "goal directed" strategies of our earlier system and are inspired directly by strategies from Dijkstra and Gries.

7 Conclusions

As stated earlier, the primary goal of our tool is to provide a basis for investigating the formal derivation of programs from specifications. Our immediate aim is to be able to work through examples given in texts such as [Gries, 1981], [Dromey, 1989], [Kaldewaij, 1990] and [Morgan, 1990], and to allow us to derive alternative algorithms for the same problem. The tool has now reached a stage where it is quite usable for performing small derivations such as these. The immediate prerequisite for deriving a wider range of algorithms is the development of more comprehensive theories and more powerful tactics.

The major question still to be addressed is whether the formal derivation approach embodied in the refinement calculus, and the type of tool support embodied in our tool, will scale up to larger problems. Our experience to date shows that the user needs to carefully plan out most of the derivation in advance, otherwise considerable time is wasted redoing refinement steps because of mistakes in earlier steps. This is partly because of the inflexibility of the tool, and we are addressing this problem by providing more flexibility in the way the user interacts with the tool, such as our facilities for backing up and redoing earlier steps. It is also partly due to the nature of the refinement calculus, where a refinement step such as introducing a loop often requires several preparatory steps to introduce a local variable, modify preconditions, etc. As indicated above, we are attempting to address this problem by the use of derived rules and tactics.

Acknowledgements

We wish to thank Dave Carrington, Cliff Jones, Hans Litteck and an anonymous referee for their helpful and encouraging comments on the paper. Ray Nickson's work was supported by a University Grants Committee Postgraduate Scholarship. Part of this work was done while Mark Utting held a Visiting Lectureship at Victoria University of Wellington. This work was also supported by a Victoria University of Wellington Internal Research Grant.

References

[Abrial *et al.*, 1991] J.-R. Abrial, S. T. Davies, M. K. O. Lee, D. S. Neilson, P. N. Scharbach and I. H. Sørensen, *The B Method*, BP Research, Sunbury Research Centre, U.K., 1991.

[Back, 1988] R. J. R. Back, "A Calculus of Refinements for Program Derivations", *Acta Informatica*, **25**:593–624, 1988.

[Back, 1991] R. J. R. Back, "Refinement Diagrams", *Proceedings Fourth Refinement Workshop*, Cambridge, 9–11 January, 1991, British Computer Society.

[Back and von Wright, 1990] R. J. R. Back and J. von Wright, "Refinement Concepts Formalised in Higher Order Logic", *Formal Aspects of Computing*, **2**:247–272, 1990.

[Bauer *et al.*, 1985] F. L. Bauer *et al.* (The CIP Language Group), *The Munich Project CIP, Volume I: The Wide Spectrum Language CIP-L*, Springer-Verlag, Lecture Notes in Computer Science 183, 1985.

[Bauer *et al.*, 1987] F. L. Bauer *et al.* (The CIP System Group), *The Munich Project CIP, Volume II: The Program Transformation System CIP-S*, Springer-Verlag, Lecture Notes in Computer Science 292, 1987.

[Carlsson and Widén, 1988] Mats Carlsson and Johan Widén, *SICStus Prolog User's Manual*, Swedish Institute of Computer Science, 1988.

[Carrington and Robinson, 1990] D. A. Carrington and K. A. Robinson, "Tool Support for the Refinement Calculus", *Computer Aided Verification Workshop*, New Jersey, June 1990.

[Constable *et al.*, 1986] R. L. Constable *et al.*, *Implementing Mathematics with the Nuprl Proof Development System*, Prentice-Hall, 1986.

[Dijkstra, 1968] E. W. Dijkstra, "A Constructive Approach to the Problem of Program Correctness", BIT, **8**(3):181–185, 1969.

[Dijkstra, 1976] E. W. Dijkstra, *A Discipline of Programming*, Academic Press, 1976.

[Dromey, 1989] Geoff Dromey, *Program Derivation: The Development of Programs from Specifications*, Addison-Wesley, 1989.

[Ducassé and Emde, 1991] Mireille Ducassé and Anna-Maria Emde, "OPIUM: A Debugging Environment for Prolog Development and Debugging Research", *ACM Software Engineering Notes*, **16**(2):67–72, April 1991.

[Floyd, 1971] R. W. Floyd, *Towards Interactive Design of Correct Programs*, Technical Report CS-235, Stanford University, September 1971.

[Gries, 1981] David Gries, *The Science of Programming*, Springer-Verlag, 1981.

[Groves and Nickson, 1988] L. J. Groves and R. G. Nickson, *Towards a Program Derivation Editor*, Technical Report, Department of Computer Science, Victoria University of Wellington, 1988.

[Jones et al., 1991] C. B. Jones, K.D. Jones, P.A. Lindsay and R. Moore, *mural: A Formal Development Support System*, Springer-Verlag, 1991.

[Kaldewaij, 1990] Anne Kaldewaij, *Programming: The Derivation of Algorithms*, Prentice-Hall, 1990.

[Kim, 1989] Ted Kim, *XWIP Reference Manual*, University of California, Los Angeles, 1989.

[Morgan and Robinson, 1987] Carroll Morgan and Ken Robinson, "Specification Statements and Refinement", *IBM Journal of Research and Development*, **31**(5):546–555, September 1987.

[Morgan, 1989] Carroll Morgan, "Types and Invariants in the Refinement Calculus", in *Mathematics of Program Construction*, J. L. A. van de Snepscheut (Ed.), Springer Verlag, Lecture Notes in Computer Science 375, 1989, pp 363–378.

[Morgan, 1990] Carroll Morgan, *Programming from Specification*, Prentice-Hall, 1990.

[Morgan and Gardiner, 1990] Carroll Morgan and Paul Gardiner, "Data Refinement by Calculation", *Acta Informatica*, **27**:481–503, 1990.

[Morris, 1987] Joseph M. Morris, "A Theoretical Basis for Stepwise Refinement and the Programming Calculus", *Science of Computer Programming*, **9**:287–306, 1987.

[Neilson et al., 1989] M. Neilson, K. Havelund, K. R. Wagner and E. Saaman, "The RAISE Language, Method and Tools", *Formal Aspects of Computing*, **1**:85–114, 1989.

[Partsch and Steinbrüggen, 1983] H. Partsch and R. Steinbrüggen, "Program Transformation Systems", *ACM Computing Surveys*, **15**:199–236, 1983.

[Paulson, 1987] L. C. Paulson, *Logic and Computation: Interactive Proof with Cambridge LCF*, Cambridge University Press, 1987.

[Ritchie and Taylor, 1988] Brian Ritchie and Paul Taylor, *The Interactive Proof Editor: An Experiment in Interactive Theorem* (sic), Technical Report LFCS-88-61, University of Edinburgh, July, 1988.

[Scheifler and Gettys, 1986] Robert W. Scheifler and Jim Gettys, "The X Window System", *ACM Transactions on Graphics*, **5**(2):79–109, April 1986.

[Vickers, 1990] T. Vickers, "An Overview of a Refinement Editor", *5th Australian Software Engineering Conference*, May 1990, Sydney, pp. 39–44.

Revisiting Abstraction Functions For Reasoning About Concurrency

Jeannette M. Wing
School of Computer Science, Carnegie Mellon University
Pittsburgh, PA 15213 USA

Abstract

Hoare introduced abstraction functions for reasoning about abstract data types in 1972 [1]. What happens in the presence of concurrency? Reasoning about objects in a concurrent system necessitates extending the notion of abstraction functions in order to model the system's inherent nondeterminisitic behavior. My talk presented in detail the extensions required to reason about lock-free concurrent objects, used to build linearizable systems. It also discussed briefly a different extension required to reason about atomic objects, used to build fault-tolerant distributed systems.

Much of this work is joint with Maurice Herlihy and previously published in two papers [2, 3].

1 Background

Hoare introduced abstraction functions for reasoning about abstract data types in 1972 [1]. In the sequential domain, an implementation consists of an *abstract type* ABS, the type being implemented, and a *representation type* REP, the type used to implement ABS. The subset of REP values that are *legal* representations is characterized by a predicate called the *representation invariant*, **I**: REP $\rightarrow$ BOOL. The abstraction function,

A: REP $\rightarrow$ ABS

maps each representation value that satisfies the invariant to a single abstract value.

2 What happens in the presence of concurrency?

A *concurrent object* is a data object shared by concurrent processes. *Linearizability* is a correctness condition for concurrent objects defined in terms of the semantics of abstract data types. Intuitively, linearizability requires that each operation executed appear to "take effect" instantaneously and that the order of nonconcurrent operations be preserved. These two requirements allow us to describe acceptable concurrent behavior directly in terms of acceptable sequential behavior, an approach that simplifies both formal and informal reasoning about concurrent programs.

In order to prove that an implementation of a concurrent object is correct, i.e., linearizable, it is necessary to extend the notion of an abstraction function. The abstraction function must map a single representation value (that satisfies the invariant) to a *set* of abstract values:

$$\mathbf{A}\text{: REP} \rightarrow 2^{ABS}$$

The change to the range of the abstraction function results from inherent nondeterminism as defined by linearizability. Intuitively, the nondeterminism arises because at any point in time operations concurrently performed on an object may or may not have "taken effect." For each operation we want to permit the possibility that it has or has not. The paper by Herlihy and Wing [2] motivates linearizability, discusses the change to the notion of abstraction function, and walks through an example of a FIFO queue in depth.

3 What happens in the presence of concurrency and faults?

An *atomic object* is a data object shared by concurrent transactions. A transaction is a process that executes a sequence of operations where that sequence (in contrast to each individual operation) is considered an atomic unit, i.e., "all-or-nothing." A transaction may succeed, in which case all its operations take effect; or, it may fail, in which case none of its operations take effect. Faults such as lost messages and site crashes are masked as aborted (failed) transactions.

Atomicity is a correctness condition for atomic objects defined in terms of the semantics of abstract data types. It requires that all transactions that perform operations on an object be "all-or-nothing," serializable (the concurrent execution of a set of transactions must be equivalent to some sequential execution), and permanent (effects of committed transactions persist).

In order to prove that an implementation of an atomic object is correct, i.e., atomic, it is necessary to extend the notion of an abstraction function. The abstraction function must map a single representation value (that satisfies the invariant) to a *set* of *sequences* of abstract operations:

$$\mathbf{A}\text{: REP} \rightarrow 2^{OPS*}$$

where OPS is the set of operations on the abstract type, ABS. Nondeterminism (set of sequences) is inherent because any serialization should be allowed. We need to keep track of history information (sequences of operations) because the future successful completion of a transaction may require that its operations be "inserted in the middle" of a history, where the resulting history is a serialization. The paper by Wing [3], based on earlier work by Herlihy and Wing, explains in detail the model of computation for atomic objects and the extended notion of abstraction functions for reasoning about the correctness of their implementations.

References

[1] C.A.R. Hoare, "Proof of Correctness of Data Representations," *Acta Informatica*, Vol. 1, 1972, pp. 271-281.

[2] M.P. Herlihy and J.M. Wing, "Linearizability: A Correctness Condition for Concurrent Objects," *ACM TOPLAS*, Vol. 12, No. 3, July 1990, pp. 463-492.

[3] J.M. Wing, "Verifying Atomic Data Types," *International Journal of Parallel Programming*, Vol. 18, No. 5, 1989, pp. 315-357.

A case study in formally developing state-based parallel programs–the Dutch National Torus*

Xu Qiwen†
Institut für Informatik und Praktische Mathematik II
der Universität Kiel, Preußerstr. 1-9
W-2300 Kiel 1, Germany

He Jifeng‡
Oxford University Computing Laboratory
Programming Research Group
8-11 Keble Road, Oxford OX1 3QD
England, U.K.

Abstract

Recently, formal methods, both assertional (compositional) and algebraic, for developing state-based parallel programs have been studied. This paper presents one of the few not-that-trivial case studies in this area, based on the combined use of both (though mainly assertional) methods. The case study is conducted in a top-down fashion, and we demonstrate that verification can be naturally conducted at the same time as, and combined with, the design of the system.

1 Introduction

Although most of recent research in concurrency has been conducted in the communication-based setting, it has been clear that for some applications state-based (with shared-variable) programs are much more natural and for some problems even the only practical solutions. Therefore, recently there has been a renewal of interest in studying the state-based concurrency, particularly, in pursuing compositional proof methods [St90, XH91 and Jo91] based on Cliff Jones' idea of including assumptions about the interference from the other components into the specification [Jo81], and in extending to this framework the algebraic approach, formerly only studied in sequential programs [Hoare et al 87] and in communication-based concurrency [Mi89, Ho85 and Ba90].

Besides the interest of their own and other applications, algebraic laws can be used to transform a parallel program in Owicki/Gries language to equivalent sequential programs. We recently observed that if a parallel program

*Part of the research was supported by Sino-British Friendship Scholarship Scheme, while the first author was reading D.Phil. at Oxford University

†email: qxu@informatik.uni-kiel.dbp.de and qxu@prg.oxford.ac.uk

‡email: jifeng@prg.oxford.ac.uk

is equivalent to a sequential one, traditional sequential data refinement techniques, upward and downward simulation can simply carry over. (Note: A direct formulation of data refinement in state-based concurrency is also possible.)

We present a not-that-trivial case study in this paper. The problem was first raised and solved by Edsger W. Dijkstra [Di77], but the solution we have designed here is more directly inspired by [GdeRR82].

In section 2, we briefly recall some basic notations, largely taken from [XH91]. Section 3 is the case study. The paper is concluded with a short discussion in section 4.

2 Methods

2.1 An Owicki/Gries language

The language we use to describe the algorithm is taken from [OG76], which basically extends Dijkstra's language by parallel composition and a simple synchronization statement. The syntax and a brief explanation of various language structures is as follows:

$$S ::= \textit{skip} \mid X := E \mid S_1 \sqcap S_2 \mid S_1;S_2 \mid \textit{if}\, b\, \textit{then}\, S_1\, \textit{else}\, S_2\, \textit{fi} \mid \\ \textit{while}\, b\, \textit{do}\, S\, \textit{od} \mid \textit{await}\ b\ \textit{then}\ S\, \textit{end} \mid S_1 \parallel S_2.$$

The statement *skip* has no effect on any program variables, and terminates immediately. In the assignment statement, X represents a vector of variables $(x_1, ..., x_n)$, and E represents a vector of expressions $(e_1, ..., e_n)$. The execution of an assignment statement is considered as atomic, with $x_1, ..., x_n$ being set to the values computed for $e_1, ..., e_n$. The nondeterministic choice of P and Q, written as $P \sqcap Q$, behaves either like P or Q. $P;Q$ is executed by executing P first, when P terminates, executing Q. If P is blocked, then $P;Q$ is blocked until P is released. The conditional and iteration statements are denoted as usual by *if b then P else Q fi* and *while b do P od*, in which the evaluation of the boolean test b is atomic, but the environment can interrupt between the boolean test and first action from P or Q.

The above are just the usual sequential structures. The two more complicated structures are the parallel composition and the *await*-statement. In $P \parallel Q$, P and Q are executed concurrently, with atomic actions from two processes interleaving each other. $P \parallel Q$ is blocked if both processes are blocked and released if one of the processes is released. Synchronization and mutual exclusion are achieved by *await b then P end*, which in turn is the cause of a process to become blocked. When b is true, P will be executed without interruption. If P loops forever the whole process is led to a failure, while if P terminates the execution of the statement is considered to be atomic. When b does not hold, the process is blocked and can only become active again when the environment has set b to true.

Lamport's bracket notation $< P >$ is considered as a short form of *await true then P end*. Note we have lifted the restriction (in e.g., [St90, XH91]) that only local or private variables can be used in the boolean test b of the conditional and iteration statement. This reduces the number of variables that have to be introduced but the proof rules of *if* and *while* become slightly more complicated.

2.2 Specification

A specification describes what the correct behaviors of a system are. When we are only concerned with total correctness, the overall requirement can be given as a relationship between the values of variables before and after the execution of the system. However, the system can be implemented by a number of parallel components, and in order to support constructive design and modular verification, compositional methods are needed [dR85].

Cliff Jones [Jo81] observed that interference has to be specified for achieving compositionality in state-base concurrency, and has given an outline of a compositional proof system for a subset of Owicki/Gries language, which was recently extended by Ketil Stølen [St90] to the full language.

The work in our paper [XH91] was along the same line as that of Stølen's, although the exact treatment differed in a number of aspects. A specification is a tuple of five predicates:

$$(pre,\ rely,\ run,\ guar,\ post).$$

If v is the vector of state variables $(v_1, ..., v_n)$, and v' is $(v'_1, ..., v'_n)$, the parameter dependence of these predicates is given by $pre(v)$, $rely(v,\ v')$, $run(v)$, $guar(v,\ v')$ and $post(v)$.

A specification describes the conditions (usually called *Assumptions*) under which the program is used, and the expected behaviours (usually called *Commitments*) of the program when it is used under these conditions. The *Assumptions* part of a specification is composed of *pre*, *rely* and *run*, and the *Commitments* part is composed of *guar* and *post*. A program P satisfies a specification $(pre,\ rely,\ run,\ guar,\ post)$ if under the assumptions that:

1.) P will only be invoked in a state which satisfies *pre*,

2.) any sequence of consecutive environment actions satisfies *rely*, in the sense that the value of $rely(v,\ v')$ is true if v has the values of the variables in the state before this sequence of environment actions and v' has the values of the variables in the state after it,

3.) the environment will eventually establish *run* if the program is blocked,

P will ensure these commitments:

4.) any sequence of consecutive program actions satisfies *guar* in a similar sense as the rely-condition,

5.) only a finite number of steps from P is possible,

6.) once computation stops, the program has terminated, rather than being blocked, and its final states satisfy *post*.

Informally, *rely* and *guar* describe the extent of the interference which can be tolerated and respectively caused by the program. *run* is the condition to ensure the program to proceed, that is, when it is satisfied, the program can be 'unblocked'. In order to avoid writting specifications which can be satisfied by any programs, pre-condition is required not to be equivalent to *false*, namely, $\exists v.pre(v)$ should be true. Moreover, we follow Jones' suggestion assuming *rely* and *guar* are reflexive and transitive. With this restriction, the above requirements about *rely* and *guar* can be simplified as:

any action from the environment (program) satisfies *rely* (*guar*).

One might have noticed that the *post*-condition is now unary instead of binary as in [XH91]. No expressive power is lost by this, since we allow the use of auxiliary variables. In sequential programming, one may prefer the use of binary *post*-condition, but our experiments showed in the parallel case, it could lead to overloading too many interpretations to already overloaded state variables (in just one specification). Finally, we observe that if a specified program is not going to be used in parallel with any other part of the system, its specification is of the form $(pre,\ v' = v,\ true,\ true,\ post)$, which just describes the sequential input-output relationship. We write this kind of specification simply as $(pre,\ post)$.

2.3 Proof rules

We present the proof rules in this section. Since most of the rules are straightforward, we only give some explanations for the parallel and the await rules at the end.

Skip

$$\frac{pre\ \underline{stable\ when}\ rely}{skip\ \underline{sat}\ (pre,\ rely,\ true,\ (v' = v),\ pre)}$$

Here *pre* <u>*stable when*</u> *rely* is a shorthand for $\forall v,\ v'.\ pre(v) \wedge rely(v, v') \Rightarrow pre(v')$. This is necessary because we do not assume in the semantics that the first action must be taken by the system.

Nondeterminism

$$\frac{\begin{array}{l} P\ \underline{sat}\ (pre,\ rely,\ run,\ guar,\ post) \\ Q\ \underline{sat}\ (pre,\ rely,\ run,\ guar,\ post) \end{array}}{P \sqcap Q\ \underline{sat}\ (pre,\ rely,\ run,\ guar,\ post)}$$

Assignment

$$\frac{\begin{array}{l} pre \Rightarrow post[E/X] \\ \lceil X' = E \rceil \Rightarrow guar \\ pre\ \underline{stable\ when}\ rely \\ post\ \underline{stable\ when}\ rely \end{array}}{X := E\ \underline{sat}\ (pre,\ rely,\ true,\ guar,\ post)}$$

Here $\lceil X' = E \rceil \hat{=} (X' = E) \wedge \forall y \in (v - X).\, y' = y$.

Composition

$$\frac{\begin{array}{l} P \ \underline{sat}\ (pre,\ rely,\ run,\ guar,\ mid) \\ Q \ \underline{sat}\ (mid,\ rely,\ run,\ guar,\ post) \end{array}}{P;Q \ \underline{sat}\ (pre,\ rely,\ run,\ guar,\ post)}$$

Conditional

$$\frac{\begin{array}{l} pre\ \underline{stable\ when}\ rely \\ P \ \underline{sat}\ (pre \wedge b,\ rely,\ run,\ guar,\ post) \\ Q \ \underline{sat}\ (pre \wedge \neg b,\ rely,\ run,\ guar,\ post) \end{array}}{if\ b\ then\ P\ else\ Q\ fi \ \underline{sat}\ (pre,\ rely,\ run,\ guar,\ post)}$$

Iteration

$$\frac{\begin{array}{l} (Inv(\alpha) \wedge \alpha > 0) \Rightarrow b \\ Inv(0) \Rightarrow \neg b \\ (Inv(\alpha) \wedge rely) \Rightarrow \exists \beta \leq \alpha.\, Inv(\beta)' \\ P \ \underline{sat}\ (Inv(\alpha) \wedge \alpha > 0,\ rely,\ run,\ guar,\ \exists \beta < \alpha.\, Inv(\beta)) \end{array}}{while\ b\ do\ P\ od \ \underline{sat}\ (\exists \alpha.\, Inv(\alpha),\ rely,\ run,\ guar,\ Inv(0))}$$

For a formula F, which could be a predicate or a function, F' stands for the formula from F with all the unprimed variables in it replaced by the same variables primed. Here α and β range over a set of ordinal numbers, of which 0 is the minimal member. Ordinal-valued (instead of integer-valued) loop counters are necessary here for proving termination, because the nondeterminism caused by the environment can be unbounded.

Parallel

$$\frac{\begin{array}{l} (post_1 \Rightarrow run_2) \wedge (post_2 \Rightarrow run_1) \wedge (run_1 \vee run_2) \\ (rely \vee guar_1) \Rightarrow rely_2 \\ (rely \vee guar_2) \Rightarrow rely_1 \\ (guar_1 \vee guar_2) \Rightarrow guar \\ P \ \underline{sat}\ (pre,\ rely_1,\ run \wedge run_1,\ guar_1,\ post_1) \\ Q \ \underline{sat}\ (pre,\ rely_2,\ run \wedge run_2,\ guar_2,\ post_2) \end{array}}{P \parallel Q \ \underline{sat}\ (pre,\ rely,\ run,\ guar,\ post_1 \wedge post_2)}$$

Await

$$\frac{\begin{array}{l} pre\ \underline{stable\ when}\ rely \\ post\ \underline{stable\ when}\ rely \\ P\ \underline{sat}\ (pre \wedge b \wedge y = v,\ v' = v \wedge y' = y,\ true,\ true,\ \ guar(y/v,\ v/v') \wedge post) \end{array}}{await\ b\ then\ P\ end \ \underline{sat}\ (pre,\ rely,\ pre \Rightarrow b,\ guar,\ post)}$$

Here y is a fresh variable vector.

Auxiliary variable

$$\frac{\begin{array}{l} \forall v.\exists z.pre_1 \wedge \forall v, v', z.\exists z'.rely_1((v, z),\ (v', z')) \\ P \ \underline{sat}\ (pre \wedge pre_1,\ rely \wedge rely_1,\ run,\ guar,\ post) \end{array}}{P \backslash z \ \underline{sat}\ (pre,\ rely,\ run,\ guar,\ post)}$$

,provided $z \cap freevar\ (pre,\ rely,\ run,\ guar\ post) = \emptyset$.

Here z is a list of auxiliary variables. Auxiliary variables do not influence the control flow of the program, therefore they only appear in the lefthand side of the assignment or in the righthand but then the corresponding element in the lefthand is also an auxiliary variable. In order to be able to remove the auxiliary variables in z, which may not contain all the auxiliary variables, we require that if a variable of z is in the righthand of an assignment, the corresponding auxiliary variable in the lefthand is also one of z. Moreover, we stipulate auxiliary variables are only updated at the same time as the program variables. Syntactically, auxiliary variables only appear in multi-assignment or *await* statements involving also some program variables.

In this rule, *pre*, *rely*, *run*, *guar* and *post* do not contain free occurrences of any variables in z, while pre_1 and $rely_1$ do not constrain the program variables in the sense that $\forall v.\exists z.pre_1$ and $\forall v, v', z.\exists z'.rely_1((v, z), (v', z'))$ hold. Hence, pre_1 and $rely_1$ will not be equivalent to *false*, since otherwise the hypothesis P sat $(pre \wedge pre_1,\ rely \wedge rely_1,\ run,\ guar,\ post)$ will hold trivially. Here, $P \backslash z$ stands for the program with all the assignments in P to variables in z removed and any program of the form *await true then* $X := E$ *end* replaced by $X := E$.

Consequence

$$\frac{\begin{array}{l} pre \Rightarrow pre_1,\ rely \Rightarrow rely_1,\ run \Rightarrow run_1,\ guar_1 \Rightarrow guar,\ post_1 \Rightarrow post \\ P\ \underline{sat}\ (pre_1,\ rely_1,\ run_1,\ guar_1,\ post_1) \end{array}}{P\ \underline{sat}\ (pre,\ rely,\ run,\ guar,\ post)}$$

The most interesting and complicated rule is naturally the one for parallel composition. Here the program of interest is $P \parallel Q$, suppose it is put together with an overall environment R. Thus, the environment of process P consists of Q and R, and the environment of process Q consists of P and R. Therefore, process P should be able to tolerate interference from both R and Q, so the best rely-condition P can assume is $rely \vee guar_2$; for the same reason, the best rely-condition Q can assume is $rely \vee guar_1$. We now show that it is not possible for $P \parallel Q$ to deadlock, under the premises of the proof rule. Assume $P \parallel Q$ is deadlocked, then from the interpretation, the overall environment has to establish *run*. There are two possibilities here, either one of the processes is terminated and the other one is deadlocked, or both of them are deadlocked. We demonstrate that neither of the two cases can be true. Suppose P is terminated and Q is deadlocked, then $post_1$ holds, and from the premises, this implies run_2 to be true. However, from the specification of Q in the premises, $run \wedge run_2$ should be able to guarantee it to be released, therefore can not be deadlocked. Moreover, P and Q can not be both deadlocked, because it follows from the premises that either run_1 or run_2 should be true at any time, and then at least one of them is not deadlocked. It is easy to see that a computation action from $P \parallel Q$ is either an action from P or from Q, and hence it satisfies $guar_1 \vee guar_2$. Finally, both P and Q terminate in the end, so as a result, both *post*-conditions are established for the terminating states.

The *await*-rule is not difficult to understand. The *await*-body P is only executed when b is true, and is not interrupted. Furthermore, P will not deadlock simply because P does not have any *await*-statements. Therefore *await b then P* can only become blocked if b is not true, but from the specification in the conclusion part of the rule, the environment will establish $pre \Rightarrow b$ eventually when the program is blocked. This together with the pre-condition *pre* ensures b to be true, thus *await b then P* becomes active again. To the outside, the execution of P in *await b then P* is atomic, therefore the *guar*-condition is obviously satisfied. Finally, if the *post*-condition of P is not damaged by the environment, it should hold in the end as well.

The parallel rule can be extended to the case of n components

$$\frac{\begin{array}{l}(\bigwedge_{i\neq k} post_i \Rightarrow run_k) \wedge \bigvee_{i=1,\ldots n} run_i \\ (rely \vee \bigvee_{i\neq k} guar_i) \Rightarrow rely_k \\ \bigvee_{i=1,\ldots n} guar_i \Rightarrow guar \\ P_i \ \underline{sat}\ (pre,\ rely_i,\ run \wedge run_i,\ guar_i,\ post_i)\end{array}}{P_1 \parallel P_2 \parallel, \ldots, \parallel P_n \ \underline{sat}\ (pre,\ rely,\ run,\ guar,\ \bigwedge_{i=1,\ldots n} post_i)}$$

2.4 Algebraic laws

Just like sequential programs and communication-based parallel programs, state-based parallel programs are also subject to a set of elegant and rich (there are about 50 basic) laws. Since this case study is mainly based on assertional methods, we only list a number of laws related to our application here. In the following, a and b stand for assignments.

1. $P \sqcap Q = Q \sqcap P$
2. $P \sqcap (Q \sqcap R) = (P \sqcap Q) \sqcap R$
3. $P \sqcap P = P$
4. $P \parallel Q = Q \parallel P$
5. $(P \parallel Q) \parallel R = P \parallel (Q \parallel R)$
6. $P \parallel (Q \sqcap R) = (P \parallel Q) \sqcap (P \parallel R)$
7. $P \parallel skip = P$
8. $(a; P) \parallel (b; Q) = (a; (P \parallel (b; Q))) \sqcap (b; ((a; P) \parallel Q)))$
9. $X := E; X := F \sqsubseteq X := F(E/X)$
10. $(a; P) \parallel Q \sqsubseteq a; (P \parallel Q)$

Both the algebraic laws and the proof system are based on one (specification oriented) semantics [XH91, XH92], and this provides a formal justification for using them together in the development. When $P = Q$ is valid, P and Q satisfy the same class of specifications, and when $P \sqsubseteq Q$, Q satisfies any specification that P satisfies.

From the above laws, we have

$$\begin{array}{l}(a; P) \parallel (a; Q) \\ = (a; (P \parallel (a; Q))) \sqcap (a; ((a; P) \parallel Q)) \\ \sqsubseteq (a; a; (P \parallel Q)) \sqcap (a; a; (P \parallel Q)) \\ \sqsubseteq a; a; (P \parallel Q)\end{array}$$

If the righthand of the assignment a does not refer to the lefthand side, we have further

$$a; a; (P \parallel Q) \sqsubseteq a; (P \parallel Q)$$

2.5 Data refinement

Data refinement has played an important role in sequential design methods, such as VDM and Z. It is certainly desirable to extend it to parallel programming. One trivial fact is that, traditional sequential data refinement techniques, such as, upward and downward simulation simply carry over.

> **Claim.** For any parallel program, if it is equivalent to a sequential program, then data refinement can be carried out just like in the sequential setting, provided the implementation of the abstract operations is executed atomically.

More precisely, let us write $P(D)$ or $P(Dop_1, ..., Dop_n)$ for a parallel program using data type D where $Dop_1, ..., Dop_n$ are a collection of atomic operations on D. Now suppose the abstract data type is A, with $Aop_1, ..., Aop_n$ as atomic operations and the concrete data type is C, with $Cop_1, ..., Cop_n$ as the corresponding concrete operations. The theory of data refinement shows that in sequential programming, the use of the abstract data type can be replaced by the use of the concrete one, when certain simple proof obligations holds. The above Claim indicates that if there exists a sequential program, say Ps, equivalent to P, then the use of A in P can be replaced by that of C in such parallel program P, if a simulation relation can be established between A and C just by the sequential proof obligations.

Suppose that a downward simulation d holds between A and C. Then in order to ensure that the step of data replacement is correct, we are required to prove a so called ***subdistributivity*** property [HHS87].

$$
\begin{array}{ll}
P(A);d & \\
= Ps(A);d & \{\text{assumption}\} \\
\sqsubseteq d;Ps(C) & \{\text{subdistributivity for sequential case}\} \\
= d;P(C) & \{\text{assumption}\}
\end{array}
$$

> **Conjecture.** A parallel program in the interleaving model is equivalent to a sequential one.

Although this is widely accepted, no rigorous proof had been given before for Owicki/Gries language. Recently, we have proven this conjecture in an algebraic framework by showing a set of algebraic laws are sufficient to transform a parallel program to an equivalent sequential one [XH92]. Therefore, in a practical design, the programmer can refine the data just like in the sequential case, but we must emphasize the concrete operations should remain atomic, because in a parallel system, a small change of atomicity can cause totally different behaviors.

3 Case study: the Dutch National Torus

3.1 The problem and the overall specification

Suppose there are three bags $R(ed)$, $W(hite)$ and $B(lue)$, each containing a number of red, white and blue pebbles. The task is to rearrange these pebbles, so that each bag only has pebbles of its own colour, thus forming a neatly coloured Dutch National Torus.

Further, assume these bags are stored at three different places of a network, and the communication can only take place in one direction, say from R to W, W to B and B to R. Moreover, the buffers RW, WB and BR can only contain one pebble.

Roughly, the algorithm works like this. For each bag, take the pebble on its lefthand buffer and put it into the bag, and choose any pebble not of its colour, sending it out to its righthand buffer. Keep on 'rotating' pebbles like this until all the pebbles in the bag are of the right colour and there are not any pebbles in the buffers to be transferred.

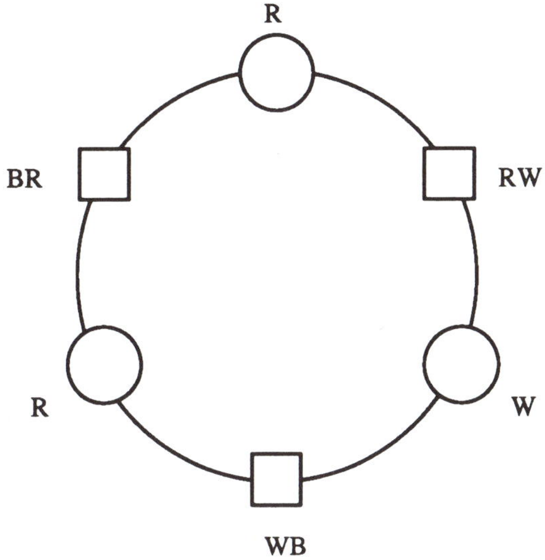

Suppose R_0, W_0 and B_0 stand for the initial values of the three bags. $All(Col, X)$ is a boolean function, denoting that all the pebbles in bag X are of the colour Col. The overall specification is:

Spec−system

$$\begin{array}{l} pre: \quad (R = R_0) \wedge (W = W_0) \wedge (B = B_0) \\ post: \quad All(Red, R) \wedge All(White, W) \wedge All(Blue, B) \\ \quad \wedge (R \cup W \cup B = R_0 \cup W_0 \cup B_0) \end{array}$$

Introduce three boolean variables l_R, l_W and l_B, and let $I1$ denote

$$(l_R \Rightarrow All(Red, R)) \wedge (l_W \Rightarrow All(White, W)) \wedge (l_B \Rightarrow All(Blue, B))$$

then the overall specification becomes:

$$pre: \quad (R = R_0) \wedge (W = W_0) \wedge (B = B_0)$$
$$post: \quad I1 \wedge l_R \wedge l_W \wedge l_B \wedge (R \cup W \cup B = R_0 \cup W_0 \cup B_0)$$

3.2 The first decomposition

The pebbles that each bag contains are of course changing during the execution of the program, but the union of the three bags together with the pebbles being transmitted along the channels should always equal to $R_0 \cup W_0 \cup B_0$, since no pebbles should be destroyed nor created by the program.

We could assign a special symbol, say ε, to a buffer to indicate that it is empty, then testing whether the buffer is empty becomes testing whether it has the value ε. Another way (more efficient when a 'pebble' is a large piece of data) is to introduce three flags e_{RW}, e_{WB} and e_{BR}, whose value is *true* when the buffer is empty and *false* when it holds valid data, i.e. a yet to be transferred pebble. Let

$$<RW> \mathrel{\widehat{=}} \{RW \mid \neg e_{RW}\}$$
$$<WB> \mathrel{\widehat{=}} \{WB \mid \neg e_{WB}\}$$
$$
 \mathrel{\widehat{=}} \{BR \mid \neg e_{BR}\},$$

then the fact that no pebble is destroyed nor created is described by the formula $I2$:

$$R \cup W \cup B \cup <RW> \cup <WB> \cup
 = R_0 \cup W_0 \cup B_0$$

Lemma 1 $I2 \wedge (e_{RW} \wedge e_{WB} \wedge e_{BR}) \Rightarrow (R \cup W \cup B = R_0 \cup W_0 \cup B_0)$

The program is now going to be implemented as:

Init;*Programbody*.

The goal of *Init* is to set initial values to the relevant variables so that $I1 \wedge I2$ holds, and its specification is therefore as follows:

Spec−Init:

$$pre: \quad (R = R_0) \wedge (W = W_0) \wedge (B = B_0)$$
$$post: \quad I1 \wedge I2.$$

The specification of *Programbody* is:

Spec−Programbody:

$$pre: \quad I1 \wedge I2$$
$$post: \quad I1 \wedge I2 \wedge l_R \wedge l_W \wedge l_B \wedge e_{RW} \wedge e_{WB} \wedge e_{BR}$$

Spec−Init can be easily implemented, for example, by the following code:

Code−Init:

$e_{RW}, e_{WB}, e_{BR} := true, true, true;$
$l_R := All(Red,\ R);$
$l_B := All(Blue,\ B);$
$l_W := All(White,\ W).$

Now our task is only to develop *Programbody*.

3.3 The second decomposition

To this end, a parallel solution, associating to each bag two processes, seems to be natural. Suppose for bag R the corresponding two processes are R_1 and R_2. R_1 repeatly checks if there is a valid pebble in R's lefthand buffer BR, and if so, moves it into R. Similarly, R_2 repeatly checks if there is a non-red pebble in R, and if so, it waits until its righthand buffer RW is empty and then move the alien pebble to RW. Therefore, a suggestion for the implementation of *Programbody* is:

$$R_1 \parallel R_2 \parallel W_1 \parallel W_2 \parallel B_1 \parallel B_2.$$

Now we have to figure out a specification for each process and show that the proof obligations in the parallel rule hold. Obviously, each process will contain a loop structure, but since at this stage we only have a vague idea how they are going to work, we postpone the more detailed consideration for a while and first try to obtain a rather rough specification for each process. These specifications have to be modified when more precise design decisions have been taken.

Considering the specification of R_1, we can simply take the *pre*-condition as that of *Spec–Programbody*. As already suggested earlier, we would like $I1 \wedge I2$ to be invariant, so $I1 \Rightarrow I1'$ and $I2 \Rightarrow I2'$ should be in the *rely*-condition. Notice that when the lefthand buffer BR has a valid pebble, namely, when $\neg e_{BR}$ holds, the pebble should stay there until moved by R_1 itself. Therefore we expect $\neg e_{BR} \Rightarrow \neg e'_{BR}$ is also in the *rely*-condition. We then tentatively fix the *rely*-condition as

$$(I1 \Rightarrow I1') \wedge (I2 \Rightarrow I2') \wedge (\neg e_{BR} \Rightarrow \neg e'_{BR}).$$

Having reached this stage, we can quite easily see what the *guar*-condition should be by considering what the other processes will rely on, since these processes are all similar or symmetrical. Therefore one expects $(I1 \Rightarrow I1') \wedge (I2 \Rightarrow I2')$ is required. It is easy to see that R_1 has nothing to do directly with RW, W, WB, and B, hence it can obviously guarantee $(e'_{RW} = e_{RW}) \wedge (l'_W = l_W) \wedge (e'_{WB} = e_{WB}) \wedge (l'_B = l_B)$, which we abbreviate as $I(RW, W, WB, B)$. Process R_2 is the only process to send out R's non-red pebble, so R_1 should guarantee $\neg l_R \Rightarrow \neg l'_R$ (meaning that if there is one non-red pebble in R, then after one step from R_1, there is still one non-red pebble in R). Putting these together, the *guar*-condition becomes:

$$(I1 \Rightarrow I1') \wedge (I2 \Rightarrow I2') \wedge I(RW, W, WB, B) \wedge (\neg l_R \Rightarrow \neg l'_R).$$

Now we try to work out what the *run*-condition should be. R_1 will only have to wait if BR is empty and some of the pebbles have not reached their bags. R_1 can go ahead when $\neg e_{BR}$ or $l_R \wedge l_W \wedge l_B \wedge e_{RW} \wedge e_{WB} \wedge e_{BR}$ holds, and in the former case move the corresponding pebble to R, while in the later case just terminate. Therefore, the *run*-condition is

$$\neg e_{BR} \vee (l_R \wedge l_W \wedge l_B \wedge e_{RW} \wedge e_{WB} \wedge e_{BR}).$$

The *post*-condition can just take that of *Spec–Programbody*, that is,

$$I1 \wedge I2 \wedge l_R \wedge l_W \wedge l_B \wedge e_{RW} \wedge e_{WB} \wedge e_{BR}.$$

In summary, the specification of process R_1 is as follows:

Spec$-R_1$:

$$\begin{array}{rl} pre: & I1 \wedge I2 \\ rely: & (I1 \Rightarrow I1') \wedge (I2 \Rightarrow I2') \wedge (\neg e_{BR} \Rightarrow \neg e'_{BR}) \\ run: & \neg e_{BR} \vee (l_R \wedge l_W \wedge l_B \wedge e_{RW} \wedge e_{WB} \wedge e_{BR}) \\ guar: & (I1 \Rightarrow I1') \wedge (I2 \Rightarrow I2') \wedge I(RW,\ W,\ WB,\ B) \wedge (\neg l_R \Rightarrow \neg l'_R) \\ post: & I1 \wedge I2 \wedge l_R \wedge l_W \wedge l_B \wedge e_{RW} \wedge e_{WB} \wedge e_{BR}. \end{array}$$

From the discussion, it is clear that the specification of process R_2 is:

Spec$-R_2$:

$$\begin{array}{rl} pre: & I1 \wedge I2 \\ rely: & (I1 \Rightarrow I1') \wedge (I2 \Rightarrow I2') \wedge (\neg l_R \Rightarrow \neg l'_R) \\ run: & (\neg l_R \wedge e_{RW}) \vee (l_R \wedge l_W \wedge l_B \wedge e_{RW} \wedge e_{WB} \wedge e_{BR}) \\ guar: & (I1 \Rightarrow I1') \wedge (I2 \Rightarrow I2') \wedge I(W,\ WB,\ B,\ BR) \wedge (\neg e_{RW} \Rightarrow \neg e'_{RW}) \\ post: & I1 \wedge I2 \wedge l_R \wedge l_W \wedge l_B \wedge e_{RW} \wedge e_{WB} \wedge e_{BR}. \end{array}$$

3.4 Modification of the last level specifications

Let us consider the question when a process, say R_1, can terminate. The main problem left is to design a '*convergence function*' to ensure the termination of the loop. Consider a red pebble in W, it has to be moved four times (to W, WB, B and BR) before getting into R, so for this pebble, its 'distance' to the bag which it belongs is 4. Similarly, the distance of a red pebble in WB, B and BR is 3, 2 and 1 respectively.

The pebble in RW should never be red, because RW is initially empty and a red pebble should not be sent out from R, which is the only bag that can transmit a pebble to RW. Let $num(col, X)$ denotes the number of the pebbles of colour *col* in X, then the following function E gives the numbers of the moves to be carried out.

$$\begin{array}{l} E = 5 \times num(Red, <RW>) + 4 \times num(Red, W) + 3 \times num(Red, <WB>) \\ +2 \times num(Red, B) + num(Red, <BR>) + 5 \times num(White, <WB>) \\ +4 \times num(White, B) + 3 \times num(White, <BR>) + 2 \times num(White, R) \\ +num(White, <RW>) + 5 \times num(Blue, <BR>) + 4 \times num(Blue, R) \\ +3 \times num(Blue, <RW>) + 2 \times num(Blue, W) + num(Blue, <WB>) \end{array}$$

Lemma 2 $E = 0 \Leftrightarrow l_R \wedge l_W \wedge l_B \wedge e_{RW} \wedge e_{WB} \wedge e_{BR}$.

Clearly, $E' \leq E$ ensures that pebbles on the whole are moved only closer to their bags, therefore when all the pebbles have reached their bags, they will remain there.

Lemma 3

$$\begin{array}{l} E' \leq E \\ \Rightarrow ((l_R \wedge l_W \wedge l_B \wedge e_{RW} \wedge e_{WB} \wedge e_{BR}) \Rightarrow (l'_R \wedge l'_W \wedge l'_B \wedge e'_{RW} \wedge e'_{WB} \wedge e'_{BR})). \end{array}$$

The above reasoning indicates that $E' \leq E$ should be in the *rely*, and consequently *guar* conditions.

Now we are ready to consider some details of the implementation. One standard technique in sequential programming to construct a *while*-statement from its specification is to take part of the *post*-condition and use its negative as the boolean test. One can do the same in parallel programming. One choice might be to take e_{BR} from the *post*-condition, but a little thought shows that R_1 can not terminate simply when e_{BR} is *true*, because although this indicates that the buffer BR is currently empty, there may well be a red pebble in W, which has to be passed to BR and moved by R_1 to R later. A better solution is to take the whole $l_R \wedge l_W \wedge l_B \wedge e_{RW} \wedge e_{WB} \wedge e_{BR}$ from the *post*-condition. Testing a long boolean expression is not efficient, and therefore a new variable b is introduced. It is assigned the value of the expression and the testing is performed on it instead.

In order to use the *while*-rule, we have to find an invariant, and this is quite easy now:

$$Inv(\alpha) \hat{=} \begin{cases} I1 \wedge I2 \wedge (\alpha = 2 \times E) & \text{if } E > 0 \\ I1 \wedge I2 \wedge (\alpha = 1) & \text{if } E = 0 \wedge \neg b \\ I1 \wedge I2 \wedge (\alpha = 0) & \text{if } E = 0 \wedge b \end{cases}$$

The proof obligations in the *while* rule require $(Inv(\alpha) \wedge rely) \Rightarrow \exists \beta \leq \alpha.\, Inv(\beta)'$. This is ensured if $b \Rightarrow b'$ is also in the *rely* condition, as shown by the following lemma:

Lemma 4 $(Inv(\alpha) \wedge (E' \leq E) \wedge (b \Rightarrow b')) \Rightarrow \exists \beta \leq \alpha.\, Inv(\beta)'$.

Thus, the specifications of R_1 and R_2 (in which predicates are indexed by 1 and 2 respectively, in order to check the proof obligations by the generalized parallel rule) are modified accordingly:

Spec$-R_1$:

pre_1 : $I1 \wedge I2$
$rely_1$: $(I1 \Rightarrow I1') \wedge (I2 \Rightarrow I2') \wedge (\neg e_{BR} \Rightarrow \neg e'_{BR})$
$\quad \wedge (b \Rightarrow b') \wedge (E' \leq E)$
run_1 : $\neg e_{BR} \vee (l_R \wedge l_W \wedge l_B \wedge e_{RW} \wedge e_{WB} \wedge e_{BR})$
$guar_1$: $(I1 \Rightarrow I1') \wedge (I2 \Rightarrow I2') \wedge I(RW, W, WB, B) \wedge (\neg l_R \Rightarrow \neg l'_R)$
$\quad \wedge (b \Rightarrow b') \wedge (E' \leq E)$
$post_1$: $I1 \wedge I2 \wedge l_R \wedge l_W \wedge l_B \wedge e_{RW} \wedge e_{WB} \wedge e_{BR}$

Spec$-R_2$:

pre_2 : $I1 \wedge I2$
$rely_2$: $(I1 \Rightarrow I1') \wedge (I2 \Rightarrow I2') \wedge (\neg l_R \Rightarrow \neg l'_R)$
$\quad \wedge (b \Rightarrow b') \wedge (E' \leq E)$
run_2 : $(\neg l_R \wedge e_{RW}) \vee (l_R \wedge l_W \wedge l_B \wedge e_{RW} \wedge e_{WB} \wedge e_{BR})$
$guar_2$: $(I1 \Rightarrow I1') \wedge (I2 \Rightarrow I2') \wedge I(W, WB, B, BR) \wedge (\neg e_{RW} \Rightarrow \neg e'_{RW})$
$\quad \wedge (b \Rightarrow b') \wedge (E' \leq E)$
$post_2$: $I1 \wedge I2 \wedge l_R \wedge l_W \wedge l_B \wedge e_{RW} \wedge e_{WB} \wedge e_{BR}$

The specifications of W_1, W_2, B_1 and B_2 (whose constitute predicates are indexed by 3, 4, 5 and 6 respectively), are similar, so we are not going to write them out, but some details can be seen from the verification step, which is to show

$$R_1 \parallel R_2 \parallel W_1 \parallel W_2 \parallel B_1 \parallel B_2 \ \underline{sat} \ Spec{-}Programbody,$$

by checking the proof obligations in the generalized parallel rule. Now *rely*, *run* and *guar* are $v' = v$, *true* and *true* respectively, thus the proof obligations are reduced to:

$$\begin{array}{l} 1).\ (\bigwedge_{i \neq k} post_i \Rightarrow run_k) \wedge \bigvee_{i=1,\ldots,6} run_i \\ 2).\ \bigvee_{i \neq k} guar_i \Rightarrow rely_k \end{array}$$

The first holds because the following trivial lemma.

Lemma 5 (*a*). $post_i \Rightarrow run_k \quad i,k = 1,\ldots,6.$ (*b*). $\bigvee_{i=1,\ldots,6} run_i$

For 2), it is necessary to check each process separately. Here we show the case of $\bigvee_{i \neq 1} guar_i \Rightarrow rely_1$. Since $\forall i = 2,\ldots,6.\, guar_i \Rightarrow (I1 \Rightarrow I1') \wedge (I2 \Rightarrow I2') \wedge (E' \leq E) \wedge (b \Rightarrow b')$, we only have to show the following lemma.

Lemma 6 $\forall i = 2,\ldots,6.\, guar_i \Rightarrow (\neg e_{BR} \Rightarrow \neg e'_{BR})$

The proof is trivial:

$$\begin{array}{l} guar_2 \Rightarrow I(W,\ WB,\ B,\ BR) \Rightarrow (\neg e_{BR} \Rightarrow \neg e'_{BR}) \\ guar_3 \Rightarrow I(WB,\ B,\ BR,\ R) \Rightarrow (\neg e_{BR} \Rightarrow \neg e'_{BR}) \\ guar_4 \Rightarrow I(B,\ BR,\ R,\ RW) \Rightarrow (\neg e_{BR} \Rightarrow \neg e'_{BR}) \\ guar_5 \Rightarrow I(BR,\ R,\ RW,\ W) \Rightarrow (\neg e_{BR} \Rightarrow \neg e'_{BR}) \\ guar_6 \Rightarrow (\neg e_{BR} \Rightarrow \neg e'_{BR}). \end{array}$$

3.5 Two small decompositions

From now on, the *rely*, *run* and *guar* conditions in each specification are not changed, so we can concentrate on the *pre* and *post* conditions, and record development and verification in a 'proof-outline-style'. For R_1, this result is:

$$\begin{array}{l} \{I1 \wedge I2\} \\ b := l_R \wedge l_W \wedge l_B \wedge e_{RW} \wedge e_{WB} \wedge e_{BR}; \\ \{\exists \alpha.\, Inv(\alpha)\} \\ \mathit{while}\ \neg b\ \mathit{do} \\ \quad \{Inv(\alpha) \wedge \alpha > 0\} \\ \quad R_1{-}body \\ \quad \{\exists \beta < \alpha. Inv(\beta)\} \\ \mathit{od} \\ \{Inv(0)\} \\ \{I1 \wedge I2 \wedge l_R \wedge l_W \wedge l_B \wedge e_{RW} \wedge e_{WB} \wedge e_{BR}\}. \end{array}$$

The remaining proof obligations are:

$$\begin{array}{l} (Inv(\alpha) \wedge \alpha > 0) \Rightarrow \neg b \\ Inv(0) \Rightarrow b \\ Inv(0) \Rightarrow (I1 \wedge I2 \wedge l_R \wedge l_W \wedge l_B \wedge e_{RW} \wedge e_{WB} \wedge e_{BR}), \end{array}$$

and they follow directly from the definition and lemma 4.

3.6 A small step of transformation

Since all the six processes begin with the same assignment statement, and the righthand of the assignment does not refer to the lefthand side, it can be moved outside, based on the algebraic law. More precisely, let $\widehat{R_1}, ..., \widehat{B_2}$ denote the rest parts of $R_1, ..., B_2$ with the beginning assignments removed, then the resulting system is:

$$(b := l_R \wedge l_W \wedge l_B \wedge e_{RW} \wedge e_{WB} \wedge e_{BR}); (\widehat{R_1} \parallel \widehat{R_2} \parallel \widehat{W_1} \parallel \widehat{W_2} \parallel \widehat{B_1} \parallel \widehat{B_2}).$$

Soundness of the law indicates that it satisfies the same specification, which in this case is *Spec−Programbody*.

3.7 Implementation

One could carry on decomposing the specification of R_1*—body*, but when a carefully planned design has reached such a detailed level, it is possible to try out an implementation directly and show it is correct with respect to the specification.

Code$-R_1-$*body*:

$\{Inv(\alpha_0) \wedge \alpha_0 > 0\}$
await $(l_R \wedge l_W \wedge l_B \wedge e_{RW} \wedge e_{WB} \wedge e_{BR}) \vee \neg e_{BR}$ *then skip end*;
$\{Inv(\alpha) \wedge (\alpha \leq 1 \vee (1 < \alpha \leq \alpha_0 \wedge \neg e_{BR})) \wedge \alpha_0 > 0\}$
if $\neg e_{BR}$ *then*
  $\{Inv(\alpha) \wedge \alpha \leq \alpha_0 \wedge \alpha_0 > 0 \wedge \neg e_{BR}\}$
  $< R, e_{BR} := R \cup \{BR\}, true;$
  if $col(BR) \neq red$ *then* $l_R :=$ *false fi* $>$
  $\{Inv(\alpha) \wedge \alpha < \alpha_0 \wedge \alpha_0 > 0\}$
fi;
$\{Inv(\alpha) \wedge (\alpha \leq 1 \vee \alpha < \alpha_0) \wedge \alpha_0 > 0\}$
$b := l_R \wedge l_W \wedge l_B \wedge e_{RW} \wedge e_{WB} \wedge e_{BR}$
$\{Inv(\alpha) \wedge (\alpha = 0 \vee \alpha < \alpha_0) \wedge \alpha_0 > 0\}$
$\{Inv(\alpha) \wedge (\alpha < \alpha_0)\}$.

The development of other processes are similar. We list the complete programs of $\widehat{R_1}$ and $\widehat{R_2}$ below.

Code$-\widehat{R_1}$

while $\neg b$ *do*
  await $(l_R \wedge l_W \wedge l_B \wedge e_{RW} \wedge e_{WB} \wedge e_{BR}) \vee \neg e_{BR}$ *then skip end*;
  if $\neg e_{BR}$ *then*
    $< R, e_{BR} := R \cup \{BR\}, true;$
    if $col(BR) \neq red$ *then* $l_R :=$ *false fi* $>$;
  fi;
  $b := l_R \wedge l_W \wedge l_B \wedge e_{RW} \wedge e_{WB} \wedge e_{BR}$
od

$Code-\widehat{R_2}$

$while\ \neg b\ do$
$\quad await\ (l_R \wedge l_W \wedge l_B \wedge e_{RW} \wedge e_{WB} \wedge e_{BR}) \vee (\neg l_R \wedge e_{RW})\ then\ skip\ end$
$\quad if\ \neg l_R\ then$
$\quad\quad RW := choose(White\&Blue,\ R);$
$\quad\quad < R, e_{RW} := R - \{RW\}, false;$
$\quad\quad if\ All(red,\ R)\ then\ l_R := true\ fi >;$
$\quad fi;$
$\quad b := l_R \wedge l_W \wedge l_B \wedge e_{RW} \wedge e_{WB} \wedge e_{BR}$
$od.$

This implementation is still at a rather high level, because a data type *bag* with four operations $X := X \cup \{u\}$, $X := X - \{u\}$, $choose(col1\&col2,\ X)$ and $All(col,\ X)$ on it is used. The first two operations stand respectively for inserting and deleting a pebble. The third and the fourth are two expressions, with $choose(col1\&col2,\ X)$ denoting an arbitrary pebble from X of colour either $col1$ or $col2$ and $All(col,\ X)$ denoting whether pebbles in X are all of colour col. Their formal definitions are straightforward and therefore omitted here.

3.8 Data refinement

In order to execute the program on a computer, the abstract data type *bag* must be replaced by a more concrete one.

One solution well known in the sequential programming is to refine it by a linked list, with the abstraction function or simulation relation mapping the list to a bag whose elements are just those stored in the list. For each abstract operation there must be a concrete one, so for example, corresponding to the abstract operations $X := X \cup \{u\}$, there is a concrete operation

$< new(r);$
$r.element := u;$
$last.next := r;$
$last := r >$

The theory of data refinement shows that in sequential programming, the use of the abstract data type can be replaced by the use of the concrete one, when certain simple proof obligations holds. Our observation indicates that for the kind of parallel program for which that exists an equivalent sequential one in a language covered by the sequential data refinement theory, sequential data refinement methods also apply. Therefore, for our program, when the implementation of its operation is executed atomically, the use of abstract data type *bag* can be replaced by that of the linked list. This is a favourite implementation in sequential data refinement, and the proof obligations have been reported many times.

This step of data refinement could of course be performed at the top level, then it would just be a normal sequential data refinement and we do not have to worry about the validity of it. However, this would result in much more complicated specifications and hence make the development much more difficult.

There is one difference between sequential and concurrent data refinement: in concurrent data refinement atomicity must be strictly preserved, and in our example, this has been clearly indicated by the use of brackets in the concrete operations. In sequential data refinement, it does not matter whether the abstract operation is replaced by a single (atomic) concrete operation or by a piece of concrete program, since in sequential programming, $< P >$ is always equivalent to P, for any program P. (This is why the bracket notation simply does not exist there at all).

This of course does not mean that atomicity can never be changed. What we are saying is only that atomicity refinement is in general not possible, but for special cases where operations satisfy certain commutativity conditions, atomicity can indeed be refined. This has already been studied in, for example, [Back, LS89], but those results may have to be modified before being used here, since the correctness concern is not exactly the same.

4 Conclusion

In this paper, a stepwise development of a parallel algorithm has been carefully presented. We have devoted a large part of the paper to explain the process of finding each development step, guided by the formal systems. A formal method enthusiast would possibly claim this algorithm is derived purely by the use of the formal methods, but in order to be honest, we have to admit from time to time in the development process, we have used intuitive thinking. On the other hand, our intuitive thinking had led to a couple of incorrect designs, which were only detected when we tried to verify that step. Our experiments showed that state-based parallel programs (with shared-variables) are usually more subtle than the communication-based ones (for example, consider why the brackets are necessary in R_1 and R_2). Without formal verification, we would have little confidence even in the correctness of an algorithm like this. Our case study demonstrated that verification can be naturally conducted at the same time as, and combined with, the design of the system. This constructive approach is only possible due to the compositionality of the methods.

Acknowledgement We are grateful to Ketil Stølen for many communications, and to Willem-Paul de Roever and referees for comments which lead to many improvements. We also like to thank Antonio Cau and Jos Coenen for interest and discussions on related topics. This work is partly supported by the Esprit Basic Research Action PROCOS.

References

[Ap84] K.R. Apt. Ten years of Hoare's logic: a survey-part II: nondeterminism. *Theoretical Computer Science* 28 83-109 1984.

[AP86] K.R. Apt and G.D. Plotkin. countable nondeterminism and random assignment. *Journal of the ACM 33* 4 724-767 1986.

[Ba90] J.C.M. Baeten. *Process Algebra.* Cambridge Univ Press, 1990.

[Di77] E. W. Dijkstra. An exercise inspired by the Dutch National Flag. EWD-608, Burroughs, Nuenen, the Netherlands 1977.

[dR85] W.P. de Roever. The quest for compositionality. in *Proc:IFIP Working Conf. The Role of Abstract Models in Computer Science*North-Holland, 1985.

[HHS87] C.A.R. Hoare, He, Jifeng and J.W. Sanders. Prespecification in Data Refinement. IPL,25 71-76 1987.

[Ho85] C.A.R. Hoare. *Communicating Sequential Processes.* Prentice Hall, London. 1985.

[Hoare et al 87] C.A.R. Hoare et al. Laws of programming. *Commun. ACM 30,* 8 672-686 1987.

[GdeRR82] R. T. Gerth, W.P. de Roever and M. Roncken. A study in distributed systems and Dutch patriotism. In M. Joseph (editor) *Proc. of the 2nd conf. on Foundations of Software Technology and Theoretical Computer Science.* Bangalore, India 1982.

[Jo81] C.B. Jones. Development methods for computer programs including a notion of interference. Dphil. Thesis, Oxford University Computing Laboratory, 1981.

[Jo91] C.B. Jones. Interference resumed. in P. Bailes, editor, *Australian Software Engineering Research 1991.*

[LS89] L. Lamport and F.B. Schneider. Pretending atomicity. Research report 29, Digital System Research Center 1989.

[Mi89] R. Milner. *Communication and Concurrency.* Prentice-Hall International Series in Computer Science, 1989.

[OG76] S. Owicki and D. Gries. An axiomatic proof technique for parallel programs. *Acta Inform. 6* 319-340 Springer-Verlag 1976.

[St90] K. Stølen. *Development of Parallel Programs on Shared Datastructures.* Ph.D Thesis, Computer Science Department, Manchester University, 1990.

[St91] K. Stølen. An attempt to reason about shared-state concurrency in the style of VDM. in S. Prehn and W. J. Toetenel, editors, *Proceedings of VDM 91*, LNCS 551, Springer-Verlag, 1991.

[XH91] Xu Qiwen and He Jifeng. A theory of state-based parallel programming: Part 1. in J. Morris, editor, *Proceedings of BCS FACS 4th Refinement Workshop* January 1991, Cambridge, Springer-Verlag.

[XH92] Xu Qiwen and He Jifeng. Laws of parallel programming. Manuscript, 1992.

Proving Total Correctness with Respect to a Fair (Shared-State) Parallel Language

Ketil Stølen*

Institut für Informatik, der Technischen Universität,
Munich, Germany

Abstract

A method for proving programs totally correct with respect to an unconditionally fair (shared-state) parallel language is presented. The method is compositional and well-suited for top-down program development. It does not depend upon temporal logic, and program transformation is not employed. A number of examples are given.

1 Introduction

The two most well-known approaches to proving fair termination are the *explicit schedulers* method and the *helpful directions* method. The explicit schedulers method [Par81] transforms a fair termination problem into an ordinary nondeterministic termination problem by augmenting the code with statements in such a way that the new program simulates exactly all fair computations of the old program.

The helpful directions method is based upon choosing helpful directions at intermediate stages. There are two variants of this approach. One bases the selection upon a rank, where each rank has its own set of helpful directions [GFMdR85], while the other employs a state predicate to determine the helpful directions [LPS81]. A third way of reasoning about fairness is to use temporal logic, as in for example [GPSS80].

The approach described in this paper does not employ any of the techniques mentioned above, although it is to some degree related to the helpful directions method. In the style of LSP [Stø90], [Stø91a], [Stø91b] rely- and guarantee-conditions are used to characterise interference, while a wait-condition is employed to select helpful paths. Auxiliary variables are needed. However, they are not first implemented and thereafter removed, as for example in the Owicki/Gries method [OG76]. Instead the use of auxiliary variables is 'simulated' in the deduction rules.

The next section, Section 2, defines the basic programming language. The syntax and meaning of specifications are the topics of Section 3, while the most important deduction-rules are explained in Section 4. Section 5 consists of a number of examples. Finally, Section 6 indicates some extensions and compares the method to other methods known from the literature.

*Author's address: Institute für Informatik, der Technischen Universität, Postfach 20 24 20, Arcisstrasse 21, D-8000 München 2, Germany. Email address: stoelen@informatik.tu-muenchen.de

2 Programming Language

The object of this section is to characterise the programming language, both at syntactic and semantic level. A *program*'s context-independent syntax is characterised in the well-known BNF-notation: given that $\langle vl\rangle$, $\langle el\rangle$, $\langle dl\rangle$ and $\langle ts\rangle$ denote respectively a list of variables, a list of expressions, a list of variable declarations, and a Boolean test, then any program is of the form $\langle pg\rangle$, where

$$\begin{aligned}
\langle pg\rangle &::= \langle as\rangle|\langle bl\rangle|\langle sc\rangle|\langle if\rangle|\langle wd\rangle|\langle pr\rangle\\
\langle as\rangle &::= \langle vl\rangle := \langle el\rangle\\
\langle bl\rangle &::= \mathsf{blo}\ \langle dl\rangle\ \mathsf{in}\ \langle pg\rangle\ \mathsf{olb}\\
\langle sc\rangle &::= \langle pg\rangle; \langle pg\rangle\\
\langle if\rangle &::= \mathsf{if}\ \langle ts\rangle\ \mathsf{then}\ \langle pg\rangle\ \mathsf{else}\ \langle pg\rangle\ \mathsf{fi}\\
\langle wd\rangle &::= \mathsf{while}\ \langle ts\rangle\ \mathsf{do}\ \langle pg\rangle\ \mathsf{od}\\
\langle pr\rangle &::= \{\langle pg\rangle \parallel \langle pg\rangle\}
\end{aligned}$$

The main structure of a program is characterised above. However, a syntactically correct program is also required to satisfy some supplementary constraints. First of all, with respect to the assignment-statement $\langle as\rangle$, it is required that the two lists have the same number of elements, that the j'th variable in the first list is of the same type as the j'th expression in the second, and that the same variable does not occur in the variable list more than once.

The block-statement $\langle bl\rangle$ allows for the declaration of variables $\langle dl\rangle$. To avoid tedious complications due to name clashes: for any program z, a variable x may occur in maximum one of z's declaration lists and only once in the same list. Moreover, if x occurs in the declaration list of one of z's block-statements z', then all occurrences of x in z are in z'.

A program variable x is *local* with respect to a program z, if it occurs in a declaration list in z. Otherwise, x is *global* with respect to z. This means of course that a variable x which is local with respect to a program z, may be global with respect to some of z's subprograms.

In LSP [Stø90] variables occurring in the Boolean test of an if- or a while-statement are constrained from being accessed by any other program running in parallel. In this paper there is no such constraint.

The programming language is given operational semantics in the style of [Acz83]. A *state* is a mapping of all programming variables to values, while a *configuration* is a pair of the form $\langle z, s\rangle$, where z is a program or the *empty program* ϵ, and s is a state. Moreover, s_ϑ denotes the state s restricted to the set of variables ϑ, while $s \models b$ means that the Boolean expression b is true in the state s.

An *external* transition is the least binary relation on configurations such that

- $\langle z, s_1\rangle \xrightarrow{e} \langle z, s_2\rangle$,

while an *internal* transition is the least binary relation on configurations such that either

- $\langle v := r, s\rangle \xrightarrow{i} \langle \epsilon, s(^v_r)\rangle$, where $s(^v_r)$ denotes the state that is obtained from s, by mapping the variables v to the values of r in the state s, and leaving all other maplets unchanged,

- $\langle$blo d in z olb$, s_1\rangle \xrightarrow{i} \langle z, s_2\rangle$, where s_2 denotes a state that is obtained from s_1, by mapping the variables in d to randomly chosen type-correct values, and leaving all other maplets unchanged,
- $\langle z_1; z_2, s_1\rangle \xrightarrow{i} \langle z_2, s_2\rangle$ if $\langle z_1, s_1\rangle \xrightarrow{i} \langle \epsilon, s_2\rangle$,
- $\langle z_1; z_2, s_1\rangle \xrightarrow{i} \langle z_3; z_2, s_2\rangle$ if $\langle z_1, s_1\rangle \xrightarrow{i} \langle z_3, s_2\rangle$ and $z_3 \neq \epsilon$,
- $\langle$if b then z_1 else z_2 fi$, s\rangle \xrightarrow{i} \langle z_1, s\rangle$ if $s \models b$,
- $\langle$if b then z_1 else z_2 fi$, s\rangle \xrightarrow{i} \langle z_2, s\rangle$ if $s \models \neg b$,
- $\langle$while b do z od$, s\rangle \xrightarrow{i} \langle z;$ while b do z od$, s\rangle$ if $s \models b$,
- $\langle$while b do z od$, s\rangle \xrightarrow{i} \langle \epsilon, s\rangle$ if $s \models \neg b$,
- $\langle \{z_1 \parallel z_2\}, s_1\rangle \xrightarrow{i} \langle z_2, s_2\rangle$ if $\langle z_1, s_1\rangle \xrightarrow{i} \langle \epsilon, s_2\rangle$,
- $\langle \{z_1 \parallel z_2\}, s_1\rangle \xrightarrow{i} \langle z_1, s_2\rangle$ if $\langle z_2, s_1\rangle \xrightarrow{i} \langle \epsilon, s_2\rangle$,
- $\langle \{z_1 \parallel z_2\}, s_1\rangle \xrightarrow{i} \langle \{z_3 \parallel z_2\}, s_2\rangle$ if $\langle z_1, s_1\rangle \xrightarrow{i} \langle z_3, s_2\rangle$ and $z_3 \neq \epsilon$,
- $\langle \{z_1 \parallel z_2\}, s_1\rangle \xrightarrow{i} \langle \{z_1 \parallel z_3\}, s_2\rangle$ if $\langle z_2, s_1\rangle \xrightarrow{i} \langle z_3, s_2\rangle$ and $z_3 \neq \epsilon$.

The above definition is of course sensible only if expressions in assignment-statements and Boolean tests never evaluate to 'undefined'. Thus, all functions occurring in expressions must be required to be total.

It follows from the definition that Boolean tests and assignment-statements are atomic. The empty program ϵ models *termination*.

In the rest of the paper skip will be used as an alias for the assignment of an empty list of expressions to an empty list of variables.

Definition 1 *A* computation *of a program z_1 is an infinite sequence of the form*

$$\langle z_1, s_1\rangle \xrightarrow{l_1} \langle z_2, s_2\rangle \xrightarrow{l_2} \dots \xrightarrow{l_{k-1}} \langle z_k, s_k\rangle \xrightarrow{l_k} \dots,$$

where for all $j \geq 1$, $\langle z_j, s_j\rangle \xrightarrow{l_j} \langle z_{j+1}, s_{j+1}\rangle$ is either an external or an internal transition, and no external transition changes the values of z_1's local variables.

If σ is a computation of z, the idea is that an internal transition represents an atomic step due to z, while an external transition represents an atomic step due to z's *environment*, in other words, due to the other programs running in parallel with z.

Given a computation σ, $Z(\sigma)$, $S(\sigma)$ and $L(\sigma)$ are the projection functions to sequences of programs, states and transition labels respectively, and for all $j \geq 1$, $Z(\sigma_j)$, $S(\sigma_j)$, $L(\sigma_j)$ and σ_j denote respectively the j'th program, the j'th state, the j'th transition label and the j'th configuration. $\sigma(j, \dots, \infty)$ denotes the result of removing the $j-1$ first transitions.

Two computations (or prefixes of computations) σ of z_1 and σ' of z_2 are *compatible*, if $\{z_1 \parallel z_2\}$ is a program, $S(\sigma) = S(\sigma')$ and for all $j \geq 1$, $L(\sigma_j) = L(\sigma'_j)$ implies $L(\sigma_j) = e$. More informally, σ of z_1 and σ' of z_2 are compatible, if there is no clash of variable names which restricts z_1 and z_2 from being composed in parallel (see restriction on local variable names above), and for all n: the state in the n'th component of σ is equal to the state in the n'th component of σ', if the n'th transition in σ is internal then the n'th transition in σ' is external, and if the n'th transition in σ' is internal then the n'th transition in σ is external. The reason for the two last constraints is of course that z_2 is a part of z_1's environment, and z_1 is a part of z_2's environment, thus an internal transition in σ must correspond to an external transition in σ', and the other way around.

For example, given three assignment-statements z_1, z_2 and z_3, the two computations

$$\langle z_1; z_2, s_1\rangle \xrightarrow{i} \langle z_2, s_2\rangle \xrightarrow{i} \langle \epsilon, s_3\rangle \xrightarrow{e} \sigma,$$
$$\langle z_3, s_1\rangle \xrightarrow{i} \langle \epsilon, s_2\rangle \xrightarrow{e} \langle \epsilon, s_3\rangle \xrightarrow{e} \sigma$$

are not compatible, because they both start with an internal transition. However,

$$\langle z_1; z_2, s_1\rangle \xrightarrow{i} \langle z_2, s_2\rangle \xrightarrow{e} \langle z_2, s_3\rangle \xrightarrow{e} \langle z_2, s_4\rangle \xrightarrow{i} \langle \epsilon, s_5\rangle \xrightarrow{e} \sigma,$$
$$\langle z_3, s_1\rangle \xrightarrow{e} \langle z_3, s_2\rangle \xrightarrow{i} \langle \epsilon, s_3\rangle \xrightarrow{e} \langle \epsilon, s_4\rangle \xrightarrow{e} \langle \epsilon, s_5\rangle \xrightarrow{e} \sigma$$

are compatible, and they can be *composed* into a unique computation

$$\langle \{z_1; z_2 \parallel z_3\}, s_1\rangle \xrightarrow{i} \langle \{z_2 \parallel z_3\}, s_2\rangle \xrightarrow{i} \langle z_2, s_3\rangle \xrightarrow{e} \langle z_2, s_4\rangle \xrightarrow{i} \langle \epsilon, s_5\rangle \xrightarrow{e} \sigma$$

of $\{z_1; z_2 \parallel z_3\}$, by composing the program part of each configuration, and making a transition internal iff one of the two component transitions are internal.

More generally, for any pair of compatible computations σ and σ', let $\sigma \bowtie \sigma'$ denote

$$\langle z_1, s_1\rangle \xrightarrow{l_1} \langle z_2, s_2\rangle \xrightarrow{l_2} \ldots \xrightarrow{l_{k-1}} \langle z_k, s_k\rangle \xrightarrow{l_k} \ldots,$$

where for all $j \geq 1$,

- $s_j = S(\sigma_j)$,
- $z_j = \{Z(\sigma_j) \parallel Z(\sigma'_j)\}$ if $Z(\sigma_j) \neq \epsilon$ and $Z(\sigma'_j) \neq \epsilon$,
- $z_j = Z(\sigma_j)$ if $Z(\sigma'_j) = \epsilon$,
- $z_j = Z(\sigma'_j)$ if $Z(\sigma_j) = \epsilon$,
- $l_j = e$ if $L(\sigma_j) = e$ and $L(\sigma'_j) = e$,
- $l_j = i$ if $L(\sigma_j) = i$ or $L(\sigma'_j) = i$.

It is straightforward to show that:

Proposition 1 *For any pair of compatible computations σ of z_1 and σ' of z_2, $\sigma \bowtie \sigma'$ is uniquely determined by the definition above, and $\sigma \bowtie \sigma'$ is a computation of $\{z_1 \parallel z_2\}$.*

Moreover, it is also easy to prove that:

Proposition 2 *For any computation σ of $\{z_1 \parallel z_2\}$, there are two unique compatible computations σ' of z_1 and σ'' of z_2, such that $\sigma = \sigma' \bowtie \sigma''$.*

So far no fairness constraint has been introduced. This means for example that if z_1 and z_2 denote respectively the programs

$$b := \mathsf{true}, \qquad\qquad \mathsf{while}\ \neg b\ \mathsf{do\ skip\ od},$$

then there is no guarantee that $\{z_1 \parallel z_2\}$ terminates even if the program is executed in an environment which is restricted from changing the truth-value of b. There are two reasons for this:

- $\{z_1 \parallel z_2\}$ may be infinitely overtaken by the environment, as for example in the computation:

  $$\langle\{z_1 \parallel z_2\}, s_1\rangle \xrightarrow{e} \langle\{z_1 \parallel z_2\}, s_2\rangle \xrightarrow{e} \ \ldots\ \xrightarrow{e} \langle\{z_1 \parallel z_2\}, s_j\rangle \xrightarrow{e} \ \ldots\ .$$

  In this particular computation all transitions are external. However, more generally, a computation suffers from this type of unfairness if it has only finitely many internal transitions and the empty program is never reached (it does not terminate).

- z_1 may be infinitely overtaken by z_2. This is for example the case in the computation:

  $$\langle\{z_1 \parallel z_2\}, s\rangle \xrightarrow{i} \langle\{z_1 \parallel \mathsf{skip}; z_2\}, s\rangle \xrightarrow{i} \langle\{z_1 \parallel z_2\}, s\rangle \xrightarrow{i} \langle\{z_1 \parallel \mathsf{skip}; z_2\}, s\rangle \xrightarrow{i} \\ \ldots \xrightarrow{i} \langle\{z_1 \parallel z_2\}, s\rangle \xrightarrow{i} \langle\{z_1 \parallel \mathsf{skip}; z_2\}, s\rangle \xrightarrow{i} \ \ldots\ .$$

  In the general case, a computation which suffers from this type of unfairness, has infinitely many internal transitions. Moreover, from a certain point, at least one *process* is infinitely overtaken.

Informally, a computation is *unconditionally fair* iff each process, which becomes executable at some point in the computation, either terminates or performs infinitely many internal transitions. Observe that this excludes both unfairness due to infinite overtaking by the overall environment, and unfairness which occurs when one process is infinitely overtaken by another process. (What is called unconditional fairness in this paper is inspired by the definition of impartiality in [LPS81].)

To give a more formal definition, let $<$ be a binary relation on computations such that $\sigma < \sigma'$ iff $S(\sigma) = S(\sigma')$, $L(\sigma) = L(\sigma')$, and there is a (non-empty) program z such that for all $j \geq 1$, $Z(\sigma_j); z = Z(\sigma'_j)$. Moreover, $\sigma \leq \sigma'$ means that $\sigma < \sigma'$ or $\sigma = \sigma'$. Clearly, for any computation σ, there is a minimal computation σ', such that $\sigma' \leq \sigma$ and for all computations σ'', if $\sigma'' < \sigma$ then $\sigma' \leq \sigma''$. Moreover, a computation σ is unconditionally fair iff its minimal computation σ' is unconditionally fair. For example a computation of the form

$$\langle z_1; z, s_1 \rangle \xrightarrow{l_1} \langle z_2; z, s_2 \rangle \xrightarrow{l_2} \ldots \xrightarrow{l_{j-1}} \langle z_j; z, s_j \rangle \xrightarrow{l_j} \ldots,$$

where the subprogram z never becomes executable, is unconditionally fair if the computation

$$\langle z_1, s_1 \rangle \xrightarrow{l_1} \langle z_2, s_2 \rangle \xrightarrow{l_2} \ldots \xrightarrow{l_{j-1}} \langle z_j, s_j \rangle \xrightarrow{l_j} \ldots$$

is unconditionally fair.

It remains to state what it means for a minimal computation σ to be unconditionally fair. There are two cases: first of all, if there are two computations σ', σ'' and a $j \geq 1$, such that $Z(\sigma'_1) \neq \epsilon$, $Z(\sigma''_1) \neq \epsilon$ and $\sigma' \bowtie \sigma'' = \sigma(j, \ldots, \infty)$, then σ is unconditionally fair iff both σ' and σ'' are unconditionally fair. On the other hand, if σ cannot be decomposed in such a way, then σ is unconditionally fair iff σ terminates or σ has infinitely many internal transitions.

Definition 2 *Given a computation σ, if there is a computation σ', such that $\sigma' < \sigma$ then*

- *σ is unconditionally fair iff σ' is unconditionally fair,*

else if there are two computations σ', σ'' and a $j \geq 1$, such that $Z(\sigma'_1) \neq \epsilon$, $Z(\sigma''_1) \neq \epsilon$ and $\sigma' \bowtie \sigma'' = \sigma(j, \ldots, \infty)$ then

- *σ is unconditionally fair iff both σ' and σ'' are unconditionally fair,*

else

- *σ is unconditionally fair iff either*
  - *there is a $j \geq 1$, such that $Z(\sigma_j) = \epsilon$, or*
  - *for all $j \geq 1$, there is a $k \geq j$, such that $L(\sigma_k) = i$.*

Observe that propositions 1 and 2 also hold for unconditionally fair computations.

Definition 3 *Given a program z, let $cp_u(z)$ be the set of all unconditionally fair computations σ, such that $Z(\sigma_1) = z$.*

The definition above not only constrains the programming language's parallel construct to be unconditionally fair, but also restricts the actual program from being *infinitely overtaken* by the overall environment. The latter restriction can be thought of as an assumption about the environment built into the semantics.

It may be argued that it would have been more correct to state this assumption at the specification level as an assumption about the environment (in other words as an additional assumption in definition 4. In that case, the definition of unconditional fairness can be weakened to allow for infinite overtaking by the overall environment. However, this distinction is not of any great practical importance since the deduction rules are exactly the same for both interpretations.

3 Specified Programs

A specification is of the form $(\vartheta, \alpha) :: (P, R, W, G, E)$, where ϑ is a finite set of programming variables, α is a finite set of auxiliary variables, the *pre-condition* P, and the *wait-condition* W are unary predicates, and the *rely-condition* R, the *guarantee-condition* G, and the *effect-condition* E are binary predicates. For any unary predicate U, $s \models U$ means that U is true in the state s. Moreover, for any binary predicate B, $(s_1, s_2) \models B$ means that B is true for the pair of states (s_1, s_2).

The *global state* is the state restricted to $\vartheta \cup \alpha$. It is required that $\vartheta \cap \alpha = \emptyset$, and that P, R, W, G and E constrain only the variables in $\vartheta \cup \alpha$. This means for example, that if there are two states s, s', such that $s \models P$ and $s_{\vartheta \cup \alpha} = s'_{\vartheta \cup \alpha}$, then $s' \models P$.

Predicates will often be characterised by first order formulas. In the case of binary predicates *hooked* variables (as in VDM [Jon90]) are employed to refer to the 'older' state. To avoid excessive use of parentheses it is assumed that $\Rightarrow$ has lower priority than $\wedge$ and $\vee$, which again have lower priority than $|$, which has lower priority than all other operator symbols. This means for example that $(a \wedge b) \Rightarrow c$ can be simplified to $a \wedge b \Rightarrow c$.

A specification states a number of assumptions about the environment. First of all, the initial state is assumed to satisfy the pre-condition. Secondly, it is assumed that any external transition, which changes the global state, satisfies the rely-condition. For example, given the rely-condition $x < \overleftarrow{x} \wedge y = \overleftarrow{y}$, it is assumed that the environment will never change the value of y. Moreover, if the environment assigns a new value to x, then this value will be less than or equal to the variable's previous value. The assumptions are summed up in the definition below:

Definition 4 *Given a set of variables ϑ, and pre- and rely-conditions P, R, then $ext(\vartheta, P, R)$ denotes the set of all computations σ, such that:*

- $S(\sigma_1) \models P$,
- *for all $j \geq 1$, if $L(\sigma_j) = e$ and $S(\sigma_j)_\vartheta \neq S(\sigma_{j+1})_\vartheta$ then*
  - $(S(\sigma_j), S(\sigma_{j+1})) \models R$.

A specification is not only stating assumptions about the environment, but also commitments to the implementation. Given an environment which satisfies the assumptions, then an implementation is required either to *busy-wait* forever in states which satisfy the wait-condition or to *terminate*. Moreover, any internal transition, which changes the global state, is required to satisfy the guarantee-condition. Finally, if the implementation terminates, then the overall effect is constrained to satisfy the effect-condition. External transitions both before the first internal transition and after the last are included in the overall effect. This means that given the rely-condition $x > \overleftarrow{x}$, the strongest effect-condition for the program skip is $x \geq \overleftarrow{x}$. The commitments are summed up below:

Definition 5 *Given a set of variables ϑ, and wait-, guarantee- and effect-conditions W, G, E, then $int(\vartheta, W, G, E)$ denotes the set of all computations σ, such that:*

- *there is a $j \geq 1$, such that for all $k \geq j$, $S(\sigma_k) \models W$, or there is a $j \geq 1$, such that $Z(\sigma_j) = \epsilon$,*
- *for all $j \geq 1$, if $L(\sigma_j) = i$ and $S(\sigma_j)_\vartheta \neq S(\sigma_{j+1})_\vartheta$ then*
  - $(S(\sigma_j), S(\sigma_{j+1})) \models G$,
- *for all $j \geq 1$, if $Z(\sigma_j) = \epsilon$ then $(S(\sigma_1), S(\sigma_j)) \models E$.*

(As in LSP, see [Stø91b], it is also possible to interpret the wait-condition as an assumption about the environment. In that case the environment is assumed always eventually to provide a state which falsifies the wait-condition, while the implementation is required to terminate. The deduction rules are exactly the same for both interpretations.)

A *specified program* is a pair consisting of a program z and a specification $(\vartheta, \alpha) :: (P, R, W, G, E)$, written

$$z \ \underline{\text{sat}} \ (\vartheta, \alpha) :: (P, R, W, G, E).$$

It is required that for any variable x occurring in z, x is an element of ϑ iff x is global with respect to z. Moreover, any variable occurring in z is restricted from being an element of α.

If the set of auxiliary variables is empty, it is now straightforward to characterise what it means for a specified program to be valid: namely that any program computation which satisfies the environment assumptions, also satisfies the commitments to the implementation. More formally:

Definition 6 $\models_u$ z $\underline{\text{sat}}$ $(\vartheta, \emptyset) :: (P, R, W, G, E)$ *iff* $ext(\vartheta, P, R) \cap cp_u(z) \subseteq int(\vartheta, W, G, E)$.

So far very little has been said about the use of auxiliary variables. Auxiliary variables are employed to increase the expressiveness. For example, without auxiliary variables many 'correct' developments are excluded because sufficiently strong intermediate predicates cannot be expressed.

In the Owicki/Gries method [OG76] (and in many other approaches) auxiliary variables are first implemented as ordinary programming variables and thereafter removed. The reason why this strategy is chosen by Owicki/Gries, is that they conduct their proofs in several iterations, and one way to 'remember' the auxiliary structure from one iteration to the next is to store it in terms of program code. They first conduct a proof in the style of ordinary Hoare-logic, then they prove freedom from interference and so on, and the auxiliary structure is implemented in order to ensure that it remains unchanged from the first to the last iteration. In the method presented in this paper, there is only one proof iteration and therefore no need to 'remember' the auxiliary structure. Thus, the use of auxiliary variables can be 'simulated' in the deduction rules. Note that there are no constraints on the type of an auxiliary variable. For example the user is not restricted to reason in terms of full histories (history variables, traces etc.), but is instead free to define the auxiliary structure he prefers.

To characterise validity when the set of auxiliary variables is non-empty, it is necessary to introduce some new notation. If l and k are finite lists, then $\#l$ denotes the number of elements in l, $\langle l \rangle$ denotes the set of elements in l, $l \circ k$ denotes the result of prefixing k with l, while l_n, where $1 \leq n \leq \#l$, denotes the n'th element of l. Finally, $a \leftarrow_{(\vartheta,\alpha)} u$ iff a is a list of variables, u is a list of expressions, and ϑ and α are two sets of variables, such that $\#a = \#u$, $\langle a \rangle \subseteq \alpha$, and for all $1 \leq j \leq \#a$, any variable occurring in u_j is an element of $\vartheta \cup \{a_j\}$.

An *augmentation* with respect to two sets of variables ϑ and α, is the least binary relation $\overset{(\vartheta,\alpha)}{\hookrightarrow}$ on programs such that either:

- $v := r \overset{(\vartheta,\alpha)}{\hookrightarrow} v \circ a := r \circ u$, where
  - $a \leftarrow_{(\vartheta,\alpha)} u$,
- blo $x_1 : T_1, \ldots, x_n : T_n$ in z olb $\overset{(\vartheta,\alpha)}{\hookrightarrow}$ blo $x_1 : T_1, \ldots, x_n : T_n$ in z' olb, where
  - $z \overset{(\vartheta \cup \bigcup_{j=1}^{n}\{x_j\},\alpha)}{\hookrightarrow} z'$,
- $z_1; z_2 \overset{(\vartheta,\alpha)}{\hookrightarrow} z_1'; z_2'$, where
  - $z_1 \overset{(\vartheta,\alpha)}{\hookrightarrow} z_1'$ and $z_2 \overset{(\vartheta,\alpha)}{\hookrightarrow} z_2'$,
- if b then z_1 else z_2 fi $\overset{(\vartheta,\alpha)}{\hookrightarrow}$ blo b' : B in $b' \circ a := b \circ u$; if b' then z_1' else z_2' fi olb, where
  - $b' \notin \vartheta \cup \alpha$, $a \leftarrow_{(\vartheta,\alpha)} u$, $z_1 \overset{(\vartheta,\alpha)}{\hookrightarrow} z_1'$, and $z_2 \overset{(\vartheta,\alpha)}{\hookrightarrow} z_2'$,
- while b do z od $\overset{(\vartheta,\alpha)}{\hookrightarrow}$ blo b' : B in $b' \circ a := b \circ u$; while b' do z'; $b' \circ a := b \circ u$ od olb, where
  - $b' \notin \vartheta \cup \alpha$, $a \leftarrow_{(\vartheta,\alpha)} u$ and $z \overset{(\vartheta,\alpha)}{\hookrightarrow} z'$,
- $\{z_1 \parallel z_2\} \overset{(\vartheta,\alpha)}{\hookrightarrow} \{z_1' \parallel z_2'\}$, where
  - $z_1 \overset{(\vartheta,\alpha)}{\hookrightarrow} z_1'$ and $z_2 \overset{(\vartheta,\alpha)}{\hookrightarrow} z_2'$.

The idea is that $z_1 \overset{(\vartheta,\alpha)}{\hookrightarrow} z_2$ if z_2 can be obtained from z_1 by adding auxiliary structure with respect to a set of programming variables ϑ and a set of auxiliary variables α. The augmentation of an assignment statment allows a possibly empty list of auxiliary variables to be updated in the same atomic step as r is assigned to v. The additional constraint $a \leftarrow_{(\vartheta,\alpha)} u$ is needed to make sure that the elements of a really are auxiliary variables, and that the different auxiliary variables do not depend upon each other. The latter requirement makes it possible to remove some auxiliary variables from a specified program without having to remove all the auxiliary variables. This requirement states that if an auxiliary variable occurs on the left-hand side of an assignment-statement, the only auxiliary variable that may occur in the corresponding expression on the right-hand side is the very same variable. However, an assignment to an auxiliary variable may have any number of elements of ϑ in its right-hand side expression.

The block-statement is used in the augmentations of if- and while-statements to allow auxiliary variables to be updated in the same atomic step as the Boolean test is evaluated. Note that the introduced Boolean variable is local and can therefore not be accessed by the environment. Thus the augmentations of if- and while-statements do not significantly change their external behaviour. An internal transition represents either the execution of a declaration list in a block-statement, a Boolean test in an if- or a while-statement, or an assignment-statement. Since the former is 'independent' of the state in which it takes place, it is enough to update auxiliary variables in connection with the execution of Boolean tests and assignment-statements.

Observe that the definition of an augmentation does not restrict the auxiliary variables to be of a particular type. For example, if z_1 denotes the program

```
if x = 0 then
     x := 1
else
     while x ≤ 0 do x := x + 1 od
fi
```

and z_2 denotes the program

```
blo b1 : B in
     b1, a := x = 0, a + 1;
     if b1 then
          x, a := 1, a + 1
     else
          blo b2 : B in
               b2, a := x ≤ 0, a + 1;
               while b2 do x, a := x + 1, a + 1; b2, a := x ≤ 0, a + 1 od
          olb
     fi
olb
```

then $z_1 \overset{(\{x\},\{a\})}{\hookrightarrow} z_2$.

It may be argued that the definition of an augmentation is rather complicated and hard to remember. However, augmentations are only used to characterise the semantics of a specified program and is not something the user needs to worry about in order to apply the method. For example, augmentations do not occur in the deduction rules.

It is now possible to define what it means for a specified program to be valid when the set of auxiliary variables is non-empty: namely that the program can be augmented with auxiliary structure in such a way that any program computation which satisfies the environment assumptions, also satisfies the commitments to the implementation. More formally:

Definition 7 $\models_u z_1$ $\underline{\text{sat}}$ $(\vartheta, \alpha) :: (P, R, W, G, E)$ *iff there is a program* z_2*, such that* $z_1 \overset{(\vartheta,\alpha)}{\hookrightarrow} z_2$ *and* $\models_u z_2$ $\underline{\text{sat}}$ $(\vartheta \cup \alpha, \emptyset) :: (P, R, W, G, E)$.

4 Deduction Rules

The next step is to define a logic, called LSP_u, for the deduction of valid specified programs. The consequence-, assignment-, sequential-, while- and parallel-rules are explained in detail below. The remaining rules needed to prove semantic completeness together with some useful adaptation rules are listed in the appendix.

Given a list of expressions r, a set of variables ϑ, a unary predicate B, and two binary predicates C and D, then $\overleftarrow{r}$ denotes the list of expressions that can be obtained from r by hooking all free variables in r; $\overleftarrow{B}$ denotes a binary predicate such that $(s, s') \models \overleftarrow{B}$ iff $s \models B$; I_ϑ denotes the predicate $\bigwedge_{v \in \vartheta} v = \overleftarrow{v}$, while $C|D$ denotes the relational composition of C and D, in other words, $(s, s') \models C|D$ iff there is a state s'' such that $(s, s'') \models C$ and $(s'', s') \models D$. Moreover, C^+ denotes the transitive closure of C, while C^* denotes the reflexive and transitive closure of C. Finally, C is well-founded iff there is no infinite sequence of states $s_1 s_2 \ldots s_k \ldots$ such that for all $j \geq 1$, $(s_j, s_{j+1}) \models C$.

The *consequence-rule*

$$\frac{\begin{array}{l} P_2 \Rightarrow P_1 \\ R_2 \Rightarrow R_1 \\ W_1 \Rightarrow W_2 \\ G_1 \Rightarrow G_2 \\ E_1 \Rightarrow E_2 \\ z \ \underline{\text{sat}} \ (\vartheta, \alpha) :: (P_1, R_1, W_1, G_1, E_1) \end{array}}{z \ \underline{\text{sat}} \ (\vartheta, \alpha) :: (P_2, R_2, W_2, G_2, E_2)}$$

is straightforward. It basically states that it is sound to strengthen the assumptions and weaken the commitments.

The first version of the *assignment-rule*

$$\frac{\begin{array}{l} \overleftarrow{P} \wedge R \Rightarrow P \\ \overleftarrow{P} \wedge v = \overleftarrow{r} \wedge I_{\vartheta \setminus \{v\}} \Rightarrow (G \vee I_\vartheta) \wedge E \end{array}}{v := r \ \underline{\text{sat}} \ (\vartheta, \emptyset) :: (P, R, \mathsf{false}, G, R^* | E | R^*)}$$

is sufficient whenever the set of auxiliary variables is empty. Any unconditionally fair computation is of the form

$$\langle v := r, s_1\rangle \xrightarrow{e} \ldots \xrightarrow{e} \langle v := r, s_k\rangle \xrightarrow{i} \langle \epsilon, s_{k+1}\rangle \xrightarrow{e} \ldots \xrightarrow{e} \langle \epsilon, s_n\rangle \xrightarrow{e} \ldots .$$

Thus, the statement will always terminate, and there is only one internal transition. Moreover, since the initial state is assumed to satisfy P and any external transition, which changes the global state, is assumed to satisfy R, it follows from the first premise that $s_k \models P$ and that $(s_k, s_{k+1}) \models \overleftarrow{P} \wedge v = \overleftarrow{r} \wedge I_{\vartheta \setminus \langle v\rangle}$. But then, it is clear from the second premise that $(s_k, s_{k+1}) \models G \vee I_\vartheta$, and that for all $l > k$, $(s_1, s_l) \models R^*|E|R^*$, which proves that the rule is sound.

In the general case, the execution of an assignment-statement $v := r$ corresponds to the execution of an assignment-statement of the form $v \circ a := r \circ u$, where $a \leftarrow_{(\vartheta,\alpha)} u$. Thus, the rule

$$\frac{\begin{array}{l}\overleftarrow{P} \wedge R \Rightarrow P \\ \overleftarrow{P} \wedge v = \overleftarrow{r} \wedge I_{\vartheta\setminus\langle v\rangle} \wedge a = \overleftarrow{u} \wedge I_{\alpha\setminus\langle a\rangle} \Rightarrow (G \vee I_{\vartheta\cup\alpha}) \wedge E\end{array}}{v := r \ \underline{\text{sat}}\ (\vartheta, \alpha) :: (P, R, \mathsf{false}, G, R^*|E|R^*)} \qquad a \leftarrow_{(\vartheta,\alpha)} u$$

is sufficient. The only real difference from above is that the premise guarantees that the assignment-statement can be augmented with auxiliary structure in such a way that the specified changes to both the auxiliary variables and the programming variables will indeed take place. Moreover, since **skip** is an alias for the assignment of an empty list of expressions to an empty list of variables, the *skip-rule*

$$\frac{\begin{array}{l}\overleftarrow{P} \wedge R \Rightarrow P \\ \overleftarrow{P} \wedge I_\vartheta \wedge a = \overleftarrow{u} \wedge I_{\alpha\setminus\langle a\rangle} \Rightarrow (G \vee I_{\vartheta\cup\alpha}) \wedge E\end{array}}{\mathsf{skip}\ \underline{\text{sat}}\ (\vartheta, \alpha) :: (P, R, \mathsf{false}, G, R^*|E|R^*)} \qquad a \leftarrow_{(\vartheta,\alpha)} u$$

follows as a special case.

The *sequential-rule*

$$\frac{\begin{array}{l}z_1 \ \underline{\text{sat}}\ (\vartheta, \alpha) :: (P_1, R, W, G, P_2 \wedge E_1) \\ z_2 \ \underline{\text{sat}}\ (\vartheta, \alpha) :: (P_2, R, W, G, E_2)\end{array}}{z_1; z_2 \ \underline{\text{sat}}\ (\vartheta, \alpha) :: (P_1, R, W, G, E_1|E_2)}$$

depends upon the fact that the first component's effect-condition implies the second component's pre-condition. This explains why P_2 occurs in the effect-condition of the first premise. Since an effect-condition covers interference both before the first internal transition and after the last, it follows from the two premises that the overall effect is characterised by $E_1|E_2$.

The *while-rule*

$$\frac{\begin{array}{l}\overleftarrow{P} \wedge R \Rightarrow P \\ E^{+} \wedge (R \vee G)^{*}|(I_{\vartheta} \wedge \neg W)|(R \vee G)^{*} \textit{ is well–founded} \\ z \ \underline{\text{sat}}\ (\vartheta, \emptyset) :: (P \wedge b, R, W, G, P \wedge E)\end{array}}{\text{while } b \text{ do } z \text{ od } \underline{\text{sat}}\ (\vartheta, \emptyset) :: (P, R, W, G, R^{*}|(E^{*} \wedge \neg b)|R^{*})}$$

can be used when the set of auxiliary variables is empty. The unary predicate P can be thought of as an invariant which is true whenever the Boolean test b is evaluated. Since the conclusion's pre-condition restricts the initial state to satisfy P, and since it follows from the first premise that P is maintained by the environment, it follows that P is true when the Boolean test is evaluated for the first time. The occurrence of P in the effect-condition of the third premise implies that P is also true at any later evaluation of the Boolean test.

It follows from the third premise that the binary predicate E characterises the overall effect of executing the body of the while loop under the given environment assumptions. But then it is clear that the overall effect of the while-statement satisfies $R^{*}|(E^{+} \wedge \neg b)|R^{*}$ if the loop iterates at least once, while the overall effect satisfies $R^{*}|(I_{\vartheta} \wedge \neg b)|R^{*}$ otherwise. This explains the conclusion's effect-condition. That any internal transition either leaves the state unchanged or satisfies G also follows from the third premise.

Note that $\wedge$ is the main symbol of the well-founded predicate in the second premise. To prove that this premise implies that the statement terminates unless it ends up busy-waiting in W, assume there is a non-terminating computation (a computation where the empty program is never reached)

$$\sigma \in ext(\vartheta, P, R) \cap cp_{u}(\text{while } b \text{ do } z \text{ od})$$

such that for all $j \geq 1$, there is a $k \geq j$, which satisfies $S(\sigma_k) \models \neg W$. It follows from the third premise that there is an infinite sequence of natural numbers $n_1 < n_2 < \ldots < n_k < \ldots$, such that for all $j \geq 1$,

$$(S(\sigma_{n_j}), S(\sigma_{n_{j+1}})) \models E.$$

But then, since by assumption $\neg W$ is true infinitely often, and since the overall effect of any finite sequence of external and internal transitions satisfies $(R \vee G)^{*}$, it follows that there is an infinite sequence of natural numbers $m_1 < m_2 < \ldots < m_k < \ldots$, such that for all $j \geq 1$,

$$(S(\sigma_{m_j}), S(\sigma_{m_{j+1}})) \models E^{+} \wedge (R \vee G)^{*}|(I_{\vartheta} \wedge \neg W)|(R \vee G)^{*}.$$

This contradicts the second premise. Thus, the statement terminates or ends up busy-waiting in W.

In the general case the following rule

$$\frac{\begin{array}{l}\overleftarrow{P_1} \wedge R \Rightarrow P_1 \\ (E_1|E_2)^+ \wedge (R \vee G)^*|(I_{\vartheta \cup \alpha} \wedge \neg W)|(R \vee G)^* \textit{ is well-founded} \\ \textsf{skip } \underline{\text{sat}}\ (\vartheta, \alpha) :: (P_1, \textsf{false}, \textsf{false}, G, P_2 \wedge E_1) \\ z\ \underline{\text{sat}}\ (\vartheta, \alpha) :: (P_2 \wedge b, R, W, G, P_1 \wedge E_2)\end{array}}{\textsf{while } b \textsf{ do } z \textsf{ od } \underline{\text{sat}}\ (\vartheta, \alpha) :: (P_1, R, W, G, R^*|(E_1|E_2)^*|(E_1 \wedge \neg b)|R^*)}$$

is needed. Remember that the execution of **while** b **do** z **od** corresponds to the execution of a program of the form

$$\textsf{blo } b' : \textsf{B in } b' \circ a := b \circ u; \textsf{while } b' \textsf{ do } z'; b' \circ a := b \circ u \textsf{ od olb},$$

where $a \leftarrow_{(\vartheta,\alpha)} u$ and $z \overset{(\vartheta,\alpha)}{\hookrightarrow} z'$. The third premise simulates the evaluation of the Boolean test. Thus, the overall effect satisfies $R^*|(E_1|E_2)^+|(E_1 \wedge \neg b)|R^*$ if the loop iterates at least once, and $R^*|(E_1 \wedge \neg b)|R^*$ otherwise.

To grasp the intuition behind the *parallel-rule*, consider first the rule

$$\frac{\begin{array}{l} z_1\ \underline{\text{sat}}\ (\vartheta, \alpha) :: (P, R \vee G_2, \textsf{false}, G_1, E_1) \\ z_2\ \underline{\text{sat}}\ (\vartheta, \alpha) :: (P, R \vee G_1, \textsf{false}, G_2, E_2)\end{array}}{\{z_1 \parallel z_2\}\ \underline{\text{sat}}\ (\vartheta, \alpha) :: (P, R, \textsf{false}, G_1 \vee G_2, E_1 \wedge E_2)}$$

which is sufficient whenever both component programs terminate. Observe that the rely-condition of the first premise allows any interference due to z_2 (given the actual assumptions about the overall environment), and similarly that the rely-condition of the second premise allows any interference due to z_1. Thus since an effect-condition covers interference both before the first internal transition and after the last, it is clear from the two premises that $\{z_1 \parallel z_2\}$ terminates, that any internal transition, which changes the global state, satisfies $G_1 \vee G_2$, and that the overall effect satisfies $E_1 \wedge E_2$.

The next version of the parallel-rule

$$\frac{\begin{array}{l} \neg(W_1 \wedge E_2) \wedge \neg(W_2 \wedge E_1) \wedge \neg(W_1 \wedge W_2) \\ z_1\ \underline{\text{sat}}\ (\vartheta, \alpha) :: (P, R \vee G_2, W_1, G_1, E_1) \\ z_2\ \underline{\text{sat}}\ (\vartheta, \alpha) :: (P, R \vee G_1, W_2, G_2, E_2)\end{array}}{\{z_1 \parallel z_2\}\ \underline{\text{sat}}\ (\vartheta, \alpha) :: (P, R, \textsf{false}, G_1 \vee G_2, E_1 \wedge E_2)}$$

is sufficient whenever the overall program $\{z_1 \parallel z_2\}$ terminates. It follows from the second premise that z_1 can end up busy-waiting only in W_1, when executed in an environment characterised by P and $R \vee G_2$. Moreover, the third premise implies that z_2 can end up busy-waiting only in W_2, when executed in an environment characterised by P and $R \vee G_1$. But then, since the first premise implies that z_1 cannot be busy-waiting after z_2 has terminated, that z_2 cannot be busy-waiting after z_1 has terminated, and that z_1 and z_2 cannot be busy waiting at the same time, it follows that $\{z_1 \parallel z_2\}$ is guaranteed to terminate in an environment characterised by P and R.

It is now easy to extend the rule to deal with the general case:

$$\frac{\begin{array}{l}\neg(W_1 \wedge E_2) \wedge \neg(W_2 \wedge E_1) \wedge \neg(W_1 \wedge W_2)\\ z_1 \ \underline{\text{sat}}\ (\vartheta, \alpha) :: (P, R \vee G_2, W \vee W_1, G_1, E_1)\\ z_2 \ \underline{\text{sat}}\ (\vartheta, \alpha) :: (P, R \vee G_1, W \vee W_2, G_2, E_2)\end{array}}{\{z_1 \parallel z_2\} \ \underline{\text{sat}}\ (\vartheta, \alpha) :: (P, R, W, G_1 \vee G_2, E_1 \wedge E_2)}$$

The idea is that W characterises the states in which the overall program is allowed to end up busy-waiting.

This rule can of course be generalised further to deal with more than two processes:

$$\frac{\begin{array}{l}\neg(W_j \wedge \bigwedge_{k=1,k\neq j}^{m}(W_k \vee E_k))_{1\leq j\leq m}\\ z_j \ \underline{\text{sat}}\ (\vartheta, \alpha) :: (P, R \vee \bigvee_{k=1,k\neq j}^{m} G_k, W \vee W_j, G_j, E_j)_{1\leq j\leq m}\end{array}}{\|_{j=1}^{m} z_j \ \underline{\text{sat}}\ (\vartheta, \alpha) :: (P, R, W, \bigvee_{j=1}^{m} G_j, \bigwedge_{j=1}^{m} E_j)}$$

Here, $\|_{j=1}^{m} z_j$ denotes any program that can be obtained from $z_1 \parallel \ldots \parallel z_m$ by adding curly brackets. The 'first' premise ensures that whenever process j busy-waits in a state s such that $s \models \neg W \wedge W_j$, then there is at least one other process which has not terminated and is not busy-waiting. This rule is 'deducible' from the basic rules of LSP$_u$.

5 Examples

Examples where a logic of this type is employed for the development of non-trivial programs can be found in [Stø90], [Stø91a], [XH92]. Moreover, it is shown in [Stø90], [Stø91b] how auxiliary variables can be used both as a specification tool to eliminate undesirable implementations, and as a verification tool to make it possible to prove that an already finished program satisfies a certain specification. The object here is to apply LSP$_u$ to prove fair termination.

Let z_1 and z_2 denote the programs

$$b := \mathsf{true}, \qquad\qquad \mathsf{while}\ \neg b\ \mathsf{do\ skip\ od}.$$

It should be obvious that

$$\models_u \{z_1 \parallel z_2\} \ \underline{\text{sat}}\ (\{b\}, \emptyset) :: (\mathsf{true}, \overleftarrow{b} \Rightarrow b, \mathsf{false}, \mathsf{true}, \mathsf{true}).$$

This follows easily by the consequence- and parallel-rules, if

$$\vdash_u z_1 \ \underline{\text{sat}}\ (\{b\}, \emptyset) :: (\mathsf{true}, \overleftarrow{b} \Rightarrow b, \mathsf{false}, \overleftarrow{b} \Rightarrow b, b),$$
$$\vdash_u z_2 \ \underline{\text{sat}}\ (\{b\}, \emptyset) :: (\mathsf{true}, \overleftarrow{b} \Rightarrow b, \neg b, \overleftarrow{b} \Rightarrow b, \mathsf{true}).$$

(For any specified program ψ, $\vdash_u \psi$ iff ψ is provable in LSP$_u$.) The first of these specified programs can be deduced by the consequence- and assignment-rules. The second follows by the pre-, consequence- and while-rules, since

$$\vdash_u \textsf{skip } \underline{\textsf{sat}}\ (\{b\}, \emptyset) :: (\neg b, \overleftarrow{b} \Rightarrow b, \neg b, \overleftarrow{b} \Rightarrow b, \textsf{true}),$$

and it is clear that

$$\neg \overleftarrow{b} \wedge (\overleftarrow{b} \Rightarrow b) | ((\overleftarrow{b} \Leftrightarrow b) \wedge b) | (\overleftarrow{b} \Rightarrow b)$$

is well-founded.

A slightly more complicated synchronisation is dealt with in the next example. Let z_1 and z_2 denote the programs

while $n > 0$ **do**
  if n mod $2 = 0$ **then** $n := n - 1$ **else skip fi**
od,

while $n > 0$ **do**
  if n mod $2 = 1$ **then** $n := n - 1$ **else skip fi**
od.

Given that $n > 0$, the program z_1 may reduce the value of n by 1 if n is even, while z_2 may subtract 1 from n if n is odd. Thus, it should be clear that

$$\models_u \{z_1 \parallel z_2\}\ \underline{\textsf{sat}}\ (\{n\}, \emptyset) :: (\textsf{true}, n < \overleftarrow{n}, \textsf{false}, \textsf{true}, n \leq 0).$$

Moreover, this follows by the consequence- and parallel-rules if

$$\vdash_u z_1\ \underline{\textsf{sat}}\ (\{n\}, \emptyset) :: (\textsf{true}, n < \overleftarrow{n}, n \bmod 2 = 1 \wedge n > 0, n < \overleftarrow{n}, n \leq 0),$$
$$\vdash_u z_2\ \underline{\textsf{sat}}\ (\{n\}, \emptyset) :: (\textsf{true}, n < \overleftarrow{n}, n \bmod 2 = 0 \wedge n > 0, n < \overleftarrow{n}, n \leq 0).$$

The first of these can be deduced by the pre-, consequence-, assignment-, if- and while-rules since it can easily be proved that z_1's if-statement satisfies

$$(\{n\}, \emptyset) :: (n > 0, n < \overleftarrow{n},$$
$$n \bmod 2 = 1 \wedge n > 0, n < \overleftarrow{n}, \overleftarrow{n} \bmod 2 = 0 \Rightarrow n < \overleftarrow{n})$$

and

$$\overleftarrow{n} > 0 \wedge (\overleftarrow{n} \bmod 2 = 0 \Rightarrow n < \overleftarrow{n}) \wedge$$
$$(n \leq \overleftarrow{n}) | (n = \overleftarrow{n} \wedge (n \bmod 2 = 0 \vee n \leq 0)) | (n \leq \overleftarrow{n})$$

is well-founded. Not surprisingly, z_2 can be proved to satisfy its specification in a similar way.

Finally, to indicate how LSP_u can be used for the design of programs in a top-down style, let g be a function, such that $\models \exists y \in Z : g(y) = 0$, and consider the task of designing a program z which satisfies

$$\vdash_u z\ \underline{\textsf{sat}}\ (\{x\}, \emptyset) :: (\textsf{true}, \textsf{false}, \textsf{false}, \textsf{true}, g(x) = 0).$$

One sensible decomposition strategy is two split the searching into two parallel processes z_1 and z_2 dealing with respectively the non-negative and the negative integers. This means that z should be of the form

$$\mathsf{blo}\ f : \mathsf{B}\ \mathsf{in}\ f := \mathsf{false}; \{z_1 \parallel z_2\}\ \mathsf{olb},$$

where the Boolean flag f is to be switched on when the appropriate argument is found. Clearly, any atomic step after f has been initialised is required to satisfy the *binary* invariant

$$(\overleftarrow{f} \Rightarrow f) \wedge (f \Rightarrow g(x) = 0),$$

from now on denoted by in. Moreover, it follows by the effect-, consequence-, assignment-, sequential- and block-rules that this is a valid implementation of z if

$$\vdash_u \{z_1 \parallel z_2\}\ \underline{\mathrm{sat}}\ (\{x, f\}, \emptyset) :: (\neg f, in, \mathsf{false}, in, f),$$

which again can be deduced by the consequence- and parallel-rules if

$$\vdash z_1\ \underline{\mathrm{sat}}\ (\{x, f\}, \emptyset) :: (\neg f, in, (\forall y \in Z : y \geq 0 \Rightarrow g(y) \neq 0) \wedge \neg f, in, f),$$
$$\vdash z_2\ \underline{\mathrm{sat}}\ (\{x, f\}, \emptyset) :: (\neg f, in, (\forall y \in Z : y < 0 \Rightarrow g(y) \neq 0) \wedge \neg f, in, f).$$

Moreover, the consequence-, assignment-, sequential- and block-rules imply that

$$\mathsf{blo}\ x' : Z\ \mathsf{in}\ x' := 0; z_1'\ \mathsf{olb}$$

is a valid decomposition of z_1 if

$$z_1'\ \underline{\mathrm{sat}}\ (\{x, f, x'\}, \emptyset) :: (\neg f \wedge x' = 0, in \wedge x' = \overleftarrow{x'},$$
$$(\forall y \in Z : y \geq 0 \Rightarrow g(y) \neq 0) \wedge \neg f, in, f).$$

Finally, since

$$(\neg \overleftarrow{f} \wedge \overleftarrow{x'} \geq 0 \wedge (\forall y \in Z : 0 \leq y < \overleftarrow{x'} \Rightarrow f(y) \neq 0) \wedge$$
$$(g(\overleftarrow{x'}) = 0 \Rightarrow f) \wedge (g(\overleftarrow{x'}) \neq 0 \Rightarrow x' = \overleftarrow{x'} + 1))^+ \wedge$$
$$in|(x = \overleftarrow{x} \wedge (f \Leftrightarrow \overleftarrow{f}) \wedge x' = \overleftarrow{x'} \wedge (\exists y \in Z : y \geq 0 \wedge g(y) = 0 \vee f))|in$$

is well-founded, it can be deduced by the pre-, consequence-, assignment-, if- and while-rules that

$$\mathsf{while}\ \neg f\ \mathsf{do}\ \mathsf{if}\ g(x') = 0\ \mathsf{then}\ f, x := \mathsf{true}, x'\ \mathsf{else}\ x' := x' + 1\ \mathsf{fi}\ \mathsf{od}$$

is a correct implementation of z_1'. A program which implements z_2 can be designed in a similar style.

6 Discussion

Rules for proving fair termination with respect to a set of transition functions $\{f_1, \ldots, f_m\}$ assosiated with m processes are described in [LPS81]. A state predicate is used to characterise helpful directions in the same way as LSP_u employs a wait-condition to select helpful execution paths of the while-statement's body. Rules for fair termination with respect to a set of transition functions are also given in [APS84]. These rules are based upon explicit scheduling.

Explicit scheduling is also used in [OA86], but in a less abstract setting. Unfortunately, the method depends upon a freedom from interference test which can be carried out only after the component processes have been implemented and their proofs have been constructed. This is unacceptable when designing large software products in a top-down style, because erroneous design decisions, taken early in the design process, may remain undetected until the whole program is complete. In the worst case, everything that depends upon such mistakes will have to be thrown away.

To avoid problems of this type a proof method should satisfy what is known as the principle of ***compositionality*** [dR85], [Zwi89] — namely that a program's specification always can be verified on the basis of the specifications of its constituent components, without knowledge of the interior program structure of those components.

The methods in [BKP84] and [Lam85] are based upon temporal logic. They are both compositional and non-transformational. Moreover, they can be used to prove total correctness with respect to the type of programming language discussed above. However, due to lack of published examples, it is not clear how useful they are when it comes to practical program development. One obvious difference, with respect to the approach presented in this paper, is that these logics have a much wider application area — they can for example be used for the design of non-terminating programs with respect to general liveness properties. Some very general compositional parallel-rules are proposed in [Sta85] and [AL90].

LSP is a compositional formal method specially designed for top-down development of totally correct shared-state parallel programs. LSP can be thought of as a compositional reformulation of the Owicki/Gries method [OG76], and also as an extension of Jones' rely/guarantee approach [Jon83]. A related system is described in [XH91]. Examples where LSP is used for the development of non-trivial programs can be found in [Stø90], [Stø91a]. In [Stø90] it is also explained how LSP can be extended to deal with partial functions and guarded commands.

This paper shows how LSP can be modified to allow for the design of programs, whose correctness depends upon busy-waiting. Only unconditional fairness is discussed here. However, systems for weak and strong fairness can be formulated in a similar style. The author is currently working on a paper which deals with both unconditional, weak and strong fairness. This paper will include soundness and semantic completeness proofs for the formal system presented above.

7 Acknowledgements

I would like to thank my PhD supervisor Cliff B. Jones for his help and support. I am also indebted to Howard Barringer and Xu Qiwen. A special thanks goes to Mathai Joseph whose comments led to many improvements.

The research reported in this paper was carried out at the Department of Computer Science, Manchester University with financial support from the Norwegian Research Council for Science and the Humanities and the Wolfson Foundation.

References

[Acz83] P. Aczel. On an inference rule for parallel composition. Unpublished Paper, February 1983.

[AL90] M. Abadi and L. Lamport. Composing specifications. Technical Report 66, Digital, Palo Alto, 1990.

[APS84] K. R. Apt, A. Pnueli, and J. Stavi. Fair termination revisited with delay. *Theoretical Computer Science*, 33:65–84, 1984.

[BKP84] H. Barringer, R. Kuiper, and A. Pnueli. Now you may compose temporal logic specifications. In *Proc. Sixteenth ACM Symposium on Theory of Computing*, pages 51–63, 1984.

[dR85] W. P. de Roever. The quest for compositionality, formal models in programming. In F. J. Neuhold and G. Chroust, editors, *Proc. IFIP 85*, pages 181–205, 1985.

[GFMdR85] O. Grumberg, N. Francez, J.A. Makowsky, and W. P. de Roever. A proof rule for fair termination of guarded commands. *Information and Control*, 66:83–102, 1985.

[GPSS80] D. Gabbay, A. Pnueli, S. Shelah, and J. Stavi. On the temporal analysis of fairness. In *Proc. 7th ACM-POPL*, 1980.

[Jon83] C. B. Jones. Specification and design of (parallel) programs. In Mason R.E.A., editor, *Proc. Information Processing 83*, pages 321–331, 1983.

[Jon90] C. B. Jones. *Systematic Software Development Using VDM, Second Edition*. Prentice-Hall International, 1990.

[Lam85] L. Lamport. An axiomatic semantics of concurrent programming languages. In K. R. Apt, editor, *Logics and Models of Concurrent Systems*. NATO ASI Series, Vol. F13, 1985.

[LPS81] D. Lehmann, A. Pnueli, and J. Stavi. Impartiality, justice and fairness: The ethics of concurrent termination. In *Proc. Automata, Languages, and Programming, Lecture Notes in Computer Science 115*, pages 264–277, 1981.

[OA86] E. R. Olderog and K. R. Apt. Fairness in parallel programs: The transformational approach. Technical Report 86-1, Liens, 1986.

[OG76] S. Owicki and D. Gries. An axiomatic proof technique for parallel programs. *Acta Informatica*, 6:319–340, 1976.

[Par81] D. Park. A predicate transformer for weak fair iteration. In *Proc. 6th IBM Symp. on Math. Foundation of Computer Science*, 1981.

[Sta85] E. W. Stark. A proof technique for rely/guarantee properties. In S. N. Maheshwari, editor, *Proc. 5th Conference on the Foundation of Software Technology and Theoretical Computer Science, Lecture Notes in Computer Science 206*, pages 369–391, 1985.

[Stø90] K. Stølen. *Development of Parallel Programs on Shared Data-Structures.* PhD thesis, University of Manchester, 1990. Also available as technical report UMCS-91-1-1, University of Manchester.

[Stø91a] K. Stølen. An attempt to reason about shared-state concurrency in the style of VDM. In S. Prehn and W. J. Toetenel, editors, *Proc. VDM'91, Lecture Notes in Computer Science 552*, pages 324–342, 1991. Also available as technical report UMCS-91-7-1, University of Manchester.

[Stø91b] K. Stølen. A method for the development of totally correct shared-state parallel programs. In J. C. M. Baeten and J. F. Groote, editors, *Proc. CONCUR'91, Lecture Notes in Computer Science 527*, pages 510–525, 1991. Also available as technical report UMCS-91-6-1, University of Manchester.

[XH91] Q. Xu and J. He. A theory of state-based parallel programming by refinement:part 1. In J. Morris and R. C. Shaw, editors, *Proc. 4th BCS-FACS Refinement Workshop*, 1991.

[XH92] Q. Xu and J. He. A case study in formally developing state-based parallel programs — the dutch national torus. In C. B. Jones and R. C. Shaw, editors, *Proc. 5th BCS-FACS Refinement Workshop*, 1992.

[Zwi89] J. Zwiers. *Compositionality, Concurrency and Partial Correctness: Proof Theories for Networks of Processes and Their Relationship*, volume 321 of *Lecture Notes in Computer Science*. Springer-Verlag, 1989.

Additional Rules Needed to Prove Semantic Completeness

if ::

$$\frac{\begin{array}{l}\overleftarrow{P_1} \wedge R \Rightarrow P_1 \\ \mathsf{skip}\ \underline{\mathsf{sat}}\ (\vartheta, \alpha) :: (P_1, \mathsf{false}, \mathsf{false}, G, P_2 \wedge E_1) \\ z_1\ \underline{\mathsf{sat}}\ (\vartheta, \alpha) :: (P_2 \wedge b, R, W, G, E_2) \\ z_2\ \underline{\mathsf{sat}}\ (\vartheta, \alpha) :: (P_2 \wedge \neg b, R, W, G, E_2)\end{array}}{\mathsf{if}\ b\ \mathsf{then}\ z_1\ \mathsf{else}\ z_2\ \mathsf{fi}\ \underline{\mathsf{sat}}\ (\vartheta, \alpha) :: (P_1, R, W, G, R^*|E_1|E_2)}$$

block ::

$$\frac{z\ \underline{\mathsf{sat}}\ (\vartheta, \alpha) :: (P, R \wedge \bigwedge_{j=1}^{n} x_j = \overleftarrow{x_j}, W, G, E)}{\mathsf{blo}\ x_1 : T_1, \ldots, x_n : T_n\ \mathsf{in}\ z\ \mathsf{olb}\ \underline{\mathsf{sat}}\ (\vartheta \setminus \bigcup_{j=1}^{n} \{x_j\}, \alpha) :: (P, R, W, G, E)}$$

elimination ::

$$\frac{\begin{array}{l} x \notin \vartheta \\ z\ \underline{\mathsf{sat}}\ (\vartheta, \alpha) :: (P, R, W, G, E)\end{array}}{z\ \underline{\mathsf{sat}}\ (\vartheta, \alpha \setminus \{x\}) :: (\exists x : P, \forall \overleftarrow{x} : \exists x : R, W, G, E)}$$

pre ::

$$\frac{z\ \underline{\mathsf{sat}}\ (\vartheta, \alpha) :: (P, R, W, G, E)}{z\ \underline{\mathsf{sat}}\ (\vartheta, \alpha) :: (P, R, W, G, \overleftarrow{P} \wedge E)}$$

Some Useful Adaptation Rules

effect ::

$$\frac{z\ \underline{\mathsf{sat}}\ (\vartheta, \alpha) :: (P, R, W, G, E)}{z\ \underline{\mathsf{sat}}\ (\vartheta, \alpha) :: (P, R, W, G, E \wedge (R \vee G)^*)}$$

rely ::

$$\frac{z\ \underline{\mathsf{sat}}\ (\vartheta, \alpha) :: (P, R, W, G, E)}{z\ \underline{\mathsf{sat}}\ (\vartheta, \alpha) :: (P, R^*, W, G, E)}$$

invariant ::

$$\frac{\begin{array}{l} P \Rightarrow K \\ \overleftarrow{K} \wedge (R \vee G) \Rightarrow K \\ z\ \underline{\mathsf{sat}}\ (\vartheta, \alpha) :: (P, R, W, G, E)\end{array}}{z\ \underline{\mathsf{sat}}\ (\vartheta, \alpha) :: (P, R, K \wedge W, \overleftarrow{K} \wedge G, E)}$$

stutter ::

$$\frac{z\ \underline{\text{sat}}\ (\vartheta, \alpha) :: (P, R, W, G, E)}{z\ \underline{\text{sat}}\ (\vartheta, \alpha) :: (P, R \vee I_{\vartheta \cup \alpha}, W, G, E)}$$

glo ::

$$\frac{\begin{array}{l} x \notin \vartheta \cup \alpha \\ z\ \underline{\text{sat}}\ (\vartheta, \alpha) :: (P, R, W, G, E) \end{array}}{z\ \underline{\text{sat}}\ (\vartheta \cup \{x\}, \alpha) :: (P, R, W, G \wedge x = \overleftarrow{x}, E)}$$

aux ::

$$\frac{\begin{array}{l} x \notin \vartheta \cup \alpha \\ z\ \underline{\text{sat}}\ (\vartheta, \alpha) :: (P, R, W, G, E) \end{array}}{z\ \underline{\text{sat}}\ (\vartheta, \alpha \cup \{x\}) :: (P, R, W, G \wedge x = \overleftarrow{x}, E)}$$

A Note on Compositional Refinement

J. Zwiers*
University of Twente
P.O. Box 217
7500 AE Enschede, The Netherlands

J. Coenen†
Dept. of Math. and Computing Science
Eindhoven University of Technology
P.O. Box 513
5600 MB Eindhoven, The Netherlands

W.-P. de Roever‡
Institut für Informatik und Praktische Mathematik
Christian-Albrechts-Universität zu Kiel
D-2300 Kiel 1, Germany

Abstract

Implementing a (concurrent) program P often requires changing the syntactic structure of P at various levels. We argue and illustrate that in such a situation a natural framework for implementation correctness requires a more general notion of refinement than that of [HHS87], a notion which involves the introduction of separate refinement relations for P's various abstract components. An outline is given of a formal framework for proving implementation correctness that involves these notions.

1 Introduction

Transformational program development, in all its fashions, has become one of the main ways to construct sequential, parallel, and distributed systems. During such a development one constructs a sequence of more and more refined systems Q, R, S, etc. According to some suitable notion of implementation, system Q is implemented by its successor R, which is itself implemented by S etc. In its simplest form, program transformation relies on algebraic equalities of the form $S = T$ or on implementation relations of the form $S \sqsubseteq T$ (*S is refined by T*).

An important property of transformations based on inequalities is that it is relatively easy to incorporate *specification* and *verification* based-on program

*E-mail: zwiers@cs.utwente.nl

†Supported by NWO/SION project 612-316-022: "Fault Tolerance: Paradigms, Models, Logics, Construction." E-mail: wsinjosc@win.tue.nl

‡Partially supported by ESPRIT project 3096: "SPEC." E-mail: wpr@informatik.uni-kiel.dbp.de

logics. Such specifications have the form $S \sqsupseteq \chi$, often denoted in this context by S **sat** χ, where S is a system as before, but where χ is a formula of some appropriate program logic [Z89]. Within this framework it is natural to apply process operations '*op*' not only to processes S but also to logic specifications φ or combinations of processes and specifications, resulting in so called *mixed terms* [Z89, O91]. This admits a transformational approach where an initial logical specification is transformed gradually into an implementation as a process. During each step in such a development trajectory one replaces one subterm by another subterm. One of the following three situations applies to each replacement of a subterm by another.

- A *specification* φ is replaced by *process* S such that $S \sqsupseteq \varphi$.
- A *process* S is replaced by another *process* T such that $T \sqsupseteq S$.
- A *specification* φ is replaced by another *specification* ψ such that $\psi \sqsupseteq \varphi$, i.e. $\psi \rightarrow \varphi$ should be a logically valid implication.

It is possible to go one step further in this integration of processes and program logics, by introducing a *single, unified* language of terms that can be composed by means of operations originating from process languages, such as parallel or sequential composition as well as by means of *logical* operations from propositional logic and predicate calculus [ZdR89]. So not only can specifications be combined by means of process operations, but also can processes be combined by means of logic operations such as conjunction. Apart from being more uniform this approach has technical advantages such as the possibility to define more complex process operations by means of simpler logical and process operations. An example is the definition of various forms of parallel composition of processes in terms of logical conjunction and a few simple process operations such as relabeling of actions or projection of communication histories [ZdR89]. Another advantage of the integration of processes and logic is the possibility to deal with higher order constructs such as predicate transformers in a natural way, completely inside a single unified framework. As we rely heavily on such techniques because it also turns out to be the proper framework for expressing and proving reification, we introduce such a unified language in the appendix.

The use of the term reification rather than refinement emphasizes the use of simulation techniques to justify the transformation steps of the development process. Such general techniques are based on *simulation* of an 'abstract' high level specification A by a more concrete lower level implementation C. The idea originates from the well known techniques for data reification, where the relation between abstract and concrete is specified by means of so called abstraction functions, also called retrieve functions, mapping concrete data to abstract data. Data reification can be generalized to simulation where a retrieve function maps complete computations, also called 'runs', from the concrete level to the more abstract level. This is based on the assumption that systems S can *semantically* be interpreted as sets of runs of the system. This view is consistent with many models of computation, both for sequential and concurrent systems. Typical examples are the CSP trace, ready set and failure models, where a run coincides with a finite communication history, possibly decorated or augmented with information concerning termination and deadlock behaviour. Other examples are that of the set of, labeled or unlabeled, state sequences associated with state-transition systems, the runs as defined for Petri nets and event structures, and the traces as introduced by Mazurkiewicz. But maybe the simplest example is the classical model for sequential nondeterministic programs as binary relations on states, where each initial/final state pair (s_0, s_1) represents one possible computation. Retrieve functions ρ which are defined on single states, mapping states s_c of the C system to states $s_a = \rho(s_c)$ of the A system, can be extended straightforwardly to abstraction functions ρ on runs, in the form of state sequences $\sigma_C = (s_0, s_1, s_2, \ldots)$, by pointwise applying ρ. Hence,

$$\sigma_A = (\rho(s_0), \rho(s_1), \rho(s_2), \ldots) .$$

Similarly, ρ is then extended to an operation on *sets of runs*, by applying ρ pointwise to each run in turn:

$$\rho(C) \triangleq \{\sigma_A \mid \exists_{\sigma_C \in C}(\sigma_A = \rho(\sigma_C))\} .$$

Intuitively, system C implements A or as we will say, *refines* A with respect to retrieve function ρ, if for any possible C run there is a corresponding, i.e. ρ related, A run. This is easily expressed by the following requirement.

$$\rho(C) \subseteq A \tag{1}$$

Note that for the special case that ρ is the identity function, this boils down to $C \subseteq A$, that is, we are back at the simpler form of implementation for mixed terms discussed above. In this case we simply say that C *refines* A.

Although it might not be apparent from (1), it can be shown, see [CdRZ91] that the verification conditions for functional data reification in VDM amount to the same as (1). Data refinement as discussed in [R81] and on pp. 221–222 of [J90] is slightly more general than functional reification in that it allows abstraction *relations* α rather than retrieve *functions* ρ between concrete and abstract data. This means that one particular concrete value can represent several abstract values, a desirable property when dealing with implementation bias. [1] When dealing with abstraction relations α the refinement relation between systems can be formulated as follows.

Definition 1.1 *(Strong simulation)*
System C *strongly simulates* system A with respect to relation α if

$$\alpha(C) \subseteq A$$

□

A slightly more general notion of simulation is given in the next definition.

Definition 1.2 *(Weak simulation)*
System C *weakly simulates* system A with respect to α if

$$C \subseteq \alpha^{-1}(A)$$

□

[1] A specification is said to be implementation biased if it includes more implementation detail than strictly necessary (see e.g. [J90]).

Strong simulation requires that for any C run σ_C *all* α related runs σ_A are possible runs for the abstract system A. Weak simulation only requires that there is *at least one* such α related run that is also a possible run for A. Clearly weak simulation is more liberal than strong simulation, because $\alpha(C) \subseteq A \Rightarrow C \subseteq \alpha^{-1}(A)$ if (and only if) α is *total*, but $C \subseteq \alpha^{-1}(A) \Rightarrow \alpha(C) \subseteq A$ if (and only if) α is *functional*. Whereas retrieve *functions* are not adequate when considering implementation bias, requiring totality is not a real limitation. After all, it is only required that the abstraction relation is total with respect to the admissible states of the concrete data type, which can be achieved by strengthening the data invariant part of the representation invariant that characterizes the abstraction relation.

Both strong and weak simulation are defined in terms of abstraction relations on the level of *computations.* As it turns out, the well known notions of upward and downward simulation are not of this form, i.e. cannot be understood in terms of abstraction relations operating on computations. What *is* possible however is to characterize upward and downward simulation of A by C by means of inequalities of the following form:

$$C \subseteq F_\alpha(A) \qquad \text{(downward simulation)}$$

$$C \subseteq G_\alpha(A) \qquad \text{(upward simulation)}$$

The operations F_α and G_α transform processes, i.e. they transform sets of computations, and are defined in [HHS87], relying on weakest prespecifications and strongest postspecifications. Within our unified language they can be expressed in terms of relational composition $X \fatsemi Y$, weakest preconditions $[X]Y$ and the leads-to operator $X \leadsto Y$, as follows:

$$F_\alpha(X) = \alpha^{-1} \leadsto (X \fatsemi \alpha^{-1}),$$

$$G_\alpha(X) = [\alpha](\alpha \fatsemi X).$$

Next we note that both weak and strong simulation can be formulated as inequalities of this form. For weak simulation as defined above this is already the case, and the inequality for strong simulation is expressible in our language as

$$C \subseteq \alpha^R(A),$$

where α^R denotes the *right adjoint* of α. We therefore define in general refinement of A by C with respect to F as the inequality

$$C \subseteq F(A).$$

Departing from this definition of refinement we define in this paper a generalization of it to what can be called *compositional refinement*.
Compositional refinement does not treat abstract and concrete programs as monolithic entities but rather takes their decomposition into smaller programs into account. A limited form of compositionality has been defined in [HHS87], where it it is called *subdistributivity*. An operator F as above sub-distributes over some n-ary language operator *op* iff

$$F(op(X_1, \ldots, X_n)) \supseteq op(F(X_1), \ldots, F(X_n)).$$

Subdistributivity guarantees the following for refinement of complete programs of the form $P(A_1, \ldots, A_m)$ that are built up by means of subdistributive operations from some set of basic programs $A_1, \ldots, A_m$: If each of the A_i is refined by C_i with respect to F, then the whole program $P(A_1, \ldots, A_m)$ is refined by $P(C_1, \ldots, C_m)$ with respect to F. Subdistributivity allows refinement of basic abstract program A_i by means of basic concrete program C_i. But it does not allow for refinement of the (parameterized) abstract program $P(X_1, \ldots, X_m)$ to a 'concrete' program $Q(X_1, \ldots, X_n)$. In this paper we give a precise definition of such 'context refinements' and we provide examples thereof.

Related to context refinement is the idea of a *varying abstraction relation*. The basic idea is that different components of a program might be refined with respect to different abstraction relations, one for each component, rather than using a uniform abstraction relation for the whole program. A very simple example of a varying abstraction relation is provided by variable or channel hiding contexts that are used to declare *local* abstract and concrete variables and (CSP style) channels. The general picture here is that we have an abstract program operating on abstract variables a say, and an implementing program C operating on corresponding concrete variables c, where C refines A with respect to abstraction relation α, i.e. $C \subseteq \alpha^{-1}(A)$. The two programs are placed in contexts $H_A(X)$ and $H_C(Y)$ that declare the a or c as local variables and initialize, and possibly even finialize, those variables. For appropriate contexts we then have that from $C \subseteq \alpha^{-1}(A)$ it follows that $H_C(C) \subseteq H_A(A)$. We regard this as context refinement, where $H_A(X)$ is refined by $H_C(Y)$ and where the abstraction relation α for the components X and Y has been replaced by the *identity* relation on the outer level. In general we do not require the identity at the outer level or 'interface level' as refinement relation; a nontrivial choice for refinement at the interface level enables us to formalize so called *interface refinement.* In the paper we treat an example of context refinement for a communication protocol where there is a shift from rather complicated abstraction functions for components to a relatively simple abstraction function for the interface.

Our definition of compositional refinement takes both context refinement and varying abstraction relations into account. It can be formulated as a simple weak homomorphism property. We say that a program (context) $A(X_1, \ldots, X_n)$ is refined by another program (context) $C(Y_1, \ldots, Y_n)$ with respect to F_0 (for the outer level) and $F_1, \ldots, F_n$ (for the components) iff

$$C(F_1(X_1), \ldots, F_n(X_n)) \subseteq F_0(A(X_1, \ldots, X_n)),$$

for all $X_1, \ldots, X_n$.

The outline of the remainder of this report is as follows. In section 2 we first discuss the rôle of compositionality in refinement and its relation with the notion of subdistributivity in [HHS87]. We give an example that illustrates how the refinement relation ρ between the overall abstract program and the concrete program may be *different* from the refinement relations ρ_i between their (concurrent) abstract and concrete components A_i resp. C_i. Secondly, we introduce a refinement notion which generalizes subdistributivity by allowing *context re-*

finements. This is illustrated by an example based on the self-stabilizing snapshot algorithm of Katz and Perry [KP90]. In the appendix we present a theory that unifies several refinement methods for both sequential and concurrent programs within one framework. The theory is related to calculus of [HH87] and [HHS87]. Furthermore the theory is applied to the examples of section 2.

2 Compositional refinement

An important question for transformational techniques in general is how they combine with a modular style of system development. Transformations should be *vertically* composable as well as *horizontally* composable. Vertical composability or *transitivity* is the property that if a system A can be transformed into a system B which in turn can be transformed into C then the immediate step from A to C is also a legal transformation. This requirement is readily satisfied for most transformation techniques, including simulation where we rely on composability of retrieve functions. Horizontal composability or *compositionality* requires that if a system $S(S_1, \ldots, S_n)$ can be decomposed into parts $S_1, \ldots, S_n$ and a top level part $S(\ldots)$, then implementing the parts yields also an implementation of the whole. To be more precise, let $S = S(X_1, \ldots, X_n)$ be a program term with free variables $X_1, \ldots, X_n$, for which other programs, say $S_1, \ldots, S_n$ can be substituted which we denote formally as $S[S_1/X_1, \ldots, S_n/X_n]$ and more informally as $S(S_1, \ldots, S_n)$. Then, if S_i is implemented by T_i, for $i = 1, \ldots, n$, compositionality requires that $S(S_1, \ldots, S_n)$ is implemented by $S(T_1, \ldots, T_n)$.

For simple algebraic equalities between processes the requirements of vertical and horizontal composability are readily satisfied, because equality is transitive and substitutive:

$$\begin{array}{ll} \text{if } \; Q = R \text{ and } R = S & \text{then } Q = S, \text{ and} \\ \text{if } \; S_i = T_i \text{ for } i = 1, \ldots, n & \text{then } S(S_1, \ldots, S_n) = S(T_1, \ldots, T_n). \end{array}$$

More complex transformational techniques rely on implementation relations in the form of inequalities between processes rather than equalities. For implementation relations of the form $S \subseteq T$ horizontal composability is guaranteed when programs are built up from smaller parts by means of *monotonic* operations. For systems denoting sets of 'runs' — the implementation relation $S \sqsubseteq T$ denotes the set inclusion $T \subseteq S$ — this means that an operation 'op' satisfies the following property.

$$\text{if } \; T_i \subseteq S_i \text{ for } i = 1, \ldots, n \quad \text{then } op(T_1, \ldots, T_n) \subseteq op(S_1, \ldots, S_n).$$

Vertical composability follows from the transitivity of the subset relation.

Next we consider the composability requirements that were posed above for refinement notions based on simulation. Again, vertical composability causes no problems: if R refines Q with respect to α_1 and S refines R with respect to α_2 than S refines Q with respect to $\alpha_1 \circ \alpha_2$:

$$\begin{array}{ll} \text{if} & R \subseteq \alpha_1^{-1}(Q) \text{ and } S \subseteq \alpha_2^{-1}(R) \\ \text{then} & S \subseteq (\alpha_1 \circ \alpha_2)^{-1}(Q) \end{array}$$

Horizontal composability, however, is not so simple. From $S_i \subseteq \alpha^{-1}(T_i)$ for $i = 1, \ldots, n$ it does in general *not* follow that $S(S_1, \ldots, S_n) \subseteq \alpha^{-1}(S(T_1, \ldots, T_n))$. A notorious counterexample is sequential composition: $\alpha^{-1}(S_i) \subseteq T_i$, $(i = 1, 2)$, does not necessarily guarantee that $\alpha^{-1}(S_1); \alpha^{-1}(S_2) \subseteq T_1; T_2$, unless some restrictions are imposed upon α (c.f. [CdRZ91]). What we need here is a property related to the notion of *subdistributivity* as introduced in [HHS87].

Subdistributivity of relation α for some n-ary program operation op means that for any systems $S_1, \ldots, S_n$ the following inequality holds:

$$op(\alpha^{-1}(S_1), \ldots, \alpha^{-1}(S_n)) \subseteq \alpha^{-1}(op(S_1, \ldots, S_n)) \ .$$

If $S(X_1, \ldots, X_n)$ is built with monotonic subdistributive operations only, then it follows easily that

$$\begin{array}{ll} \text{if} & C_i \subseteq \alpha^{-1}(A_i) \text{ for } i = 1, \ldots, n \\ \text{then} & S(C_1, \ldots, C_n) \subseteq \alpha^{-1}(S(A_1, \ldots, A_n)). \end{array}$$

So, subdistributivity forms the basis of the compositional treatment of *data refinement* in [HHS87], where abstract operations A_i on abstract data within program S, are implemented by concrete operations C_i, operating on concrete data. Concrete operations of C_i, resp. abstract operations of A_i, can be considered as atomic operations in the syntax trees of $S(C_1, \ldots, C_n)$, resp. $S(A_1, \ldots, A_n)$. I.e. apart from their atoms these trees have the same syntactic structure.

However, in some situations a more general notion of subdistributivity is required that allows the refinement relation ρ between the overall abstract and concrete programs to be *different* from the refinement relations ρ_i between the concrete and abstract components C_i resp. A_i. This is illustrated in the following example.

Example 2.1
Consider the an abstract communication medium MED_A where messages $m_1 m_2 \ldots m_k$ enter MED_A via some channel in_A and leave via channel out_A. Messages cannot get lost or duplicated, but they can leave MED_A in a different order than they entered it. We want to sketch a few development steps, both *vertically*, by refining the representation of messages and *horizontally*, by indicating how an abstract medium could be built up from a sender process that routes messages via a number of (lower level) channels to a receiver process that merges them into a single stream which leaves the communication module through a buffer. What we want to illustrate is that a relatively simple message representation for the *interface* of the whole module has to be replaced by a more complicated representation inside. Moreover, the *context* that puts together the sender, the channels and the receiver has to be refined into a more complicated context that includes a sliding window process. Thus we see here an example of context refinement with a varying abstraction relation.

First we consider a 'vertical' development step, where MED_A is refined into a more concrete one MED_C. For this refined medium MED_C we take into account that abstract messages m_i, which can be of arbitrary length, are to be split into sequences of fixed-length packets $\pi(m_i) = p_i^1 p_i^2 \ldots p_i^{k_i}$ for the concrete level. The channels in_A and out_A are for the concrete level replaced by similar channels in_C and out_C, and an abstract message m traveling along in_A or out_A is replaced by the sequence $\pi(m)$ that travels along in_C or out_C. We specify a simple protocol that requires that packets for a given message enter and leave MED_C *as a contiguous, ordered sequence*. In order to reconstruct a message from its packets we assume that each packet p_i^j carries a message identification as well as the total number of packets for that message. The relation between the abstract the concrete level is easily formalized by a retrieve function ρ, mapping communication *histories* for in_C and out_C to abstract communication histories. For a history h of the form $\pi(m_1)\pi(m_2)\cdots\pi(m_n)$ we define $\rho(h) = m_1, m_2, \ldots m_n$. If h' is a history like h as above except that for the last message only a few packets have been communicated we can isolate the longest prefix h'' of h' of 'complete' messages and we define $\rho(h') = \rho(h'')$. This retrieve function ρ forms the basis for an abstraction relation α that relates the complete concrete behaviour, i.e. the combined history h_C for the in_C and out_C channels together, to the complete abstract behaviour h_A, thus:

$$\alpha(h_C, h_A) \text{ iff } (h_A|in_A) = \rho(h_C|in_C) \text{ and } (h_A|out_A) = \rho(h_C|out_C).$$

Note that α is functional, in that there is at most one h_A value for any h_C value, which will be denoted by $\alpha(h_C)$. For histories h_C that do not conform to the protocola introduced above the value of $\alpha(h_C)$ is not defined.
We can now specify the required *interface refinement* as follows:

$$MED_C \subseteq \alpha^{-1}(MED_A).$$

Due to the fact that α is a partial function this can also be rephrased as the requirements that α is *defined* for all MED_C histories and moreover that

$$\alpha(MED_C) \subseteq MED_A.$$

We remark that ρ (and α) map histories to histories and that a mapping from (single) concrete communications to abstract ones does not suffice.

Thus far we have described a rather standard simulation relation for concurrent programs. Note that the refinement relation defines the representation of messages on the module *interface* only; nothing is said yet about message representation inside the module. In fact this representation is determined only after some 'horizontal' development steps are made, where we develop the medium *on the abstract level*, i.e. without taking any message representation into account. Then, after this horizontal development, *compositional refinement* comes in when we refine abstract internal messages. The idea of the horizontal step is that we use standard *process refinement* techniques to implement the abstract communication medium as a network of processes consisting of a router and a merge process communicating via an asynchronous network consisting of a number of (virtual) channels. Because the messages may be routed through the network via different routes, it is possible that they are received out of order. We can describe this by means of a program in a CSP style process language:

$$(NET_A)\backslash\{Vin_A(i), Vout_A(i), Bin_A\} \text{ where}$$

$$NET_A \triangleq ROUTER_A \parallel VCHANNELS_A \parallel MERGER_A \parallel BUFFER_A,$$

$$VCHANNELS_A \triangleq VCHAN_A(1) \parallel VCHAN_A(2) \parallel \cdots.$$

The (synchronous) transfer of messages from one component to another can be described by means of CSP style communication via CSP channels. We remark here that CSP communication channels should not be confused with communication media such as MED_A or the $VCHAN$ channels. CSP communication is used here exclusively as a *mathematical* device to describe the transfer of messages from one component to another, whereas processes like $VCHAN_A(i)$ are (simplified) models of certain components of communication networks or distributed operating systems. The CSP 'channels' connected to these processes are as follows:

$$chan(ROUTER_A) = \{in_A, Vin_A(1), Vin_A(2), \ldots\}$$

$$chan(VCHAN_A(i)) = \{Vin_A(i), Vout_A(i)\}$$

$$chan(MERGER_A) = \{Bin_A, Vout_A(1), Vout_A(2), \ldots\}$$

$$chan(BUFFER_A) = \{Bin_A, out_A\}$$

Except for the in_A and out_A channels, all these channels are *hidden* by the CSP hiding construct "$X \backslash \{Vin_A(i), Vout_A(i), Bin_A\}$". The idea of the design is that incoming messages are forwarded by the ROUTER via one of the VCHANs which act as communication media, of limited capacity and with a low reliability. The ROUTER should take such capacities and potential failures into account and distribute incoming messages in an appropriate way. The MERGER collects the messages from all VCHANs and sends them all via the *Bin* channel towards the BUFFER which in turn delivers them via out_A. Due to nondeterministically determined delays in the reception of messages that are sent via different VCHANs the order of messages might indeed get lost, as is allowed by the specification. It is not difficult to specify processes like $ROUTER_A$, and to show correctness of the MED_A implementation as above on the basis of these component specifications. One might then continue this 'horizontal' development, by implementing the component processes. At some moment though this has to be followed by a 'vertical' stage, where we take the representation of messages by sequences of packets into account. During this vertical stage a component such as $ROUTER_A$ is replaced by a component $ROUTER_C$ that behaves much like $ROUTER_A$ except that it operates on packets rather than messages. At first look we might use essentially the same abstraction relation α to relate the concrete internal level to the abstract level. (This 'generic' α should relate, by means of the ρ function, not only in_C and out_C to in_A and out_A but also the concrete *internal* channels to their abstract counterparts.) A correct solution could then be specified by the requiring that $ROUTER_C \subseteq \alpha^{-1}(ROUTER_A)$, and similarly for the other components. For in that case the subdistributivity of the CSP parallel composition and hiding constructs would guarantee that $MED_C \subseteq \alpha^{-1}(MED_A)$, as required.

The problem with this proposed solution is that it assumes that the low level $VCHAN$ processes preserve the ordering of messages, which is quite unrealistic, and moreover forces us to send all packets for some particular message via

the same $VCHAN$ virtual channel. If we drop the assumption on order preservation and allow the $ROUTER$ to arbitrarily distribute packets the protocol specified above is no longer obeyed, since in general the packets for a message will leave MED_C via out_C out of order and non-contiguous, i.e. intermixed with packets belonging to other messages.
Informally one sees that we can correct the situation by tagging packets with a sequence number and replacing the abstract $BUFFER_A$ process by a process SW implementing a *sliding window protocol*. That is, rather than merely buffering packets, SW will delay incoming packets until it has received all packets for some message and will then deliver all of them, in order and consecutively, via out_C.

For this more sophisticated solution we can no longer use ρ (and α) as the abstraction function for the *internal* behaviours. Rather we define a more complex variation γ of ρ that in some sense incorporates a specification of a sliding window protocol in that it extracts the abstract messages from a 'shuffled' sequence of packets. (For those sequences that *do* conform to our protocol, γ and ρ are *both* defined and yield equal results).

Let $\#h$ denote the length of a communication history h and $h\backslash\{p_1, p_2, \ldots\}$ a variant of the hiding operation, that removes the indicated messages $p_1, p_2, \ldots$ from h. then we define:

$$\gamma(\epsilon) = \epsilon$$

$$\gamma(h) = \begin{cases} m_l\, \gamma(h\backslash\{p_l^j \mid 1 \le j \le k_l\}) & , \begin{array}{l}\text{if there exists an } n : 1 \le n \le \#h\text{:}\\ \{p_l^j \mid 1 \le j \le k_l\} \subseteq \{h_i \mid 1 \le i \le n\}\\ \text{and for all } i : 1 \le i \le \#h\\ \{p_i^j \mid 1 \le j \le k_i\} \not\subseteq \{h_j \mid 1 \le j < n\}^2\end{array} \\ \epsilon & , \text{otherwise.} \end{cases}$$

As an example, suppose $\pi(m_1) = p_1^1 p_1^2$ and $\pi(m_2) = p_2^1$ and $p_1^1 p_1^2 p_2^1$ is transmitted via in_C, corresponding to $\rho(p_1^1 p_1^2 p_2^1) = m_1 m_2$ via in_A. On channel Bin_C the sliding window may receive sequences $p_1^1 p_1^2 p_2^1$ and $p_2^1 p_1^1 p_1^2$ representing $m_1 m_2$ and $m_2 m_1$ respectively, and which would be legal output for the out_C channel. It may also receive a sequence such as $p_1^2 p_2^1 p_1^1$, which is not allowed on out_C, and for which ρ is not defined. The γ function *is* defined for all three sequences, e.g. $\gamma(p_1^2 p_2^1 p_1^1)$ is computed as follows:

$$\begin{array}{rll} & \gamma(p_1^2 p_2^1 p_1^1) & \\ = & m_2\, \gamma(p_1^2 p_2^1 p_1^1 \backslash \{p_2^1\}) & \text{, choose } n = 2 \\ = & m_2\, \gamma(p_1^2 p_1^1) & \text{, definition of hiding} \\ = & m_2\, m_1\, \gamma(p_1^2 p_1^1 \backslash \{p_1^1, p_1^2\}) & \text{, choose } n = 2 \\ = & m_2\, m_1\, \gamma(\epsilon) & \text{, definition of hiding} \\ = & m_2\, m_1 & \end{array}$$

Thus, γ maps h_C to the abstract history h_A such that message $h_A(i)$ is the ith completely received message. Based on γ we formulate a β relation defined on

[2] One chooses n to be the minimal value for which there exists an index l such that all packets of m_l are received.

the complete internal behaviour. For example, for the $MERGER$ component we define

$$\beta(h_C, h_A) \text{ iff}$$

$$(h_A|\{Vout_A(1), Vout_A(2), \ldots\}) = \gamma(h_C|\{Vout_C(1), Vout_C(2), \ldots\}) \text{ and}$$

$$(h_A|Bin_A) = \gamma(h_C|Bin_C).$$

The criterium for correct refinement of $MERGER_A$ by $MERGER_C$ is then formulated as expected:

$$MERGER_C \subseteq \beta^{-1}(MERGER_A),$$

and similar requirements for the $ROUTER$ and $VCHAN$ components. Subdistributivity is now sufficient to conclude that we have also

$$(INT_C) \subseteq \beta^{-1}(INT_A).$$

where

$$INT_A \triangleq (ROUTER_A \parallel VCHANNELS_A \parallel MERGER_A) \text{ and where}$$

$$INT_C \triangleq (ROUTER_C \parallel VCHANNELS_C \parallel MERGER_C).$$

Finally, we define *contexts* for INT_A and INT_C:

$$Ctx_A(X) \triangleq (X \parallel BUFFER) \backslash \{Vin_A(i), Vout_A(i), Bin_A\}$$

$$Ctx_C(Y) \triangleq (Y \parallel SW) \backslash \{Vin_C(i), Vout_C(i), Bin_C\}$$

What we claim here is that context Ctx_C *refines* Ctx_A in the following sense:

$$Y \subseteq \beta^{-1}(X) \Rightarrow Ctx_C(Y) \subseteq \alpha^{-1}(Ctx_A(X)), \text{ for all } X, Y.$$

This property can be formulated equivalently as:

$$Ctx_C(\beta^{-1}(X)) \subseteq \alpha^{-1}(Ctx_A(X)), \text{ for all } X.$$

A proof of this claim will be sketched below, after the formal definition of compositional refinement. From the claim and the refinement relation between INT_A and INT_C it then easily follows that

$$Ctx_C(INT_C) \subseteq \alpha^{-1}(Ctx_A(INT_A)).$$

(Which shows the correctness of the whole design).

What the example shows is that the usual definition of program simulation, which assumes a uniform choice for the retrieve function, is not appropriate within a compositional set-up. For although the γ and β functions *could* have been used at the *interface* level too, such is exactly the situation one wants to avoid by the principle of 'separation of concerns': the (simple) ρ and α functions are all that is needed to specify the externally observable behaviour of the communication module, and any complexity related to internal detail is to be avoided for that purpose. Moreover, one might decide later on to re-implement the module much better than our proposal, *while retaining our refined interface*.
(End of example)

We define a more general notion of refinement, avoiding the limitation signalled above by introducing separate refinement relations for every component. Moreover, the definition is in terms of *context refinement*.

Definition 2.1 *(Compositional Refinement)*

We say that $S_0(X_1, \ldots, X_n)$ is refined by $T_0(Y_1, \ldots, Y_n)$ with respect to F_0 and $F_1, \ldots, F_n$ iff

$$T_0(F_1(X_1), \ldots, F_n(X_n)) \subseteq F_0(S_0(X_1, \ldots, X_n)),$$

for all $X_1, \ldots, X_n$.
□

In this paper we mainly concentrate on the case where F_j is of the form α_j^{-1}. We repeat the definition for this special case:

Definition 2.2 *(Compositional Refinement based on Weak Simulation)*

System $S_0(X_1, \ldots, X_n)$ is refined by $T_0(Y_1, \ldots, Y_n)$ with respect to relations α_0 and $\alpha_1, \ldots, \alpha_n$ iff

$$\alpha_0^{-1}(S_0(X_1, \ldots, X_n) \supseteq T_0(\alpha_1^{-1}(X_1), \ldots, \alpha_n^{-1}(X_n)))$$

for all $X_1, \ldots, X_n$.
□

For the simple case that S_0 and T_0 contain no free variables, our definition coincides with the notion of weak simulation introduced in definition 1.2.

Another important special case is that where S_0 equals T_0 and where $F_0 = F_1 = \cdots = F_n$. This is essentially subdistributivity of F_0 for S_0, where we extend this latter notion to complete terms $S_0(X_1, \ldots, X_n)$, rather than just operations $op(X_1, \ldots, X_n)$.
We already noticed that data refinement in the sense of [HHS87] implies a transformation of programs in which only their (atomic) data structure operations are replaced. The reason for this is that although subdistributivity admits implementation of operations or subprograms within a context S, it does not admit transformation of the *context* S itself. For concurrency, this situation is not satisfactory, because there are many cases where one's intuitive notion of implementation implies a change of context. For instance, take Milner's suggestion (in [M80]) to implement shared variable concurrency using communication based concurrency by modelling shared variables as separate concurrent processes, whose communications correspond to read and write operations. Here, the added shared variable modelling processes are put in parallel with the top syntactic level of the appropriately transformed shared variable program, implying a syntactic change at various levels. Another example of such a context change is contained in [Z90], which gives a correctness proof of a reification where the sequential abstract operations of a program are implemented by concurrent versions, more specifically, where abstract operations are replaced by communications with concurrent processes, implementing the

data structures involved in concurrent fashion and running in parallel with the appropriately transformed original program.

Some basic properties of compositional refinement are contained in the following theorems, which we present in the form appropriate for weak simulation.

Theorem 2.3 *(Refinement for monotonic terms)*
Let $T_0(Y_1, \ldots Y_n)$ be monotonic in each of its Y_i variables. Then $S_0(X_1, \ldots, X_n)$ is refined by $T_0(Y_1, \ldots, Y_n)$ with respect to relations α_0 and $\alpha_1, \ldots, \alpha_n$ if for all $Y_1, \ldots, Y_n$ and all $X_1, \ldots, X_n$:

$$(\bigwedge_{i=1..n} Y_i \subseteq \alpha_i^{-1}(X_i)) \Rightarrow T_0(Y_1, \ldots, Y_n) \subseteq \alpha_0^{-1}(S_0(X_1, \ldots, X_n)).$$

■

Theorem 2.4 *(Horizontal composability)*
Let the following conditions be satisfied.

- $S_0(X_1, \ldots, X_n)$ is refined by $T_0(X_1, \ldots, X_n)$ with respect to α_0 and $\alpha_1, \ldots, \alpha_r$
- $S_i(Y_1, \ldots, Y_m)$ is refined by $T_i(Y_1, \ldots, Y_m)$ with respect to α_i and $\beta_1, \ldots, \beta_m$, for $i = 1, \ldots, n$. (We assume here that the variables of each of the systems S_i is contained in a common list $Y_1, \ldots, Y_m$.)
- T_0 is monotonic in each of the X_i variables.

Then the composed system

$$S_0(S_1(Y_1, \ldots, Y_m), \ldots, S_n(Y_1, \ldots, Y_m))$$

is refined by

$$T_0(T_1(Y_1, \ldots, Y_m), \ldots, T_n(Y_1, \ldots, Y_m))$$

with respect to α_0 and $\beta_1, \ldots, \beta_m$.
■

Our definition of compositional refinement is rather general and moreover formulated in terms of parameterized, i.e. higher order, programs. Thus it might seem complicated to prove refinement on the basis of actual program texts and assertional specifications. For concrete specification- and programming languages it is possible though to have simpler criteria for checking the refinement conditions. We give a sketch of this for the case of CSP style processes and assertional trace specifications, within a "Programs as Predicates" setting [Ho85],[ZdR89]. That is, we use a mixed formalism that includes both processes and specifications as special case.

An assertional trace specification of a process P is a (first order) formula $\chi(h)$ with a special designated variable h denoting the communication history of the specification. The programs as predicates paradigm can be paraphrased as follows. Programs P can *semantically* be regarded as predicates on traces too, which we sometimes indicate by the notation $P(h)$. (*Syntactically* though, the h variable does not occur at all in the program text of P.)

A *context* $Ctx(X_1, \ldots, X_n)$ can be regarded in this way as a predicate of the form $\chi(h_1, \ldots, h_n, h)$, where the h_i denote traces of the components X_i, and where the last variable h denotes the trace of Ctx put around those components. Proof systems such as [Z89], [ZdR89] allow one to prove implications of the form $P(h) \rightarrow \chi(h)$. Such implications denote exactly the same as $P \subseteq \chi$ in the notation of this paper, i.e. program P should satisfy specification χ.

Now for predicates as above, there is a simple characterization for inverse images of the form $\alpha^{-1}(\chi)$, by means of substitution:

Lemma 2.5
For functions α and predicates $\chi(h)$ on (abstract) traces:

$$\alpha^{-1}(\chi(h)) = \chi(\alpha(h))$$

(Note that the variable h on the left hand side denotes the abstract trace, whereas the h on the right hand side denotes the concrete counterpart.) ■

Assume that we want to prove that some context $Ctx_A(X_1, \ldots, X_n)$ is refined by $Ctx_C(Y_1, \ldots, Y_n)$ with respect to α and $\beta_1, \ldots, \beta_n$. Furthermore, assume that we have *equivalent* predicates χ_A and χ_C for Ctx_A and Ctx_C. The refinement condition of the form

$$Ctx_C(\beta_1^{-1}(X_1), \ldots, \beta_n^{-1}(X_n)) \subseteq \alpha^{-1}(Ctx_A(X_1, \ldots, X_n))$$

can then be rewritten as follows:

$$\forall h \left(\exists h_1, \ldots, h_n (\bigwedge_{i=1..n} X_i(\beta_i(h_i)) \wedge \chi_C(h_1, \ldots, h_n, h)) \rightarrow \right.$$

$$\left. \exists t_1, \ldots, t_n (\bigwedge_{i=1..n} X_i(t_i) \wedge \chi_A(t_1, \ldots, t_n, \alpha(h)) \right)$$

This implication should be valid for all $X_1, \ldots, X_n$. A sufficient condition for the implication to hold is obtained by choosing $t_i = \beta_i(h_i)$, followed by simplification of the formula:

$$\forall h\, (\forall h_1, \ldots, h_n (\chi_C(h_1, \ldots, h_n, h) \rightarrow \chi_A(\beta_1(h_1), \ldots, \beta_n(h_n), \alpha(h)))) .$$

What we have shown is the following theorem:

Theorem 2.6 *Compositional Refinement for Trace Specifications*
For trace predicates $\chi_A(h_1, \ldots, h_n, h)$ and $\chi_C(h_1, \ldots, h_n, h)$ a sufficient condition for refinement of Ctx_A by Ctx_C with respect to α and $\beta_1, \ldots, \beta_n$ is:

$$\forall h\, (\forall h_1, \ldots, h_n (\chi_C(h_1, \ldots, h_n, h) \rightarrow \chi_A(\beta_1(h_1), \ldots, \beta_n(h_n), \alpha(h)))) .$$

■

Example 2.2
As an example we consider the contexts introduced at the end of example of the communication medium. We recall the definition of these contexts:

$$Ctx_A(X) \triangleq (X \parallel BUFFER)\backslash\{Vin_A(i), Vout_A(i), Bin_A\}$$

$$Ctx_C(Y) \triangleq (Y \parallel SW)\backslash\{Vin_C(i), Vout_C(i), Bin_C\}$$

Techniques as for instance discussed in [Z89] allow one to prove equivalence of these contexts with the following predicates:

$$\chi_A(h_1, h) \triangleq \exists t'(h = (t'|\{in_A, out_A\}) \wedge chan(t') = \{in_A, out_A, Bin_A\}$$

$$\wedge\, (t'|\{in_A, Bin_A\}) = h_1 \wedge out_A \leq (t'|Bin_A))$$

and:

$$\chi_C(h_1, h) \triangleq \exists h'(h = (h'|\{in_C, out_C\}) \wedge chan(h') = \{in_C, out_C, Bin_C\}$$

$$\wedge\, (h'|\{in_A, Bin_A\}) = h_1 \wedge out_C \leq \gamma(t'|Bin_C))$$

What has to be shown to prove the refinement relation that we claimed at the end of the previous example can now be reduced to the following straightforward verification condition:

$$\forall h_1, h(\chi_C(h_1, h) \;\rightarrow\; \chi_A(\beta(h_1), \alpha(h)),$$

where α and β are the abstraction relations introduced in the example. **(End of example)**

Finally we provide another example of context refinement, which can be considered a special case of compositional refinement.

Example 2.3 *(Self-stabilizing snapshot algorithm of [KP90])*
Consider a distributed system in which processes communicate by asynchronous message passing via directed channels. The communication network is strongly connected, and the channels are FIFO buffers of sufficient capacity. The *global state* of a distributed system is the product of all the local states plus the contents of the channels. An *accurate snapshot* is defined as follows [KP90].

> *At any global state σ, a process is said to have an* accurate snapshot *of σ' if local variables of the process contain a representation of a global state that is a* possible *successor of σ' and a* possible *predecessor of σ.*[3]

[3]It is implicitly understood that σ and σ' are states within the same computation.

Snapshots may be used, for example, to detect wether a distributed algorithm has terminated or to retrieve information contained in the local states of the processes.

In [CL85] Chandy and Lamport presented the algorithm for obtaining accurate snapshots, which is used as a basis for the 'StableSnap' algorithm of Katz and Perry [KP90]. We will briefly outline the Chandy-Lamport algorithm. For a more complete discussion of the algorithm and its correctness argument we refer to [CL85,D83]. Process P_0 may invoke the snapshot algorithm by recording its local state and sending a *marker* along each outgoing channel. From this moment on the process records for each incoming channel the messages it receives. On receiving a marker along an incoming channel c a process P_i executes the subroutine $CL(c)$ (algorithm 1). If process P_0 has received all reports, it may

```
IF Pi has not yet recorded its local state
   THEN Pi records its local state and starts recording
        the incoming messages on channel c;
        Pi sends a marker on each outgoing channel
   ELSE Pi stops recording the incoming messages on channel c
FI;
IF Pi has stopped recording the messages on all incoming channels
   THEN Pi sends a report to P0
FI
```

Algorithm 1: $CL(c)$ (Snapshot, [CL85]).

initiate another snapshot. Let CL_i denote the snapshot algorithm for process P_i and $\frac{S}{T}$ denote the superposition (or superimposition), see e.g. [BF88], of program S upon T, then the distributed system $P_0 \parallel \cdots \parallel P_{n-1}$ is transformed into

$$\frac{CL_0}{P_0} \parallel \cdots \parallel \frac{CL_{n-1}}{P_{n-1}} \; .$$

The structure of this system can be described by

$$C(P_0, \ldots, P_{n-1}, CL_0, \ldots, CL_{n-1}) \; , \qquad (2)$$

where the *context* $C(X_0, \ldots, X_{n-1}, Y_0, \ldots, Y_{n-1})$ is defined as

$$\frac{Y_0}{X_0} \parallel \cdots \parallel \frac{Y_{n-1}}{X_{n-1}} \; .$$

We describe an algorithm called 'StableSnap' that can be viewed as a refinement of (2), where the context $C(X_0, \ldots, X_{n-1}, Y_0, \ldots, Y_{n-1})$ is transformed into
$K(X_0, \ldots, X_{n-1}, Y_0, \ldots, Y_{n-1})$, thereby leaving $P_0, \ldots, P_{n-1}$ and $CL_0, \ldots, CL_{n-1}$ unchanged. So, the resulting system can be described as

$$K(P_0, \ldots, P_{n-1}, CL_0, \ldots, CL_{n-1}) \; . \qquad (3)$$

Compositional refinement allows one to show a refinement relation between $C(X_0,\ldots,X_{n-1},Y_0,\ldots,Y_{n-1})$ and $K(X_0,\ldots,X_{n-1},Y_0,\ldots,Y_{n-1})$ without paying attention to the structure of P_i and CL_i $(i = 1,\ldots,n)$, all in order to prove that (2) is refined by (3). Similarly, one could refine P_i into some process P_i' or CL_i into CL_i' $(i = 1,\ldots,n)$. Subdistributivity as in [HH87] would allow only these latter refinements, but *not* context refinement.

The 'StableSnap' algorithm is a *self-stabilizing* snapshot algorithm based upon the Chandy-Lamport algorithm. Paraphrasing Katz and Perry, a self-stabilizing program is a program that eventually resumes normal behaviour even if its execution is initiated from an illegal state. In this sense a self-stabilizing program can tolerate transient faults. Following [KP90], $sem(P)$ denotes the set of all possible execution sequences of P for arbitrary initial states. Let $legsem(P)$ denote the subset of $sem(P)$ with all execution sequences starting in *legitimate* initial states (initial states satisfying some characteristic predicate.) Given the definitions for self-stabilization:

> *Program P is* self-stabilizing *if each sequence in $sem(P)$ has a non-empty suffix that is identical to a suffix of some sequence in $legsem(P)$,*

and program extension:

> *Program Q is an* extension *of program P if for each global state in $legsem(Q)$ there is a projection onto all variables and messages of P such that the resulting set of sequences is identical to $legsem(P)$, upto stuttering,* [4]

a program Q is defined to be a *self-stabilizing extension* of program P if Q is self-stabilizing and also an extension of P (see [KP90]).

Below we give a brief description of the core of the 'StableSnap' algorithm. Each *round* of the 'StableSnap' algorithm is initiated by process P_0 by sending a marker on each outgoing channel. Process P_0 may initiate a new round at any time. A round ends when process P_0 has received a *report* for that round from all processes. Due to the lack of synchronization each process may be involved in a different round, Therefore it is assumed that each marker and report contains the round number of the originating process at the moment of sending. Upon receiving a marker via channel c a process P_i invokes the algorithm $KP(c)$ (algorithm 2). A distributed system $P_0 \parallel \cdots \parallel P_{n-1}$ is transformed by superposition of the 'StableSnap' algorithm into

$$\frac{KP_0(CL_0)}{P_0} \parallel \cdots \parallel \frac{KP_{n-1}(CL_{n-1})}{P_{n-1}},$$

where $KP_i(CL_i)$ means that KP_i uses the subroutines of CL_i.

It can be shown, c.f. [KP90], that a distributed system $StableSnap(X_1 \parallel \cdots \parallel X_k)$ obtained by superposition of the 'StableSnap' algorithm is a self-stabilizing extension of the system *Snapshot* $(X_1 \parallel \cdots \parallel X_k)$, that is obtained by superposing the Chandy-Lamport algorithm upon $X_1 \parallel \cdots \parallel X_k$. Let π be the function

[4] A sequence is stuttering if there exist two identical consecutive states in that sequence.

```
IF Pi is recording this channel and
   the marker has the same round number as Pi
   THEN start CL(c);
        IF Pi stopped recording all channels
           THEN send a report to process P0
        FI
   ELSE IF the marker was received before
           THEN skip
           ELSE IF the marker has a higher round number than Pi
                   THEN propagate the marker along all channels;
                        adapt the round number and restart CL(c)
                   ELSE propagate the marker along all channels;
                        IF Pi stopped recording all channels
                           THEN send a report to process P0
                        FI
                FI
        FI
FI
```

Algorithm 2: $KP(c)$ (StableSnap, [KP90]).

that maps each execution sequence s of 'StableSnap' to the unique execution sequence s' obtained by first projecting the states of s to the variables and messages of 'Snapshot' and then removing duplicate immediate-successors of states. Then from the fact that 'StableSnap' is an extension of 'Snapshot' it follows that

$$\hat{\pi}^{-1}(legsem(Snapshot)) = legsem(StableSnap) ,$$

where $\hat{\pi}^{-1}$ is defined by

$$\hat{\pi}^{-1}(\Sigma) \triangleq \{s \mid s' = \pi(s),\ s' \in \Sigma\} .$$

Furthermore, let κ be the relation that relates all execution sequences s with each execution sequence s' that is a non-empty suffix of s then $\hat{\kappa}^{-1}$ is defined by

$$\hat{\kappa}^{-1}(\Sigma) \triangleq \{s \mid (s, s') \in \kappa,\ s' \in \Sigma\} .$$

Given the fact that 'StableSnap' is self-stabilizing w.r.t. 'Snapshot', it follows that ($legsem(X) \subseteq sem(X)$ for all X)

$$\hat{\pi}^{-1}(\hat{\kappa}^{-1}(sem(Snapshot))) \supseteq sem(StableSnap) ,$$

It is easily seen that the $Snapshot(X_1 \parallel \cdots \parallel X_k)$ context is refined by the context $StableSnap(X_1 \parallel \cdots \parallel X_k)$ if one chooses $\alpha_0 = (\kappa \circ \pi)$ and for α_i ($i = 1, \ldots, k$) the identity relation in definition 2.1.

The superposed programs can only affect its own variables, but not variables of the underlying program. Furthermore, the underlying program and the

superposed program can identify whether a message belongs to the underlying or the superposed program, so that no interference can occur. These restrictions guarantee that the superposed program can not block or affect the control of the underlying program. Therefore we may conclude that (this kind of) superposition is monotonic. Because superposition is monotonic, it follows from theorem 2.4 that if we replace the macro's of the Chandy-Lamport algorithm by correct implementations, then that will not affect the correctness of the Katz-Perry algorithm, *independently* of the underlying program.
(End of example)

3 Conclusions

We discussed the rôle of compositionality in refinement and argued that a more general notion of refinement than subdistributivity is needed for compositional refinement. The motivation for such a generalized notion of refinement was illustrated by some non-trivial examples.

Furthermore, we introduced a general framework that unifies several refinement methods for sequential and concurrent programs. The expressive power of the resulting theory has been investigated, which resulted in the conclusion that several well-known theories, such as the prespecification calculus, are embedded within the theory.

A Formal framework

In this section we sketch some of the underlying principles and techniques that are used throughout the paper. One of the problems that we encountered when studying the literature on reification and simulation was the large variety of theories and methods being proposed, both for sequential and for parallel systems. Quite often there is a strong relationship between methods, and it is one of our aims to clarify such relationships. For sequential systems we presented a more uniform framework for several well known reification methods in [CdRZ91]. For instance, it was shown how Reynolds' reification method and VDM-style reification can be related within one predicate transformer framework. Here we extend these results by proposing a language that allows for the formulation of several definitions of simulation, such as upwards or downwards simulation, applicable to both sequential and parallel systems. The language resembles more classical formalisms such as predicate transformer calculi and the relational calculus. It differs from these formalisms in that we make a clear distinction between *composition* of relations and predicate transformers on the one hand and *sequential composition* of programs on the other hand. For instance, in a trace-based formalism we use binary retrieve relations to map concrete communication histories to abstract histories. Composing such relations does not correspond to the sequential composition operator of the programming language. For the latter operation amounts to *concatenation of histories*. However, the predicate transformer framework for sequential programs is embedded in the theory below as a special case in which programs denote binary relations on states. To deal with concurrent programs we use relations not on states but on complete computations, which we sometimes refer to as *generalized states*. In [Z89] a predicate transformer theory and formalism for concurrency based on this notion of generalized states is developed which indicates the wide range of applicability of predicate transformer concepts and which is subsumed in the formalism presented below.

The theory is defined relative to two basic types, viz. $\mathcal{S}tate$ and $\mathcal{C}omp$. The elements $\mathcal{S}tate$ are (generalized) states and the elements of $\mathcal{C}omp$ are computations. For types $\tau_1, \ldots, \tau_n$ the type $\mathcal{R}el$ is defined by

$$\mathcal{R}el(\tau_1, \ldots, \tau_n) \triangleq \mathcal{P}(\tau_1 \times \cdots \times \tau_n) .$$

Thus the elements of $\mathcal{R}el$ are relations. In case of a unary relation we use $\mathcal{S}et(\tau)$ rather than $\mathcal{R}el(\tau)$. The type $\mathcal{T}rans$ is only defined for non-basic types τ_1 and τ_2:

$$\mathcal{T}rans(\tau_1, \tau_2) \triangleq \tau_1 \longrightarrow \tau_2$$

The elements of $\mathcal{T}rans$ are called transformers, because predicate transformers turn out to be special elements of $\mathcal{T}rans$. Besides elements of the types defined above, the theory also includes a class of formulae, which will be discussed later.

Definition A.1 *(Relations)*
Relations are defined inductively as follows.

- Let χ be a n-place predicate on tuples in $\tau_1 \times \cdots \times \tau_n$, then

  $$\{(t_1, \ldots, t_n) \in \tau_1 \times \cdots \times \tau_n \mid \chi(t_1, \ldots, t_n)\}$$

  is a relation of type $\mathcal{R}el(\tau_1, \ldots, \tau_n)$.

- Let R be a relation of type $\mathcal{R}el(\tau_1, \ldots, \tau_n)$, then
  - the complement $\neg R \triangleq \bar{R}$ is a relation of type $\mathcal{R}el(\tau_1, \ldots, \tau_n)$.
  - the converse R^{-1} is a relation of type $\mathcal{R}el(\tau_n, \ldots, \tau_1)$.

- Let R_1 and R_2 be relations of type $\mathcal{R}el(\tau_1, \ldots, \tau_n)$, then the union $R_1 \vee R_2 \triangleq R_1 \cup R_2$ and the intersection $R_1 \wedge R_2 \triangleq R_1 \cap R_2$ are relations of type $\mathcal{R}el(\tau_1, \ldots, \tau_n)$.

- Let R_1 be a relation of type $\mathcal{R}el(\tau_1, \ldots, \tau_{n-1}, \tau_n)$ and R_2 be a relation of type $\mathcal{R}el(\tau_n, \tau_{n+1}, \ldots, \tau_{n+m})$, then their composition $R_1 \mathbin{;} R_2 \triangleq R_2 \circ R_1$ is a relation of type $\mathcal{R}el(\tau_1, \ldots \tau_{n-1}, \tau_{n+1}, \ldots \tau_{n+m})$.

- A special case of the previous definition is the *relational image* $R(\!|S|\!)$, which abbreviates $S \mathbin{;} R$. We employ this abbreviation when S is a unary relation, i.e. a set. So if R is a relation of type $\mathcal{R}el(\tau_1, \tau_2, \ldots, \tau_n)$ and S is of type $\mathcal{S}et(\tau_1)$, then the relational image $R(\!|S|\!)$ is a relation of type $\mathcal{R}el(\tau_2, \ldots, \tau_n)$.

- Let T be a transformer of type $\tau_1 \longrightarrow \tau_2$, and let R be a relation of type τ_1 then $T(R)$ is a relation of type τ_2.

□

Notice the notation $R_1 \fatsemi R_2$ for composition of relations. Although we do not present any particular programming language here, we denote sequential composition of programs by $S_1 ; S_2$. As explained above, the two operations coincide only for the case of ***sequential*** programs, where $S_1 ; S_2$ (also) denotes relational composition.

Definition A.2 *(Transformers)*
For non-basic types $\tau_1, \tau_2 \ldots$ transformers are defined inductively as follows.

- Let X be a variable of type τ_1 and R be of type τ_2, possibly with free occurrences of X, then $\lambda X.R$ is a transformer of type $\tau_1 \rightarrow \tau_2$.
- Let T_1 and T_2 be transformers of type $\tau_1 \rightarrow \tau_2$, then
  - $T_1 \wedge T_2$ and $T_1 \vee T_2$, respectively defined by
    $(T_1 \wedge T_2)(X) \triangleq T_1(X) \wedge T_2(X)$ and
    $(T_1 \vee T_2)(X) \triangleq T_1(X) \vee T_2(X)$,
    are transformers of type $\tau_1 \rightarrow \tau_2$.
  - Likewise, $\neg T_1$ is a transformer of type $\tau_1 \rightarrow \tau_2$.
- Let T_1 be a transformer of type $\tau_1 \rightarrow \tau_2$ and T_2 be a transformer of type $\tau_2 \rightarrow \tau_3$, then $T_2 \circ T_1$ is a transformer of type $\tau_1 \rightarrow \tau_3$.
- Let T be a transformer of type $\tau_1 \rightarrow \tau_2$ then the adjoint transformer $T^\dagger$ is defined by

  $$T^\dagger(X) \triangleq \bigcup\{Y \mid T(Y) \subseteq X\}.$$

  It is a transformer of type $\tau_2 \rightarrow \tau_1$.

□

Because the definitions above are very general, we will discuss some more specific cases of transformers, that capture some of the more familiar (predicate) transformers.

If R is of type $\mathcal{R}el(\tau_1, \tau_2)$ and S of type $\mathcal{S}et(\tau_1)$, then $R(\!|S|\!)$ is the ***strongest postcondition*** of type $\mathcal{S}et(\tau_1)$.

$T^\dagger(X)$ is easily seen to be the largest Y such that $T(Y) \subseteq X$. For the cases of interest T can be assumed to be completely additive (c.a.), i.e.

$$T(\bigcup\{X \mid \ldots X \ldots\}) = \bigcup\{T(X) \mid \ldots X \ldots\}.$$

In that case $T^\dagger$ is also characterized by the following property of right adjoints:

$$T(X) \subseteq Y \text{ if and only if } X \subseteq T^\dagger(Y).$$

The use of the adjoint operation is that it allows for a uniform definition of several distinct predicate transformers, such as weakest preconditions, weakest prespecifications, generalizations thereof for concurrency, the weakest postspecification and the related 'leads to' transformer. We provide some of the details. Let R be a relation of type $\mathcal{R}el(\tau_1, \ldots, \tau_{n+1})$. Furthermore, let X resp. Y be a variable of type $\mathcal{R}el(\tau_1, \ldots, \tau_n, \tau_{n+2}, \ldots, \tau_{n+m})$ resp. $\mathcal{R}el(\tau_{n+1}, \ldots, \tau_{n+m})$. We define the so called 'leads to' transformer $\lambda X.R \rightsquigarrow X$ of type:

$$\mathcal{R}el(\tau_1, \ldots, \tau_n, \tau_{n+2}, \ldots, \tau_{n+m}) \to \mathcal{R}el(\tau_{n+1}, \ldots, \tau_{n+m}),$$

as the adjoint of $R \mathbin{;} Y$, i.e.

$$\lambda X.R \rightsquigarrow X \triangleq (\lambda Y.R \mathbin{;} Y)^{\dagger} .$$

This definition includes the following well known transformers as special cases.

- If R is of type $\mathcal{S}et(\tau_1)$ and S of type $\mathcal{S}et(\tau_2)$, then $R \rightsquigarrow S$ is the 'leads to' relation of type $\mathcal{R}el(\tau_1, \tau_2)$. If we interpret R and S as precondition and postcondition of a Hoare style formula, then $R \rightsquigarrow S$ is the largest program (i.e. relation) that satisfies that Hoare formula.
- If R is of type $\mathcal{R}el(\tau_1, \tau_2)$ and S of type $\mathcal{R}el(\tau_1, \tau_3)$, then $R \rightsquigarrow S$ is the *weakest postspecification* S/R of Hoare and He [HH87] of type $\mathcal{R}el(\tau_2, \tau_3)$, (take $n = 1$ and $m = 2$ in the above definition.)

For relation R of type $\mathcal{R}el(\tau_1, \ldots, \tau_n)$ and variables X and Y respectively of type $\mathcal{R}el(\tau_{n+1}, \ldots, \tau_{n+m}, \tau_2, \ldots, \tau_n)$ and $\mathcal{R}el(\tau_{n+1}, \ldots, \tau_{n+m}, \tau_1)$, the transformer $[R]$ of type $\mathcal{R}el(\tau_{n+1}, \ldots, \tau_{n+m}, \tau_2, \ldots, \tau_n) \to \mathcal{R}el(\tau_{n+1}, \ldots, \tau_{n+m}, \tau_1)$ is defined as the adjoint of $Y \mathbin{;} R$, i.e.

$$\lambda X.[R]X \triangleq (\lambda Y.Y \mathbin{;} R)^{\dagger} .$$

The following special cases may be more familiar.

- Taking $m = 0$ and $n = 2$ in the above definition, if R is of type $\mathcal{R}el(\tau_1, \tau_2)$ and S is of type $\mathcal{S}et(\tau_2)$, then $[R]S$ denotes the *weakest precondition* transformer of type $\mathcal{S}et(\tau_1)$.
- And if R is of type $\mathcal{R}el(\tau_2, \tau_3)$ and S is of type $\mathcal{R}el(\tau_1, \tau_3)$, then $[R]S$ is the *weakest prespecification* $R\backslash S$ of [HH87] of type $\mathcal{R}el(\tau_1, \tau_2)$.

The transformer $\langle R \rangle$ is as usual defined as the dual of $[R]$, i.e. $\langle R \rangle X \triangleq \neg[R]\neg X$. The purpose of this transformer in theories for reification has been explained in [CdRZ91]. It has the so called 'angelicness' property, which can be formulated as

$$\langle S \vee T \rangle = \langle S \rangle \vee \langle T \rangle$$

Such transformers appear for instance in work by Ralph Back [BvW89]. Back does not make a clear notational distinction between transformers of the form $[S]$ and of the form $\langle S \rangle$. Consequently he must introduce angelic statements, such as the angelic choice operators '$\diamond$' satisfying the (surprising) law

$$[S \diamond T] = [S] \vee [T] .$$

A related construct is the angelic assignment of [BvW89] which is used in work on refinement. Such angelic constructs cannot be explained on the level of relations, i.e. if we model statements as binary relations, then the operation $S \diamond T$ does not exist. For example the statement $x := a \diamond x := b$ has the following properties.

$$[x := a \diamond x := b](x = a) \equiv \mathsf{true} \tag{4}$$
$$[x := a \diamond x := b](x = b) \equiv \mathsf{true} \tag{5}$$

From (4) it follows immediately that $[\![x := a \diamond x := b]\!] \subseteq \{(s_0, s_1) \mid s_1(x) = a\}$, and likewise from (5) it follows that $[\![x := a \diamond x := b]\!] \subseteq \{(s_0, s_1) \mid s_1(x) = b\}$. Hence, for all a and b such that $a \neq b$ it follows that $[\![x := a \diamond x := b]\!] = \emptyset$. For this reason we prefer a theory based on a combined use of the box and diamond operators $[S]$ and $\langle S \rangle$.

Definition A.3 *(Formulae)*
The syntactic class $\mathcal{F}orm$ of (correctness) formulae is defined as follows.

- Let R_1 and R_2 be relations of type $\mathcal{R}el(\tau_1, \ldots, \tau_n)$, then $R_1 \subseteq R_2$ is a formula.

- Let $F_1 \in \mathcal{F}orm$ and $F_2 \in \mathcal{F}orm$, then $F_1 \rightarrow F_2$ and $F_1 \wedge F_2$ are formulae with the obvious interpretation.

- Let X be a variable of type $\mathcal{R}el(\tau_1, \ldots, \tau_n)$ and F be a formula with free occurrences of X, then $\forall X.F(X)$ is a formula. The formula $\forall X.F(X)$ is true if $F(R)$ is true for all relations R of type $\mathcal{R}el(\tau_1, \ldots, \tau_n)$, and false otherwise.

□

We will use abbreviations such as $\exists X.F(X)$ with the usual interpretation.

Some special formulae can be defined as follows. For relations R_1, R_2, and R_3 of type $\mathcal{R}el(\tau_1, \ldots, \tau_n)$, $\mathcal{R}el(\tau_n, \ldots, \tau_{n+m})$, and $\mathcal{R}el(\tau_1, \ldots, \tau_{n-1}, \tau_{n+1}, \ldots \tau_{n+m})$ we define *generalized Hoare formulae*

$$(R_1)\ R_2\ (R_3) \triangleq R_1 \mathbin{⨾} R_2 \subseteq R_3\ .$$

In case that R_1, R_2, and R_3 resp. are of type $\mathcal{S}et(\tau_1)$, $\mathcal{R}el(\tau_1, \tau_2)$, and $\mathcal{S}et(\tau_2)$, then $(R_1)\ R_2\ (R_3)$ coincides with the classical Hoare-style correctness formula $\{R_1\}\ R_2\ \{R_3\}$ (c.f. [CdRZ91]). In a similar way [CdRZ91] VDM-style (partial) correctness formulae can also be defined.

As a last example of the expressive power of this framework, we demonstrate how the theory of [HHS87] can be embedded in our theory. A relation C *downward simulates* relation A w.r.t. simulation relation R if

$$R \mathbin{⨾} C \subseteq A \mathbin{⨾} R\ .$$

Following [HHS87] we define the transformer F_R by

$$F_R(X) \triangleq R \rightsquigarrow (X \mathbin{⨾} R)\ .$$

From the definition of $\leadsto$ it follows that

$$R \fatsemi F_R(A) \subseteq A \fatsemi R \,.$$

Thus $F_R(A)$ is the largest relation that downward simulates A with respect to R. Because, in the prespecification calculus '$\fatsemi$' coincides with ';', this is a generalized version of F_R as defined in [HHS87]. In a similar way we can also define the transformer G_S for *upward simulation*, c.f. [HHS87,CdRZ91].

References

[BF88] Bougé L & Francez N. *A Compositional Approach to Superimposition.* Proc. of the 15th Symp. on Principles of Programming Languages, pp. 240–249, 1988.

[BvW89] Back RJR & von Wright J. *A Lattice-theoretical Basis for a Specification Language.* Proc. of the conf. on Mathematics of Program Construction, LNCS 375, van de Snepscheut (Ed.) Springer 1989.

[CL85] Chandy KM & Lamport L. *Distributed Snapshots: Determining Global States of Distributed Systems.* ACM Transactions on Computer Systems 3(1):63–75, 1985.

[CdRZ91] Coenen J, de Roever WP & Zwiers J. *Assertional Data Reification Proofs: Survey and Perspective.* Proc. of the 4th BCS-FACS Refinement Workshop, Workshops in Computing, pp. 97–114, Springer-Verlag 1991.

[D83] Dijkstra E.W. *The Distributed Snapshot of K.M. Chandy and L. Lamport.* EWD864a.

[Ho85] Hoare C.A.R. *Programs are predicates.* in Mathematical Logic and Programming Languages, Hoare and Shepherdson(eds), Prentice-Hall, 1985.

[HH87] Hoare CAR & He J. *The Weakest Prespecification.* Information Processing Letters 24:127–132, 1987.

[HHS87] Hoare CAR, He J & Sanders JW. *Prespecification in Data Refinement.* Information Processing Letters 25:71–76, 1987.

[J90] Jones CB. *Systematic Software Development using VDM.* Prentice-Hall 1990 (2nd edition).

[KP90] Katz S & Perry JP. *Self-Stabilizing Extensions for Message-passing Systems.* Proc. of the 9th Symp. on Principles of Distributed Computing, pp. 91–101, 1990.

[M80] Milner R. *A Calculus of Communicating Systems.* LNCS 92, Springer-Verlag 1980.

[O91] Olderog ER. *Nets, Terms, and Formulas.* Cambridge Tracts in Computer Science 23, Cambridge University Press 1991.

[R81] Reynolds JC. *The Craft of Programming.* Prentice-Hall 1981.

[Z89] Zwiers J. *Compositionality, Concurrency, and Partial Correctness: Proof Theories for Networks of Processes, and their Relationship.* LNCS 321, Springer-Verlag 1989.

[Z90] Zwiers J. *Refining Data to Processes.* Proc. of VDM '90, LNCS 428, pp. 352–369, Springer-Verlag 1990.

[ZdR89] Zwiers J & de Roever WP. *Predicates are Predicate Transformers: a Unified Compositional Theory for Concurrency.* Proc. of the 8th Symp. on Principles of Distributed Computing, pp. 265–279, 1989.

Implementing Promoted Operations in Z

J.C.P. Woodcock
Oxford University

Abstract

We describe the *promotion* technique in Z. Some of its formal properties have been investigated, and it has been shown how to perform data refinement on promoted operations. In this paper, we show how promotion is closely allied to procedures and their parameters. We take the most commonly used form of promotion, and show that it may be implemented using call-by-reference parameters.

1 Introduction

In this paper we describe a technique for structuring large descriptions. It is called *promotion,* and it is a way of composing and factoring specifications in the Z notation [1]. Promotion has been used extensively in the IBM CICS specification to structure large descriptions, and was devised originally by [4]. There it was called *framing,* because it is evocative of placing a frame around a picture: only what is inside the frame may change; what is outside must remain unaffected by an operation. This is still the best way of understanding promotion. As we shall see, we focus on a small part of a system, and then enlarge our view to encompass the whole picture. The first formal treatment of promotion appeared in [5]; this work is continued and extended in [2].[1]

In the first section, we discuss how to factor and compose operations, and give three different examples of the promotion technique. In the second section we give the definition of what constitutes a promotion, and distinguish between free and constrained promotions. Finally, we consider how a particular form of promotion might be implemented.

2 Factoring Operations

Suppose that we have the following definitions:

Local

$s : \mathbb{P}\,\mathbb{N}$

Global

$f : Name \rightarrowtail\!\!\!\!\!\rightarrow Local$

[1]The examples in the first part of this paper are due to Peter Lupton.

This kind of thing happens very often in specifications: the global state contains multiple, indexed instances of the local state. Now suppose that we want an operation that updates a particular local value in the global state:

$$\begin{array}{|l}\hline \multicolumn{1}{l}{Add_G} \\ \Delta Global \\ n? : Name \\ x? : \mathbb{N} \\ \hline n? \in \operatorname{dom} f \\ f' = f \oplus \{n? \mapsto (f\ n?).s \cup \{x?\}\} \\ \hline \end{array}$$

We must supply the index $n?$ and the new value, but it is difficult to see exactly what is being done to the local state indexed by $n?$; this problem is exacerbated if the update is any more complicated than this simple addition of an input. Furthermore, there are likely to be several operations of this kind.

In order to expose more clearly what is going on, the global operation may be factored into a local operation and a mixed operation:

$$\begin{array}{|l}\hline \multicolumn{1}{l}{Add_L} \\ \Delta Local \\ x? : \mathbb{N} \\ \hline s' = s \cup \{x?\} \\ \hline \end{array}$$

$$\begin{array}{|l}\hline \multicolumn{1}{l}{Update} \\ \Delta Global \\ \Delta Local \\ n? : Name \\ \hline n? \in \operatorname{dom} f \\ \theta Local = f\ n? \\ f' = f \oplus \{n? \mapsto \theta Local'\} \\ \hline \end{array}$$

The local operation explains what happens to the local state; the global operation expalains how changes in a local state are incorporated into the global state. The governing principle here is that of separation of concerns: there are two factors in the operation, and we have described them separately. Now our global operation may be composed from these factors with a little bit of schema calculus:

$$Add_G \mathrel{\widehat{=}} \exists \Delta Local \bullet Update \wedge Add_L.$$

2.1 Examples of Promotion

The example that we have just seen is often encountered: the global state consists of a partial function into instances of the local state. Of course, this is not the only possibility. In this section we describe two more examples to illustrate promotion.

2.1.1 Sequence

Suppose that we need a stack in our specification. The stack contains *Local* values, where *Local* contains a natural number, amongst other things:

$$\begin{array}{|l}\hline \textit{Local} \\ n : \mathbb{N} \\ \ldots \\ \hline \ldots \\ \hline \end{array}$$

A stack is just a sequence of *Local* values, but we further require that the contents of the stack are ordered:

$$\begin{array}{|l}\hline \textit{Global} \\ \textit{stack} : \mathrm{seq}\,\textit{Local} \\ \hline \forall\, i, j : \mathrm{dom}\,\textit{stack} \mid i < j \bullet (\textit{stack}\ i).n < (\textit{stack}\ j).n \\ \hline \end{array}$$

The following mixed operation will promote operations on a local state to operations on a stack:

$$\begin{array}{|l}\hline \textit{Update} \\ \Delta \textit{Global} \\ \Delta \textit{Local} \\ \hline \#\textit{stack} > 0 \\ \theta \textit{Local} = \textit{head stack} \\ \textit{stack}' = \langle \theta \textit{Local}' \rangle \frown \textit{tail stack} \\ \hline \end{array}$$

The predicate says that the stack must be non-empty, and that changes are made to the element on the top of the stack only.

2.1.2 Relation

Suppose that we are specifying an electronic mail system, and that we have already specified a *MailBox*, and its attendent operations. Now we turn to the description of a *MailSystem*. *MailBox*es are indexed by *Address*, but a person may have several addresses, and an address may be associated with several people. Our system state is

$$\begin{array}{|l}\hline \textit{MailSystem} \\ \textit{people} : \textit{Name} \leftrightarrow \textit{Address} \\ \textit{mbox} : \textit{Address} \rightarrow\!\!\!\!\!\!\rightarrow\!\!\!\!\!\!\!\mapsto \textit{MailBox} \\ \hline \end{array}$$

Now, when an incoming message is destined for a particular name $n?$, it is quite correct to put it in any one of the mailboxes whose address corresponds to $n?$. The following mixed operation promotes operations on a *MailBox* to a *MailSystem*; it responds with the address used:

$$
\begin{array}{|l}
\multicolumn{1}{l}{\_\, Update \,\rule{30em}{0.4pt}} \\
\Delta MailSystem \\
\Delta MailBox \\
n? : Name \\
a! : Address \\
\hline
n? \mapsto a! \in people \\
a! \in \operatorname{dom} mbox \\
\theta MailBox = mbox\ a! \\
mbox' = mbox \oplus \{a! \mapsto \theta MailBox'\} \\
\hline
\end{array}
$$

3 Promotion

We can now give a definition of promotion. Suppose that we have

- a local state L;
- a global state G that is given in terms of the local state;
- a local operation Op, that operates on L;
- a mixed operation Φ, that operates on both L and G.

Then, Φ **promotes** Op to the global operation

$$\exists \Delta L \bullet \Phi \wedge Op$$

which operates on the global state G.

A promotion is **free** when the mixed operation used satisfies

$$\exists L'; G' \bullet \Phi \Rightarrow \forall L' \bullet \exists G' \bullet \Phi.$$

This means that if the update Φ is possible at all, then it must be possible for all outcomes of the local state. The value of this is that Φ will fit with any local operation that maintains the state invariant on L. A promotion that does not satisfy the freeness condition is called **constrained**.

Promotion enjoys a number of pleasing properties, one of the most important of which is the following.

Theorem 1 [promoted precondition] If Op is promoted in the above way, so that we have

$$\Phi Op \mathrel{\widehat{=}} \exists \Delta L \bullet \Phi \wedge Op,$$

then ΦOp satisfies

$$\text{pre}\ \Phi Op = \exists L \bullet \text{pre}\ \Phi \wedge \text{pre}\ Op.$$

□

4 Implementing promotion

Suppose that we have the following definitions. *Op* is a local operation on the state L, and Φ promotes it to the global state G which indexes local states using a partial function:

$$
\begin{array}{|l}
\hline
\textbf{\textit{G}} \\
f : X \twoheadrightarrow L \\
\hline
\end{array}
$$

$$
\begin{array}{|l}
\hline
\Phi \\
\Delta G \\
\Delta L \\
x? : X \\
\hline
x? \in \operatorname{dom} f \\
\theta L = f\ x? \\
\{x?\} \ntriangleleft f' = \{x?\} \ntriangleleft f \\
f'\ x? = \theta L' \\
\hline
\end{array}
$$

Notice that the precondition of this mixed operation is

$$
\begin{array}{|l}
\hline
\text{pre } \Phi \\
G \\
L \\
x? : X \\
\hline
x? \in \operatorname{dom} f \\
\theta L = f\ x? \\
\hline
\end{array}
$$

This means that we have a good simplification of the precondition of the promoted operation.

Lemma 1 [simplification] Given the definitions, we have that

$$\text{pre } \Phi Op = [\, G;\, x? : X \mid x? \in \operatorname{dom} f \wedge (\text{pre } Op)[\theta L := f\ x?]\,]$$

Proof

$$
\begin{array}{l}
\text{pre } \Phi Op \\
= \textit{“by the promoted precondition theorem”} \\
\exists\, L \bullet \text{pre } \Phi \wedge \text{pre } Op \\
= \textit{“by simplification”} \\
\exists\, L \bullet [\, G;\, L;\, x? : X \mid x? \in \operatorname{dom} f \wedge \theta L = f\ x? \wedge \text{pre } Op\,] \\
= \textit{“by the one-point rule”} \\
[\, G;\, x? : X \mid x? \in \operatorname{dom} f \wedge f\ x? \in L \wedge (\text{pre } Op)[\theta L := f\ x?]\,] \\
= \textit{“by the definition of } G\textit{, and that } f\ x? \textit{ is defined”} \\
[\, G;\, x? : X \mid x? \in \operatorname{dom} f \wedge (\text{pre } Op)[\theta L := f\ x?]\,]
\end{array}
$$

□

ZRC is a refinement calculus for Z [6], based closely on Morgan's refinement calculus [3]. An important feature of ZRC is the separation of pre- and postconditions, ready for refinement. The translation between schemas and so-called specification statements is given by (for Op, an operation on the state S):

$$Op =$$

$$\mathbf{con}\,\alpha S \bullet$$
$$\quad \alpha S' : \left[\left(\begin{array}{l} \mathrm{pre}\ Op \\ \Xi S \end{array} \right), Op \right]$$

Thus, both the precondition and the postcondition become predicates (in dashed variables) of single states. The logical constant S is used to preserve before-values so that they may be referred to in the postcondition. This translation has the virtue that it is close to the Z schema (postconditions use no decoration when referring to before-variables, and dashes when referring to after-variables.

Value-result substitution in programming languages involves the replacing of one variable—the *formal* parameter—by another variable—the *actual* parameter. In our little programming language, it is written

$$prog[\mathbf{value\,result}\, f := a]$$

The rule for value-result parametrisation in ZRC is

$$\begin{array}{l}
\mathbf{begin} \\
\quad \mathbf{con}\,\alpha A \bullet \\
\quad\quad \alpha G', \alpha A' : \left[\left(\begin{array}{l} pre[\theta F' := \theta A'] \\ \theta A = \theta A' \end{array} \right), post[\theta F, \theta F' := \theta A, \theta A'] \right] \\
\mathbf{end} \\
\sqsubseteq \\
[\mathbf{value\,result}\, F := A] \bullet \\
\quad \mathbf{begin} \\
\quad\quad \mathbf{con}\,\alpha F \bullet \\
\quad\quad\quad \alpha G', \alpha F' : \left[\left(\begin{array}{l} pre \\ \theta F = \theta F' \end{array} \right), post \right] \\
\quad \mathbf{end}
\end{array}$$

This rule is best understood backwards. The result is a program that is value-result parametrised: it refers to a local state F. When it is used, the actual parameter (A) is systematically substituted for the formal parameter (F). Thus, if we have a specification that embodies that substitution, then we must "undo" this substitution in order to obtain the parametrised implementation.

Now, consider the implementation of ΦOp. The idea is to transform it so that we can apply the value-result parametrisation rule. To this end, we introduce a temporary variable t to play the rôle of the actual parameter variable. The variable t must be initialised with the value $f\,x?$, and finally its value must be inserted into the partial function f at the appropriate point $x?$.

ΦOp

$=$ *"by translation into specification statement"*

$$\mathbf{con}\ \alpha G \bullet$$

$$\alpha G' : \left[\begin{pmatrix} \text{pre}\ \Phi Op \\ \theta G = \theta G' \end{pmatrix}, \begin{pmatrix} \exists \Delta L \bullet \\ \quad x? \in \operatorname{dom} f \\ \quad \theta L = f\ x? \\ \quad \{x?\} \lhd f' = \{x?\} \lhd f \\ \quad f'\ x? = \theta L' \\ \quad Op \end{pmatrix} \right]$$

$\sqsubseteq$ $\mathbf{var}\ t \bullet$

$$\alpha G', t' : \left[\begin{pmatrix} \text{pre}\ \Phi Op \\ \theta G = \theta G' \end{pmatrix}, \begin{pmatrix} \exists \Delta L \bullet \\ \quad x? \in \operatorname{dom} f \\ \quad \theta L = f\ x? \\ \quad \{x?\} \lhd f' = \{x?\} \lhd f \\ \quad f'\ x? = \theta L' \\ \quad Op \end{pmatrix} \right]$$

$\sqsubseteq$ *"sequential composition"*

$$\alpha G', t' : \left[\begin{pmatrix} \text{pre}\ \Phi Op \\ \theta G = \theta G' \end{pmatrix}, \begin{pmatrix} \text{pre}\ \Phi Op \\ \theta G = \theta G' \\ t' = (f'\ x?) \end{pmatrix} \right]; \qquad [\lhd]$$

$$\alpha G', t' : \left[\begin{pmatrix} \text{pre}\ \Phi Op \\ \theta G = \theta G' \\ t' = (f'\ x?) \end{pmatrix}, \begin{pmatrix} \exists \Delta L \bullet \\ \quad x? \in \operatorname{dom} f \\ \quad \theta L = f\ x? \\ \quad \{x?\} \lhd f' = \{x?\} \lhd f \\ \quad f'\ x? = \theta L' \\ \quad Op \end{pmatrix} \right] \qquad [i]$$

$\sqsubseteq$ *"assignment"*

$t := f\ x?$

$[i] =$ *"by the promoted precondition theorem"*

$$\alpha G', t' : \left[\begin{pmatrix} \exists L \bullet \\ \quad \text{pre}\ \Phi \\ \quad \text{pre}\ Op \\ \theta G = \theta G' \\ t' = (f'\ x?) \end{pmatrix}, \begin{pmatrix} \exists \Delta L \bullet \\ \quad x? \in \operatorname{dom} f \\ \quad \theta L = f\ x? \\ \quad \{x?\} \lhd f' = \{x?\} \lhd f \\ \quad f'\ x? = \theta L' \\ \quad Op \end{pmatrix} \right]$$

$=$ *"by the simplification lemma"*

$$\alpha G', t' : \left[\begin{pmatrix} x? \in \operatorname{dom} f \\ (\text{pre}\ Op)[\theta L := (f\ x?)] \\ \theta G = \theta G' \\ t' = (f'\ x?) \end{pmatrix}, \begin{pmatrix} \exists \Delta L \bullet \\ \quad x? \in \operatorname{dom} f \\ \quad \theta L = f\ x? \\ \quad \{x?\} \lhd f' = \{x?\} \lhd f \\ \quad f'\ x? = \theta L' \\ \quad Op \end{pmatrix} \right]$$

= *"by two applications of the one-point rule"*

$$\alpha G', t' : \left[\begin{pmatrix} x? \in \operatorname{dom} f \\ (\text{pre } Op)[\theta L := t] \\ \theta G = \theta G' \\ t' = (f' \, x?) \end{pmatrix}, \begin{pmatrix} x? \in \operatorname{dom} f \\ \{x?\} \lhd f' = \{x?\} \lhd f \\ Op[\theta L, \theta L' := (f \, x?), (f' \, x?)] \end{pmatrix} \right]$$

⊑ *"strengthen postcondition"*

(The final value of t is undetermined; let's make it $f' \, x?$.)

$$\alpha G', t' : \left[\begin{pmatrix} x? \in \operatorname{dom} f \\ (\text{pre } Op)[\theta L := t] \\ \theta G = \theta G' \\ t' = (f' \, x?) \end{pmatrix}, \begin{pmatrix} \{x?\} \lhd f' = \{x?\} \lhd f \\ Op[\theta L, \theta L' := (f \, x?), t'] \\ t' = f' \, x? \end{pmatrix} \right]$$

⊑ *"following assignment"*

(Updating f in this way will make sure that $t' = f' \, x?$, and that no other part of f changes.)

$$\alpha G', t' : \left[\begin{pmatrix} x? \in \operatorname{dom} f \\ (\text{pre } Op)[\theta L := t] \\ \theta G = \theta G' \\ t' = (f' \, x?) \end{pmatrix}, Op[\theta L, \theta L' := (f \, x?), t'] \right]; \qquad [\lhd]$$

$$f := f \oplus \{x? \mapsto t\}$$

⊑ *"logical constant introduction"*

(We introduce t so that we can refer in the postcondition to the value of t' before this specification statement.)

con t •

$$\alpha G', t' : \left[\begin{pmatrix} x? \in \operatorname{dom} f \\ (\text{pre } Op)[\theta L := t] \\ \theta G = \theta G' \\ t' = (f' \, x?) \\ t = t' \end{pmatrix}, Op[\theta L, \theta L' := (f \, x?), t'] \right]$$

⊑ *"strengthen postcondition"*

(We change the expression $f \, x?$ in the postcondition into t.)

$$\alpha G', t' : \left[\begin{pmatrix} x? \in \operatorname{dom} f \\ (\text{pre } Op)[\theta L := t] \\ \theta G = \theta G' \\ t' = (f' \, x?) \\ t = t' \end{pmatrix}, Op[\theta L, \theta L' := t, t'] \right]$$

= *"by a property of substitution"*

$$\alpha G', t' : \left[\begin{pmatrix} \begin{pmatrix} x? \in \operatorname{dom} f \\ (\text{pre } Op)[\theta L := \theta L'] \\ \theta G = \theta G' \\ \theta L' = (f' \, x?) \end{pmatrix} [\theta L' := t'] \\ t = t' \end{pmatrix}, Op[\theta L, \theta L' := t, t'] \right]$$

$\sqsubseteq$ [**value result** $\theta L := t$] •

begin con αL •

$$\alpha G', \alpha L' : \left[\left(\begin{array}{l} x? \in \operatorname{dom} f \\ (\operatorname{pre} Op)[\theta L := \theta L'] \\ \theta G = \theta G' \\ \theta L' = (f'\, x?) \\ \theta L = \theta L' \end{array} \right), Op \right]$$

end

$\sqsubseteq$ *"contract frame"*

(The global state is no longer referred to in the postcondition; therefore we can contract the frame and forget about it.)

$$\alpha L' : \left[\left(\begin{array}{l} x? \in \operatorname{dom} f \\ (\operatorname{pre} Op)[\theta L := \theta L'] \\ \theta G = \theta G' \\ \theta L' = (f'\, x?) \\ \theta L = \theta L' \end{array} \right), Op \right]$$

$\sqsubseteq$ *"weaken precondition"*

(The precondition carries some assumptions that we no longer need: get rid of them.)

$$\alpha L' : \left[\left(\begin{array}{l} \operatorname{pre} Op \\ \theta L = \theta L' \end{array} \right), Op \right]$$

$=$ *"by translation"*

Op

Now, if we gather up the code that we have developed, then we find that we have

ΦOp

$\sqsubseteq$

con αG •
    begin
        var t •
            $t := f\, x?$;
            con t •
                Op[**value result** $\theta L := t$];
            $f := f \oplus \{x? \mapsto t\}$
    end

$\sqsubseteq$ *"eliminating redundant logical constants"*

$$
\begin{array}{l}
\textbf{begin} \\
\quad \textbf{var}\ t \bullet \\
\qquad t := f\ x?; \\
\qquad Op[\textbf{value result}\ \theta L := t]; \\
\qquad f := f \oplus \{x? \mapsto t\} \\
\textbf{end}
\end{array}
$$

$\sqsubseteq$ *"eliminating t"*

(The variable t is declared, then initialised, then held constant; we can eliminate it by replacing each applied occurrence by $f\ x?$, since f does not change until after the last mention of t.)

$Op[\textbf{value result}\ \theta L := f\ x?]$

Thus, the promoted operation is implemented simply a procedure call and value-result parametrisation. Notice that in the absence of aliasing, value-result parametrisation is equivalent to call-by-reference. This is useful, since it gives an efficient way of passing our global data structure as a parameter.

The algorithm refinement of *Op* can now take place independently of the development of the rest of the code.

5 Summary

Our basic result is that promotion in Z can be implemented using simple, traditional subroutine mechanisms. Of course, it might not be the best way to implement a given specification, since it is not always desirable that a program follow the structure of its specification. However, it does match our programming intuitions about what we are doing with promotion.

Acknowledgments

This work has been inspired by the many discussions on promotion that I have had with Peter Lupton, amongst others, at IBM UK Laboratories at Hursley Park. Paul Gardiner and Stephen Brien made valuable comments that have helped to improve the paper.

References

[1] S. Brien, *Z Base Standard*, Version 0.5, Oxford University Computing Laboratory (1992).

[2] P.J. Lupton, "Promoting Forward Simulation", *Procs 5th Annual Z User Meeting,* Springer-Verlag (1991).

[3] Carroll Morgan, *Programming from Specifications*, Prentice Hall, 1991.

[4] Carroll Morgan & B.A. Sufrin, "Specification of the UNIX filing system", *IEEE Transactions on Software Engineering,* **SE-10**(2): 128–142 1984.

The technique of promotion, or framing, was originally devised to help structure this specification of the UNIX filing system.

[5] J.C.P. Woodcock, "Mathematics as a Management Tool: Proof Rules for Promotion", in *Software Engineering for Large Software Systems,* (B.A. Kitchenham, Editor), Elsevier Applied Science (1990).

This paper explores some of the properties of promotion, and give some proof rules for calculating the preconditions of promoted operations.

[6] J.C.P. Woodcock, *Using Standard Z: Specification, Proof and Refinement,* Prentice Hall *to appear.*

A Rules from ZRC

In this appendix, we give a few of the rules for refinement of specification statements in ZRC. They are drawn from [6], and are based on the refinement calculus of Morgan [3]. They differ in that they use Z, particularly schemas, and that the rules below do not use Morgan's zero-subscript convention. In general, they are pairs of predicates, a precondition and a postcondition; each is a predicate on a single (dashed) state. Logical constants are used to refer to before-values in the postcondition.

A.1 Local variable introduction

$w : [pre, post]$
$\sqsubseteq$
begin
  var $x : T \bullet$
    $w, x' : [pre, post]$
end.

A.2 Logical Constant introduction

If $pre \Rightarrow (\exists c : T \bullet pre_2)$, and
c does not occur free in $w : [pre, post]$,then
$w : [pre, post]$
$\sqsubseteq$
con $c : T \bullet$
  $w : [pre_2, post]$

A.3 Sequential composition

$w, x : [pre, post]$
$\sqsubseteq$
$x : [pre, mid]$;
$w, x : [mid, post]$

A.4 Strengthen postcondition

If $pre[w' := W] \wedge post_2 \Rightarrow post_1$, then

begin
    con W •
        $w : [pre, post_1]$
end

$\sqsubseteq$

begin
    con W •
        $w : [pre, post_2]$
end

Author Index

Published in 1990–91

AI and Cognitive Science '89, Dublin City University, Eire, 14–15 September 1989
A. F. Smeaton and G. McDermott (Eds.)

Specification and Verification of Concurrent Systems, University of Stirling, Scotland, 6–8 July 1988
C. Rattray (Ed.)

Semantics for Concurrency, Proceedings of the International BCS-FACS Workshop, Sponsored by Logic for IT (S.E.R.C.), University of Leicester, UK, 23–25 July 1990
M. Z. Kwiatkowska, M. W. Shields and R. M. Thomas (Eds.)

Functional Programming, Glasgow 1989, Proceedings of the 1989 Glasgow Workshop, Fraserburgh, Scotland, 21–23 August 1989
K. Davis and J. Hughes (Eds.)

Persistent Object Systems, Proceedings of the Third International Workshop, Newcastle, Australia, 10–13 January 1989
J. Rosenberg and D. Koch (Eds.)

Z User Workshop, Oxford, 1989, Proceedings of the Fourth Annual Z User Meeting, Oxford, 15 December 1989
J. E. Nicholls (Ed.)

Formal Methods for Trustworthy Computer Systems (FM89), Halifax, Canada, 23–27 July 1989
Dan Craigen (Editor) and Karen Summerskill (Assistant Editor)

Security and Persistence, Proceedings of the International Workshop on Computer Architecture to Support Security and Persistence of Information, Bremen, West Germany, 8–11 May 1990
John Rosenberg and J. Leslie Keedy (Eds.)

Women into Computing: Selected Papers 1988–1990
Gillian Lovegrove and Barbara Segal (Eds.)

3rd Refinement Workshop (organised by BCS-FACS, and sponsored by IBM UK Laboratories, Hursley Park and the Programming Research Group, University of Oxford), Hursley Park, 9–11 January 1990
Carroll Morgan and J. C. P. Woodcock (Eds.)

Designing Correct Circuits, Workshop jointly organised by the Universities of Oxford and Glasgow, Oxford, 26–28 September 1990
Geraint Jones and Mary Sheeran (Eds.)

Functional Programming, Glasgow 1990, Proceedings of the 1990 Glasgow Workshop on Functional Programming, Ullapool, Scotland, 13–15 August 1990
Simon L. Peyton Jones, Graham Hutton and Carsten Kehler Holst (Eds.)

4th Refinement Workshop, Proceedings of the 4th Refinement Workshop, organised by BCS-FACS, Cambridge, 9–11 January 1991
Joseph M. Morris and Roger C. Shaw (Eds.)

AI and Cognitive Science '90, University of Ulster at Jordanstown, 20–21 September 1990
Michael F. McTear and Norman Creaney (Eds.)

Software Re-use, Utrecht 1989, Proceedings of the Software Re-use Workshop, Utrecht, The Netherlands, 23–24 November 1989
Liesbeth Dusink and Patrick Hall (Eds.)

Z User Workshop, 1990, Proceedings of the Fifth Annual Z User Meeting, Oxford, 17–18 December 1990
J.E. Nicholls (Ed.)

IV Higher Order Workshop, Banff 1990
Proceedings of the IV Higher Order Workshop, Banff, Alberta, Canada, 10–14 September 1990
Graham Birtwistle (Ed.)

Printing: Weihert-Druck GmbH, Darmstadt
Binding: Buchbinderei Schäffer, Grünstadt